W9-CNU-877

Popular Science
HOMEOWNER'S ENCYCLOPEDIA

FULLER & DEES
TIMES MIRROR
New York • Los Angeles • Montgomery

Contributing Authors

RONALD M. BENREY *Rochester, Michigan*	***Electrical Wiring; Home Air Conditioning.***
GEORGE DANIELS *Danbury, Connecticut*	***Piers, Floats, Docks, & Boathouses; Upholstery.***
RICHARD DAY *Palomar Mt., California*	***Automotive Systems; Caulking; Chain Sawing.***
R. J. DECRISTOFORO *Los Altos Hills, California*	***Construction; Power Tools; Workshops***
WILLIAM C. EYMANN *Palo Alto, California*	***Photography.***
RUDOLF GRAF and GEORGE WHALEN *New Rochelle, New York*	***Alarm Systems; Heating Systems; Wall Papering; Outdoor Lighting; Lawnmowers; Batteries.***
JAY HEDDEN *Kansas City, Missouri*	***Footings & Foundations; Framing; Hardware; Floor Construction.***
LYNN HILTS *Chicago, Illinois*	***Paints & Painting.***
DARRELL HUFF *Carmel, California*	***Acoustics & Sound Control; Kitchen Design & Planning; Energy Saving Tips; Suspended Ceilings; Fireplaces.***

3734 Atlanta Highway, Montgomery, Alabama 36109

Library of Congress Cataloging in Publication Data
Main entry under title: Popular Science Homeowner's Encyclopedia

1. Dwellings — Maintenance and repair — Amateurs' manuals. 2. Repairing — Amateurs' manuals. 3. Do-it-yourself work. I. Title: Homeowner's encyclopedia.
TH4817.3.P66 643'.7'03 74-19190
Complete Set ISBN 0-87197-070-8
Volume I ISBN 0-87197-071-6

Contributing Authors

INFORDATA INTERNATIONAL, INC.
Chicago, Illinois
Automation; Stereo Systems; Safety; Decorating.

MORRIS KRIEGER
Brooklyn, New York
Plumbing Systems; Drainage Systems.

DON MEADOWS
Montgomery, Alabama
Drapery Hardware.

DONALD MEYERS
Shoreham, New York
Brick & Stone Work; Concrete; Patio Construction; Porch Construction; Dormer Construction.

JACK PAYNE
Franklin Lakes, New Jersey
Boat Construction.

EVAN POWELL
Greenville, South Carolina
Appliances; TV Repairs & Troubleshooting.

MORTON SHULTZ
Middlesex, New Jersey
Room Additions; Cabinetmaking.

DAVE VIGREN
New York City
Boats & Boating; Insect & Pest Control; Lawns & Gardens.

The authors listed above contributed not only the entries mentioned, but also many other informative articles, photographs and illustrations to the POPULAR SCIENCE HOMEOWNER'S ENCYCLOPEDIA.

SPECIAL RECOGNITION to Sears, Roebuck & Co for permission to use material from their SIMPLIFIED ELECTRICAL WIRING

EDITORIAL DIRECTOR
JoAnne Rogers

PROJECT EDITORS
Gordon Girod
Elaine Pannell

ART DIRECTOR
George J. Alexandres

PRODUCTION DIRECTOR
William J. Holmes

Introduction

The POPULAR SCIENCE HOMEOWNER'S ENCYCLOPEDIA, which you now hold in your hand, is a reference work designed for the entire family. Alphabetically-arranged entries cover most possible home repair and improvement situations. An extensive system of cross-references eliminates the need for an index by providing immediate suggestions for related and additional information. Hundreds of line drawings, and color and black and white photographs, illustrate and explain material discussed in the entries. A special section on PROJECTS provides plans, materials, and step-by-step building instructions for a variety of home construction projects.

Popular Science

HOMEOWNER'S ENCYCLOPEDIA

Abrasives

The most commonly found abrasives for use in the home workshop are such *natural* ones as garnet, flint (quartz), and emery, and such *artificial* ones as aluminum oxide and silicon carbide. The natural ones are mined like any mineral while the artificial ones are essentially products of an electric furnace. The aluminum oxide is fused bauxite; the silicon carbide results from a sand-coke fusion.

Each of the abrasives is especially good for a particular application, but in practice overlaps do exist. A particular grit in one abrasive will often do the job when the best abrasive is not available. It is a good idea to know the abrasives and what they are best used for. Then, when you must, you can improvise, but wisely.

Types of Abrasives

Aluminum oxide is available with either paper or cloth backing. The cloth backing is always stronger and more flexible. It can be used dry or with a lubricant; is excellent for machine sanding of wood, plastics and metal; and can take a lot of abuse. The paper backing can be used on machines but is generally recommended for hand work. Aluminum oxide is probably the most popular abrasive today for all-around shop use.

Silicon carbide is excellent for wet sanding either by hand or machine. You can use it on undercoats and primers as well as on uncoated surfaces. You'll find in most cases that it is the best abrasive to use on metals. It comes with a paper backing but is waterproof. It's ideal for very fine work such as the final sanding of an auto-body repair job to get glass-smooth finish.

Emery is another good metal abrasive that is fine for polishing jobs and for initial steps like removing rust and scale. It may be used either dry or with a lubricant.

Garnet is very good for wood sanding, is available with a paper backing and is used dry. It's a fairly good all-purpose shop paper even though aluminum oxide is favored over it for power tool use.

Flint is the least durable of the abrasives and comes with a paper backing. It is cheap and, therefore, often used on preliminary work when you know the job will result in quick clogging. Although it is not made for power sanding, you can cut up standard sheets for use with a pad sander. It is never used for wet sanding.

In order of hardness, the abrasives can be listed as follows: silicone carbide, aluminum oxide, emery, garnet and flint.

The least expensive abrasives are the natural ones. The synthetics cost more but they last longer.

Sizes

The grit number of an abrasive is actually a *mesh number* indicating the particular size wire or silk screen that was used to filter the abrasive material during the manufacturing process. For example, particles that pass through a number twelve screen would total twelve to the inch if they were lined up. When the screen control

TYPE	VERY FINE	FINE	MEDIUM	COARSE	VERY COARSE
flint	4/0	2/0-3/0	1/0-$\frac{1}{2}$	1-2	$2\frac{1}{2}$-$3\frac{1}{2}$
garnet	6/0-10/0	3/0-5/0	1/0-2/0	1/2-$1\frac{1}{2}$	2-3
aluminum oxide and silicon carbide	220-360	120-180	80-100	40-60	24-36

This chart groups different abrasives into five classes of word grit-descriptions and indicates the numbers of the grits that fall in each.

The grit of the abrasive paper has to do with the size of the abrasive particles. "Coarse," "medium," and "fine" are general classifications. Within each, there is an assortment of grit sizes. See the corresponding charts.

becomes impractical because of the size of the particles, then fairly complex flotation systems are used to accomplish the same thing. Grit sizes can go from the No. 12, which is the coarsest, to No. 600, which is the finest.

The resulting smoothness of a project depends on the grit you use. The No. 12 would produce results similar to what you would get by rubbing wood with tiny, sharp stones. Using No. 600 is almost like rubbing with flour. The usual recommendation of working through progressively finer grits of paper until you achieve the smoothness you want is good, but the critical factor is the choice of the grit you start with. Many manufacturers of abrasive materials simplify the grading system by using words instead of, or in addition to, mesh sizes. The words can go from "extra coarse" to "extra fine," and relying on them for general shop use isn't really out of line.

Remember that abrasives are cutting tools. They do their job by removing material almost like tiny chisels. The "chisel" you start with will leave minute ridges and grooves that you must

ABRASIVE	USE	GRIT ROUGH	 MEDIUM	 FINE	REMARKS
aluminum oxide	hardwood aluminum copper steel ivory plastic	2 1/2-1 1/2 40 40-50 24-30 60-80 50-80	1/2-1/0 60-80 80-100 60-80 100-120 120-180	2/0-3/0 100 100-120 100 120-280 240	Manufactured, brown color, bauxite base, more costly than garnet but usually cheaper to use per unit of work
garnet	hardwood softwood composition board plastic horn	2 1/2-1 1/2 1 1/2-1 1 1/2-1 50-80 1 1/2	1/2-1/0 1/0 1/2 120-180 1/2-1/0	2/0-3/0 2/0 1/0 240 2/0-3/0	Natural mineral, red color, harder and sharper than flint
silicon carbide	glass cast iron	50-60 24-30	100-120 60-80	12-320 100	Manufactured, harder but more brittle than aluminum oxide, very fast cutting
flint	removing paint, old finishes	3-1 1/2	1/2-1/0		Natural hard form of quartz, low cost, use on jobs that clog the paper quickly

Here are suggestions that will help you select a type and a grit for a particular material and finish. Which grit you start with has much to do with the original state of the surface you work on.

8/0 = 280	3/0 = 120	$1^1/_2$ = 40
7/0 = 240	2/0 = 100	2 = 36
6/0 = 220	0 = 80	$2^1/_2$ = 30
5/0 = 180	$^1/_2$ = 60	3 = 24
4/0 = 150	1 = 50	

Here are the number equivalents of the various grit sizes.

MATERIAL	FIRST STEP	SECOND STEP	FINAL
oak	$2^1/_2$-$1^1/_2$	$^1/_2$-1/0	2/0-4/0
maple	$2^1/_2$-1	$^1/_2$-1/0	2/0-4/0
maple (curly)	$2^1/_2$-$1^1/_2$	$^1/_2$-1/0	2/0-4/0
birch	$2^1/_2$-1	$^1/_2$-1/0	2/0-4/0
mahogany	$2^1/_2$-$1^1/_2$	$^1/_2$-1/0	2/0-3/0
walnut	$2^1/_2$-$1^1/_2$	$^1/_2$-1/0	2/0-4/0
fir	$1^1/_2$-1	$^1/_2$-1/0	2/0
pine	$1^1/_2$-1	1/0	2/0
gum	$2^1/_2$-$1^1/_2$	$^1/_2$-1/0	2/0-3/0
willow	2	$^1/_2$-1/0	2/0
cypress	$2^1/_2$-$1^1/_2$	$^1/_2$-1/0	2/0
plaster			5/0-8/0
hardboard		3/0-4/0	5/0-7/0

Here are grit sizes to choose for various materials. If the material is fairly smooth to begin with, you can skip the first step.

remove with smaller "chisels." Always start with the least coarse abrasive that will do the job. With today's materials, it's not likely that you will have to go beyond a "medium" classification, which would encompass grits from about No. 60 to No. 100.

Beyond this first grit, if you want a truly professional job, you will find it unwise to make jumps exceeding two grit sizes. If you go beyond this, you may find that the finer grits will not remove the ridges and furrows left by the initial sanding. The surface might feel smooth to your hand, but there will be crevices that will be revealed when you apply stain. These imperfections will also occur when you have done considerable cross-grain sanding and insufficient with-the-grain sanding. In the extreme, and especially with a belt sander, the flaws will emerge as cross-grain swirls. Do cross-grain work, regardless of the grit of the paper, only when you wish to remove material fast. For the desired smoothness, do the bulk of the work by stroking with the grain.

Coatings

When abrasive particles are placed in a close-packed formation, the descriptive term is "closed coat." The result is a fast-cutting and durable abrasive surface but one that can clog easily under certain conditions. When abrasive particles are applied with spaces between so that only about 50% to 70% of the backing is covered, the product is called "open coat." This type won't cut as fast as a closed-coat design simply because there aren't as many abrasive particles. On the other hand, it will not clog as quickly.

Closed coats cut faster, are more durable and do a smoother job. Open coats are best for soft materials, gummy materials and for finish removal chores.

Care of Abrasives

The cost of abrasive materials can add up if you are too casual with how you use them and neglect some simple maintenance chores. When the paper becomes worn so that it doesn't cut anymore, you have no choice but to discard it. However, a coarse-grit paper, for example, used to the point where it no longer does the job it was designed for can be used further as a finer grit.

Dry cleaning with a brush will slow the accumulation of stubborn waste on an abrasive surface. When the accumulation is powdery and loose, a bristle brush will do. When the accumulation is thick, a wire brush may be used. Work the brush in all directions to re-expose the sharp cutting grains. When you are doing such work on a power tool, don't work with the machine running or you will soon have a

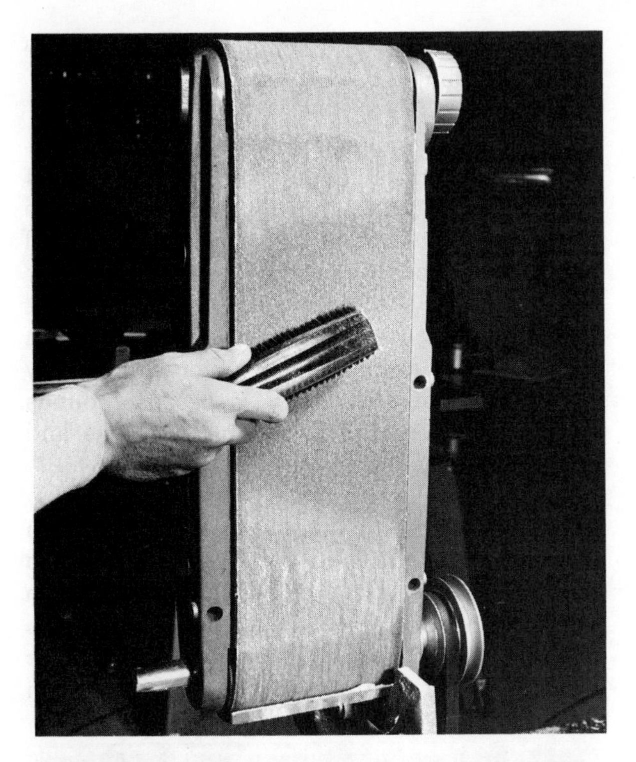

Frequent "dry cleaning" with a brush will help prevent buildup of grit-clogging waste. Use a circular motion with the belt stationary. A soft brush will do the job when the waste is loose, especially on fine papers.

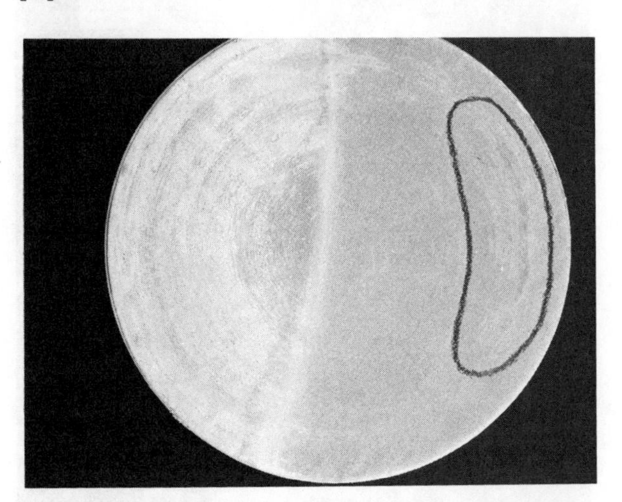

In some situations you'll find spots that will not wash out. Such spots can be the result of uneven mounting of the disc. Despite these areas, there can still be much surface left on an abrasive that can be used.

"brushless" brush. Instead, rotate the belt sander or the disc sander by hand as you scrub out the wood dust.

Many times you can double the useful life of an abrasive belt by scrubbing it in lukewarm, sudsy water. Rub vigorously with a stiff brush to work waste out of the valleys. Use a cloth to mop off the excess moisture and then place the belt back on the machine to dry. Another method is to stretch the washed belt lightly between two pipes or poles correctly spaced in holes drilled in a board. If the belt shrinks, readjust the machine tension to compensate.

Remove accumulations of pitch that cause slick spots on the belt with a brush that you have soaked in turpentine. Use a circular motion; then stroke in one direction to throw off the solvent and dirt. Quickly pat dry with a cloth before the solvent can penetrate the backing.

Accident Prevention

[SEE SAFETY.]

Accordion-Fold Door

An accordion-fold door is a folding door made of vinyl-coated materials which are attached to a metal framework. They save space in closets that is wasted by swinging doors. These doors may be used to divide rooms or to close off certain sections of large areas. *SEE ALSO FOLDING DOORS.*

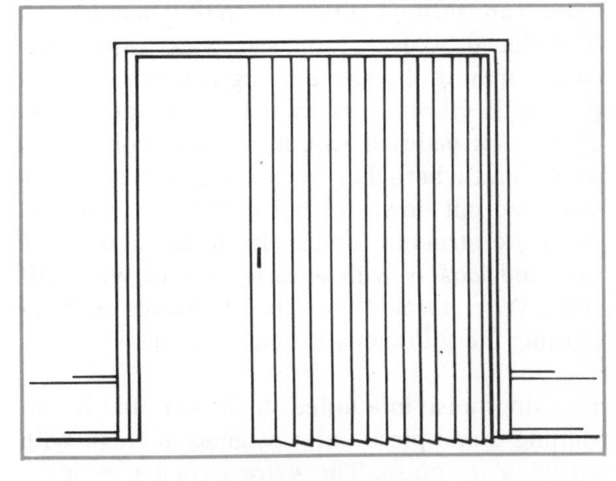

Accordion-Fold Door

Acoustics & Sound Control

Noise is one of the most disturbing forms of pollution in our crowded modern world. As well as acute discomfort, it can produce fatigue and even actual illness. Controlling noise in your home can take three principal forms: *First* is prevention. This is the quickest and simplest, but is limited in its possibilities. *Second* is within-a-room absorption. Within limits this is rather easy to accomplish, too, with soft or porous surfaces. But it does not solve the major problem of keeping what is happening outdoors or in another room from coming through a wall or floor and bothering you. That requires the *third* form of control, the kind referred to as soundproofing.

PREVENTION AND DEADENING

Begin your sound control program by preventing extra noise. Oil squeaky motors and hinges. Place any vibrating appliances on rubber pads and use mechanical door closers or buffers to prevent slamming doors. A number of these measures may add up to a surprisingly quieter house.

In new construction or extensive additions or remodeling, prevent much more noise, especially in respect to plumbing. Unpleasant plumbing noises are caused by vibration when water runs through pipes. Much of this noise can be reduced by using large size water pipes. The same amount of water passing through a 1 inch pipe will vibrate less than in a 3/4 inch pipe. Heavy felt padding around pipes at connecting points and where they touch the house structure will also cut down on noise. Pipes suspended from the structure under the house should be fastened loosely with wire instead of with stiff rods. Wire permits the pipe to vibrate without passing the vibrations through the joists.

Flushing noise in a toilet can be avoided by installing a one-piece unit designed to flush with virtually no noise. The extra expense is more than justified, since a toilet is usually near a bedroom or close to a room where guests are being entertained.

Another functional source of noise in the modern house is its ventilating devices. The type of fans selected and where and how they are placed will determine how serious a decibel problem they create.

Obviously you cannot eliminate all noise. Even rooms which are relatively quiet within may sound noisy at times. This is because sounds bounce off the hard, reflective surfaces and come back at you from several directions.

When people are talking in an empty room you can hear their words as they speak and then, a fraction of a second later, you hear them again bouncing off floor, ceiling, and walls. The echo and the words as spoken blend together. It is difficult to talk comfortably or listen to music in

Acoustic effectiveness no longer means an industrial look. These tiles have a surface designed to hide the functional perforations and are the first such product in which the individual squares blend. This type of ceiling, fit in appearance for any room and especially to be desired in a noisy one, can be suspended to produce a lower ceiling where wanted.

an empty room. To stop the echo there are several things that can be done. Add rugs, upholstered furniture, or heavy draperies until the sound level is comfortable. Excessive absorption of sound, of course, will give a dead feeling to the room.

Kitchens are notoriously noisy rooms because of their many slick hard surfaces which bounce back sound. A typical home during busy meal preparation periods may be more nerve-wracking and noisier than a downtown city street at rush hour.

The most common problem is caused by reverberation. Sound waves bounce off the hard surfaces of a room — windows, doors, walls, counters, cabinets, furniture, ceilings, and from working appliances — bouncing back and forth again and again in a split second until the sound builds up to an annoying level.

Using Acoustical Tiles

Reverberation lends itself to a simple solution. Acoustical ceilings, which can absorb between 55 and 75 percent of the sound waves striking their surfaces, will effectively stop echoing. However, confusion continues to exist over which ceilings may carry the name *acoustical*. It is important to know what is meant by this somewhat elastic term. Otherwise you risk purchasing an item assumed to be truly acoustical to discover that the product does not perform to your expectations.

All ceiling tiles or suspended ceiling panels deaden noise to some degree, but all do not merit being called acoustical. Only those tiles and panels that have been engineered by their makers to absorb specified quantities of sound, usually more than 50 percent, are entitled to this label.

Two of the most popular methods of giving acoustical properties to mass-produced ceilings are with fissures or perforations or both. These have the further benefit of being readily apparent, so there is no question about the product's acoustical nature. Some fissures simulate the distressed look of elegant travertine marble.

The secret of an acoustic ceiling is fissures or perforations or both in the tile. Those tiny perforations are noise traps.

Perforations may be tiny pinpricks or relatively large holes, and they may form a design or be nearly hidden by it. Sound waves entering these surface interruptions cause the air already inside to be set in motion. This causes friction, and much of the sound wave's energy is turned into heat. Depending on the type of product and method of installation, an acoustical ceiling frequently absorbs one-half to three-quarters of the sound waves striking it.

Since the ceiling is usually a room's largest uncluttered area, it is the logical place to put acoustical material. While carpets are excellent for muffling impact noises, furnishings and occupants often shield the flooring from acting efficiently to reduce more prevalent airborne sounds (stereo, kitchen appliances, etc.).

By using acoustical ceilings, *buffer zones* can be set up to intercept sound before it can spread. An acoustical buffer zone in the dining room would reduce kitchen noise heard in the living room by 40 percent. Prevent hallways or passageways from acting like speaking tubes by using acoustical ceilings to absorb sound.

Put in place with adhesive or staples, acoustic ceiling tiles are a do-it-yourself favorite. They are especially useful during a remodeling that includes adding a recreation room in the basement where noise protection is wanted for rooms above.

Home improvement dealers now stock a selection of different types of acoustical ceilings in many new decorator styles. Wood fiber acoustical ceilings are inexpensive, but remarkably efficient, sound traps. Mineral fiber ceilings cost a bit more, but offer the added benefit of incombustibility. Recently developed is a ceiling tile made of a blend of natural and synthetic fibers combining the advantages of the two materials. Priced at the level of a good grade wood fiber ceiling, the new tiles, like their mineral fiber counterparts, won't burn and are not affected by changes in temperature or humidity.

Ceiling tiles and suspended ceilings, the other major category, require no great skill to install. Acoustical tiles can be cemented directly to an existing ceiling, if it is in good condition. Otherwise it is necessary to apply furring strips to the old ceiling and staple the tiles to these strips of wood.

Suspended ceilings, on the other hand, consist of larger acoustical panels resting in a metal grid network which is hung from the overhead by wires. This type of acoustical ceiling is particularly suitable for hiding unsightly ducts, rafters, or wiring without losing accessibility.

Acoustical ceilings are not priced prohibitively for modest noise-control budgets, either. For an average 10' x 15' room, excluding labor, one could be installed for about $36 for the least expensive acoustical tile to $60 for the very best suspended ceiling, including custom framework.

Besides absorbing noise, ceiling tiles should help to prevent the passage of the remaining sound into adjoining parts of the house. This problem can be acute, such as in the case of a bedroom located above an active family room.

The denser the composition of the tile, the better it will keep sound from spreading to other areas. The densest acoustical tiles sold in this country are made from mineral fiber or wood fiber. Other materials, such as glass fiber, are more porous and allow the sound to slip through with greater ease.

A consumer trying to decide between two competing types of tile should balance density with sound absorption. The absorbency of an acoustical tile is shown by its *noise reduction coefficient* rating, or NRC, which the dealer should be able to provide for each item in stock. Technical as it seems, NRC can be readily understood as the percentage of sound striking the surface of the tile that will be absorbed. A spread of more than 10 NRC points (for example, a .50 tile and a .70 tile) indicates a definite increase in sound absorption for the higher-rated product. Any narrower gap is more difficult for the ear to detect. In some cases, the consumer might wish to settle for a lower NRC rating in a higher density tile if he is concerned with blocking noise out as he is with absorbing it. All acoustical tiles are efficient sound absorbers when compared to ceilings.

Preventing Noise Transmission

To stop noise from passing from one room to another, larger measures often must be taken. This is especially true when the transmission is through a wall.

To tackle this problem first determine how the sound enters by placing an ear close to each point where sound may be transmitted to the room. Check such places as through floor, ceiling, wall, through the air, through heat ducts, plumbing pipes, or along floor joists. You will note, of course, that noise travels easily through lightweight materials and passes through a small opening as readily as through a large one. Do not think that you can prevent sound from passing from one room to the next by placing a sound absorbing surface on the wall of a room.

Materials that are good absorbers of sound within a room are poor sound insulators between two rooms.

It is true, however, that heavy insulation is more effective than a light insulation material.

Materials such as rock wool, fiber glass, or loose fill insulation are heat insulators and do little or no good when it comes to keeping sounds from traveling through. At most, an insulating blanket is a useful auxiliary in a heavy wall of the kinds described below. Two or three thicknesses of gypsum board will help keep sound from being transmitted through walls, and are helpful in keeping sound from passing through a ceiling from one floor to another.

Sometimes sound seems to be coming through a door when actually it may be coming under the door. Tuck a heavy rug at the bottom or edges of the door. If this stops most of the sound, insulate the door soundwise by placing rubber or felt strips around the edge of the door. A slab door is more soundproof than a hollow core door. Best of all is a sand-filled hollow core door. Plywood nailed across a panel door helps to soundproof it.

How Materials Compare

The following are insulating materials you could use between rooms, in the order of their effectiveness: Solid masonry such as brick or cement blocks, concrete are best; or heavy plaster is very effective.

One or more thicknesses of gypsum board with air space between layers will prevent sound transmission. Wood is less effective, but plywood, because of its layers of glue and cross-grain layers, is better than the same thickness of paneling.

A bookcase wall or a closet, often used as a sound barrier between rooms, is over-rated as a noise insulator. The closet wall is a barrier only because a number of layers of cloth do absorb sound, but this is an absorptive lightweight type of insulator which does not work effectively. A closet wall, empty of any clothing at all, can better control sound if you place strips of felt or rubber around doors, which should be heavy also. Books, because of their density, make good individual sound insulators, but in a bookcase wall there is still space above and around books through which sound travels easily. A bookcase wall will work more effectively if it is detached from the wall behind it.

When you add a recreation room in your basement, you may create a new problem. Using it may be no fun if users must constantly be concerned about disturbing the rest of the family upstairs.

Noise from Outside

Open windows are usually the source of most noise entering the house. The mere act of closing any windows in a noisy area will be helpful. Double insulating glass will cut down on outside noise level problems, but not unless the adjoining wall is also well insulated against noise. Dense trees such as conifers and thick shrubs will keep sound waves from the street away from the house, as will a concrete wall or a good high hedge. An outdoor patio, uncomfortable because of street noises, can be insulated by a fence plus plantings and the addition of a recirculating fountain which will add splashing sounds without wasting water.

The most effective measures are possible, naturally, only when you are doing extensive remodeling, adding a room, or building a new house. Then you can approach the problem scientifically. Begin by trying to isolate noisy areas such as the playroom from living room and master bedroom from wherever TV listening will be most frequent.

You can also make use of sound-controlling wall floor systems. Keep in mind, first of all, that materials designed to muffle sound within a room or to insulate against heat loss and gain are limited in their value as sound barriers. To stop the penetration of sound you must interpose bulk or mass, which generally means heavy materials. Masonry is ordinarily quite effective, since even so-called lightweight concrete blocks are a relatively heavy building material. Gypsum-board products are also helpful since they offer good weight and solidity in a conveniently usable form. The density and mass of plywood and hardboard make them other good candidates.

There are two basic measurements you will need to know about to plan sound-control methods. One of these is the familiar *decibel.* It is a measure of the intensity of loudness of sound.

More directly useful to you is the factor called STC, which means *sound-transmission class.* It is a measure, not of the loudness of sound, but of how much a given wall or other barrier reduces the intensity of sound passing through it. It measures *total* effect of a wall or floor, since this effect depends on arrangement of parts and on the method of framing as well as on the sheet materials used. Therefore, you can reduce sound transmission by isolating one side of a wall from the other, as well as by interposing bulk.

What a given STC means in your home can be judged from these examples of classes: STC 25: through such a wall, normal speech can be fairly easily understood. An STC in the 20's is considered very poor. STC 30: loud speech can be understood fairly well. STC 35: loud speech audible but not intelligible. STC 42: loud speech audible as a murmur. STC 45: must strain to hear loud speech. STC 48: some loud speech barely audible. STC in the 50's is regarded as excellent.

Building a Noise-Resisting Wall

When you are faced with the job of erecting an effective sound barrier, the question comes down to how to achieve an adequate STC. The methods most feasible in frame construction are the following, any one of them, or two or more used in combination: Interpose a sheet of heavy material on one or both sides of the framing. Laminate a second sheet, preferably of different material, over the first. Place a sound-muffling material, such as blanket insulation of the type used to keep a house warm, within the frame wall. Separate the two sides of the wall so that it becomes two walls without sound-transmitting contact between them. Instead of hanging the wall surface material directly on the framing, first put up resilient channels (horizontally, 2 feet on center) and fasten to them.

Now fasten the 1/4 inch sound-deadening board to the furring strips. Place it horizontally, using panel adhesive and cement-coated 5d nails. Put one nail at each corner as a minimum. The 1/2 inch gypsum board should go up vertically over the sound-deadening board. Use panel adhesive and, at the corners, 4d coated nails. The result is a solid, sound-resisting base for taping and painting or for the installation of prefinished plywood paneling.

Alternative methods can be worked out for sound control of existing walls, using adaptations of the methods for new construction that follow.

To build a sound-controlling wall, first place 2 x 4 sole and then toenail 2 x 4 studs to it 16 inches on center.

Studs must be properly vertical to insure that edges of sound-deadening board will fall upon them.

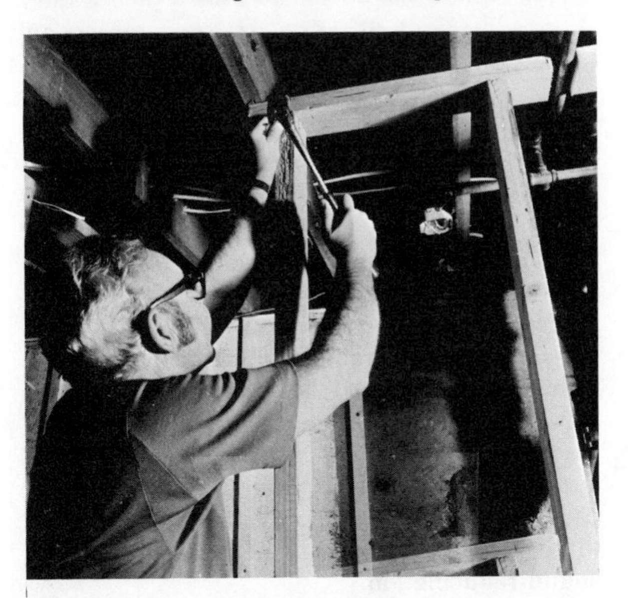

Toenail studs to plate. Note that plate is cut in two for pipe, permissible with nonloadbearing wall.

If you are working with a masonry wall, provide 1 x 2 nailing strips instead. Use a stud gun if concrete nails will not work—or use construction adhesive.

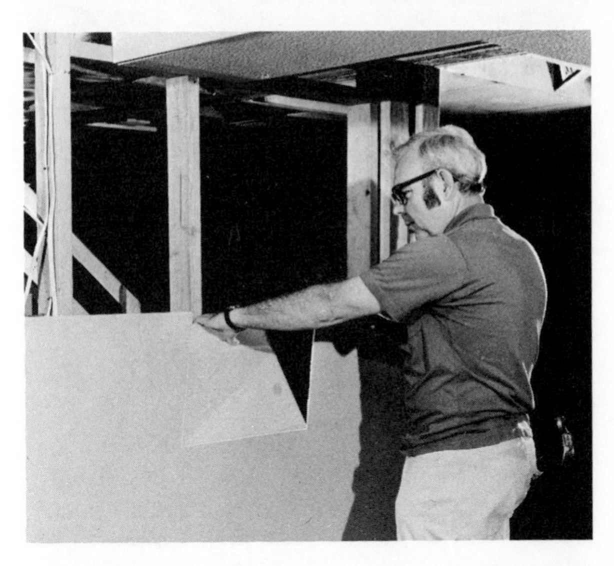

Sound-deadener is 1/4 inch gypsum board. Cut it by scoring with sharp knife and breaking section out.

To give you a wide variety of choice, Western Wood Products Association has compiled 18 partition systems you might choose from in building a wall, whether in a new home or in remodeling or adding to a house.

These systems are in three groups. The first uses ordinary framing of the 2 x 4's. The second occupies about two inches more space, since the plates are 2 x 6's to permit staggered studs. Walls in the third group use slightly thicker framing, based on double plates of 2 x 3's spaced about 1 inch apart.

The American Hardboard Association has created some wall systems using hardboard, which

Apply panel adhesive to studs, sole and plate. This gun type is supplied by Georgia-Pacific, maker of the sound-deadening board.

Gypsum board goes up into place and is nailed as a supplement to the adhesive. Application is horizontal because next layer will be plywood applied vertically.

have been evaluated in terms of Sound Transmission Class. If you put 1/4 inch hardboard directly on the studs on both sides of the wall, you will not get much sound reduction. The rating of STC 36 is as good as you could get with 1/2 inch gypsum board. However, it is better than you could get with 1/2 inch plaster over gyp-

With adhesive, only a few nails are needed. Note use of 2 x 4 scrap as foot lever to hold panel for nailing.

sum lath (STC 33) and much better than the 28 that prefinished Lauan (Philippine mahogany) plywood produces.

Perhaps the best system is one that produces an STC of 54 by using staggered studs — 2 x 4's 16 inches on center with 2 x 6 sole and cap. This is the same kind of framing in the chart for walls numbered from 7 to 11. Between the studs weave a 2 inch mineral-wool blanket with vapor barrier. Then on each side of the wall apply 1/2 inch gypsum board, completing the barrier with caulking around the edges. It is always important to seal up leaks around the perimeter of any sound-reducing job.

To produce the STC of 54, complete the job with a layer of 1/4 inch hardboard on each side, laminated to the drywall. If this is prefinished hardboard, the wall is completed.

Floor-Ceiling Noise

Sometimes the sound-transmission problem is a vertical one as between one floor and another of a home. As mentioned earlier, acoustical tiles installed in the ceiling are one approach.

Cementing on plywood will complete the acoustic wall. Sprayed black line is to prevent white show-through at joints.

Panel adhesive is applied an inch or two from all edge positions of plywood, as well as in zigzag pattern.

A second is reduction of impact sounds, usually footsteps overhead. A heavy carpet helps, as does heavy carpet padding. A further help is a sub-base under the padding and on top of the subfloor. Better than ordinary underlayment is a softer material, such as panels of fiber board. Care must be taken, however, not to use very soft materials where heavy furniture could dent it severely.

Softwood plywood with heavy texture has somewhat more sound-muffling effect than smooth-finished hardwood has. A couple of nails at top of panel act as a hinge.

Along with all these methods of reducing sound production and transmission, there is one further option that sometimes works when nothing else will. It is sound-masking. A neutral or pleasant sound can be produced within a room to make intruding sounds no longer noticeable. Falling or bubbling water, as mentioned earlier, is one such sound. Music is, of course, the masking sound most often used.

New Walls

If you are building a new wall, about the *least* sound-resistant method you can use is to apply thin plywood paneling directly to the studs on both sides. One of the easiest methods is to apply 1/2 inch gypsum board to one or both sides first. It is readily available, and gives the most results for expense incurred.

A hinge makes it possible to pull panel away from adhesive briefly to let it dry before panel is pressed back again.

Installation of first panel is completed by addition of nails at bottom, elsewhere only if they seem needed.

A comparatively simple method that will produce excellent sound-deadening requires furring strips plus two layers of gypsum board. This is quite effective even if only one side of the wall is being treated. Begin by nailing strips to the old wall, or attaching them with panel adhesive. You might use either 1 x 2 lumber or strips of plywood 3/8" x 17/8". Put the first strip at floor line and others horizontally every 16 inches. Add vertical strips every 4 feet to support the edges of the sound-deadening board. (Like most gypsum-board products, this commonly comes in 4 x 8 sheets.) Leave about 1/4 inch space between these vertical strips and the horizontal ones, to allow for ventilation. The furring reduces sound transmission by creating an air pocket between the existing wall and the sound-deadening board.

SOUND CONTROL IN NEW CONSTRUCTION

When buying or building a new home, or remodeling an older one, the homeowner needs to be aware of these suggestions to control sound. They have been worked out by architects concerned with noise control.

Place noisy rooms or busy ones so they face the street; reserve the quieter orientations for bedrooms and living rooms. Any big windows, especially in living rooms, should face toward your own lot, not the street. Except as demanded by ventilation needs, try to avoid bedroom windows that face streets.

Preserve as many existing trees and shrubs as possible to shield the house from street and neighbor noises. A yard wall, six feet high if permissible, is an excellent noise barrier between street and deck or patio area.

Quiet and noisy zones of the house should be separated. If possible place the bedrooms in one wing, living areas in another with a buffer zone between.

The front entrance should open into a hall which buffers the living room from street sounds. Weather stripping around the door perimeter will reduce outside sounds, and wall areas around it should be heavily battened with acoustical materials.

Avoid long straight hallways which become sound tunnels. A bend or two in the hall plus walls lined with acoustical material will mitigate sound transmission. Neither a family room nor bedrooms should open directly on a hall to the living room.

Straight stairways are an acoustical menace. Give them a bend, a landing, and access to a short hall in order to cut down sound paths. Padded stair carpet plus insulation in walls adjoining staircases helps, too.

Sounds *should* bounce off the walls in a room where music is played, but cushions, carpets, and soft furnishings are needed to absorb the sound.

Closet walls filled with clothing are effective noise barriers, provided the closet doors are solid core and well sealed.

Bathroom noises can be reduced between walls, especially when two bathrooms are back to back, by construction of two, rather than the usual single, studs between walls.

Most effective of all sound barriers is a good thick fireplace wall. Place it on an inside wall next to a bedroom if possible.

Acoustical treatment will help the most to cut down on reverberation and reduce the piercing sharpness of workshop sounds to other rooms. Check all the appliances for vibration noise. Merely installing felt or rubber pads can do a great deal to reduce noise in kitchen and laundry.

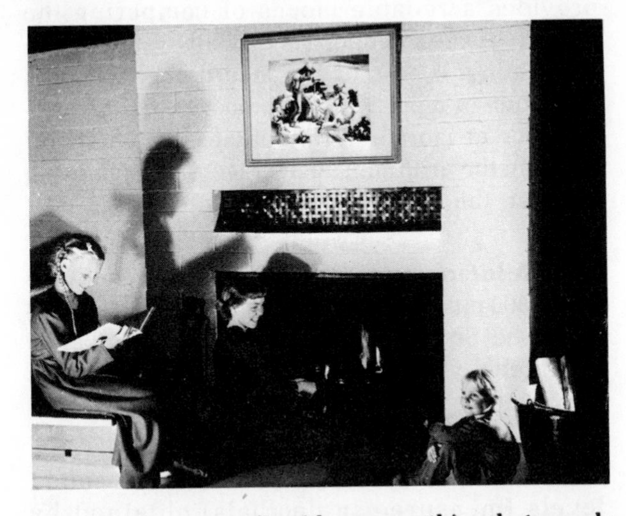

More than a cozy fireside scene, this photograph shows a peace-keeper in the home: a wall that is an effective sound barrier. Masonry blocks 8 inches thick keep noise from passing from living room to parents' bedroom beyond. The rough-faced block has some sound-muffling value within the room as well.

SOUND CONTROL PROBLEMS AND SOLUTIONS

When electrical outlets are placed back to back in partition walls, sound is permitted to travel easily from room to room. If you are remodeling, place one of the receptacles in the next stud cavity. If not remodeling, remove the cover plate, pack insulation in the wall cavity around the receptacle. Caulking around the receptacle helps too.

Back-to-back medicine cabinets in adjoining bathrooms conduct sound from one room to another. If possible, remove the cabinets and place insulation batts in the resulting cavity. Close the opening and face it with gypsum wallboard and mirrors. If this solution is not feasible, remove only one of the cabinets and reposition it in some other part of the room. Place insulation in the resulting cavity.

Doors joining one unit to the next unit which permit sound to leak to other parts of the home can be replaced with a solid core door. Sealing around the perimeters with a vinyl gasket is also helpful.

Remove base and ceiling moldings and caulk at both ceiling and floor line with a nonhardening type acoustical sealant to stop sound leaks at top and bottom plates of walls and partitions.

Unless a television jack is used, the best TV reception is through an exterior wall. They should not be backed up to adjoining interior walls thus preventing the sound from carrying.

THE VOCABULARY OF ACOUSTICS AND SOUND CONTROL

Airborne noise: Noise radiated into the air — voices, music, barking dogs, typewriters and jackhammers.

Attenuation (sound isolation, sound insulation): The reduction in the intensity of sound. Attenuation is measured in decibels.

Background Noise Level: Noise level of the environment, created by street traffic, trains, mechanical equipment, etc. An objective of noise control is to reduce the sound transmitted to a level below the background noise level.

Caulk, Seal: A permanent, elastic type adhesive or sealant used to prevent sound leaks through cracks, joints or other openings.

Decibel: A unit used for measuring the intensity (loudness) of sound. The easiest way to identify sound pressure levels is to compare them to sounds which we recognize readily. For example, the sound of soft radio music heard in a quiet home would be at approximately the 35 decibel level. The sound in a noisy office or department store would be at approximately the 60 decibel level. Average conversation is in the 40 to 60 decibel range.

Flanking: Noise transmitted indirectly around a sound barrier rather than directly through it, such as noise traveling from one room up into a plenum space, then down into another room.

Frequency: The number of sound waves per second produced by the source of sound. Audible frequencies ranged from 20 cycles per second (cps) to 20,000 cps. Middle "C," for example, is 262 cps.

Gypsum Sound Deadening Board: A new incombustible ¼ inch thick gypsum board, designed to reduce sound transmission in wall and floor-ceiling assemblies economically.

Impact Insulation Class (IIC): The sound transmission loss performance of a floor/ceiling assembly designated by a single number. Rating is determined by laboratory testing, based on use of "tapping" machine. The higher the number, the better the resistance to impact noise. (This same testing standard is used by the U.S. Department of Housing and Urban Development.)

Impact Noise Rating (INR): Formerly used as testing criteria, however, the (IIC) has replaced this rating. Both INR and IIC measurements are based on noise caused by footsteps. A minus rating means poor performance. The higher the plus rating, the better the performance.

Leak or Sound Leak: Sound passing through a crack or other opening in an assembly.

Noise: Unwanted sound.

Sound: A pressure wave that travels outward in all directions from its source at a speed of 1,120 feet per second. Sound may also be the source, or the sensation experienced in the ears when pressure waves strike the eardrums.

Sound Absorption: The absorption of the energy of sound waves by a porous or soft, limp material. Carpeting and upholstered furniture will help absorb sound within a room, whereas hard walls, floors and ceiling surfaces will reflect sound.

Sound Deadening Fiberboard: A low density product designed to reduce sound transmission in wall and floor-and-ceiling systems.

Sound Level: The loudness or intensity of sound, measured in decibels.

Sound Transmission Class (STC): The sound transmission loss performance of a partition designated by a single number. The STC rating provides a reliable means of comparing the noise reduction properties of wall systems. The STC rating, by use of a standard curve, lowers the rating of a partition with poor sound characteristics at isolated frequencies which is not done by the arithmetical average. The higher the number, the better the sound control.

Speech Interference Zone: The frequency range (500-2800 cps) which includes average conversation. The Speech Interference Zone number is obtained by averaging the transmission loss curve between 500 and 2800 cps.

Transmission Loss: The difference in sound levels (measured in decibels) obtained by measuring the sound intensity on both sides of a wall assembly with a noise source on one side.

Transmitted Noise Level: The sound that passes through a wall.

Acrylic Resin Glue

Synthetic acrylic resin glue, sometimes referred to as plastic resin glue, comes in powder form and must be mixed with a liquid. It is usually sold in twin containers, one with powder and one with liquid. The setting time of this glue is determined by the proportions used when combining the two ingredients. When gluing with a heavy assembly of woods, clamping is definitely necessary. The bonding power of this glue reaches three tons per square inch.

Acrylic resin glue is water resistant, heat resistant, stain resistant, colorless and easily handled. It is excellent for gluing hard and softwoods, and it is particularly good as a gap filler. A word of caution, however; in some instances there is a possibility of damage to plastics, rubber and lacquers. During hot weather, it is a good idea to keep the resin glue in a container surrounded with ice cubes to stretch working time. *SEE ALSO ADHESIVES.*

Additions

[SEE ROOM ADDITIONS.]

Address Light

The pushbutton for your doorbell places at your disposal an ever-ready source of electricity that supplies power to an elegant address light which adds convenience and a quiet to every home. There is no need for extra wiring. It only requires two inconspicuous wires from the pushbutton to the address light which produces an even, low intensity light that silhouettes your house number. The low voltage bulbs in the address light are always on except when the pushbutton is pressed. They are not visible during daylight.

Address Light

HOW IT WORKS

The transformer is always ready to power your bell, buzzer or chime. A touch on the pushbutton activates the circuit and at all other times the electrical circuit is idle, or open. At that time the full transformer voltage (typically 10 volts for a bell or buzzer and 16 volts for a chime) is available across the two contact screws of the pushbutton. You can use this ready voltage and all of the existing wiring to power the 'address light. The bulbs must not draw too much current so the bell or the chime will be activated. So, the address light uses minimum bulbs that require only two volts at a current of 60 milliampere (60 thousandths of an ampere) for full light output. Five bulbs are used for a 10V bell circuit and eight bulbs needed for a chime that has a 16-volt transformer. The five-bulb arrangement can also be used at 16 volts provided a 100 ohm five-watt resistor is added to absorb the extra 6 volts.

The bulbs and resistor (if it is needed) are electrically connected in series. The sockets are mounted in front of a curved silvered section made from a 12 fluid-ounce frozen orange juice container which is an efficient light reflector. Aluminum foil on cardboard can also be used. Sockets are attached to the reflector with screws and nuts. The screw for the center socket(s) also goes through the back of the case and thereby holds the lamp/reflector assembly securely in place.

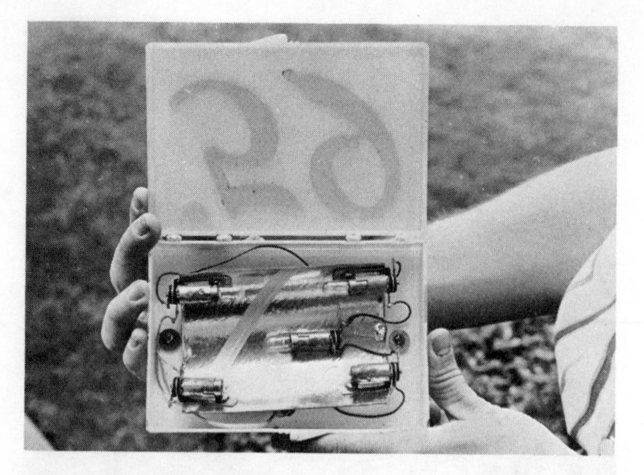

The lamp/reflector assembly is housed in an acrylic box with a clear cover that is readily available in any hardware or notion store. But first every inside surface of the box, except the cover, is spray-painted to make it opaque. If you can get a box that has an opaque bottom and a clear cover, so much the better. The cover gets a *light* dusting of a suitable color of spray paint to make it translucent. (The purchased numerals, made of metal or plastic, are then pasted to the front outside surface of the box.)

The two screws which hold the address light to the house and the wires to the pushbutton both go through rubber grommets for weather protection. Other mounting means may be dictated by the location selected for the address light.

To wire the address light connect the two wires from the unit to the screws on the pushbutton. That's all there is to it.

Wiring Diagrams

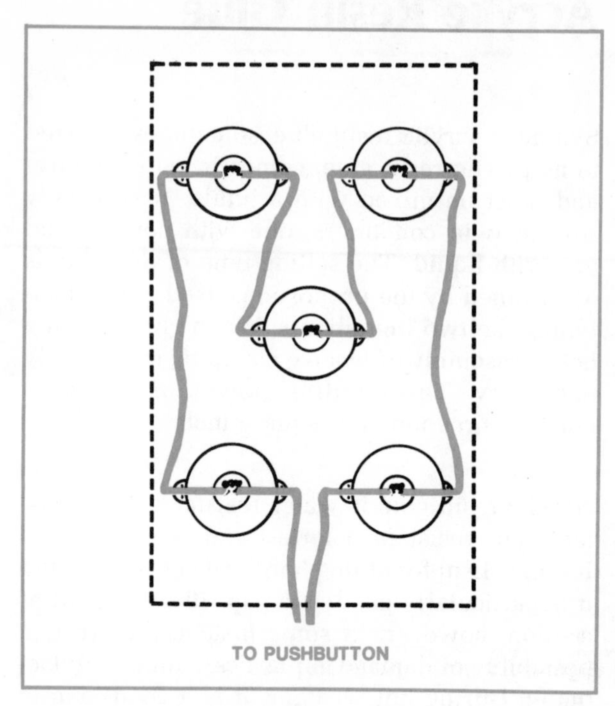

Five-bulb arrangement for use with 10 volt bell transformer

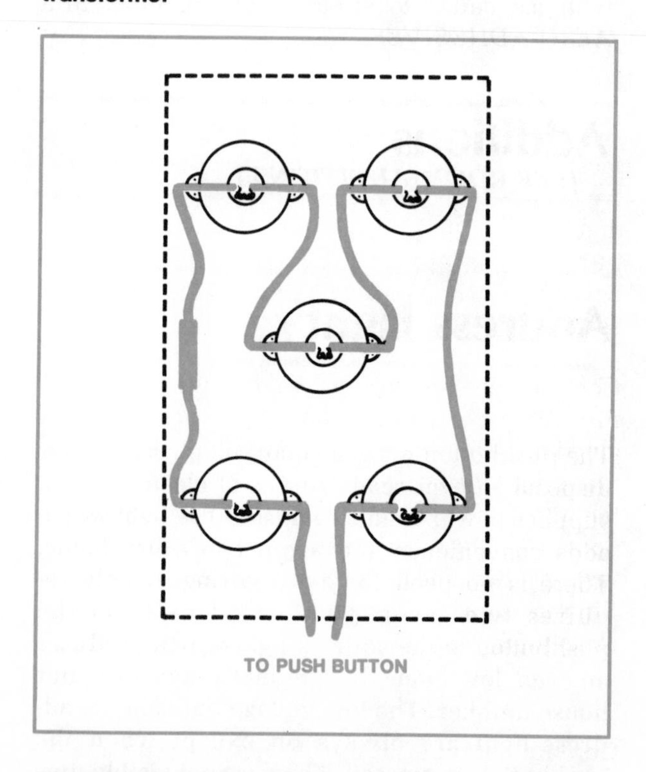

Alternate five-bulb plus resistor (see text) arrangement for use with 16 volt chime transformer

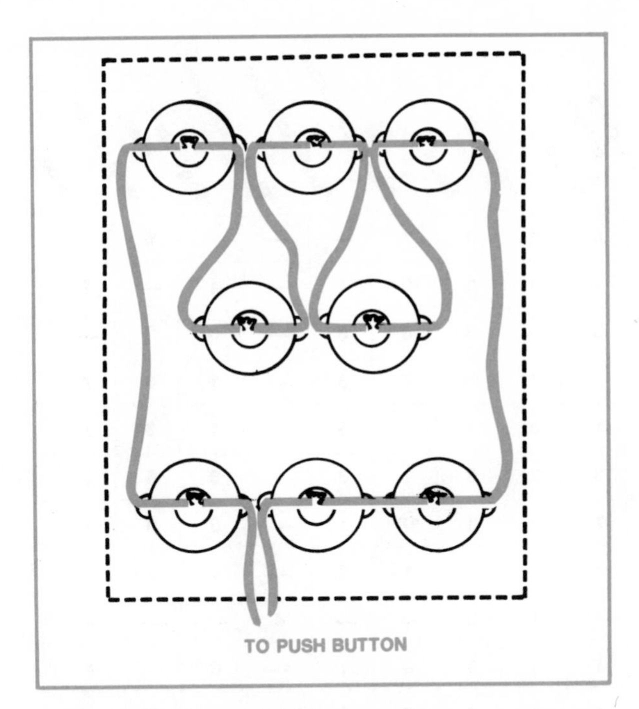

Eight-bulb arrangement for use with 16 volt chime transformer

Adhesives

Adhesives are substances that bond two surfaces together. They may be classified into ten types: contact cements, resorcinol and formaldehyde glues, epoxy glues, mastics, latex base adhesives, rubber base adhesives, polyvinyl resin adhesives, plastic glues, silicone sealants, gums and pastes.

Certain rules apply to all work with adhesives. First, to insure a secure bond, the surfaces to be glued must be clean, dry and well-fitted. Second, to hold well, the adhesive must be suitable for the use intended, e.g., a waterproof glue for outdoor use. Third, to insure a secure joint, some form of clamping or fastening device is required. Finally, follow the manufacturer's directions closely for best results.

CONTACT CEMENTS

Contact cements bond on contact (hence the name.) Positioning of materials must be accurate the first time. Once the pieces are joined, they cannot be moved to adjust the fit because about two-thirds of the full bond strength is present on contact. Contact cements are used to bond plastic laminate to counter tops; or metal, polyurethane foam, or hardboard to wood.

Excess cement at joints or on finish surfaces may be removed with lacquer thinner or nail polish remover. Contact cement is not a satisfactory structural adhesive in furniture making, but is suitable for applying finish laminates or veneers to well-constructed cabinets.

Resorcinol and Formaldehyde Glues

Resorcinol and formaldehyde glues should be used in joints needing great structural strength. Resorcinol glue is an excellent choice for boat building and outdoor furniture construction because it is completely waterproof and, when cured, stronger than wood. Formaldehydes are restricted to interior use because they are water soluble. The homeowner must mix both of these glues.

EPOXY GLUE

Epoxies are purchased in two-part containers and must also be mixed by the homeowner. When the resin and the hardner are mixed in equal parts, epoxies become one of the strongest glues available. The glue sets by chemical action rather than solvent evaporation; therefore all of the material applied contributes to the bond.

Almost anything may be glued with epoxies; however they are particularly effective in joining metal to metal, and in making usable repairs to china and pottery. (Dishes repaired with epoxies may be washed in hot, soapy water without affecting the glue joint). Because they are relatively expensive, epoxies are more suitable for gluing small areas. Large objects can best be glued with resorcinol, casein or other wood glues.

MASTICS

Mastic adhesives are used to bond floor tile, wall paneling or ceiling paneling. Mastics provide a good bond to cement, ceramic tile, asphalt or hardboard.

ADHESIVE USE CHART

	Acoustic tile	Carpets	China, glass, pottery	Drywall	Hardboard	Metal	Paper, cardboard	Plastic laminate	Plastic wall tile	Vinyl fabric	Vinyl sheet and tile	Wood
Acoustic tile	4	—	—	4	4	1	1	—	—	—	6	4
Carpets	—	5	—	1	1	1	5	1	—	1	—	1
China, glass, pottery	—	—	3	3	—	3	6	3	—	6	6	—
Drywall	—	—	3	7	1	3	7	3	—	1	6	7
Hardboard	1	—	—	1	3	3	1	3	—	1	6	7
Metal	1	—	3	3	3	3	1	3	—	6	6	3
Paper, cardboard	1	5	6	7	1	1	10	1	—	6	6	1
Plastic laminate	1	—	3	3	3	3	1	3	—	1	6	3
Plastic wall tile	—	—	—	4	4	6	—	—	4	—	—	4
Vinyl fabric	—	1	6	1	1	8	6	1	—	6	—	1
Vinyl sheet and tile	6	—	6	4	4	6	6	6	—	—	6	4
Wood	4	—	—	7	2	3	1	3	—	1	6	2

HOW TO USE TABLE: Select one material to be glued in left hand column. Go across page until column of other material to be glued is located. That number corresponds to the sequence of adhesives in this article (*1* is contact cement, *2* is resorcinol and formaldehyde glue). That adhesive should work well for those materials.

This adhesive is found in two general types: rubber resin (synthetic rubbers in solvents) and synthetic latex (latex in a water-base solution). Rubber resin mastics are available in tubes for caulking guns.

LATEX BASE ADHESIVES

Latex base adhesives are available in tubes and cans for fastening cardboard, paper, fabric or carpet. Their flexible, strong bonds withstand soap-and-water cleaning, but not dry cleaning. Before setting, excess or spilled adhesive may be removed with soap and water. After setting, the adhesives may be softened or removed with lighter fluid.

RUBBER BASE ADHESIVES

Rubber base adhesives cannot be used for structural bonds. In unstressed areas, rubber based adhesives provide satisfactory bonds of paper to wallboard, rubber to rubber and wood to concrete. These adhesives also may be used to repair pottery. Nail polish remover will dissolve excess adhesive.

POLYVINYL RESIN ADHESIVES

Polyvinyl resin adhesives are the familiar household "white glues" packaged in flexible plastic bottles. Water soluble, PVA adhesives should be used only for interior gluing. These adhesives are white when applied, but dry clear. They are excellent all-purpose household glues (allowing for their lack of water resistance and low stress resistance).

PLASTIC GLUES

Plastic glues are commonly known as *airplane glue* or *model making glue.* Care should be taken to note the two types of plastic glue. Plastic glue sold in small bottles in model shops or kits is actually a plastic solvent. When applied to the model parts, it dissolves a thin surface layer of plastic and actually welds the two parts together. The more common plastic glue found in tubes, possibly labeled as cellulose nitrate cement, is the more common and probably more useful household glue. This latter glue in addition to its model making use, can be used to glue glass, wood, plastic and most ornamental objects. On highly porous material two coats of glue may be necessary for a good bond. Plastic glue, because of the toxic solvent fumes, should be used only in a well-ventilated area.

SILICONE SEALANTS

Silicone sealants are used more as adhesive gap fillers than as actual glues. These sealants are most commonly used to fill the gap in joints around sinks, basins, and bathtubs.

GUMS AND PASTES

Gums and pastes, with two exceptions, are suitable only for joining paper, cardboard or leather. Casein glue and hide glue, the two exceptions, are traditional furniture glues. They provide strong joints, and hold for many years. Certain difficulty in preparing and using casein and hide glues have caused them to be less popular in furniture construction with the development of resorcinol and other glues. The more common gums and pastes are rubber cements, flour pastes and starch pastes. Many wallpaper pastes would be found in this classification. Water will clean up most adhesives of this type.

Adjustable Wrenches

Adjustable open-end wrenches take the place of the thumb and forefinger in loosening and tightening certain square and hexagonal-shaped nuts and fittings. The jaws on these adjustable wrenches are set between 22½ and 30 degrees, allowing a smaller working area than needed for a monkey wrench, for example.

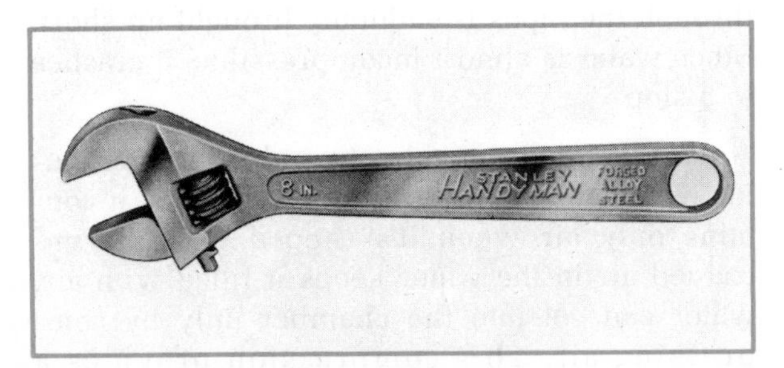

Adjustable Wrench

Adjustable open-end wrenches save time, also, because they adjust to fit the various sizes of the hex and square-shaped nuts and fittings without ruining them by rounding off the corners.

In using the adjustable open-end wrenches, there is often a question of whether to turn the wrench handle toward or away from the moveable jaw without breaking the wrench. But, the advantage of the adjustable wrench is its ability to be used in tight spots where it can be flipped over in order to take many short swings of the handle to unscrew the fitting. If the wrench has "forged" or "drop-forged" on the handle, then it is unlikely that the wrench can be broken with the bare hands, whether the handle is turned toward or away from the moveable jaw. One caution, though — if possible, always pull on a wrench handle rather than push; and if pushing is unavoidable, be careful not to smash your knuckles. *SEE ALSO HAND TOOLS.*

Adze

An adze is a long-handled cutting implement similar to an axe, but with the thin, arched blades set at right angles to the handle like that of a hoe. This shaping and finishing hand tool is used principally for rough-finishing wood. Always sharpen the blade on the concave side. *SEE ALSO HAND TOOLS.*

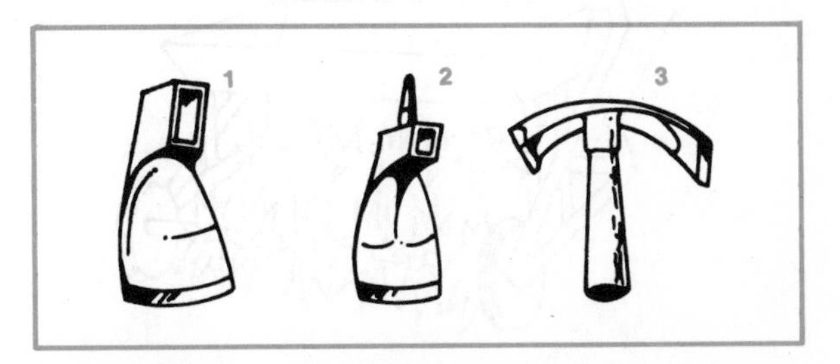

(1) Carpenter's adze with flat head, (2) ship carpenter's adze with spur, (3) cooper's adze.

Aerators

The home handyman should become familiar with the two types of aerators. First, there is the type that is used with water faucets in the home, and secondly, there is the type that is used with lawnmowers.

When used with water faucets, aerators are attached to the spout of the faucet to prevent splashing. The unit mixes air with the running water so that the water will cling to, rather than splash or bounce off the sink surface.

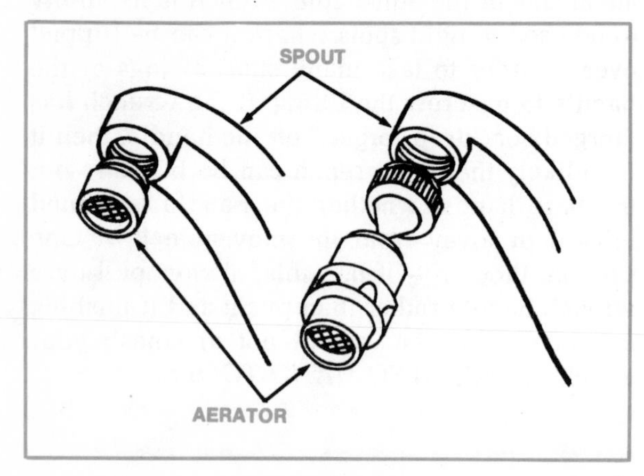

Faucet Aerator

Lawn Aerator

Various models of water aerators are available, depending upon the kind and size of spout fixture to which the unit attaches.

The second kind of aerator can be used in caring for lawns and gardens. The turf aerator perforates tightly compacted earth for better penetration of air, water, and fertilizer.

While commercial turf aerators are available, the average homeowner will find more suitable the smaller units that attach to hand or power mowers. *SEE ALSO LAWNS & GARDENS.*

A-Frame Cabin

[SEE VACATION HOMES.]

A-Frame Sawhorse

[SEE SAWHORSE CONSTRUCTION.]

Aggregate

[SEE CONCRETE.]

Air Chamber

An air chamber is a capped branch of pipe a little over a foot long, used to eliminate the crashing bang you sometimes hear when you turn off a faucet quickly.

This bang, which plumbers call *water hammer* is caused by the fact that the water, coursing through the pipes is suddenly brought up short. Since water is almost incompressible, it crashes to a stop.

An air chamber extends upward from the regular water pipe, close to the faucet. Since it contains only air when it's capped, and the entrained air in the water keeps it filled with air, water can get into the chamber only by compressing air. This compression provides a cushion that eliminates the water hammer.

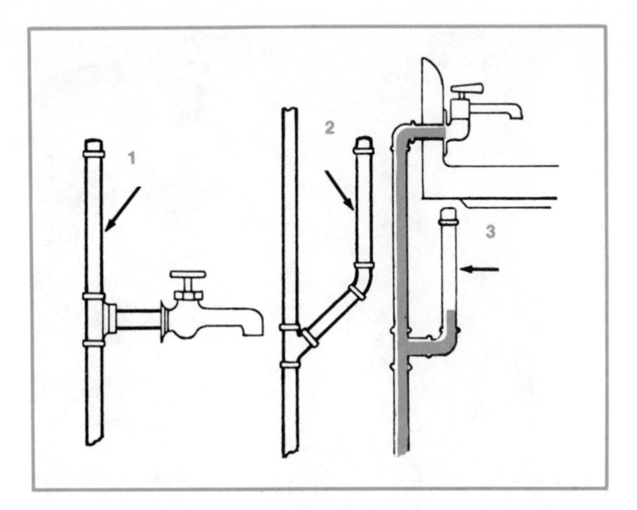

An air chamber may be located (1) just above faucet on inside of wall, (2) on vertical run, (3) or under sink.

Unless you know exactly what these vertical, dead-end pipes are, you may think they are just evidence of false starts by a plumber who changed his mind about extending the water pipes. *SEE ALSO PLUMBING REPAIRS.*

Air Conditioner Repair

Air conditioners maintain a designated temperature in an entire room or even a house. They operate by passing air from this area across the evaporator coil where heat units are absorbed. Heat is given off through the condenser located outside the home.

The portion of the air conditioner that extends into the room is the evaporator section. There is a separate fan for the evaporator and one for the condenser, although both fans are often driven by the same double-shaft motor. The air is pulled in one of the grills of the air conditioner and forced out the other while it is in operation. Most of these units are designed to keep the fans and blowers operating even when the thermostat has cycled the compressor off. There are good reasons for this. It keeps cold air from settling near floor level and keeps the room more comfortable.

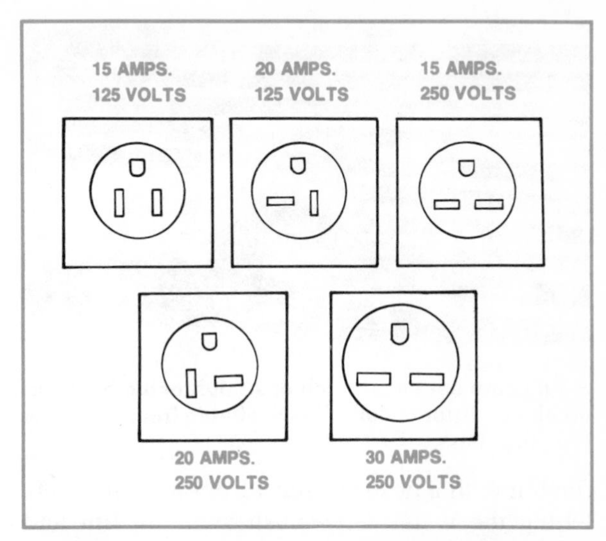

Air conditioner plugs are varied to suit capacity of unit. Never change from one type plug to another. Use correct size circuit and the proper receptacle for air conditioners.

Although the evaporator coils are normally operated at temperatures above freezing, they can begin to ice if blockage in air flow occurs. This can happen if a filter becomes clogged, or if a filter allows lint and dirt to pass through and accumulate on the coils of the air conditioner. To clean an air conditioner filter, first check and see if it is the washable-foam type as many are. If so,

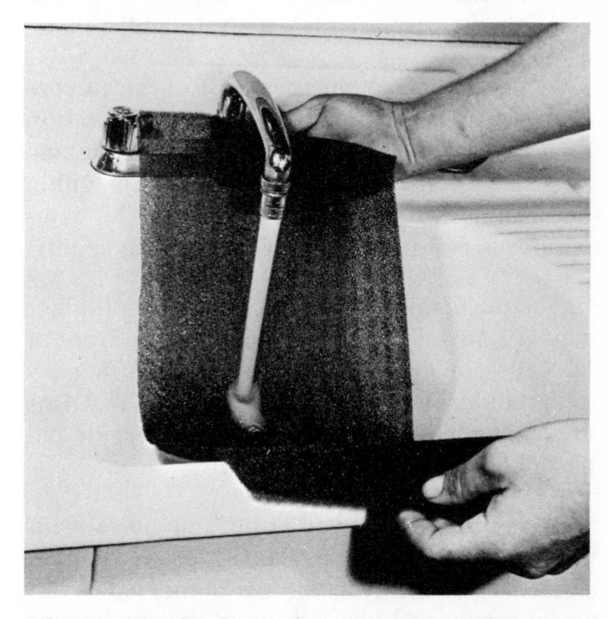

Filters must be kept clean on air conditioners. Washable type can be removed and cleaned at sink as required.

A fin comb does a good job of straightening bent fins on air conditioner coils. It is available from refrigeration suppliers.

flush it with a hose or faucet from the back side, letting the water force push away all lint and dirt. Then rinse it out thoroughly under a faucet and allow it to dry before reinstalling in the air conditioner. Other models have a disposable, fiberglass type filter which must be replaced. The size filter your unit uses will be printed on the old filter.

If the coils have become blocked with dirt it is necessary to use a cleaner. Spray a household cleaner on, let it stand for a few minutes, then spray some fresh water on to wash both the cleaner and dirt away. If fins are bent, you can obtain a fin comb, a device which can be pulled along the fins of the coil, to help straighten them.

Keep the louvers on the room side of the air conditioner turned upwards. The air circulation then tends to be forced towards the ceiling and falls toward floor level, keeping the air within the room in constant motion and the temperatures more even from floor level to ceiling.

Check the condenser side of the air conditioner as well. Any shrubbery which grows in front of the coils can block air flow and reduce efficiency and should be pruned away. Be sure that fins and coils on the condenser side are straight and clean also.

You may notice a hissing or buzzing noise from the area of the condenser fan. Most water that condenses on the evaporator is channeled to run to a sump located just in front of the condenser. The condenser fan has a "slinger ring" built around it which picks up the water and throws it

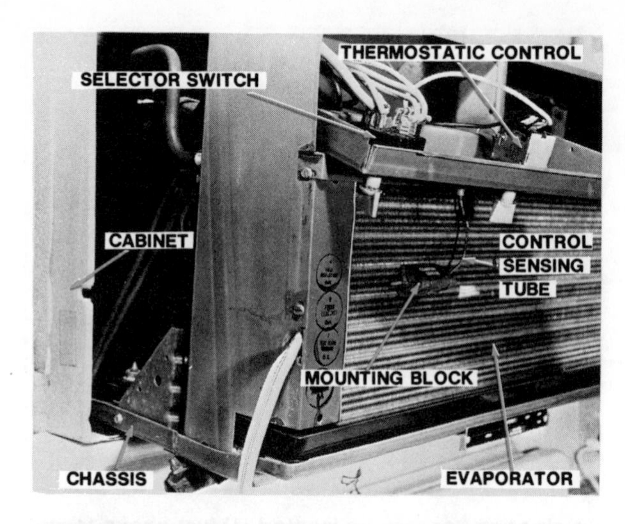

When air conditioner has slide-out chassis, remove front panel and slide the chassis forward for servicing. Oil the fan motor, if ports are provided, at the beginning of the season.

against the hot condenser. It serves two purposes: increases the efficiency of the air conditioner by some 10 to 20% to some estimates, and it helps to evaporate the excess moisture. Remember to unplug the unit and remove all power from the circuit wherever you are checking it.

Some air conditioning blower motors require lubrication. To do this, unplug the unit and remove the inside grill. Most units have a slide-out chassis, which can simply be pulled forward to release it from the outer cabinet. Look for any plugs or oil ports on the condenser fan motor. If they have them, apply about three drops of SAE-20 non-detergent motor oil or the lubricant recommended by the manufacturer.

Switches and wiring components on air conditioners must be tested with a continuity tester to see if they are in good order. Many air conditioning systems use a large running capacitor and often a starting capacitor as well for the compressor. Before these are tested, they must first be discharged by using a 20,000 ohm, two-watt, wire-wound resistor wrapped in tape. Be sure and do this *before* the capacitor is handled in any way as the capacitor acts as a storehouse for electricity and can store a dangerous and, possibly fatal, electrical charge. It must be handled

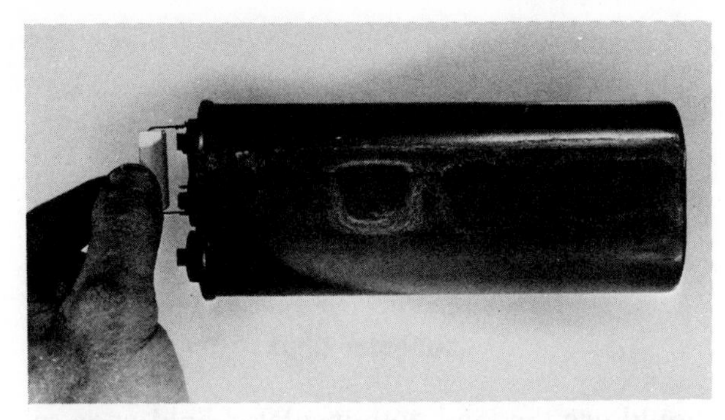

A large capacitor such as this can store up quite a jolt. They must be discharged with 20,000 ohm two-watt wire-wound resistor for handling or testing. Resistor and exposed leads should be wrapped in tape. They were left exposed here for photo.

with care. When a chassis is pulled from the front of an air conditioning unit, it is wise to clean any passageways through which water flows to the condenser. Sometimes these can become blocked with algae. A thorough washing, followed by a rinse with household ammonia, should eliminate the algae and prevent its growth.

Air Conditioning

[SEE AUTOMOBILE AIR CONDITIONING & HEATING & HOME AIR CONDITIONING.]

Air-drying Cement

Air-drying cement handles like a sandmix, dries in a few hours, and will not set under water. *SEE ALSO CONCRETE*

Air Pipe

The distribution mechanism of a warm-air heating system is composed of air pipe, or ductwork. Air pipe begins its route through the heating system from either the furnace plenum (the warm air storage unit) or from an extended plenum. Air pipe may be round or rectangular and is made from aluminum or galvanized steel. Round air pipe is available in six and eight inch diameters (also larger and smaller ones) and in two and five feet lengths. Round air pipe provides for easy installation but has limited use. Rectangular ducts are commonly used for large installations and where plans for air conditioning installations are included. *SEE ALSO HEATING SYSTEMS.*

Alarm Systems

[SEE HOME ALARM SYSTEMS.]

Aliphatic Resin Glue

Aliphatic resin glue resembles a heavy cream and comes in squeeze bottles which are ready to use. It is water-resistant for the interior use. This glue is best used for indoor woodworking jobs and repairs in the household. *SEE ALSO ADHESIVES.*

Alkyd

Alkyd is a classification for paints having synthetic alkyd resins rather than oils as a base. These paints are available in both enamel and flat finishes and rank above the more conventional oil paints in quality. Alkyd resin based paints dry rapidly. They have excellent color and gloss retention. They are also tough, durable and easy to apply. Because alkyd based paints are odorless, they should be thinned with an odorless solvent. *SEE ALSO PAINTS & PAINTING.*

Allen Screw

The Allen screw has a head with a hexagonal socket instead of the slot found in most wood or sheet metal screws. These screws act to bolt metal parts together and are adjusted with an Allen wrench. *SEE ALSO FASTENERS.*

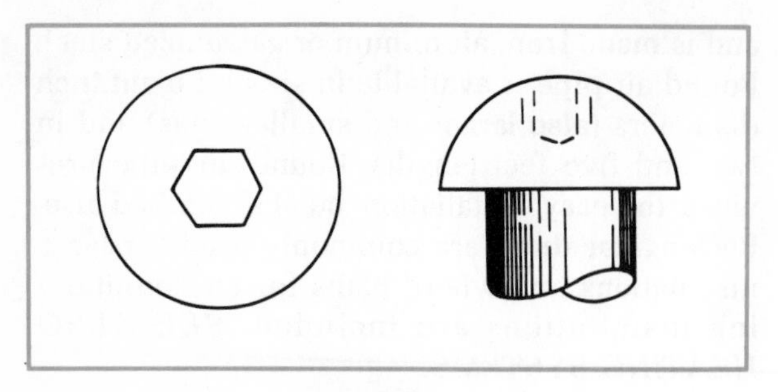

Allen Screw

Allen Wrench

The Allen wrench, often called a hex or key wrench, adjusts Allen screws and other headless setscrews. These wrenches are available in sets containing sizes to fit every size setscrew. Because the most-often used Allen wrenches are frequently misplaced, it is a good idea to buy a set with inseparable keys. Allen heads are also available to fit socket wrench sets. *SEE ALSO HAND TOOLS.*

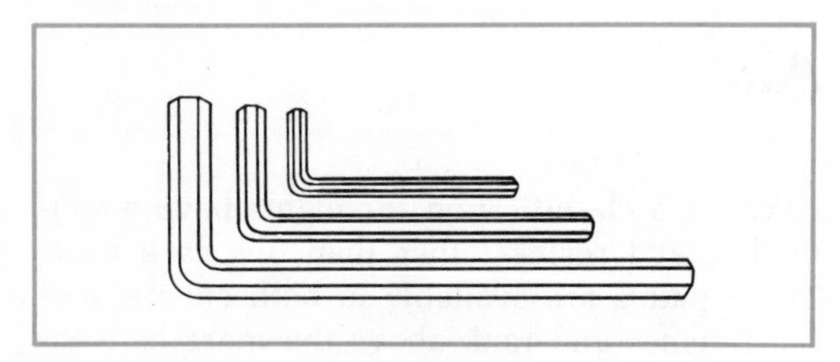

Allen Wrench

Alligator Clips

Alligator clips are fasteners which have sawlike notches along their edges. They are used mainly with T.V. and radio wires as temporary hook-ups, and may be used on electrical test boards for testing battery and bell wiring.

When testing normal electrical lines in the household, the average handyman needs to avoid the open contacts. When using these clips while the current is on, the advanced handyman

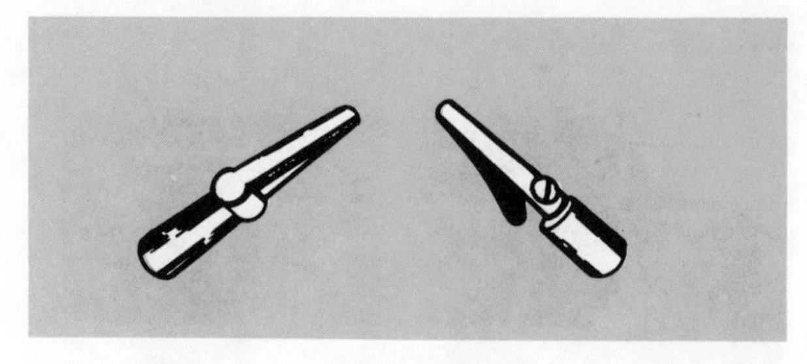

Alligator Clips

should use the kind with insulated hold-ends so that he will not be in contact with exposed ends.

Alligatoring

Alligatoring is a defect in a painted surface characterized by cracks and crazes in the paint film that resembles the hide of an alligator. The defect often goes all the way to the original surface. One painting error that causes this problem is spreading too much paint onto a damp, greasy or resinous surface. Another mistake is applying multiple coats of paint over an already improperly chalked surface. This causes the new paint to build up too thickly, not accommodating the swelling and shrinking of the wood.

If alligatoring covers a great deal of painted surface, and especially when it has begun to affect the original surface, the repair job can be a tough and costly one, as the entire surface has to be stripped down to the bare wood, sanded as smoothly as possible, dusted, primed and repainted. Often it is just as reasonable to have the house re-sided, and avoid the repair process altogether. *SEE ALSO PAINTS & PAINTING.*

All-Purpose Portable Tools Table

You can't beat the convenience of portable tools in any work situation where it's better to apply the tool to the job, but the reverse is also true.

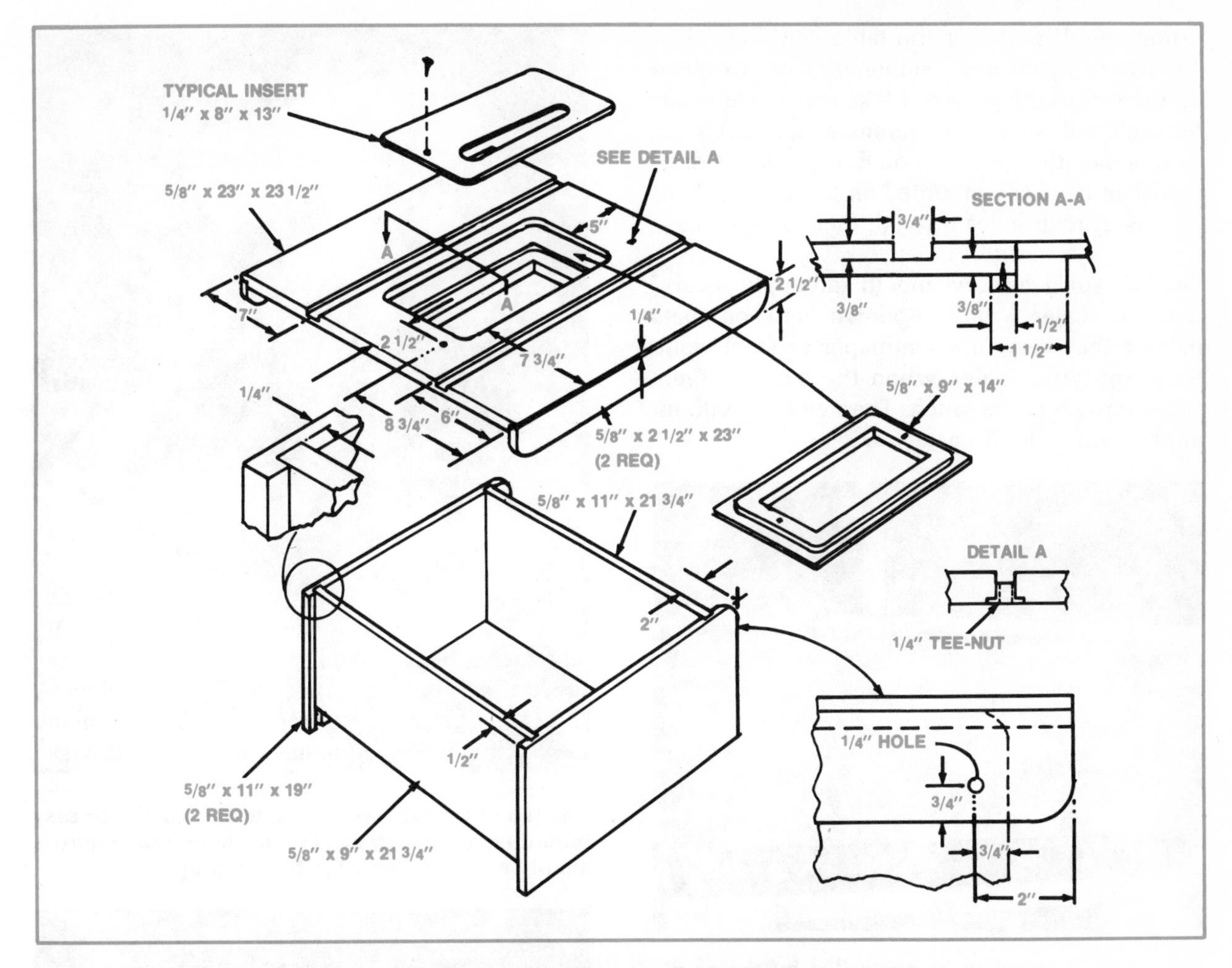

Construction details of the basic table. A hardboard covered plywood is a good choice for material because it takes abuse and will hold up a long time.

Quite often it's easier to work more precisely when the tool is stationary and you apply the work to it. With this multi-purpose table, you can convert your portable tools to stationary tools.

Picture the table as a sturdy box with a hinged top. The big 23" x 23$^1/_2$" top provides more useful working surface than most 8" circular saws. It is completely portable; you can set it on a bench or even a pair of saw-horses that are spanned with a sheet of plywood. You can also organize it around a freestanding unit of its own. A system of interchangeable inserts provides for the use of each hand-held power tool.

Most of the construction work can be done with portable tools. Form dadoes with your cutoff saw by setting blade projection to the required depth and make repeat, overlapping passes to achieve the width. A straightedge, clamped to the work, will guide the saw to assure parallel cuts.

For slots, drill a series of overlapping holes on a common center line and then clean up with a file. Internal cutouts are easy to do with a sabre saw.

You want to be careful to keep the dadoes in the table top parallel to the table opening and to the table sides. These grooves will be guides for the miter gauge so accuracy of the finished machine relates strongly to the care you use when making it. Since the end result can be a lifetime tool, it pays to use extra time to make it correctly.

Complete all parts for the table saw first; then you can use your new "stationary saw" to speed up the rest of the project. Make a separate insert for each tool you plan to mount, adapting it to accommodate the specific tool. Except for the drill, tools can be easily mounted on the underside of the insert with holes through their baseplates.

Sand all surfaces very smooth and apply several coats of sealer with a rubdown between coats using either very fine sandpaper or steel wool. Stop applying sealer when the surface feels supersmooth to the touch. Then end up with an application of hard paste wax.

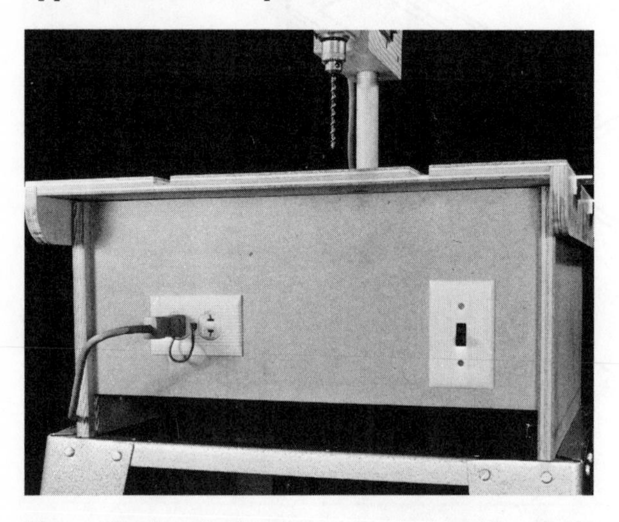

The outlet is wired to be controlled by the on-off switch. Tool switches are locked in the "on" position, and the cords are plugged into the outlet. Therefore, you control tool activity with the table switch.

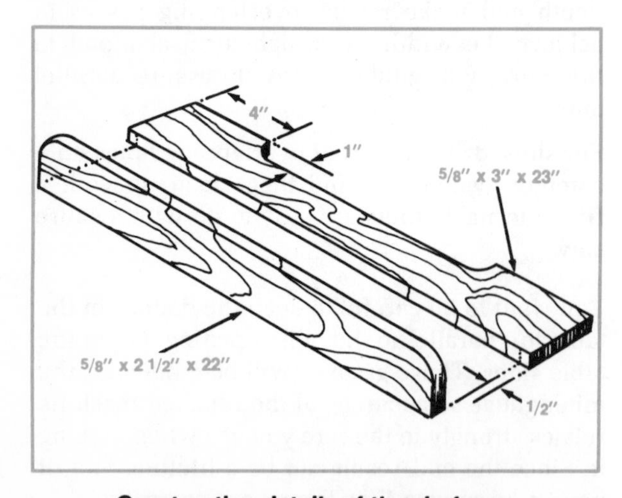

Construction details of the rip fence.

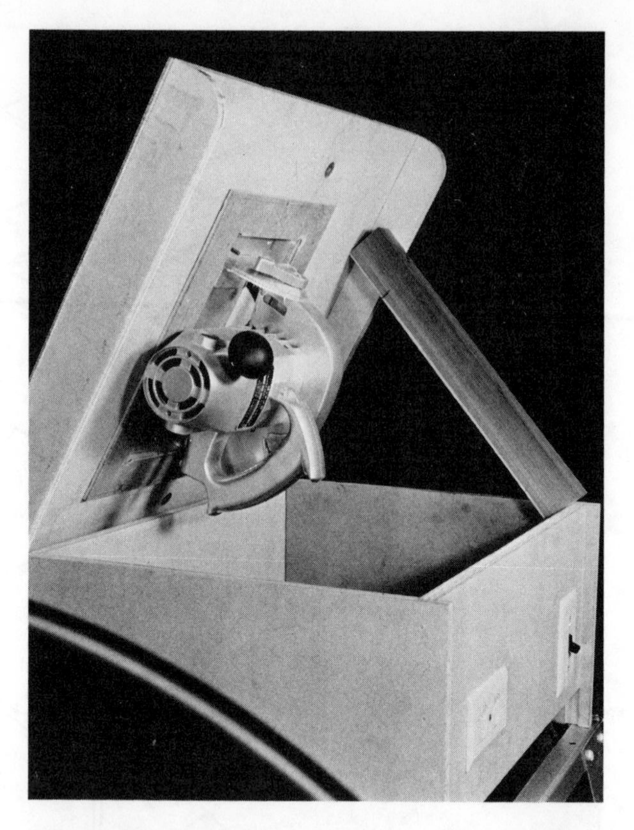

The top of the table pivots on two 1/4" bolts for easy mounting of any tool. The stick in the photo is simply a prop to keep the table top up.

The rip fence is used by setting it parallel to the saw blade and clamping it in place. It becomes a very efficient table saw with a work surface that is larger than those of many of the smaller table saws you can buy.

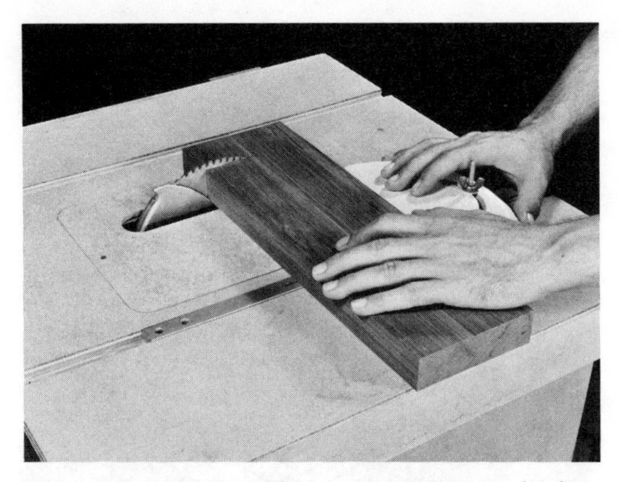

The miter gauge is used for crosscutting or mitering. If you wish, you can mark the miter-gauge head for various settings. You can even buy a ready-made miter gauge and cut the table slots to suit.

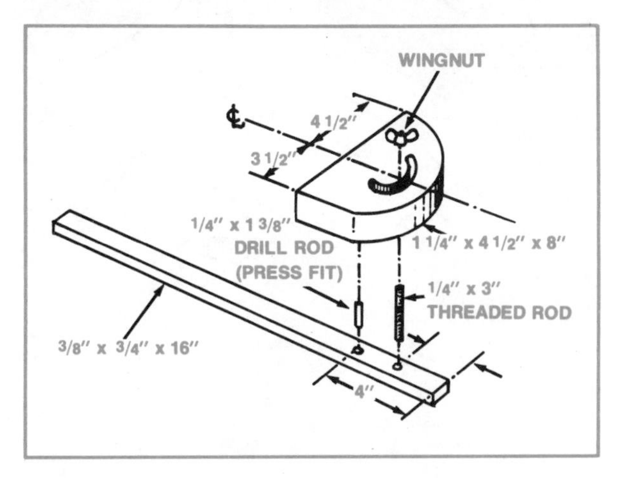

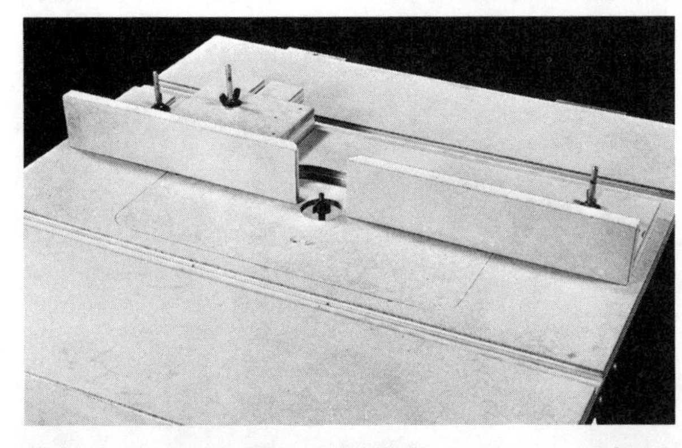

This arrangement for use of the router provides a good shaper setup. The fences are individually adjustable; depth of cut is achieved by working the router's own mechanism, as you would when using it freehand.

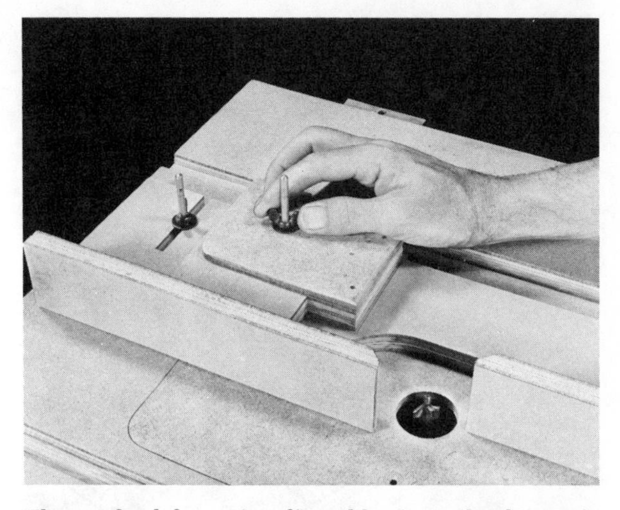

The outfeed fence is adjustable. In a "back" position, it is in line with the infeed fence.

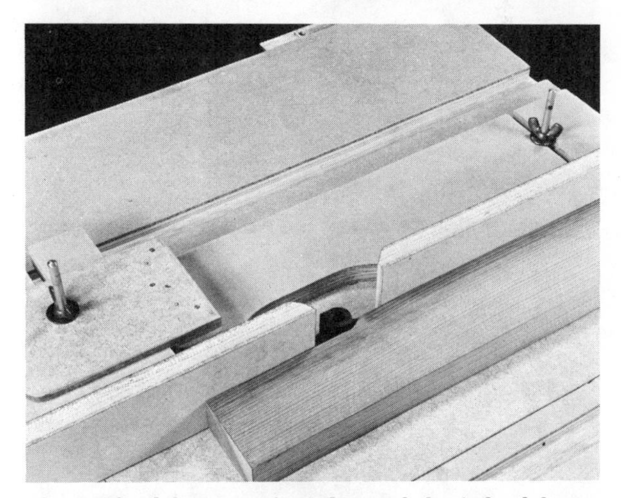

The outfeed fence projects beyond the infeed fence by the depth of the cut to allow for it when the entire edge of the stock is to be removed.

Adjust the fence as a unit to set for depth of cut when only a portion of the stock edge is to be removed by the cut.

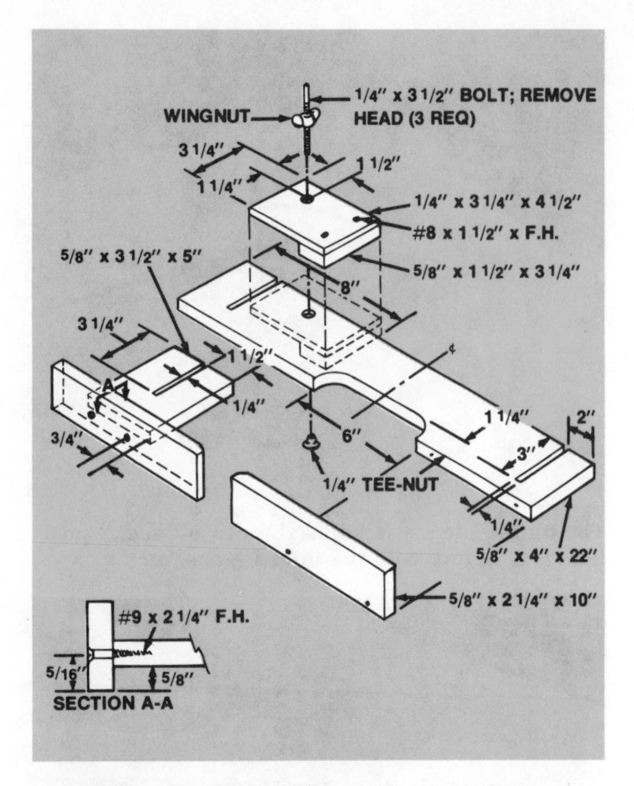

Construction details of the router-shaper setup.

Small drum sanders may be mounted in the router for light sanding jobs; but since the speed of any router is excessive for such work, apply very light pressure. You can experiment with other type cutters, such as burrs and flies.

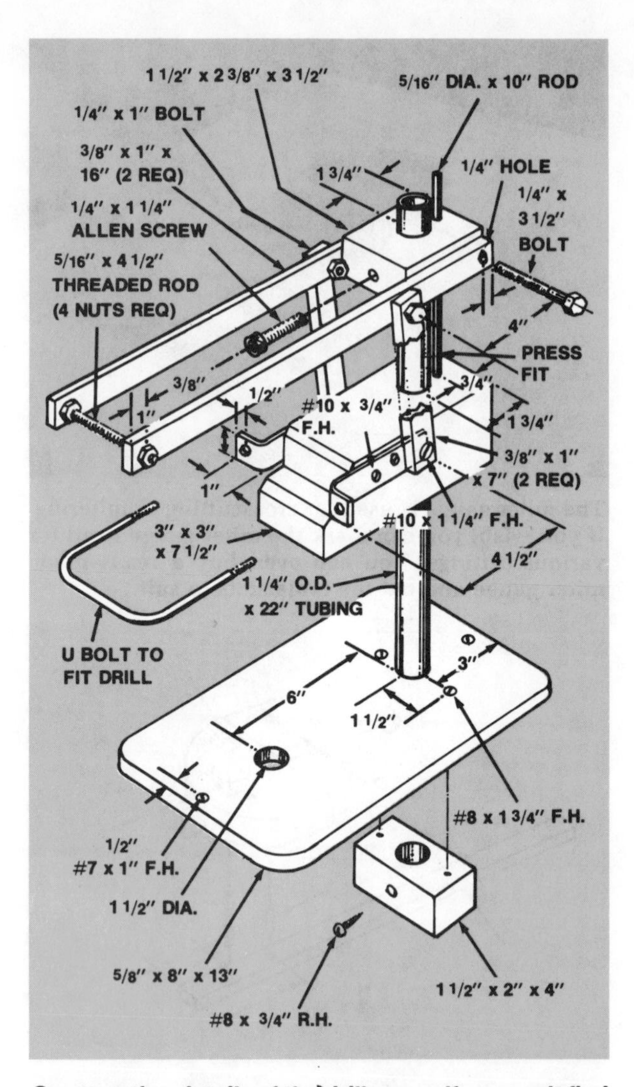

Construction details of the drill press. If you can't find a U-bolt that works correctly for you, you can easily bend one up out of threaded rod. Make the hole in the mounting block so that the column fits in it tightly.

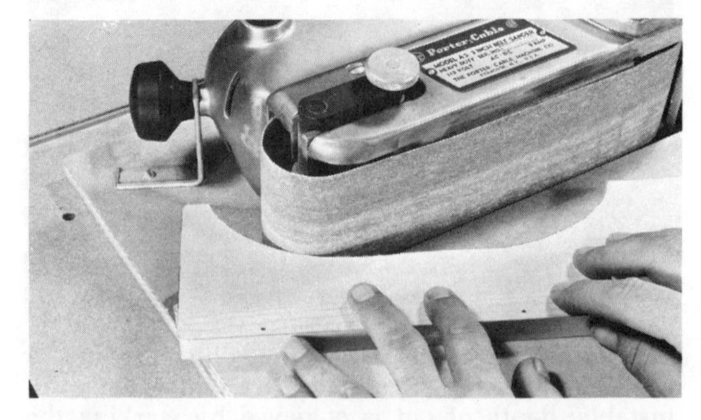

Use the front end of the sander to smooth inside curves.

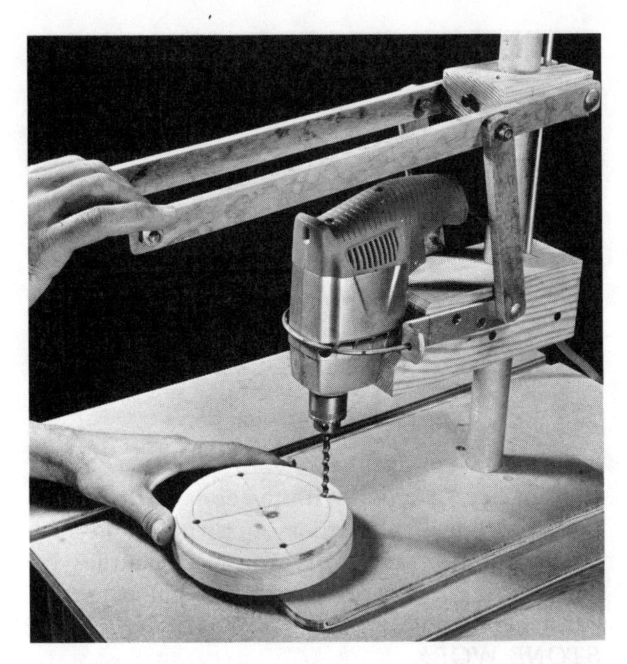

The drill press design may have to be modified in some details to fit your drill, but the basic design will work for most models. Shape the front end of the drill mounting block to fit the case of your particular tool. Use a U bolt to hold your drill to the mounting block.

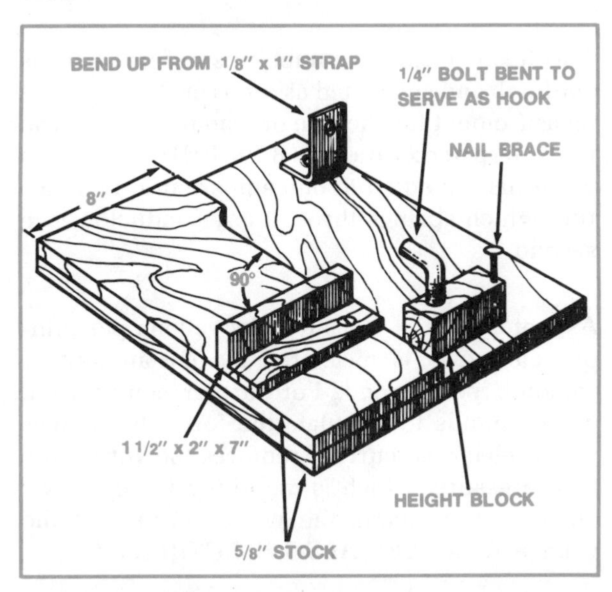

The belt sander has a mounting of its own, but a standard insert can be attached to the underside so the assembly can be fitted easily to the table. Raised work surface follows belt contour for sanding curves. Bend a piece of $^1/_8$" strap steel to the shape shown and drill a hole through the vertical leg to fit the knob-base. You can make the L-shaped holddown from a $^1/_4$" bolt.

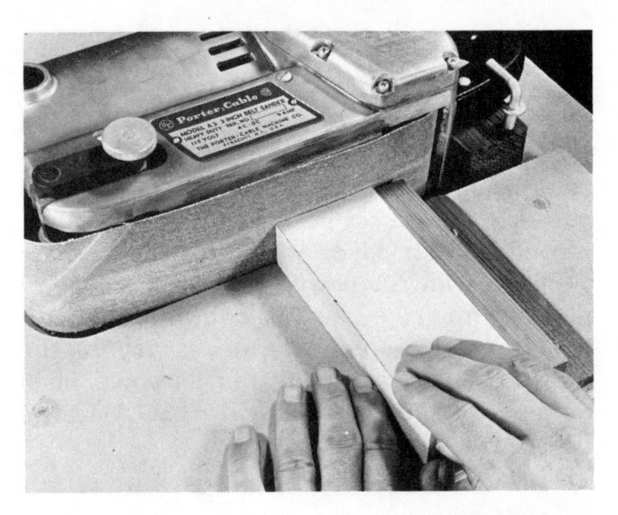

A detachable stop is a valuable addition to the sander setup. Angle between it and the abrasive surface should be 90° so the sanded ends will be square.

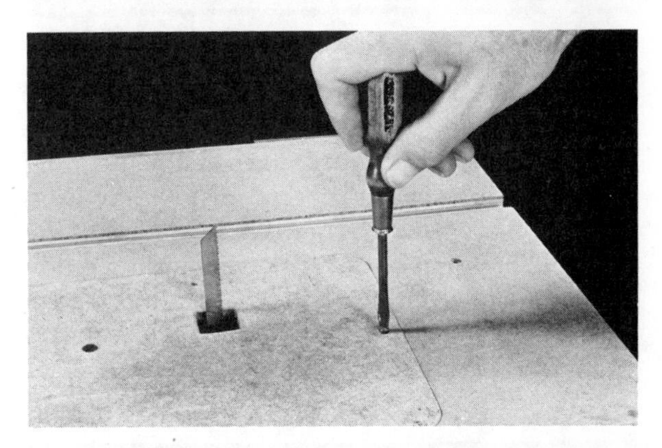

Mounting a portable jigsaw to the underside of a table insert gives you a very efficient stationary saber-sawing setup.

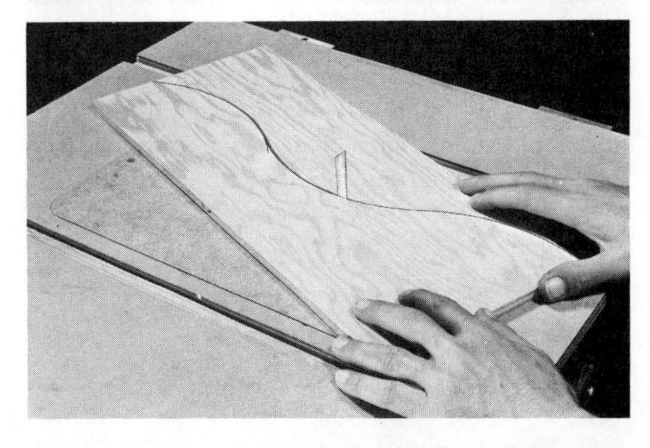

All the blades you normally use in the saber saw can be utilized when the tool is mounted in the table. In this position the blade cuts on the "down" stroke so good side of stock should be facing upwards.

Alternating Current

Alternating current (AC) is a type of electrical current that reverses itself 60 times (cycles) per second. Most modern wiring installations are supplied with AC power because this type of current must be used in conjunction with transformers which are necessary in the transportation of electricity from the power plant to the wiring installation. *SEE ALSO WIRING SYSTEMS, ELECTRICAL.*

Aluminum Oxide

Aluminum oxide is a hard, tough synthetic abrasive made by fusing bauxite clay in an electric furnace. This very sharp and fast-cutting abrasive is fast becoming the most widely-used material for making sandpaper. Made in the form of sheets, belts and disks, aluminum oxide is used extensively for polishing stainless steel and for finishing high-carbon steel and bronze. *SEE ALSO ABRASIVES.*

Alundum Wheel

An alundum wheel is a grinding wheel which contains aluminum oxide, a man-made abrasive that is extremely hard. This wheel may be used for most any sharpening job. *SEE ALSO TOOL SHARPENING.*

American Bond

American Bond is a masonry term used to describe a brick laying pattern, known also as *common bond.* In this pattern, which is called a *header row,* every fifth to seventh course (or row) of bricks is laid with the ends of the bricks facing forward. The other courses are laid with the side edges facing forward. These courses are called *stretchers.* This bricklaying pattern is the easiest and cheapest to lay. *SEE ALSO BRICK & STONE WORK.*

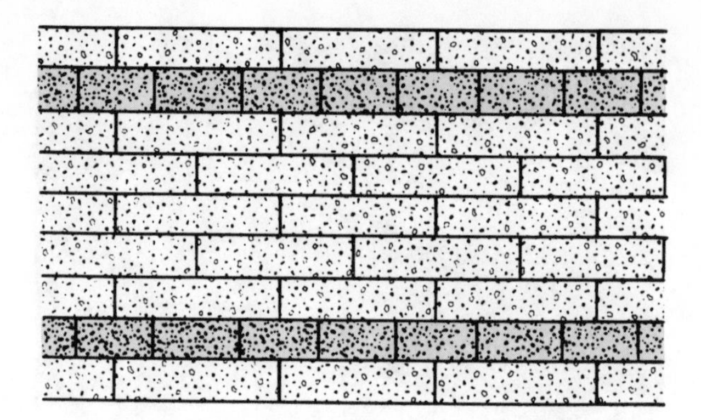

American or common bond.

Ampere

The term *ampere,* sometimes referred to as *coulomb* and shortened as *amps* or *A,* is a unit of measurement for the rate or amount of electrical flow. Approximately 6.28 billion billion electrons are equal to one ampere of direct current which springs through any conductor each second.

As water flow is measured by gallons per minute, electricity is measured by one ampere or coulomb per second. For further comparison, using pounds to calculate the force that moves water, electrical current requires the very same type pressure, which is measured in volts. The amperes flow along the wires because of the voltage force. *SEE ALSO ELECTRICITY.*

Amplifier

An amplifier is an electronic device used in phonographs, radio or TV to produce an increased sound volume and/or sound quality. The amplifier magnifies or multiplies the weak electrical signal (sound) from the instrument, allowing for operation of one or more loudspeakers, which convert the magnified electrical signals into audible sound waves. *SEE ALSO STEREO SYSTEMS.*

Anchor Bolts

Anchor bolts are square-headed fasteners used to secure stock to masonry or wood. An anchor bolt is used frequently to secure fence posts to concrete. It is more commonly used to fasten wood sills to foundations. Sills are held in place by washers and nuts put over the anchor bolts. *SEE ALSO FASTENERS.*

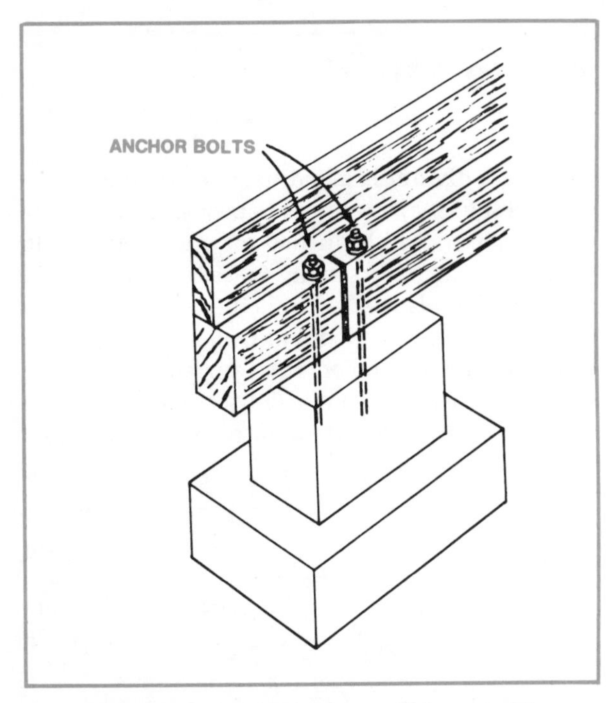

Anchor bolt used to secure sill to concrete.

Anchors

Anchors are used to keep a boat from moving due to tides, currents or winds. Most anchors are

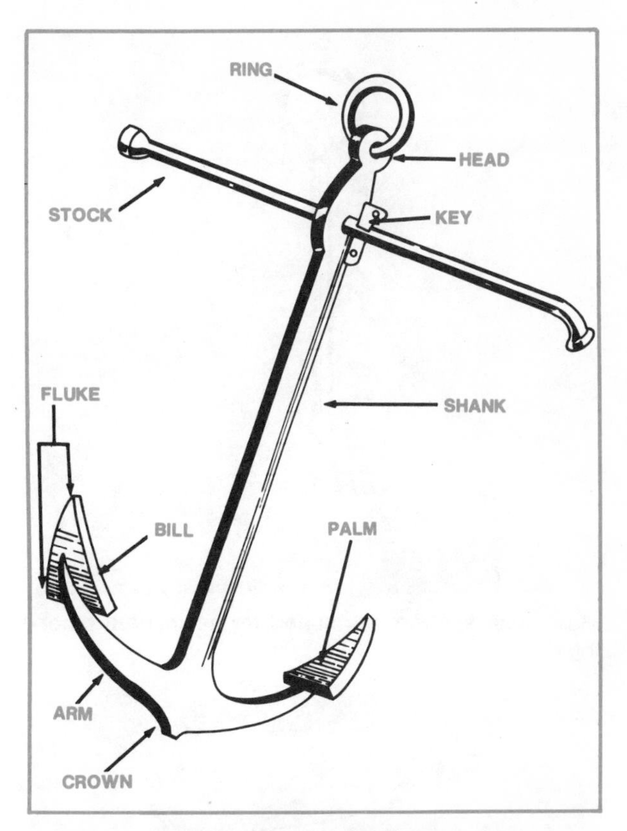

Yachtsman Anchor Parts

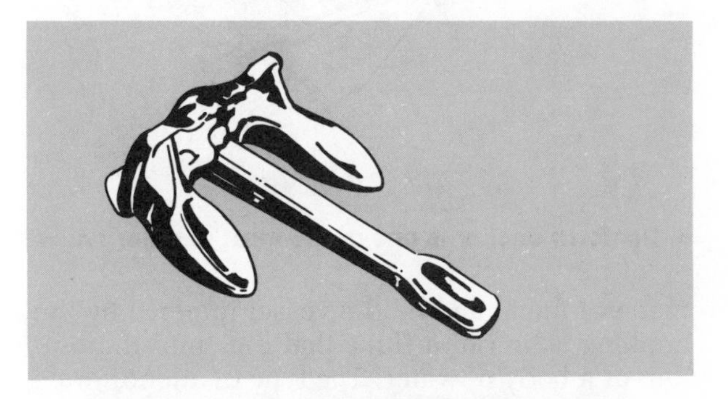

A navy, or stockless, anchor has no stock.

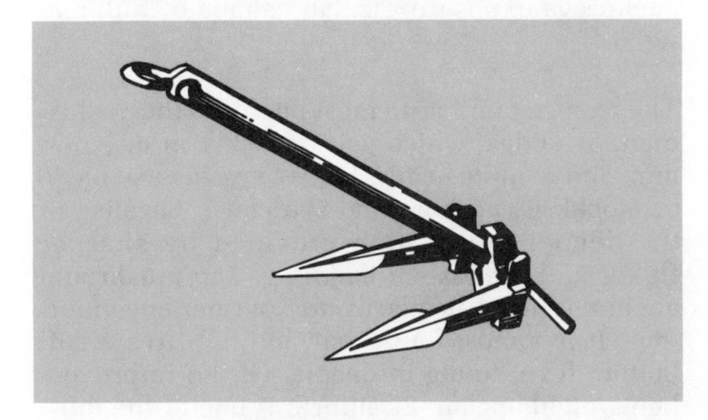

An improved version of a navy anchor is a sea claw.

Mushroom anchors are suited for permanent moorings.

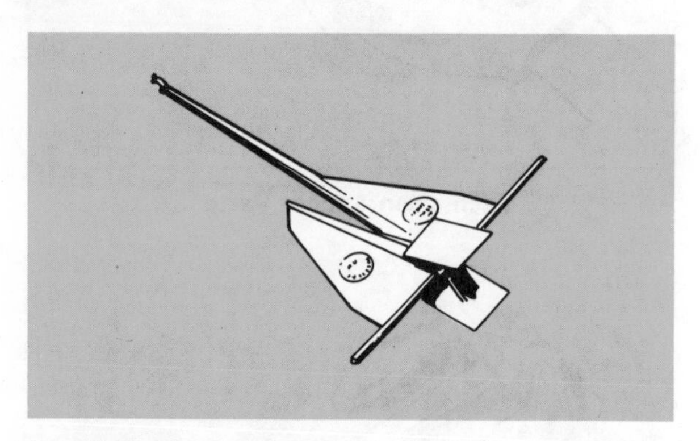

A Danforth anchor is one of the most popular types.

made of metal and hold a vessel in place by the hooking action of a fluke that digs into the bottom of a body of water. The type of anchor to be used depends on factors such as type of bottom, anchorage exposure, size and shape of hull and wind.

The anchor familiar to most people is the yachtsman, or kedge, which grips quickly in any bottom, and is quite heavy. Larger vessels use navy, or stockless, anchors and sea claws because of the deeper penetration provided by sharper flukes and the ease of handling. The mushroom anchor is used primarily for permanent moorings. It is almost foul-proof, but requires a soft bottom for it to dig in deeply. Of the improved, lightweight anchors, Danforth is one of the most popular because of its deep and quick penetration provided by longer flukes and its ease of handling and storage. *SEE ALSO RECREATIONAL BOATS & BOATING.*

Anchors & Fasteners

[SEE FASTENERS.]

Angle Bead

An angle bead is a vertical bead made of wood or metal, which is placed on exterior angles of plastered walls for protection. This bead, which is also called a staff bead, is used to conceal the joint made by two walls where they meet at right angles. *SEE ALSO MOLDING & TRIM.*

Angle Divider

The angle divider is an adjustable wood measuring tool that serves many purposes. As with a T-bevel, it is possible to use an angle divider to transfer a specific angle to several pieces of work. It also bisects, or finds the center of angles formed where two pieces of wood meet to form a joint. When working on a flat surface, the square blade may also be used as a try square in testing corners and joints for squareness. *SEE ALSO HAND TOOLS.*

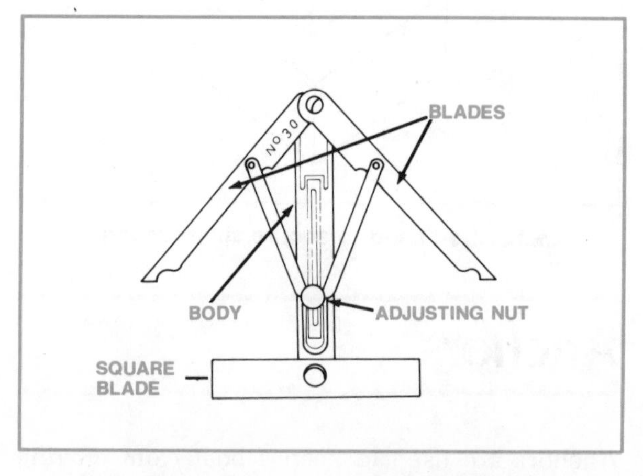

Basic parts of an angle divider.

Angle Iron

An angle iron is a fastener with pre-drilled holes, usually made of steel and bent so that the sides form a 90° angle. They are available in decorative finishes and can be found in hardware stores.

Also known as corner braces, these mending plates are available in different sizes and thicknesses, and used in reinforcing and repairing wood furniture joints. They are attached with

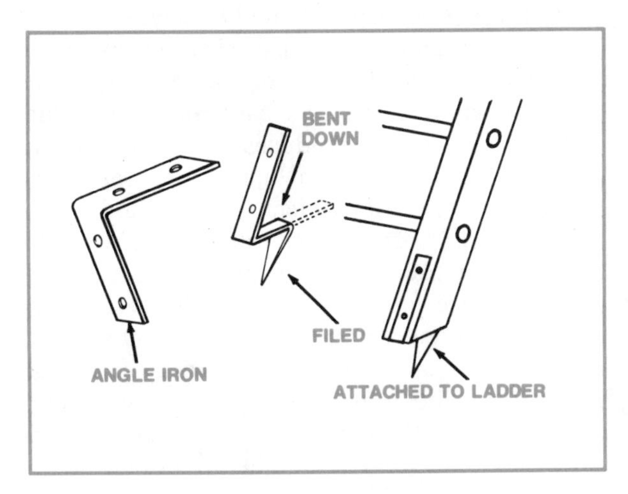

One use of an Angle Iron

flathead screws, which tighten in flush with the metal surface of the iron. They can be placed either inside or outside the joint.

Angle irons are also used in joining metal to metal or metal to wood. Sheet metal screws or flathead bolts and nuts are used when joining metal pieces together.

Angle irons can fulfill other needs around the household, when used with a little imagination. In ladder safety, for example, one side of both irons is bent down at a right angle, and filed to a point, forming a 'Z' shape in the brace. The brace is then attached to the ladder so that the point sticks into the ground when the ladder is placed upright, keeping the ladder steady.

Angle-Sprayed Texture Plywood

Angle-sprayed textured plywood changes character and color as your view of it changes. A straight-on view shows an equal combination of color and wood finish; a view from the angle sprayed shows nearly solid color; the view from the opposite angle reveals mostly wood finish. Produce this effect on straited plywood by spraying close to the surface at a flat angle. The spray hits and colors one side of the texture, while the opposite side stays light. Two colors sprayed from opposite angles will also give a striking effect.

Angle Valve

[SEE SHUT-OFF VALVE.]

Annual Rings

Annual rings, also known as growth rings, are layers of wood which normally form around the center of the tree trunk each year (or growth period) and, in cross-section, indicate the age of the tree.

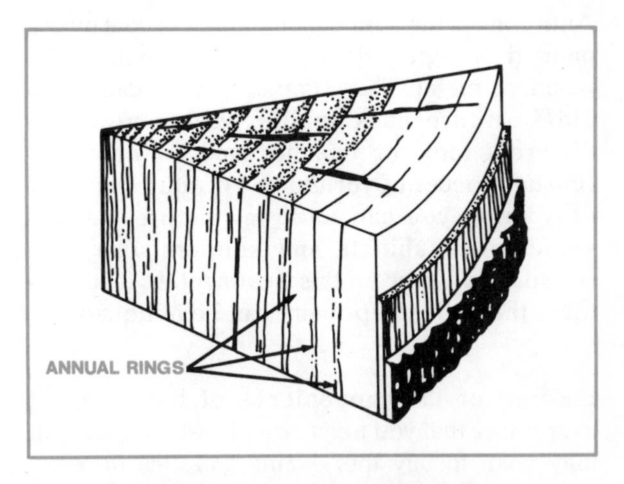

Annual rings shown in cross-section.

Antifreeze

Antifreeze is a substance added to liquids to lower their freezing points. It is used in automobile radiators and in home plumbing systems.

In automobile radiators, antifreeze is mixed with water using proportions based on the lowest temperature expected in an area. For example, if the temperature is predicted to drop to 0°, the ratio of antifreeze to water should be 33 percent antifreeze to 67 percent water. Most cans of antifreeze have instructions for mixing. In recent years, antifreeze has been recommended for year-round use in an automobile's cooling system also. The high boiling point of antifreeze helps prevent radiators from boiling over in the summer.

In home plumbing systems, traps should be drained and then filled with premixed automobile antifreeze to protect them from freezing if the home will be unheated during the winter season.

Antiquing

Antiquing is the application of a glaze coat over a painted background to mellow the look of the wood or metal. This simple process can bring old furniture back to life with a new and different look, or can be used on new, unfinished pieces of furniture. Furniture isn't the only thing you can antique; picture frames, woodwork, cabinets and shutters also look beautiful when given this treatment. In fact, anything that will accept paint can be antiqued.

Because of the convenience of having most everything that you need already assembled, you may wish to buy the glazing supplies in a kit. However, many workers prefer to buy the materials separately. This method will enable you to make use of items already on hand. The following is an example of what is included in the standard antiquing kit purchased at your paint store; color base under-coat (latex- or oil-base), color glaze, a step-by-step instruction booklet, 2 paint brushes, steel wool, cheesecloth and sandpaper. If you intend to assemble your own materials or if you intend to use the kit, you will also need the following items: pliers and screwdriver, paint thinner, varnish, a tack rag, masking tape, drop cloth or newspapers, a wood filler and wipe-up rags.

The standard antique glaze is made by mixing 3 parts turpentine, 1 part boiled linseed oil and 1 part color (pigment). One part clear varnish may be substituted for the linseed oil. Use any color that will complement the base-coat color. The use of raw sienna produces a warm reddish tone, raw umber adds a lighter tone for light-toned paint and lampblack gives a dull tone which works best on dark or strong colors. We suggest that you use oil pigment, if possible. If you must use the more common universal colorant (the pigment carried by most paint stores), allow 1 or 2 hours after mixing (with occasional stirring) for the "universal liquid" to evaporate. If this liquid is not allowed to evaporate, it could be strong enough to soften the undercoat.

If you have purchased an assembled antiquing kit, read and follow the manufacturer's directions carefully. If you are using the separate items and have them assembled, you are ready to proceed with the steps outlined below.

PREPARING THE SURFACE

Remove or mask (cover) all hardware — hinges, handles, or drawer pulls. Use paint thinner to remove wax, polish, dirt and grease. Scratches, nicks and gouges can be filled with wood filler and sanded to a smooth finish. If you prefer the "aged" look that these defects lend, then don't fill them. Badly scarred tops may be left as naturally distressed finishes. Use fine sandpaper on any cracked or peeled surface, sanding the edges well to minimize the outline of any film breaks on the surface. It is not necessary to

Courtesy of SPRED Paints by Glidden

remove old finishes unless they are in poor condition. A quick rub with the fine sandpaper makes the undercoat go on more smoothly and cover better. Wipe away all dust with a tack rag.

APPLYING THE UNDERCOAT

Brush on the undercoat in short, overlapping strokes. Apply liberally, first brushing across the grain, then with the grain to assure even coverage. Allow this coat to dry thoroughly (1 to 4 hours for a latex-base paint, 24 hours for an oil-base enamel), then check to be certain that the old finish does not show through. If it does show, apply another coat of base paint, then allow this to dry completely before going to the next step.

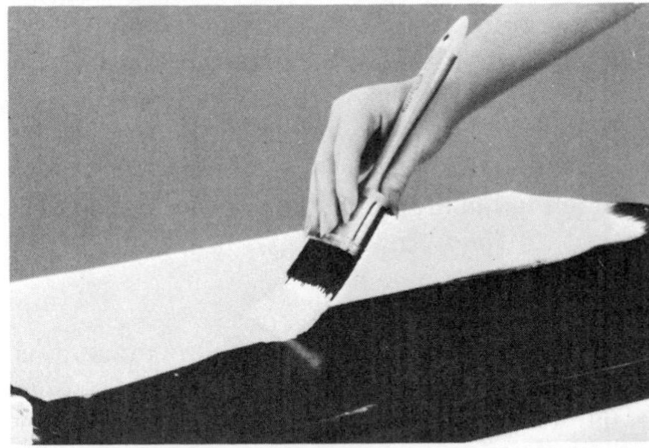

Courtesy of SPRED Paints by Glidden

APPLYING THE GLAZE

Apply the glaze liberally with a brush. Most glazes on the market today are formulated to set slowly enabling you to apply it to a complete surface before wiping. However, be sure to check the manufacturer's instructions. If you are using a glaze which *you* prepared, spread some on a small concealed area and check setting time. For large pieces, such as chests, it is best to glaze a small area at a time. Smaller pieces can usually be glazed completely before wiping.

Courtesy of SPRED Paints by Glidden

WIPING THE GLAZE

Wipe, working from the middle toward the edges. Glaze traces left in minute depressions on the surface are part of the desired effect. If you are not satisfied with the effects achieved, simply wipe the glaze off with a lint-free cloth saturated with paint thinner and start again.

Unusual patterns can be achieved by using different types of wiping materials. To achieve the look of wood grain, use a clean, dry, fairly stiff paint brush, spreading the glaze in long

Courtesy of SPRED Paints by Glidden

straight strokes on a partially wiped surface. The effects of stippling (speckles or flecks) can be obtained by dabbing the partially wiped glaze with the bristles of a brush. For a marbleized finish, crumple a sheet of plastic wrap, spread it on the glaze, then peel it off. For yet a different effect, spatter the glaze onto the surface with a broom, toothbrush or vegetable brush. Experiment with other materials such as newspaper, a sponge or carpeting until you achieve the pattern desired. Allow the glaze to dry completely (usually 1 to 2 days) before using.

FINISHING WITH VARNISH

This step is not necessary except for surfaces that are exposed to unusually tough wear. Apply a clear varnish after the glaze has completely dried. This should be applied without over-brushing, since the glazed surface may soften and streak. *SEE ALSO PAINTS & PAINTING.*

Courtesy of SPRED Paints by Glidden

Anvil

An anvil is a heavy steel or iron block used as a base when hammering or forging metalwork. It usually has a pointed or conical end which is used for shaping curved pieces of metal. The opposite end is rectangular shaped. The face, or working surface of the anvil, usually contains a square and a round hole which are utilized when working with cutting chisels. Some modern vises now come equipped with an anvil as part of the vise. An anvil should be placed on a strong timber or masonry foundation.

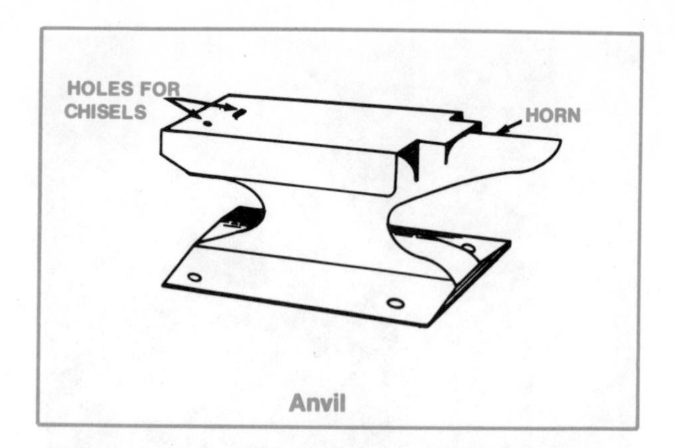

Anvil

Appalachian Hardwood

The beautiful and rugged mountains which extend from Maryland to Georgia comprise what is known as the Appalachian Hardwood Region. It has been recognized, both legally and botanically, as a distinct timber-producing area.

"Appalachian" is not a trade name. It describes high quality hardwoods of fine grain, uniform texture and distinctive character. In the Appalachian Mountains abundant rainfall, good soil and topography that promotes good drainage, combine a condition well suited to the growing of quality timber for which the area is justly famous.

When viewing the forested areas of the country, the dominating factors of the past are readily evident. Where the lumbermen dominated the economy, vast areas of forest land containing millions of feet of sawtimber still cover great parts of the area. Where agriculture has been the dominating factor, the land has been necessarily cleared for food crops and pasture, and little of the forest land remains.

In the Appalachian Region, where the mountains are not well suited to agriculture, except in some of the river valleys and fringe areas, timber operations have been an important segment of the economy for many years. Today, forests cover about two-thirds of the area and continue to support important forest industries. Cutting has not destroyed the forests.

Wood is traditionally modern and its warmth, beauty, character and interest never grows old. On the market place about 35% of the production of Appalachian Hardwoods goes into the manufacture of furniture; some 14% into flooring; about 11 % into architectural woodwork and housing; about 22% into industrial uses as pallets and containers and laminated trailer floors and the balance in others such as railroad ties and mine timbers. Interiors in the home include paneling, flooring, trim and cabinets. *SEE ALSO WOOD IDENTIFICATION.*

Courtesy of Appalachian Hardwood Manufacturers, Inc., High Point, N. C.

Appliance Repair, Major

Much of our life style today centers to a large extent around the appliances in our home. These appliances have reduced and in some cases eliminated the heavy chores of housekeeping. It is expensive to operate these appliances and even more costly to repair them. Both are good reasons to learn all you can about the appliances.

If you learn enough about your appliances, there is a very good chance that you can remedy a large majority of problems that may arise with them. You can also learn proper usage and maintenance which will prolong the life of the appliance.

Before beginning work on an appliance, become familiar with the way the equipment operates. This is essential to any sort of repair or maintenance. The best way to learn about the appliance is to study the information that is supplied with it.

Keep in mind that basic differences exist not only among brands but among individual models of the same brand of appliance. This is not intended to be a step-by-step servicing procedure as found in a service manual. However, if you apply the information and learn about your particular appliance, it helps you solve problems yourself as they arise, know how to take care of an appliance and to maintain it properly and, hopefully, allow you to realize why certain steps or procedures are necessary.

This information should be helpful to you even though you don't carry out any actual service work. This is true because a better understanding of the appliance leads to better habits of usage and preventive maintenance. It also makes it easier to place the service call and to make observations which can help the service technician to bring the correct parts and equipment the first time he comes.

One other thing that should be emphasized is that more than one-third of all service calls made by technicians each year are due to problems not related to the machine. Most of these relate to such things as blown fuses, appliances that are unplugged, or failure to use the machine correctly. Moreover, the instruction manual that comes with most appliances contains fairly detailed information about what to do if your particular appliance doesn't work. A quick check of this information can help eliminate service calls.

Replacing a fuse can often save a service call. Know the fuses which protect appliance circuits and install a good fuse even if old one doesn't appear to be blown, sometimes appearances are deceiving. Use time-delay type fuses on circuits with motors connected to them. Turn power off by pulling main switch before handling fuse. It is a good idea to stand on a board or other insulating material.

To reset a circuit breaker, first flip it to the off position and then all the way back to the on position. If it again trips, immediately check the appliance for a short circuit or ground.

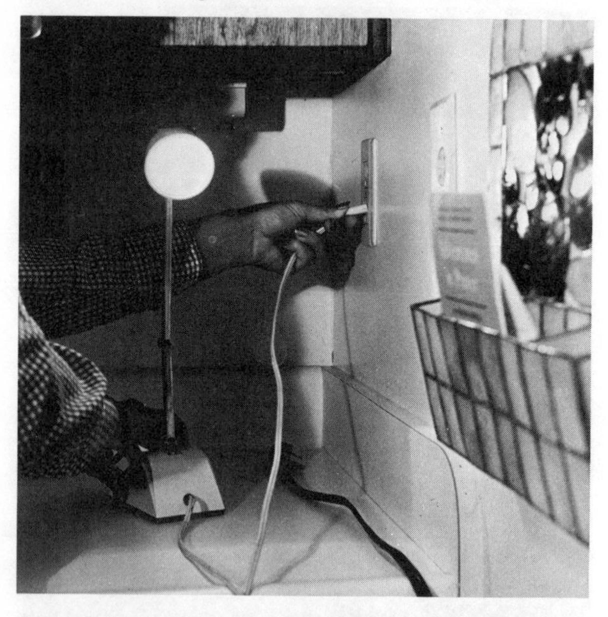

One of the easiest tests is to plug a small table lamp into the receptacle when an appliance fails to operate. If lamp lights, you know that voltage is reaching the receptacle. The fuse and/or circuit breaker is good in this case.

One of the best ways to be sure that a call is not unnecessary is to first check to see that power is reaching the appliance. In the case of 115-volt appliances this is easily done by plugging a table lamp into the receptacle. If the light operates, you know that power is reaching it. In the case of 230 volt appliances, such as a clothes dryer and some air conditioners, the unit might operate partially. In a dryer, for example, the motor might operate, the lights burn and the drum revolve. This is because the 230-volt single-phase residential circuit is actually composed of two 115 volt circuits. There is a separate fuse on each one of the hot lines that feed this circuit. If one of these fuses is blown the dryer will run but not heat, since the heating element is the only portion of the dryer that is connected across the 230-volt circuit. A reasonably reliable way to check for this problem is to remove the fuse block or turn off the switch where the fuses are located for the particular appliance. If the fuses give no indication that they are blown, reverse the two fuses that are in the fuse holders. If the symptoms change, for example if the dryer then quits running all together, you can be certain that the fuse is the problem. Don't overlook the fact that one side of a double-pole circuit breaker may be faulty, too.

Circuits that use two fuses (like this dryer circuit) can be deceiving. Sometimes one fuse can be blown, letting the unit partially operate. To be sure, replace both fuses with new fuses as a check.

Most of the necessary tools will probably already be in the home workshop. You will need a set of screwdrivers (both Phillips and standard),

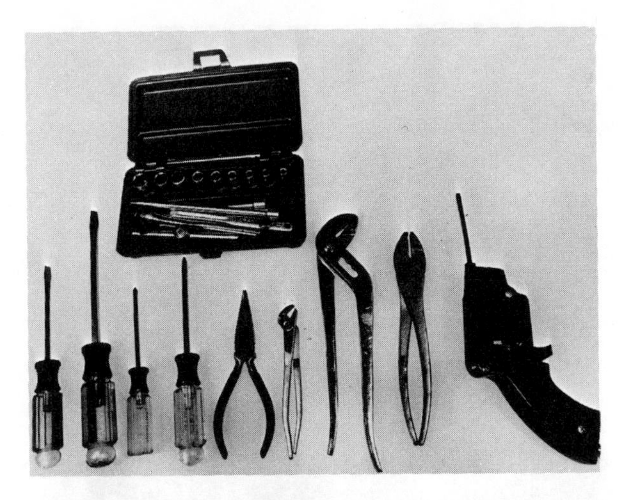

A set of tools like these can take care of most problems that arise with home appliance. 1/4" socket set is at rear. At front, left to right, are screwdrivers, 1/4" and 3/8" bits, #1 Phillips, #2 Phillips, long-nose pliers, small and large slip-joint pliers, hose clamp pliers and soldering iron.

Volt-ohm-meter (VOM) like the one shown at right is big help in remedying appliance problems. Small battery-powered continuity tester seen at left can be helpful also. Light comes on when circuit is complete.

a set of pliers (preferably slip-joint type), an assortment of wrenches and a few specialized tools such as a soldering gun and a pair of hose clamp pliers. The latter can be obtained at most automotive and appliance parts distributors.

One other piece of equipment which is really necessary for serious appliance repairs is a volt-ohm-meter (VOM). The VOM is almost indispensable for appliance repairs. You can buy a good volt-ohm-meter for anywhere from $10 to $25, however, many appliance repairs discussed in this book will not require this equipment. If what you learn here should lead to a deeper interest in appliance repairs, you would be well advised to purchase one of those less expensive VOMs and obtain more detailed information about appliance repairs.

It will often be necessary to buy a repair part to replace the one that is worn or damaged. Usually the best first step is to contact the dealer who sold you the appliance or the servicing agent that he recommended.

Authorized agencies usually have a rather complete stock of parts for their particular brand of appliances. Some cities have appliance parts distributors which act as regional distributors for several major brands of appliances. They will have not only a complete stock of repair parts, but often accessory parts and kits as well. In any case it is best to use parts authorized by the factory for your particular model or to those recommended by an authorized distributor or by knowledgeable service technicians.

Be sure that you need a repair part before purchasing it, as most parts distributors and dealers will not accept a part for refund once it has been taken from the premises. Many unskilled technicians can damage a part when installing it or connect it up incorrectly, causing internal damage.

When installing a part several wires which are usually color-coded may be connected to a switch. Make a sketch of the placement of that wiring. Often, symbols are used on the switches and wiring to make sure that the correct wire is connected to its corresponding terminal. If you have any doubt, make your own symbol by placing a piece of tape around each wire and number the wire. Make a drawing of the switch and number its terminals before you take the switch off or remove the wires from the old switch. If both parts are identical (sometimes there are variations in replacement parts especially when modifications have been made), this works well.

Lettering by this timer terminal denotes wire terminal number which is to be attached. Wire can be located by color markings on insulation of wire, or by a wiring diagram of appliance.

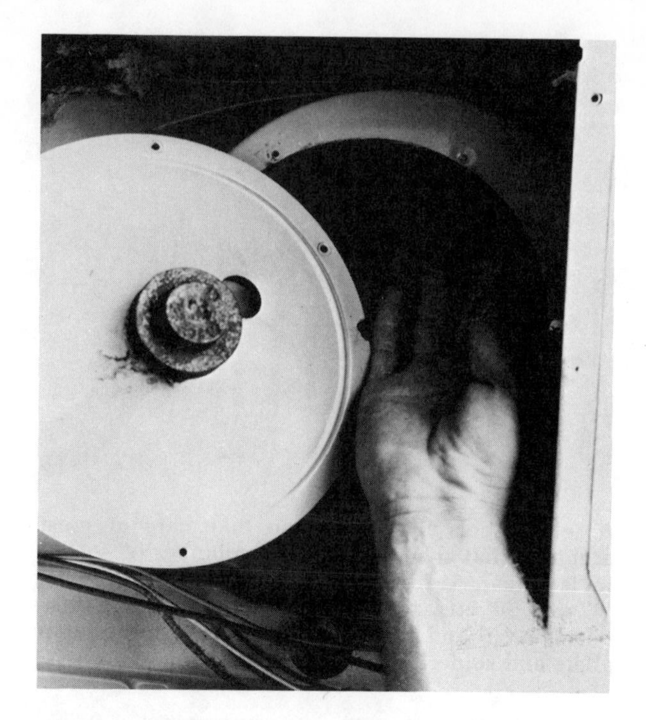

Sharp edges behind sheet metal panels like this can cause cuts. Use care when working within any appliance.

To locate a part, contact a factory authorized dealer or distributor, tell him the part you need and give him any identifying numbers that are on the old part as well as the model number of your machine, which will be found on a stamped metal tag. The tag is usually located on the back or on the bottom toe plate of the appliance. You might also mention the symptoms of the problem that you are having. Often dealers will be able to give you advice which can be helpful.

Don't underestimate the safety factors that are involved in any good job of appliance repair. The primary one is electrical. The current found in most household circuits is very capable of causing a serious, or even fatal, shock hazard. For this reason, none of the procedures outlined should ever be attempted with the appliance plugged in. When tests are recommended, they can be made with a simple continuity tester, or the VOM using resistance checks. Even when a voltage check must be made, it can be done by turning the power off, clipping the meter leads to the line, turning the power on, noting the reading of the meter, then turning the power back off before disconnecting the meter leads. There is no need to touch an appliance for servicing while it is connected to the power. Don't attempt it. Before removing any access panels or otherwise inspecting an appliance and disassembling in any way, be sure that it is unplugged.

Other potential dangers are the danger of cuts and breaks caused by sharp edges on sheet metal, a slipping screwdriver or tool or by a hand being caught in a belt. To reduce the possibility of any danger, again the appliance should always be turned off and unplugged when it is being checked. If you are on guard for sharp edges you are not likely to have problems with them. Handling tools correctly helps eliminate a lot of the danger. Finally, never get your hands or any part of your body near any part that's moving, even during normal operation of the machine.

Most modern appliances are made with polarized or grounded cords. On these cords the third (round) prong on the plug is slightly longer than the others and enters the receptacle first. If the

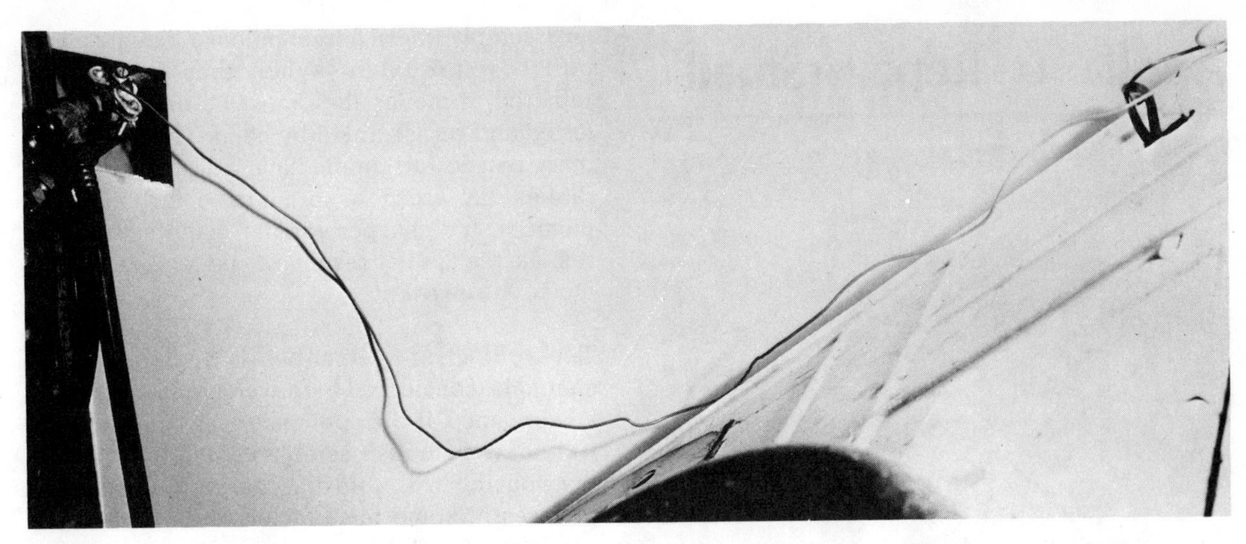

A jumper wire from appliance to water line is always a good safety investment. Clamp for the water line can be obtained from any electrical supply house.

receptacle is properly grounded, a connection is made from the cabinet of the machine to the grounded conductor in the line. This greatly increases the safety in using such appliances since any electrical faults (such as a ground from the wiring harness to the cabinet of the appliance) would follow the shortest path to ground. This would be out the grounding conductor rather than through the body of a person who should happen to touch the appliance. If your receptacles are properly wired and connected this is a great safety feature. If there is any doubt about the existence of a good ground on your own wiring, it's not a bad idea to run a separate wire from any screw (first scrape away any paint beneath) on the cabinet of the machine and attach the opposite end of this wire to the nearest cold water line with a grounding clamp made for the purpose, which can be purchased at any electrical supply store. Place a jumper wire around any plastic fittings on water heater, water meter, etc. Never cut this third member off a polarized cord. If you don't have grounded receptacles, it is wise to have them installed by a qualified electrician. *SEE ALSO: AIR CONDITIONER REPAIR; CLOTHES DRYER REPAIR; DEHUMIDIFIER; DISHWASHER REPAIR; FREEZER; GARBAGE DISPOSAL REPAIR; RANGES & OVENS; REFRIGERATION APPLIANCES; REFRIGERATOR REPAIR; WASHING MACHINE REPAIR.*

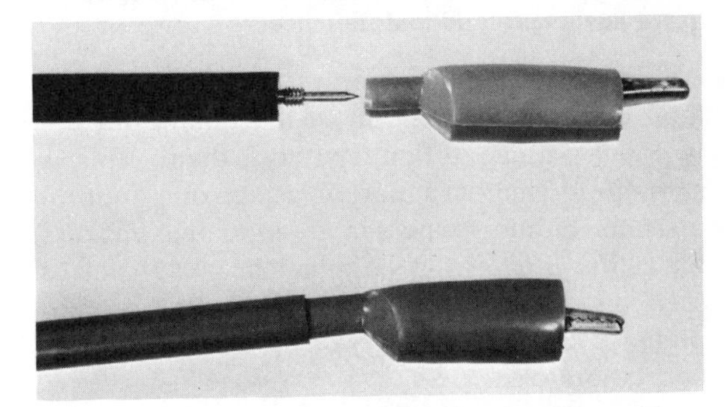

Clip leads such as these on volt-ohm-meter are helpful in making resistance tests, and are absolutely imperative for voltage tests.

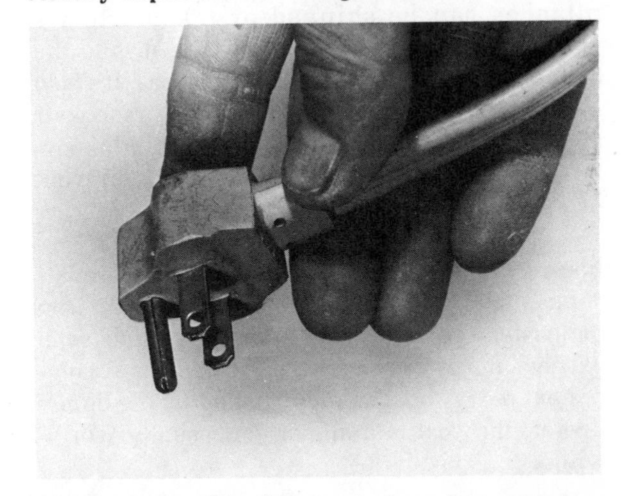

Polarized plug like this one is for safety purposes. Never defeat it by cutting third (round) prong from plug.

Appliance Repair, Small

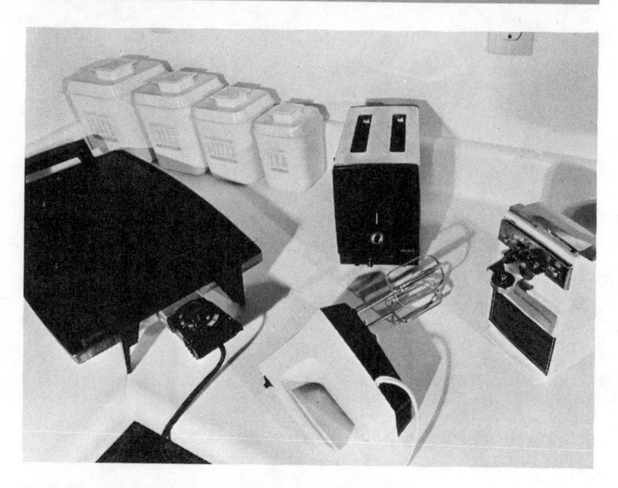

Small appliances do big jobs at little cost, but do require basic care and maintenance.

Appliances account for only a small fraction of total energy consumption in the home, but life would be quite difficult without them. This is something that is apparent when one fails to operate. Home owners and appliance makers have this problem in common because each is concerned with economical repairs to these appliances in the face of skyrocketing materials and labors cost.

Makers cope with this problem in various ways. Many have regional service centers to which appliances can be shipped or taken when a problem occurs and in many cases, it is to the owner's advantage to use these services. It's also a good idea to know how to make repairs to your appliances. Certainly the owner should know how to use them and maintain them to prevent problems from arising.

Because of these spiraling labor costs in repair shops, having a small appliance such as an iron or toaster repaired often approaches and even exceeds the price of a new one. But if a new component part is bought and installed by the homeowner, the cost is minimal and usually worthwhile.

Manufacturers have something of the same problem. Small appliances can be turned out on an assembly line at a tremendous rate with a low unit cost for labor. When they have to be repaired, it means they must be disassembled, tested and reassembled by hand. This is the primary reason for "immediate replacement" warranties that are now so common for small appliances. It's cheaper for the manufacturers to replace the appliances than to pay a skilled technician to rework it.

The subject of warranties is something that should be considered before attempting to repair an appliance. If the appliance is still in warranty it is not wise to disassemble it. Simply removing the housing will void the warranty on the appliances of some manufacturers. But when the product is out of warranty, it is often not economical to repair it unless you do it yourself.

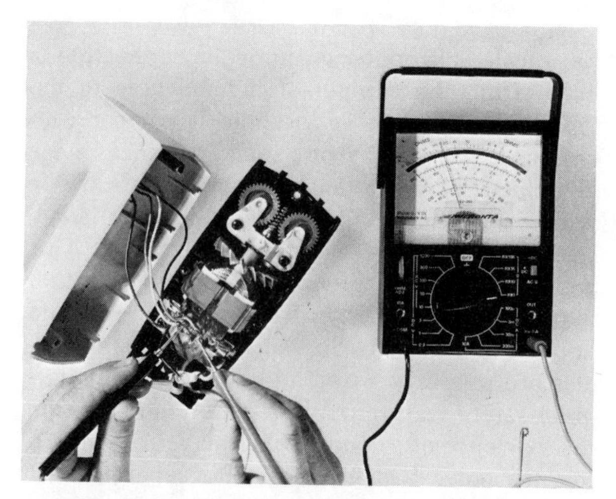

Volt-ohm-meter or continuity checker can be used to test condition of an appliance component with equipment unplugged.

Before an appliance can be maintained and repaired, the owner should have a basic idea of the way in which that appliance operates. This is the principle upon which the information here is given and it is all-important. Certain tips are given which will allow disassembling the appliance and to make a decision about the repairs involved. Hand tools needed will be a screwdriver assortment (one should have a quarter-inch bit, and one with an eighth-inch bit plus various others); phillips screwdrivers numbers one and two; pliers, longnose pliers and a small set of sockets or wrenches. Once a few repairs have been made, you may want to add a volt-ohm-meter (VOM), since this expands the capabilities of diagnosis many times over. *(SEE VOLT-OHM-METER.)*

The guide that follows is intended to better acquaint you with your home appliances and help you diagnose and repair problems that arise, using primarily your own power of deductions and your knowledge of the manner in which the appliance operates. Hopefully you will also pick up a lot of pointers that will guide you in using the appliance to greater advantage and in a manner which will help to prolong its useful life.

When you have located the problem you will likely need to obtain a repair part for the appliance. This may not be an easy job. The best bet is to first check with one of the servicing dealers who sells or services the particular appliance. If he doesn't have the part, he should be able to steer you to a good source for it. In many cities there are one or more service agencies who perform only servicing work, and that only for certain brands. In the case of small appliances, a single agent might service as many as ten or fifteen various brands. Most of these dealers are more than happy to sell you parts. They'll be listed in the yellow pages of the telephone book under the heading *Electric Appliances — Small — Repairing.* A word of caution; be sure of your diagnosis before you purchase a part for an appliance. Most dealers are reluctant to take them back once they have left the premises.

When servicing any electrical household equipment, never attempt to remove a housing or service it in any way without first unplugging it. Be sure that all the power is removed from the equipment that you are working on. The 115 volt power supply found in homes can be dangerous indeed and don't let anyone tell you otherwise. Treated with respect, it is one of the finest servants we have; if abused, it can cause injury and even death. There is no reason to have power applied to any appliance or any circuit when it's being serviced.

The primary reason the VOM is recommended for making continuity checks in electric appliances is to enable the homeowner to check the appliance without endangering himself. If you are lacking one, and if you don't feel the expense is justified, you can make or purchase a buzzer or light by using a standard dry cell battery to check continuity of most appliance components. It's a short project and the cost would be minimal.

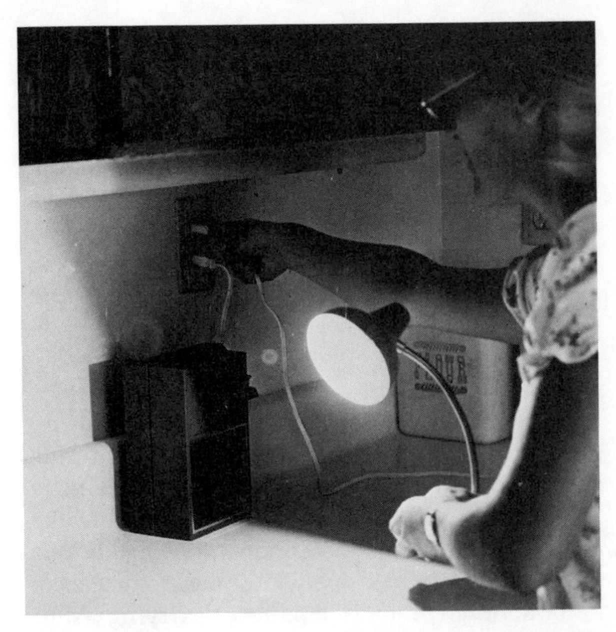

Plug table lamp into receptacle and check for presence of voltage when an appliance fails to operate. If light doesn't come on, look at fuse or circuit breaker.

If you watch carefully what the appliance is doing and listen for any unusual sounds, you can very easily pinpoint the problem — *if* you understand how the appliance operates and the principles which are involved. These are the things stressed here. Step by step instruction procedure would require separate handling for practically every brand and model of small appliance that is on the market. If you understand generally the way in which it operates, you can apply this knowledge to the appliance and come up with the answer to the problem.

This theory helps you to achieve the most from what you know about appliance repair. It can save you money, and it can save you time and inconvenience during a period when an appliance would otherwise be down and possibly waiting in a repair shop.

One of the first problems you will encounter when you attempt to disassemble a small appliance is finding a means of getting it apart. Disassembling is often difficult since stylists tend to hide the little clips and screws that hold the appliance together. Locating them is not always easy. Look carefully under knobs, trim strips and any covers that seem to be accessible and removable. As each appliance is pictured and mentioned, you will see some common ways in which this is done.

Soldering techniques are important, and they are sometimes necessary in making appliance repairs. To solder a wire properly, first remove the insulation carefully without cutting into the conductor. Anytime the conductor is nicked, its diameter is reduced which in turn reduces the amount of current it is capable of carrying. After the insulation is removed, make a firm mechanical connection with the wire and the part to be joined, which may be a quick-disconnect terminal or another length of wire.

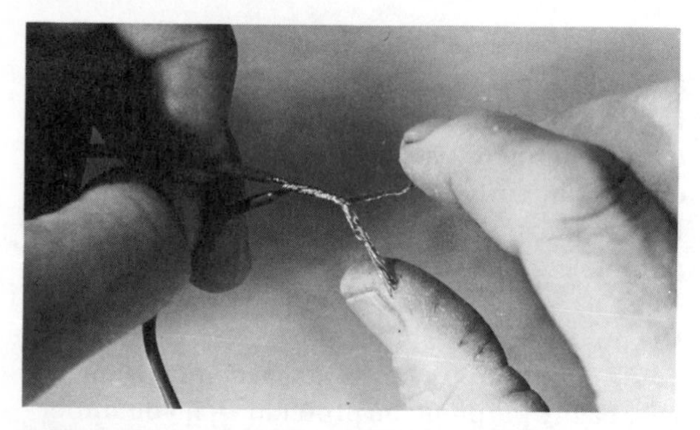

Wiring splices must have good mechanical connections before solder joint can be made. The one shown above is called the "pigtail" splice.

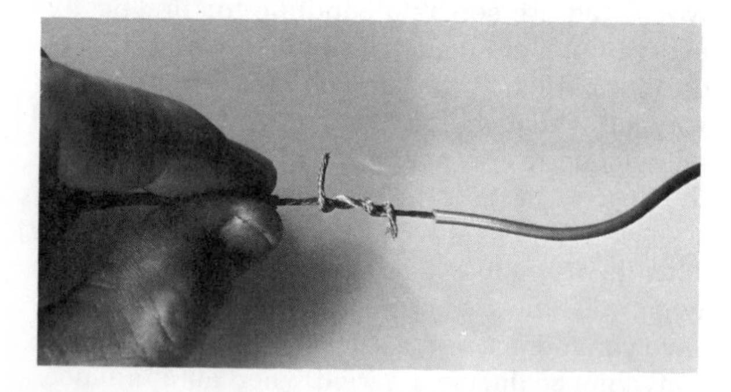

This splice shown here is the "Western Union" splice.

Two types of splices are used in the soldering process to join wires. One is called the pigtail splice and the other is the Western Union splice. They are both illustrated in the accompanying photographs.

When the joint is filled with solder, remove it but continue to hold the gun on the joint for a few seconds to let the flux boil away. Then remove the gun, being very careful not to move the joint for a few seconds. You'll see a slight change in the appearance of the joint as it hardens. If you move the joint too soon, it results in what is known as "cold solder joint", which is weak. The tiny fractures make the solder take on a dull, brittle appearance which you will recognize.

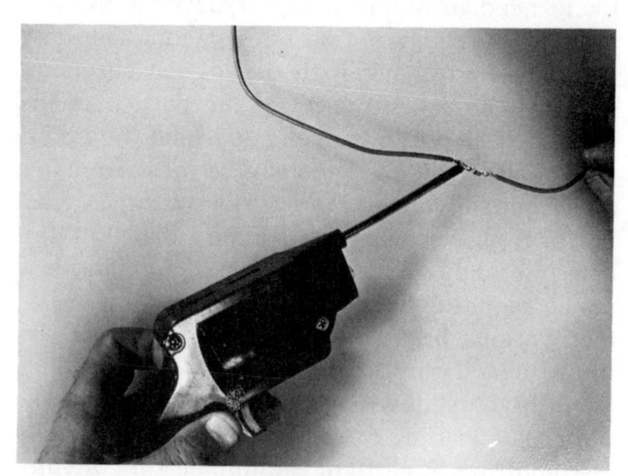

A small soldering gun (this one has 75 watts capacity) is suitable for most appliance repair jobs. Begin by touching tip of gun to work as shown above.

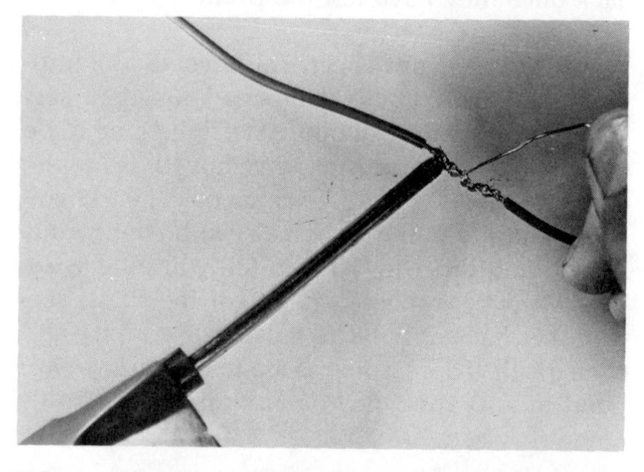

When work is heated thoroughly, touch solder to the tip of the work, not to the tip of the gun. Solder will tend to flow toward the gun. Trim the wire edges when the soldering job is done.

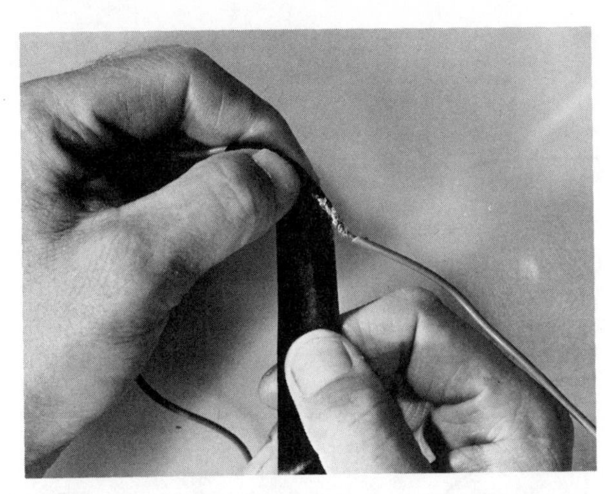

To tape a soldered splice, be sure to pull the tape tightly as you are wrapping the joint. Overlap each layer about a quarter-inch.

When the soldering is completed, taping is usually necessary. This is something that should be practiced along with soldering. Several brands of good quality plastic electrical tape are available, which make a clean, neat job of this. The trick is to stretch the tape carefully as you wind it across the joint. The stretch will conform exactly to the shape and size of the material underneath. If it's loose and has openings between the wraps, it should be redone.

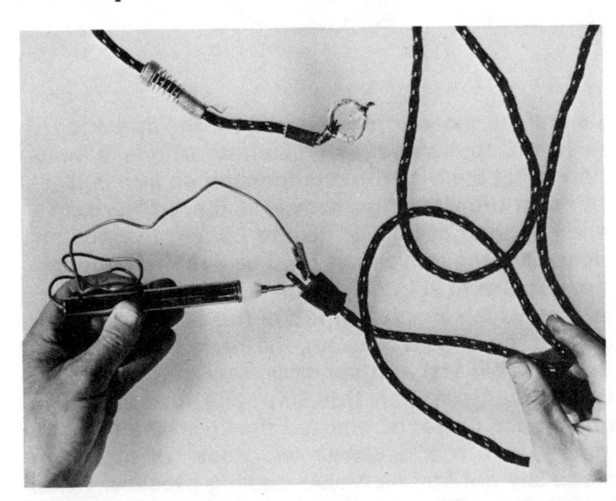

Appliance cords are easily tested by removing them from the appliance and clipping both ends together. Then attach an ohmmeter or continuity tester across the two prongs of the plug. Finally, twist, bend, and flex the cord along its entire length. If continuity light comes on or if meter needle drops, the cord is defective and should be replaced. Tester shown above has battery-powered light.

Often problems with small home appliances lie in the cord itself. These should be checked carefully. For a complete and thorough check you will need a volt-ohm-meter or some device to indicate continuity.

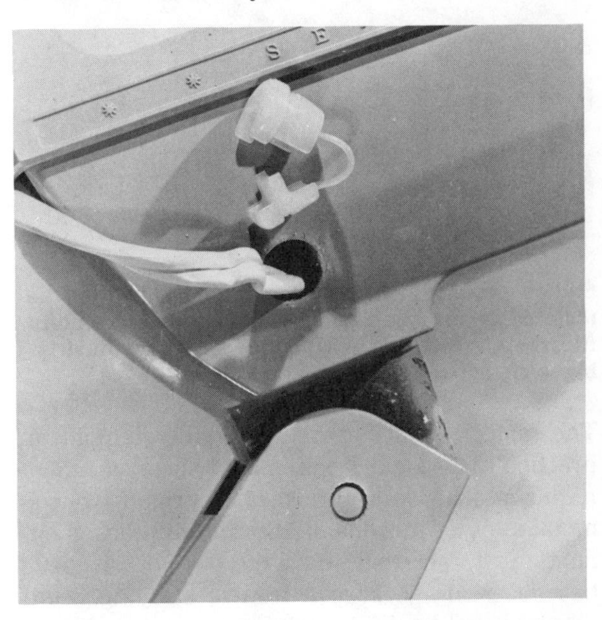

Area of strain relief (shown removed in this photo) is suspect location for internal break in cord.

Sometimes you will be able to see the problem with the cord. Breaks often occur near the plug and at the strain relief, the clamp that holds the conductor tightly to the frame of the appliance. A tug at these weak points, with the appliance unplugged, will often reveal these breaks, even if they are beneath the outer insulation of the cord. The terminals where the cord attaches to the appliance are sometimes at fault also, inspect them carefully.

If a break occurs at the plug or if the insulation of the cord is worn, it is wise to replace the entire cord with a new one. When repairing heating type appliances, be sure to use heat-resistant cords especially made for the purpose.

Small appliances can be divided into two classes: heating devices and motor driven devices. Some, such as small electric heaters with a blower, are a combination of the two. Dividing them into these catagories helps to facilitate the repairs on each one.

Switch contacts in small appliances can often be restored to use by cleaning with automotive point file, then burnishing or polishing surface with striking surface from matchbook.

The material that forms the heating element in practically all small heating appliances is called *nichrom*. This is a wire that is formed from a metal alloy of nickel and chromium. It has good heating characteristics and the physical properties necessary to keep it from destroying itself when heated by the electrical current that passes through it.

These elements are found in two forms. The first is called an open-type element because the heating element is visible and accessible. The wire itself is usually found in a coil form, but in some appliances such as room heaters, hair dryers and other devices where space is at a premium the material is found in a flat ribbon-like form.

The model number plate of the appliance will usually list the wattage of the heating element. If it is the coil type of nichrom wire, it can be purchased from an appliance repair center in the coil. It is also available in bulk form. A certain length of a particular diameter of nichrome will give it a certain electrical resistance, and from this the wattage of the element can be determined. Before you put it into the appliance you just have to measure the old element and stretch the length of bulk nichrome to the same length.

When stretching nichrome wire, stretch the entire length at one time. Take the nichrome and fasten one end securely to a nail or screw. Hold the other end with a pair of pliers and pull until

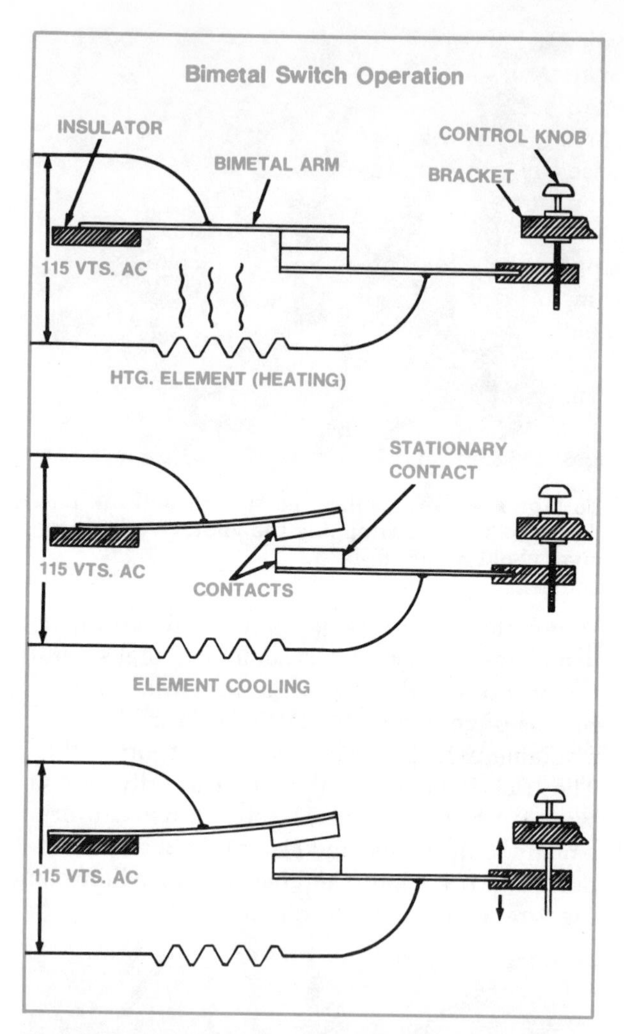

Bimetal thermostats are important to the operation of all home appliances. A typical adjustable bimetal thermostat such as the one found in an iron is illustrated in the drawings above. In the first drawing, when voltage is applied to the circuit, the heating element of the iron comes on. The heat from the element begins to act upon the bimetal arm of the thermostat, which is actually part of the electrical circuit also. In the middle drawing, the heat is sufficient to bend the bimetal arm upwards, enough to open the two contacts. When this happens, the circuit is broken and power is removed from the element. The bimetal arm reacts slowly and does not close immediately but begins a slow cooling process. When it's cooled sufficiently, it again closes the contacts and the cycle is repeated. In the bottom drawing you see how this effect is used to obtain an adjustable temperature range. The stationary contact is mounted so that it can move up and down on a threaded shaft. When it is in the upper position, more heat is required to warp the bimetal arm sufficiently to break contact. In a lower position, less heat is required.

you reach the desired length. Don't stand in front of the wire, for if it should come loose, it can snap back at you like a spring. This method insures that the wire is evenly stretched — otherwise hot spots will result and it will burn out prematurely.

Appliances that use heating elements must have some means of controlling the heat from this element. The device that does this is called a thermostat. In small appliances it usually takes the form of a bimetal thermostat. With the bimetal, two pieces of unlike metals are bonded or fused together under high temperature so that they appear to be one piece of metal. However, the different metals also have different rates of expansion when they are heated. The one that expands the most tends to push the other one up, causing a bowing effect as the metal bends. This action can be used to open and close a set of electrical contacts, which in turn opens and closes the circuit. Many bimetals are made in disc form, and the disc snaps back and forth like a child's "cricket" toy. Bimetal controls can be manufactured to very close tolerances. Many are adjustable and take the form of a leaf. Some are made at fixed temperatures and are not adjustable.

Several types of motors are used in motor driven appliances. Most common is the universal motor, so named because it will operate on either alternating or direct current. The rotor or spinning part of the motor has windings just like the stationary or field part of the motor. They are connected together by a series of carbon brushes that conduct the current from one to the other. These brushes are a source of wear, and must be replaced after a certain amount of running time depending upon the particular appliance. If a motor driven appliance fails to operate, look for these brushes. Often they have a cap on the outside of the housing and simply removing this with a screwdriver will allow them to be checked. They're held tightly against the commutator of the motor by a spring. *SEE ALSO AUTOMATIC COFFEE MAKER REPAIR; BLENDER REPAIR; CAST THERMOSTATIC HEATING APPLIANCES; ELECTRIC BLANKET REPAIR; ELECTRIC CAN OPENER REPAIR; ELECTRIC CLOCKS REPAIR; ELECTRIC FAN REPAIR; ELECTRIC HAIR SETTER REPAIR; ELECTRIC IRON REPAIR; ELECTRIC KNIFE REPAIR; ELECTRIC SHAVER REPAIR; ELECTRIC SHOE POLISH REPAIR; ELECTRIC TOASTER REPAIR; FLOOR POLISHER REPAIR; FOOD MIXER REPAIR; HAIR DRYER REPAIR; HEATING PAD REPAIR; HOT PLATE REPAIR; POPCORN POPPER REPAIR; PORTABLE ELECTRIC HEATER REPAIR; PORTABLE HUMIDIFIER REPAIR; ROASTER OVEN REPAIR; STYLING COMB REPAIR; VACUUM CLEANER REPAIR; VAPORIZERS & BOTTLE WARMERS REPAIR; WAFFLE IRON REPAIR.*

Appliance Symbols

On blueprints, appliance symbols are used to designate where appliances will be installed. For ease in preparing and reading plans, symbols are used rather than complicated scale drawings of appliances. *SEE ALSO BLUEPRINTS.*

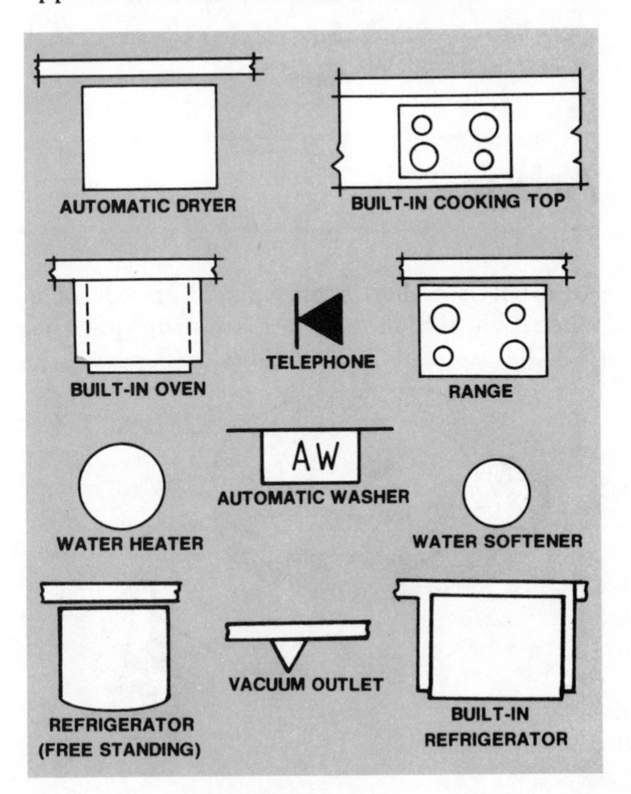

Appliance Symbols

Apron

The apron is a decorative molding located under the inside sill of a window frame so that it is flush with the interior wall. Its purpose is both decorative and practical because it covers the opening between the window frame and the interior wall, preventing drafts and heat loss. *SEE ALSO MOLDING & TRIM.*

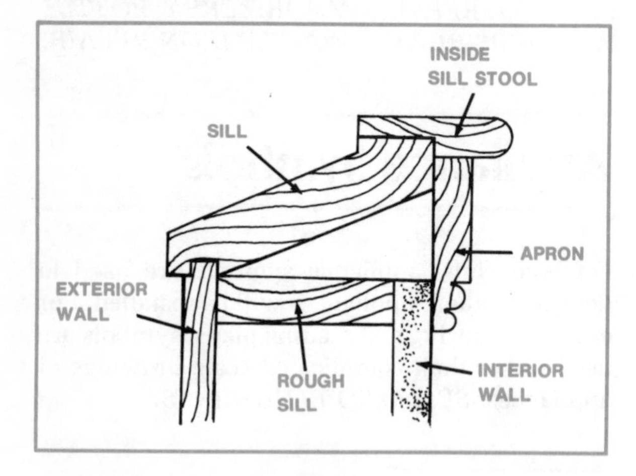

Apron

Arbor

An arbor is a short shaft, spindle or axle of a wheel on which another rotating part is

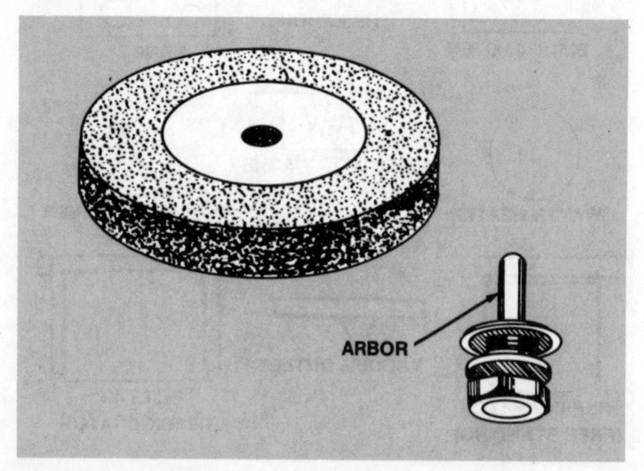

Grinding wheel and arbor (arrow).

An Aluminum Arbor

mounted. The arbor on a cutting machine holds work that is to be cut.

The term arbor also applies to vine-supporting wooden latticework which usually covers a path, or to a bower of vines or branches.

Arbor & Trellis

Often the names "arbor" and "trellis" are used interchangeably. Arbor, however, is a heavier archway structure which should be strong enough to support the weight of shrubs, vines or flowers. Unlike the trellis, the arbor may be used to enclose passageway. A latticework made of

Trellis Arbor

wooden strips which supports climbing plants is called a trellis. Although a fence, wall, house or garage may support it, this lighter structure may be built to stand on its own. *SEE ALSO LAWNS & GARDENS.*

Arc Welding

[SEE WELDING AND WELDING EQUIPMENT.]

Architect's Scale

Architect's scales, like the ones shown, are used by the architect in scaling his drawings to size. Each division on the rule represents 1 foot, which is divided into 12 parts, each equal to 1 inch. *SEE ALSO DRAFTING EQUIPMENT.*

Architectural Symbols

Architectural symbols are used to represent building materials and other items on blueprints. Although plans are drawn to scale, some items cannot be represented easily or clearly by scale drawings. Therefore, commonly accepted symbols are used. *SEE ALSO BLUEPRINTS.*

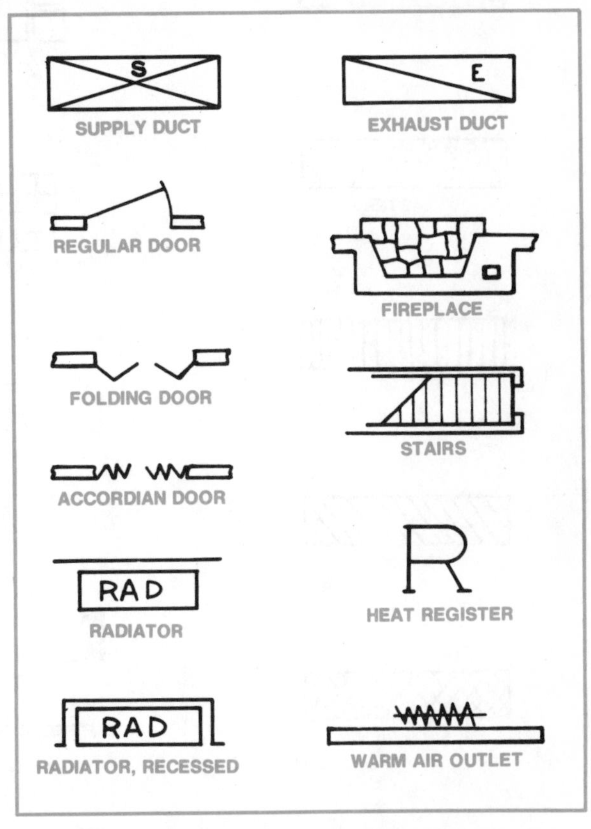

Some commonly used architectural symbols.

Courtesy of Fairgate Rule Company, Inc.

36″ ARCHITECT'S SCALE (triangular)

YOU CAN MEASURE UP TO 383 FEET . . .
without moving the rule when you use the 3/32″ inch to the foot scale. This is what we call "easy measuring".

Scales: 3/32, 3/16, 3/8, 3/4, 1-1/2, 3, 1/2, 1, 1/8, 1/4 inch to the foot. Inches: 16ths (36″).

(three sides) Code: AS-036 Size: 36″ x .84″ x .84″ x .84″

6″ ARCHITECT'S SCALE (flat)

Scales: 1/2, 1, 1/8, 1/4 inch to the foot.

Code: AS-006

Size: 6″ x 3/4″

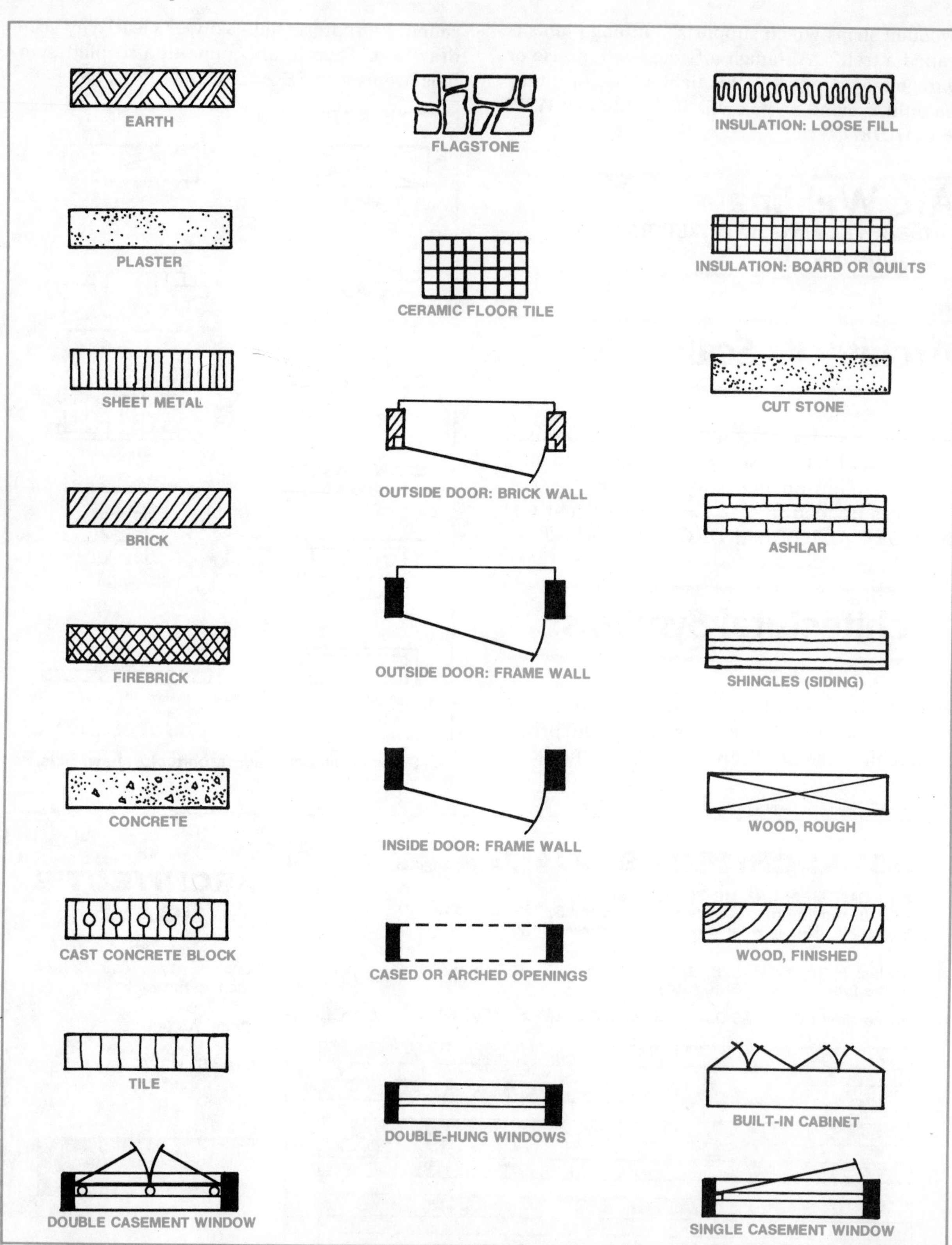

Architectural Symbols.

Archway

An archway is the structural frame around an opening, which may serve as support for a wall or other weight above it. The most common styles of archways are curved or round, with a rectangular door frame. These may be used as dividers between rooms or as entrance halls. *SEE ALSO WALL & CEILING CONSTRUCTION.*

Curved Archway

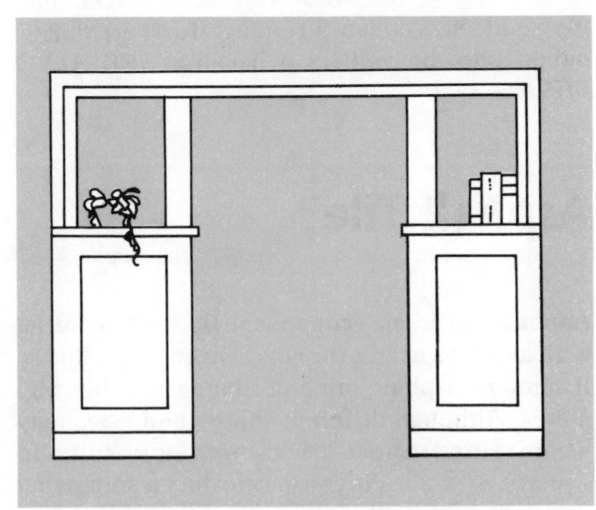

Rectangular Door Frame Archway

Areaway

A sunken space providing access, air or light to a basement is referred to as an *areaway.*

Armature

The armature is a revolving or movable part of a motor, consisting of wires wound around an iron core. The armature rests on a rotor which is made to turn by the action of the armature. As electric current passes through the wire windings, two electromagnetic fields develop. The armature is positioned so that "like poles" are facing. As these like poles repel each other and cause the armature to move one quarter turn, the unlike poles then attract and cause another quarter turn. By reversing the current, the electromagnetic field is reversed. The final two quarter turns are accomplished by the same magnetic forces. *SEE ALSO ELECTRIC MOTORS.*

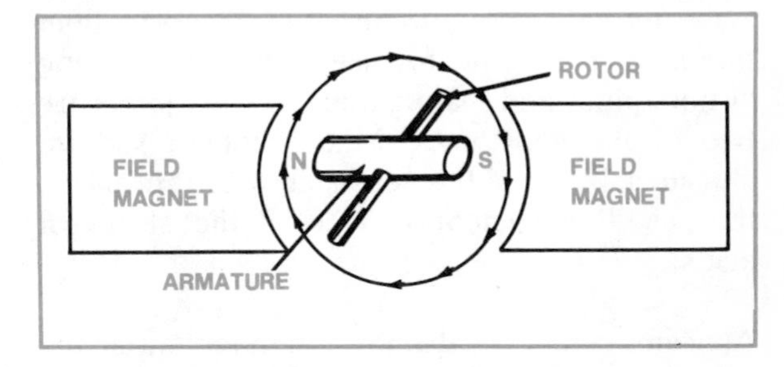

Armature's relation to major parts of motor.

Armored Cable

Armored cable is the type of cable referred to by the National Electrical Code as Type AC, and is commonly known by such trade names as BX, Flexsteel, etc. It consists of two or three individual wires, assembled into a cable and housed by spiral-wound steel armor. Heavy, tough paper is overwrapped between the wires and the flexible outer shield. This cable should only be used indoors in permanently dry locations. *SEE ALSO WIRE SIZES & TYPES.*

Arris

An arris is the sharp edge or salient angle formed by the meeting of two surfaces (whether plain or curved), used especially in moldings.

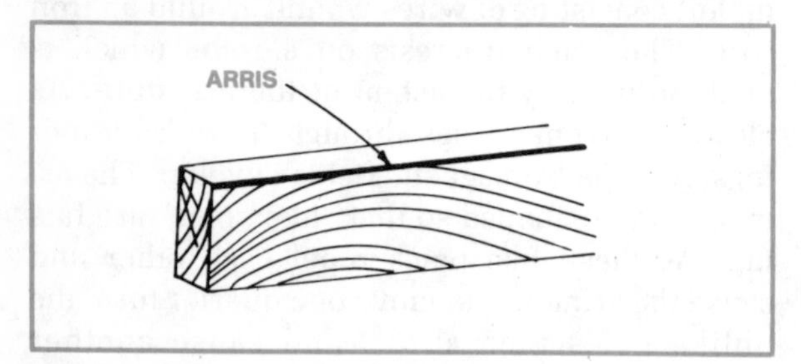

Asbestos Cement

Asbestos cement is purchased in dry form, then mixed with a liquid for use. Insulating heating system pipes and sealing flue-chimney joints are two of its many uses. Mixed with a sodium silicate solution to the consistency of thin paste, the resulting cement will resist the strongest acids.

Asbestos cement is also used in the manufacturing of exterior wallboard and shingles, making them durable, attractive, and suitable for any type sidewall surface. Because of their physical properties, asbestos-cement shingles are recommended for use in areas where smoke, smog and chemicals pollute the atmosphere.

Asphalt

Asphalt is of great commercial value because it is used in road building, waterproofing, roofing, floor tiling and automobile manufacturing. It is an organic material that is sticky, black or brown in color, with a consistency ranging from heavy liquid to solid. The chemical composition of asphalt is too variable and complex to be precisely determined.

Asphalt is obtained either from natural sources or the distillation of petroleum. Asphalt obtained from natural sources often contains minerals while petroleum asphalt does not. Other than this difference, the two sources resemble each other in all respects.

Asphalt Roofing Materials

[SEE ROOFING MATERIALS.]

Asphalt Siding

Asphalt siding is a remodeling material, second in popularity only to aluminum siding. It is a fibrous board impregnated with asphalt, having a granular surface in a variety of designs. The board (purchased in shingles, block, or squares) is fastened to the wall with nails driven into plywood or wooden stripping (furring) that is nailed into the wall as a backing. *SEE ALSO SIDING.*

Asphalt Tile

Asphalt tile is an economical flooring material which can be used over concrete or wood floors. It contains asphalt, mineral fibers and other pigments. Although different shapes and sizes may be obtained, these tiles come generally in squares 9″ x 9″. Vinyl-asbestos tile, a somewhat more expensive alternative, is easier to maintain, due to its grease resistance and lasting color.

Asphaltum Paint

Asphaltum paint is made from natural, solid bituminous asphalt. It is used for general metal maintenance where long range protection is unnecessary. This paint is an excellent off-season protection for farm equipment. Apply to a clean, dry surface with a brush, roller or spray gun. When spraying, thin it slightly with a paint thinner. Asphaltum paint has a high resistance to water and dries to a glossy sheen in approximately two hours. *SEE ALSO PAINTS & PAINTING.*

Astragal

An astragal is a small molding of rounded surface (generally from one half to three quarters of a circle) attached to one of a pair of folding doors or a window sash to prevent them swinging through. It is also used with sliding doors to insure a tighter fitting where the doors meet. *SEE ALSO MOLDING AND TRIM.*

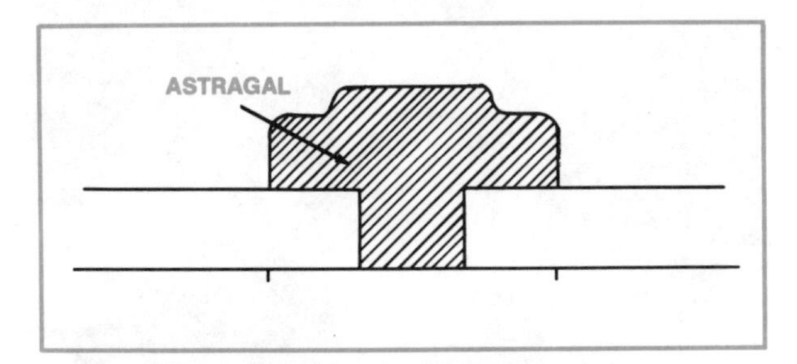

One use of an Astragal.

Attic Remodeling

[SEE REMODELING.]

Auger

[SEE SNAKE, PLUMBER'S.]

Auger Bit

The auger bit, a woodworking tool, is used solely for boring holes. Available in diameters from 3/16'' to 1'', they are graduated by 1/16''. Gimlet bits, drills or awls are used if a hole smaller than 3/16'' is needed. Expansive or Forstner bits are used to bore a hole larger than 1''.

The size of auger bits is indicated by a single number representing sixteenths of an inch and stamped on the squared end of the shank. Thus, the number 8 means it will bore a hole 8/16'' or 1/2'' in diameter.

Five basic parts of an auger bit include cutters, screw, spurs, twist and shank. The spurs make a downward cut in the wood while the cutters are removing material between screw and spur. The twist carries removed material upward to clear the path for cutting.

There are two critical differences in standard auger bit features — the single and double thread. The sharp, threaded feed screw protruding from the center of the bit is made in single thread form (threads farther apart) for fast boring in green or gummy wood. Since it has only one spur and cutting edge, the single thread type can clear itself readily of chips which result in construction work. While the double thread form (threads close together) for seasoned or soft woods works slower, it makes a more accurate and smoother hole and is preferable for cabinetmaking.

Essentially auger bits are for use in a hand brace only. The chuck end of their shank has a square taper. The business end has a screw point. The point pulls the bit into the work, minimizing the pressure you have to apply. Hand-drilling is largely obsolete, so you aren't likely to have much use for this type of bit.

However, there are auger bits made for use in electric drills. Often used by plumbers and other professionals, they come in sizes from 3/4'' to 1 1/2'', are available at mill supply houses, and are

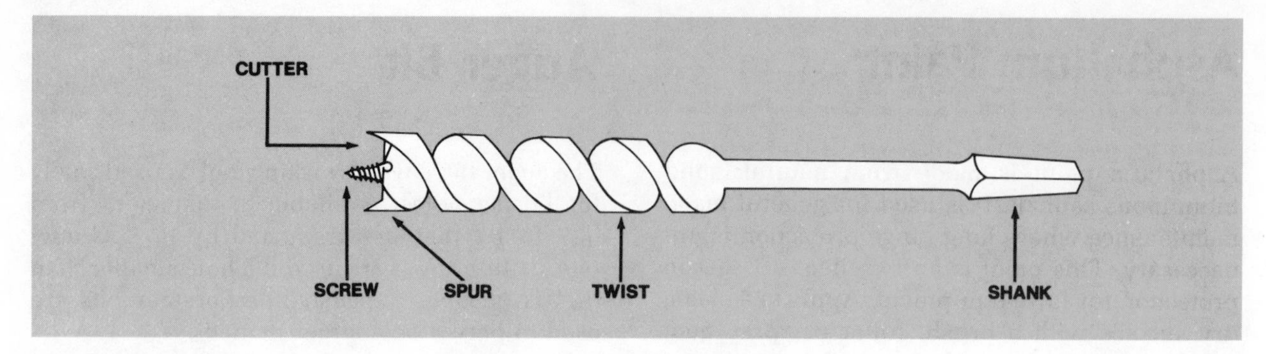

Basic Parts of an Auger Bit

somewhat expensive. They are made for use in 1/2" chucks. Power auger bits pull into wood with amazing speed, and are not easy for the inexperienced to control.

You can modify a hand-brace auger bit for use in an electric drill. First, cut off the square shank. Second, file off most of the threads on the screw point to reduce the speed of its self-feed and make drilling more controllable.

Sharpening an auger bit is a simple matter with a small mill file or a bit file made for the purpose. You will notice that the two cutting edges are beveled like chisels on the surface nearest the tang of the bit. File this surface only to restore a cutting edge. A few strokes usually do the job. Sharpen the spurs by filing on the inside surface only. You can give a final keenness to both by whetting with a small slipstone. The job is not critical, but try to keep the edges of spurs and cutting edges even. Don't file heavily on one, lightly on the other. *SEE ALSO HAND TOOLS.*

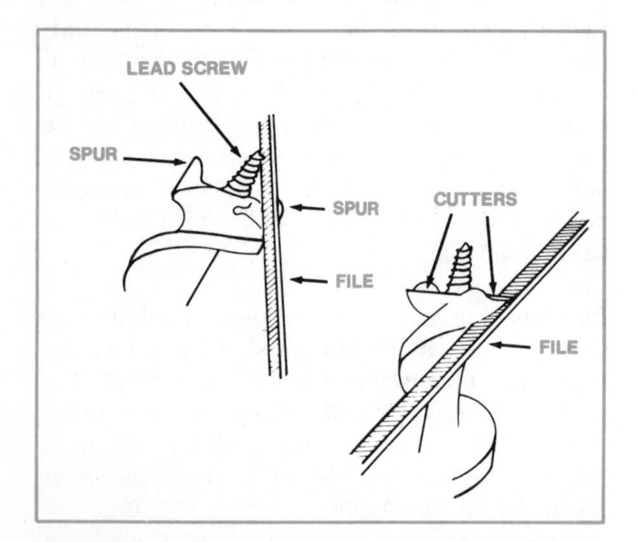

When sharpening an auger bit, sharpen only inside of spur edges (left) and never file any part of lead screw. When sharpening cutters (right), file only the surface nearest the shank. Like a chisel, the cutters must have only a single bevel.

Automatic Coffee Maker Repair

Courtesy of General Electric Company

When you fill a percolator with water and plug it in, you may think that the percolator is heating the entire tank of water which then boils up through the coffee grounds. Actually only a small amount of water at the bottom of the tube is being heated at any given time. The tube is designed so that a small washer or passageway

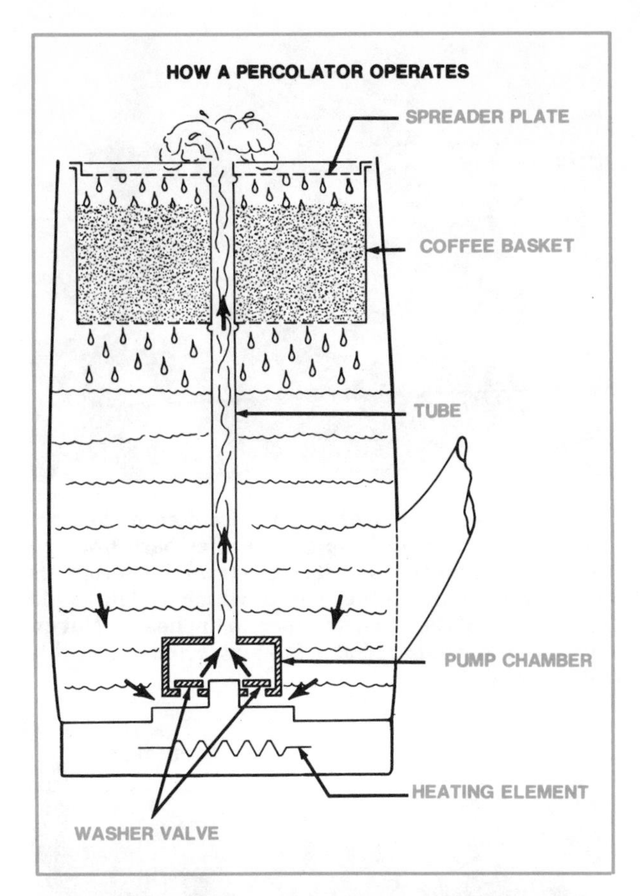

The mechanical operation of the percolator is visible in the next drawing. The heat from the element is concentrated in an area just below the pump chamber. The chamber is designed so that water can flow into it easily but cannot flow back out into the reservoir. In this illustration a washer acts as a check valve. When this water is heated, it expands and is pushed up the tube and out the top onto the spreader plate, where it falls down to the coffee in the basket and back into the reservoir. As soon as this water is displaced, the check valve opens and more water flows in from the reservoir to take its place. A clogged or oily washer valve or pump chamber or a restricted tube can impair the operation of the coffee maker. It's important to clean these components regularly.

acts as a valve, allowing water to flow into the tube but not out at the bottom where it comes in.

When the water is heated, it boils. Since it cannot go out the bottom of the tube, it has to go out the top. As soon as the water is displaced, more water comes in through the passageway at the bottom to take its place. The water that leaves the top of the tube then filters back through the coffee grounds and into the tank in the bottom.

After repeatedly forcing the water from the reservoir across the coffee grounds, the coffee gradually develops the correct strength and the water in the reservoir has become warmer. A thermostat mounted to the bottom of the reservoir senses the temperature. At a certain temperature (which is also proportional to the amount of brewing that has taken place) the thermostat shuts the main heater off. In many units, a warming heater or auxiliary heater is turned on at this time to keep the coffee in the reservoir warm.

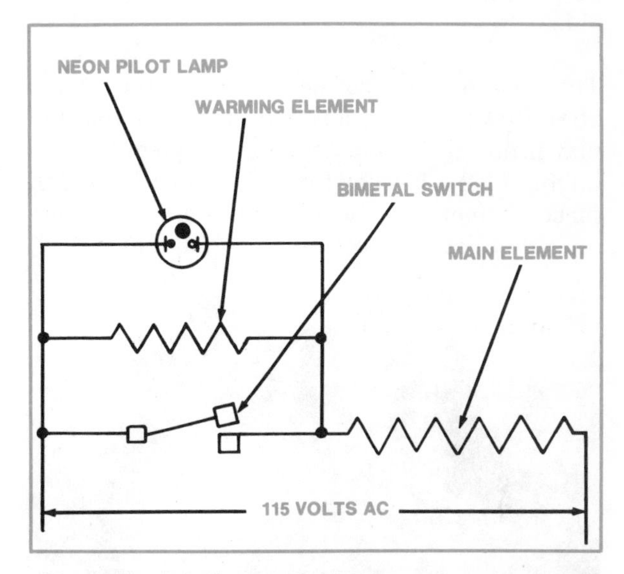

In a typical automatic percolator circuit the bimetal switch or thermostat controls the main heating element. As the temperature of the water in the reservoir of the percolator becomes warmer, a point is reached where the bimetal switch opens. Up to this point, the switch is shunting the circuit around the neon pilot light and the warming element. But when the switch opens, the circuit is completed through these two components using the main element as one of the conductors. Normally the heat given off by the warming element is sufficient to maintain temperatures in the reservoir. The thermostat will not reset until cold water is put into the percolator for the next brewing cycle.

It's important to keep all of the water-containing parts of the percolator clean, since coffee has a high oil content. This is easier said than done, however, because soap will often leave a bad taste in the percolator, leaving the cure worse than the ailment. One solution is to soak the reservoir and the removable parts of the coffee maker in a solution of water and baking soda, then rinse carefully and reassemble. Done regularly, this will keep the coffee fresh-tasting and the coffee maker clean.

Coffee maker problems can arise in several areas. If the unit is completely inoperable, check the receptacle with a table lamp to see if voltage is reaching it. With the coffee maker unplugged, check the plug at the cord and at the connection at the coffee maker if a detachable cord is used. If not, check the area of the strain relief. If the coffee maker still doesn't operate, take a look inside.

The base of most coffee makers is removable after first removing any thermostat knobs that may protrude from it. Look for a large nut on the bottom of the base or for screws that hold it in place. Sometimes these screws are the same ones that hold the feet to the coffee maker.

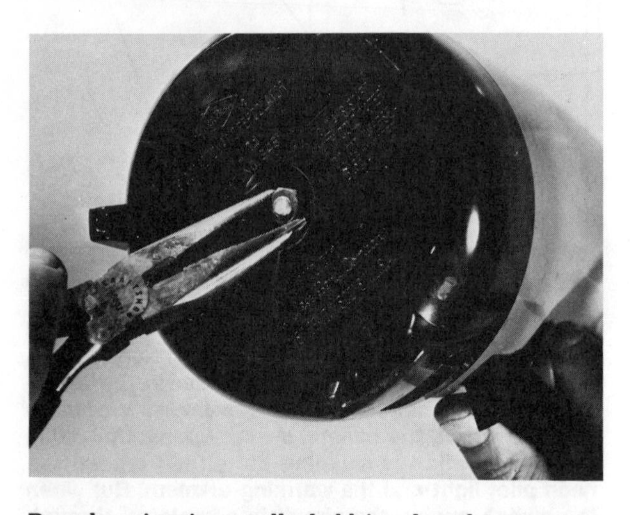

Base housing is usually held in place by a nut or screws. Long-nose pliers may be required if nut is deeply recessed.

With the base removed, you should be able to locate the terminals of the heating element, the thermostat contacts, and usually a pilot light as well. The thermostat contacts should be fairly clean, not corroded or pitted. If they are, this may be the problem. Clean them with an automotive point file and polish them with a stick of hardwood or a striking surface from a book of paper matches. Look for any loose or broken wiring. Since a heating element is used here, the wiring will most likely be the heat

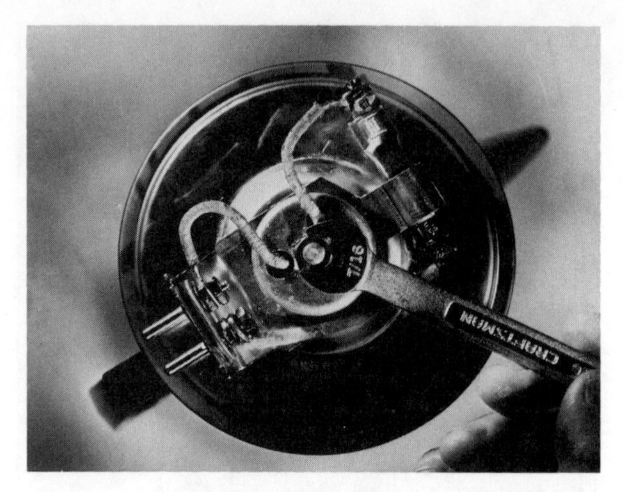

Electric components of a typical coffee maker are visible in the view from below after base housing has been removed. Circuit comes from line terminals through the bimetal thermostat, which is clamped to the bottom of the base, and then to the heater. Nut on which stud retains heater is being removed in this photograph.

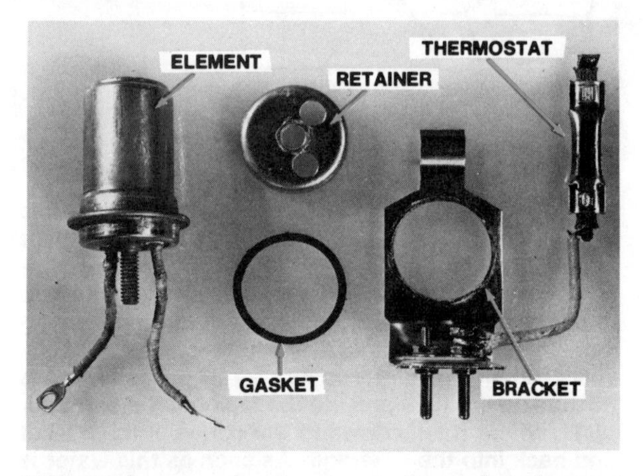

With stud removed all components can be taken out of percolator. Gaskets should be replaced at any time element is removed.

resistant type and this should also be used for replacement purposes. If any terminals are corroded or burned be sure and polish all parts of the connections until they are bright and shiny before replacing the terminal. Once in place be sure that all are snug and tight.

If you should suspect that a thermostat needs calibrating you can probably do it. Then test the coffee maker by tasting the resulting brew. Calibration screws will probably be located on the bimetal arm if an adjustable thermostat is used. A routine inspection should show which way to turn a particular screw. If the coffee is strong the thermostat is likely to be overheating. If it is too weak, it is underheating. A thermostat that wanders very far from calibration should be replaced.

While checking the thermostat, be sure it is also mounted securely to the base where it can sense the temperature of the coffee within the reservoir. If a thermostat has poor contact with the base, the heat transfer will be minimal and the calibration will be thrown off.

How a Drip-Filter Coffee Maker Works

MAIN ELEMENT

WARMING ELEMENT

Operation of a drip-filter coffee maker is similar, but there are two major differences. Water being heated is kept entirely separate from that which is already brewed. The water flows into the heating chamber, where the temperature is closely controlled by a bimetal thermostat clamped to the side. As water heats, it is forced up the tube and out the spout where it falls across the coffee. A filter in the bowl of the coffee container controls the rate at which the water passes through. The coffee which drips through into the serving container is not diluted and is ready to drink as soon as it passes through. A warming element built into the base keeps the coffee at serving temperature. The main element in the heating chamber is usually an enclosed type.

The heating element is usually not visible. It may be located in a small metal tube or it may be located at the bottom of the base. Some heating elements are removed from the inside of the reservoir. If a gasket is used between the reservoir and an element, it should be replaced each time the element is removed.

A coffee maker that has been immersed in water could easily retain enough water to cause a

Drip-filter coffee maker is becoming a popular appliance. Begin disassembly by removing spout from reservoir as shown.

Bottom of coffee maker can be removed after unplugging. Four screws and nut hold this cover in place.

shocking condition. Shocking can also be caused by a grounded element or any grounded conductor within an appliance. If this problem arises, check carefully with a VOM to locate the problem. Be sure that it is completely free of grounds before putting it back into service.

A new type of coffee maker that is becoming quite popular is the drip-filter type coffee maker. In this unit the reservoir is separate from the coffee container. The water enters a heating chamber, is heated and displaced across the grounds. It drips through the grounds and is filtered before entering the glass container. For the most part, servicing recommendations and trouble shooting would be the same except that

With cover removed location of the components inside is visible. Reservoir is held in place with two screws.

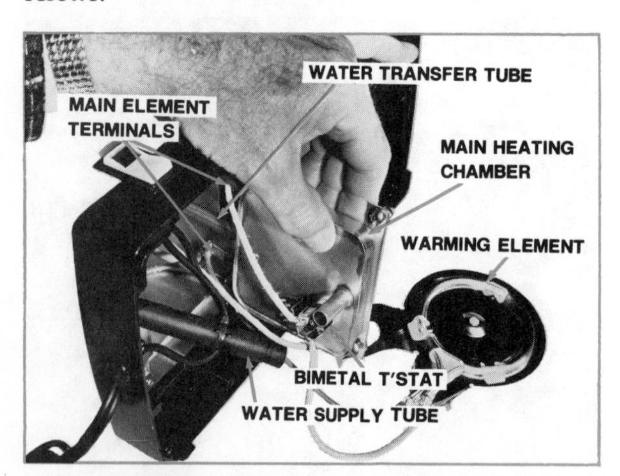

When screws are loosened, pump chamber can be pulled free. Note bimetal limit switch clamped to pump.

the warming heater is entirely separate from the main heater, which is located in the chamber that displaces the water. A small bimetal-type thermostat is clamped to the heating chamber to turn the main heater off when the water supply is gone. *SEE ALSO APPLIANCE REPAIR, SMALL.*

Heating element is built into pump area, can be tested at terminals seen above. Element is not visible. Warming element can be checked without removing.

Automatic Garage Door

[SEE GARAGE DOOR OPENER.]

Automation

Automation can make life safer and more convenient. Until recently, some of these devices were only available for commercial use. But consumer demand for conveniences led to the availability of automatic and remote-controlled devices that turn your lights on and off, open garage doors, start a fire in your fireplace or turn on the power in your vacation home. The only limitations to these and many more conveniences are your imagination and budget.

CENTRALIZED MUSIC-INTERCOM SYSTEMS

The music-intercom system is rapidly becoming a common household feature, especially in newly constructed homes where units can easily be installed. An intercom, doorbell, door opener and speaker, AM-FM radio, phonograph and tape recording facilities, message taping, fire and/or burglar alarm, morning wake-up alarm are some of the options open to the homeowner. These highly versatile intercom-music systems are also available with stereo options which are adaptable to your present turntable and tape recorder. Before making any purchase, it is a good idea to write down all the features desired for your system. Buy a master control unit that is large enough to accommodate the options desired and add them later.

The master control is usually placed in a key room such as the kitchen or family room. Satellite intercoms, each with its own volume control, can be put in as many as a dozen rooms. Turning down the volume will not cut out the intercom and door speaker circuits in the unit. The master control of the music-intercom system is available in a wall-mounted model or in a cabinet that matches existing modular components.

TIMERS

Portable timers have been available for years to control lights and time sun lamps and heat lamps. A model that plugs in flush against a wall outlet is a favorite for use with electric coffeemakers. Another type turns off the TV set should you fall asleep. A newer model timer automatically turns on house lights at staggered on-off times so that the lights won't come on at the same time each night. Another version can be hooked up to open and close electrically operated drapes.

The permanent variety of time switch is usually mounted in a rugged metal box for installation against an inside or outside wall. These models are intended for heavy electrical loads such as controlling major appliances, heating plants and general area lighting. They are connected directly to the circuit breaker panel. Special features such as extra screw-on trippers permit multiple on-off cycles every 24 hours.

A permanent time switch for a furnace enables you to lower the temperature of your home during sleeping hours and raise it back to a warmer setting by the time your family is ready to get up in the morning. Another kind of permanent time switch for controlling lights and small appliances is finished in several decorator colors. It mounts directly into a wall outlet box and matches the color scheme of the room.

Clock timers for almost any purpose and photo-electric cells offer the homeowner a remarkable range of practical uses in and around the house.

A seven-day timer enables you to control on-off times individually for each day of the week. Although this timer is intended primarily for commercial use, the owner of a vacation home can use it to turn on the heating plant and refrigerator in his weekend retreat. Another type of timer adjusts itself according to the length of day caused by seasonal changes.

Another convenience is a time switch which is wired to your sprinkler pump or master control valve. It will turn the lawn sprinklers on or off at the times you set and provide different watering schedules for three different areas. You can choose a model with a seven-day cycle or a twelve-day cycle.

A timer that turns off appliances is a practical energy saver. Just set it for the amount of time you want the appliance to operate from fifteen minutes to six hours. The unit can be used to control operating times of such items as fans, vaporizers and most commonly TV sets.

In choosing a portable or permanent timer, consider how it will be used. The less expensive models are usually less complicated and limited to lower watt output, the more expensive types usually have higher wattage ratings and offer extra features which may not be necessary.

PHOTO ELECTRIC CELLS

Photo electric controls are available in a variety of models to suit a householder's needs. A small portable version plugs directly into a wall outlet and can be used to control lights anywhere as long as outside light conditions can activate it. Another model screws into a lamp socket. More permanent photo electric controls are available which fit into electric boxes or in a special housing that mounts on an outside wall or on top of a post light. Some exterior lights come already equipped with their own photo control unit.

Be sure the photo control unit you buy does not respond to casual or intermittent light. To keep them from responding to intermittent light, many photo controls are equipped with a built-in delay that keeps them from being activated by any light source of less than twenty seconds duration. Other models have directional louvers that enable the photo cell to respond only to light conditions directly overhead.

For tighter control over a photo-control unit, use it in conjunction with an ordinary light switch. The disadvantage to this setup is that you must remember to turn the switch back on again the next day. You can also purchase a unit that incorporates an override switch or reset button. The model with the reset button offers the most versatility. It will turn your lights on at dusk and off at dawn, but you have the choice of cutting the power any time in between. The reset button will automatically recycle the control for the next day.

Build An Automatic Light Control

An expensive device that you can build yourself automatically turns on your garage or yard lights as you drive into the garage. From the time your headlights activate the unit, you have three minutes before it gives the lights a warning flicker and gradually dims them out.

The materials for this automatic light control are available at an electronic supply house. They might also have material for the 3″ x 4″ x 5″ cabinet that houses the unit.

The completed light control plugs into any wall outlet and will accept a light source up to 800 watts. A 1/4 inch grommet holds the light-operated rectifier (LSCR) to the front panel. To prevent extraneous light from activating the unit, keep the rectifier as close as possible to the rear of the grommet.

A manual control is available by adding a bell button to the circuit. Connect the bell wires to the points marked A and B on the diagram. For more *on* time, substitute the capacitor marked C2 for one with a higher value. For example, a 20mfd capacitor will give you six minutes of light.

Set the completed control where your headlights will hit it. Connect the unit to a power source and plug the garage lights into the back. Adjust the sensitivity (Rl) so the light comes on just when hit by the headlights. Keep the control out of any location where it might be activated by direct sunlight.

The automatic light controller can be adapted to other uses such as holding on the lights as you leave the basement or laundry area.

AUTOMATIC BURGLAR ALARMS

Until recently, conventional burglar alarm systems required that someone be there to hear them. That problem can now be solved with a device that will make a phone call when an intruder enters.

This latest security device connects to your telephone and to almost any kind of alarm system. A series of switches programs the unit to

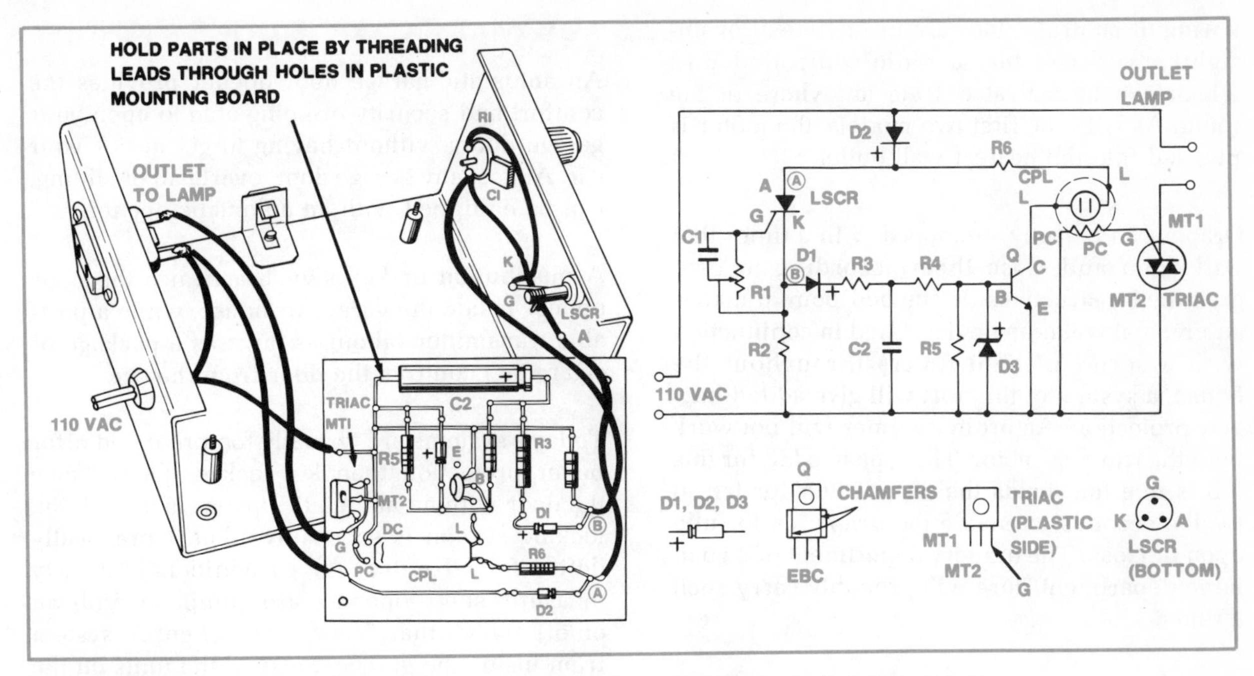

The materials for this automatic light control device may be purchased at almost any electronic shop.

place a call to a neighbor or to the local police station. When a prowler trips any of the activating devices, this unit will dial the number you have programmed into it. If the line is busy, it will call again and again, until the call gets through. At this point it will perform one or all of the following: it will transmit a series of coded tones, play a pre-recorded message for help (through an optional tape deck) and/or activate a microphone that allows the listener to hear the activity. This device can also be connected to a fire alarm system and programmed to call for help when the smoke or fire detection system is activated.

PUSHBUTTON DRAPERIES

Draperies or curtains that operate automatically are a welcome convenience in any household. A traverse rod that comes with a tiny built-in motor that moves along the traverse track can now be purchased. Any existing draperies with a traverse rod can be readily converted to remote control operation. The electric motor that does the work replaces the floor-mounted cord pulley and is hidden behind the drapes. The motor is activated by a switch mounted in the wall or by a tiny switching device attached to the motor by a long flexible power cable. If you feel that electric

Parts List

C1 — 0.1mfd capacitor
C2 — 10mfd 150 V capacitor
R1 — 1-meg. carb. potentiometer
R2 — 82,000-ohm, 1/2w resistor
R3 — 390-ohm, 1w resistor
R4 — 2.2-megohm, 1/2w resistor
R5 — 560,000-ohm, 1/2w resistor
R6 — 22,000-ohm, 1/2w resistor
D1, D2 — Diode (Motorola HEP 156 or equiv.)
D3 — Zener diode, 6.2V (Motorola HEP 103 or eq.)
Q — High-voltage transistor (eqv. Motorola HEP S3022)
LSCR — Light-op. SCR, 200V (eqv. Radio Shack 276-1081)
Triac — Mot. HEP R1725 or eqv.
CPL — eqv. Light coupler Sigma 301T1-120A1 (SW Tech. Prod., 219 W. Rhapsody, San Antonio, Tex.)
Perforated circuit board — 4″ x 5″

wiring or control cables are inconvenient or unsightly, you can buy a radio-controlled unit which can be activated from anywhere in the room. As with the first two models, the motor is plugged into the nearest wall outlet.

Drapes can be fully automated with a timer that will open and close them according to programmed instructions. In the bedroom, it makes an unusual wake-up device. Used in conjunction with a series of light timers throughout the house, a system of this sort will give added burglar protection. An ordinary timer will not work with the traverse motor. The type needed for this job is one that holds the on position for ten to twelve seconds to enable the draperies to fully open or close. The drapery department of a good large department store will probably carry such a timer.

FIREPLACE FIRE STARTERS

Devices available today make it possible to convert your present wood-burning fireplace into an automatic gas-operated unit that is so realistic it is almost impossible to tell it from the genuine article. Burning gas filtering through a pan of silicone granules or vermiculite causes the material to glow like embers. Ceramic logs or large volcanic rocks are set on top of the pan to achieve the realistic result.

Converting a fireplace to an automatic one is not complicated. If you already have a gas kindler, it is even simpler. Automatic gas units are available in kit form from most fireplace supply stores. To assemble the kit, run the gas line into the fireplace. Connect the burner pan, pilot light and igniter. Next, run the control cable to the control switch. The small heat-activated generator in the igniter allows you to place the switch anywhere within a distance of 50 feet from the fireplace. You can also set up your automatic fireplace to turn itself on when the room temperature drops. Just substitute a thermostat for the switch. Fill the pan with the granules provided. Place the grate over the pan and load it with cement logs or volcanic rock. Light the pilot and the operation is complete.

AUTOMATIC GARAGE DOOR OPENERS

An automatic garage door opener provides the comfort and security of being able to open your garage doors without having to get out of your car. Almost any garage door, overhead or sliding, can be equipped with an automatic opener.

A pushbutton or key switch activates the door opener inside the garage or house, while a portable transmitter (about as large as a package of cigarettes) controls the door from the car.

Today's systems are virtually foolproof and offer better protection than key-locked doors. Once the door with an automatic opener is closed, the locking system is so positive that it practically defies forced entry. As an additional security measure, some openers are equipped with an on/off switch that deactivates the entire system from inside the garage. Most all the units on the market incorporate a safety clutch that keeps the door from closing if it encounters some obstacle.

Door openers come in a chain drive or screw drive models. Prices vary, depending on optional features that can include key switches, automatic interval light and the number of transmitters desired. Some units are capable of lifting doors that weigh up to 250 pounds.

Automatic openers have been adapted to other uses as well. The screw-driver version can be set up to control overhead patio canopies and sliding roofs. It can also be used as a source of power to move large between-room partitions or to construct dumbwaiters.

A typical garage door system is shown here. Mechanical and electrical connections are similar to the majority of closers commonly available.

A guide to features which are desirable in choosing a garage door opener are: A motor and power train which are powerful enough to raise a heavy door (up to 200 lbs.) Sufficient illumination for a two car garage, preferably with an independent switch. A light delay system which allows adequate time for a security check and reaching the garage light switch (2 or 3 minutes is sufficient).

A manual over-ride provision. A positive automatic locking device for protection against forced entry. An instant reverse of mechanism to avoid damage to both obstructing objects and opener. A circuit provision to stop door at any convenient point and an instant-reverse switch cutoff for the last few inches, as a guard against activation by snow buildup. Engineering to allow as many do-it-yourself repairs and adjustments as possible.

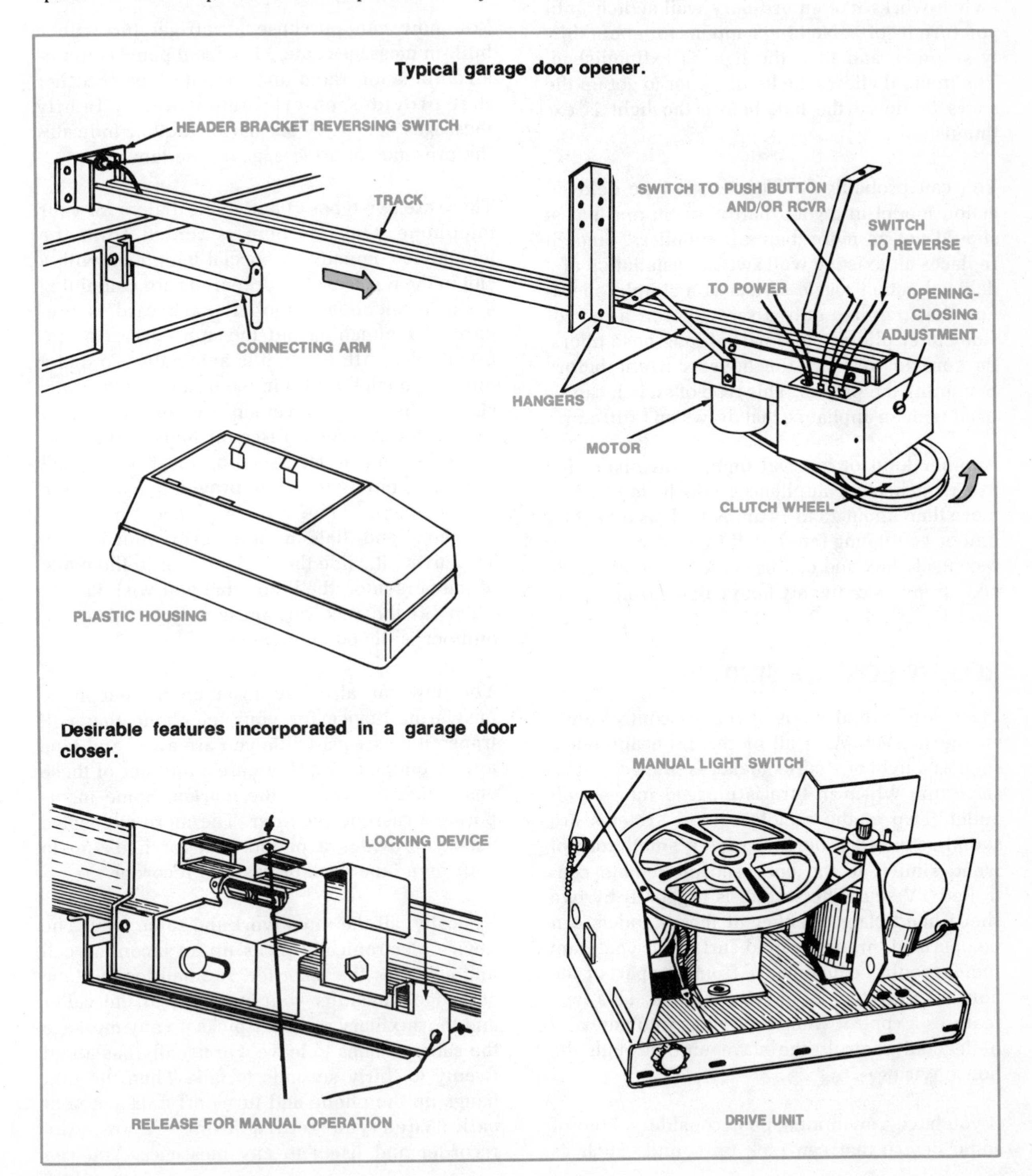

DELAYED ACTION SWITCHES

The installation of a delayed-action wall switch for your hall or basement lights is an easy and economical do-it-yourself project. A delay action switch works like an ordinary wall switch until you turn it "off". Nothing happens for about thirty seconds, and then the light is extinguished. The interval allows the homeowner to get up the stairs or down the hall before the light is extinguished.

You can probably find the toggle-type delayed action model in a good hardware store. Its cost should not be more than a few dollars. Since it replaces an existing wall switch, installation of a delayed action toggle switch is a simple operation that requires only a screwdriver, a pair of side cutter pliers, and a pair of long-nose pliers. Be sure to turn off the house current before beginning the project. This type of switch can be used with an appliance that draws up to 10 amps.

Another kind of interval timer is available for use with heavier appliances which don't draw more than about 13 to 14 amps such as a heating unit or ventilating fan. It will fit into an ordinary receptacle box and can be set for intervals up to sixty minutes or twenty hours, depending on the model.

REMOTE CONTROL SYSTEMS

There are several kinds of remote control units on the market. With all of them, an appliance such as a light or a coffeemaker is plugged into a slave unit which in turn is plugged into a wall outlet. Two of the remote control systems are sound-activated. The first uses a small control wand similar to the one used on remote controlled TV sets. The second is triggered by two sharp hand claps. Neither of these models can be operated through a solid surface. If you want remote control convenience from any part of the house, a third type of unit is available. This type features a control wand that plugs into any wall outlet and controls the slave unit through the house wiring.

If you have a swimming pool, consider a kind of sonic device that can pick up sounds such as splashing. The same system can also be used to detect motion in a room and can be hooked into most burglar alarm systems.

OTHER FORMS OF AUTOMATION

You now can purchase a refrigerator with a built-in message center. The front panel contains a combination radio and cassette tape recorder that provides entertainment and a family messages center. A special *on* button indicates the presence of a message on the tape.

There are two types of automatic dialers for your telephone. One of them is rented from the telephone company. A special telephone with a slot in the top accepts a prepared card containing a single telephone number. Each card is prepared by punching out the appropriate perforated holes. After that, it is automatic. To dial a number, push the card into the slot. Another version of the same convenience is available from your local electronic discount house. Programming the unit involves coding most often used telephone numbers on the provided deck with a special pencil. The unit is placed under the telephone and dials the number of your choice. To activate it, slide the deck pointer to the name of the person on the index that you wish to call. Then lift the receiver, press a button and the number is dialed automatically.

You now can also buy an automatic telephone answering device for your telephone that will transmit messages while you are away and tape any incoming calls. There are a number of these answering devices on the market. Some incorporate a cassette recorder. The more expensive variety provides a phono jack for hook up to your own tape deck or cassette recorder.

Basically, all the units work the same way. The device electronically picks up an incoming call and activates the recorder. A small looped tape cartridge transmits your message to the caller and the auxiliary recorder picks up any message the caller wishes to leave. He usually has about twenty to thirty seconds to talk. Then the unit hangs up the phone and turns off until the next call. When you return home, rewind the recorder and listen to any messages. You can also purchase a companion unit that enables you to telephone from anywhere in the country to receive any messages waiting for you. When you hang up the telephone, the at-home unit waits for the next call.

Automobile Air Conditioning and Heating

Auto heating and air conditioning systems operate on the same principle. Heat is moved from a hotter to a cooler medium. With the heating system, that hotter medium is engine coolant right from the water jacket. The cooler medium is the car's interior air or outside air that is brought in fresh and heated. In air conditioning, the hotter medium is the interior of the car and the cooler medium is refrigerant inside the system.

HEATING SYSTEMS

Most cars use hot-water heating. Hot engine coolant is pumped by the engine's water pump out of the top of the water jacket and through 5/8 inch diameter rubber heater hoses to a heater core. The heater core is much like a small radiator with myriad passages for coolant to flow through while giving up some of its heat. A squirrel-cage blower motor driven by a small DC electric motor sends air through the heater core's air passages and out of heater openings to warm the car as you drive. Coolant leaves the heater core, runs through a return heater hose and to the suction side of the water pump.

Heat Control

Two methods of heater temperature control are used. Both are operated by the temperature lever on the dashboard's heater control panel. In one method a cable-operated restricting valve in the hot-water line between engine and heater core is closed for less heat. In the other, called the blend-air system, a duct damper is used to blend heated air with cold, fresh air from outside the car. This method gives closer temperature control. The heater has a blower fan with a selection speed. On some modern cars the blower runs on low speed at all times to keep fresh air circulating.

Another control on some heaters permits you to select whether you will heat with inside air or bring in fresh air and heat it. Fresh-air heating is more comfortable and reduces window fogging. Hot-air from the heater core is carried up behind the instrument panel and released against the windshield for defrosting purposes. A defroster control diverts heater output to defrosting.

Heater Controls

Most heater valves and diverter doors are worked remotely by flexible cables. A few cars also use vacuum-operated valves moved by what are called *vacuum pots.* Some cars are beginning to use automatic heating and air conditioning temperature controls like those in the home. While they offer comfort at its best, these systems are not easy to service, and should be maintained by a professional technician.

Heating Problems

Control cables consist of an outer wire-wound housing and an inner hardened-wire control. The housing is clamped at both ends with the wire free to slide inside it. Through lack of lubrication or through kinking, heater control cables can tighten up and the control becomes hard to move. If forced, the cable can be bent or broken or the housing can even be pulled out of its hold-down clamp. You'll have to lie on the floor of the car to find and fix a problem cable.

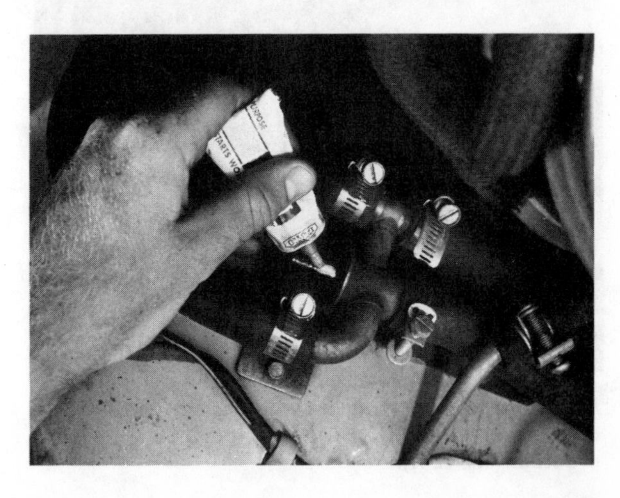

If the housing doesn't have an outer covering, oil the wire by flowing fine machine oil onto the housing and it will find its way inside. If the inner cable breaks, get a whole new cable from the car dealer and install it. If it is simply bent, you can quickly straighten it with a pair of slip-joint pliers. Cable adjustment is done by loosening the clamp and sliding the housing either toward the end to lengthen the action or away from the end to shorten the action. Tighten the clamp and test.

Sometimes a temperature-control restricting valve gums up and becomes hard to work. The valve should be replaced before the flexible cable breaks from the strain. Some restricting valves are built into the heater and require that the whole heater must be removed in order to adjust them. On this type, valve replacement becomes a professional job.

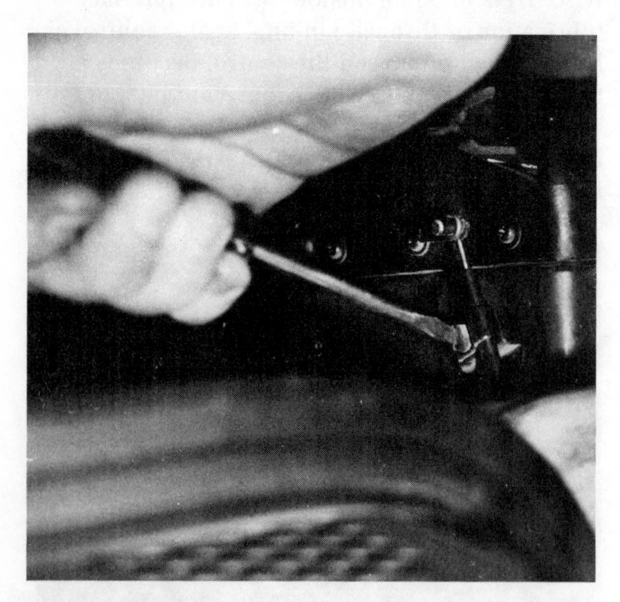

Adjusting flexible control cables to damper doors in the heater/defroster unit may correct a heating problem (see text).

No-Heat Condition

To correct a car heater that won't warm the car sufficiently consider the following factors. First of all, be sure that the car interior is well sealed. Air leaks around doors and windows can make the output of a new heater seem weak. Give your car doors the paper test. Close them on a strip of paper cut from a grocery bag and then try to pull the strip out. It should resist. If it slides easily, the weatherstripping is not making good contact at that spot. Try all around every door. Plug up the holes by slicing off the weatherstripping in these spots and cementing an additional piece of stripping underneath to make it thicker. Seal holes in the engine firewall with house weatherstrip caulking cord. Balled up and pressed into openings, this material remains flexible.

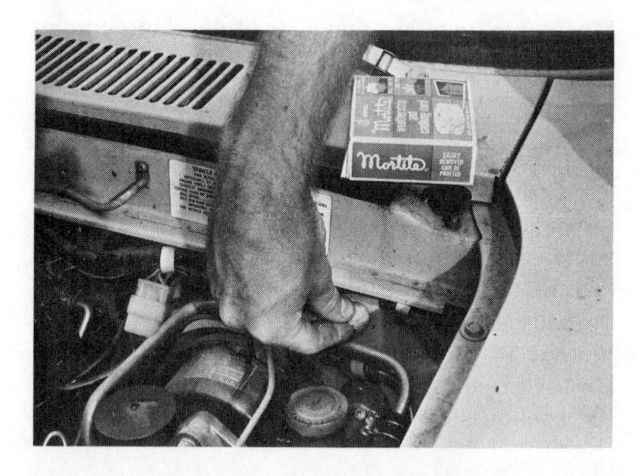

Check coolant level in the radiator. If it is too low, it will affect heater output. Refilling corrects the problem. Restricted flow of coolant can cause a lack of heat as well. Check both heater hoses for kinks. Pinch them; if they're hard and brittle or soft and gummy, they should be replaced. Generally, heater hoses more than a few years old are suspect. Replace if they look cracked or worn. Remove one and peer into it. If swelled rubber is reducing its diameter, replace it.

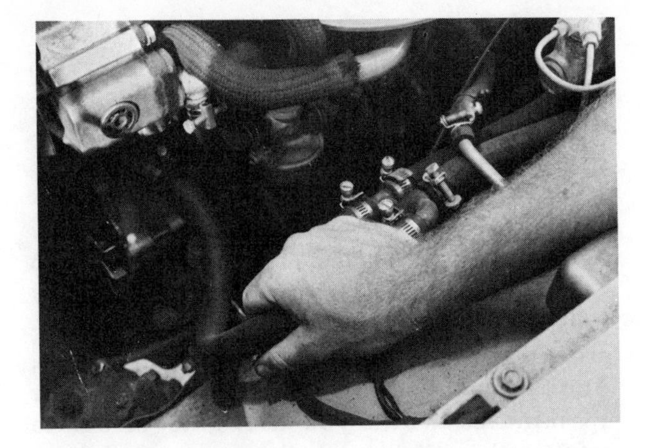

The most likely spot for a coolant-flow restriction is in the heater core. Sediment collects there and can easily block off some of the coolant passages. Reverse-flushing is the cure. Professionals use pressurized air/water equipment, but you can try a home-style reverse-flush yourself. To do it, drain the cooling system into a pan. Drain until you can remove the engine end of both heater hoses without losing coolant. Tape the end of a garden hose to the end of the water pump's heater hose and turn on the water full force. This should blow most collected sediment out through the other heater hose, which should be open. If this treatment doesn't help, you will need a professional reverse-flush.

If there is a flow restriction in the restricting valve, replace it.

One more heater check is of the blend-air damper door. If its cable is improperly adjusted

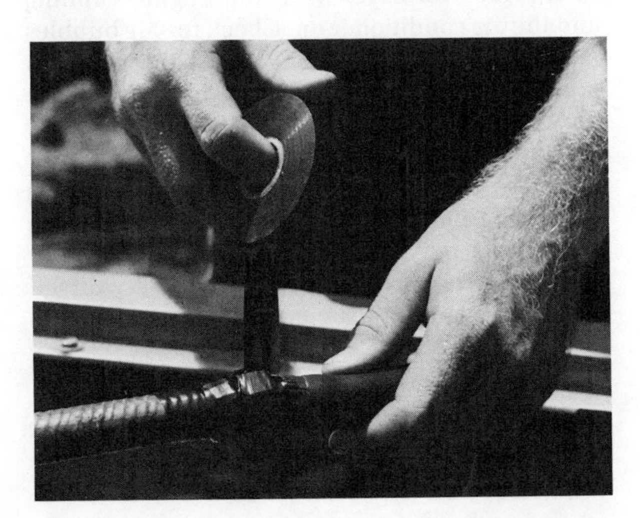

or has slipped, the damper may not move to its high-heat position. A simple cable adjustment will cure it.

Coolant Too Cool

A common cause of low heater output is not in the heater, but in the engine. Either a low-temperature thermostat has been installed in the engine water outlet or the thermostat has failed in an open position. In either case, the engine runs too cool and never produces the hot coolant needed to make a heater work properly. The dashboard temperature gauge may or may not read too low. Modern emissions controlled cars often use a single high-temperature thermostat all year round. Older cars used the high-temperature thermostat in the winter and called for a lower-temperature one in the summer. Consult your owner's manual for the temperature range thermostat you should use in winter. Installing the right one should make the heater work like new. (See the section on cooling systems for more on thermostat service.)

Blown Fuse

To correct an inoperative blower motor, simply locate the blower fuse and chances are you will find it has blown. Very possibly, no short-circuit is involved, but the fuse blew because it became overheated from long blower operation. Most times replacing the fuse will start the blower working again. If there is a short-circuit, it will have to be traced down and fixed before a new fuse will work. Check the blower switch, wiring, and motor.

In a case of too much heat, first check the blend-air valve. It may not be closing off enough heated air. If your car uses a restricting valve for heat regulation, check that for full-opening.

AIR CONDITIONING

Automotive air conditioning works like a home refrigerator, but uses the automobile engine for power. It also dehumidifies as well as cools.

The average auto air conditioning system has five components: compressor, condenser, receiver/dryer with sight glass, expansion valve and evaporator. The system also contains a refrigerant called Freon 12 that flows among them as either a liquid or a gas. Pressurized and cooled, it is a liquid, then when it is evaporated it becomes a gas. In so doing the refrigerant absorbs heat, much like rubbing alcohol evaporating from a feverish forehead. The compressor is a small pump which is belt-driven by the engine through a magnetic clutch. The condenser, the exterior heat-removing portion of the system, is located in the air stream ahead of the radiator. The receiver/dryer stores excess refrigerant and removes moisture from it. The expansion valve regulates the flow of refrigerant to the evaporator. The evaporator chills as Freon liquid turns to Freon gas. A blower forces air through the evaporator coils and out the air-conditioning ducts.

How The Air Conditioner Works

Freon 12 is a gas as it is drawn into the compressor. The compressor squeezes it into the condenser as a hot compressed gas. Heat is taken out by ambient air flowing through the condenser, cooling the gas and turning it to a liquid. The liquid is then pushed through the receiver/dryer by pressure from the compressor and on through the expansion valve where the air pressure is lower and flows on into the evaporator where the liquid turns back into a gas which, in turn, goes back to the compressor to begin the refrigeration cycle all over again.

In some systems, cooling temperature is controlled by a lever that opens and closes the expansion valve. In these, the compressor cycles on and off as needed to keep pressure in the system. In other systems the compressor runs continuously and temperature is governed by mixing cooled and heated air in a blend-air chamber. Some systems let you cool with either outside or recirculated inside air. For maximum cooling, use inside air, otherwise it is better to use outside air.

Refrigeration oil circulates through the system with refrigerant to lubricate the compressor and keep the expansion valve functioning.

In time, tiny leaks can lose enough refrigerant to affect car cooling and you will notice that the car doesn't get as cool as it once did. A professional can quickly tell whether the system leaks. He uses what is called a halide torch. Its flame changes color in the presence of minute concentrations of Freon.

You can prevent air-conditioning problems by three maintenance steps: (1) Use a soft brush to keep dead insects which will restrict heat flow brushed off the condenser. (2) Keep the compressor drive belt adjusted to proper tension. And (3) run the air conditioner once a month for 15 minutes while you drive, to circulate refrigeration oil through the system and keep compressor and expansion valve lubricated.

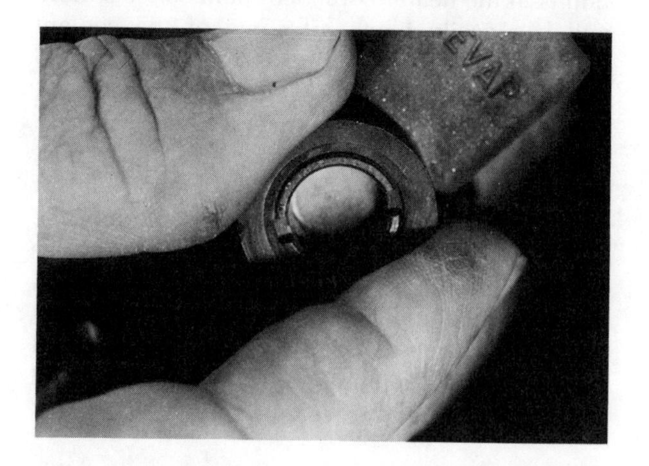

Troubleshooting

If you suspect that the air conditioner's cooling power is waning, look into the sight glass on top of the receiver/dryer with the engine running and the air conditioner on. Check for air bubbles in the refrigerant as it flows past the glass. (It may need to be wiped clean). There should be none, and the glass should be clear. If there is air in the system, the glass will look milky as the air bubbles rush past. Such a system needs bleeding and recharging. Oil streaks on the glass mean that all the refrigerant has leaked out. In either case, take the car to a garage as do-it-yourself recharging is not recommended.

Measuring Air Temperature

One other check you can make to tell whether the system is cooling as it should: Run the engine at a fast idle (about 1500 rpm) with the air condi-

tioner on full cold and the blower on low speed. Place a thermometer in one of the cold-air outlets where it will read out the temperature of the chilled air. This should be between 38 and 45 degrees F. depending on outside air temperature and humidity. If it is higher, the system probably needs recharging.

Recharging

The professional who recharges your car's air-conditioning system will use a manifold gauge set with two pressure gauges, and four or five puncture cans of Freon 12 refrigerant. The number of cans of refrigerant he adds depends on how low the system is and how much it holds. There is no way to tell until he fills it. The maximum weight of refrigerant your car's system holds is stamped on the compressor's identification plate. It definitely will need no more than that. One can of Freon 12 contains 14 ounces of refrigerant.

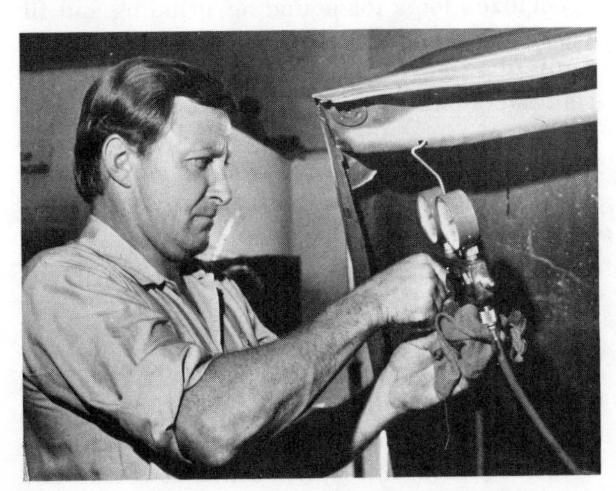

The manifold set is connected into two service valves which act like tire valves and are protected by knurled metal caps. The caps are removed for access, high-pressure-side and low-pressure-side hoses are hooked up, and the system is charged through the low side. The mechanic will charge with the air conditioner running until the high-side gauge reads a near-normal pressure of 120 to 180 psi (it depends on temperature). The low-side pressure should be a normal 15 to 30 psi. Pressures will normalize and the sight glass will clear soon as the system is full. He will add about half a pound more and stop.

Humidity Effects

High moisture content (humidity) makes the air harder to cool. Humidity can even reach the point where the evaporator ices up from condensed moisture. Then no more cool air can be delivered and the unit must be turned off to permit melting. Later, run it on a slightly higher temperature setting to prevent further icing. Once every season, check the evaporator drain hose to be sure that the condensate drains under the car, not on the floor.

Excess moisture inside the refrigeration system can freeze in the expansion valve and stop its action. This can only be cured by a professional with a vacuum pump who can evacuate the moisture and recharge the system. System noises (other than leaves falling into the blower) should be diagnosed by a mechanic.

The only other service you can perform is to check the air conditioner fuse if the compressor's magnetic clutch refuses to cycle on. Watch the inner part of the compressor pulley. It should turn when the clutch engages. If there is trouble with the fuse, look for one or two 30-ampere time-delay fuses. One may be in the fuse panel, the other may be difficult to find. Look for its location in the service manual. If a replacement fuse blows, too, take the car to a professional.

A complete professional check of the system's operation, plus bleeding and recharging, usually costs less than $20, including the cost of new refrigerant.

Automobile Body Repairs

The pleasant first few months with a car that is new and looks it can be extended indefinitely now that touch-up products widely available make it easy to remove minor dents and scratches from the body of the car. A car that has suffered from bent fenders, flying gravel and the doors of other cars can regain much of the beauty with which it came from the factory.

The products to use are ones designed for the amateur without previous experience. (You will not need to be a refinisher, or even a neat hand with a brush, to use them.) For even fairly large jobs you will not need to body solder and/or use specialized tools for pounding, grinding and filing. The principal items of equipment will be putty filler that comes in a can ready to use, fine sandpaper and spray paint. For a larger job, such as one of those shown in the illustrations, you will need a file and perhaps some power sanding equipment commonly found in home workshops.

KINDS OF PAINT

For small nicks and deep scratches in the paint, the easiest thing to use is a brush, as fine and soft as possible. Paint to use with it may come in a small bottle purchased from the new-car dealer that, in some instances, will contain a brush. You

Sand the area smooth. With heavy coats of baked-on enamel, as with this classic Mercedes-Benz, power sanding with a disc will speed the job.

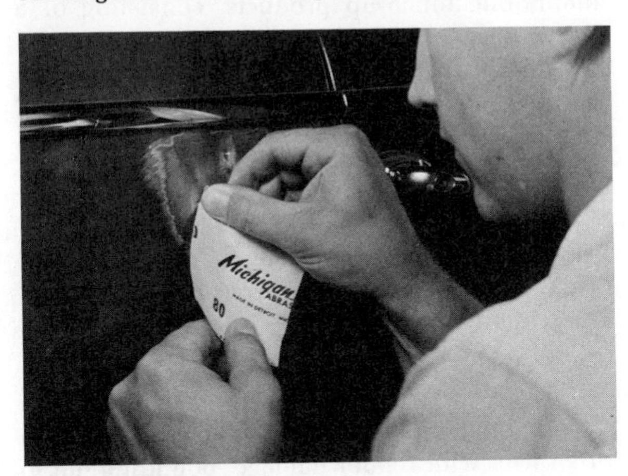

Complete the sanding by hand, feathering edges with very fine sandpaper.

may need to spray a small puddle from a self-spray can onto a piece of metal, and then dip the brush into it; or you may have to go to an auto-parts dealer and have a small supply made up for you. Dealers who handle car paints have formulas from which they can mix almost any hue of paint. You can have this made up for brushing and thin it as necessary for spraying as well.

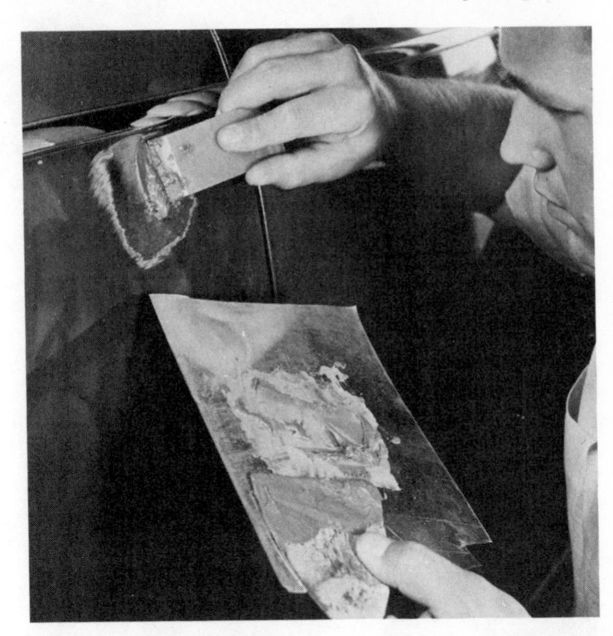

Mix plastic body filler and smooth it on with spreader supplied. Mix just enough; it sets in minutes.

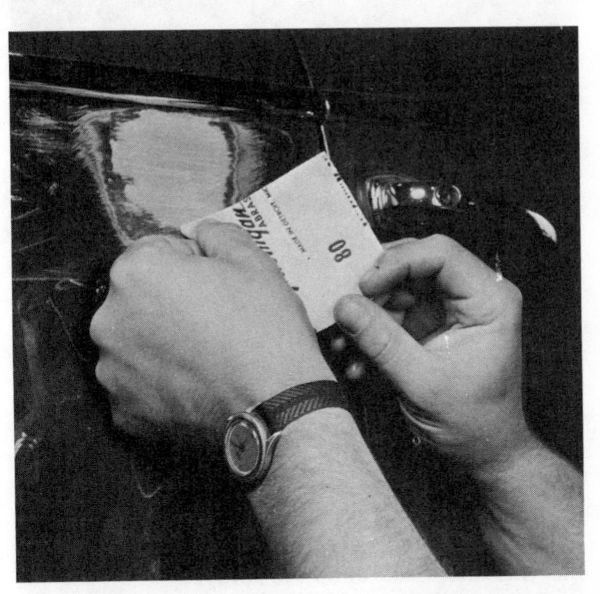

Sand again, this time to smooth the filler to the contours of the car body. Spray with gray primer.

Any but the tiniest touch-ups can be done neatly with spray methods . . . using either some kind of paint sprayer or self-spray aerosol can.

Because approximately 300 colors are now available in self-spray cans, it is likely that you can find the color name and number of your automobile's finish in the dealer's stock. This

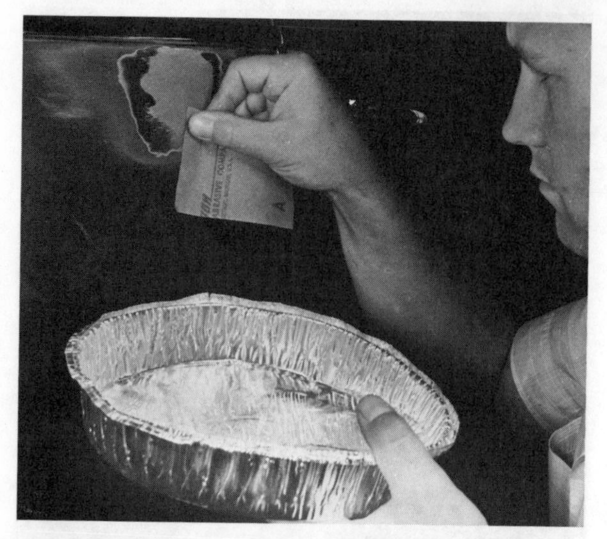

Use fine water sandpaper to smooth after prime coat. Dip paper in water (held in foil pan here).

Larger rough shield of newspaper protects neighboring areas, and reduces clean-up afterwards.

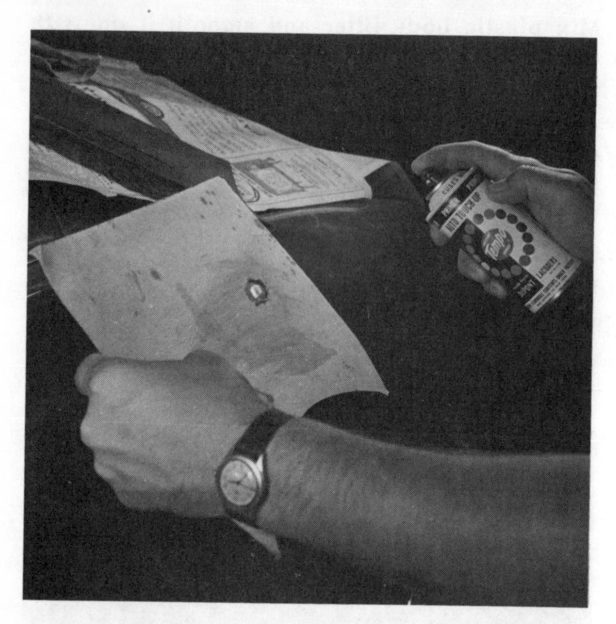

Use the same procedure to repair even a tiny dent like this one: Use a shield to spray.

self-spray touch-up paint is also made to match some outboard motors.

If you are not able to match the color of your car in pre-mixed aerosol cans there are still two paint-purchase possibilities. You can have a pint of lacquer or enamel made up for you and then use it in a spray gun. Or, if your dealer offers a comparatively new and very convenient service, you can have the paint spray-packed for you in the same sort of aerosol can used for pre-packaging.

If this spray-pack service is not available and you do not own a spray gun, there is a simple and inexpensive gun made by a leading maker of automobile touch-up products, consisting of a plastic head and nozzle placed on a small jar and powered by a can of propellant. The propellant is replaceable, and the unit has many household and arts-and-crafts uses, with adhesives, solvents, lubricants and insecticides as well as paint products.

Primers to use where bare metal is exposed are sold in self-spray cans wherever touch-up paints are available.

PREPARING THE METAL

Where dents are large and can be reached, as is often true with fender damage, pounding out to approximate shape will save on plastic filler and give it a more reliable job.

Regular auto-body tools for bumping and hammering out dents are convenient, but ordinary household tools will serve, especially where damage is minor. A carpenter's hammer used in conjunction with a wooden or rubber mallet (as shown in one of the photographs) will diminish most dents to the point where they are easily leveled by use of filler.

The next step before sanding is cleaning the surface. Wipe it free of any grease, dirt, wax or other polish with a cloth soaked in oil-free naphtha or paint thinner. Then wipe the area clean of any residue with a fresh dry cloth. Careful cleaning becomes especially important when a car has been waxed at all recently with a silicone polish. Any trace of silicone that remains on the car will produce spots in the new paint easily recognizable from their names: craters and fish eyes. If you can find any of these effects, or if you believe silicone wax has been used, you should follow a more thorough cleaning routine: Wash off the area to be painted with a good solvent (often available where touch-up supplies are sold) made for cleaning off silicones, or with oil-free naphtha. While the area is still wet, switch to dry, clean rags. Wipe the surface thoroughly, changing rags frequently. It is especially desirable to do any necessary sanding with water and sandpaper, since the water will help to keep down silicone dust. After sanding, wash off with water and dry the area thoroughly, then repeat the cleaning process.

When a dent is this large semi-paste paint remover may be needed.

SANDING

Sand the well-washed surface. Final sanding should be done with water sandpaper in a fine grade. Except where only a small spot or superficial damage is being repaired, fine sanding can be preceded by use of coarser sandpaper and power sanding equipment (see photographs) to speed up the work. Wet sanding is accomplished by dipping the sandpaper in water before using and frequently during the process to keep the abrasive paper clean and to maintain good cutting action.

After thoroughly cleaning off paint remover, polish to clean bare metal with a disc sander in an electric drill.

Sharp edges should be smoothed down or *feathered in* for about half an inch around bare spots. It is better to take more light strokes than it is to hurry the job with fewer strokes and heavy pressure. For straight or line scratches it is best to sand lightly along the scratch until the finish at the edge is very thin. Keep the sanded area as narrow as possible. Try not to cut through to bare metal at any point; bare metal requires priming, adding an extra step to the process. Finish the sanding with a light rotary motion to smooth the paint down to a feather edge. With round spots, sand in the same way but use a rotary motion only.

On edges and corners a parallel sanding motion should produce a good feather edge. Take care to sand very lightly on edges and corners since cutting will be rapid and you are trying to expose as little metal as possible. After sanding, wipe the area thoroughly with oil-free naphtha or paint thinner, preferably with a lint-free cloth. A good final clean-up step, especially if the area to be painted is large, is wiping with a tack rag.

Even an enormous cavity like this can be filled permanently with plastic body filler.

A disc sander in electric drill is used again, this time to smooth hardened filler. File and hand sanders also help.

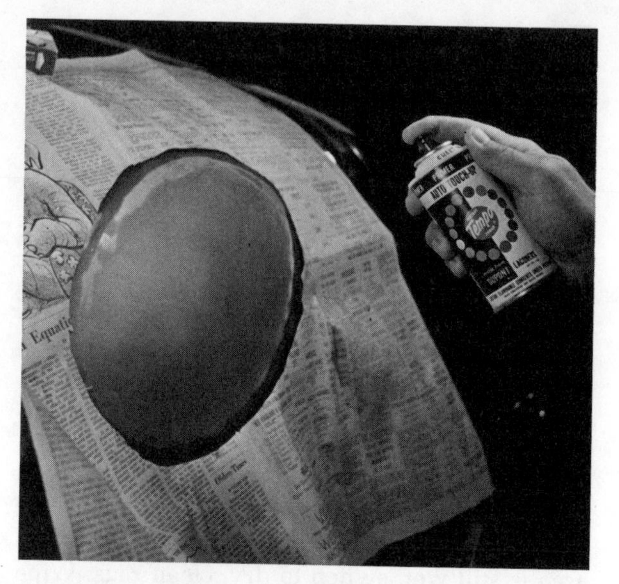

Areas around the repair should be masked to catch over-spray while gray primer is used.

With finish coat on and hardened, smoothing out with rubbing compound is all that is needed to complete the repair job.

FILLING DENTS

After sanding and cleaning, fill any dents with plastic filler of a type made for auto-body work, mixing only as much as can be used immediately. The steps in applying this plastic and shaping it are shown in the photographs.

If the repair includes a hole or a rusted-out place, use fiberglass to reinforce the plastic. Fiberglass screen for this purpose is included with many filler kits. These kits consist of the plastic filler, hardener to mix with it, fiberglass screen, sandpaper, a small tool for applying the plastic and detailed instructions.

PROTECTING SURROUNDING SURFACES

Any spray operation from primer to final coat produces some paint dust. Use newspapers held by masking tape to shield near-by surfaces, especially those that are chrome or of a different color from that being sprayed.

When painting a very small area, or when using primer, make a touch-up shield as in the photographs. If touching up a very small nick or scratch while using a shield of generous proportions, no other masking may be needed.

Use a stiff sheet of paper, cardboard or shirtboard about letter size or larger to make a touch-up shield. Cut a slit in the center of it about the size of the scratch to be painted. A small round hole will be suitable, of course, for painting a round spot. In using the shield hold it about 1 inch (perhaps half an inch if the area in question is very tiny) from the surface, lining up the hole or slot with the scratch. In painting, start to spray on one side of the hole, move across the shield past the hole, then stop the spray. Allow a few minutes between coats. Using this system allows the paint to hit the spot that needs it, with just enough overspray to blend into the original paint with a smooth feather-edge that gives no sharp lines or laps.

USING PRIMER

A primer coat is needed only if bare metal is showing or filler has been used. Its function is to insure good adhesion and long life for the finish coat.

Apply the primer with standard spray painting techniques, unless the directions on the can differ. After good coverage has been obtained, allow the final prime coat to dry at least half an hour. Then sand gently, using No. 400 water sandpaper and water. Any overspray dust from the primer should be removed from surrounding surfaces, using rubbing compound, before applying the color coat. Use oil-free naphtha or paint thinner to remove all traces of the rubbing compound. If you have a tack rag, use it to wipe the area before proceeding with the spray color coat.

SPRAY PAINTING

Make sure the color is a match. Verify the car manufacturer's paint code number on a small metal plate, usually under the hood or on the post by the driver's door. Holding the top of the spray can against the car finish will give an additional rough check on whether the color is right.

There is one compatibility problem to consider. The touch-up lacquer will go on satisfactorily over lacquer or baked-on enamel (the kinds of finishes used in automobile factories). If, however, the car has been repainted at some time with an air-dried enamel, there is a possibility that lacquer solvents could soften or lift the old finish. This problem may not happen, however, if the air-dried enamel has had at least several months to harden. To be safe, test the finish first by spraying some inconspicuous place. This test will give a chance to verify the color match as well.

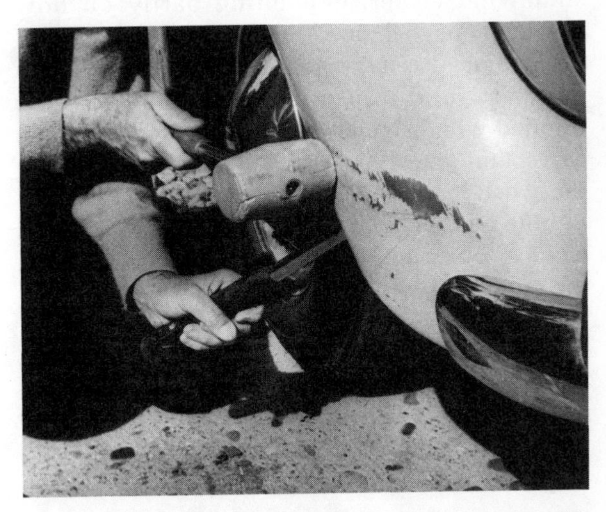

With whatever tools that are on hand, such as this carpenter's hammer and rubber mallet, beat out the dent as well as possible. Do not expect near-perfection as it is not necessary.

Sand off paint or rust down to bare, shiny metal. Feather at the edges. Use a sander or sand by hand.

Give the can of spray paint time to warm up to normal room temperature before use. Shake it thoroughly to mix the contents. It is mixing properly when you hear the metal ball clicking inside.

To be sure that the can of spray is working properly make a test run now on something like a tin can. The most important thing you will learn from this test is the ideal distance from nozzle to surface. For most spray-pack finishes this distance will be at least 6″ and perhaps 10″ or more. With some types of spray gun it will be somewhat closer, depending partly on how much you have thinned the lacquer or enamel. If the enamel has been mixed without spray-gun use particularly in mind, it may need to be thinned with as much as an equal amount of the correct thinner. If the spray nozzle is too close to the work, paint will pile up on the surface and bubble because the propellant gas has not had a chance to escape. If the nozzle is too far away, the coverage will be spotty.

Do not try to cover with a single heavy coat. That type of approach produces runs and sags. Use quick, short strokes. Give the finish time to become tacky between coats.

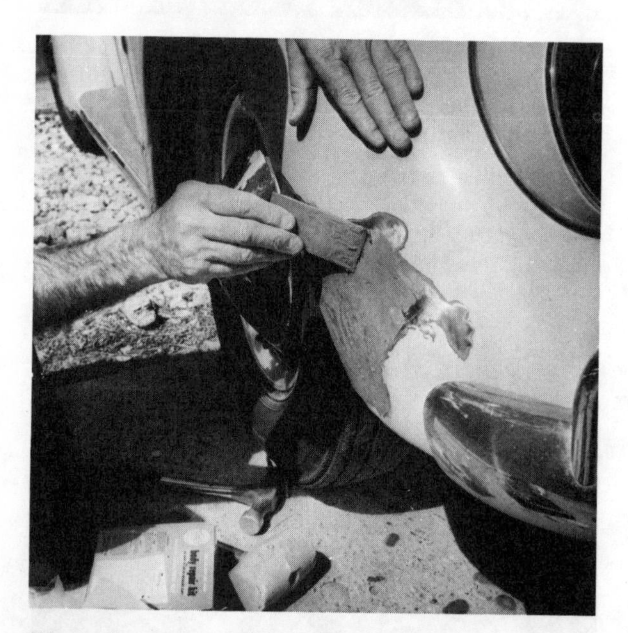

Mix body-repair plastic and spread it on, smoothing it as well as possible during application. Allow 15 minutes to dry.

Now smooth the plastic to body shape. Finishing sander speeds the job, but it can be done by hand.

Mask and spray — first with primer, then with touch-up paint. A spray gun is used here, instead of self-spray touch-up color, since color of this car was not available in prepacked paint. Job is completed by overspray with lacquer thinner.

SPRAYING METALLIC FINISHES

Glamorous high-metallic finishes found on some cars call for slightly modified techniques to produce the best match. What is in the paint can may precisely duplicate what was put on your car, yet your touch-up can fail to look the same. What is necessary is that you must apply the touch-up with the same degree of dryness that was produced during the original finishing. Otherwise, the way the metal particles align themselves in the paint film may differ and so will the appearance. To gain the desired look, practice on an inconspicuous spot in the trunk, under the hood or on a door jamb.

If the touch-up seems too dark, lighten the result in one or more of these ways: warm the car surface; warm the contents of the can by placing it in lukewarm water for a few minutes; hold the can farther away from the car; speed up the spray stroke; or increase the drying time between coats.

If the color appears too light, go the opposite way: hold the nozzle closer to the surface; slow down the spray stroke, and decrease the flash time (drying time) between coats.

LAST TOUCHES

Leveler is a solvent used to blend in any dry ring of overspray dust around the area you have touched up. It comes in a spray can, like the paint, and should be available from the same dealer. Apply it sparingly — just a light mist coat — after the finish has had time to dry. Use of leveler is not essential but it helps the appearance and, if not overused, will eliminate most of the need of rubbing.

After allowing 4 hours drying, use fine rubbing compound to remove any overspray dust that you can see on the surrounding areas. Since the methods described in this article apply also to repairing damage to the finish on appliances, it should be noted that too much rubbing is to be avoided with their porcelain-like surfaces. The overly smooth finish resulting from excessive rubbing will not match the original.

Except with very minor touch-ups it is best to allow the new finish to season for about a month before waxing.

TROUBLESHOOTING

Here are some problems and remedies one may encounter in large-scale touch-ups.

Blushing: Cloudiness appearing on the surface of the paint is usually caused by spraying in very hot and humid weather.

Craters and Fish Eyes: As described earlier, these blemishes are caused by the fact that particles left from silicones in auto polishes repel paint. Avoid by cleaning the surface thoroughly, and changing rags frequently while cleaning.

Flaking and Peeling: Poor adhesion comes from wax or grease on the car surface or prime coat. Thorough cleaning will prevent this.

Lifting: When new paint raises at once, it indicates that solvents of a previous coat are coming through. Give each coat enough time to dry.

Pinholing and Pitting: Small holes that appear on the painted surface are produced by escape of trapped propellant in self-spray lacquer. This will not happen if both the spray can and the car are warm and nozzle is held 10″ or more away during spraying.

Rough Finish: If this occurs when the spray can was held far enough away, it means the metal was not properly prepared. Be sure to sand metal, putty or primer to a good smooth finish.

Runs, Sags, Curtains: These conditions will occur only if you hesitate while spraying, or put on too heavy a coat at once. If run starts, stipple it out with fingertips and smooth over with a mist coat of spray. Runs discovered after the finish dries can generally be removed with a razor blade, then polished out or refinished.

Wrinkling: An overly heavy application of finish can cause the surface to buckle as will spraying lacquer over air-dried enamel of an earlier repair or repainting job.

Automobile Care & Maintenance

[SEE SYSTEMS, AUTOMOTIVE.]

Automobile Fuel Consumption

[SEE SYSTEMS, AUTOMOTIVE.]

Automobile Safety

[SEE DRIVING SAFETY & AUTOMOBILE INSURANCE.]

Automobile Systems

[SEE SYSTEMS, AUTOMOTIVE.]

Automobile Troubleshooting

[SEE SYSTEMS, AUTOMOTIVE.]

Awl

An awl is a pointed instrument which can easily make a pilot hole for nails, screws or brads. Primarily used when working with leather or wood, it is an appropriate tool for installing doors and door locks, fixing loose handles and fastening to wood.

If a smaller, more precise hole is required, a scratch awl is generally employed instead. A scratch awl is sharper than the common awl and can, therefore, be helpful when laying out center lines and center punching. *SEE ALSO HAND TOOLS.*

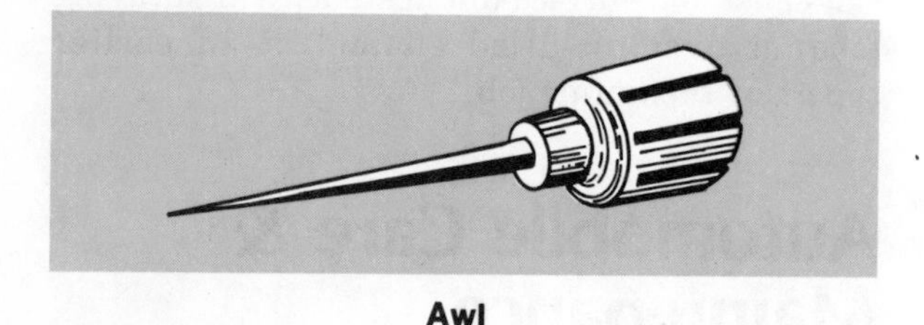

Awl

Awnings

Both home and recreational vehicle awnings are designed primarily to provide protection from the sun and rain. Most window awnings are still made of cotton canvas, but those used to cover patios and terraces are usually aluminum, fiberglass or metal.

CANVAS WINDOW AWNINGS

Window awnings have a wood, metal or steel alloy frame that can be shaped to slant at various angles, extend straight over the window or curve up and then down to cover the top half of the window. Canvas coverings for the frames are no longer restricted to solid, drab colors. Stripes add a decorative touch to any home. Some canvas awnings serve as shutters by fitting flat over the window and attaching to the window or house with one bar at each end of the awning. Window awnings keep a house cooler, cutting air conditioning costs; as well as reducing the fading and decaying of carpet, drapes and fabric-covered furniture.

PATIO & TERRACE AWNINGS

Aluminum, metal and fiberglass awnings, generally called patio covers, are more popular than canvas awnings because they are more durable and versatile. When prefinished or primed, aluminum and metal covers can be painted to match the house. Fiberglass awnings require no painting and are available in a wide range of colors. The frame of a canvas awning and a patio cover are basically made of the same materials: metal or aluminum supports and poles. However, patio covers have a higher resistance to rain, snow, sun rot and mildew than canvas awnings. Patio covers add beauty and value to a home, require no special cleaning, no storage, seldom tear and, with gutters and downspouts, provide proper water drainage. They are available in many sizes, styles and colors to suit most coverage areas and decors.

AWNINGS FOR RECREATIONAL VEHICLES

Awnings for travel trailers and recreational vehicles are becoming increasingly popular for their protection from sun and rain. These awnings generally roll up automatically into an aluminum case that is fastened to the top of one side of the trailer. Setting up these awnings is a simple operation. Pull the long tab at the center of the awning out about half way. Extend the spring arms from the side of the trailer and attach them to the chrome or aluminum awning bar in the position desired. Finish pulling the awning out for complete coverage.

Travel awnings are available in a variety of solids and stripes as well as many fabrics. The most common materials for travel awnings are canvas, vinyl, fiberglass and assorted blends.

Care of Travel Awnings

More modern canvas awnings are chemically treated on the top surface to prevent the build up of moisture and mildew. However, both sides of the awning should be lightly brushed with a medium bristle brush or whisk broom to preserve these chemicals and eliminate mildew. Using soaps and detergents, bug sprays and dry cleaning agents on canvas awnings will quickly deteriorate the special coatings and should never be used.

Vinyl laminate on canvas can be washed with a sponge or brush and mild soaps and detergents. Because water drops magnify the effect of the sun's heat and can cause premature yellowing and stiffening of the vinyl, it is better to wash the awning on a cloudy day or after sunset. Brush the underside of the awning as you would the canvas varieties.

Vinyl laminate on dacron or fiberglass is not affected by soap or bleaching solutions. Frequent hosing or washing will prevent build up of the dirt, soot and pollution that cause mildew. If stubborn stains persist, use a bleaching solution unless the awning has an additional self-cleaning coating that would be affected by harsh chemicals.

Awnings of dacron and Acrilan blends are practically mildew-proof because they are woven of inorganic threads. Clean these awnings with a sponge or brush and mild soap. They can be rolled up wet, but should be dried as soon as possible to prevent the forming of small mildew patches.

Awning Window

Structurally, an awning window is hinged at the top so that it can swing out at the bottom. It may have one or more than one framework in which the panes of glass are set. Frequently both awning windows and fixed units are used to provide a room with maximum ventilation. Several operating sashes can close on themselves or on rails separating the units if they are stacked vertically.

Cranking mechanisms or a push-bar mounted on the frame operate the sash. As the bottom of the sash moves forward, sliding friction hinges cause the top rail to come down. This so-called projected action operates most awning windows. Storm sash and screens are attached to the inside. This type of window does provide protection against rain damage while the window is open. A "ribbon" effect in which awning windows are installed side by side has proved to be quite popular. Besides allowing greater flexibility in arranging furniture along outside walls, this type of installation provides privacy for bedroom areas.

Before installing awning windows, outside clearance must be considered. Open windows must not hinder movement on walkways, porches or patios which are located adjacent to outside walls.

Maintenance and repair of awning windows includes periodic lubrication of parts, the replacement of panes and weatherstripping and window cleaning. To allow easy washing, most awning windows may be opened flat for cleaning from the inside. To replace panes, the sash must be released from the cranking mechanism and tilted flat. Once the hinges are exposed, separate them from the sides of the frame-work to allow the removal of the window. Adhesive-backed foam weatherstripping may be needed around the exterior frame of older types of awning windows. The lubrication of the cranking mechanism, scissors type linkage and sliding hinge and track is all that is required.

Backband

A backband is a narrow rabbeted molding used on the corner of a door or window casing for ornamentation or to create a heavy trim appearance. *SEE ALSO MOLDING & TRIM.*

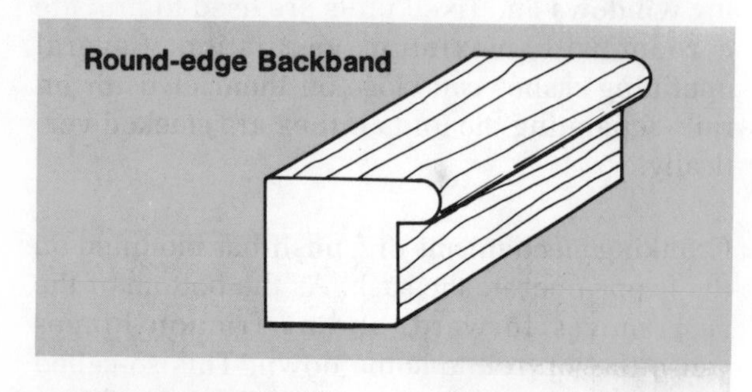

Backfill

Backfill is the term applied to the replacement of excavated earth into a pit, trench or against a foundation wall.

Before filling the excavation outside a foundation wall, the foundation should be adequately cured and waterproofed. To obtain rapid and complete drainage around basements, the backfill should be gravel, filled to within a foot of the surface.

If heavy power equipment is used to backfill, care should be taken not to damage foundation walls. Also, installed tile lines and basement windows should be protected. *SEE ALSO FOOTINGS & FOUNDATIONS.*

Backfire

Backfire is an explosion in an automobile's intake manifold, the mechanism which transports the fuel/air mixture from the carburetor to the combustion chambers. Backfire results from any of the following conditions: a lean mixture of fuel (sometimes caused by presence of dirt or water in the fuel); cold engine and presence of raw gasoline in exhaust system ("flooding") caused by pumping the gas pedal too many times while starting engine; deposits of excess carbon; leakage of unnecessary air into engine; sticking intake valves or broken valve springs; crossed sparkplug wires; loose ignition system wire; internal damage of high tension wires, which causes high voltage in the sparkplugs. *SEE ALSO SYSTEMS, AUTOMOTIVE.*

Backsaw

The backsaw derives its name from the strip of steel which runs along its back to help stiffen and reinforce it. It comes in 10- to 16-inch lengths, usually having 14 teeth to the inch. Due to its small teeth, the backsaw is used for fine, accurate cutting. It can be used with a miter box to form wood joints, and with a vise to make accurate, smooth end cuts. Tenons can be made with a backsaw by holding the work in a vise.

In sawing with the backsaw, you should begin on the waste side of the line with the handle tilted slightly upward. Start the saw kerf with a short stroke toward you and proceed with long, smooth strokes, leveling the saw as you go. Short strokes will result in a buildup of sawdust which, in turn, will cause the blade to bind. A larger type of backsaw is the miter box saw. *SEE ALSO HAND TOOLS.*

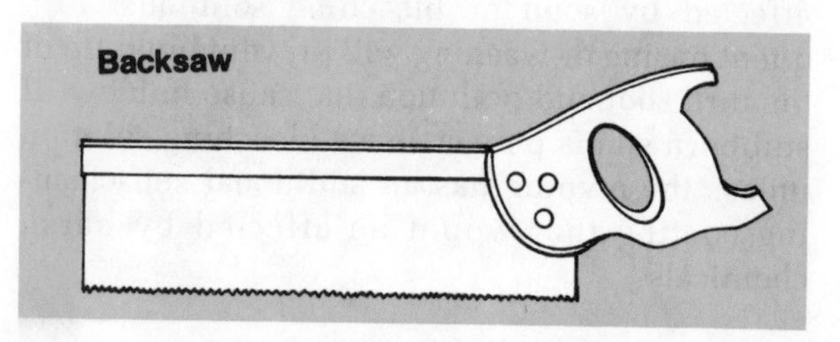

Backwired Receptacles

Backwired receptacles, unlike most receptacles which are side-wired, receive the wires through the back of the device. This convenience makes wiring outlets simpler by eliminating the need for forming loops in the wire ends that connect to the terminal screws in the receptacle.

The stripped wire ends are first inserted into the back of the receptacle, rather than the side. Then the screws, found in their normal position for side wiring, are tightened to press onto metal clamps which bring the wires into good contact.

Stripping guides are found on the surface of the receptacle to assure that the wires will be bared to the proper length, eliminating the danger of exposed wires in the connection. *SEE ALSO WIRING SYSTEMS, ELECTRICAL.*

Ball Joint Disc

The ball joint disc, a rigid type of sander, is rubber-cushioned with its shaft on a universal joint which allows the drill to tilt while the disc remains flat on a surface. Ideal for general preliminary sanding such as rough sanding and paint removal, it is especially suited to wavy surfaces on old paneling and furniture.

Even though the ball joint disc is four inches in diameter, only $1^1/_4$ inches of the disc contact the surface. Consequently, there is not much speed differential over the working area. The disc can be used flat on the work because the paper-gripping hub is recessed. Using light pressure to keep r.p.m. up, keep the disc moving and overlap successive passes slightly.

The Ball Joint Disc or Swirlaway Sander.

An overall good cabinet sander for the small shop, it is easy to use and will not scratch or dig even if the drill is tilted. This sander rides over and adapts to surface contours, smoothing without "sanding through" stain or patina of high spots. Unlike the flexible disc sander, the ball joint disc, when handled with care, can smooth wallboard seams. *SEE ALSO PORTABLE POWER TOOLS.*

Balloon Framing

Balloon framing is a type of wall construction in which the wall and corner studs are continued directly from the foundation to the plate, the horizontal structure that supports the roof rafters or trusses. This type of framing provides for the use of a reduced amount of cross-sectional lumber, thus preventing wood shrinkage,

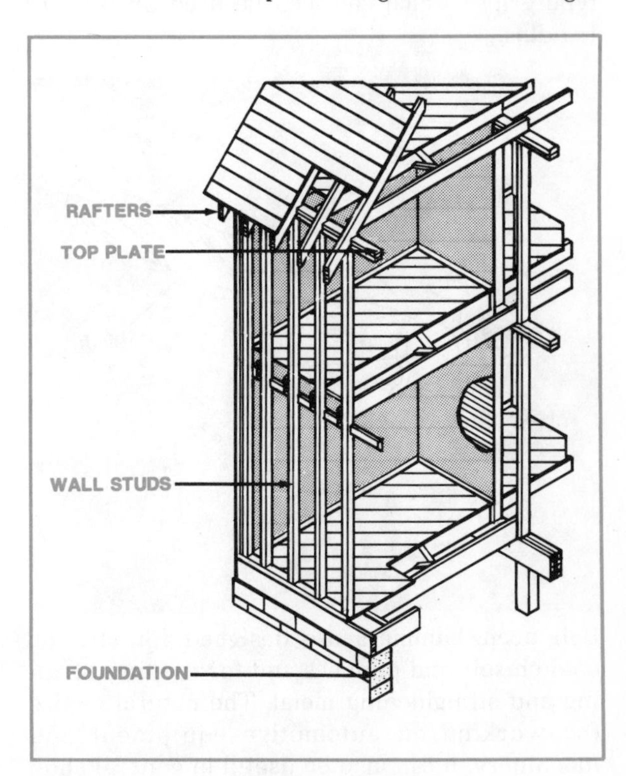

Balloon Framing

plaster cracks and other related problems. Balloon framing also includes firestopping, which is a method of using stops or blocks made of an incombustible material between the wall studs to prevent the spread of fire and smoke. These features, due to added vertical stability, make balloon framing very useful in the construction of two-story structures. *SEE ALSO WALL & CEILING CONSTRUCTION.*

Ball Peen Hammer

One of the most commonly used hammers, a ball peen hammer has a rounded, slightly crowned striking face with beveled edges and a round, ball-shaped peen opposite the face. Weights, based on the head, range from 4 to 40 ounces. A 20-ounce head is adequate for the average job. Handles may be hickory, solid or tubular steel or fiberglass. The tubular steel, solid steel and fiberglass types are generally fitted with rubber-type grips, which can also be used on hickory handles.

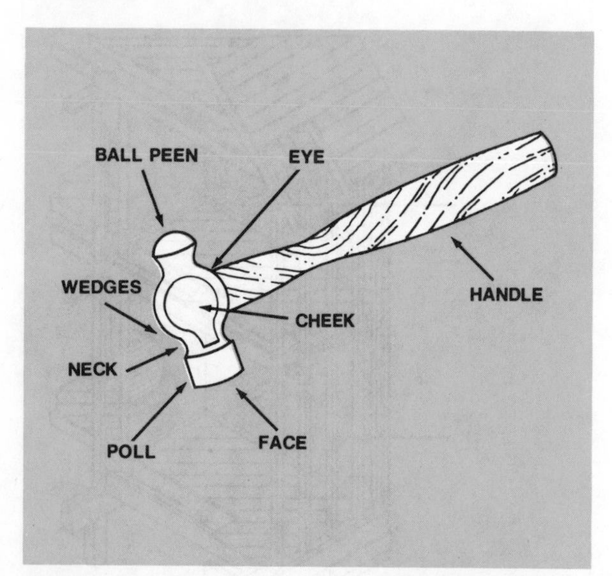

Ball peen hammers are designed for striking cold chisels and punches and for riveting, shaping and straightening metal. The natural choice for working on automotive equipment and machinery, it can also be useful in general shop work. *SEE ALSO HAND TOOLS.*

Ball Valve

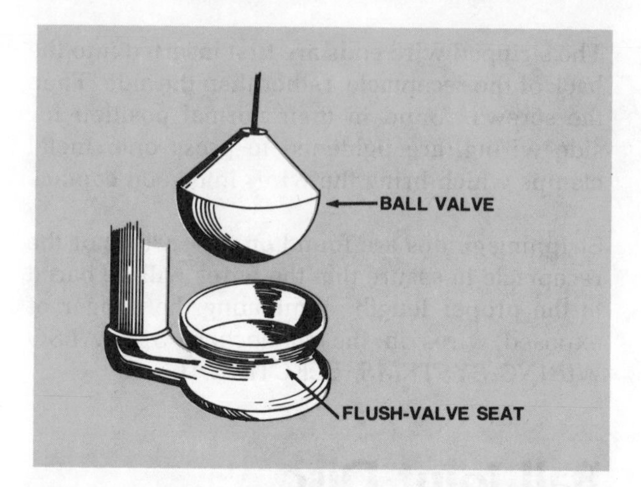

Part of a toilet tank assembly showing ball valve and seat.

A ball valve, also called a stopper ball, is a part of a toilet which opens to let water from the flush tank flow into the toilet bowl. When the handle on the flush tank is activated, the ball valve is lifted off its seat and floats upward. Water passes through an opening into the toilet bowl until the water level falls below the seat and the ball valve drops and closes the opening. The tank can then be filled again. *SEE ALSO TOILET.*

Baluster

A baluster is a vertical spindle forming part of a stairway or balcony railing. Balusters support the hand rail and are fastened between it and the stair tread. Since most stair parts are factory-produced, balusters come in standard sizes, usually 30, 33, 36 and 42 inches in overall length, and a variety of designs to meet requirements for most types of stairs. Balusters may be ordered along with other stair components from millwork dealers and will be shipped with instructions for fitting and assembly. An experienced carpenter can then assemble the stair unit on the work site. *SEE ALSO STAIR CONSTRUCTION.*

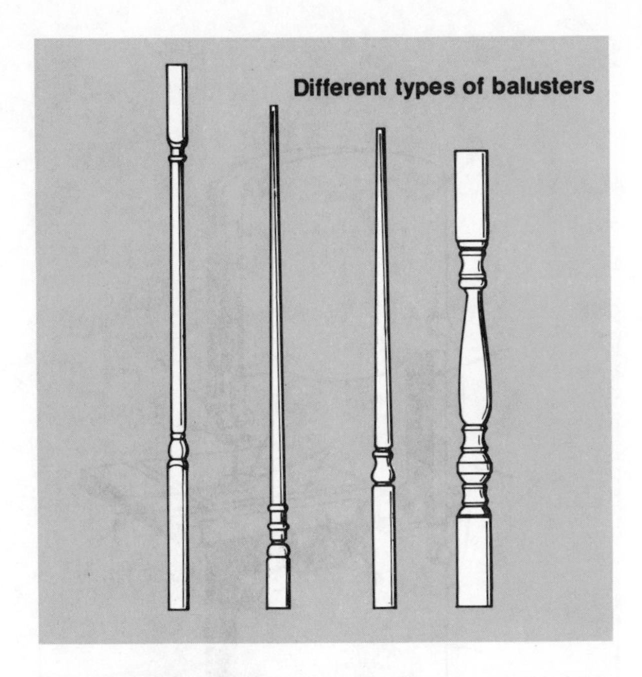

Balustrade

A balustrade is a row of stair balusters which supports the hand or stair rail, and acts as a guard or fence. The spindle-shaped balusters are situated vertically between a top and bottom rail and rest on the treads of the stairs, the horizontal boards which support the foot. *SEE ALSO STAIR CONSTRUCTION.*

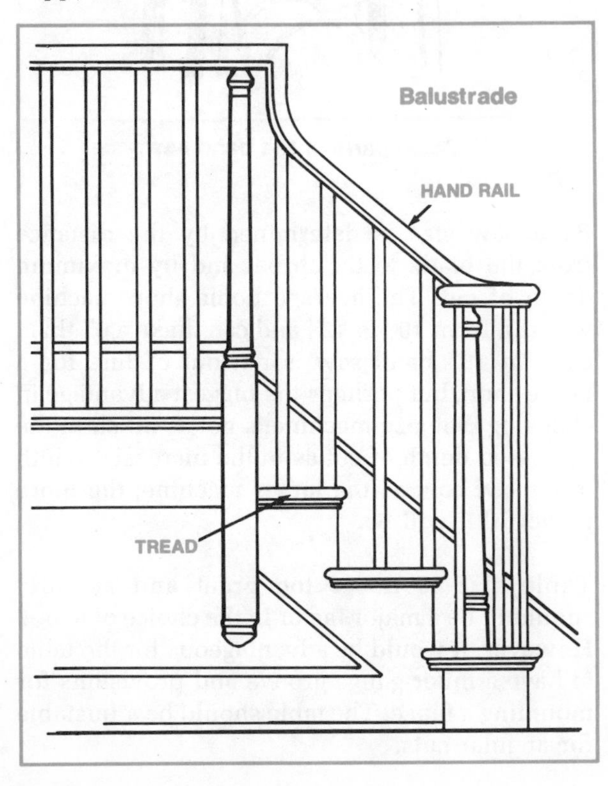

Band Clamp

Band clamps are fabric bands (canvas or nylon) attached to a crank or ratchet mechanism, and are used to simplify the assembly and glue setting of irregular shapes, such as drawers or chair rungs. Band lengths usually range from 12 to 15 feet. In clamping, the band is placed around the work, pulled snugly at the clamp body, then tightened by applying tension with the crank. *SEE ALSO HAND TOOLS.*

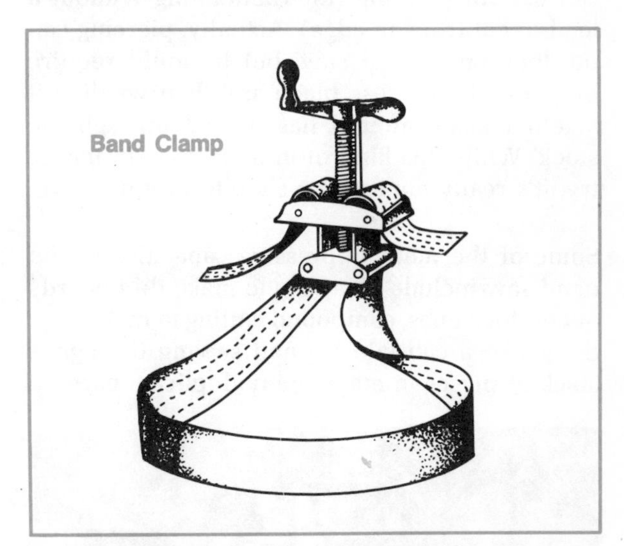

Banding

As the term applies to furniture making, banding is a thin strip of veneer or wood used to hide the edge grain of plywood or other stock. Apply banding with contact cement to smooth, square edges. Rolls of banding may be purchased at hardware stores, or you may cut your own from plywood scraps or oversized slabs. It is effective to cut the banding a bit wider than the edge, then sand it flush after application.

Band Saw

In depth-of-cut capacity and in cutting speed, the band saw is unequaled by any other home-shop woodworking machine. While you probably think of it mostly to be used for sawing curved lines, you'll discover its importance for straight-line operations and will be impressed by its ease in doing other jobs that are very difficult.

The band saw is not designed to be competition for a jigsaw even though, when it is equipped with a fine blade, the applications of the two machines can overlap. With a cut either tool can do, the band saw will do it faster. On the other hand, the jigsaw is the only stationary tool you can use for piercing (internal cutting without a lead-in cut from an edge). Actually, piercing can be done on a band saw, but it would require breaking the endless blade and then welding it together again after it has passed through the stock. While this kind of thing is done in industry, it's really not a home-shop technique.

Some of the more impressive capacities of the band saw include resawing to make thin boards out of thick ones, compound cutting to make anything like a cabriole leg and sawing through a stack of pieces to make many duplicate parts.

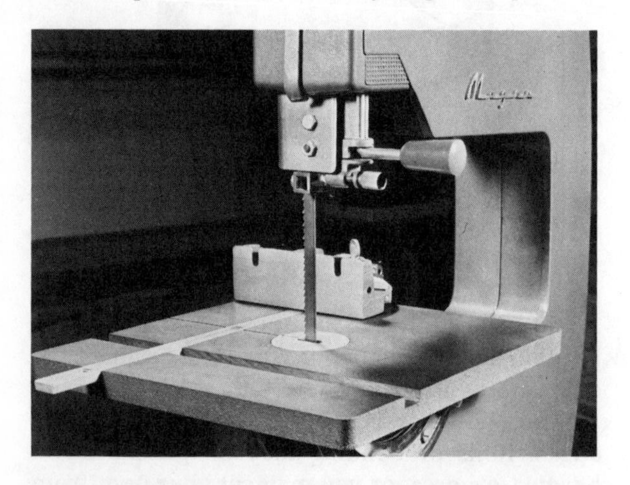

Most modern band saws have a table slot to use with a miter gauge. This one has a slot going two ways so the miter gauge (with an extension) can be used as a fence.

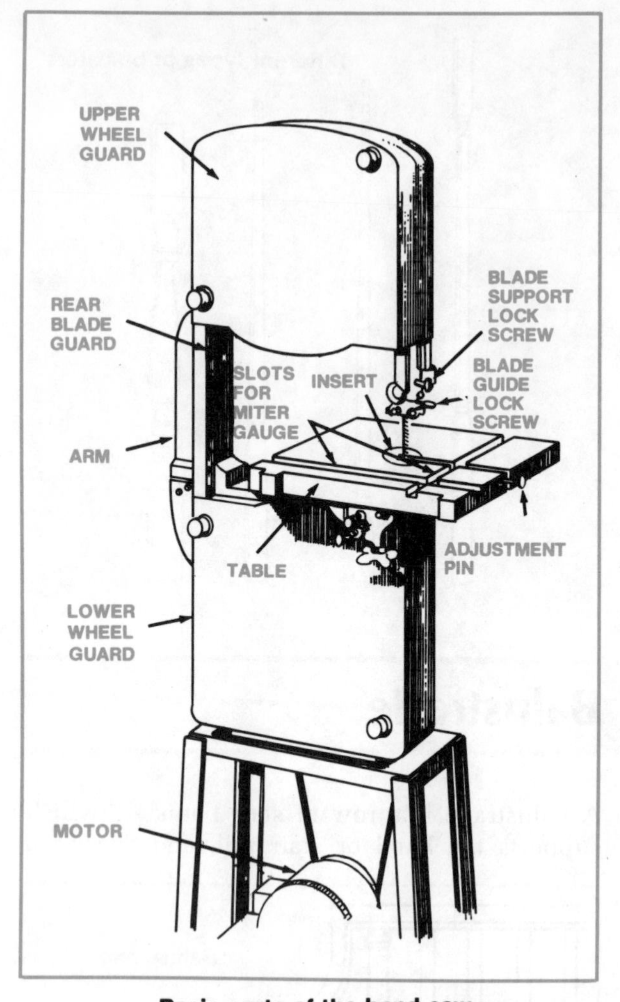

Basic parts of the band saw.

Band saw size is determined by the distance from the blade to the throat and by maximum depth of cut. The average home-shop machine will run from 10″ to 12″ and can make a 6″ thick cut. An 18″ band saw is not out of line for a home shop, but perhaps the biggest advantage in choosing that size machine is not as much in the increased depth of cut as in the increased width of cut. Of course, the larger machine, the more powerful it will be.

Table size is never too great and actually shouldn't be a major factor in the choice of a tool. However, it would be advantageous for the table to have a miter-gauge groove and provisions for mounting a fence. The table should be adjustable for angular cuts.

Blade tension is achieved by vertical adjustment of the upper wheel. Usually, it is set to markings on a built-in tension scale, as in the photo.

General Characteristics

The blade must be *tensioned* relative to its size and must *track* correctly. The tensioning is accomplished by moving the upper wheel, which is done by turning a screw, a lever or a crank (depending upon the design of the machine). Getting the correct tension is easy since most machines have built-in tension scales. You simply adjust the upper wheel until the scale pointer indicates the right setting for the blade you are mounting. If you lack the tension scale, adjust for maximum tension and then slowly slack off until you can flex the blade about 1/4" with light finger pressure. Make this test above the table with the upper blade guard raised as high as possible.

Blade tracking is usually accomplished by tilting the upper wheel so that the blade will remain centered on the wheel rims as it is turning. On some machines, the tracking is automatic. The blade moves to a correct position regardless of its width. Always go through the blade tracking routine by turning the wheels by hand.

Blade mounting, tracking and tensioning should be done with the upper and lower blade guides and backups out of the way so that these items will not interfere with the procedures and so you will be able to adjust them correctly to the new blade.

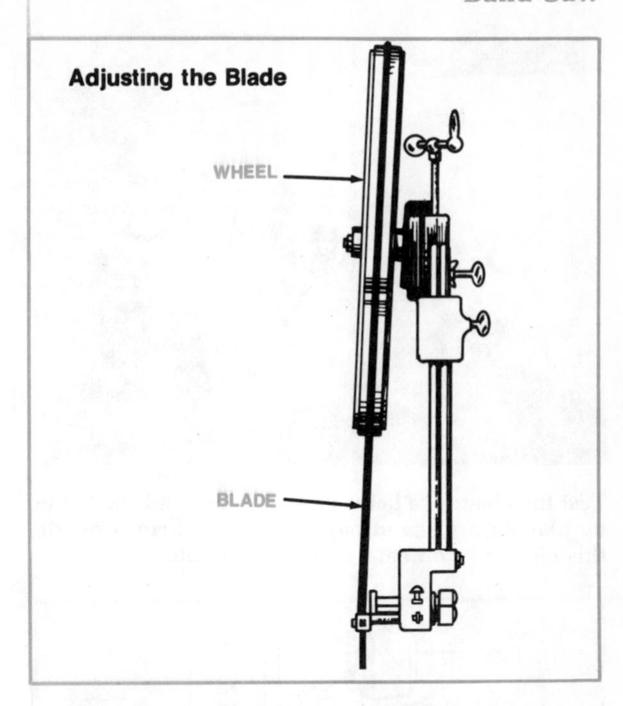

Tracking the blade is done by adjusting the upper wheel until the blade is running centered on the rim.

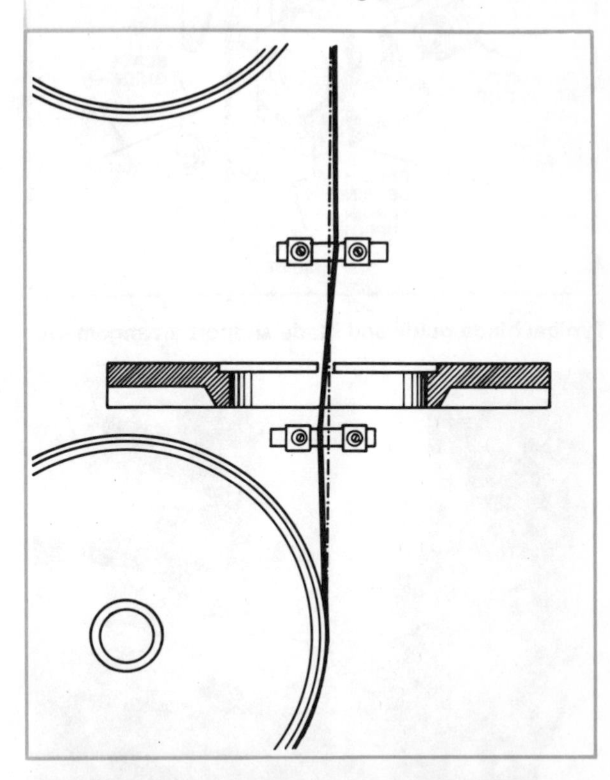

The blade guides and the blade supports should be positioned after the tracking procedure. If the guides are not set correctly, the blade can be twisted out of alignment.

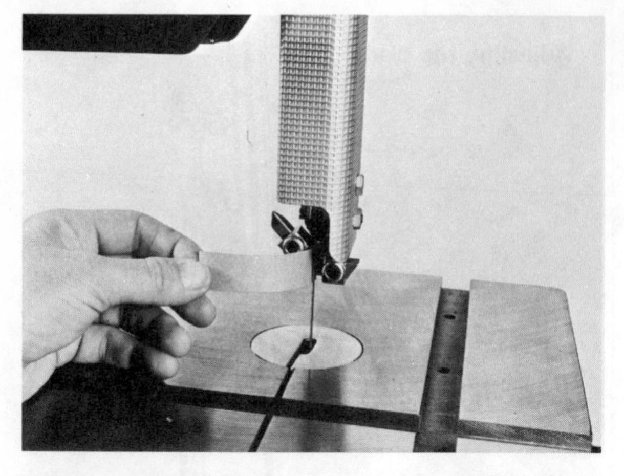

Test the clearance between the guides and the blade by placing a piece of paper between them. Provide this clearance on each side of the blade.

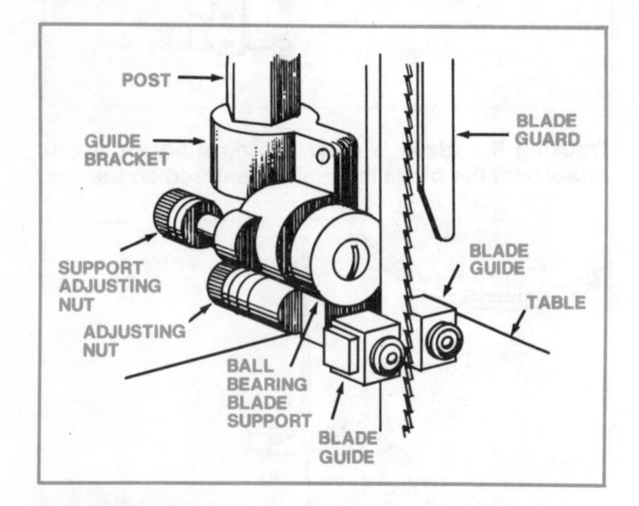

Typical blade guide and blade support arrangement.

When honing to correct lead, back up the blade with a block of wood. Apply the stone with a very light amount of pressure to the sharp side of the blade.

After the blade is mounted, the angle between it and the table should be 90°. You can check this with a square and adjust the table if necessary. Most band saws have a built-in stop for the normal table setting, and it should be fixed at this time.

The blade guides must be adjusted so they will prevent the blade from twisting without actually being in contact with the blade when it is free-running. The best way to achieve this is to use a piece of paper as a spacer when you lock the guide in position. The forward position of the guides must be adjusted to the width of the blade. Don't bring them so far forward that they contact the teeth; adjusting to depth of the space between adjacent saw teeth is fine.

The blade support (backup) should not be in contact with the blade when it is free-running. This will only contribute to blade breakage. It is best to leave a gap of 1/64" to 1/32" between the back edge of the blade and the support. In this way, the support will work only when you are cutting.

Normally, when you are making a simple cut, the kerf will be straight and parallel to the side of the table. If you feed straight and the blade runs off the line so that it becomes necessary to compensate by adjusting the feed angle, it's wise to check the blade mounting and all the guides again. If these check out well, then it's reasonable to assume that the problem is caused by something else. This can be incorrect set of the teeth, a condition that can be the result of a poor sharpening job or a saw cut that caused the blade to dull on one side. The blade does not cut in a straight line because the sharp side "leads" off. When this condition is excessive, it can be remedied only by removing the blade and having it resharpened and reset.

When the lead is slight, you can do a salvage job by lightly honing the sharp side. This procedure is not a positive approach since you are dulling the sharp side to match the other, but it can save you in a situation where you don't have a replacement blade or the time to get the mounted one fixed. You can work with the lead problem temporarily by compensating for it as you feed the stock. To do the honing, back up the blade on the dull side with a block of wood and lightly touch the sharp side with a honing stone as the blade is running.

Band Saw Blades

Blades for home-shop band saws fall into the "narrow blade category" which ranges from $^1/_8$" wide up to $^1/_2$" wide. You would not be wrong, considering routine band saw applications, if you selected a $^1/_4$" wide blade as the one you'd most like to commonly use.

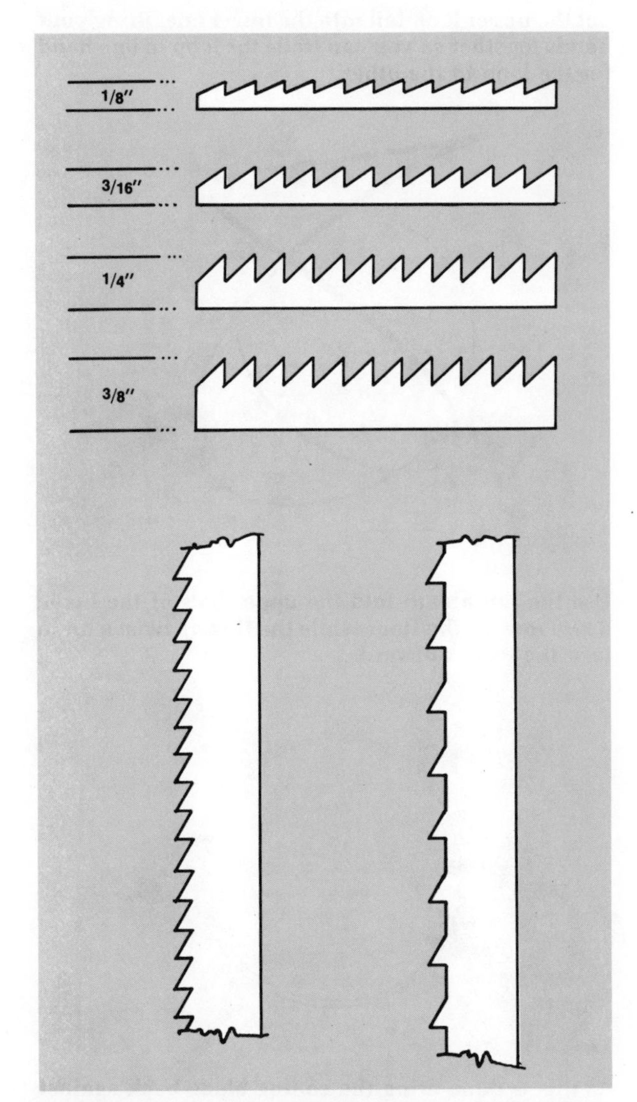

Actual size of four commonly used band-saw blades. The standard blade pattern is shown on the left. The other is a skip-tooth or "buttress" design.

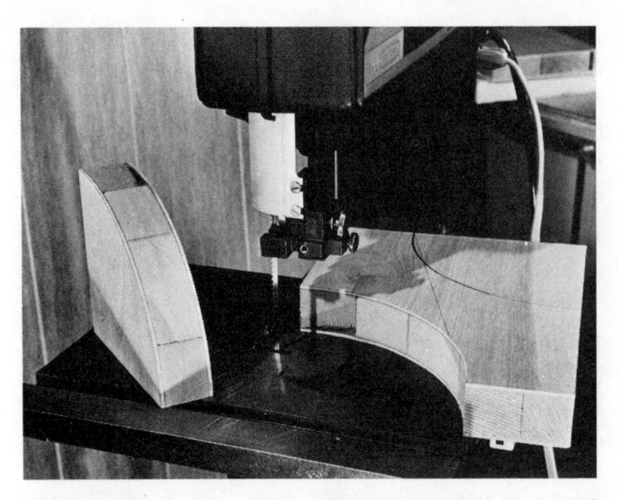

The smoothest cuts result when the blade has a lot of teeth and minimum set. When smoothness is not critical, it is better to work with a coarse blade and much set.

The two most popular blade designs are the "standard" and the "skip-tooth." The latter is so called because every other tooth is skipped. It cuts fast and throws waste out quickly. A third blade to know about is called a "roll-chip". It resembles the skip-tooth and is an excellent all-purpose blade that also does a fairly good job on plastics and metals like aluminum, including the do-it-yourself variety. A very new blade in the field is the toothless blade, but it has an edge that is coated with grits of tungsten carbide. This blade is fine for metals, ceramics and plastics; it can also be used on wood. On wood, however, cut speed is greatly reduced.

A thin blade with light set will give you the smoothest cuts while a heavy blade with heavy set provides maximum cutting speed and freedom from binding because of the wider kerf that provides more freedom for the blade.

A band saw blade will leave its mark in the cut ("washboarding"). It can be slight or so pronounced that it is impractical for some applications. This effect wouldn't bother you, for example, if you were cutting firewood; but it wouldn't be right on the edge of a cornice. Your control over the degree of washboarding rests with choice of blades. For a smooth cut, choose a blade with minimum set. The washboard effect will be minimized.

A band saw blade will cut better across the grain than with it. In the latter situation, cut speed is reduced, and there will be a tendency for the blade to follow the grain of the wood instead of a marked line. Such things will not affect your productivity, but they are band saw facts of life and you should be aware of them.

Band Saw Blade Storage

It's advisable to "fold" band saw blades and to hang them on pegs in a cabinet where they will be protected until you need them. Of course, you can hang them full-length, but this practice makes quite a demand on storage facilities. Folding isn't difficult once you get used to doing it.

After the blade is folded, tie it with a piece of string or soft wire. If you think it's going to hang unused for a long time, coat it with a light oil. Band saw blades are expensive so using them and storing them correctly can save you money.

The blades are flexible and do have considerable spring, which you will discover when you unfold them. Therefore, unfold them carefully, especially wide blades. Hold them away from your body and turn your face away.

Also, when you fold and unfold them and when you place them on the machine, be very careful not to bend them. Kinks in a blade are not easy to work with.

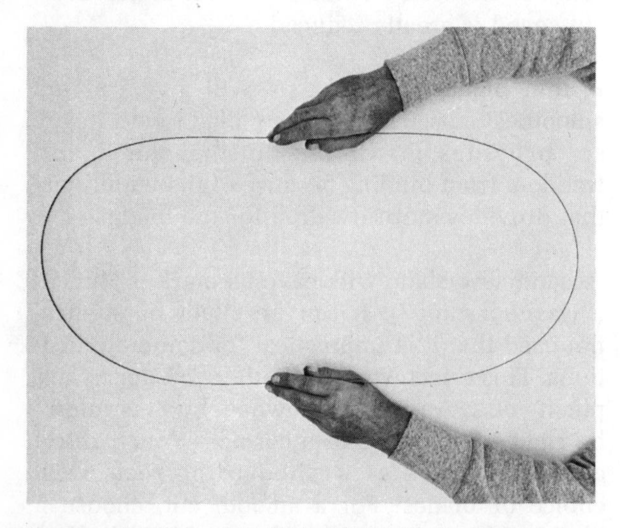

To start folding a blade, hold it with its teeth pointing away from you.

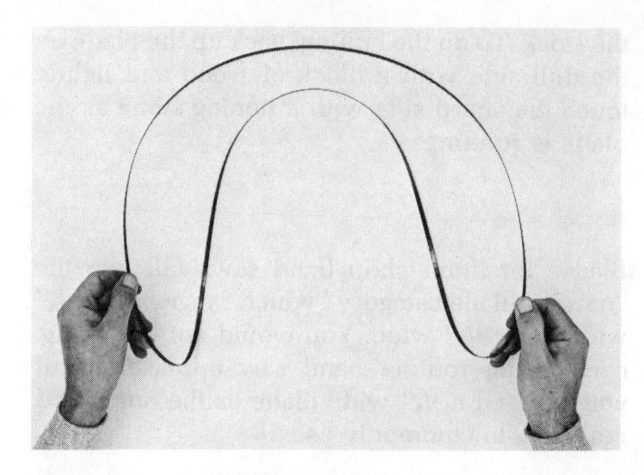

Let the upper loop fall into the lower one. Bring your hands together so you can trade the loop in one hand for the loop in the other.

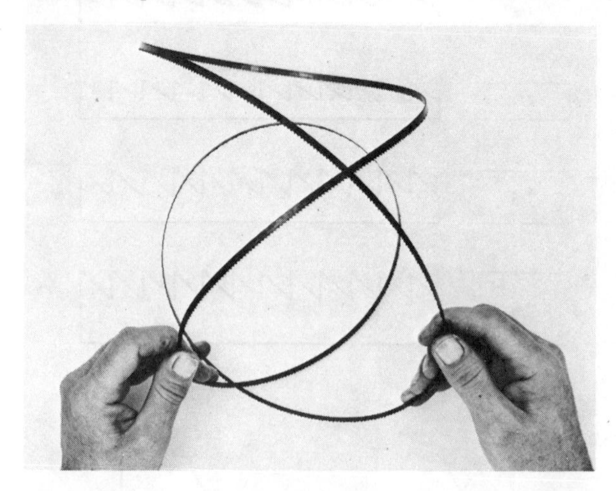

Use the thumbs to fold the upper half of the blade down toward the floor while the fingers twist a bit to turn the teeth outward.

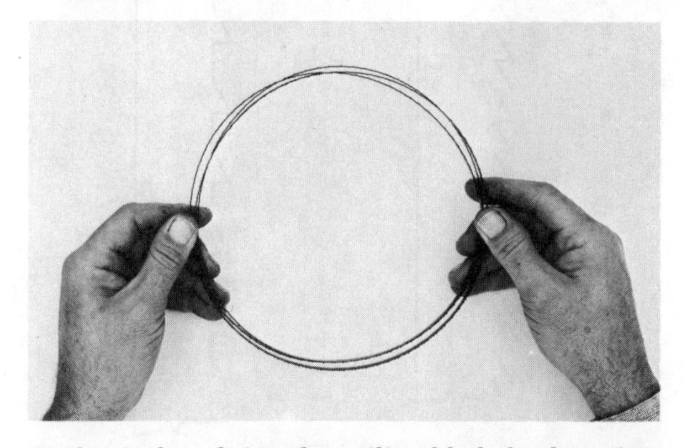

As this is done bring the coiling blade back against your body and it will fall into three uniform loops. Tie with soft wire or tape. When folding, be careful not to kink the blade.

Basics of Cutting

The usual position for band saw cutting will place you behind the left side of the table. Your left hand will be on the work doing most of the guiding while your right hand will feed the stock. The size of the work, the kind of cut and the direction of feed required will all affect how you stand and where you place your hands. There is little point in following this rule when, for example, a considerable overhang at the rear of the table makes this positioning difficult or even hazardous.

A better rule to be strict about is to keep your hands away from the blade while you keep the blade on the line. A sharp blade and a steady feed are good safety factors. Try to keep fingers of the feed hand hooked over the edge of the work. This will guard against slippage that could move your hand to a dangerous area. The sharper the blade, the less feed pressure you need; this factor also reduces the possibility of hand slippage.

Band saw cutting is basically a simple procedure, but you can easily box yourself in on some cuts so that you must saw your way out or do considerable backtracking in order to get back to the cut you want. This can happen because you get into a spot that the blade can't

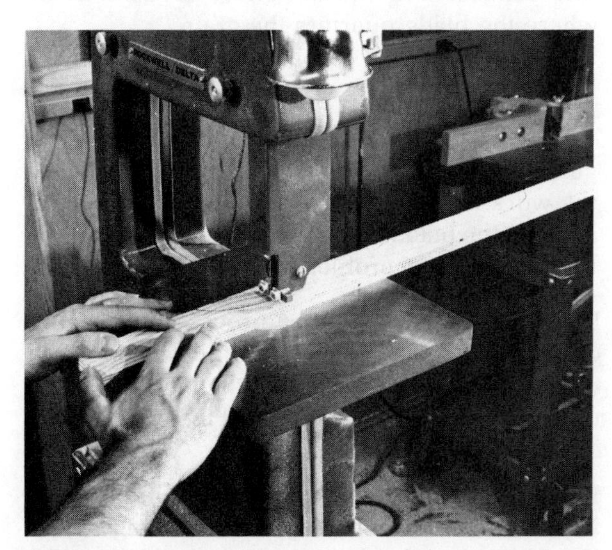

Operator's position will vary with the cut. Normal procedure calls for guiding with the left hand and feeding with the right.

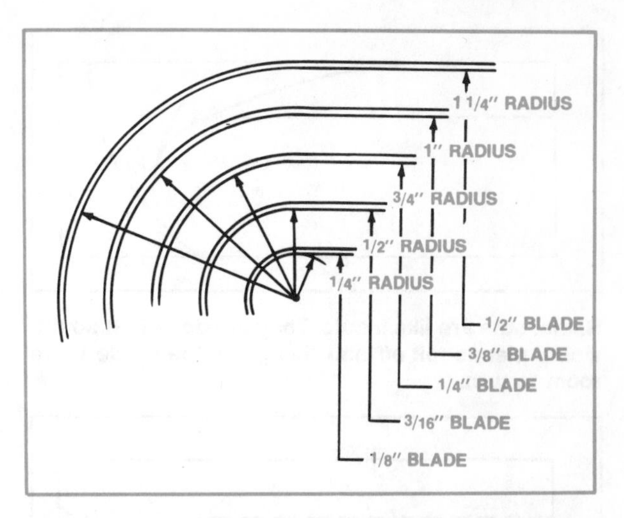

Typical turning radius of various size blades. These are not invariable since the type of blade and the amount of set are factors that effect the actual radius.

handle or because the throat of the machine interferes with feed direction.

A partial solution is to visualize the cut and plan how you will accomplish it before you do any sawing. Often, you will find that the cutting is simplified if you do the layout either totally or partially on both sides of the stock: flipping the stock can occasionally make an impossible cut possible.

On complicated jobs, it's more difficult to eliminate backtracking entirely than when the cuts are short. Frequently, it's better to saw out of a situation than it is to backtrack. This simply means leaving the cutline at a point and exiting at an edge of the stock. Then you re-enter close to the problem point and continue the job.

Corner cuts and turning holes can be done in advance with other tools in order to save time and, occasionally, material. You can form square corners with a mortising chisel or just drill holes. Drilling holes isn't a bad idea when you have many to do, especially when the turning radius is tight. This can reduce the band-saw chore to simple cutting while giving you accurate radii and smooth, drill-produced corners. In either case, whether you use square openings or holes, they must be located accurately to fit in with the design.

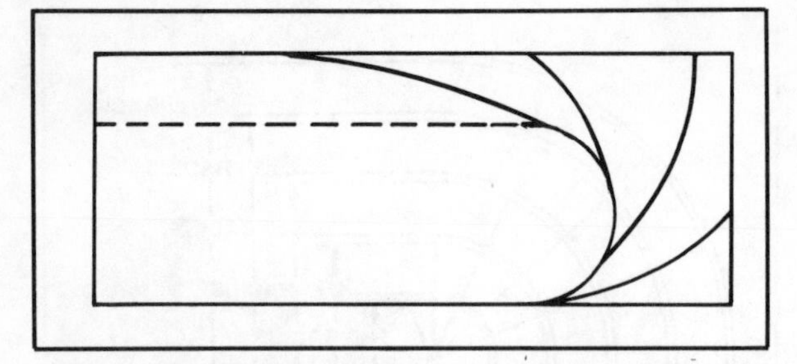

Radial cuts are like incuts. They are done first so the waste pieces fall off and this gives the blade more room to turn.

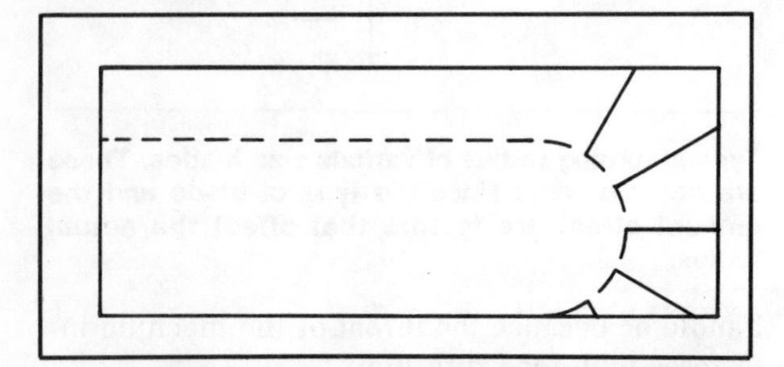

Tangential cuts means moving off the line and out of the work whenever you feel the blade begin to bind. To get the smoothest end result possible, start each new cut as carefully as possible and proceed slowly.

Radial and tangent cuts can make it possible for a blade to get around a turn it couldn't do otherwise. Radial cuts are simply cuts made from the edge of the stock to the line you have to follow. What they do is permit waste stock to fall away as you are cutting and so provide more room for the blade to turn. Tangential cuts are run-offs. You follow the line until you feel the blade is binding, move off to the edge of the stock and then come back to where you had left the line and continue to cut in similar fashion.

Freehand Cutting

When cutting freehand, you guide the band saw by hand and by sight. The bulk of what has been said so far applies to operator control over the work-to-blade relationship. The basic cutting rule is to keep the blade on the line that you have drawn. The mechanics of the machine are involved in achieving this: correct blade tension and tracking, good blade-guide settings and sharpness of the blade. Beyond this, making an accurate cut depends on providing good feed direction. It's almost like driving a car. Don't overshoot the curves. Lead into them as they come up. Slacking on feed pressure in such situations will make it easier to be accurate simply because it will provide more time to do the maneuvering.

When you approach a curve from a straight line — this applies mostly to rounding off of corners on sized stock — follow the straight edge for an inch or two before you enter the curve cut. When you do start to turn, ease up on feed so the blade can do its job.

On thick cuts the blade works harder. In such situations you should ease up on feed. When you can, use a wide blade with much set to do the job. If the cut is being done, for example, to prepare a piece of stock for lathe turning or for a part that you know will require much sanding, then the rough results of the heavy blade won't matter. When smoothness of cut of the band-saw job is critical and you choose to work with a narrow blade, be aware that the blade can bow in the cut, especially on wood that has a strong grain pattern. The only way to protect against this, other than changing to a heavy-gauge blade, is feed the work extremely slowly. The smoothness of cut on such operations, especially when you are turning a circle, will not be consistent regardless of how you feed. You'll find differences, and the roughest areas will be where the blade quarters the grain.

Basic Guided Cuts

You can use a miter gauge or a rip fence for guides on the band saw but remember that when the work is so guided, you can't compensate for lead. So the blade must be in good shape in order to work without problems.

If the band saw does not provide for a miter gauge, you can clamp a straight piece of wood to the table to act as a fence and then move a backup piece of wood along it to feed the work for the cut.

Band saw crosscuts are limited by throat interference. In a normal setup, crosscut length can't be greater than the distance from the blade to the throat. To get around this, make an angle cut as close to the line as you can get. Then make a second cut on the line. When work width permits, you can use this technique with the stock on edge. The end result is the same, but wood waste is kept to a minimum.

Another way is to offset the blade so you can feed the stock at an angle and get a straight cut without throat interference. This can be accomplished simply by making a twist-board. Cut into a piece of 3/4" stock until the kerf is about 9" or 10" long and then turn off the machine while the blade is still in the cut. Back off the guides, turn the board about 20° or 30° and clamp it to the table. The blade twists with the board, and this permits an oblique feed so you can handle longer stock. Don't use the blade guides for this operation but do use the blade supports. Such a setup is good for a limited number of cuts since the blade will tend to return to its normal position by cutting through the twist board. A more permanent answer is to make special guides that will hold the blade in the twist position.

If the band saw is equipped with a rip fence, lock it in place to obtain the cut width you need and then pass the work between it and the blade. This will be difficult to do if the blade has "lead." Actually, the heavier the blade and the more set it has, the easier it will be to do guided rip cuts.

Crosscutting to Length

On the band saw you can use the rip fence as a stop when cutting pieces to length. When the work is wide enough, simply place one end against the fence and move forward as if you were making a rip cut. On narrow work that could rock during the pass, use a backup block behind the work to do the feeding.

Angle Cuts

When a fence is used in beveling operations, position it on the right-hand side of the table so that both the fence and the work will be below the blade. The fence-table combination creates a "V" that provides excellent work support.

This setup is fine for work procedures such as chamfering, removing corners from a block that you will then spindle-turn in the lathe and ripping squares into tri-angular pieces.

When cutting circular blocks for faceplate mounting on a lathe, making the cut with the table tilted will remove much of the material you would ordinarily have to cut away with lathe chisels. The idea is especially good for lathe projects that have a taper, or for bowls.

Quite often, the fence-table setup is a good substitute for a V-block. Try it, for example, when you need to completely cut through the workpiece or when you need to slot the end of a cylinder. On such work you must be very careful to keep the wood from turning as you are making the pass.

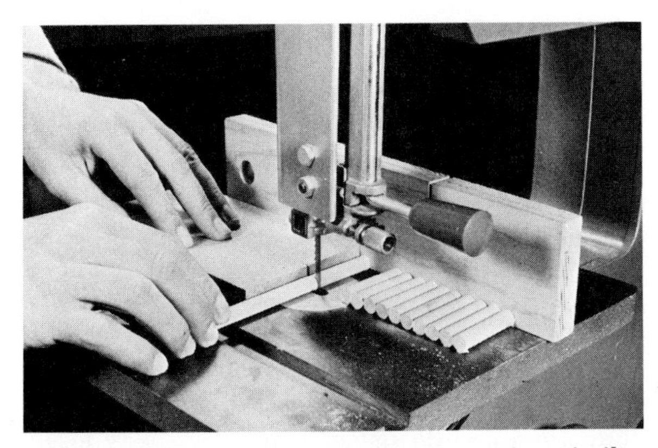

A fence may be used as a stop in cutting similar pieces. When the parts are narrow, use a back-up board to do the feeding. Push the work free of the blade before returning the backup.

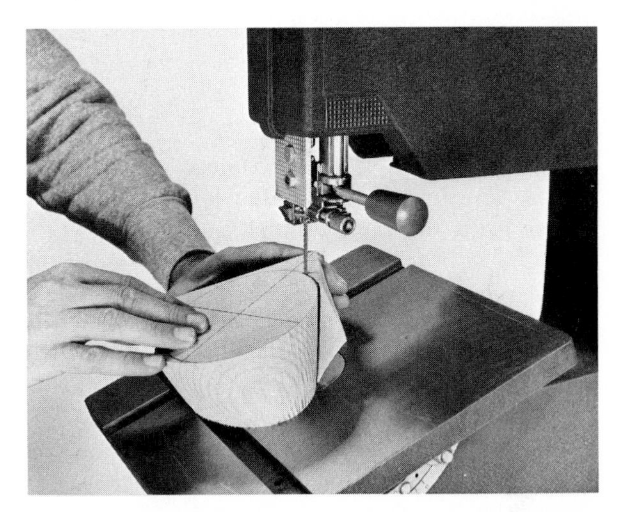

Circular cuts, with the table tilted, produce cone-shaped blocks. This is a good way to prepare stock for lathe turning.

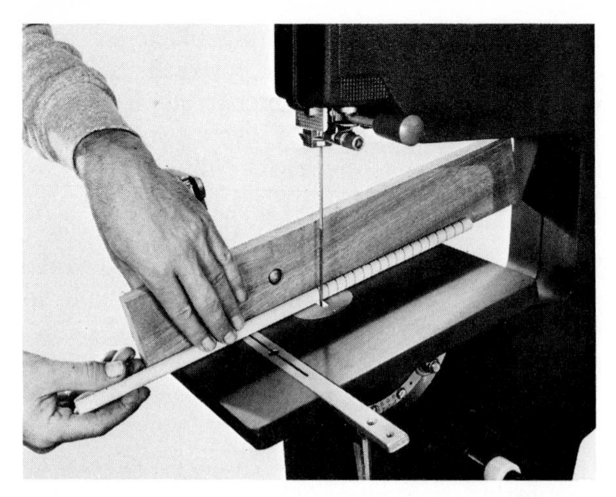

Spiral-cutting of dowels on tilted table. Spiral pitch will be constant if the work is held firmly while rotating.

Spiraling Dowels

Dowels, so treated, have superior holding power in glued joints. To do the job, tilt the band-saw table anywhere from 10° to 20° and lock the miter gauge in position as shown in the accompanying photograph. Its distance from the band-saw blade is what controls the depth of the groove. When you hold the work firmly against the miter gauge and make contact with the blade, the work will immediately begin to feed into a perfect spiral. However, don't give up hand control; the work can be twisted along the gauge faster than the blade can do the cutting. The idea is to let the work be guided automatically while you control the speed.

Resawing

Resawing is ripping a heavy board into thinner pieces. The best blade for the job is wide, has coarse teeth and plenty of set. Such a blade has enough "tail" to help keep it on a straight line and a nice wide kerf for blade room. A skip-tooth blade is recommended. This blade will not produce smooth cuts, but that is not the purpose of resawing.

On the other hand, you will often use a smaller blade because you want the smoothest cut possible or because the blade happens to be on the machine and the resaw job required doesn't justify a change. This will work but there will be more tendency for the blade to bind and to bow in the cut. A sharp blade and a slow feed are essential. Naturally, the less depth of cut involved in the job, the less critical is the blade-width factor.

Resaw jobs can be done freehand, and that is probably the method to use if the blade is not in ideal condition. Guiding the saw freehand, you can compensate to some extent for lead. After you have entered the cut and discovered that the blade is cutting fine and free, you can speed up feed as long as you keep within the blade's cutting capacity.

You can also do resaw jobs against a fence, which is a wise method when you have many pieces of equal thickness to produce. In this situation there isn't much opportunity to compensate for lead, so the blade should be a good one.

If you discover that the resaw job is putting a lot of strain on the motor, you might still be able to accomplish it if you first cut guide kerfs on the table saw. These kerfs are saw cuts on the resaw line, and they reduce the amount of material the band-saw blade must cut.

Multiple Pieces

To produce multiple pieces, preshape a thick piece of wood that you resaw into thinner, duplicate pieces or assemble thin pieces of wood into a pad and saw them all at the same time.

The resaw method involves simply drawing the shape of the part you need on the stock and then cutting it out. The shaped piece is then resawed against a fence. After the fence is adjusted to maintain the thickness of the cut, you run the preshaped part through as many times as possible, or until you have produced the number of pieces you want.

The pad method involves putting pieces of wood together in a stack and then sawing them as if they were a solid piece. The easiest way to accomplish this is to drive nails through waste areas. On a common, home-shop band saw, you can stack as many as 24 pieces of 1/4" plywood

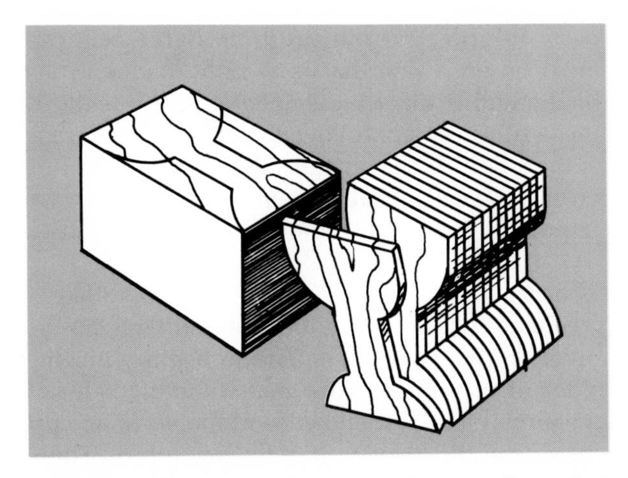

The grain pattern on each piece will depend on what side of the block the original layout and cutting were done.

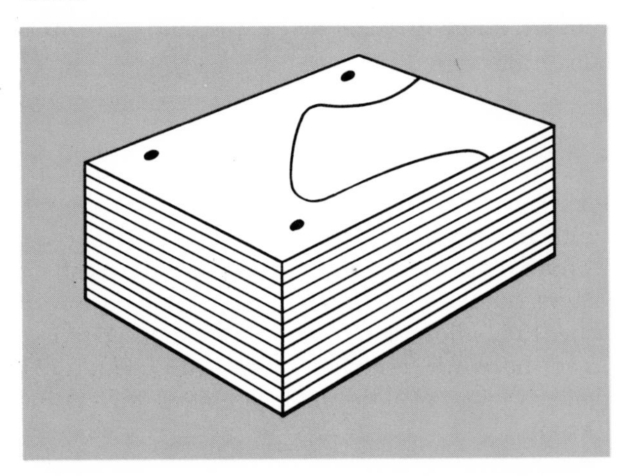

Many similar pieces can be gotten by nailing thin boards into a thick pad and sawing the combination as if it were a solid piece of wood, then separating the pieces.

and produce 24 duplicate parts in the one cutting operation.

In some situations you can use clamps to hold the pieces together as long as they don't interfere with the cutting. A little trick that can be used is to place double-faced tape between the pieces. The tape will usually hold the parts together well enough for the cutting.

Compound Cuts

Shapes that result from cuts that are made on two or more sides are classified as "compound cuts." The most common example is the cabriole leg and its variations, but the techniques may be employed to do unsymmetrical shapes and ornamental work as well as to prepare stock for lathe turning.

The basic procedure involves making a pattern of the shape you want and using it to mark two adjacent sides of the stock. Cut the work on one side, but do it to produce a minimum number of waste pieces. These are then tack-nailed back in their original positions, and the stock is cut on the second side. The waste pieces from the first cut must be replaced in order for the work to have a base and to reproduce all the original pattern markings for the second cut. When you replace them, drive the nails so the part you are cutting out will not be marred.

Pattern Sawing

Pattern sawing is required when the curves on the parts you need are not extreme. The technique to be used lets you cut duplicate pieces without having to do a layout on each and should probably be considered when the job can't be handled by either resawing a shaped piece or by pad sawing.

The idea is to set up a guide block that is undercut at one end to permit passage of the work. The end of the guide on the undercut side is notched just enough to snug the blade and is shaped in concave or convex fashion to suit the job being done. It is important for the center of the curve to be in line with the teeth of the blade.

Parts to be shaped are roughly cut to size and then tack-nailed to the pattern. When you are doing the cutting, concentrate on keeping the pattern in constant contact with the guide. Be sure on your first test cut that the blade does not cut into the pattern. If it does, make the notch in the guide arm just a bit deeper. The blade should just barely clear the pattern.

Parallel Curves

Cutting parallel curves can be as simple as following the lines that are marked on the work; and if only a few cuts are involved, that's probably the best procedure to use. However, when you have to make many of these cuts, you can set up a guide system so you can come up with as

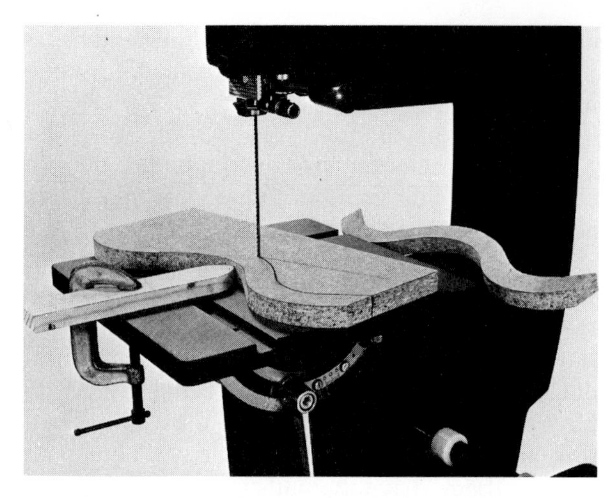

Parallel curve-cutting calls for the guide shown here. Keep the work in constant contact with the end of the guide. Of course, the blade guard is set much too high here.

many duplicate pieces as you want without having to do a layout for each.

When the curves are slight, you can use a fence to gauge the width of the cut. Make the first cut in the work freehand; make the others by passing the stock between the fence and the blade. The one important rule is to keep the arc tangent to the fence throughout the pass.

You can't use a fence as a guide when the job involves reverse curves, but a pointed guide block that you clamp to the table in line with the teeth on the blade can be used in its place. The distance between the point on the guide and the blade controls the width of the cut. It's essential to do the feeding so that contact between the guide and the side of the work is constant. With this setup, it's not likely that the cut could be oversize; but unless you handle the job carefully and feed easily, you can move off the guide. This would result in the cut being narrower than you want.

Cutting Circles

A pivot jig can be advantageous when you have many circular pieces to do; it can also be handy when you have a single oversize circular piece that might be difficult to do freehand. Any circle-cutting jig is nothing more than a pivot point around which you rotate the work to make the pass. In order for the cut to be right, the pivot must be on a line that is at right angles to the blade, and it must be aligned with the teeth. If these rules are not followed, the blade will track to the inside or the outside of the line, depending on the kind of misalignment you have. It's also important for the blade to be in good condition.

There are two ways to start the job. Make a freehand lead-in cut to the line and then set the pivot or cut the work square to begin with (the sides of the square must match the diameter of the circle) and rest one edge of the work against the side of the blade to start the procedure. There should be some pressure against the blade to begin with, and this can cause the blade to crowd a bit until it enters the cut and becomes positioned. After that, it's just a question of turning the work.

Wood Bending

On the band saw, you can do wood bending by "kerfing" or by "thinning out." You do the job with the stock on edge and angled to clear the throat. This means the kerfs will be at a slight angle, but the angled kerfs will not interfere with how they allow you to bend the wood. You can feed the work freehand, or you can use a miter gauge that is set at the angle you need to clear the throat.

Thinning out is really a resaw job that you limit to the area of the work you wish to bend. What

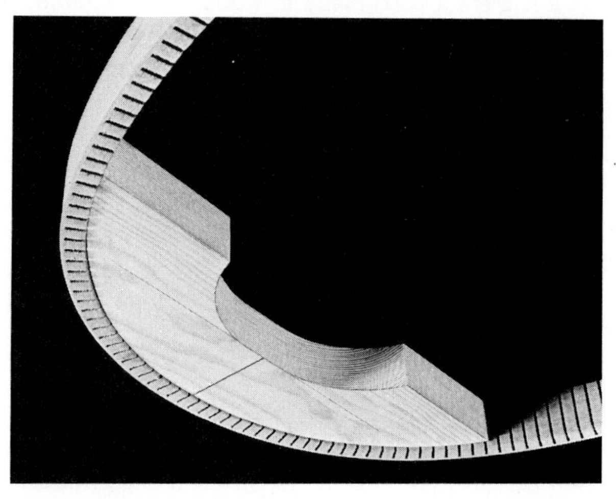

You can use the band saw to cut kerfs so that wood can be bent without having to be steamed.

you are doing is reducing the stock thickness at that point to make it flexible. Such areas are seldom used as they are since they lack strength. Instead, they are backed up with blocks. The thinned section is a "veneer" that carries the appearance, and the blocks provide the strength. For example, you would use this method for the rails of a table that has straight sides but semicircular ends.

Sanding

To set up for sanding, a special accessory kit is required that, in most cases, is used in place of the regular guides. The abrasive is an endless belt just like a band-saw blade, and it is fitted over the wheels with just enough tension to keep it tight.

The accessory kit will contain a backup plate which serves to support the belt when you move work against it. For some jobs, like contour sanding, it's possible to work without the backup plate; but you must be careful to apply the work so that you don't cause the belt to move off the wheels.

Cutting Sheet Metal

If you are working with a material like do-it-yourself aluminum, you can use a regular wood-cutting blade. For other materials, you should get either a special metal-cutting blade or a combination blade that can be used for either wood or metal. In either case, the job is done best when you use a backup board under the work. This will minimize, if not eliminate, the jagged edges that will occur when you work with the sheet metal directly on the table.

Special toothless, carbide-tipped blades can be used without the backup. The action in this case is more abrasive so the cut will be quite smooth without taking precautions. *SEE ALSO BENCH GRINDER; DRILL PRESS; JIGSAW; JOINTER; LATHE; RADIAL ARM SAW; SHAPER; STATIONARY BELT & DISC SANDER; TABLE SAW.*

Banging of Pipes

[SEE WATER HAMMER.]

Banister

A banister, or baluster, is one of the upright supports of a handrail along a staircase. However, some people think of banister as the handrail with its supporting posts. *SEE ALSO STAIR CONSTRUCTION.*

Barbecue Cart

Make the bottom frame from 1 x 4 piece. Corners can be mitered or butt-jointed. Build the 20″ x 22½″ chopping block 1¾″ thick by ripping one piece of 2 x 4, 12′ long down the center of the wide side. Cut 14 pieces 20″ long from rips. Glue so that 1¾″ sides form the block thickness (see drawing). Trim to size. It may be preferable to buy a manufactured chopping block and simply trim to size.

Cut one-inch material (¾″ actual thickness) for sides, divider, shelves and bottoms. Wood paneling, V-joint or tongue and groove boards may be used. Either glue or unitize with back braces to obtain pieces larger than available at lumber yard (see "back of door" detail). If back-brace strips are used, they can be located in line with bottom of shelf edges to give extra support to the shelves. Glue and nail sides, ends and divider to 1 x 4 bottom frame and at other appropriate joints. Nail the bottom pieces into place, then the shelves. Cut two strips from scrap material to support chopping block. Glue and nail in place. The chopping block is not fastened, but rests on these strips.

Notch or drill hole through side and into chopping block as shown on plan. The notch or hole is to accommodate either a ¾″ square x 11″ piece or a dowel (called "pullout" on the detail). The pullouts allow the tops to be supported when in folded-out position. If you do not wish to notch or drill, your dealer can supply you with hardware that will serve the same purpose.

Cut two top pieces, each edge-glued 12″ wide x 36″ long. Attach with piano hinges.

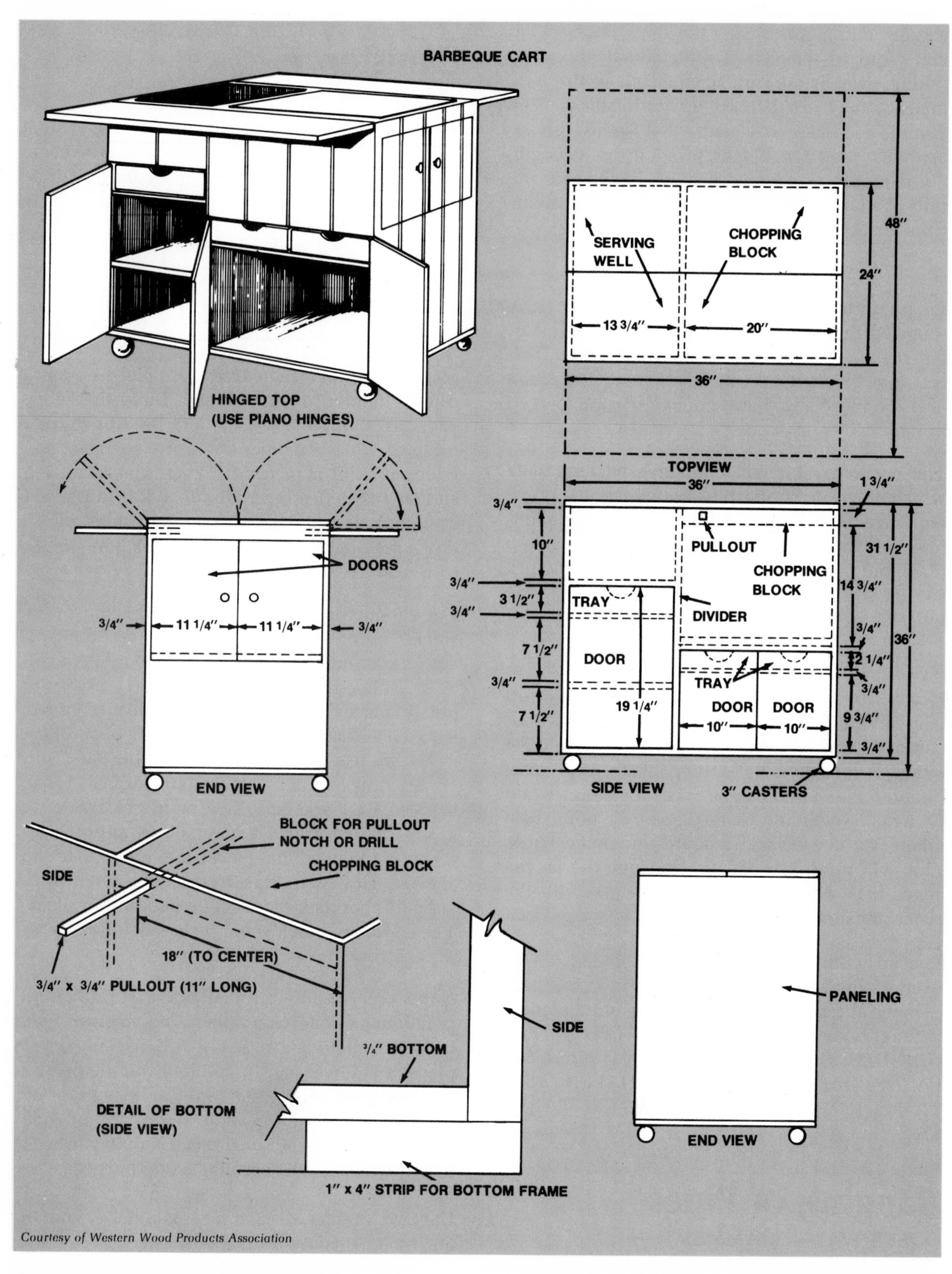

Courtesy of Western Wood Products Association

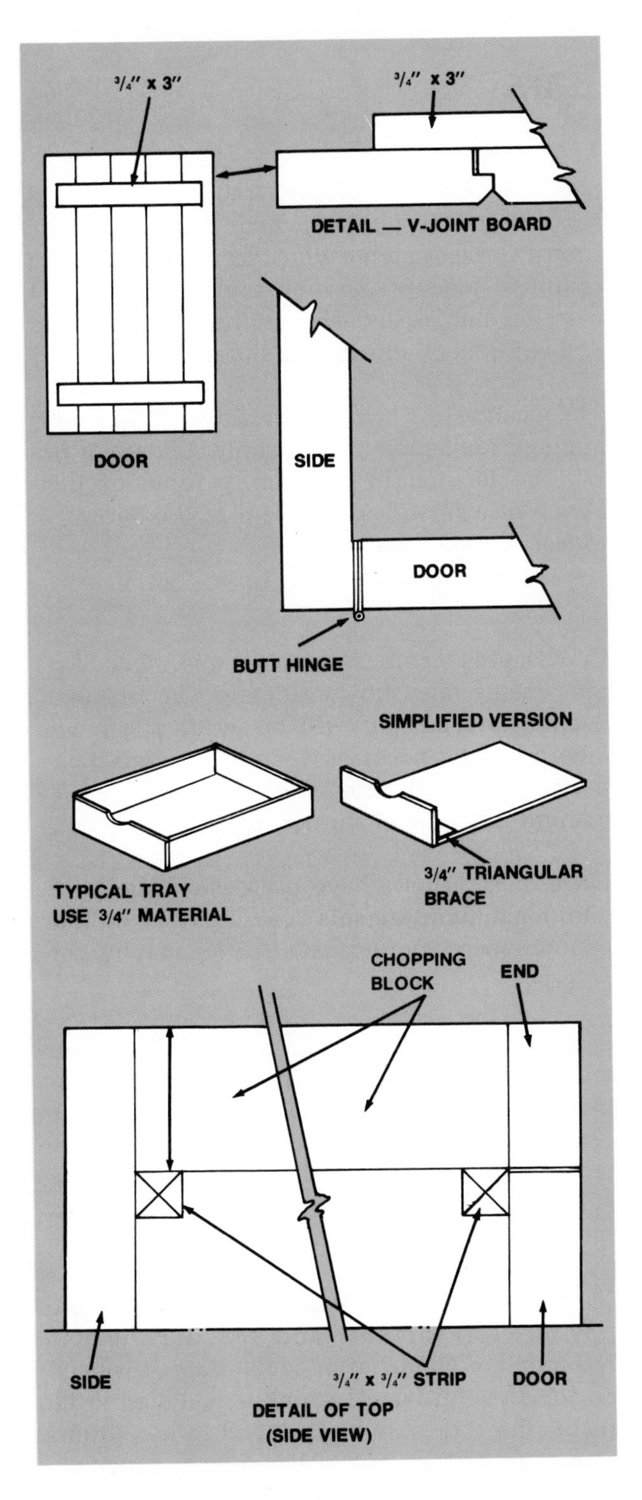

Build and install all doors using small hinges and friction or magnetic catches. (See door construction detail). Trays can be made two ways (see drawing). Build three trays as shown. The trays simply slide on previously installed shelves.

Attach four 3″ rubber wheel casters or wooden wheels to bottom for portability. For the finishing touch, the top may be covered with Formica and the serving well lined with waterproof material. Paint or stain the barbecue cart to suit yourself. *SEE ALSO PROJECTS.*

MATERIALS LIST

Standard (nominal 1″) boards are used for the most part. V-joint or tongue and groove boards may be used instead of material specified below. Wider widths can be made by edge gluing boards or paneling, where applicable.

Chopping Block: 1 piece clear, dense 2 x 4, 12′ long. Rip wide side in half, cut 7 pieces 20″ long from each half

Top: 1 piece 1 x 6, 6′ long (cut 2 pieces 36″ long)
1 piece 1 x 8, 6′ long (cut 2 pieces 36″ long)
Pair 1 x 6 and 1 x 8, edge glue, and trim for each top piece

Bottom Frame: 1 piece 1 x 4, 12′ long (cut to size, 24″ x 36″ frame)

Paneling: Width of paneling selected determines number of pieces needed. Obtain enough to cover four sides. Total area 30″ high by approximately 12″ wide (around four sides)

Doors (cut from above paneling):
1 door 13 3/4″ x 19 1/4″
2 doors 10″ x 12 3/4″
2 doors 11 1/4″ x 14 3/4″

Bottom: 1 piece 1 x 12, 6′ long (cut 3 pcs. 22 1/2″ long
1 piece 1 x 4, 2′ long (cut to 22 1/2″ length)
Pair 1 x 12 and 1 x 4, edge glue and trim for 13 3/4″ bottom piece. Pair two 1 x 12 boards, edge glue and trim for 20″ bottom piece.

Shelf: 1 piece 1 x 12, 8′ long (cut 4 pcs. 20″ long)
1 piece 1 x 12, 6′ long (cut 3 pcs. 22 1/2″ long)
1 piece 1 x 4, 6′ long (cut 3 pcs. 22 1/2″ long)
Pair 1 x 12 and 1 x 4, edge glue and trim for three 13 3/4″ shelves. Pair two 1 x 12 boards, edge glue and trim for two 20″ shelves.

Divider: 1 piece 1 x 12, 6′ long (cut two pieces 30″ long; edge glue and trim)

Three Trays: Cut 3 bottoms 21″ long from 1 piece 1 x 12, 6′ long
Cut sides, front and back from 1 piece 1 x 3, 12′ long. 1 piece 1 x 3, 6′ long

Miscellaneous: Two strips and 4 pullouts needed will come from scrap material

Hardware: 2 piano hinges, 36″ long
5 pair butt hinges
5 door pulls
4 casters with 3″ rubber wheels
2 lbs. 6d finishing nails

Barbecues

[SEE OUTDOOR BARBECUES.]

Bar Clamp

Bar clamps, which are also referred to as furniture or cabinet clamps, are available in sizes ranging in opening capacity from 2 to 8 feet. They adjust by means of a movable jaw at one end of a flat, steel bar and a crank that turns a screw at the other end.

Pipe clamps work the same as bar clamps except the jaws slide on pipe. A pipe clamp of any length can be made by buying the fixtures and using them on ordinary pipe which has been cut and threaded. Jaws can be purchased that are designed to fit $1/2$- to $3/4$-inch pipe. Because you can use any length of pipe, this arrangement offers versatility, and is an economical way to clamp large areas.

In using either of these bar-type clamps, set the fixed jaw against one side of the work, slide the movable jaw against the other side, then tighten the clamp with the hand screw. Counteract possible bending by placing one clamp above your work and one clamp below it. The pressure exerted by these clamps is tremendous, so it is recommended that scrap wood pads be used under their jaws to prevent marring. *SEE ALSO HAND TOOLS.*

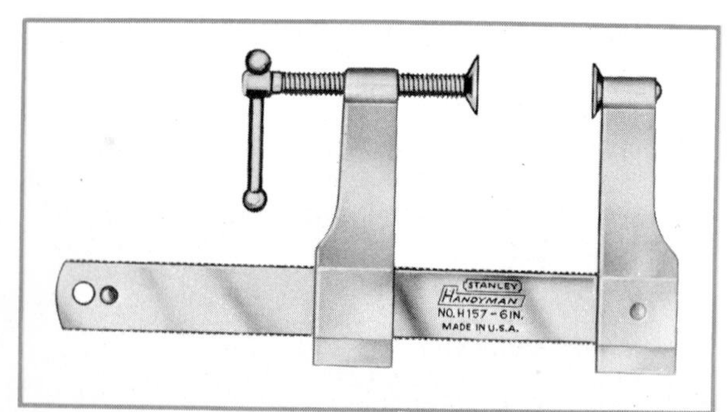

Courtesy of The Stanley Works

Bar Clamp

Bars

Bars are refreshment preparation centers that supplement the home kitchen. Bars may range from a storage cabinet with a serving counter to a complete food preparation center containing a working sink, dishwasher, refrigerator, cooktop and equipment and supply storage.

The location of a bar is determined by the entertainment demands of the family. Usually a bar will be located in the family room or den; however, a small bar may be placed wherever it makes entertaining easier.

REQUIREMENTS

In designing a refreshment bar, a number of requirements must be considered. The first is to decide how the bar will be used, which will determine the necessity for utility connections, the number of electrical outlets needed, and the amount and type of storage needed.

Once these criteria have been established, the additional requirements for access to utilities, counter space, storage, and lighting may be considered.

Access to plumbing and electrical lines is important if the bar is to contain a working, or wet, sink or have a number of electrical appliances in operation at one time. Locating a bar on a wall which contains plumbing lines and which has easy access to electrical circuits will decrease expenses and make utility connections easier.

Bar counter space must accommodate both preparing refreshments and serving them. A minimum of 36 inches of counter space is needed for a useful bar. If a sink is included in the plans, the sink may be included in the 36 inch minimum. Most home bar plans suggest a counter length between 42 and 50 inches. Addi-

Photo Courtesy: Courtesy of Karastan

A refrigerator, a wet sink, and storage are features of this built-in bar unit. Folding doors conceal the area when not in use.

Courtesy Masonite Corporation

An attractive small bar unit provides a focal point for this recreation area. The plaid of the bar canopy repeats the plaid of the screen and drapery.

tional counterspace will increase the usefulness of the bar.

Storage must accommodate bar tools and equipment, serving dishes, glasses, silverware, napkins and other necessary equipment. An inventory of the items to be stored in the bar area will enable planned storage to be designed and constructed. Efficient storage techniques (partitions for vertical storage of trays and compartmentalized drawers) will enable many entertainment items to be stored in the bar area. A concealed trash disposal area should also be provided if the space is available.

Lighting for the home bar may be classified as either working light or mood light. If the bar is located in a below-ground basement, or in a relatively dark portion of a room, some illumination for the home bartender will have to be provided. Two low-wattage (25 to 40 watt) incandescent fixtures or a small one-tube flourescent fixture will provide sufficient light for the working area. These fixtures may be fastened to a convenient surface near the work area and controller by a toggle switch mounted on the bar. A more decorative working light could be a small table lamp at one end of the bar.

Mood lighting establishes a warm, hospitable atmosphere for the bar area. Such varied arrangements as low-wattage lights behind Tiffany glass doors, ships lanterns, white globe lights, or antique lamps may be used as mood lighting. Such

Courtesy of Ethan Allen, Inc.

Drop leaves extend the bar surface of this cabinet unit. Bar equipment and serving pieces are stored behind the paneled doors.

Courtesy of Ethan Allen, Inc.

A dry sink unit serves as an attractive serving bar. With their metal-lined enclosed counter area, dry sinks are very practical service bars.

Both storage and serving space is available in this adaptation of an armoire to a refreshment bar. When not in use, the doors are closed, and a handsome storage piece graces the room.

lighting should complement the decor of either the bar area or the room in which the bar is located.

BARRING COMPLICATIONS

Probably the simplest way to gain a refreshment bar is to adapt a piece of furniture. Many end tables and low storage cabinets lend themselves readily to adaptation. Low tables containing a storage area concealed by doors are ideal small bars. A selection of bar equipment, serving pieces and napkins may be kept in the storage area, with the top of the table serving as a preparation and serving counter. A tray of glasses and an ice bucket makes this arrangement a functional refreshment bar.

Armoires, large storage pieces that have come back in favor in recent years, have sufficient internal space to create a relatively complete bar arrangement. Lower drawers or shelves can store bar equipment, trays, napkins, serving dishes and other equipment. Removal of a center shelf will provide a working counter at a convenient height. Glasses may be stored in the remaining upper shelves. The counter area and the

Courtesy Masonite Corporation

One end of a recreation room is used for this refreshment and serving bar. Beams on the bar front repeat the beaming of the ceiling.

inside back of the armoire may be covered with water-resistant roll plastic or plastic laminate.

A number of furniture manufacturers have case pieces designed to be used as bar or refreshment centers. These pieces of furniture are either low tables or chests or tall wall cabinets. The low chest designs may be used as tables or tempor-

Courtesy of Ethan Allen, Inc.

Furniture designed to serve as serving bars and storage pieces comes in a variety of furniture styles. Careful selection will ensure that the bar will add to the decor of the room.

ary seating when not in use as a refreshment center.

If the house is designed with a passthrough to the kitchen, the kitchen counter behind the passthrough may be used as a bar for entertaining, particularly if nearby cabinet space is available to store bar needs. If a new home or a kitchen remodeling is being planned, inclusion of a small sink in the immediate area of a passthrough will make the area function more efficiently as a bar.

Some home craftsmen make their bars an integral part of a recreation room, and base their decorating scheme around the bar. Other home craftsmen prefer that the bar be out of sight when not in use. Bars may be placed behind draperies, behind folding screens, behind a wall of folding doors, or inside a little-used closet. If 24 inches may be taken from the length of a recreation room, a combination storage wall and entertainment bar may be constructed across the entire end of the room. Floor to ceiling draperies, accordion-fold doors or a series of bi-fold doors may be hung in front of the entertainment wall to close it off from the rest of the room when not in use. The addition of shelves and counter space inside a little-used closet will provide a useful permanent bar.

A RUSTIC BAR

A curved bar covered with rough-textured exterior siding will provide a focal point in the corner of a recreation room. Materials needed will

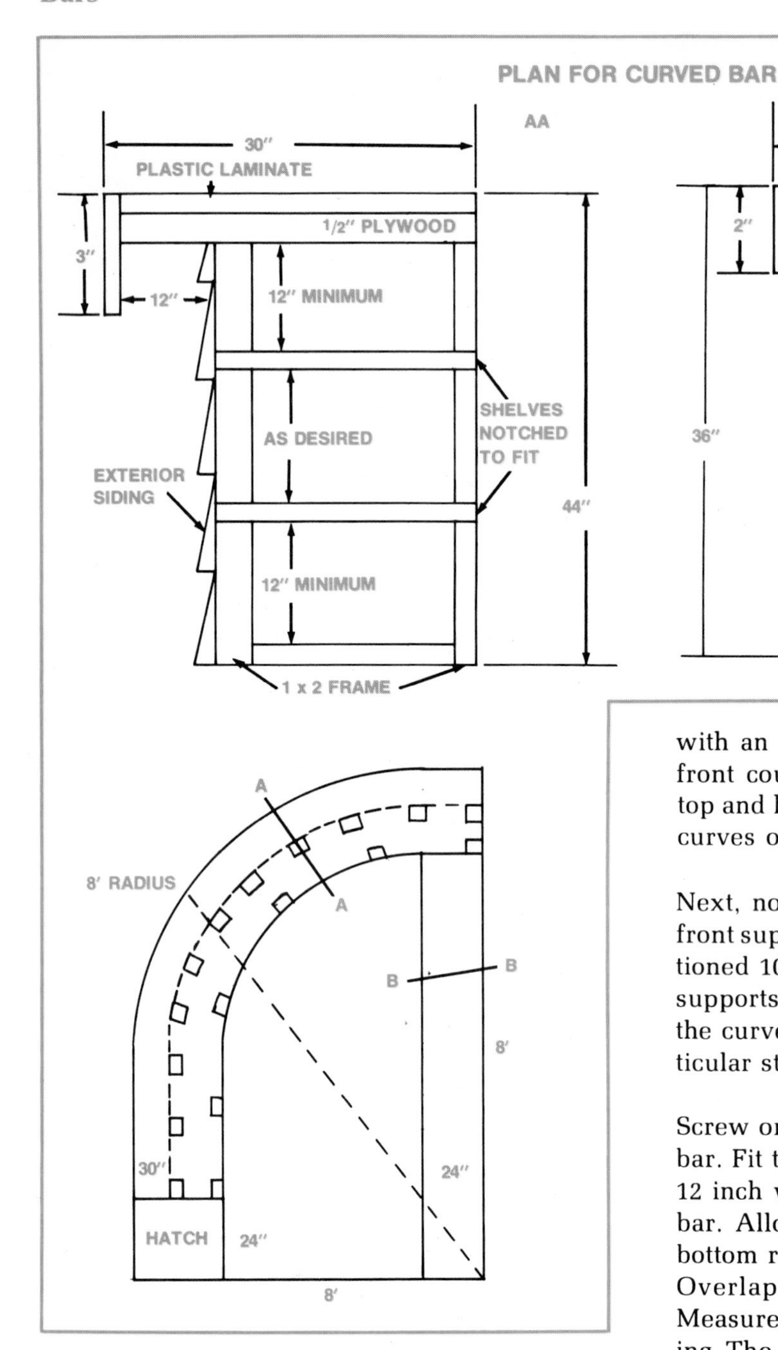

include ½ inch exterior plywood, 1 x 2 inch clear pine, rough-textured exterior siding, plastic laminate, a piano hinge and nails and screws for fasteners. Hand tools are sufficient for building the bar, although a saber saw would speed the cutting of the plywood and laminate.

First, lay out the curves of the bar top, base, and shelves on ½ inch plywood. Our bar is figured with an 8 foot radius, which gives 12½ feet of front counter space. Cut out the base, shelves, top and hatch. Using the top as pattern, mark the curves of the top on the plastic laminate.

Next, notch the base and shelves to fit the 15 front supports for the bar. The supports are positioned 10 inches on centers. If desired, the back supports should be spaced fairly evenly around the curve; however, some adjustment to fit particular storage requirements may be made.

Screw or toenail the supports to the base of the bar. Fit the shelves in place and fasten. Nail the 12 inch wide strips of siding to the front of the bar. Allow about ¼ inch clearance below the bottom row, to avoid damage if moving the bar. Overlap each row to conceal the nailheads. Measure and trim the top row to fit before nailing. The overhang of the bar top will conceal any roughness in the cut.

Position the bar top in place. Nail or screw to the supports. Countersink all fastener heads. Using glue and brads, fasten the front apron in place.

Cut out previously marked curved top from plastic laminate. Cut out front apron from laminate scrap. (If desired, a back apron may be

Courtesy Masonite Corporation

A rustic curved bar sets the decor for an informal family recreation room.

cut also.) Using contact cement, fasten laminate to top and front apron of bar.

Stain siding desired color.

Using 1 x 2 lumber and 1/2 inch plywood, build counter hatch. Cover with plastic laminate, then fasten in place using piano hinge.

The back bar, if desired, is essentially a plywood bookcase with additional supports added. Construction is similar to the curved bar. Fasten to end of curved unit and to wall to provide a rigid unit.

Baseboard

The term baseboard refers to a board or molding which is applied to the bottom of a wall to conceal the joint between the wall surface and the finish flooring. Although base trim as such is composed of two other members, base molding and base shoe, baseboard is frequently used to represent all three.

Baseboards reach completely around the room between built-ins, door openings and cabinets. An important point to remember is that coped joints should be used at internal corners while mitered joints are for external corners.

Choose the baseboard material to be installed and arrange it around the sides of the room. To save time and money, sort the pieces according to the size needed for each area. A mitered-lap joint or scarf joint is used when connecting a straight run of baseboard. Since joints must always be nailed through the wall to the studs, installing baseboard is simple if each stud is located. Record these locations initially on the

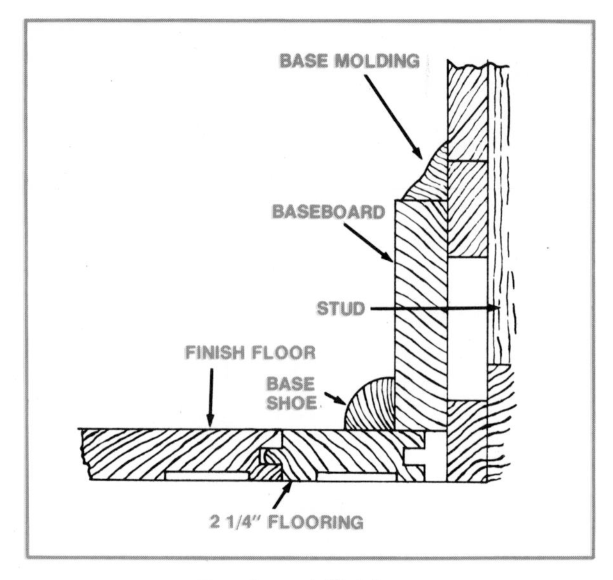

Baseboard Molding

rough floor before the plaster is applied and then on the wall covering prior to the application of the finish flooring or underlayment.

A stud can be found by tapping along the wall with a hammer. A solid sound will indicate its approximate location. However, the exact position can be determined by driving nails directly into the wall and the stud. Other studs can be located by measuring according to stud spacing (usually 16 inches O.C.).

Both the cut and fit of each section of baseboard must be correct with respect to the miter joint or cope joint specifications. Once these have been checked, the installation is simple.

Using finishing nails that can drive deep into the studs, nail the board tightly in place. It is usually easier to drive nail heads at an angle and, for right-handed workers to proceed in a counterclockwise direction around the room. In most recent construction patterns, baseboards are usually pushed against door casings. *SEE ALSO MOLDING & TRIM.*

Base Cap

Base cap is a type of molding that is applied to the top of a baseboard. *SEE ALSO MOLDING & TRIM.*

Base Coat

The base coat is the first coat of paint which is applied after the primer on a newly-built house. Some painters prefer to use a white base coat while others use the color of the final coat. When applying a one-coat paint to a house which has been painted previously, the top coat of the old paint job can become the base coat. *SEE ALSO PAINTS & PAINTING.*

Basements

[SEE FOOTINGS & FOUNDATIONS; REMODELING.]

Base Molding

A base molding is a thin strip of molding applied to the top of an unmilled baseboard to give a finished appearance or a decorative effect. It is nailed directly to the baseboard to lend a solid appearance by preventing gaps between the baseboard and the base molding. Finishing nails should be used and countersunk so that the holes may be filled with putty before the final finish is applied. *SEE ALSO MOLDING & TRIM.*

Base Shoe

The base shoe is a piece of molding much like quarter round in appearance which is placed at the bottom of the baseboard to seal the joint between the baseboard and the floor and to give a neat, finished appearance. It is fitted at the same time as the baseboard, but is not permanently installed until the floor finishing is complete. Base shoe is nailed directly to the floor or subfloor, if practicable, as baseboards may shrink causing the base shoe to lift from the floor. *SEE ALSO MOLDING & TRIM.*

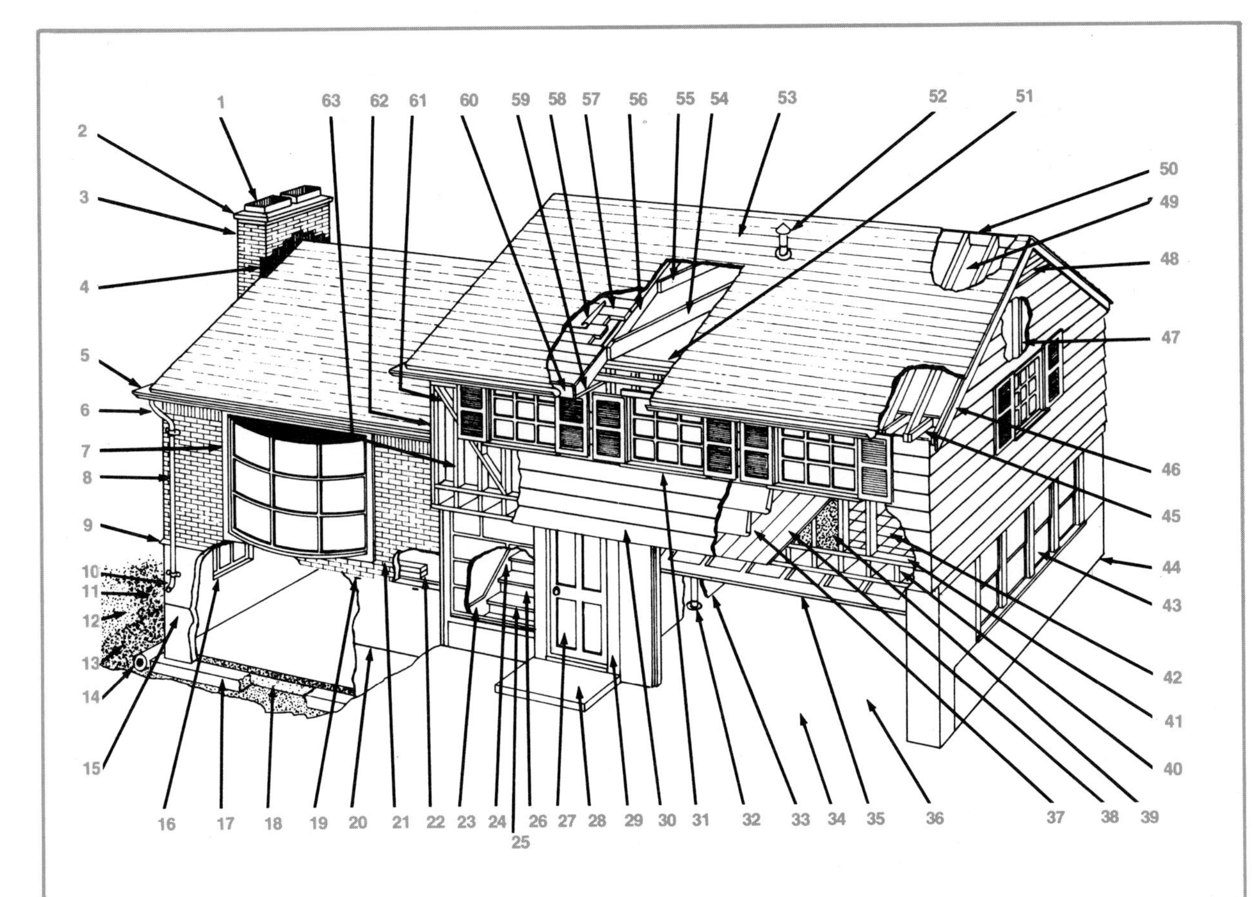

Basic Parts of a House

1. **flue**
2. **chimney cap**
3. **brickwork of chimney**
4. **chimney flashing**
5. **gutter**
6. **downspout gooseneck**
7. **window trim**
8. **leader, downspout**
9. **termite shield**
10. **downspout elbow**
11. **porous fill**
12. **topsoil**
13. **subsoil**
14. **drain tile**
15. **foundation wall**
16. **basement window**
17. **foundation wall footing**
18. **cinder fill**
19. **weep hole**
20. **waterproofing**
21. **brick veneer**
22. **sill**
23. **baseboard**
24. **stringer**
25. **stair tread**
26. **stair riser**
27. **front door**
28. **entrance platform**
29. **door trim**
30. **beveled siding**
31. **window sill**
32. **basement post (lally column)**
33. **interior trim**
34. **garage**
35. **upward-acting garage door**
36. **concrete floor or slab**
37. **building paper**
38. **diagonal sheathing**
39. **rockwool insulation**
40. **floor joist**
41. **sole plate**
42. **asphalt tile floor**
43. **double-hung window**
44. **grade**
45. **lookout**
46. **end rafter**
47. **gable stud**
48. **louver**
49. **attic space**
50. **ridge**
51. **double plate**
52. **roof ventilator**
53. **roofing shingles**
54. **ceiling joist**
55. **collar beam**
56. **rafter**
57. **roof boards**
58. **vapor barrier**
59. **soffit**
60. **fascia**
61. **corner bracing**
62. **double studding**
63. **studding**

Basin Wrench

A plumbing tool, the basin wrench, is needed to work on hard-to-reach water-supply pipes and faucets behind lavatories and sinks. Able to grip, turn and remove nuts in almost impossible areas, the basin wrench is a highly specialized tool for it can do a job that the standard tool cannot.

In most homes it is used when working on bathtub faucets that are built into the wall or installing an inplace lavatory or sink. The basin wrench has a reversible action lever that tightens or loosens the grip on the plumbing fixture. Depending on which way it's swiveled, the toothed, curved section can be removed and reinserted in the stem to work in either a clockwise or counter-clockwise direction.

For extra reinforcement, a slot in the major stem will allow the top handle to slide through. Once the top handle is in place, an additional amount of pressure may be exerted. A short length of pipe can be used over this handle for added leverage to "break" a tight joint. This should be utilized only in extreme cases.

To remove a faucet and install a new one means getting up behind the basin, and the only way to do it is with a basin wrench. It belongs in every well-equipped plumbing center. *SEE ALSO PLUMBERS TOOLS & EQUIPMENT.*

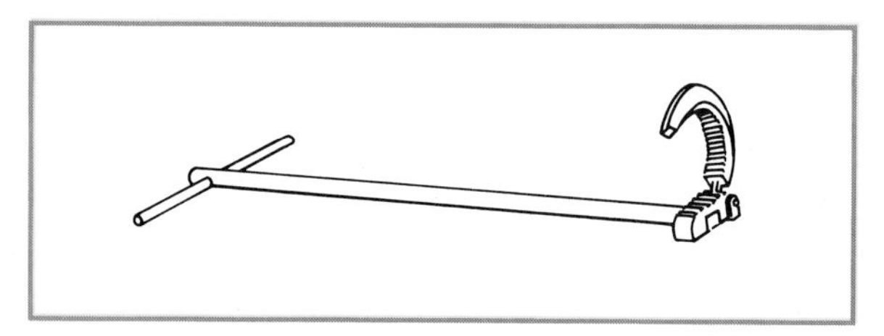

Basin Wrench

Basket-Weave Door

Dress up cabinets with attractive and easy to make basket-weave doors. They can be woven through dowels set in a grooved frame or, for a novel effect, given a two-way open weave. Thin and narrow strips of wood, veneer, plastic or cloth may be used.

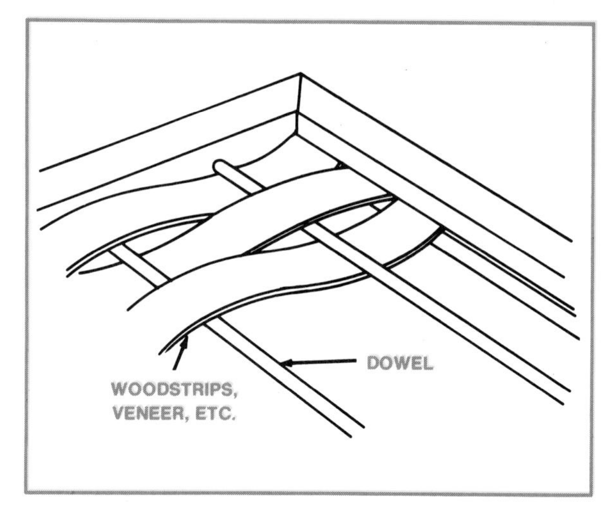

One style of basket-weave door.

Basket-Weave Fence

Basket-weave fences are often called "good neighbor" fences because they present the same good looks from either side. Besides being highly decorative, basket-weave fences are well suited to protect a windy area and provide privacy.

There are many variations of design possible. The weave can vary from very wide and open, to flat. It can be vertical or horizontal.

Once construction techniques are mastered, basket-weave fences are simple to construct. Wooden slats for weaving should be no less than ½ nor more than 1-inch thick. A popular width is 6 inches. It is a good idea to use standard lengths of lumber with 4 by 4-inch posts spaced accordingly. If you begin at the bottom and work upward, the slats can rest on each other as you work and the job will be easier. This will also enable you to get the fence as close to the ground as you want without risking miscalculation. For a strong fence, nail the slats to alternating posts.

The vertical boards that the slats are woven around are called spacers and can be various sizes depending upon the finished look desired. The smaller the spacers, the closer the weave. Rails at the top and bottom are optional, depending upon the design of the fence.

There is another version of the basket-weave fence that is easier to construct, but is not considered a "good neighbor" fence. Nail the boards to the same side of the posts, leaving just enough room for the clearance of a spacer, and weave the spacers in from the top on alternate sides of the boards. On this type fence, a top rail is commonly used. *SEE ALSO FENCES & GATES.*

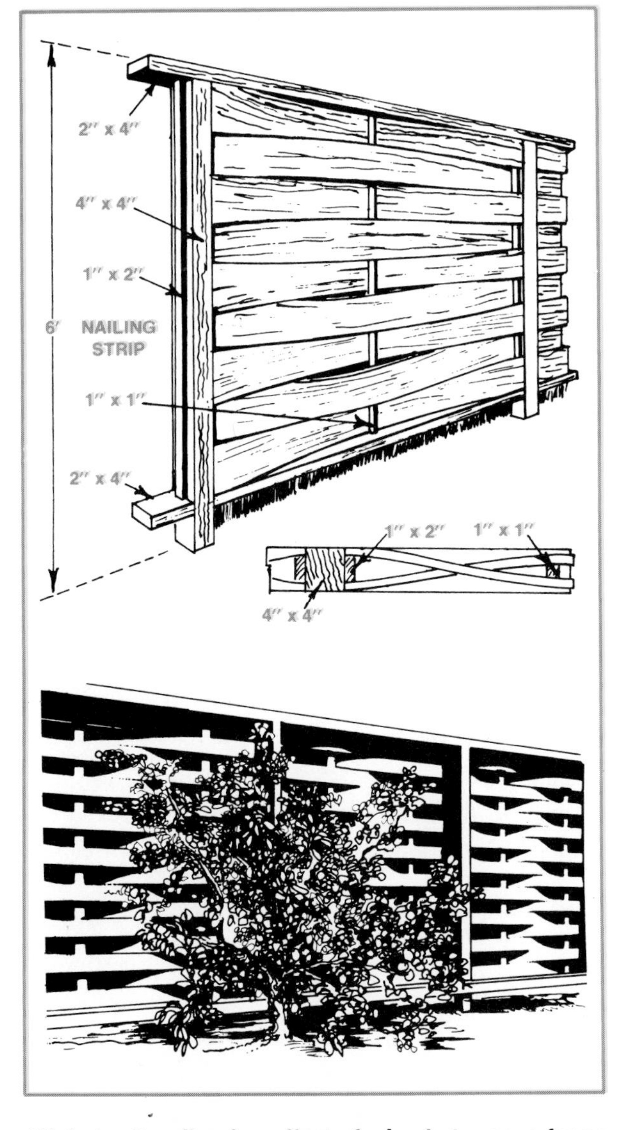

Minimize the dizzying effect of a basket-weave fence with the use of an espaliered vine.

Bass Boat

This shallow water boat for the fisherman who likes to work the weed and stump areas of his favorite lakes is easy to build. It is designed for several different power sources. An electric trolling motor or up to a three horsepower outboard may be used, or the fisherman can row it or make the paddle wheels to be driven by a small air-cooled engine.

The seating arrangement of this boat is the unique feature of the design. The fisherman can sit anywhere and face any direction and have live wells or storage wherever wanted.

To start construction, lay out the bow curve on one 1 x 12 x 12 foot piece of redwood (pine or other wood may be used, but redwood is preferred). Cut it to shape and use the first piece to trace the curve on the other three pieces. (Note that the outside pieces cover the ends of the bow 2 x 4, but the two center ones are notched to fit under the rear edge of the 2 x 4.) Cut the 10 degree angle on the stern end and lay the four pieces aside.

Cut the transom piece and the bow 2 x 4 to length and angle-cut each end 5 degrees. Measure where the two center 1 x 12's will attach to bow and transom and draw lines on each for guides.

Glue and nail the two sides to the transom and to the bow 2 x 4. Then glue and nail the two inside

Materials List

5	1" x 12" x 12'	Redwood boards - sides, transom, etc.
1	2" x 4" x 5'	Fir - bow
2	1/4" x 4' x 8'	A.C. plywood - bottom
1	1/2" x 4' x 8'	A.C. plywood - paddle sides and seats
1	1" x 3" x 4'	Oak - paddle wheel arms
1	2" x 2" x 4'	Fir - nailers
2	1" x 3" x 10'	Redwood - paddles
1 qt.		Weldwood waterproof glue
1 lb.	1" 15 gauge	Boatnails
		Assorted nails, hinges and screw eyes
6		Flange mounted bearings
1 pr.		Oarlocks and sockets

pieces to the transom and bow. Square the hull and nail and glue 2 x 2 x 10 inch blocks into each corner along the transom for additional strength.

Turn the hull upside down and plane the edges of the sides flat. Give all edges a coat of glue. Beginning at the transom, nail a sheet of 1/4 inch plywood to all edges with 1 inch galvanized boat-nails. Where the plywood ends near the bow, glue and nail a batten across the inside of the floor. Start the second sheet of 1/4 inch plywood from there to the bow. After the hull is trimmed and all glue is dry, nail the 4 keels in place and the 1 x 2 cap strips along the two sides and bow top.

Decide on the location of live wells and divide the center section off accordingly with 1 x 12's cut to fit snugly crosswise between the two center 1 x 12's. Glue and nail the cross pieces to each side and the bottom, then drill 1/2 inch holes through the bottom section to allow water to enter the well. Use the rest of the center section for dry storage. Cut 1/2 inch plywood covers for all wells and hinge them on one side.

One section may be made into a viewing box by replacing the 1/4 inch plywood bottom with a section of auto window glass, and the fisherman can look down to find fish from a glass-bottom boat. Seal it well so that it does not leak.

If the home craftsman wishes to make the paddle wheels to propel the boat, the drawings are detailed enough to show how. A stop under the wheel arms may be added so that the paddles do not go too deep in the water. Since the paddles may be made from scrap lumber or plywood, they are not dimensioned on the plan other than to suggest 3/4 inch diameter pipe for jack shaft and paddle wheel shaft. Be sure to make splash

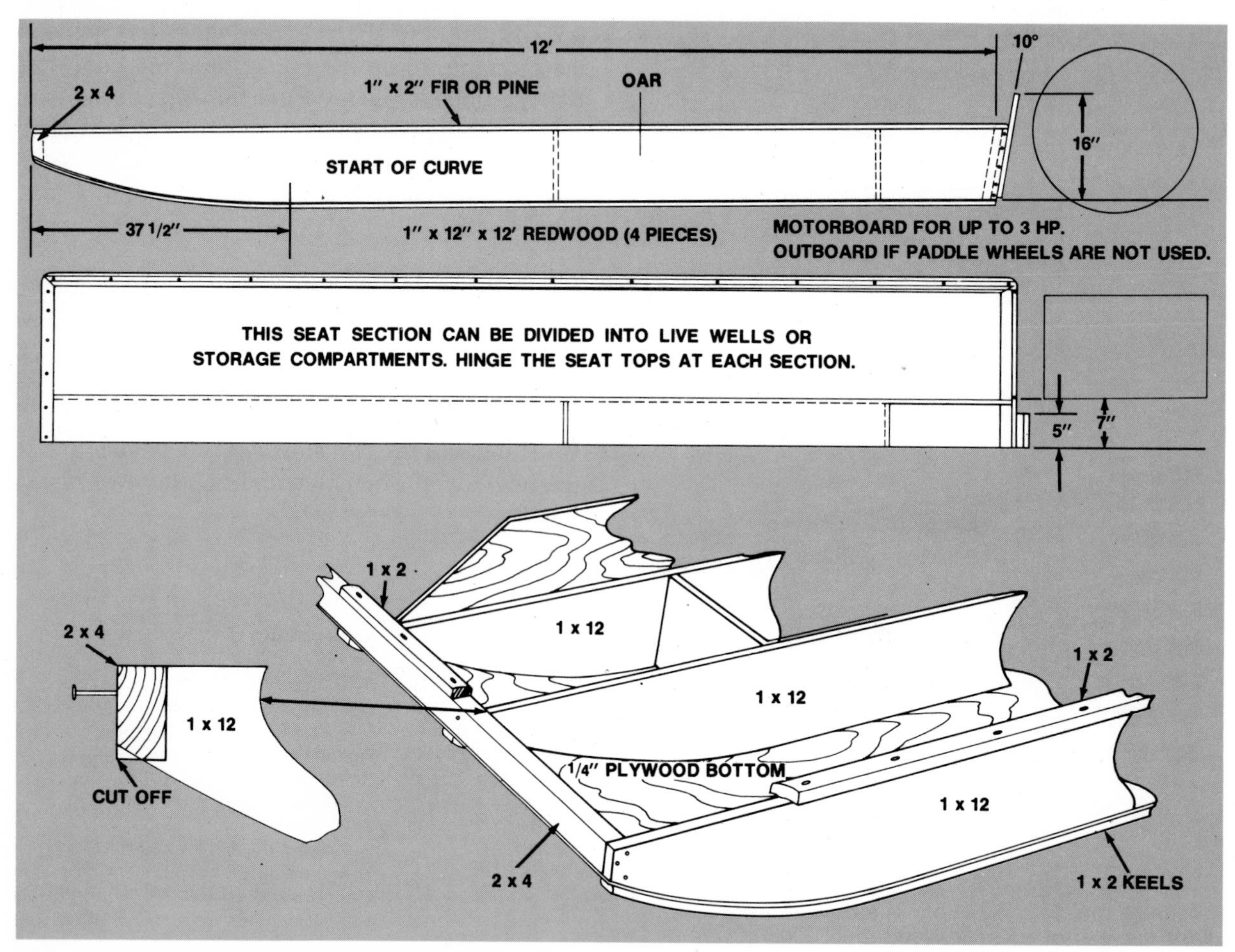

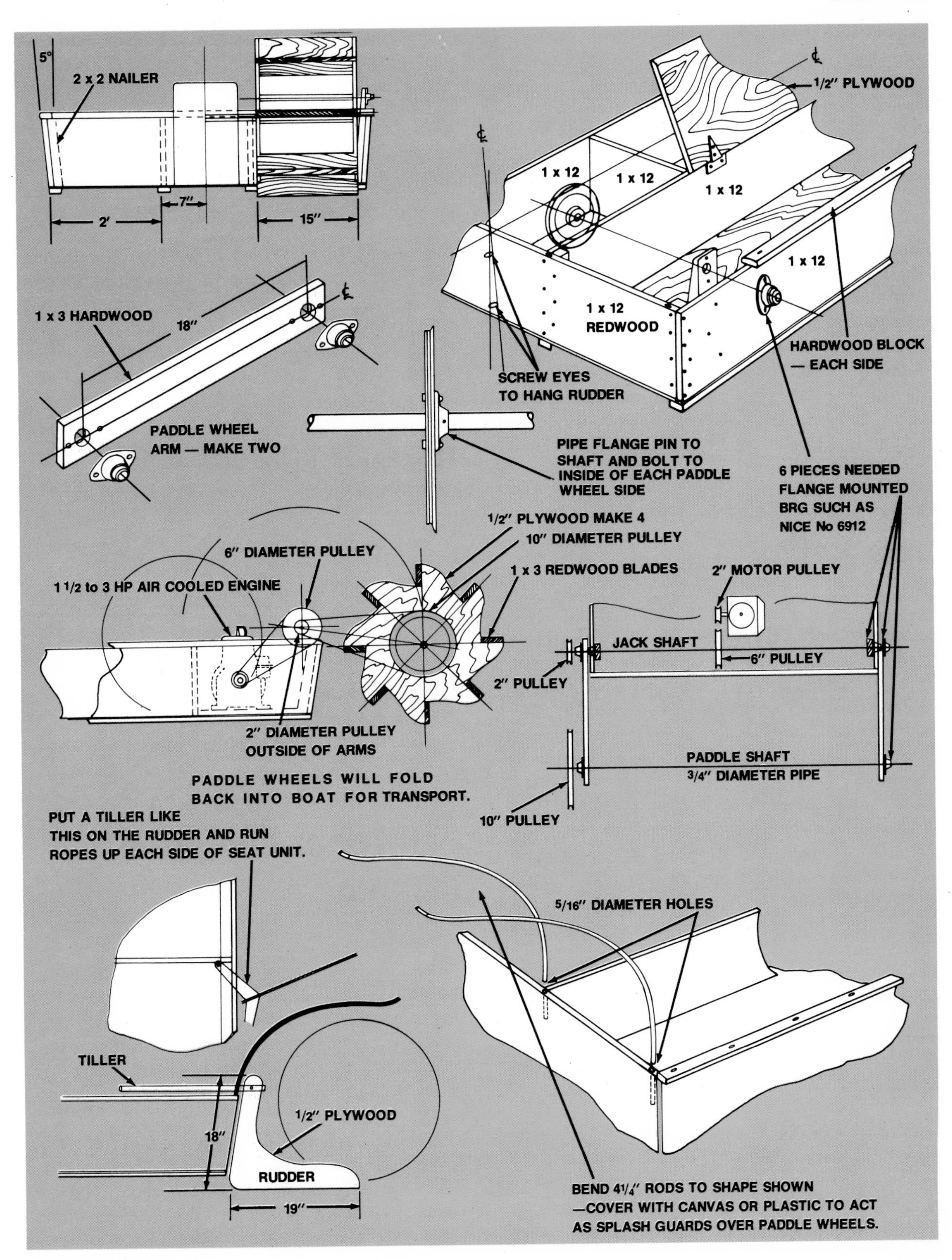
5°
2 x 2 NAILER
2'
7"
15"
1/2" PLYWOOD
1 x 12
1 x 12
1 x 12
1 x 12
1 x 12
REDWOOD
HARDWOOD BLOCK
— EACH SIDE
SCREW EYES
TO HANG RUDDER
1 x 3 HARDWOOD
18"
PADDLE WHEEL
ARM — MAKE TWO
PIPE FLANGE PIN TO
SHAFT AND BOLT TO
INSIDE OF EACH PADDLE
WHEEL SIDE
6 PIECES NEEDED
FLANGE MOUNTED
BRG SUCH AS
NICE No 6912
1/2" PLYWOOD MAKE 4
10" DIAMETER PULLEY
6" DIAMETER PULLEY
1 1/2 to 3 HP AIR COOLED ENGINE
1 x 3 REDWOOD BLADES
2" MOTOR PULLEY
JACK SHAFT
6" PULLEY
2" PULLEY
2" DIAMETER PULLEY
OUTSIDE OF ARMS
PADDLE SHAFT
3/4" DIAMETER PIPE
PADDLE WHEELS WILL FOLD
BACK INTO BOAT FOR TRANSPORT.
10" PULLEY
PUT A TILLER LIKE
THIS ON THE RUDDER AND RUN
ROPES UP EACH SIDE OF SEAT UNIT.
5/16" DIAMETER HOLES
TILLER
1/2" PLYWOOD
18"
RUDDER
19"
BEND 4 1/4" RODS TO SHAPE SHOWN
—COVER WITH CANVAS OR PLASTIC TO ACT
AS SPLASH GUARDS OVER PADDLE WHEELS.

guards over each paddle wheel. A simple removable one is illustrated in the drawings.

The air-cooled engine must be mounted on wooden rails fastened to the floor or side walls of the engine compartment. The rudder shown in the drawings is for use with the paddle wheels only.

The bass boat can be easily customized by adding a top or a place to mount a patio umbrella. Other suggestions are to install an automatic anchor mount, or insulate a section of the seat area for cold beverage storage. Each side of the boat is roomy enough to spread out a sleeping bag for overnight camping. There is no reason that, with care, a sterno stove could not be used on board. Also, the boat could be 14 feet or 16 feet long if preferred.

Bass Reflex

A bass reflex cabinet is one which allows troublemaking low-frequency notes to escape from a speaker into an air space within the cabinet itself. In so doing, it extends the bass characteristics and broadens the resonance to a moderate degree, resulting in a smoother overall sound.

A space between the actual speaker and the speaker port (opening) on the cabinet may be provided by removing the speaker and placing an ordinary faucet washer over each mounting bolt of the speaker. Replace the speaker and tighten the nuts enough to hold the speaker without producing a rattle or flattening the washers. Lining the inside of the cabinet with an insulating material will aid in stopping unnecessary vibration. *SEE ALSO STEREO SYSTEMS.*

Basswood

Basswood, the softest of the hardwoods, is a product of the American linden and the tulip tree. This straight-grained wood of light color is easy to carve, warp resistant and well suited for fretwork. The grain is very slight and often nonexistent making it a good choice for craftwork. Basswood is widely used in the manufacturing of drawing boards, moldings, cabinets and excelsior. Its characteristics make it particularly suitable as a core stock for plywood.

Basswoods may be sealed with a penetrating finish for good adhesion, but the topcoat should be varnish, shellac or lacquer. As with other fine-grained woods, the best finish is one that builds on the surface. *SEE ALSO WOOD IDENTIFICATION.*

Bastard File

A bastard file is any file that has semi-coarse teeth, as "bastard" defines the coarseness of the file and is not a type of file. *SEE ALSO HAND TOOLS.*

Bathroom Construction

[SEE BATHROOM DESIGN & PLANNING; FRAMING.]

Bathroom Design & Planning

Bathroom design may include merely changing the decor in the present bath, replacing its fixtures, or completely remodeling or modernizing it, according to family needs. The most wide-open category in planning, of course, is creating an entire bathroom for a new home.

The basic purpose of the bath should first be decided upon, whether it be for children, for the entire family, as a guest powder room, shower room or cosmetic center. In modes of design, a bath may be conservative or mod, colorful or

Courtesy of Kohler Company

A fine example of a contemporary bathroom, this luxurious design includes a $5^1/_2$ x 7 foot bathtub, with dual water controls and dual showers, a low-profile toilet and matching bidet, and a *his* and *hers* island lavatory center. The lavatory for the lady includes a shampoo fitting with spray arm, swing-away spout, and an oval-shaped basin. The mirror settings and plants give the room a spacious effect while accessories and linens blend colorfully to bring it together. The fixtures are done in sky-blue fiberglass.

subtle, economical or highly luxurious. The total design will be determined by the family's personal tastes and the amount of money they have budgeted for it.

Whether planning a bath for a new home or remodeling an old one, the budget inevitably makes part of the necessary decisions. Generally, fittings and fixtures for the bath are priced according to appearance and working performance. The more expensive ones last longer, are more attractive and have better working order.

Economy-choice fixtures from a respectable firm will be well-made, but less attractive than higher-priced types. Consider mortgage and later remodeling possibilities, as well as present expense.

The bath should coordinate with the living style of the family. Another thing to consider is the overall decorating scheme of the home as color schemes and style for the bathroom should be compatible with other rooms.

Today the bath has become an important decorating unit. There are now storage units, mirrors of all sizes, built-in color-matched plumbing fixtures, new lighting effects and private partitions for ideas in bathroom planning.

BASIC ELEMENTS OF THE BATH

There are certain elements basic to all well-planned bathrooms. Beginning with a convenient floor plan, comfort, color and storage should be kept in mind. Since fixtures are permanent furniture, they should be chosen first.

Colored fixtures are becoming more and more prevalent in modern baths. Each should be chosen from the same manufacturer because whites from different lines sometimes have different tones. Fixtures should also be chosen under the type of light in which they will be used. Fluorescent, incandescent and natural lights all have different effects. Fixtures may not look the same when they are installed if the lighting is different. Fixtures come in black or basic white as well as colors.

Bathtubs come in three basic styles. Rectangular models for family use should be at least five feet long and high enough, preferably 16 inches, to lessen chance of splash-over. Square models usually have a seat inside. Smaller square tubs are excellent for children's baths and double as a shower base for adults. Sunken tubs are more elegant looking, though difficult to clean and not practical for children. There are also more compact deeper soaking tubs. Materials for bathtubs are cast iron or formed steel with acid-resistant finishes.

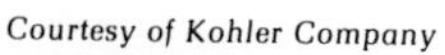

Courtesy of Kohler Company

Courtesy of Kohler Company

Triangular Lavatory

Courtesy of Kohler Company

Circular Lavatory

Courtesy of Kohler Company

Square Lavatory

Everyone new can have the luxury of a whirlpool bath with units that may be installed in a regular bathtub. Most have a simplified action to mix air and water for water action which soothes and stimulates circulation. These whirlpool attachments come in chromium or gold electroplate.

Lavatories come in many shapes: triangular, rectangular, square or circular. Most are built into units with cabinets. Some of these types are the self rimming, which requires no metal framing ring around the upper surface; under-the-counter, which is mounted beneath an opening cut into the countertop; and the integral lavatory and counter, which is seamless and smooth-surfaced. The wall hung models are usually rectangular in shape.

Toilets or water closets come in four styles, based on flushing action. Expense and performance are equated. The least expensive model is the *washdown*. It has a low water level in the tank, making cleaning difficult. Its simple washout action makes it clog more readily also.

Least expensive of the siphon-action toilets is the *reverse trap* which is moderately noisy, yet efficient. More of the interior surface of this model is covered with water. It is only slightly more expensive than the washdown.

The *siphon-jet toilet* is an improvement over the reverse-trap with its quieter flushing action and large trapway for less clogging. It has a big interior water level also.

The *low-profile,* very similar to the siphon-jet in flushing action, is a low silhouette, one-piece model. Its elegance, its almost silent flushing action and lower profile account for additional expense.

Wall-hung toilets are more expensive than one and two-piece models which attach to the floor, but the wall-hung models make cleaning easy and, therefore, save time. Triangular-tank toilets take advantage of corner space to provide more room in small spaces. Toilets are all made of vitreous china which is acid-resistant.

Courtesy of Eljer

The bidet is a companion fixture to the toilet. It is designed for the entire family for cleansing the perineal area after toilet use. The bidet user sits astride it facing the wall where hot and cold water controls are located. A soothing comfortable spray is provided for rinsing. The bowl surface is rinsed out by similar attachments. Bidets are very modern fixtures which should be considered when remodeling or designing a new bath.

Courtesy of Eljer

Shower units may be separate facilities or additional units to bathtubs. A 36 x 36 inch shower stall is the minimum size for adult use. Showers are available in enameled steel or fiberglass.

Courtesy of Kohler Company

This antique lavatory fitting brings distinctive elegance to every day living. Whatever the decor, Victorian, Early American, the Roaring 20s, this type of fitting will fit the mood.

Faucet fittings include colored handles, monograms and jewel-like tops. Gold fixtures are elegant and perfect for luxury looks although they are expensive. Single-control faucets, prevalent now for their convenience and easy cleaning, are used in showers and lavatories. Interchangeable valve units, which take the place of washers in many faucet styles, operate easily with little trouble. High brass content in fixtures makes them attractive and more durable.

COLORS

If colors are chosen for the bathroom fixtures, neutral tones might be selected for the walls and floor, however the fixture color should be duplicated in the room setting. Color builds up very quickly in small rooms. Choosing color, like everything else that goes into decorating, is a matter of personal preference. Looking at a color wheel for combinations might be helpful. Colors, such as red and green, which appear opposite each other on the wheel, are *complementary*. If they are used together, both should not be full intensity.

Analogous colors, located side-by-side on the color wheel, such as orange and yellow, might work out nicely for bright effects.

Monochromatic schemes, using one color in several different tones, tints or shades, may be put together for warm effects. The bathroom is perfect for using monochromatic harmony since it is most effective in small rooms. Also, many decorative touches can be used to change the one-color effect without adding a lot of extra expense.

Triad harmony, using three colors, may provide a nice utilization of tones equidistant from each other on the color wheel. It can be varied by using tints, tones or shades of the primary colors or by using pure hues of them.

MEDICINE CABINETS, VANITIES and MIRRORS

Medicine cabinets are notorious for holding few articles. This is one reason planning adequate storage space is so important. But medicine cabinets have their advantages in the overall decorating plan. In some homes, this storage unit is merely functional, just a box with a mirrored door or a large mirror which actually conceals the storage space. In bathroom design today there are all types of mirrors including rectangular, oval and square to enhance the room as well as to conceal bath supplies. They should be chosen to coordinate with the vanity.

Twin and tripled medicine cabinets can relieve the overload of one unit. In smaller bathrooms, corner cabinets fit nicely. If space is very tight, cabinets may be set in between wall studs. Cabinets are available in both recessed and surface-mounted styles. Surface mounts minimize wall-piercing, however, and help to retain the natural sound barrier created by wall surfaces. Many people do not consider this factor in bathroom planning.

Decorative mirrors may be arranged many different ways. Mounted on either side of a single cabinet unit, they form a three-way mirror. They may be used as sliding doors for cabinets and/or placed full length in dressing room baths.

Courtesy of Kohler Company

This elegant and festive red/pink color scheme, in a compartmented setting, features *his* and *her* lavatories for convenience, a bidet and low-profile toilet and a luxurious sunken six-foot bathtub with sloping back and safety grip rails.

Courtesy of Eljer

Mirrors have a broadening effect in any bathroom. Definite wallpaper patterns used in conjunction with large mirrors, especially horizontal designs, also provide the illusion of spaciousness in a bath.

LIGHTING & ELECTRICAL OUTLETS

Proper lighting is important in design for specific areas like vanities and medicine cabinets and for general overall illumination in the bath. Lighting arrangements should be decided upon in the blueprint stages of planning — what type is to be used and where. No-window bathrooms and colored fixtures are special considerations to keep in mind.

Developments for lighting in certain areas have been made with the new and different fixtures on the market. There are waterproof lights available for the tub and shower areas. Electrical switches for such units should be way out of reach from the fixture's user, however. Specified illumination is required in compartmented baths because of the separation in fixtures.

There are several possibilities for lighting arrangements. Lighting for vanities should be balanced to create no-shadow effects on facial features. Good choices for this area include theatrical lighting, an arrangement of lights outlining a cabinet or mirror, and soffit lighting, mounted overhead and concealed by a translucent panel. Soffit lighting puts light where it is needed without being obvious. It reflects from the counter and sink more easily also.

Light should be directed correctly to discourage blurring and brassy reflections. It is best placed above and at the sides of mirrors. While lighting from above is easier on the eyes, strip lighting for mirrors is more effective. Sidelights are said to be shadowless, and are preferred by men for shaving.

Skylighting, or natural light, is effective for creating privacy in the bath. This is good in problem areas where a window cannot be placed. Some people prefer this natural lighting in an otherwise dark room.

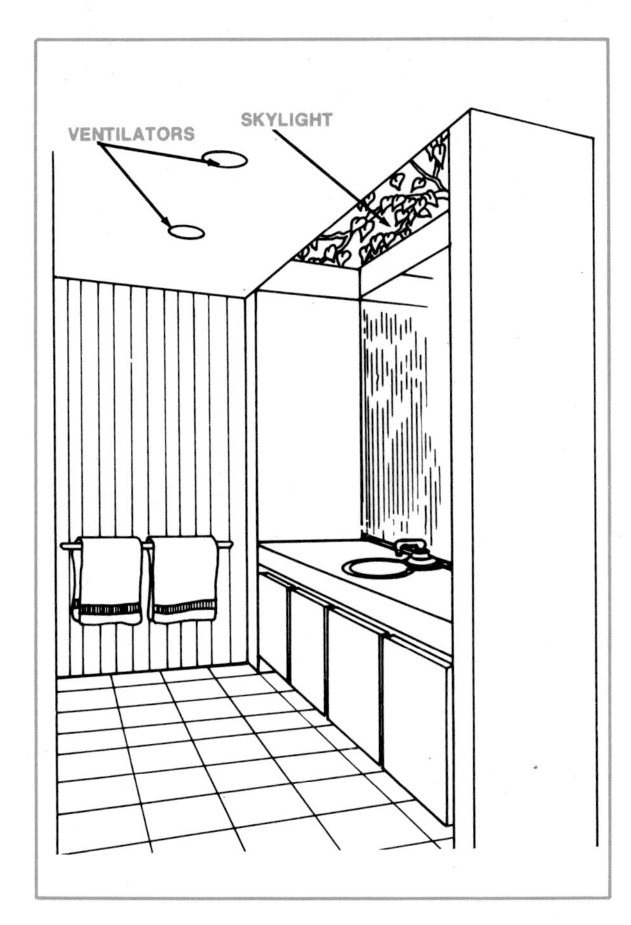

In an interior space or one which doesn't need a window because of more privacy, a skylight may be used. It is best to use ventilators with this type of light, as shown. Use of mirrors here makes the room visually larger.

Any light which cannot be looked at comfortably is too bright. Diffusing too-bright light can be done by choosing frosted bulbs and frosted glass or plastic panels set in front of incandescent bulbs. Diffusion can be helped also by light-colored walls and ceiling.

If a bathroom is chilly, light fixtures with built-in elements for heating may be installed. Some lights are combined with a fan; others can be connected with a sunlamp.

Fluorescent tubes, using only one-third of the electric current, extend light in a line at low brightness levels. On the other hand, fluorescent lights do not render color very accurately.

For the best lighting, a combination of incandescents and fluorescents, which allow for overall illumination, should be used to create a soft glow throughout the room.

It is good to plan where electrical outlets should be used when planning lighting arrangements. Appliances such as electric hair setters and curlers, which will require these outlets, should be kept in mind. Adequate storage for facial saunas, exercisers, shavers and electric toothbrushes is important, too.

WALLS and CEILINGS

Choosing wall coverings is a big factor in the overall color scheme and decoration for the bathroom.

Walls around the tub are the first consideration. Ceramic tiles, ranging from 1 x 1 inch to 9½ inch squares, are popular. The most commonly used size for wall tile is 4½ x 4½ inches, usually found in a bright glaze. Other luxury-type wall coverings are made of terrazzo tile, quarry tile and marble. If marble is used, it is good to use it for the floor and vanity top also.

Some less expensive covers are mirrored walls, vinyl products that resemble marble or tile and plastic finished or laminated hardboards. Some

Courtesy of Eljer

easily installed wall materials are reproductions of hardboard paneling in realistic woodgrains and wood paneling with a plastic finish.

Light, pastel-toned colors are best for walls rather than bordered, decorative tiles. Too much design on walls tends to overshadow other features of the room, making it necessary to choose other accessories accordingly. Light colors for walls and ceilings should especially be considered for long-range planning as they will allow flexibility in changing about or remodeling other room furnishings.

For the upper walls and ceiling, wallpaper is a neat and appealing idea. Designs to match any color can be found, often with matching fabrics for windows or a shower curtain. A water-proof liner must be used with fabric for a shower curtain. Vinyl and plastic-coated wallpapers are washable. There are some which have texture resembling wood, brick and leather.

Wallpapering a small area such as a bathroom can be inexpensive. If the room is larger, papering one wall is still very decorative. Wallpaper is priced by rolls, one equaling 35 square feet. Double-roll bolts have narrower paper, 18 to 20½ inches wide. Papers in a 28 inch width may come in a triple-roll bolt.

Paint is still a good inexpensive, easy-to-apply covering. Semigloss and latex-based are washable paints which protect against bathroom moisture. For matching fixtures and other items, paint may be custom-mixed to get exactly the right tone.

The ceiling should be completed before the walls are decorated. Papering a ceiling lowers it. Ceiling height is also minimized by wide-matching borders placed around the top part of the wall. Acoustical tile, which needs only occasional cleaning, resists great temperature changes as well.

ACCESSORIES

Linens and other accessories in a bathroom can help to make the most of set color schemes in fixtures, floors and wall. Be mindful of exactly the type of bathroom in which the accessories will be used. These items give the room its own personality, usually fitted both to the family's tastes and to the design or trend of other rooms in the home.

Accessories such as scales, tissue holders and paperholders are useful items of bathroom equipment but do not always coordinate with the decor. Some manufacturers have designed these items as built-in units which can be attractively fitted into most settings and save space as well.

Courtesy of Eljer

Courtesy of Eljer

Since accessories and linens are impermanent, the bathroom never has to get out-dated or dull-looking. In choosing linens, carpeting and other washable materials, it is best to get high-quality items. Laundered materials can wear out quickly, especially in a family bath. So think about usage, in addition to attractiveness and style, when buying washable items.

Several factors relate to the cost of towels, including size, color, pattern and depth of pile. The latest trends, of course, will be more expensive than the old standard patterns. This factor also applies to window accessories, bathmats, carpets and rugs, shower curtains and tub enclosures.

Courtesy of Kohler Company

The plant craze can apply to the bathroom, too. Some manufacturers of fixtures are now making plant boxes for toilet tank tops and other settings in the bath. The high humidity in this room makes it ideal for plant growth.

Courtesy of Kohler Company

Pictures are good accessories for setting a theme. In the family bathroom, flower prints might be used while a mud bath would look cheerful with various graphics & posters. There is no set rule on decorating ideas for the bathroom. Mirror arrangements, sculpture, towel stands, gold or chrome containers and many other items may be used.

FLOORS

The best kind of floor for the bathroom is one which requires little cleaning and is indifferent to moisture. Floor materials for the bath include ceramic tiles, marble, sheet vinyl, vinyl tile, poured floors or carpet. Matte or crystalline glazed tile is better than highly glazed wall tile for durability. Unglazed mosaic tile makes a good durable floor as does quarry tile. Shapes for floor tiles include hexagons, octagons, rectangles, large or small squares, and Spanish and Moorish patterns. Poured floors, composed of glazed polyurethane chips, are referred to as seamless because they require no waxing. Sheet vinyl, usually sold in 6-foot widths, can cover a small floor with no seams. Vinyl tiles may also be used. These range from 12 to 18 inches square and resemble marble, bamboo or parquet flooring.

For permanent installation, ceramic or plastic tiles might be used. Some of the latter come with pre-pasted backs, which are easy to install.

Carpet gives the bath a luxurious look, and is becoming more prevalent with the easy-to-care-for styles available. Indoor/outdoor carpet is good because it soaks up dampness and can be washed off with a sponge. Thicker soft-piled coverings, which are machine-washable, are very attractive. They should always be purchased with non-skid backings for safety.

Resilient floors, which come in tile or sheet materials, are easy to install. Linoleum or asphalt tile is relatively inexpensive. Though it is the best known of the resilient floors, linoleum has limitations. It can only be installed on sub-floors; it cannot be used below or at grade. But, linoleum is good for long wear and resistance to grease. Asphalt tile, while being very durable, is

more susceptible to grease and soil staining. It may be installed at any level.

HEATING & VENTILATION

Windows or exhaust fans provide ventilation for bathrooms. If a window is used for ventilation, it should not be placed above the tub. When this cannot be avoided, install an easy-to-operate window, preferably the swing-out crank type. Exhaust fans, vented to the outside, can be installed in any bathroom to prevent excessive humidity in the house. These fans may be built into light and heater units in small bathrooms. It is better to have separate wall switches for each unit, however.

When there is not a central heating system in the home, gas or wall-space heaters are needed. The wall heater should be placed in a safe position to avoid possible fire hazards. Electric heaters should be properly grounded and have a thermostat connection. Venting and a safety pilot shut-off are necessary for gas heaters. A fan-assisted ceiling heater may be good for small areas. Infrared heat lamps provide spot heating for someone using a towel after the bath or for hair drying.

BATHROOM REMODELING

Modernization, space-saving and replacing worn fixtures are some reasons for remodeling the bathroom. The make-over is often a slight change in decor but may involve an extensive detailed reconstruction of the room.

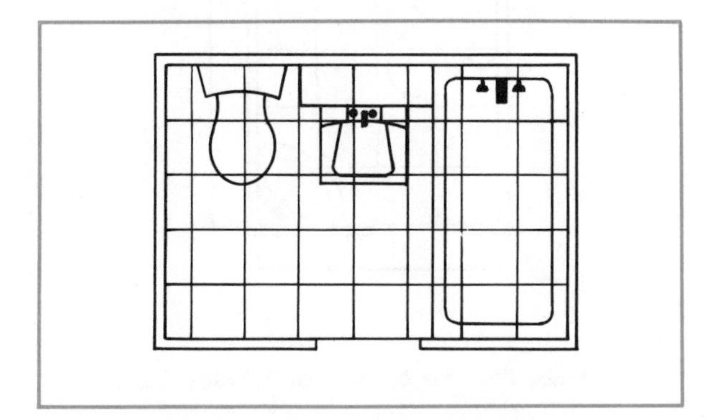

Floor Plan for One-Wall Bath

Courtesy of Eljer

This decorative one-wall bath illustrates how accessories can beautify a simple design and enhance white fixtures. The openness of these storage units allows more space for coordination of the vivid blue/green color scheme.

Complete reconstruction involves relocation of fixtures, the addition or improvement of ventilating and heating ducts, adding light fixtures, replacing flooring and wall coverings and purchasing new medicine cabinets, mirrors and other accessories.

When decisions have been made concerning the exact type of remodeling to be done, the first step is making a floor plan. It should include details on storage space and basic fixtures to indicate whether there will be enough room for them to fit into the new arrangement. A sketch of the present bath should also be made, showing sizes and shapes of room fittings. This will help in choosing new sizes for greater convenience.

ADDING A BATH

Many homes, even those with two full baths, can use another for guests or for added convenience. Finding additional space for a bathroom is not a difficult task; however, installation can be made simpler when the location is near existing plumbing. With a bit of innovation, many unique spaces in the home can be converted into bathrooms.

For a powder room, a 4 x 5′ area is sufficient. Often a small bedroom can be converted into a large bath to serve an adjoining bedroom. Powder rooms or showers may be located in a utility room or basement downstairs. The attic, especially if it has been made into a bedroom, is a good place for an extra bath as is the garage adjoining the house. A garage bath is handy for cleaning up after outdoor gardening and car repairs.

Bathroom make-overs do not have to be extravagant. New wallpapering or tiling can add much to the design of an old room at little expense. Old floor tiles may be resurfaced with mosaic tiles. Carpeting is now a practical floor cover with many indoor/outdoor types available.

Adding a sliding glass or folding door to the tub area is good for preventing mop-ups after showers. A useful change in decor, glass shower enclosures with full-length mirrors also help make the room appear larger.

This bathroom design, arranged in an island unit in the center of the room, is perfect for a 12 x 15 foot area. It includes vanities on either side of the toilet/storage area with an enclosed luxury square tub directly behind. Closets may be arranged to provide access to bedrooms and bath as well in this design. One ceiling unit above this assembly can house a vent fan, heater, lighting and shower curtain track (for the tub/shower unit). The open storage allows more versatility in room decorations.

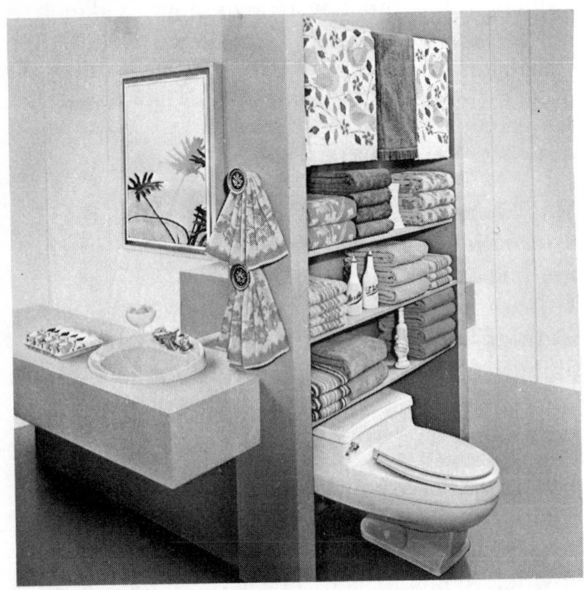

Courtesy of Eljer

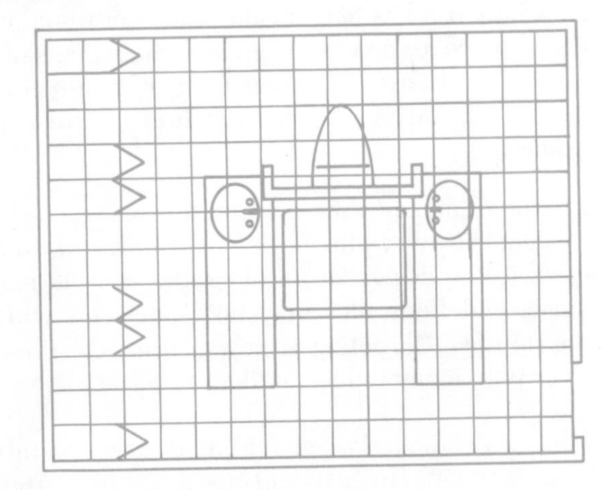

Floor Plan for An Island Bath

When a powder room is needed for the home, but there is not a lot of space available, this 4 x 4 foot bath can be installed in a storage closet, under a stairway or even in the corner of a room.

It is ideal for connecting two rooms since this particular design with cornered fixtures permits space for two doors. Mirrors are nice for visual expansion. The black/white contrast offers opportunity for varying the setting with many color accents.

Courtesy of Eljer

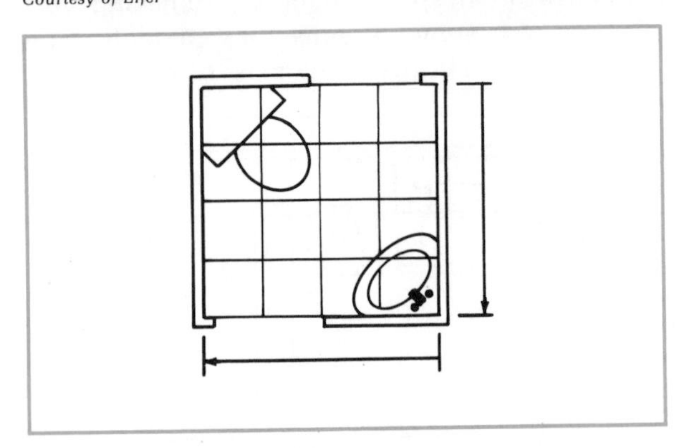

Floor Plan for 4 x 4 Foot Powder Room

The family bath should be designed to offer privacy while keeping fixtures together in a localized setting. The compartmented design is perfect for this room. The 12 x 12 foot bath shown includes lavatories, placed on opposite sides of a large counter top, with cabinetry which extends to the ceiling to house lighting fixtures. There is a medicine cabinet above each lavatory with towel-hangers on the reverse side for the other lavatory. There are two private toilet facilities, each containing storage space in a cabinet assembly. The room may provide double-access closet space for adjoining bedrooms. A primary/secondary color scheme of yellow and green is carried out in fixtures as well as accessories.

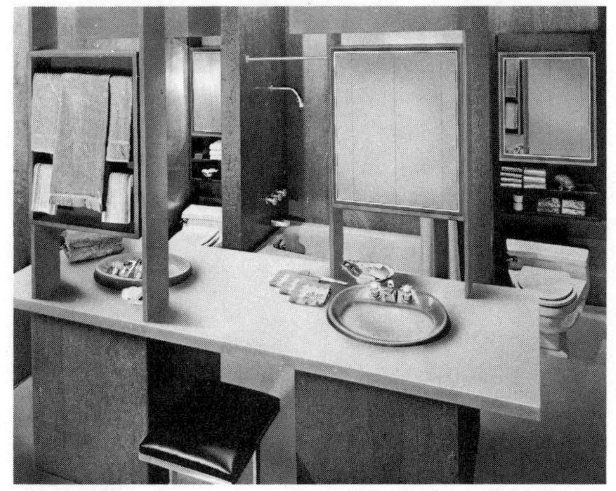

Courtesy of Eljer

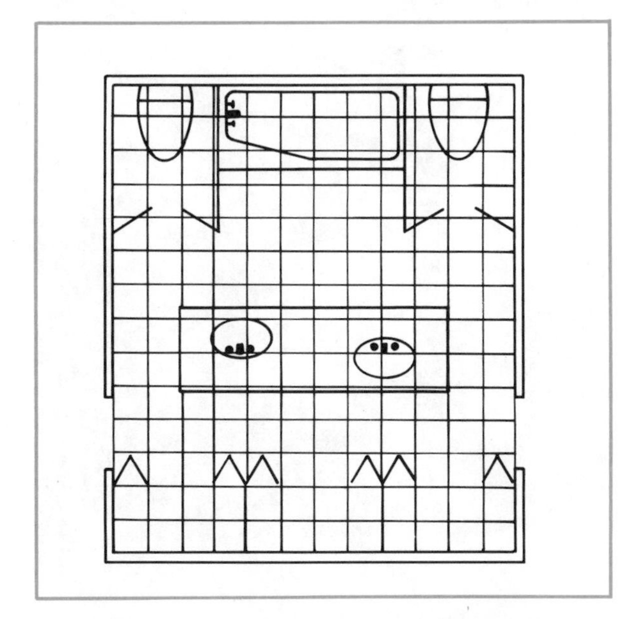

Floor Plan for Compartmented Family Bath

MODULAR BATHROOM SYSTEMS

A new idea in major remodeling is the prefabricated unit bath. The unit is inserted into the frame of the bath a section at a time. The fixtures

Courtesy of Morgan Adhesives Company

The bathroom prior to remodeling.

Courtesy of Morgan Adhesives Company

The deep grout lines were raised by scoring the old grout and then applying new grout as flush as possible with the surface of the tile.

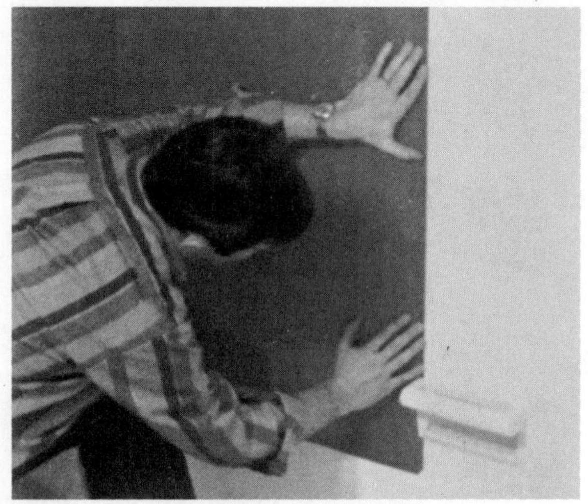

Courtesy of Morgan Adhesives Company

The red burlap wall covering is applied to the shellacked tile.

Courtesy of Morgan Adhesives Company

The white leatherette vinyl is applied to the wall.

Courtesy of Morgan Adhesives Company

Blue vinyl stripes are placed over the white leatherette.

Courtesy of Morgan Adhesives Company

A big advantage of decorating with self adhesive vinyls — no odors, solvents, or wet surfaces. The bathroom retains its functional use during the decorating process.

Courtesy of Morgan Adhesives Company

The finished project. A newly redecorated bathroom with curtains for window and shower to complete the picture.

including a lavatory, toilet, tub, shower and electrical parts are built in and ready to connect to the right systems. This type of remodeling is generally inexpensive though very modern-looking.

BATHROOM FLOOR PLANS

There are four basic floor plans to be considered in bathroom design and planning. Making the most out of available space is the most important consideration.

The One-Wall Bath is a plan suited to a room long and narrow, as narrow as 4½ feet. Here plumbing connections, drains and vents are located conveniently along one wall.

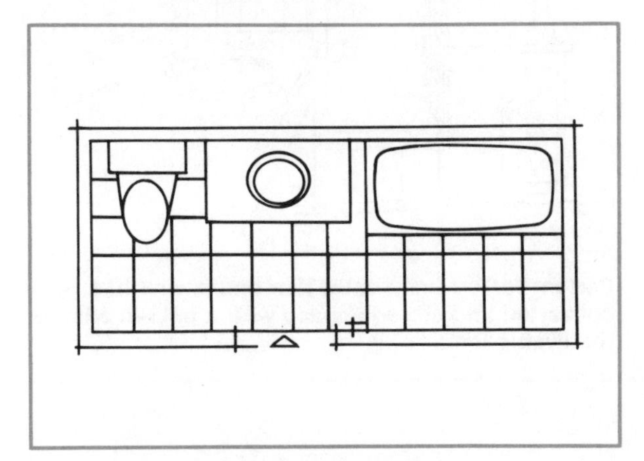

The One-Wall Bath

The L-Shaped Bathroom is the most common plan for smaller bathrooms. It provides more floor space, using one plumbing wall when the bathtub is installed on one end of the room.

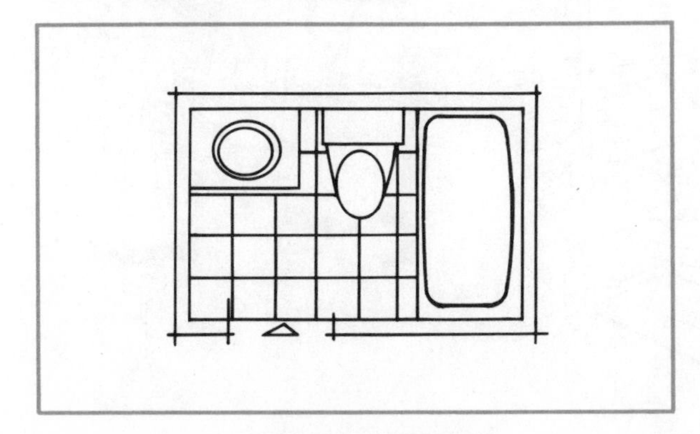

The L-Shaped Bath

The U-Shaped Bathroom most practically utilizes space in a square-shaped room. However plumbing is more complicated because it is divided and not confined to one wall.

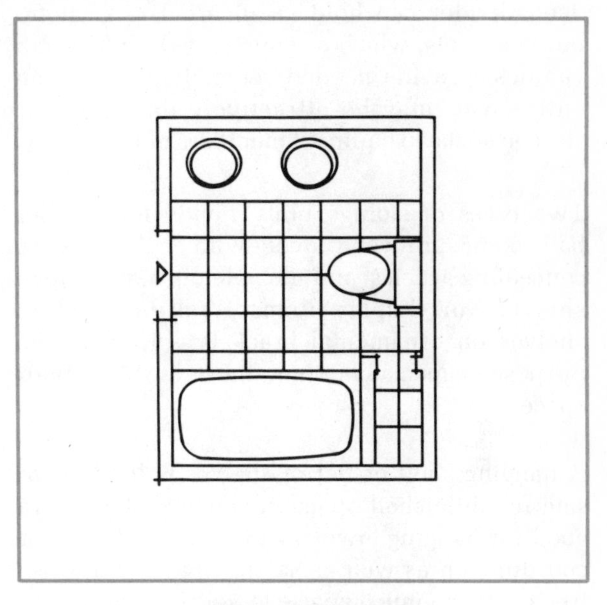

The U-Shaped Bath

The Corridor Bathroom is useful for a small bath connecting two bedrooms. This would be very suitable for a home or apartment with space for only one bath.

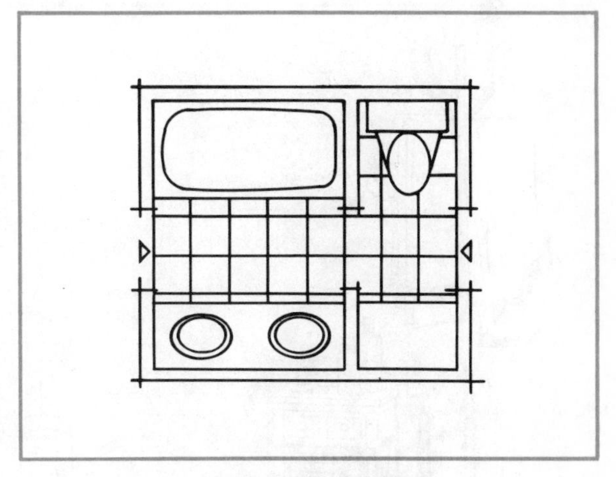

The Corridor Bath

BATHROOM STORAGE

Storage space can be found in any-sized bathroom for such articles as towels, soap, toiletries, cleaning aids and medicines.

In large bathrooms, of course, there are many choices available. Compartmenting, or using dividers in the bath, is a good idea. These dividers can even become closets. A 12-inch deep divider can hold small articles. Custom-built cabinets, which are often used underneath vanities, provide needed room. If possible, an entire wall may be attractively designed for storage space to equip all members of the family.

Two types of storage units, handy for smaller bathrooms, are wood-toned, with enclosures for concealing articles, and the pole units, with open shelves for display items. Wall-hung glass shelves on ornamental brackets will serve the purpose, especially when there is little floor space.

A hanging shelf or tier of shelves will compensate for little shelf space in cabinets. These are good for hanging towels, which can add to color coordination as well as saving space. If a towel tree takes too much space, towel rings can be attached to the wall creatively. Old-fashioned coat racks or costumers may be used for this. A couple of feet is all that is needed for a small built-in bathroom closet to house extra supplies and towels.

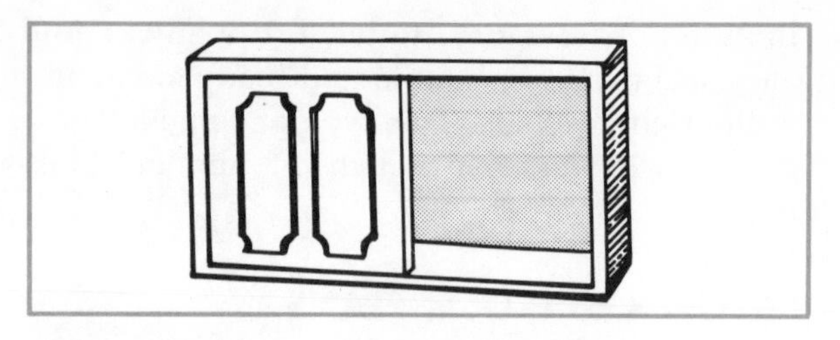

Wall cabinets with sliding doors conveniently fit into small spaces.

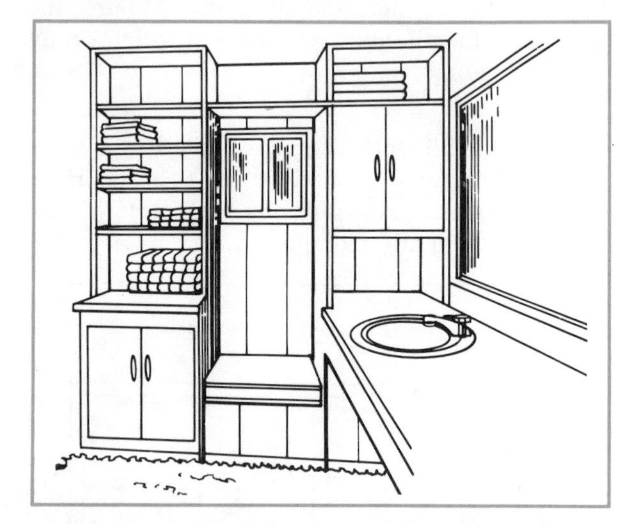

Perfect for a family bath, this entire wall has been converted into storage space with a built-in seat for the livable look.

Bathroom Fixtures

A great variety of fixtures is available for the bathroom. These fixtures can be colorfully arranged or combined to fit any size room or decorative plan, creating many style effects.

When designing a bath, choosing fixtures should be first as they are permanent furniture. Cabinets, tile or carpet, wallpaper and other decorative additions can be chosen to complement the fixtures.

Plumbing fixtures for the bath come in livable, stylish colors. Most manufacturers offer five or more different colors from which to choose. Select color combinations with care, especially in bathrooms with no windows. Fluorescent and incandescent lighting, sometimes with natural lighting combined, change the colors of fixtures.

BATHTUB

A bathtub is a fixture which is made of cast iron, formed steel or polyester (fiberglass). It ranges in length from four to six feet and in height from 12 to 16 inches. It usually has an acid-resistant porcelain enamel finish. Shapes for tubs are rectangular and square, except for soaking tubs, which are rounded. The rectangular size, or recess bath, is more useful for adults as a stretch-out tub. It is designed to be enclosed by walls on both sides and back. There are variations to the theme, however. Antique-style tubs sit upright apart from any wall attachment. There are also sunken tubs, which may be placed anywhere in the bathroom. The square-shaped receptor bath, while ideally suited for a child's bath, is also a luxury-designed shower base for adults. The soaking tub is rounded, more compact and deeper.

SHOWER

Shower units vary in size and design. The basic unit contains a shower head with fittings to control waterflow. This shower head may also be an addition to a bathtub unit or part of a one-piece bathtub-shower combination. Shower units are compacted, extended or circular. Modern features of a shower unit, especially in the new modules, include built-in contoured soap dishes, built-in seats or shelves and low or high grab bars for accident prevention. A unique idea for showers, introduced from Europe, is the telephone or personal hand shower which can be used while either standing up or sitting in the bathtub. This hand-contoured shower head may be directed at any angle and is useful for shampooing or for bathing children. The telephone shower also prevents women's hair from getting wet if placed in the unit as an extra addition to the existing head. Another newer feature, the non-scald valve is specially designed to keep the water temperature stable preventing scalding or icy waterflow. It does not allow interference from other water fixtures used simultaneously.

TOILET

A toilet, sometimes referred to as a water closet, is a bowl-shaped fixture which is designed to flush out waste. Most home toilets have a tank and bowl. When water lines leading to a fixture are too small to provide water needed quickly, a tank is necessary. The tank provides storage for an ample water supply to get proper flushing action. The tank has inner mechanisms which contribute to flushing, but the design of the bowl is also important. A toilet bowl is either round or elongated, also called extended rim.

The elongated bowl is more attractive and easier to clean because of its large interior water surface. There are four basic kinds of toilets, characterized and priced by their flushing actions.

The *washdown* type is the least expensive, noisiest and least efficient. It has a simple washing action and leaves a low water level in the bowl which makes cleaning difficult.

The *reverse trap* is the least expensive of the siphoning-action toilets. It is noisy, but efficient. This type is less likely to clog up and has more water in the bowl than the washdown.

The *siphon jet* is an improvement over the reverse-trap. It, too, has a large water surface in the bowl, but its quick siphoning action and quieter flushing make it a little more expensive.

Probably the most expensive toilet built today is the *low profile,* a one-piece, siphoning-action type. It has almost silent flushing and none of its interior surfaces are left dry.

Off-the-floor toilets make floor cleaning less difficult. These require a special *chair carrier* of metal inside the wall. Recently on the market are triangular-shaped toilets which save floor space by utilizing corners.

Newer devices for toilets include buttons instead of handles for flushing and venting devices in the flush mechanism. These vents help to keep rooms fresh. Water flowing in the flush cycle creates a partial vacuum in the bowl. The vacuum draws air and odors through holes in the flushing rim into the toilet's discharge outlet and vent pipe where they escape.

BIDET

The bidet, the most modern fixture for personal hygiene, is used for cleansing the perineal area of the body after toilet use. It is a companion of the toilet, usually located next to it in the bathroom. A bidet user sits astride the bowl facing controls which regulate water volume and temperature. Installing one does not require additional plumbing and is beneficial for all family members.

LAVATORY

The lavatory, or washbasin, makes water available in the bathroom for cleansing the hands and face. It comes in many different shapes; round, oval, rectangular or triangular. It can be fitted over or under a counter top or hung from the wall. Lavatories are made of vitreous china, cast iron, formed steel and plastic and marble. Newer features of the lavatory include shampoo fittings, lotion dispensers, swing-away spouts and spray attachments.

FAUCET

A faucet is a fitting or mechanical device which controls water entering or leaving a fixture. Lavatory faucets are of several types. The washer-type deck faucet is equipped with two handles and a valve for water flow and varies in size. Disc valve faucets are washerless and operate by one handle or knob. Faucet handles are usually made of metal or translucent material. Modern faucets may have an aerator attachment with a vacuum-like action to make an even water flow.

HOW TO CARE FOR BATHROOM FIXTURES

Bathroom fixtures require regular washing with soap and water. Harsh abrasives should not be used for cleaning as they will scratch surfaces, nor should acid or bleach-based cleansers be used because they dull the gloss. If the glossy surface of the porcelain or china is worn away it encourages staining.

Photographic developing solutions can badly stain fixtures, as well as dripping faucets which may create hard-water mineral deposits on lavatory basins. Stain-removing agents, such as mild abrasives and some milder laundry soaps mixed with warm water and a dash of kerosene, should be used for cleaning. They are not harmful to surfaces. Care should be taken to protect bathtub finishes by placing mats in the tub before use. Overloaded medicine cabinets are another threat to fixtures. Sometimes contents of these cabinets fall out and crack or stain the lavatory below. *SEE ALSO PLUMBING FIXTURES.*

Bathroom Plumbing

[SEE PLUMBING SYSTEMS.]

Bathroom Remodeling

[SEE BATHROOM DESIGN & PLANNING.]

Bathroom Sauna

[SEE SAUNA.]

Bathroom Wiring
[SEE WIRING SYSTEMS, ELECTRICAL]

Bathtub Drains
[SEE PLUMBING SYSTEMS.]

Bathtub Wall Kit Installation

Adding a look of elegance to the bathroom, while providing practical and durable wall and counter surfaces, can be accomplished by either the handy amateur or professional by using Du Pont's *Corian* bathtub wall kit.

The basic parts of the kit are four panels of Du Pont's marble-like *Corian* sheet, each a quarter-inch thick and 57 inches high. There are two end panels and two back corner panels, plus a center wall strip which overlaps the two back panels for a handsome sculptured effect. The panels may be installed in new construction or over existing tile walls.

To complete the bathroom, a matching *Corian* vanity top and bowl are also available. These modern products combine the look of elegance with no-nonsense, easy-care features. Hard and non-porous, *Corian* resists scratches, mars and stains, and normally wipes clean with a damp cloth or sponge. Even tough stains, including that of the forgotten cigarette, are easily removed with an abrasive household cleanser.

Both the bathtub wall kit and the one-piece vanity top and bowl are available in three colors: Dawn Beige and Olive Mist, each having delicate veins of color running throughout, and Cameo White, a solid color. They may be obtained from a building and plumbing supply dealer and from kitchen and bath installer-fabricators.

Here are the step-by-step instructions:

1. Read the instructions through. Be sure you understand every step.

Courtesy of Du Pont

2. Open your *Corian* Bathtub Wall Kit and trial fit the panels around the tub enclosure. This will show whether end panels should butt against wall or against back wall corner panels. Options give you a leeway or 1/4 inch in positioning the end panels for perfect fit across the end of the tub.

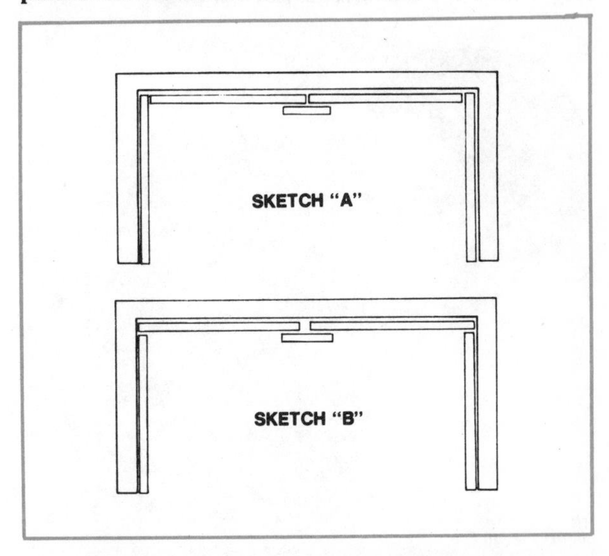

In sketch A, the end panels are installed first — snug to the back wall. The back wall panels are then butted to the end panels. This procedure is described in these instructions. In alternate sketch B, the back wall panels are installed first snug to the end walls. The end panels are then butted to the back wall panels.

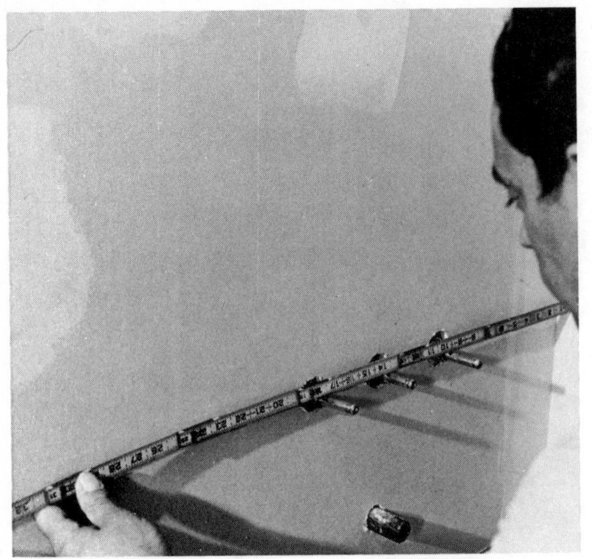

Courtesy of Du Pont

3. With the wall ready for installation, measure the position on the wall of all projecting fixtures. Chart the location of all holes that must be made in the end sheet.

4. Mark the openings required with a pencil.

5. Drill small holes in each opening to be cut out.

6. With sabre saw, cut a hole approximately 1/2" larger than the diameter of each fitting.

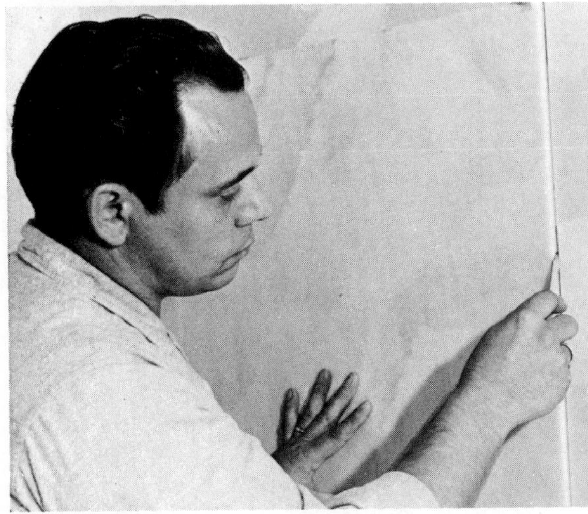

Courtesy of Du Pont

7-8. Determine the location of the soap dish, if planned. (Note: soap dish must be located in one of the back wall corner panels and not interfere with the back wall center strip.) Mark location and shape on sheet. Drill hole and cut required opening with sabre saw. Measure and outline with pencil area to be covered as a guide for applying adhesive.

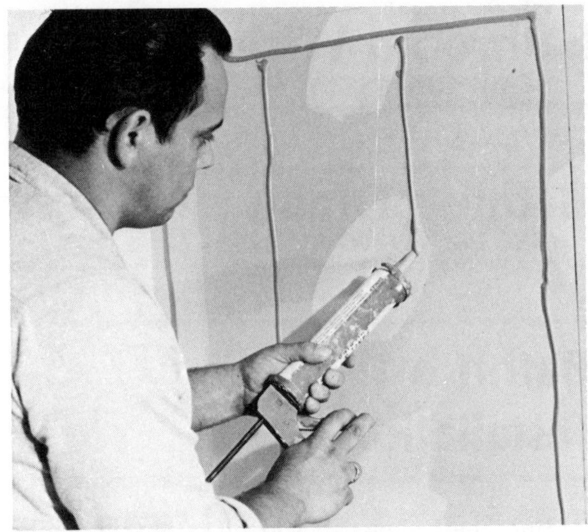

Courtesy of Du Pont

9. Apply adhesive to end wall, running beads across top and bottom, four beads from top to bottom, 6 inches to 8 inches apart. Also run a bead around each plumbing opening.

10. Install the sheet within 5-7 minutes after applying adhesives, pressing it firmly against the adhesive and making sure that good overall contact is obtained with the adhesive beads.

11. After positioning, pull the panel away from the wall for two minutes to allow the adhesive solvent to vent. Note that the adhesive has spread and will grip wide areas of both *Corian* and wall.

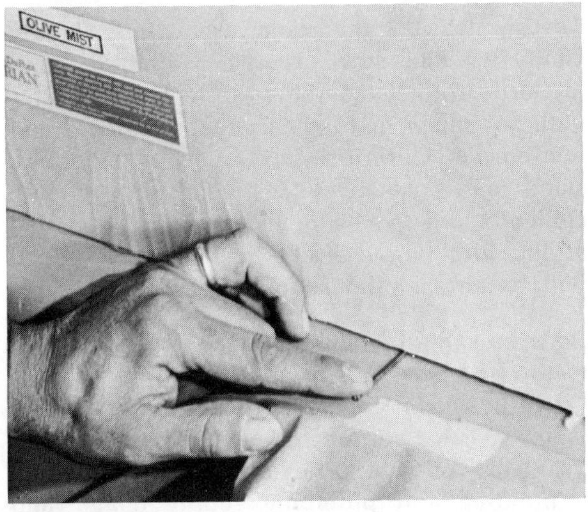

Courtesy of Du Pont

12. After positioning the sheet, place finishing nails (about 6-penny size) at either end of the tub where the sheet has been installed so that space will be available for caulking. In the same manner, install the other end wall panel.

13. Apply adhesive to area to be covered by back wall corner panel, running beads across the top and bottom, and four beads from top to bottom, the same as for the end panels. Run a bead around soap dish opening, if needed. Install back wall corner panel, using nail shims. Install the second back wall corner panel in the same manner.

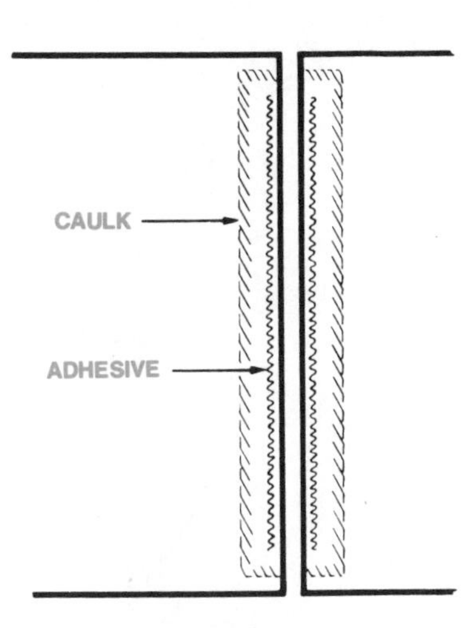

14-15. Round off the exposed edges of the back wall center strip with fine sandpaper as desired. Mark position of the back wall center strip on the two back wall panels with a pencil. Apply both adhesive and caulk as shown in the sketch.

16. Install the *Corian* back wall center strip and press into adhesive and caulk. Install soap dish, if planned, using adhesive or other fastening recommended by the manufacturer.

17. Remove shim nails under panels.

Courtesy of Du Pont

18. Caulk the opening between panels and top of tub.

19. Caulk corners where panels meet, also run a bead of caulk along top of panels, along side of edges of back wall center strip and outside edges of end panels.

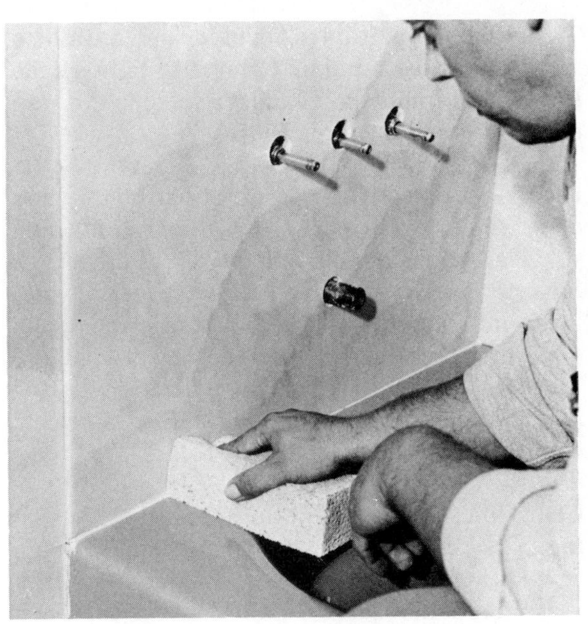

Courtesy of Du Pont

20. Smooth all caulk seams with damp sponge for a neat, finished appearance.

Batten

Often called cleats or bats, battens are narrow strips of wood or metal placed across joints to prevent warping, to strengthen or to hold the boards together. *SEE ALSO MOLDING & TRIM.*

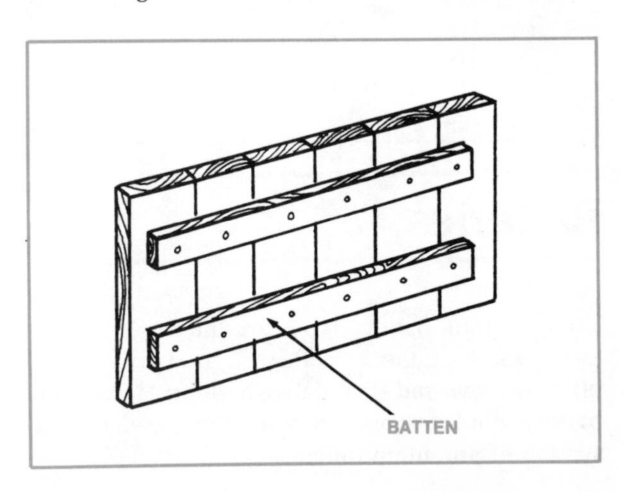

Batter Boards

The temporary frames leveled and nailed to stakes at the corner of an excavation to mark the lines of the foundation and to help keep the wall plumb are called *batter boards*.

Locate the exact corners of the structure and drive small layout stakes into the ground; then set small nails or tacks into the top of the stakes for exact measurements. At least 4 feet beyond the foundation lines, drive 2 x 4 stakes and attach 1 x 6 or wider batter boards in a level position. They should be attached at a convenient working height. Braces should be used if the soil is loose, or if they are higher than 3 feet.

Using lines and a plumb bob, pull the lines so they pass directly over the layout stakes. Use a saw kerf to mark the exact spot where the lines cross the batter boards. Pull the lines taut, run them around the board and through the saw kerf several times; then fasten with nails. *SEE ALSO FOOTINGS & FOUNDATIONS.*

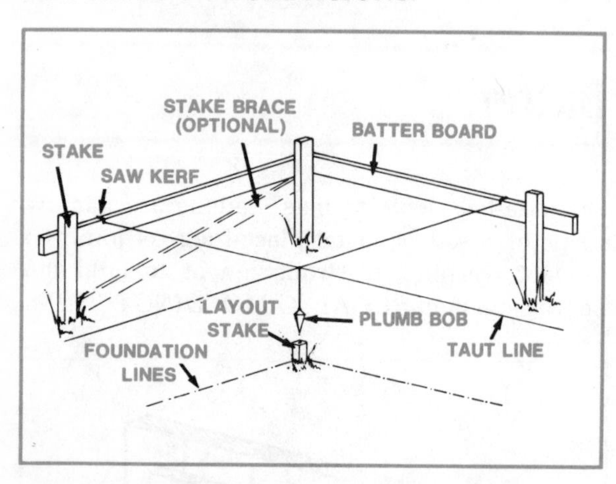

Batteries

Two common battery types are the dry cell battery, which is the D cell used in various appliances, toys and flashlights, and the 12-volt car battery, the foremost component in the electrical system of an automobile.

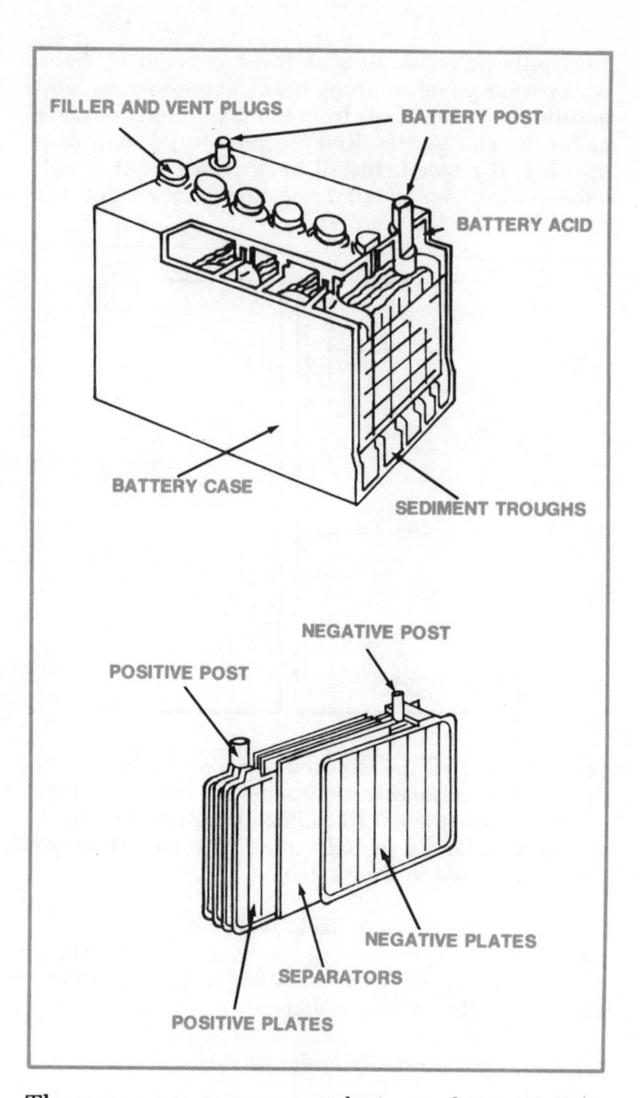

There are many types and sizes of D cell batteries available. The four main classifications are the zinc-carbon cells, available in leakproof and not-leakproof types, alkaline cells, mercury cells, and rechargeable nickel-cadmium batteries. Different types of batteries are used according to the amount of power required, the length of time this power is needed, and the length of time the battery can be stored without losing power. For example, mercury batteries are most efficient for use in hearing aids, electric watches and transistor radios, where low power is needed for long periods of time. Alkaline cells are most useful when high power is needed for short, intermittent time periods, such as in flashbulbs or strobelights. Zinc-carbon cells have a moderately short life, and are manufactured in three basic categories — photoflash, transistor applications, and general purpose, each used for the purpose specified. The nickel-cadmium cells have an indefinite life period if recharged through an AC outlet after every use. Alkaline, zinc-carbon, and mercury cells are also rechargeable. Several rechargers for these cells are manufactured.

The 12-volt auto battery is composed of six compartments, or cells. Each cell contains seven to fifteen plates, which are filled with a specially formulated lead. The plates are submerged in electrolyte, a mixture of sulphuric acid and water. The flow of electric current is caused by the reaction of the electrolyte on the plates. The battery supplies this current as it is needed by the car.

Water must be added periodically to maintain the electrolyte at the proper level. An underfilled battery causes the exposed plate parts to harden and become chemically inactive. An overfilled battery results in corrosion of the battery support mechanism by spilled electrolyte. *SEE ALSO SYSTEMS, AUTOMOTIVE*

Battery Chargers

Battery chargers are an inexpensive way to postpone the need for a new battery, whether in your car, flashlight or transistor radio. The two major types of chargers are those intended for automobile batteries and those used for batteries which go in flashlights, toys and small appliances.

Automobile battery chargers are of two types, each with its own specific purpose. The quicker battery charger is commonly a temporary measure which it used to get a run-down battery recharged enough to start the engine. This involves a quick surge of electricity, and while this method may be necessary in certain emergencies, it should be avoided if possible. If it is necessary to use a fast charge, the automobile owner should know that the spurt of electricity may ruin an old battery that might have been revitalized by a slow or "trickle" charger. He should also be sure that all electrical accessories such as the radio are turned off, as the surge of electricity may burn them out. Better still, protect the accessories by disconnecting the battery cables before hooking up the charger and keep them disconnected until the charger is removed.

A much preferred method of charging an automobile battery is the "trickle" charge. This charger takes about 12 to 16 hours to completely charge a battery, depending on how run-down the battery is. If the charger is not equipped with an automatic shut-off, a specific gravity reading should be taken every two hours until the specific gravity no longer increases. A "trickle" charger helps to prevent the battery plates from being coated with lead sulfate which can lead to an internal short circuit. The frustration of a car that won't start on a cold winter morning will not be a problem of the car owner who remembers to hook up his car to a slow "trickle" charger the night before.

Toys and flashlights can expect a much longer life with the use of a smaller battery charger. It is best to use rechargeable nickel-cadmium batteries as they hold a charge longer and can be recharged many more times than a regular flashlight cell. However, rather than waste the batteries which you are presently using, recharge them until they will no longer hold a charge, and then replace them with the longer lived nickel-cadmium variety. It is best to recharge a battery before its charge has been totally exhausted. It is most important to follow the manufacturer's directions as to the placement of batteries in the charger.

In addition to the better-known types of battery chargers, there are also the direct-supply power chargers which are plugged directly into toys and small appliances. There is also available from electronic stores and mail-order supply houses an adapter for transistor radios which involves some simple rewiring of the earphone jack to allow direct recharging of 9-volt transistor batteries.

Finally, owners of hearing aids can fashion a home-made type of charger to give their mercury batteries a boost from a regular flashlight cell.

This is accomplished by the use of a bronze or copper wire which is bent in an oblong 0-shape with the ends of the wire touching the bottom. It should be snug enough to hold a mercury hearing aid cell tightly to the center post. The cell will take a charge on only one side, so the owner will have to experiment to see which side this is. Many times the rechargeable side is marked with an X. It is also advisable to start with a new battery and new mercury cells and recharge them alternately each day. A slight hum indicates the cell needs a few hours rest before reuse.

Bay

As the term applies to the handyman, a bay is one of the spaces or intervals into which a building plan is divided by piers, columns or division walls.

Bay Window

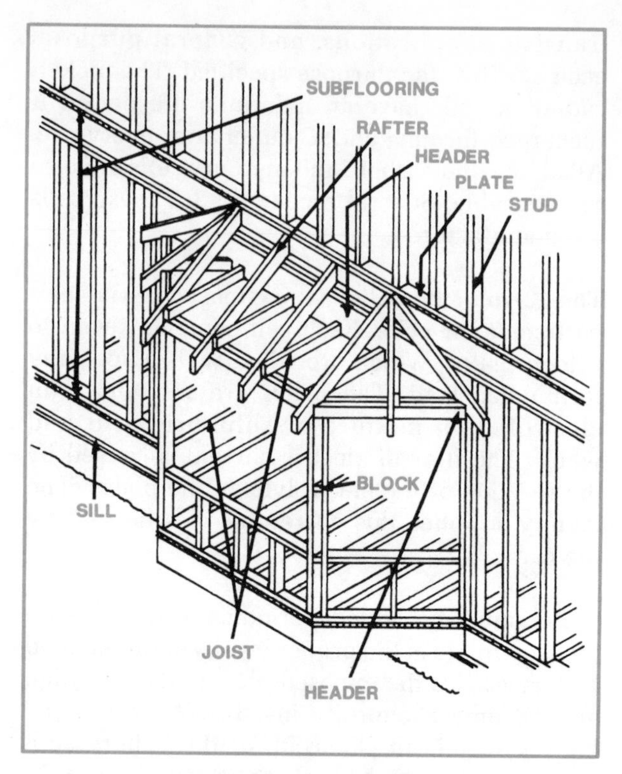

Bay Window Framing

The bay window, a rectangular, curved or polygonal window or series of windows, projects outward from the wall of a building. Usually supported on a foundation extending beyond the main framing, it forms a bay or recess in the room.

Living room and dining room areas are normally where bay windows are desired. Although there is a very wide variation in taste and architectural expression, the space required for a bay window should be only a certain portion of the entire floor space. Through the use of good design, a bay window can add both charm and decorative value to your home.

Quite suitable for a houseplant collection display, it can also serve as an attractive seating area and storage cabinet. A plain wooden bench running the length of the bay window can be made to fit its contour. Pad the seat with a piece of foam rubber or old bed comforter. Then cover it with a fabric that will blend with the decor of your room. A roomy storage compartment can be made from the empty space between the seat and the floor. By building-in a wood wall with hinged or sliding doors underneath the seat, this space can be transformed into useful cabinet space. *SEE ALSO PORCH & BAY FRAMING.*

Beach House

[SEE HOUSE DESIGNS.]

Bead, Beading

Beading is a type of decorative molding which is rounded and contains a small groove. Beading is used to cover joints both in house construction and in furniture making. Wall joints employ beading to cover and reinforce paneling and wall board at corners and at joint breaks. A beaded

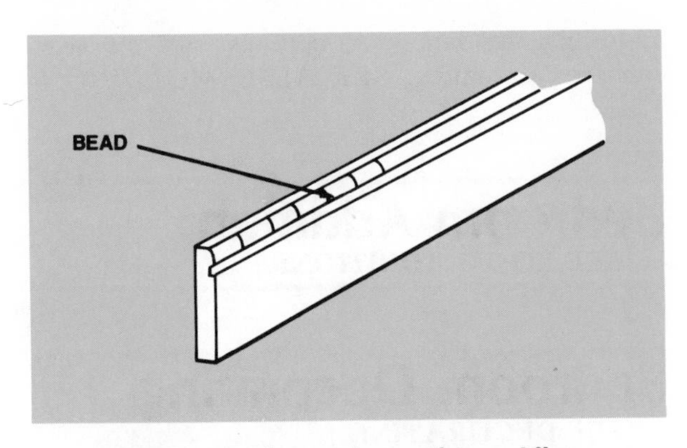

Beading used as a decorative molding.

ceiling conceals the joint between the wall and ceiling. Table tops sometimes contain a beaded edge for decorative effect. *SEE ALSO MOLDING & TRIM.*

Beading Bit

A beading bit is used in conjunction with a router to form a decorative edge in making furniture of various periods.

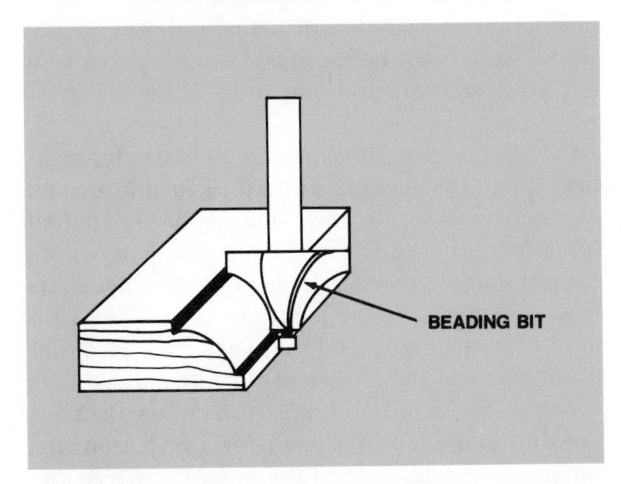

A beading bit makes a decorative edge on furniture.

Beams

Beams, an inclusive term for joists, girders, rafters and purlins, are structural members used between posts, columns or walls. Sizes are based on the space between supports, deflection permitted and the load the beams must carry. Solid timbers are recommended when beam sizes are small or when a rustic appearance is desired. Available in a wide range of sizes and finishes, laminated beams are usually more economical to use where high stress factors demand large sizes.

Beams for floor structures may be solid, box, glue-laminated or built-up of several pieces of timber nailed together. Occasionally, the built-up beams are formed with spacer blocks between the main members.

The two basic types of beams used in beam-supported roof systems are transverse beams that are much like exposed rafters on wide spacings, and longitudinal beams (also called purlins) that run parallel to the supporting side walls and ridge beam. Because of the heavy loads they must carry and the greater distances they must span, longitudinal beams are usually larger in cross section than transverse beams. Either type of beam must be sufficiently supported by posts or stud walls that incorporate a heavy top plate. When supported on posts, the connection can be reinforced with a wide panel frame that extends to the top of the beam. Transverse beams can be jointed to the sides of the ridge beam and supported on top. Metal tie plates, hangers and straps are needed to absorb the horizontal thrust.

There are many types of imitation wood beams on the market today for both interior and exterior use that are economical and are specifically designed for installation by the homeowner. *SEE ALSO FLOOR CONSTRUCTION.*

Bearing Partition

A bearing partition or bearing wall supports the weight of upper structure framing members, as well as its own weight. All outside walls are bearing partitions. The studs of a bearing partition have double plates directly over them which

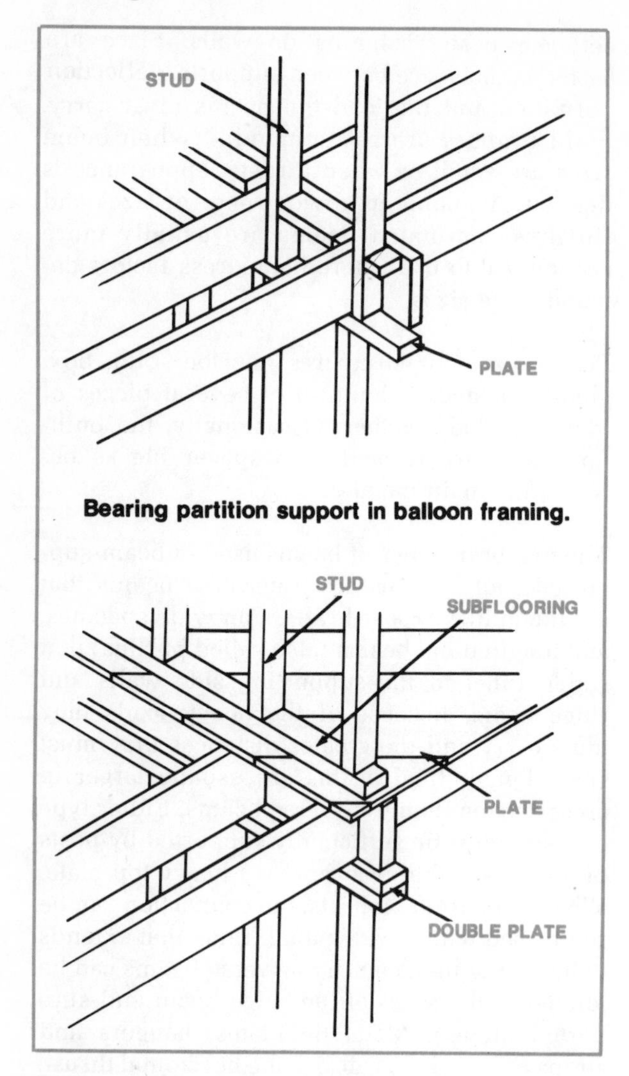

Bearing partition support in balloon framing.

Bearing partition support in platform frame construction.

bear the ceiling joists. In platform frame construction, the framing members of the second floor rest on subflooring above the bearing partition of the first floor. In balloon frame construction the second floor framing members are placed directly on the first floor bearing partition top plate. *SEE ALSO WALL & CEILING CONSTRUCTION.*

Bed Molding

Bed molding is used where two surfaces come together at an angle. A corner molding, bed molding gives beauty to ceilings, as well as to cornices or eaves. *SEE ALSO MOLDING & TRIM.*

Bedroom Addition

[SEE ROOM ADDITIONS.]

Bedroom Decorating

[SEE DECORATING.]

Beech Wood

Beech wood, a fine-textured hardwood, is hard, strong and heavy, weighing about 3.8 pounds per board foot. It can have reddish, golden brown or white heartwood. The sapwood is white. As an all-purpose, cheaper wood, beech can be worked in any direction to the grain and it has a smooth, even surface that resists wear. For these reasons, beech is used for mass-produced goods made by machine, such as chairs and exterior parts of furniture that are painted or stained obscuring the wood. Unpainted beech must be stained to give it any character, since it has an indistinct grain.

After steam treatment beech bends easily, making it ideal for the curved parts of furniture such as chair backs, armrests and legs. It is well suited for laminating and is widely used in plywood. Beech requires care in drying but once dried, its hardness makes it appropriate for rocker runners, drawer sides and runways and other interior parts of cabinets and furniture as well as for short tool handles, boxes and crates. Beech is durable enough to be used for finish flooring, but it is not suitable for outdoor use. *SEE ALSO WOOD IDENTIFICATION.*

Bell-Faced Hammer

Experienced craftsmen prefer a bell-faced hammer to one with a plain, flat face because the slightly convex striking surface minimizes marring when the nails are driven flush. Although a plain-faced hammer is easier to use, it hits the nail at an angle and bends it. With the bell-faced hammer, nail deflections are reduced because the rounded face matches the arc of the swing and provides a square, true blow. *SEE ALSO HAND TOOLS.*

Belt & Disc Sander

[SEE PORTABLE POWER TOOLS; STATIONARY BELT & DISC SANDER.]

Belt & Pad Sander

[SEE PORTABLE POWER TOOLS.]

Bench Grinder

While the bench grinder can be a very versatile tool, its main function in a woodworking shop is to renew the worn edges and maintain the sharp edges of cutting tools. These cutting tools may be hand tools such as butt wood chisels or power-driven cutters such as jointer knives and twist drills.

A parting tool is easy to do by just renewing the "V" on the side of the wheel. Keep the tool level and be sure to grind an equal amount on both edges. Hone after grinding.

The function of the grinder as a safety tool is often overlooked. With a grinder, you are more likely to keep tools sharp, and sharp tools mean better and safer work. In addition, you are more likely to remove burrs from the head of a cold chisel or even a nail hammer before they can become dangerous projectiles.

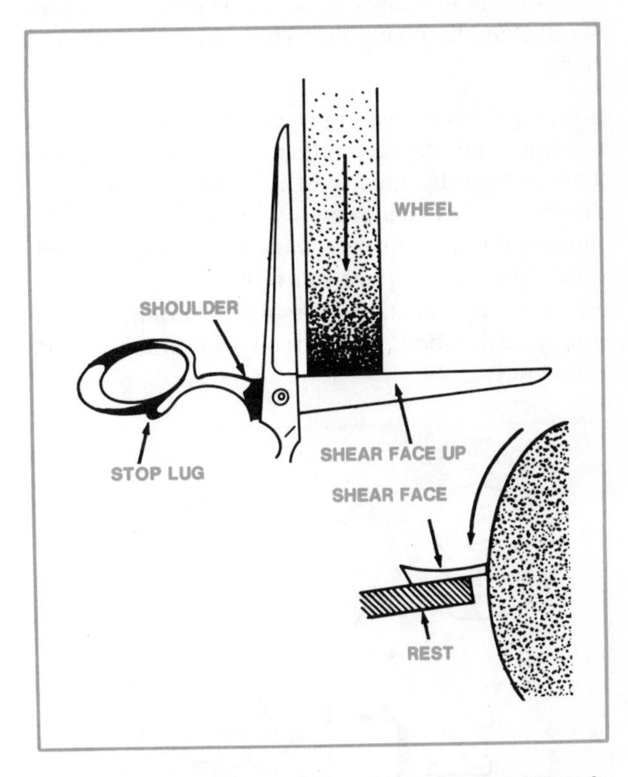

Do scissors and shears on a fine grit wheel that is square across the face. Make very light passes and keep the motion uniform to guarantee a straight cutting edge. Such tools should be honed after grinding.

It's true that you can drive grinding wheels on other tools such as the drill press, the radial arm saw, the lathe, or even the table saw. With proper precautions these temporary setups can be used efficiently. But a good grinder is the one tool that is specifically designed for the job, and for optimum results there really is no substitute.

General Characteristics

The most popular grinder is a self-contained unit that resembles a double-shaft motor. However, it is so encased with covers, guards and shields that the only areas exposed are those parts of the grinding wheels that you need to see in order to work.

The bench grinder is a plug-in-and-use unit that you bolt down to an existing bench or mount on a special bench that you make or buy as an accessory. The word "pedestal" in the name of the tool merely indicates a particular design of floor stand (usually heavy-duty) on which the grinder rests.

Some grinders are belt driven. A pulley is mounted on the shaft that drives the wheels. This pulley, by means of a V-belt, connects to another pulley that is on a separate motor shaft. Such units are cheaper than the self-contained ones, but they require more mounting room. In addition, by the time you add a motor, extra pulley and V-belt, you're really not much ahead financially.

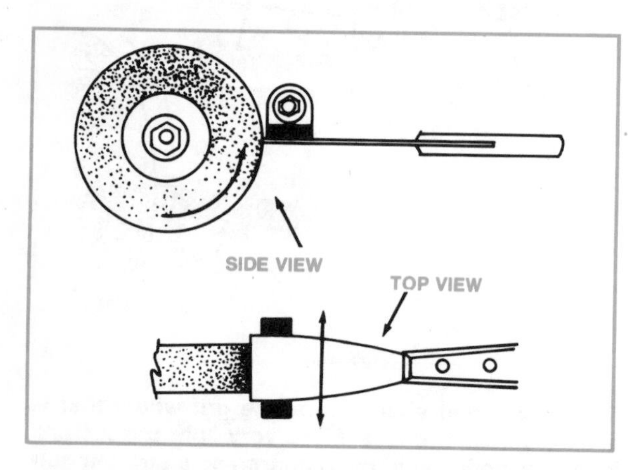

All you want to do with a putty knife is square off the edge — then remove burrs and smooth the end by working on an oilstone. Thin materials like this overheat easily, so use a delicate touch.

A grinder is often thought of in relation to its polishing head. This polishing head unit does have a horizontal shaft and you can mount grinding wheels on it, but it does not approach being a safe grinder. Many manufacturers will tell you specifically that the polishing head they show in a catalog is not for grinding.

The size of the grinder is listed in terms of wheel diameter. For example, if it's called a 7″ grinder, you know it is designed to turn 7″ grinding wheels. Home shop sizes run from 5″ to 7″ with motor horsepower ranging from 1/4 to 1/2. When

This jointer-knife jig spans across both wheels so both or either of the grits can be used. The bevel on the guide must be shaped to provide the correct angle on the knife. Check this with a protractor.

you get into 8″ wheels and motor horsepower 3/4″ or more, you are entering the heavy-duty area where the tool is designed for continuous production work in places such as machine shops and garages.

Regardless of the size of the tool, it should be equipped with strong wheel covers, eye shields (preferably adjustable) and adjustable tool rests. If it has a water tray and a flexible gooseneck lamp, so much the better. Such extras as spark arresters, exhaust outlets and adjustable spark deflectors are good to have and will be found on the higher priced units.

Five-inch bench grinder drives two vitrified aluminum oxide grinding wheels at about 3,400 rpm. Main purpose of the grinder in the home woodworking shop is to keep tools sharp, but it can also be used to drive wire brushes and buffing wheels.

When you situate any grinder, be sure to bolt it solidly to a good, strong support. The less vibration you have the easier it will be to do work well.

Wheels

A grinding wheel is made of abrasive grains that are bonded together by means of a special material. Each of the grains is a cutting tool that becomes dull as it does its job and finally tears loose so another sharp grain can take over. The makeup of any wheel involves five factors: the abrasive, the grain, the grade, the structure, and the bond.

The abrasive is the material that does the cutting. Most of the wheels supplied with home-type grinders are of aluminum oxide. This is good for grinding all materials that have a high tensile strength such as high speed steel and carbon steels. Silicon carbide is good for working on low tensile strength materials like brass, bronze, gray iron, aluminum, and copper.

The grain has to do with abrasive grit size, and there are as many categories here as you will find in common sandpaper. "Coarse" grits will run from No. 12 to No. 24. "Medium" grits will run from No. 30 to No. 60. "Fine" grits will run from No. 70 to No. 120. Even finer grits in the "very fine" and "flour size" categories can run from No. 150 to No. 600.

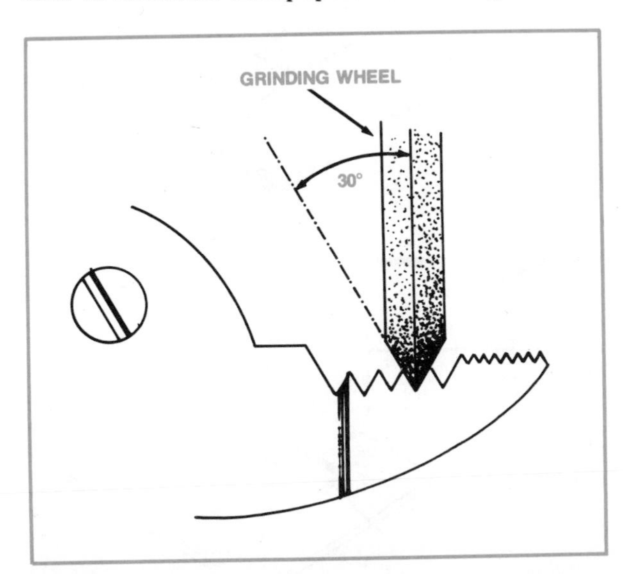

Grinding wheels may be shaped, or purchased preshaped to do special jobs. This one renews the serrations in pliers' jaw. More common wheels are square- or round-edged. Cup wheels are good for sharpening tools like gouges and roundnose lathe chisels.

Wheels supplied as standard equipment with the grinder you buy usually fall into the general medium category, even when they are listed as coarse. The coarse (sometimes called out as a "medium coarse") will be about a No. 36, and the medium (sometimes called out as a "medium fine") will be about a No. 60. These grit sizes in aluminum oxide are very good for all-purpose wood-shop work.

The grade of a wheel has to do with the bond, which can run from very soft to very hard. Hard wheels hold abrasives together even under extreme pressure while soft wheels permit them to loosen easily. In general, hard wheels are used for grinding soft materials while the soft wheels are used on hard materials. Between the two extremes, a medium-hard grade, is best for average work.

In essence, structure refers to the spacing of the grains throughout the wheel. Hard, brittle materials are handled best on wheels with abrasive grains that are closely spaced. Wheels with widely spaced grains do better with soft materials that tend to clog the abrasive.

The bond refers to the material that is used to hold the abrasive grains together. For our purposes, we are concerned with a vitrified bond which consists of special clays and other ceramic materials. The bond material and the abrasive grains are fused at high temperatures to form a glasslike mass. The result is a high-strength, porous wheel with a cool cutting action. The vitrified bond is excellent for general-purpose grinding.

Safety and Care of Wheels

Never run a grinding wheel faster than the speed that is listed on the flange. Excessive speed will generate destructive heat and will also subject the wheel to centrifugal force that it may not be able to withstand. Both conditions can result in wheel breakage.

Test a wheel for cracks before you mount it. Do a visual check for chipped edges and cracks that you can see, then mount the wheel on a rod that you pass through the arbor hole and tap the wheel gently on the side with a piece of wood. The wheel will ring clear if it is in good condition. A dull thud may indicate the presence of a crack that can't be seen by eye. If it happens, don't take any chances; discard the wheel.

Good grinding wheels have metal bushings and are fit tightly on the spindle. However, they must not be so tight that you have to hammer them on or so loose that they will not run true. Washers made of blotting paper should be placed on each side between the wheel and the flanges. Be sure the diameter of the paper washers is not less than the diameter of the flanges. The purpose of the paper washers is to equalize the pressure on the sides of the wheel.

Tighten lock nuts only as tight as they have to be to secure the wheel. Excessive pressure can cause the wheel to break. After the wheel is mounted and all guards replaced, let the wheel run idle for a minute or so as you stand to one side.

Always adjust the tool rests so they are within 1/8" of the wheel. This will reduce the possibility of getting the work wedged between the rest and the wheel. Whenever possible, work on the face of the wheel. Working on the side of the wheel is necessary for many jobs but inspect frequently to be sure you do not reduce wheel thickness to the point where further use becomes hazardous.

Wear safety goggles or a good face mask on all grinding operations even if the job is simple such as touching up a screwdriver tip. Metal grinding creates sparks so keep the area around the grinder clean. Let the wheel come up to full speed before you apply the work.

To Dress a Wheel

"Dressing" a wheel can be done to renew sharpness or to true up the face of the wheel. The most common type of dresser is a mechanical one with star wheels that revolve as the tool is pressed against the wheel. To use it, set the tool rest so the gap between it and the face of the grinding wheel is just enough so the heel of the dresser can brace against the forward edge of the tool rest. Tilt the handle of the dresser up at a slight angle but do not make contact with the grinding wheel until after you have turned on the motor. Press the dresser easily against the turning wheel until you get a bite; then move slowly from side to side across the wheel. A small bite and many passes is better than a big bite and one pass.

It takes a little experience to do this job. Work cautiously, hold the dresser with force on the tool rest, do not use excessive pressure against the grinding wheel, and you'll soon master the technique.

Job Possibilities

If you have to remove metal from metal, the job can probably be done on the grinder as long as it's feasible to apply the work to the tool. Welded joints can be smoothed; round or square bar

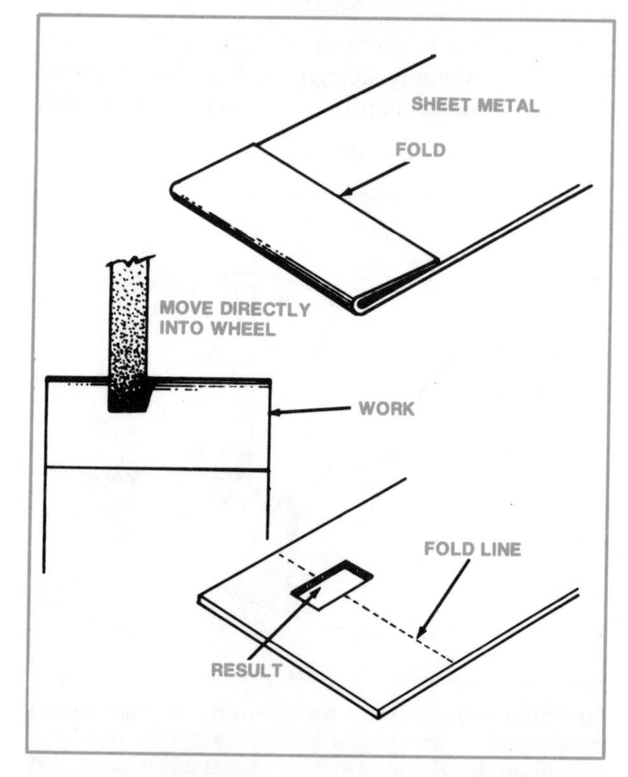

The technique to use to create a square hole in sheet metal. Don't make the fold too sharp or the sheet metal may crack when it is unfolded after grinding.

stock can be scored on an edge of the wheel as a preliminary step to hack-sawing or cutting with a chisel. Burrs that form on the hammer end of cold chisels can be ground away. You can even do such jobs as forming a square opening in metal tubing simply by moving the tube directly into the face of the wheel. A similar job can be done on sheet metals if you fold the metal. Then, with the fold line forward, move the work straight into the wheel. When you unfold the metal, you have a square opening. Of course the thickness of the wheel dictates the minimum cut. You can do wider cuts by making more than one pass, but you can't make narrower ones.

When you must point or bevel or just chamfer an end on bar stock, do it this way if the work-size permits. Both the drill and the wheel are turning.

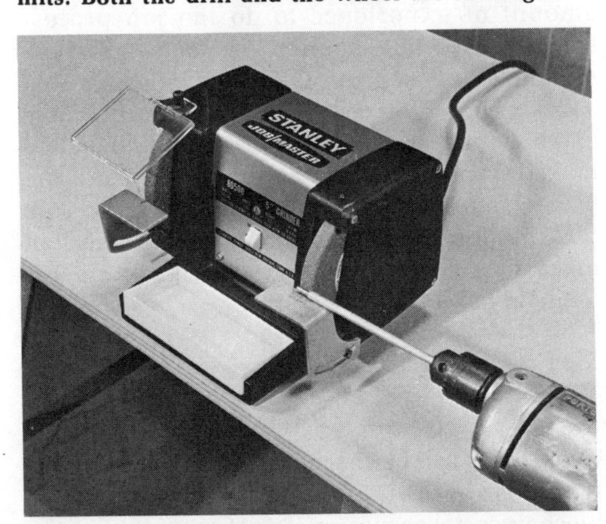

The same technique can be used to reduce diameter. Keep pressure very light. Be sure to provide for minimum clearance between tool rest and face of the wheel.

Working with a portable drill facilitates pointing rods and even reducing end diameters. Chuck the rod in the drill and let it spin as you apply it to the turning wheel. It isn't necessary to apply a lot of pressure, but it is a good idea to avoid using just one spot on the wheel. Working in this manner will usually produce more accurate results than if you tried to do it freehand.

Hollow-Ground Edges

Creating a hollow-ground edge is easy to do on the face of the wheel simply because the wheel shape produces the hollow-ground form automatically. The tool must be held at an angle with the work edge against the upper part of the

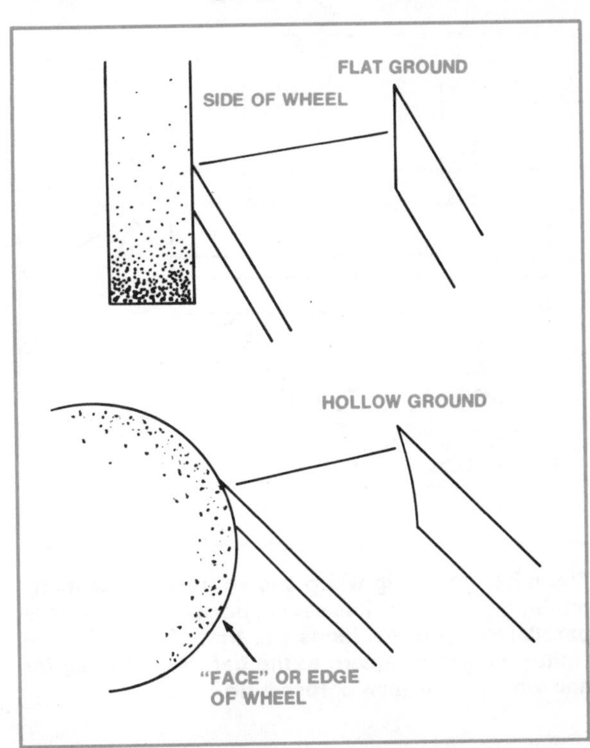

Hollow-grinding is done on the face of the wheel — flat-grinding on the side. In each case, the more acute the angle between tool and wheel, the longer the bevel will be. See text for cautions about wheel-side use.

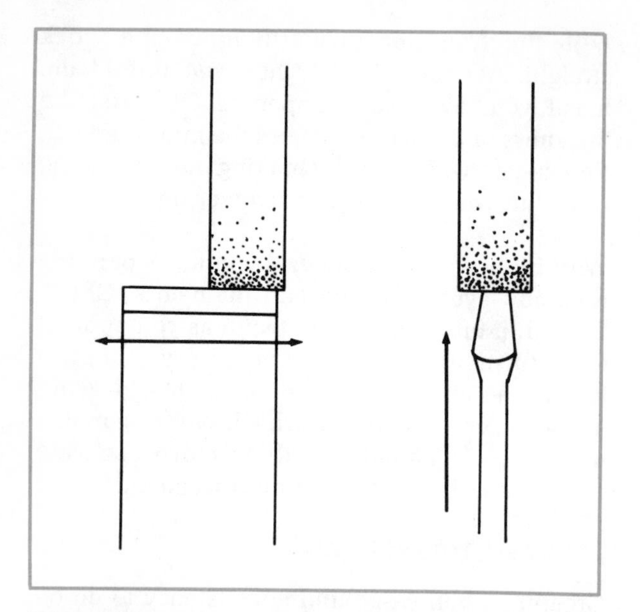

To square an edge, move the blade parallel to the face of the wheel. When the edge is narrow, such as the tip of a screwdriver, it can be moved directly forward into the wheel. Remove the least amount that will do the job.

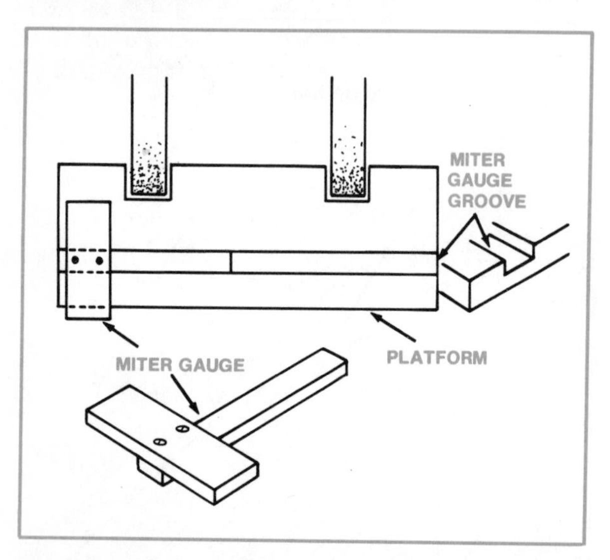

The miter gauge jig will prove very useful for many grinding jobs. When it is set up, be sure the groove is parallel to the wheel faces and that the head of the "miter gauge" is square to the bar. Make the jig for one wheel or to span across both.

wheel. The more acute the angle, the longer the cutting edge will be. Many times, it's possible to rest the blade of whatever you are sharpening against the rear edge of the tool rest and to use this contact as a pivot to bring the cutting edge of the tool forward. Take light touches until the grinding is complete.

Flat bevels are best done on the side of the wheel. In all cases, keep the metal cool. Have water on hand so you can quench the item frequently. Allowing the metal to get too hot can destroy the temper of the tool.

Working Across the Wheel Face

To renew a straight edge, work on the face of the wheel. If the work is wider than the wheel thickness, then you must pass laterally while keeping the work edge parallel to the face of the wheel. If the work edge is narrow, you can move the work directly forward.

To do this kind of work with more accuracy than you might be able to achieve freehand, make the miter-gauge jig shown in the accompanying sketch. This jig is no more than a platform with a groove cut to receive the bar of a right-angle guide. You can make it for one wheel or long enough to span across both tool rests. Attach it with clamps or drill a few holes through the tool rests so you can secure this jig and others like it with wood screws driven up through the bottom.

Using jigs with the grinder is very important. Anything that can be sharpened can be sharpened freehand, but it takes a considerable amount of experience to do the job professionally. Creating holders for tools will help eliminate human error. Quite a few jigs are sold as accessories for the grinder. Some are simple and hold only a few tools; some are complex and make it possible to hold objects that range from plane blades to scissors. Special ones are sold for sharpening twist drills. Anytime you can make a job easier or better by buying or making a jig, do so.

Tips on Sharpening

Twist Drills

Twist drills can be sharpened freehand, but it's a tricky job that even some experienced mechanics never master. To get some idea of the proper technique, choose a new, 1/2" twist drill and go through the following procedure with the grinding wheel still.

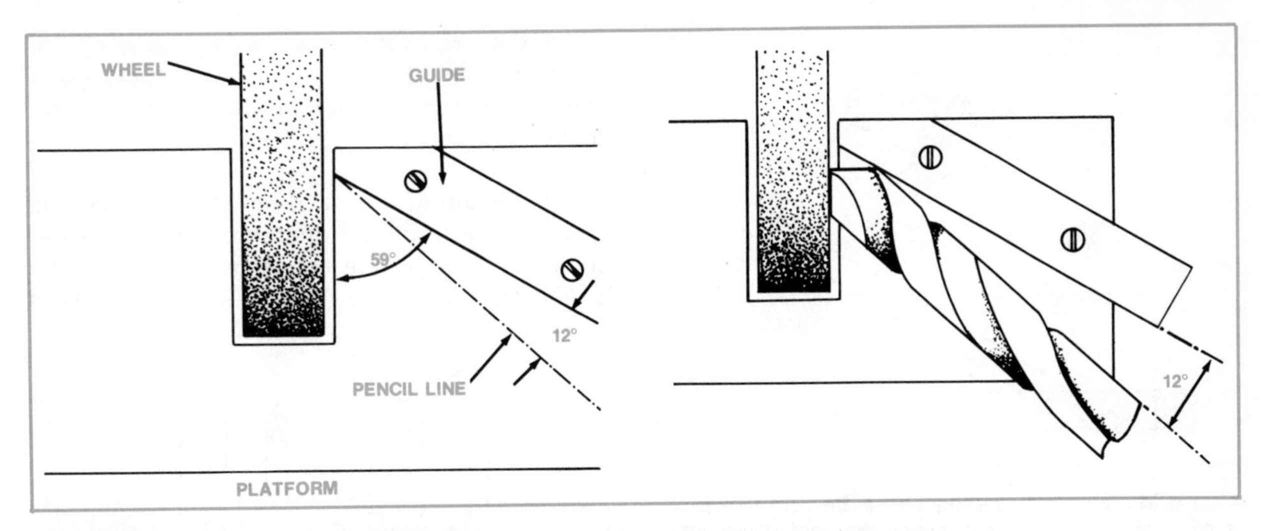

This simple jig (left) will provide a lot of help when sharpening twist drills. To use it, position the drill (right) and make a small clockwise turn as the drill is moved away from the guide block and bring it parallel to the pencil mark. Try this with a new drill and the wheel still a few times to get the feel of it.

Hold the drill near the cutting edge between the thumb and index finger of your left hand. Hold the shank end of the drill between the thumb and index finger of your right hand. Place the drill on the tool rest so its center line makes the required angle with the face of the wheel, and then slightly lower the shank end. Since you are working with a new drill, it will be easy to gauge the angle simply by placing the cutting edge of the drill flat against the face of the wheel.

Advance the drill to place its heel against the grinding wheel and then, in a combination action, slowly raise the shank end of the drill while you use your left-hand fingers to twist the drill in a counterclockwise direction until the grinding approaches the cutting edge. Don't exert a lot of pressure; don't try to work too fast. After you have gone through this procedure a dozen times or so with a new drill, test your skill by sharpening an old one.

Another possibility is to make the jig shown in the accompanying sketch and work against the side of the wheel. To use the jig, place the drill so the cutting lip is against the side of the wheel and the body of the drill is against the guide block. To do the sharpening, the drill is rotated as it is swung to a position that is parallel to the pencil line. Here too, in order to do a good job, it's wise to go through the procedure with a brand new, large size drill and with the wheel stationary. Doing this a few times will give you the feel of what is involved. Naturally, the angle of the guide must be changed if the point angle of the drill is not 59°.

Wood chisels

These tools cut best when they are square across the cutting edge and have a hollow-ground bevel.

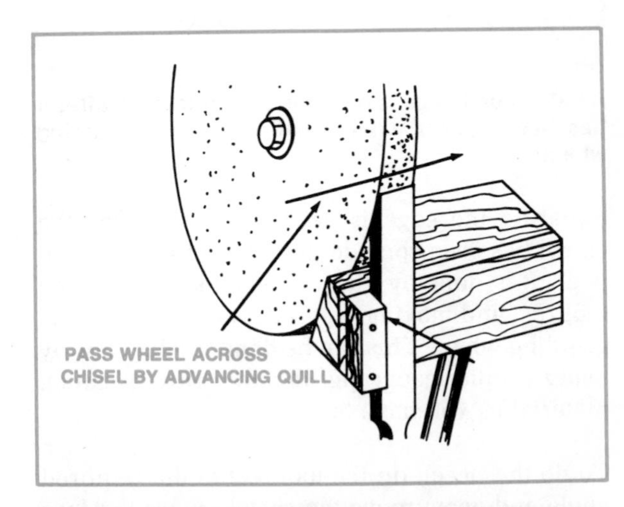

On a ShopSmith, clamp the wood chisel to the guide and do the grinding by advancing the quill. On a conventional grinder, pass the chisel back and forth across the face of the wheel.

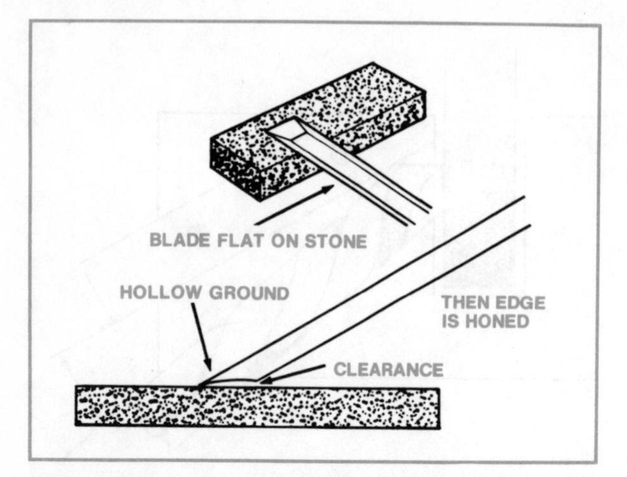

After grinding, hone as shown here. Be sure to maintain the slight clearance between the heel of the cutting edge and the stone when you are honing the bevel.

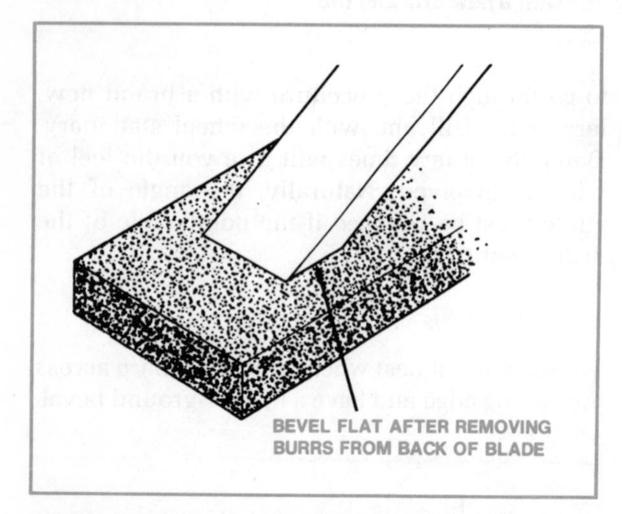

A flat-ground edge is honed in similar fashion after it has been shaped on the flat side of the grinding wheel.

Squaring the edge is necessary only after the chisel has seen considerable use and knicks appear. It is done by placing the chisel flat on the tool rest and moving it parallel to the face of the grinding wheel. This can be done freehand or by using a miter-gauge jig. Remove only as much material as you have to.

To do the bevel, tilt the tool rest to the required angle and again move the chisel across the face of the wheel. If the chisel is narrow enough, the lateral motion may not be necessary. Another method is to make a special guide block that provides the necessary bevel angle. The length of the bevel should be about twice the thickness of the chisel; this usually produces about a 30° angle.

Some amount of burr will be left on the cutting edge, so the grinding operation should be followed by honing the chisel by hand on a flat stone. This should be done with the chisel tilted

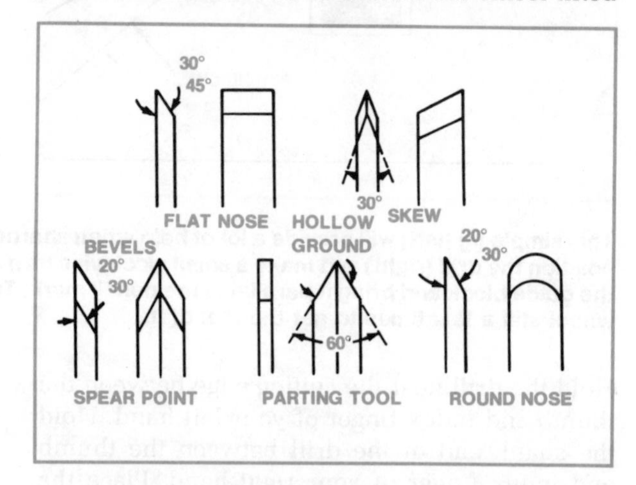

Wood-turning chisels are ground to angles shown here. All bevels are ground flat except for that of the parting tool, which always has a hollow-ground bevel.

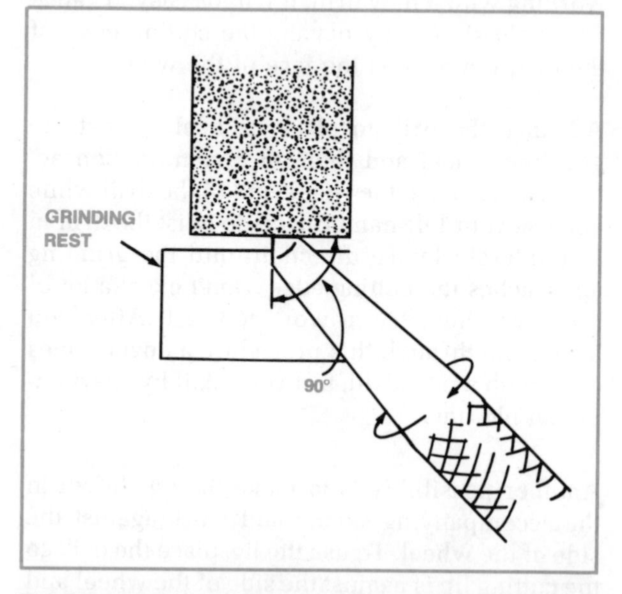

To do a punch, adjust the tool rest to the correct angle (the original angle on the punch) and then simply rotate it against the turning wheel to make the end symmetrical. Grind away only as much as you have to. Avoid overheating.

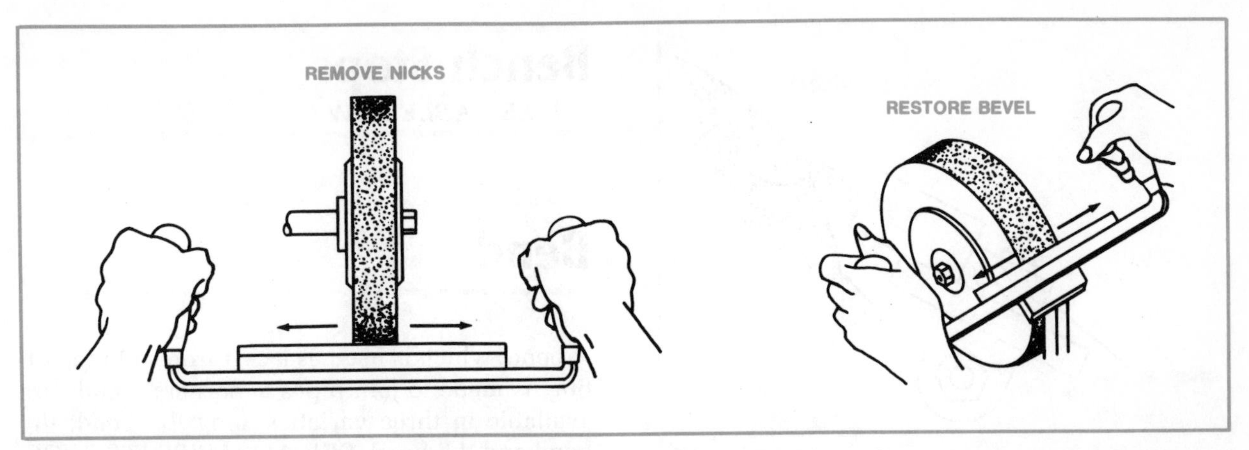

A draw knife can be ground with a single or a double bevel. It will be easy to maintain the original bevel since there are sure to be unworn portions at each end of the blade. Use light pressure in this operation.

on its bevel but with a little extra tilt to get some clearance between the heel of the cutting edge and the stone. The chisel should also be level but resting on the back surface of the blade. Alternate between the two positions until all the burrs are gone and the edge is keen enough to cut a hair.

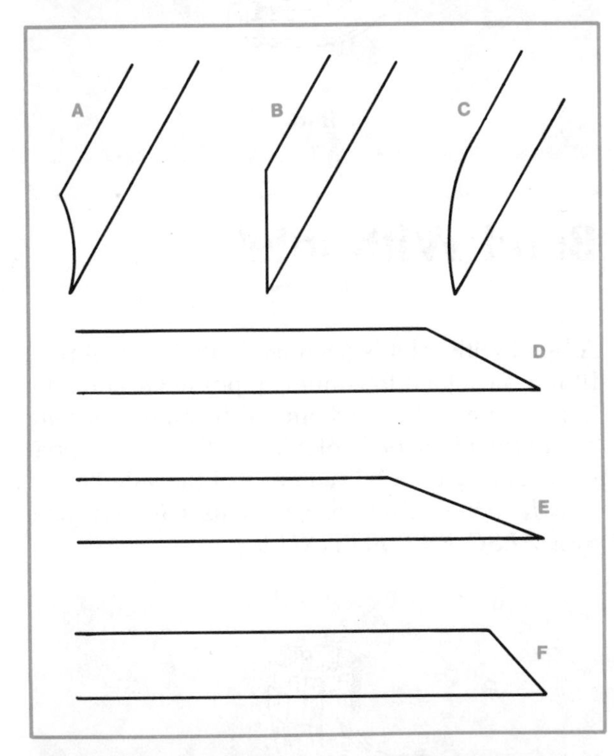

A-(hollow ground) and B-(flat ground) show good ways to shape a cutting edge. It must never be rounded as in-C. This can result from poor grinding. The bevel length should be about 2x the chisel thickness (D). A longer bevel (E) might work better on soft woods but it will knick and dull easily. The edge should never be blunt as in (F).

The honing operation actually produces a secondary bevel that does a beautiful cutting job. When you use chisels with care, the honing can be repeated quite a few times before it becomes necessary to go through the grinding procedure again.

All of the information in this section applies to hand-plane blades and similar items, as well as to wood butt chisels.

Jointer Knives

Jointer knives are done much like chisels, but it's not recommended that you try to do them freehand. Instead, work with one of the two jigs shown in the illustrations. One jig spans across both wheels of the grinder and offers the advantage of being able to go from coarse grinding to fine grinding without a jig change. Of course, if the knife is in fairly good shape to begin with, you can confine the grinding to the less coarse wheel.

The second jig employs a sliding block that has been kerfed at the correct knife angle. The knife must fit snugly in the kerf before you do the grinding. This is especially important because three knives are involved. If you don't grind them carefully, the knives will be of different width and, because of the knife-adjustment method employed by some jointers,

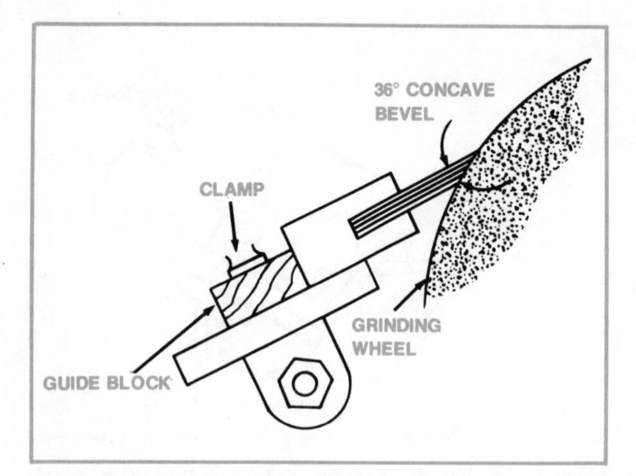

This jointer-knife jig employs a sliding hardwood holder that grips the knife securely. When making a second pass, do not change the position of the guide block. Instead, place a piece of paper between guide block and knife holder.

you will end up cutting with just one or two of the knives.

When you use the jigs, be sure that you go through each grinding procedure on each knife before you make any jig change. This assumes that more than one pass will be required to create a new edge. No matter what, keep the cuts extremely light and do not permit the knives to become overheated. You can do honing on the knives after grinding or between grindings as described for wood chisels but don't overdo the secondary bevel since this will weaken the cutting edge. Also, check the jointer entry to see how knives may be honed while they are mounted in the machine. *SEE ALSO DRILL PRESS; JIGSAW; JOINTER; LATHE; RADIAL ARM SAW; SHAPER; STATIONARY BELT AND DISC SANDER; TABLE SAW.*

Bench Mark

A bench mark is a post, block or other object fixed to the ground by surveyors to indicate a definite point from which observations are made. Bench mark also refers to a reference point from which any kind of measurements can be made.

Bench Stops

[SEE TABLE SAW.]

Bend

A bend, which is used as a cast-iron soil pipe fitting, is made to join pipes at corners. Bends are available in three varieties: long 1/4" bend, 1/4" bend and 1/8" bend. *SEE ALSO PIPE FITTINGS.*

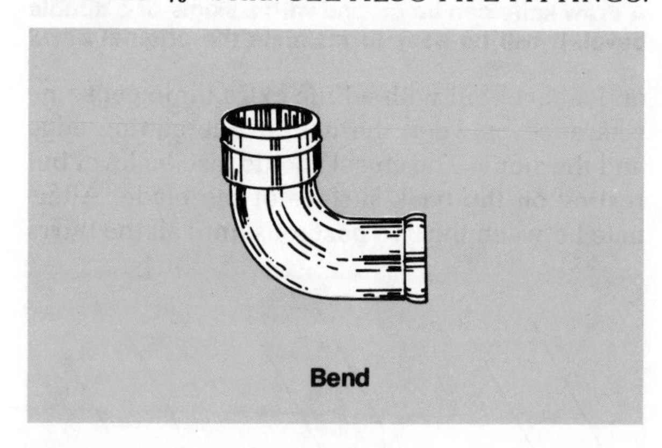

Bend

Bend With Inlet

A bend with inlet is used as a cast-iron soil pipe fitting. Designed to connect pipes at corners, the bend with inlet has an additional opening smaller than the ends of a bend. This extra opening is nearly parallel with one of the side bends. The 1/4" bend with inlet is the most common size. *SEE ALSO PIPE FITTINGS.*

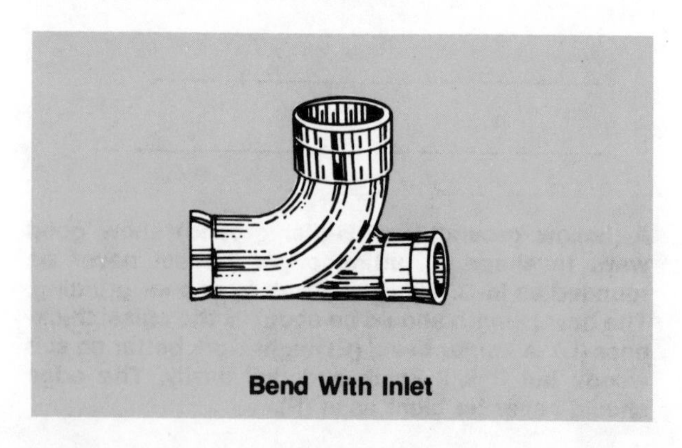

Bend With Inlet

Bevel Angles

[SEE BEVELS.]

Bevels

Beveling is a process of cutting, sawing or sanding a piece of stock or other material so that the surface or edge is at an angle less than or more than a right angle. Beveling is used for decorative purposes and also to prevent an edge from splintering. A bevel or bevel square, is also a hand tool used to lay out and check angles. The tool consists of a six to 12-inch steel blade, and a handle containing a locking screw. The blade slides and rotates in this handle and may be set and locked at an angle of one to 179 degrees. The angle is determined with a protractor or by fitting the tool to an already beveled surface.

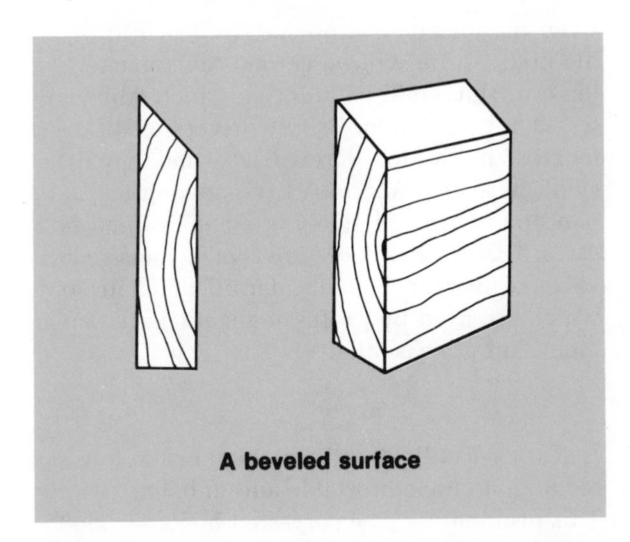

A beveled surface

Bevel Siding

Bevel siding is clapboard or weatherboard used as finishing siding on the exterior of a structure. The siding is beveled on the face from 1/8 inch at the upper edge to 3/8 inch at the lower edge. It is usually manufactured in various widths by resawing dry, square-surfaced boards diagonally to produce two wedge-shaped pieces. Install with the thick lower edge overlapping the thinner upper edge of the one below. *SEE ALSO SIDING.*

Bevel Square

The bevel square, sometimes called the sliding T bevel, can be used to lay out and test the angle of a bevel. The blade on this square can be set at any angle from 1° to 179° and locked there by means of a thumbscrew. You can set it on work and adjust its blade to match the exact angle required for a perfect fit. *SEE ALSO HAND TOOLS.*

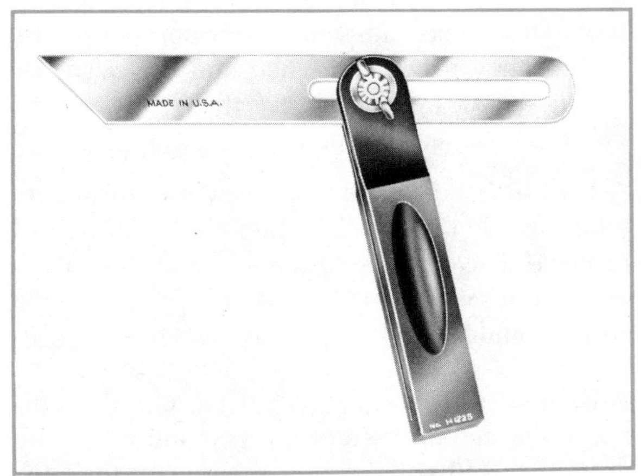

Courtesy of The Stanley Works

Bevel Square

Bicycle Maintenance & Repair

Bicycle maintenance and repair is essential to safe and enjoyable cycling. Most maintenance procedures can be done by the bikeowner. However, bicycles with derailleurs and coaster brakes should be taken to a bicycle repair shop for expert repair work.

MAINTENANCE

Tightening, oiling and cleaning are important preventive measures. Start at the front of the bike, check and tighten the post nut of the handlebars and work through the entire vehicle to the reflectors on the back fender. Take special care to have the proper amount of tension on cables and chains. If the brakes grab, or stop short, or the brake levers compress too easily, the tension on the cable needs to be adjusted until the cable responds to pressure on the brake lever smoothly. Chains are correctly adjusted when the pedal crank turns smoothly. Do not tighten the chain as a solution to pedal crank problems, rather examine the crank for any possible trouble. Readjust the chain if all the parts of the crank seem to be working properly.

The handlebar stem, front fork, hubs, chain, crank and sprockets will require oiling with 20 or 30 weight oil at least once a month. Rusted bolts should be dampened with penetrating oil so that they can be loosened and removed. Do not oil cables or brake shoes that work by friction of metal against metal.

A bike may be cleaned by spraying thoroughly with a garden hose. This simple procedure will protect the cycle from corrosive wear due to grit and grime. A coat of car polish will keep the bike shining and will add extra protection.

Adequate air pressure for tires, usually embossed on the tire's sidewall, will add to the life of the tire and will provide a more comfortable, safer ride. Bald or worn tires are prone to air leakage or blow outs. Whenever a tire has worn so that the tread is no longer obvious, the tire should be replaced.

Accessories

Bike accessories are an aid to safe cycling if they are used properly. Rear mirrors, flags and headlamps are common examples. When precautions are not taken to keep these accessories away from the face, they can become dangerous hazards. The high-backed sissy bars have no place on a bicycle saddle. In the event of an accident, they make it impossible for the rider to quickly free himself of the bike without injury. Handlegrips should always be used on the handlebars in order to prevent serious injury should the rider fall forward on them.

Night riding is fun and safe with the proper safety gear which should include a headlamp, a flag and a bright reflector. Flashlights are poor substitutes for headlamps because they do not allow the freedom of both hands. Headlamps should be attached to the center front of the handlebars, out of the rider's line of vision. Flags should be mounted on a rod of approximately five feet in length so that they wave no lower than the height of the rider's head. If the bike does not have a reflector on the rear fender, place one there, so the bike will be obvious from the rear at night. Side reflectors attached to the spokes are becoming increasingly popular. Reflective clothing should also be worn at night. Most communities have ordinances that specify night riding accessories and equipment.

REPAIR

Even the mechanical novice can learn to repair his bike. There will be certain tools needed for the job which will include: a six inch adjustable wrench, two standard screwdrivers of different lengths, a Phillips screwdriver and a pair of small, vise-grip pliers. A tire-patching kit and a hand pump are relatively inexpensive and handy for fixing flats. There are special tools such as valve core wrenches and derailleur chain tools which are used by professionals that are convenient, but not essential.

Adjusting the Seat

A seat, or saddle, that is too high or too low can result in an uncomfortable and unbalanced ride. This problem may be corrected by loosening the post nut located on the frame directly below the saddle and pulling up or pushing down on the saddle. The adjustment is correct if the heel rests comfortably on the pedal in the down position. After the saddle has been adjusted, remember to retighten the post nut.

The tilt of the saddle affects the body pressure placed on the handlebars; and if it is wrong will eventually lead to a stiff back or arm cramps. Also, an incorrectly tilted saddle will make steer-

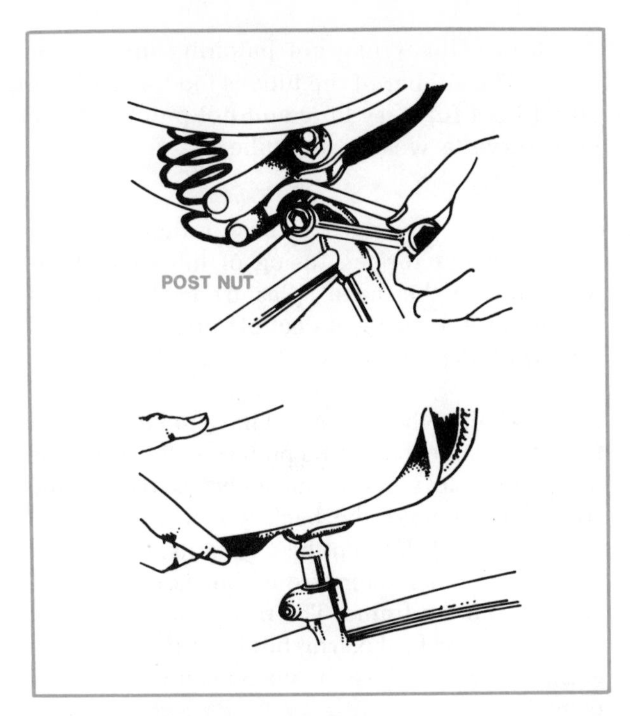

Adjusting the Saddle Height

ing difficult. Adjust the saddle tilt by loosening the nut of the saddle clamp and raising or lowering the nose of the saddle to a comfortable slant. Then, tighten the clamp nut to prevent the saddle from slipping out of adjustment.

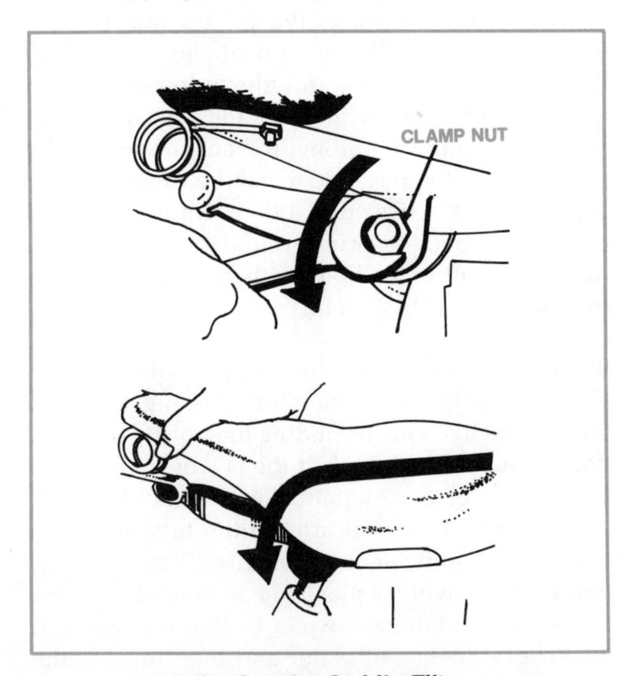

Adjusting the Saddle Tilt

Adjusting the Handlebars

The handlebars may also be adjusted to suit the rider. To adjust the height of the handlebars, loosen the handlebar post nut and gently tap on it with a hammer, driving down the taper nut. Stand in front of the bike, straddling the front wheel and grip the handlebars with one hand on each side of its center. Twist and pull or push the bars in the desired direction. Realign the handlebars so that they are centered over the front wheel and tighten the post nut.

Adjusting the tilt is a matter of loosening the handlebar clamp, making the tilt adjustment and tightening the bolt. The tilt is right when the rider can reach the handlegrips comfortably with the body leaning slightly forward.

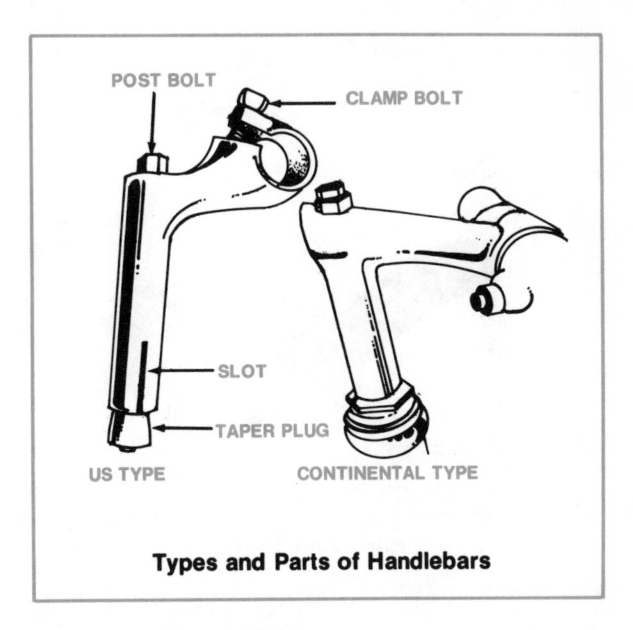

Types and Parts of Handlebars

Replacing Handgrips

Although seemingly insignificant, the handlegrips are an important safety feature. The grips keep the hands from sweating and slipping and also prevent chafing. Also, the handlegrips help to guard against a dangerous injury in the event of a fall on the handlebars. If the handgrips come off or become cracked and worn, they should be replaced. First roughen the handlebar with a piece of emery cloth, starting about six inches from the end. Then, spread gasket cement evenly over the rough area and along the inside of the handlegrip. Slip the grip onto the end of the handlebar and adjust it so that the finger ridges are directly underneath the handlebar.

There are many good arguments for taping handlebars instead of using handlegrips. Chiefly, this technique allows for several ways of gripping the handles. Begin the tape on an underside. Wrap it tightly around the handles at a slant, overlapping a quarter of an inch. Tuck the tape into the bar at the ends, and insert a plug which will secure the tape. The tape comes in many different colors to match the color of the bike.

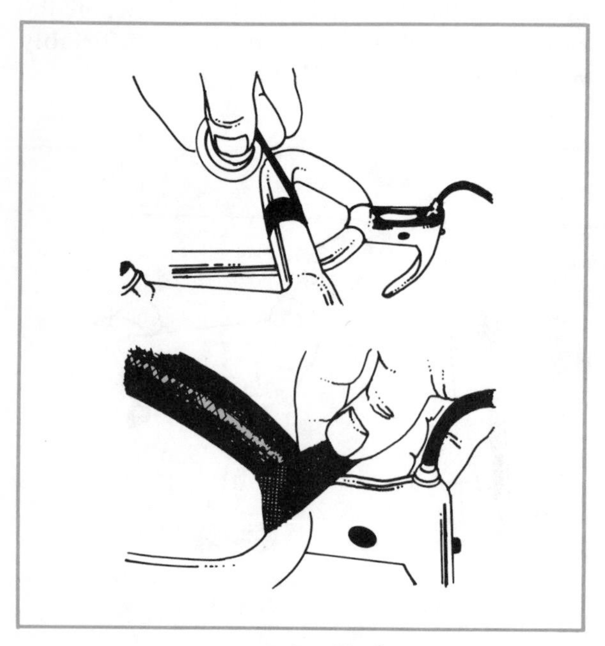

Handlebar Taping

Flat Tires

Flat tires are generally caused by either punctures or leaky valve cores. If the tube seems to be losing air, test the valve for leaks by putting a drop of water over the end of the valve stem and looking for bubbles. Tighten the valve core if there are any bubbles. The valve stem can not be replaced because there are not tubeless tires for bicycles. However, a valve core may be purchased and inserted into a valve stem with a special tool.

There are two methods of tube repair, commonly called patching: hot or fusion patching and cold patching. Never use hot patching on bicycle tubes. The rubber of the tube is too thin to withstand heat for very long and hot patching will only serve to weaken the tube.

Cold patching involves no heat, rather a rubber based cement for the fusion of the small hole. Most cold patches have a plastic back for protecting the mastic surface. Peel off this backing before applying the patch.

Although the wheel does not have to be removed from the frame to repair a puncture, there will be more room to work if the wheel is free of the frame. To remove the back wheel, remove the brake arm nut. Loosen the axle nuts, but do not completely take them from the axle. Slip the wheel from the frame. The front wheel does not have a coaster brake arm, but the axle nuts have to be removed before the wheel can be removed from the frame.

After the wheel has been lifted from the frame, check for visible signs of a puncture or a tack or nail. If a sharp object is found, mark the tire and rim at that spot before separating the two from each other. This will make it easier to find the location of the hole after the cause of the flat has been removed. Remove the valve stem nut and valve core to let the air out of the tube. Then press the tire with the thumbs to loosen it from the rim on both sides and pull the edge of the tire from the rim by rolling it back opposite the valve. Now it is possible to get the fingers under the edge of the tire so that they can pull the rest of the tire over the rim around the wheel. Slip the valve out of its hole in the rim and remove the tube from the wheel.

If the cause of the flat tire is not visible, inflate the tube slightly and listen for a hissing sound. A more effective way of finding the hole is to check for air bubbles while the tube is wet. Either running water or a container of water may be used. Gently pour water all around the tube until the air bubbles indicate the puncture. A more popular method involves placing a portion of the tube in a large container of water so that it is covered by several inches of water and then turning the tube until tell-tale bubbles indicate the hole.

To patch a tube, clean a surface about the size and shape of a half dollar around the puncture with gasoline and roughen it with a scraper. Apply rubber cement to the area, making sure that a generous amount is over the hole. Let the cement dry to a tacky surface, then apply the patch. It is important to rub the patch with a special roller in order to remove any air between the patch and tube, making sure of absolute contact between them. If a roller tool is not available, the edge of a quarter or other large coin works well.

These are the steps for repairing a puncture:

Find and mark the hole.

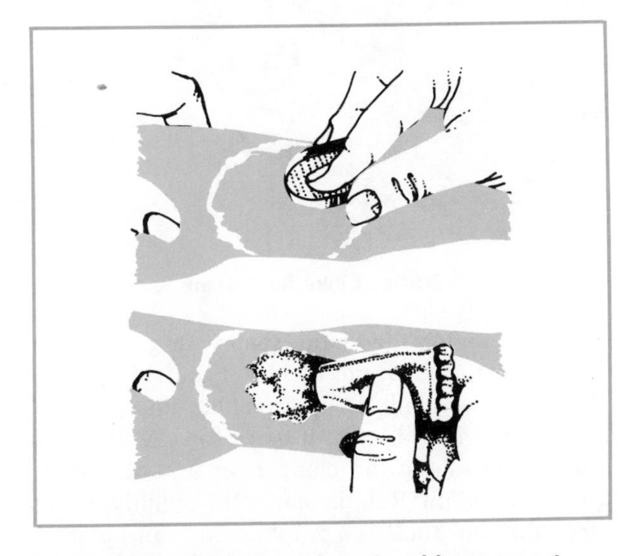

Clean the hole and apply rubber cement.

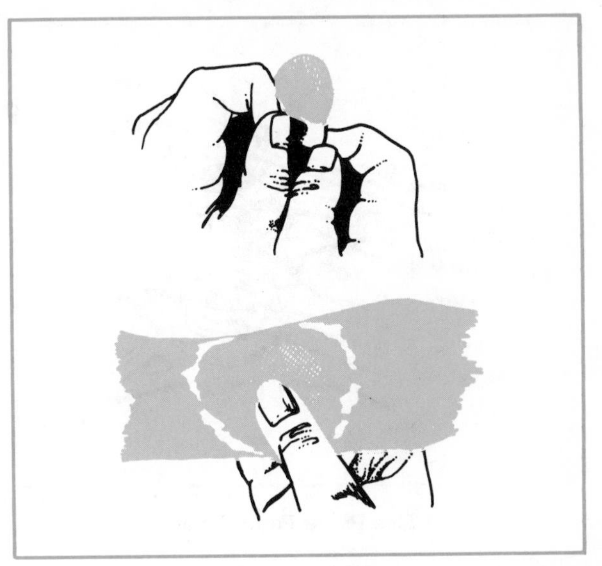

Apply the patch.

Replace the tube in the following manner: feel the inside surface of the tire and outside surface of the rim for tacks or stubs that might prick the tube and cause another puncture. For extra protection, use a rim strip to line the rim before installing the tube. Sprinkle talcum powder along the inside of the tire to lessen friction between the tire and tube. Inflate the tube enough to get the wrinkles and kinks out of it and, starting at the valve stem, slide the tube between the rim and tire. Press the tire back inside the rim edges and inflate it to about five pounds. Simultaneously bounce and turn the tire to evenly distribute the air and remove kinks. Then inflate the tire to the appropriate pressure marked on its side and put it back onto the frame.

Pedal Cranks

The pedal crank will periodically (about once a year) require lubricating to insure smooth and proper performance. Remove the left crank by removing the lock nut and lock washer. The ball-bearing retainers can then be unseated. Clean the parts with kerosene, gasoline, or other type of cleaning fluid, by soaking them overnight and rinsing them several times in different containers of clean liquid to be certain that no grit, grease or foreign matter has worked its way into the bearings. The cleaning should be done on a

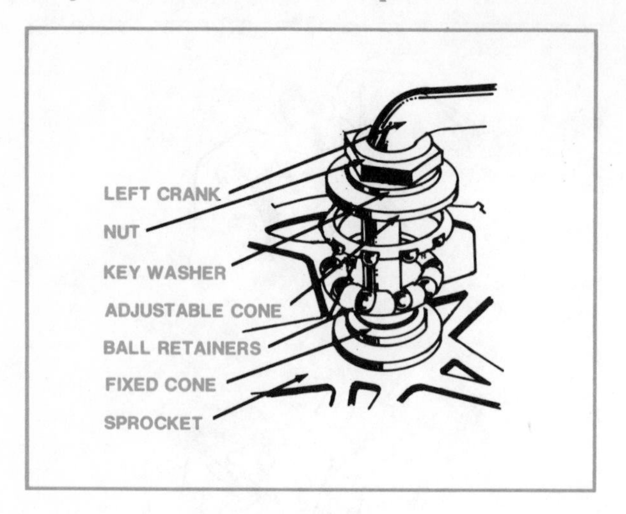

A One Piece Pedal Crank

smooth hard surface to cut down on grit. Do not clean bearings on a cloth stretched over a grassy surface! Coat the ball-bearing retainers liberally with ball-bearing or axle grease and carefully replace all parts.

Front Fork

The front fork usually does not need replacement unless it has been bent in an accident. However, the bearings will operate better if cleaned and greased annually. The handlebar post, front wheel and fender must be removed in sequence before the front fork can be taken from the bike as the fork helps to hold all of these parts onto the frame.

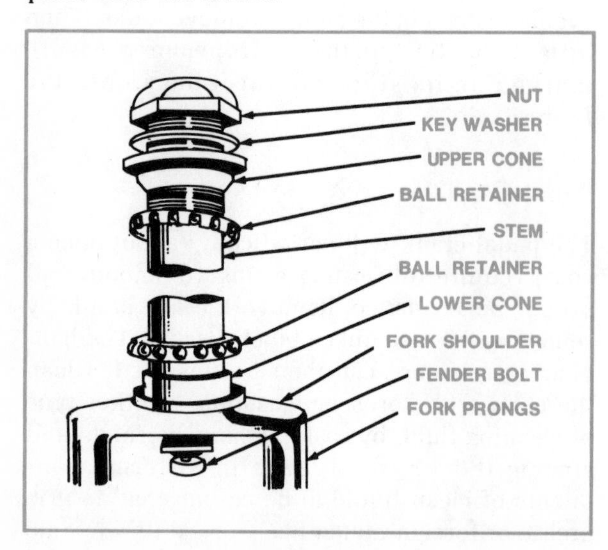

Front Fork

To clean and grease the fork, unscrew the nut, key washer and cone. Lifting the cone will free the ball-bearing retainers which may then be slipped out. The procedure of cleaning and greasing the crank bearings apply to the fork bearings, also. The cleaned fork is reassembled and replaced by retracing the steps of disassembly. Replace the front fender, wheel and handlebars.

The Chain

The chain will rust or dry out from prolonged wear and exposure to weather, dirt and grime. During the annual overhaul of the bike, remove, clean and lubricate the chain.

There will be one specific link in the chain, appropriately called the starter link, that is disconnected so that the chain can be removed. There are various types, but two of the most common are those held together by tension and those held together with a split-spring lock. Derailleur chains come apart with a rivet-removing tool that pushes the rivet out to allow for disconnection.

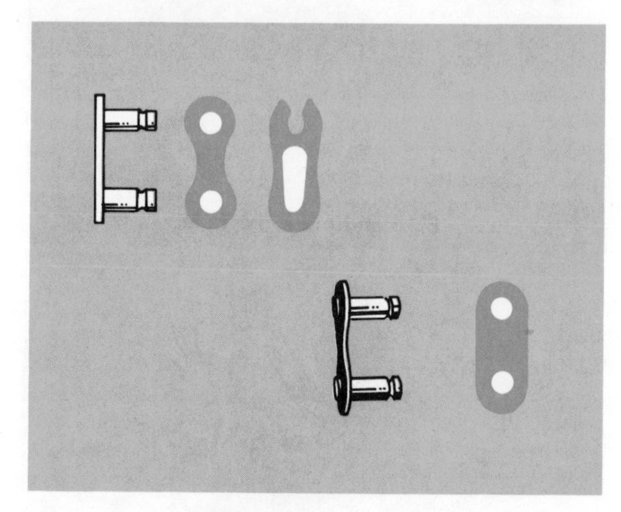

Starter Links for Chains

After removing the chain, soak it in gasoline or kerosene for a couple of hours and blot it dry with a rag or cloth. Drop the chain into a can of 30 weight oil and leave it there for several minutes. Then, hang the chain over a container to drain overnight. Rub the chain thoroughly with a dry lubricant such as a graphite stick and place it back onto the bike, reconnecting the starter links.

Brakes

Coaster brakes are located inside the hub of the back wheel. There are a number of varieties of brakes that assemble differently according to the brand used. Adjustment and repair of brakes are involved and should be done by a professional, or the manufacturer of the brake should be consulted.

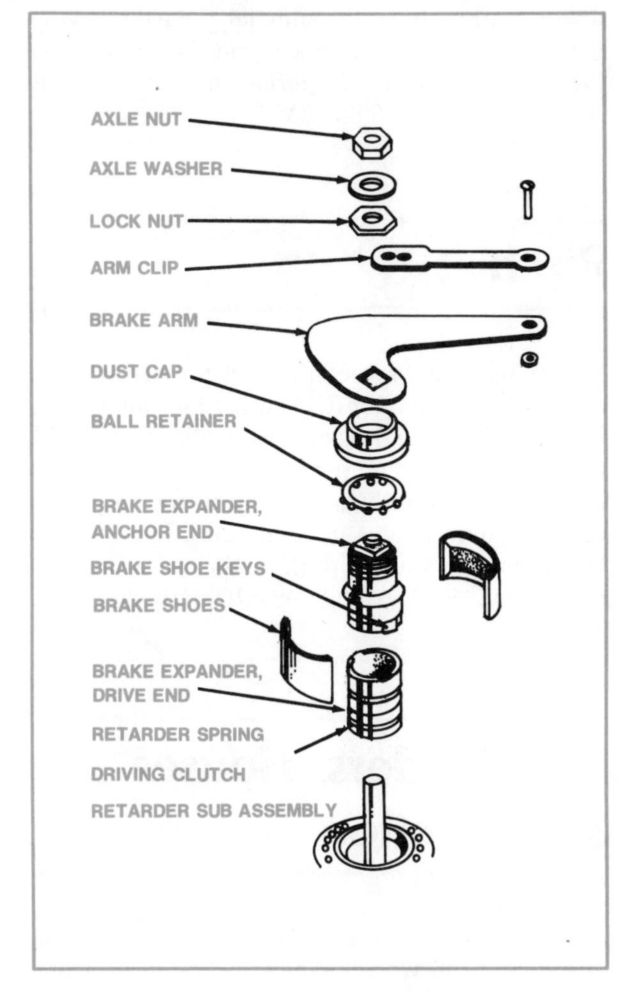

A Type of Coaster Brake

Rim brakes are found on most geared bicycles. To adjust the rim brakes that are of the side-pull variety, unscrew or tighten the lock nut which is located near the entry of cable to brake lever until the brake clamps are within 3/16 of an inch of touching the wheel. Center-pull brakes have a cable-adjusting barrel or adjust with a nut near the brake clamps. The specifications are the same.

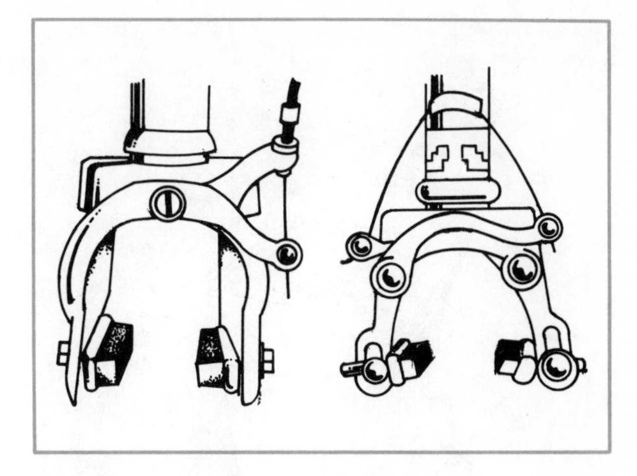

Rim or Hand Brakes

Bid

A bid is a statement of what one would give or take to supply materials, equipment, an entire structure or sections of a structure.

Bidet

Bidets are becoming a more familiar bathroom fixture in the United States than they once were. Used in conjunction with and located near the toilet, the bidet is used to cleanse the genitourinary area. Using a bidet after using the toilet is beneficial in preventing irritations and external infections in the perineal area. The soothing and cleansing effect of the running water is also helpful in caring for post-operative patients and the elderly. A mechanical stopper allows the water to fill the basin for sitz-bath usage if desired.

The user sits astride the bidet facing the wall and the water controls and activates the rinse-spray attachment manually. After usage, a transfer valve permits the water to enter through the flushing rim to thoroughly rinse the inner surface of the bowl.

The installation of the bidet requires some additional plumbing and as some bidets are not stan-

Bidet

dard size, manufacturer's suggestions concerning connection data and complete dimensions should be followed. *SEE ALSO PLUMBING FIXTURES.*

Bi-fold Doors

[SEE FOLDING DOORS.]

Bimetallic Strip

A bimetallic strip or simply *bimetal* is a heating system temperature control device used to operate oil burners, room thermostats and other appliances. It is composed of a double layer of metal strips, with each strip made of a different metal. When heated, one surface expands more quickly than the other, and arches toward the other, which expands more slowly. The opposite reaction occurs when the strip is cooled. Because of this temperature-responsive characteristic, a bimetal strip is used to operate on-off switches in many heating systems. When cooled, the strip arches one way and makes an electrical contact that turns on the switch. When heated, it arches the other way and turns off the switch. When a thermostat dial is turned up or down, it actually moves the electrical contact closer to or farther from the strip. In other words, if the heat is set to come on when the temperature in the room is 70 degrees, the bimetal is moved close to an electrical contact, and doesn't have to be cooled very much before it bends close enough to turn off the switch. If it is set for the heat to come on at a lower temperature, the bimetal is farther away from the electrical contact and must reach a lower temperature to operate the switch. *SEE ALSO HEATING SYSTEMS.*

Birch

Yellow birch and sweet birch are the two species of this wood commonly used for interior woodworking. Because they are strong, hard and hold their shape well, both are excellent for use in rails, doors, moldings and furniture. Birch is used to some extent in its natural, light finish, but often it is stained dark similar to walnut or mahogany. *SEE ALSO WOOD IDENTIFICATION.*

Bird Feeders, Houses & Protection

Attracting and feeding birds is a favorite pastime throughout the world. Watching the birds from the egg stage to the time they leave parental care and studying their nesting, rearing and habits can be fascinating as well as educational. Not only is this hobby entertaining, but it is also beneficial in providing food, shelter and protection for the birds.

Some of the simplest household projects to build are bird houses and feeders. Most anyone with a minimum of tools and materials can complete one of these projects with ease.

BIRD FEEDERS

Bird feeders benefit birds most in the winter. Since this is when fewer natural foods are available and air temperatures are lower, supplemental feeding is most necessary. Once begun, feeding should not decrease during these months. A constant supply of food should be maintained until the cold weather is over and spring has arrived. If feeding is stopped during severe weather, birds accustomed to relying upon the feeders might starve. Summer feeding is of less value since natural food is readily available.

Nesting Shelter or Shelf

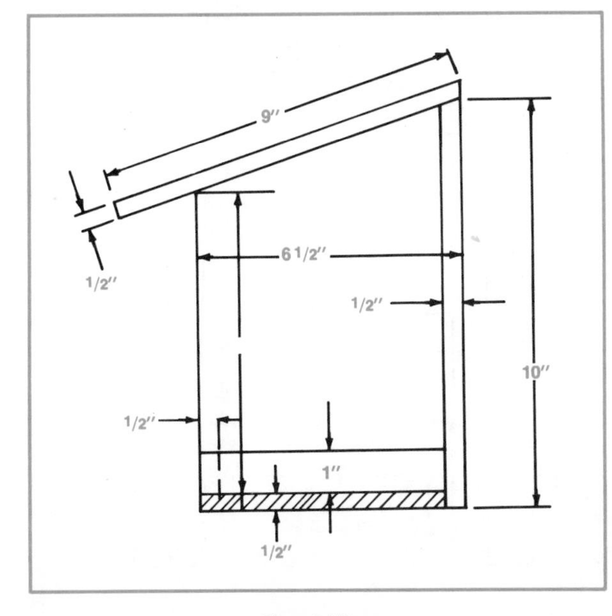

Front View

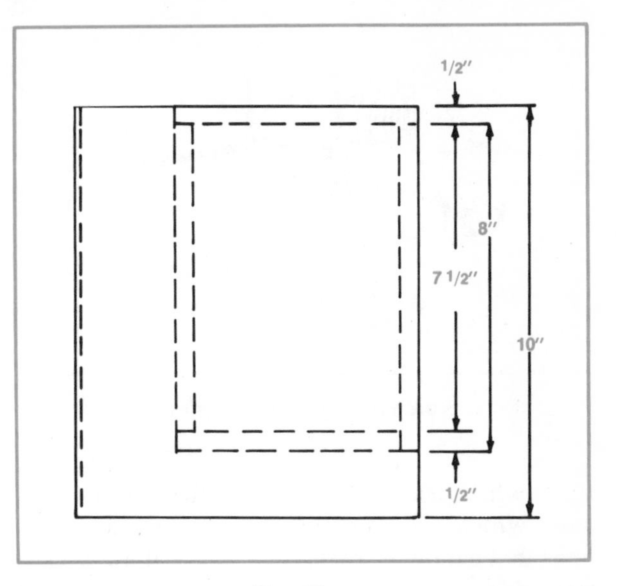

Top View

The simplest bird feeder is a plain wooden shelf at least one square foot. However, the food will be better protected if the shelf has three walls and a roof. Cautious birds will use the feeder more freely if glass panes, which permit a clearer view of any approaching danger, are set in each wall.

The open side of the feeder should face the direction from which driving rain or snow is least likely to come. An effective method of achieving this is a weather vane type feeder. This has a projecting tail that causes it to pivot like a weather vane and keeps the open side. Away from the wind, thus protecting the food. A wooden coping should be placed around the edge to restrict the amount of feed which is scratched out.

A fully opened pine cone will make a simple feeder. Dip it in heated fat or spread it with peanut butter and hang it by string from tree branches. Short sections of soft-wood branches about three or four inches thick may have several one-inch holes bored into them and be filled with suet or peanut butter to serve as a feeder also. These can be attached to the floor of the feeder or suspended from a tree limb. Mesh bags, cloths or onion sacks can be filled with suet scraps and hung from a tree branch as well.

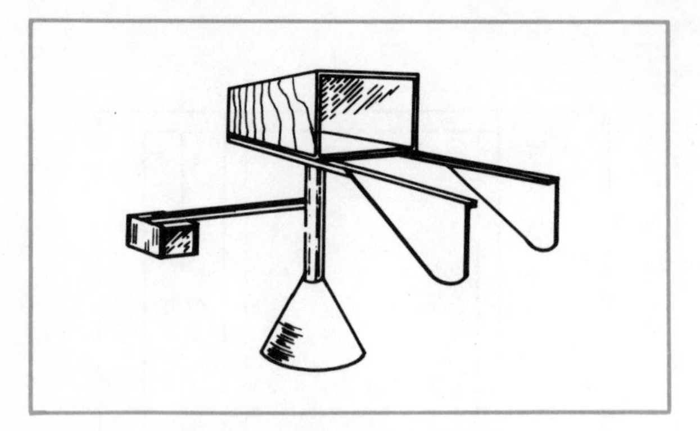

Weather Vane Bird Feeder

Birds which use feeders fall into two groups: the ones which are primarily seed eaters and the ones that eat other foods. The seed eaters are attracted by millet, cracked corn, sunflower, oats and other grains. Other foods which attract birds include such things as any table scraps, bread crumbs, crackers, broken dog biscuits, pumpkin seeds and sugar water with peanut butter, a favorite. Commercial bird feeding mixtures or various poultry feeds are often used in feeders.

The location of the bird feeder is best determined by the birds. If birds are not using it within a few weeks, move it to a new location. Protection from cats, dogs, squirrels and other animals is essential when locating the feeder.

BIRD HOUSES

Because particular bird houses attract certain species of birds, the choice of a specific design is essential. When building a bird house, certain principles of construction, location and design should be observed to make the nesting facilities safer and more comfortable for the birds. A well-built bird house should be durable, rainproof, cool and readily accessible for cleaning.

Wood is the best building material for bird houses. Pine, yellow poplar, hardwoods and cypress are the materials preferred for building a bird house. Although all are easily workable, cypress is the most durable. Sawmill waste, which are rough slabs with bark on them, furnishes satisfactory and inexpensive material for rustic houses.

Cylindrical-Shaped Rustic House

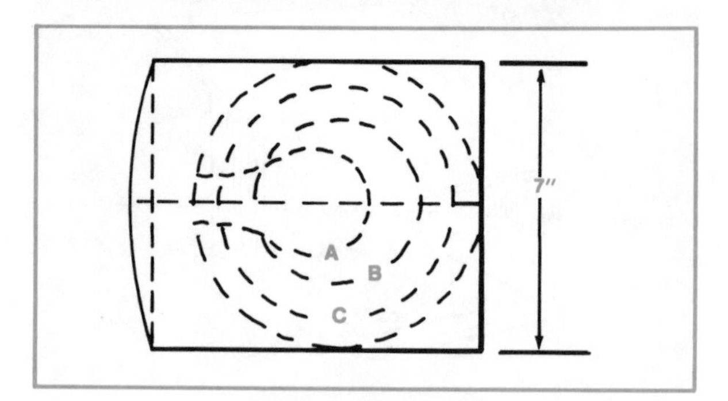

Top View

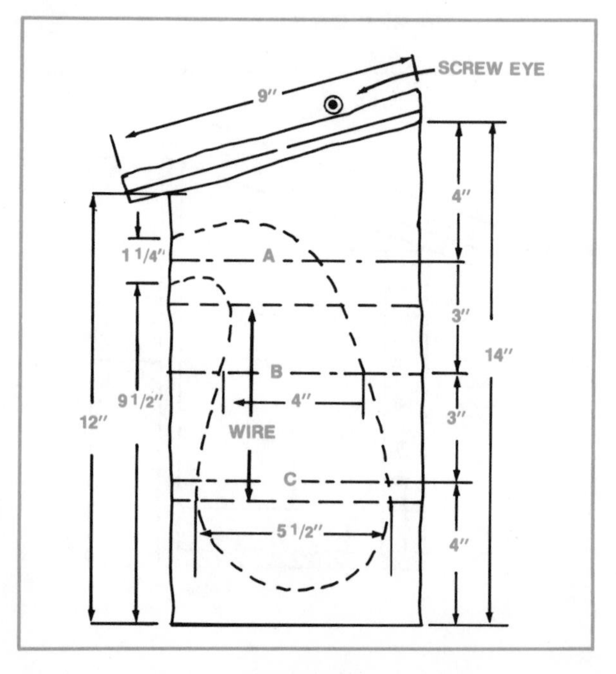

Side View

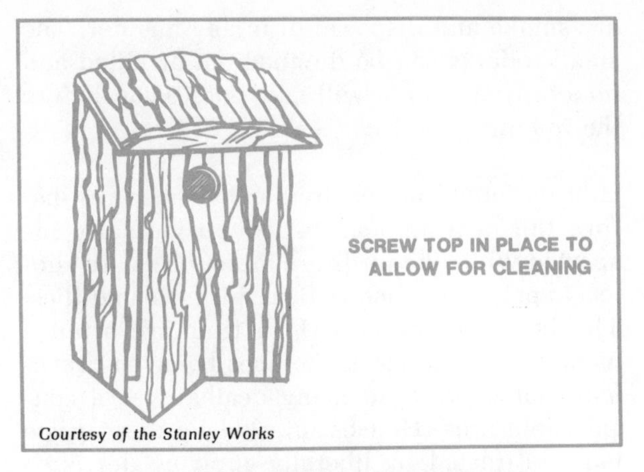

Rectangular-Shaped Rustic House

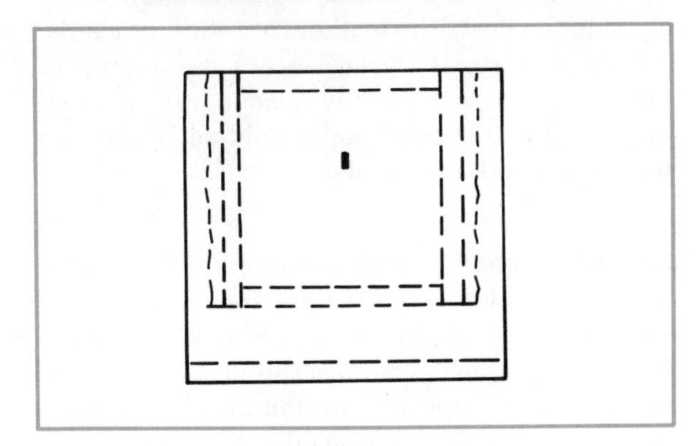

Top View

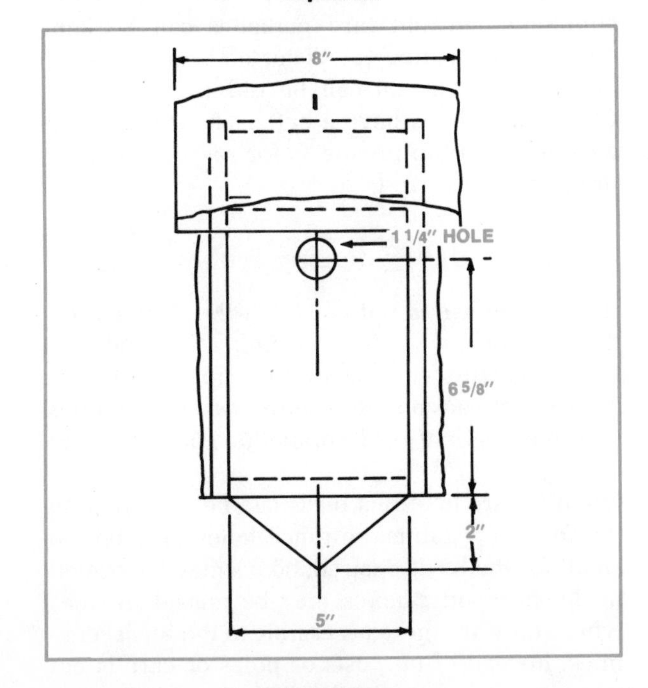

Front View

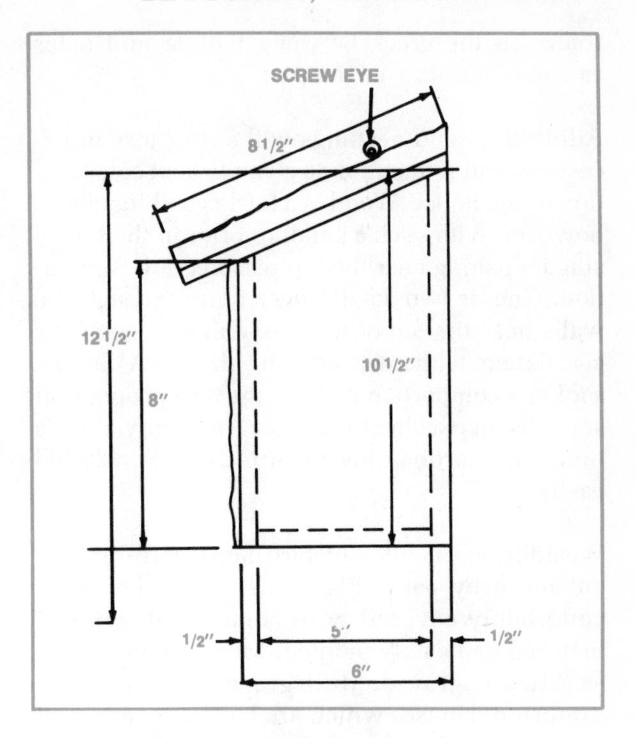

Side View

Because metal becomes intensely hot when exposed to the sun's rays, it should be avoided, except when building special houses, such as martin boxes. Pottery nest boxes are favorable, but they cannot be made easily in the average home workshop. Nest boxes constructed of tar paper or similar products are impractical for some of the larger houses and have no particular advantage over wooden ones.

To shed water readily, roofs should be built with a sufficient pitch. If the roof is practically level or level, a groove can be cut across the under face of the overhanging part to prevent water from draining into the house. Extend the overhang three inches to protect the entrance hole from driving rain. To help keep water out, the cavity hole may be drilled at an upward slant. A strip of metal or roofing paper often helps to make the ridge of the next box thoroughly waterproof.

In areas where there is freezing weather in the winter, bird houses will last longer if the sides are prolonged beyond the bottom of the box This will drain off water that otherwise might freeze in the crack between bottom and sides causing them to wedge apart.

Adult birds and nestlings will suffer less in excessive heat if attention is given to cool construction of the house. Wood is a fairly good insulator; however, with such a small interior in the box, a single opening near the top permits little ventilation. One or two small auger holes through the walls near the top of the box will give some air circulation without producing drafts. A double roof or a compartment above the nest proper will serve as an excellent insulator. In colony houses built for martins, this feature can be included easily.

Weathering qualities of bird houses are greatly enhanced by paint. Flat roofs should be either completely covered with some weatherproof material or heavily painted. Modest tones, such as brown, gray or dull green, are normally preferred. Houses which are located in exposed positions, such as martin houses, may be painted to reflect heat. Bird houses should be repainted every three to four years.

Inspecting and Cleaning Bird Houses

All bird houses should be placed so that they are readily accessible and built to be easily opened and cleaned. An opened box is a great aid in studying birds. Other arrangements may be used to permit inspection of the nest, such as having a pane of glass which slides in a groove just beneath the removable side. This glass permits observations without subjecting the birds to exposure or disturbing the nest material.

Building all bird houses so they can be opened readily for inspection is important. This feature is a necessity in regions infested by gypsy moth, since all possible hiding places for the egg masses of this species must be examined. The tussock moth and other insect pests may also place their eggs or cocoons in bird houses. Having the boxes regularly inspected and cleansed of all intruders, including mud daubers and paper wasps, bees, mice and flying squirrels, is helpful for the owner as well as the birds. The insects can be stunned by fumes of carbon bisulfide, carbon tetrachloride, sulfur or ordinary smoke and disposed of in any manner. The small rodents can be dumped out or killed and hopefully the birds will take possession before the rodents return.

Houses should be repaired and cleaned just before the nesting season and periodically inspected while the birds are there. Birds are subject to parasites, such as fleas, bird lice and flies. The larvae of certain flesh flies are often a menace to nestlings, sometimes being so prevalent that they cause many deaths over a considerable area. Houses infested by these pests may be treated by liberally applying derris or pyrethrum powder with special attention being given to the nest. The feathers of nestlings can be powdered also. If fly larvae are discovered in time, any that are actually attached to the nestlings may be removed and a mild antiseptic can be applied to the wounds.

Nest boxes should be cleaned immediately after broods have left, even if the parent birds show signs of preparing the house for another family. Old eggs and dead nestlings should be discarded and parasites kept to a minimum. The material removed should be placed on a paper and burned. Sanitation of houses can be profitably supplemented and bird parasites can be kept down by providing for water and dust or sand baths. Body vermin can be reduced this way. Clean nest boxes have a better chance of being occupied and the prospects for rearing the next brood are improved.

Attracting and Protecting Problems

If a bird house is not occupied the first season that it is erected, this is no indication that it is faulty in construction or improperly placed. There may already be more nesting facilities than the resident bird population can fill.

Often failure to attract birds can be attributed to the following faults: entrance holes may be too small for the birds desired; boxes may be located in dense woods; boxes may be placed in trees where they are more accessible to the birds' enemies, instead of on posts or poles or care is not taken to protect the birds nesting in boxes.

NESTING BOX DIMENSIONS FOR VARIOUS SPECIES OF BIRDS

Species	Cavity Floor	Cavity Depth	Entrance Above Floor	Diameter of Entrance	Height Above Ground[1]
	Inches	Inches	Inches	Inches	Feet
Bluebird	5 x 5	8	6	1½	5-10
Robin	6 x 8	8	(2)	(2)	6-15
Chickadee	4 x 4	8-10	6-8	1⅛	6-15
Titmouse	4 x 4	8-10	6-8	1¼	6-15
Nuthatch	4 x 4	8-10	6-8	1¼	12-20
House wren	4 x 4	6-8	1-6	1-1¼	6-10
Bewick's wren	4 x 4	6-8	1-6	1-1¼	6-10
Carolina wren	4 x 4	6-8	1-6	1½	6-10
Violet-green swallow	5 x 5	6	1-5	1½	10-15
Tree swallow	5 x 5	6	1-5	1½	10-15
Barn swallow	6 x 6	6	(2)	(2)	8-12
Purple martin	6 x 6	6	1	2½	15-20
Prothonotary warbler	6 x 6	6	4	1½	2-4
Starling	6 x 6	16-18	14-16	2	10-25
Phoebe	6 x 6	6	(2)	(2)	8-12
Crested flycatcher	6 x 6	8-10	6-8	2	8-20
Flicker	7 x 7	16-18	14-16	2½	6-20
Golden-fronted woodpecker	6 x 6	12-15	9-12	2	12-20
Red-headed woodpecker	6 x 6	12-15	9-12	2	12-20
Downy woodpecker	4 x 4	9-12	6-8	1¼	6-20
Hairy woodpecker	6 x 6	12-15	9-12	1½	12-20
Screech owl	8 x 8	12-15	9-12	3	10-30
Saw-whet owl	6 x 6	10-12	8-10	2½	12-20
Barn owl	10 x 18	15-18	4	6	12-18
Sparrow hawk	8 x 8	12-15	9-12	3	10-30
Wood duck	10 x 18	10-24	12-16	4	10-20

[1] Many experiements show that boxes at moderate heights mostly within reach of a man on the ground, are readily accepted by many birds.

[2] One or more sides open.

Courtesy of The Stanley Works

Entrance holes for bird houses are usually near the top to keep the mother bird concealed while nesting. Hole sizes vary with the size of the birds, such as the average hole size for a blue bird is 1½ inches while the average hole size for a wren is only one inch. The lumber used, if dressed, should be roughened, grooved or cleated to help young birds climb into the opening. Perches at the entrances are not required; they frequently seem to offer more assistance to enemies than the occupants.

To be easily accessible, bird houses should be fairly low and not beyond the reach of an available ladder.

Inevitably, those located higher will be neglected. Bird houses are usually built from eight to 15 feet above the ground. They should not be located in dense woods. Birds' houses seem to be more acceptable when placed on poles rather than on trees. If possible, they should be placed in partial sunlight, having the opening away from prevailing winds.

Because birds insist on territorial rights, especially in competition with members of the same species, a large number of boxes should not be placed on a limited area. If houses are too close together, conflicts between birds may result in no houses being occupied. The purple martin is the only native gregarious species that nests colonies in bird boxes. The houses for colonies of these birds should be on poles separated from trees or buildings. Tree swallows are also sociable and several individual boxes for them may be near each other.

Popular enemies of birds include mainly cats, dogs, squirrels, mice and other birds, such as house sparrows and house wrens. To help protect birds, a sheetmetal guard which encircles the supporting tree or pole or iron pipes could be used to prevent cats, mice, squirrels, raccoons and opossums from climbing the tree. Keeping dogs and cats away from the birds' area will help in the protection also. Discouraging any house sparrow or European starling nesting will give other species of birds an opportunity to nest in the area. They usually will not bother boxes that are within five feet of the ground. Blue jays, grackles, magpies and crows occasionally destroy eggs and young birds of other species, but seldom will they interfere with the nests inside the boxes.

HOW TO ATTRACT DIFFERENT TYPES OF BIRDS

Certain birds are attracted to particular houses for many reasons such as the size, dimensions, height and the type of house. In order to attract birds to an area, certain designs and materials necessary to build the houses are important as well as the location of the boxes.

Bluebirds and Sparrows

Bluebirds are among the least particular of bird tenants. There are various styles of boxes which will meet their needs when built to the proper dimensions and well situated. Houses of rustic construction are also acceptable to these colorful birds. Bluebirds are also partial to abandoned orchards, or nest boxes placed either in trees or on nearby fence posts, provided measures are taken to prevent attack by cats. A rather open and sunlit situation is preferable. The nest material consists mainly of dry grasses. Where house sparrows are numerous, competition for the boxes can sometimes be alleviated if they are mounted four or five feet above the ground, rather than the normally recommended five to ten feet.

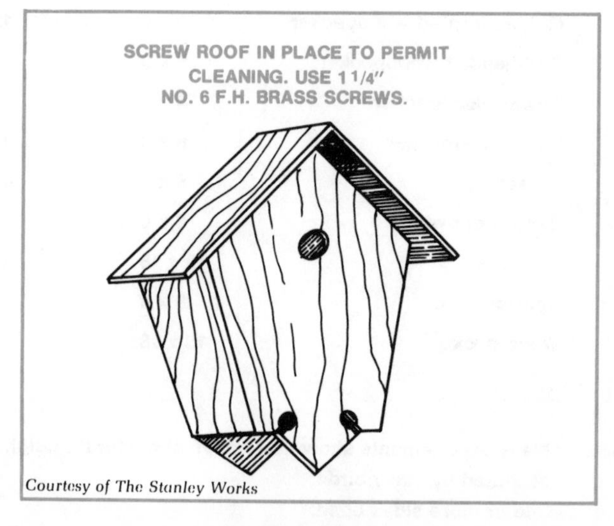

Courtesy of The Stanley Works

Bluebird House

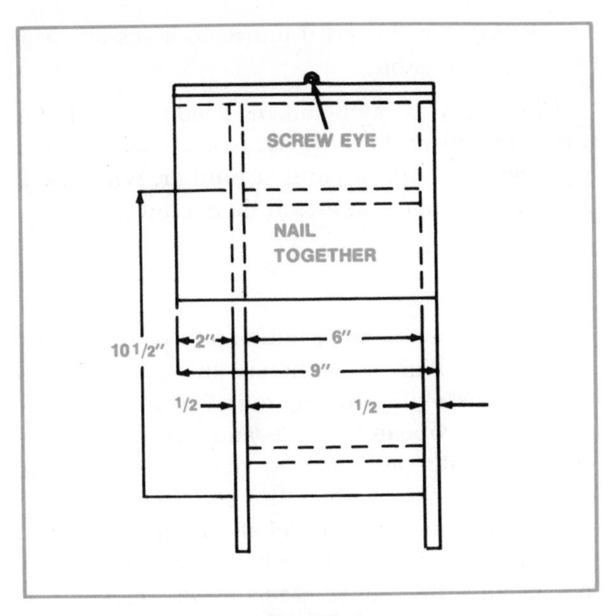

Side View

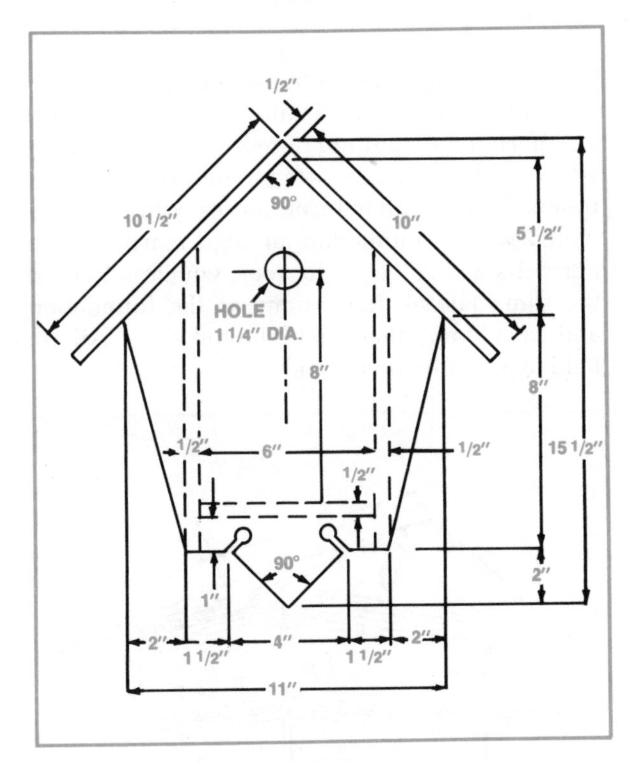

Front View

Robins, Catbirds and Thrashes

When natural sites such as well-formed crotches are absent, robins may use nesting platforms built for them. Catbirds and brown thrashers use similar nesting shelters.

These boxes should be made either. of weathered lumber or of the rustic type and placed in partly shaded spots along the main branches of trees or in the shelter of the overhanging eaves of a shed or porch roof. The birds will gather their nesting material from natural sources. However, in dry weather periods, they may be aided by wetting a spot of bare clay nearby to supply the mud used in the foundation of their nests.

Wrens

Wrens are the least fastiduous of the hole-nesting birds. Almost any kind of cavity will meet their needs, although small sized boxes with a

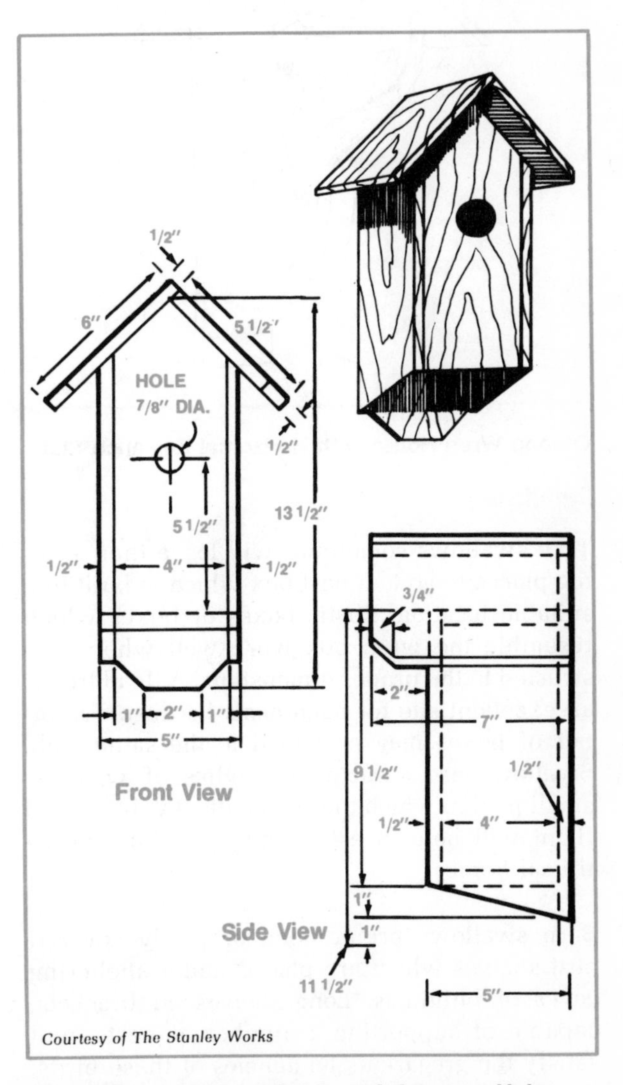

Courtesy of The Stanley Works

Oblong Wren House with Round Entrance Hole

horizontal slot instead of a round hole for an entrance are best for wrens. Birdhouses either of smooth lumber or of the rustic type are preferred. Almost any partly sunlit spot around the dooryard or orchard is agreeable to wrens. A supply of slender twigs about three inches long, placed in a handy spot will aid the birds in collecting nest material. An abundance of wren houses is desirable, because frequently these birds will leave one or more unfinished nests before completing one that they like.

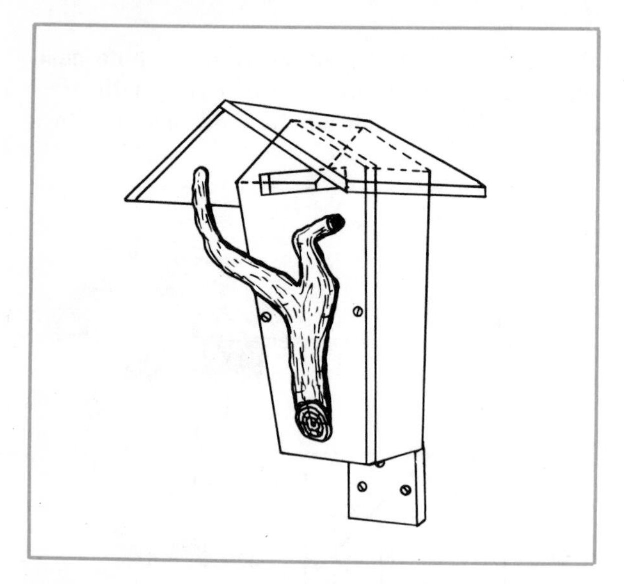

Oblong Wren House with Horizontal Entrance Slot

Swallows

Tree swallows sometimes will leave their nesting places to go to a nest box which is built in a suitable location. Rustic boxes or boxes which resemble the wren box work well when constructed to the proper dimensions. A dead tree is an excellent site for such nests because a number of boxes may be nailed to the same stub. Swallows are attracted to bodies of water; a small pool in which they can bathe by dipping in flight will help in establishing a colony in artificial homes.

Barn swallows prefer open or partly covered nest shelves which are placed under sheltering eaves of buildings. Long shelves on brackets, capable of supporting a number of nests, will satisfy the gregarious tendencies of these birds. Similar shelves under the roofs of barns or sheds will be utilized if entrance holes are provided in the gables.

Cliff swallows may be encouraged to nest under overhanging roofs by providing a narrow shelf or cleat of rough unpainted lumber, which will give them a place to attach their mud nests.

Martins

The gregarious nesting habits of purple martins give the builder of the house an opportunity to employ his skill and ingenuity in construction. Because European starlings and house sparrows are constantly attracted to martin houses, the entrances to the nest cavities should be blocked or the house should be taken down and stored during the period of the year when martins do not occupy the house. Martins are capable of maintaining their property rights during nesting season.

When building a martin house for a growing colony, make each story a unit. The uniform size will permit the addition of more stories as needed. A colony may be started in one story of eight rooms, building on to three stories with 24 rooms which will accommodate enough martins for a normal-sized colony. The roof, which is built to the same lateral dimensions as the foundation and each story, attaches to the top story. All are held together by hooks and screw eyes. To clean,

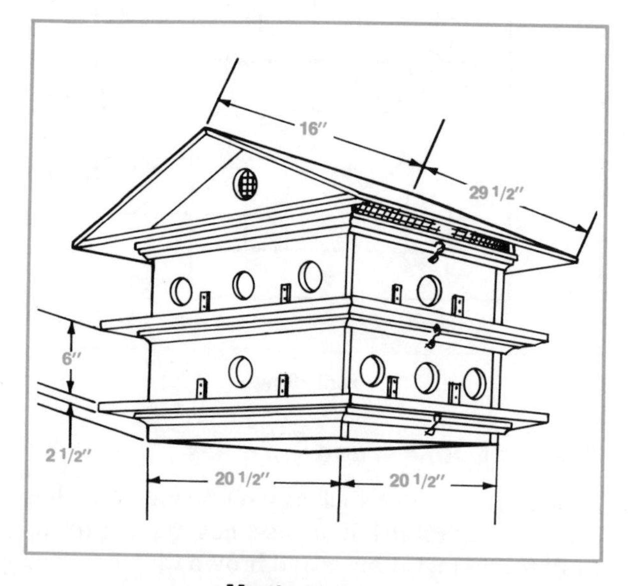

Martin House

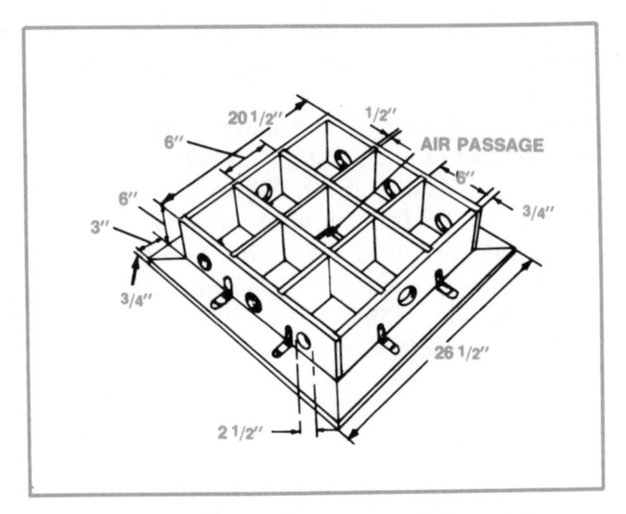

A One-Story Section of a Martin House

simply take the house apart and dump out the debris.

The temperature within the house is kept down by air circulation through the passage, which is formed by cutting out the floors of what would be central compartments. The roof, which is raised slightly above the top of the upper story, also permits the passage of air from the central shaft.

The entire house with its support may be arranged for lowering in the ground, or if the pole is set firmly in the ground, a ladder leaned against it will permit taking down the house section by section. If built of soft pine, a two-story house of this kind will weigh about 65 pounds.

Houses for martins should be located in open spaces and are usually painted white with neat trimming of another color. Like other birds, these birds are attracted by water. If a pond or stream is nearby, the probability of their establishing colonies will be increased.

The material for the walls and floors should be 3/4 inch thick with the roof and interior partitions being 1/2 inch thick. Lightweight roofing paper cut into shingles makes an efficient and neat roof covering. When facilities for gluing are available, the three inch porches may be made as extensions of the floors; otherwise, they may be attached with angle irons.

A guard rail completely surrounding each of the porches may help prevent young martins from falling before they are old enough to fly. A 1/2 inch diameter dowel elevated 3/4 inches above the outside edge of the porch helps keep young martins safe as they totter around.

Woodland Birds

Chickadees, titmice and nuthatches have similar needs. Being creatures of the woodland, they seem to prefer rustic homes. However, they will live in boxes made of weathered lumber built similar to an oblong wren house in design. Old orchards and the borders of woodlands are favorite locations for nest boxes of these birds. Chickadees often nest within a few feet of the ground, while nuthatches and titmice prefer a site of medium or considerable elevation. Food stations providing suet and nut meats placed on nearby trees will attract these birds, but keep in mind that these stations may also attract predators.

Creepers and Warblers

Brown creepers of the northern U.S. find small bark-covered houses, which closely fit to the trunks of trees, attractive. Creepers often nest behind curved pieces of bark fastened to the trunk of a living tree. Warblers sometimes nest over water in the southern swamps and are readily attracted to nest boxes.

Finches

Although house finches do not normally nest in boxes, they occasionally will use homes of simple design, like the wren house. Orchards or dooryards with a lot of shrubbery, where sunshine alternates with cool shadows, are the house finch's favorite habitat. Nest boxes may be placed in trees or on posts or attached to buildings.

Phoebes

Since phoebes enjoy being around water, the broad timbers beneath a bridge are a good location for a house. Once they have settled in an area, they will return to it each year. Nesting sites in the shape of shelves are the best kind. These may be placed on the wall just within the large open doorway of a barn, or higher along the rafters and even outside beneath the eaves, where they may get protection from above. In more exposed situations, nest shelters, like robins use, may be built.

Flycatchers

A relative of the phoebe is the crested flycatcher, whose original nesting sites were old woodpecker holes and natural cavities in trees. Boxes made of weathered or dull-painted lumber or from natural stubs or slabs may be substituted for these holes. When the boxes made from natural stubs are placed in typical situations, such as in orchards, open woodlands or in trees in pastures, they have greater appeal than the homes made of lumber.

Woodpeckers

Of all the woodpeckers, flickers respond most readily to artificial nest boxes. They will use boxes made of painted or weathered lumber if other conditions are satisfactory. Oblong boxes built to proper dimensions are preferred. A roughened interior is preferable to a smooth one because it permits the growing young to clamber up to the entrance.

Coarse sawdust, ground cork or small chips should cover the bottom of the box to a depth of one or two inches. This is done so that the birds may shape a cavity for the eggs. The chips also assist the birds in keeping the nest clean. If the chips or sawdust are not furnished, the birds may try scratching up the box to produce their own supply.

Flicker boxes should be placed above any immediately surrounding foilage. A dead tree stub or a pole of the desired height makes an excellent support.

Building boxes for flickers may be a means of preventing hole damage caused by the birds' attempts to make a home.

Red-headed woodpeckers will sometimes occupy man-made homes. Boxes made from a natural stub are most acceptable, although barkcovered boxes will serve the purpose also. They should be placed above foilage or near oak groves.

Downy and hairy woodpeckers have similar needs except for a slight difference in the size of nest cavity and entrance. Boxes covered with bark or made from natural stubs or slabs are sometimes accepted when attached to the tree trunk which is not densely shaded. Fine chips should be placed in the box's floor. Open woodland or an orchard is a good site for the nests.

Owls

Screech owls will use nesting facilities provided by man. Oblong wren type boxes made of weathered lumber and stained a dull color or covered with bark are acceptable. An apple orchard or a grove is an excellent site for screech owl boxes. The birds will supply the small amount of wood and feathers needed to make a nest.

Barn owls may be found in Southern and Central states. They often nest in barn lofts, towers or off-shore duck blinds. Simple wooden boxes of appropriate dimensions, resembling the oblong wren house, will meet the needs of these owls. The boxes may be attached to trunks of rather large trees or placed in barn cupolas or other secluded spots on buildings. *SEE ALSO PROJECTS.*

Courtesy for Bird Feeders, Houses & Protection:
Fish and Wildlife Service
U.S. Department of the Interior
Washington D.C.

Bird's Mouth

The bird's mouth is a cut or notch at the end of a roofing rafter which rests on the wall plate and anchors the rafter. This type of cut is used when a section of the rafter extends beyond the wall plate. This extension is called a tail or overhang. To saw a bird's mouth, a plumb cut line is drawn and sawed on one end of the stock. The run of the rafter, or the distance from the outside of the wall plate to the center of the ridge is measured and a seat cut is made slanting in the opposite

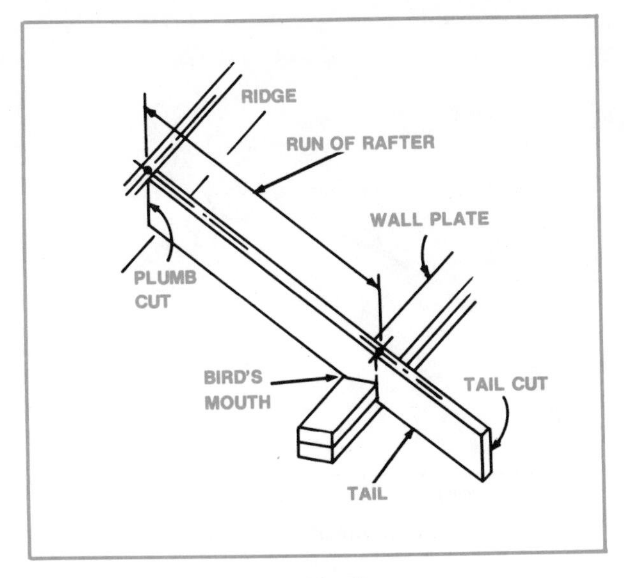

Bird's Mouth

direction from the plumb cut. The tail cut is then made, slanting in the same direction as the plumb cut and completing the bird's mouth. *SEE ALSO ROOF CONSTRUCTION.*

Bit Braces

Bit braces are the most popular types of hand drills. They are made with a bowed crank shaft and can be used to drill through many types of materials. They are handy for the homeowner who rarely does drilling and does not want to invest in a power drill. They can also be used for drilling on jobs where electricity is not readily available. Many bit braces are fitted with a ratchet which vastly increases their efficiency. Bit braces can be used with all sizes of twist drills, augers and other types of bits. *SEE ALSO HAND TOOLS.*

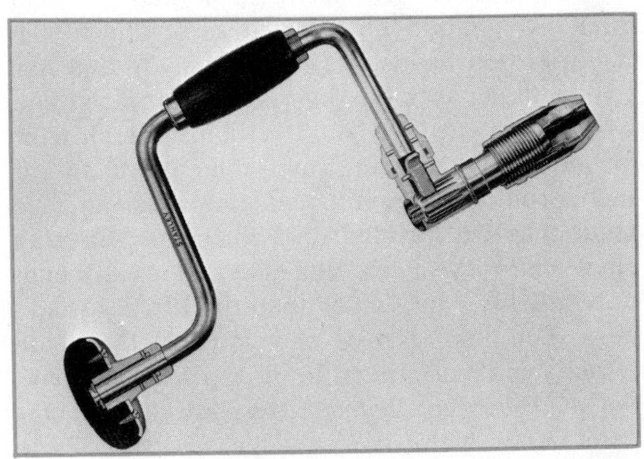

Courtesy of The Stanley Works

Bit Brace

Bits

Bits are used in hand and power drills, braces and routers for boring holes and also serve in making decorative patterns or driving a screw. All bits are not interchangeable with braces, power drills and hand drills, but some are. Twist drills can be used in hand or power drills for making holes in wood or metal. Auger bits are almost exclusively for use in a hand brace, but there are varieties made for electric drills. Masonry bits are for drilling into brick, stone, plaster, concrete, etc., and work best in power drills. Expansive bits, used in braces, not only cut holes but feed screws, also. For cutting holes up to $11^1/_2$-inches in diameter, use circle cutters. Drill points are generally for push drills. Router bits are designed for work with routers only and are not used in drills. In router work, there are ogee bits for decorative cuts, "V" grooving bits for letter and sign work, dovetail bits for making dovetail joints, besides numerous others. The best way to obtain the bits you'll use most is to purchase a matched set. *SEE ALSO HAND TOOLS; ROUTER.*

Black Swirl Finish

The workability and economy of pine makes it an ideal base for a built-up black swirl finish. This finish is formed on a gesso base, which is applied by spreading plaster of paris smoothly over the surface, then texturing with a fairly stiff, dry brush. After the plaster has hardened, apply enamel. If you want a sharp-textured finish, use only one coat of enamel; use two or three for a softer appearance. *SEE ALSO WOOD FINISHING.*

Blade Bevel Angle

The blade bevel angle is formed above the cutting edge or wedge-like part of a tool. It is sized according to the strength needed to do the cutting work. The blade bevel may be only a very slight tapering, as in a razor, or a much wider angle like the one formed above an axe wedge. On many blades, such as knives or razors, the bevel does not wear and does not need sharpening. But other tools, such as wood chisels, the blade bevel is used in the cutting or scraping process and should be sharpened. *SEE ALSO BEVELS.*

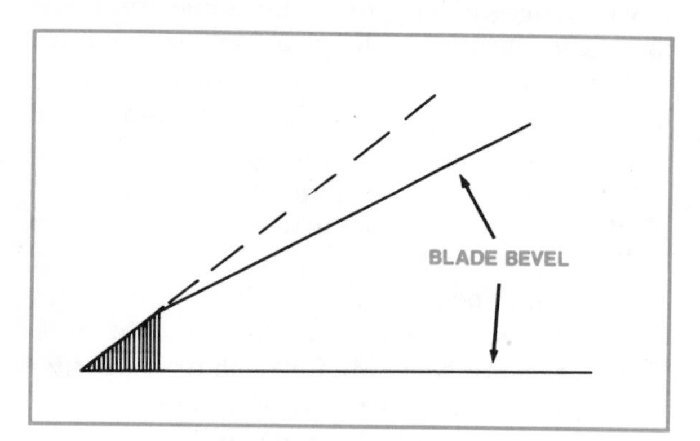

Blade Bevel Angle

Blades

Blades can be used for cutting, scraping or smoothing, depending on the one chosen. The blade in a utility knife can double as a linoleum

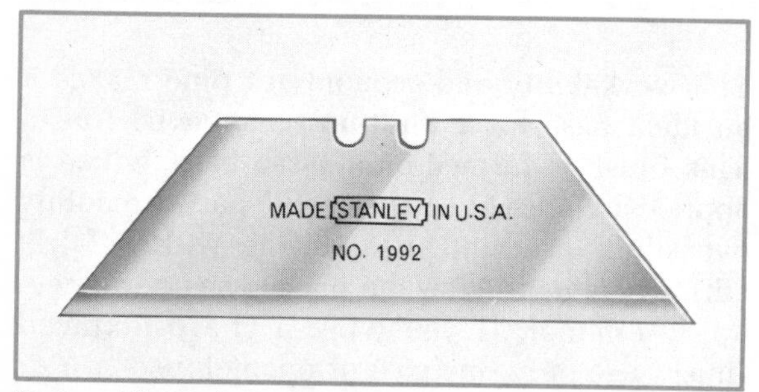

Courtesy of The Stanley Works

Utility Knife Blade

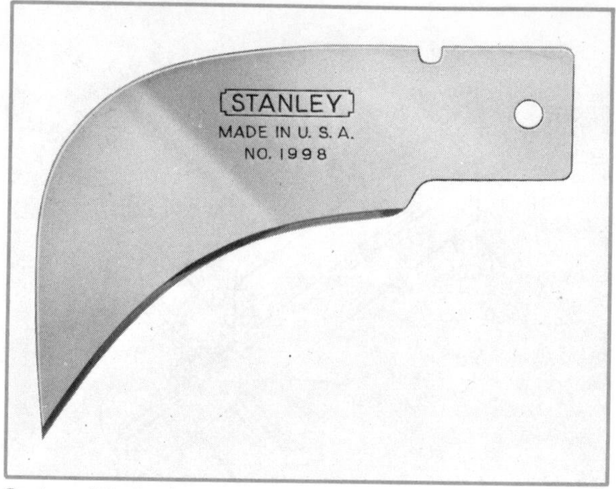

Courtesy of The Stanley Works

Linoleum Knife Blade

knife and is also good for removing paint. The drawknife blade, however, is designed only for removing excess wood. Linoleum knife blades are curved and are used primarily in cutting linoleum. The pocket knife will almost always have two blades and sometimes more. These blades are of different sizes to enable the operator to cut, scrape, whittle or sharpen in large or small areas. The blades in all knives should be sharpened frequently to maintain a good cutting edge. *SEE ALSO HAND TOOLS.*

Blade Teeth

The number of blade teeth (or points) per inch on a saw should be selected according to the material that needs to be cut. A blade that has five teeth per inch will have a coarser, faster cut, while 10 teeth per inch will give a slower, cleaner cut. A crosscut saw with eight teeth per inch provides a medium cut. Most saws have teeth that are beveled on both edges, forming small knife-like teeth, with alternating teeth bent outward for a cut wider than the blade's thickness. This insures free movement of the blade which avoids crimping. In the ripsaw, however, the teeth are not beveled; they are almost perpendicular to the cutting edge, instead. These teeth act as chisels, leaving small shavings instead of sawdust.

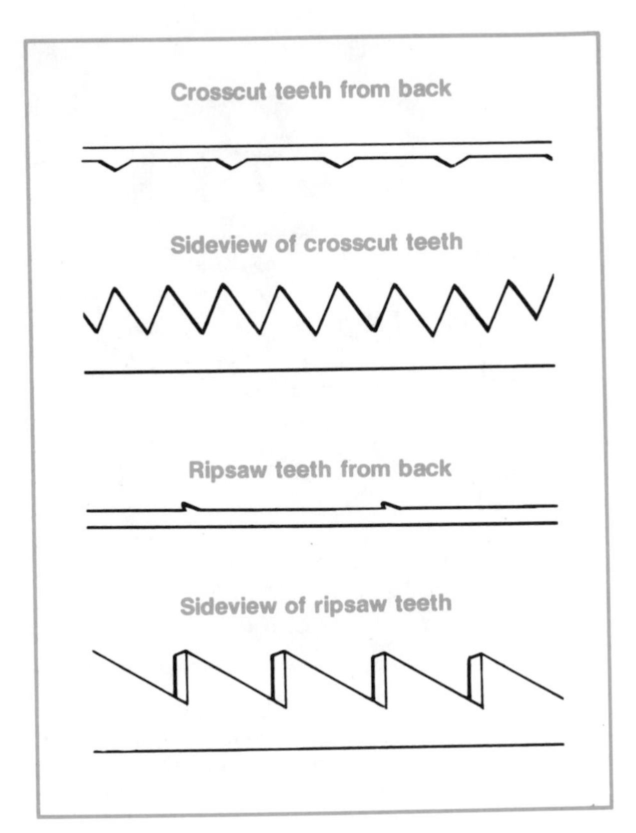

A general rule in choosing blade teeth is fine teeth for thin stock and coarse teeth for thick stock. For example, to cut a countertop sink opening, use a blade with coarse teeth, unless it is covered with a plastic laminate. In this case, use fine teeth to prevent chipping. For cutting sheet metal, select a fine-toothed blade for a smoother finish.

The teeth on most saws should be made from tempered spring steel so they can be filed and shaped. *SEE ALSO HAND TOOLS.*

Blanket Insulation

Blanket insulation is a flexible insulation made of mineral or vegetable fibers, used to provide insulation against loss of heat through conduction or convection. Proper insulation against heat, sound or vapor, installed in the walls, ceilings or roofs of homes provides for increased

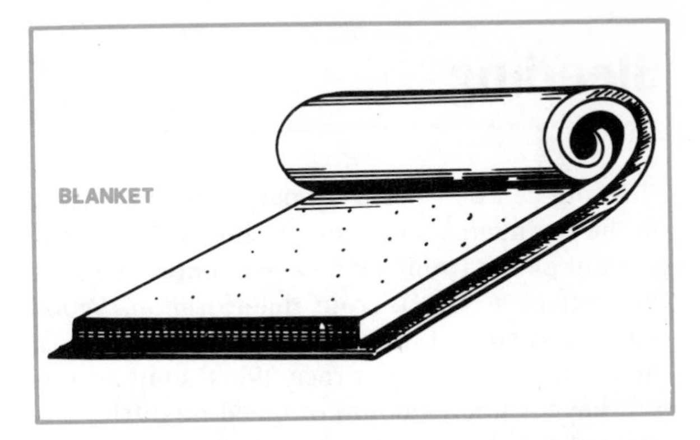

comfort as well as savings in fuel, power and equipment costs. Blanket insulation has a covering sheet usually surfaced with aluminum foil or other reflective insulation, which has a rim on each side to allow for attachment to framing members of a house. One side of the covering sheet may be asphalt-permeated to serve as a barrier against vapor. Blanket insulation is usually available in 15-inch rolls or strips of various lengths to accommodate installation between studs and joists. *SEE ALSO INSULATION.*

Bleaches & Bleaching

There are occasions when you want to make wood lighter than it is. Bleaching does this by removing some or all of its pigmentation. After bleaching, the general color of the wood is retained; only the color intensity is reduced.

Although there are many one-solution bleaches available, best results will be obtained by using the more thorough-working, two-solution ones. Following the instructions on the label, apply the first solution which chemically changes the pigments so that the second solution can remove them.

Start with a surface that is clean and free from oil, grease, dirt and the old finish (which would keep the bleach out). Finish with clear lacquer, to prevent the wood from yellowing.

Bleeding

Bleeding can be caused by paint solvents acting on the resins in some woods. This problem may prevent paints from drying and eventually cause the surface to crack from deterioration. Wood with knots should be coated with shellac to seal the resin. In spite of all precautions, some woods will have a small amount of bleeding during the first year. This will sometimes weather away, or it can often be washed off with detergent and water. *SEE ALSO PAINTS & PAINTING.*

Blemish

A defect, scar or mark on wood that affects only the surface, and tends to detract from the wood's appearance is referred to as a blemish.

Blender Repair

A blender is simply a motor-driven cutter that operates at the bottom of a glass container at varying speeds, depending upon a selection

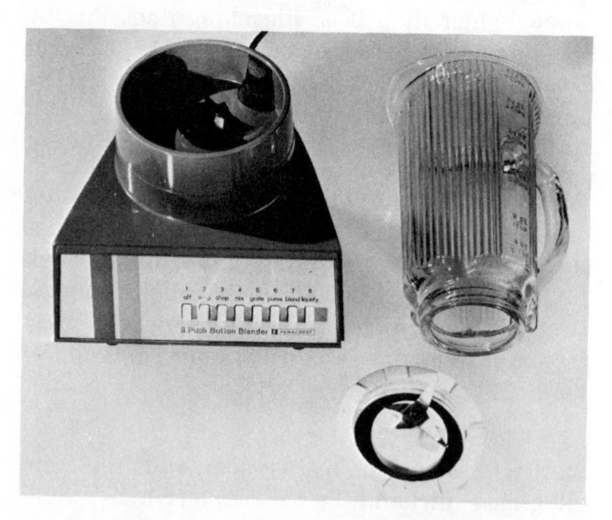

Primary parts of blender consist of motor base, container, and cutting unit, as seen above.

Coupling components are visible in this view showing base from above. When container with attached cutter unit is placed into position, the coupling halves mate to transfer power from motor to cutter unit.

usually provided by pushbuttons. The container and the shape of the cutter are designed so that the material being blended will tend to flow back into the cutter after once passing through. It's used for jobs such as cutting celery, chopping vegetables and making milkshakes. At high speeds it can be used to liquify practically all vegetables.

Other than breakage of the container, the problem you'll most likely find with a food blender will be the cutter itself. It could be a leak or damaged cutter blades. These blades can be replaced. After ordering new ones, unscrew the cutting unit from the bottom of the reservoir. Holding the coupling at the very bottom, loosen the nut or turn the shaft that holds the blades in place. Install the new ones exactly the way the old ones were removed. Use care not to dislodge or damage any of the sealing surfaces at the cutter. Handle the cutter only with heavy gloves or otherwise protect your fingers.

If the seal should leak, the same procedure is followed except the drive shaft between the coupling and the cutter is removed. Seals (if used) can then be pried away and reassembled. Be sure and reinstall any spacer washers or shims that may be used in the cutter unit. If both blade and seal appear to be damaged, the entire cutter should be replaced.

Disassembled cutter unit shows relative position of components. If cutter shaft or bearing is damaged, replace entire cutter unit. If only blade is damaged, simply release the part.

View of bottom of blender with cover removed shows position of motor and switch. Note leads going to tapped field windings in motor. The motor must be disassembled to replace brushes.

The motor coupling is simply two blocks that mate when in position. The driving one is attached directly to the motor shaft while the driven member is connected to the base of the cutter unit. The weight of the glass container is sufficient to hold the two sections of the coupling together when in place on the base.

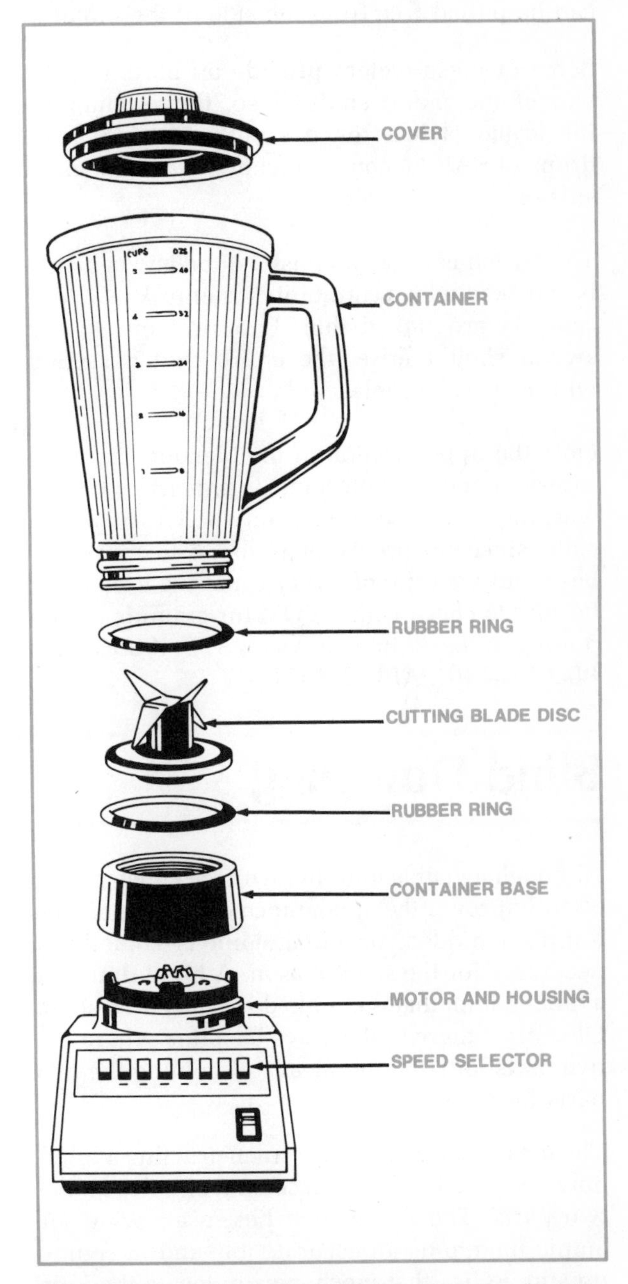

Drawing shows relative position of major blender components when blender is assembled for operation. Coupling halves separate when container is picked up off motor base.

The motor itself is usually a heavy-duty universal type motor with a number of taps to provide as many as ten or even more speeds. It's usually necessary to separate the base to make any repairs to the motor. Brushes may be held in place by removable brush clamps or by clips. After loosening a clip, the entire brush assembly can be pulled free from the side of the motor.

Some of these motors provide oil ports at each end of the motor shaft. If so, they should be lubricated at least once a year. Two or three drops of SAE-20 non-detergent motor oil should suffice.

The switch is usually a push button and can only be checked with a continuity tester or VOM. The contacts are not visible. If a problem in the switch should arise, the entire switch section will have to be replaced.

Only the upper section of the blender, the glass reservoir and the cutter unit, is immersible when washing. The base should only be wiped with a cloth since no provision is made to make the base unit waterproof. After repairing a blender, be sure to check with a VOM for grounds before putting it back into service. *SEE ALSO APPLIANCE REPAIR, SMALL.*

Blind Doweling

Although a visible joint in furniture construction often improves the appearance of a piece of furniture, a hidden, or blind, joint is sometimes necessary for the same reason. A blind dowel is a hidden joint that is easy to do in the home shop. Of course, there will always be a line where the two parts join, but the means of holding the two parts together is invisible.

The most important factor in constructing a blind dowel joint is the exact placement of holes on the two parts. The secret here lies in allowing for ample time to do an accurate job, and in setting up simple jigs that mechanically locate the hole on multiple pieces. The best method, whether for 2 or 24 pieces, is to plot the hole locations on one piece and use it as a sample for clamping

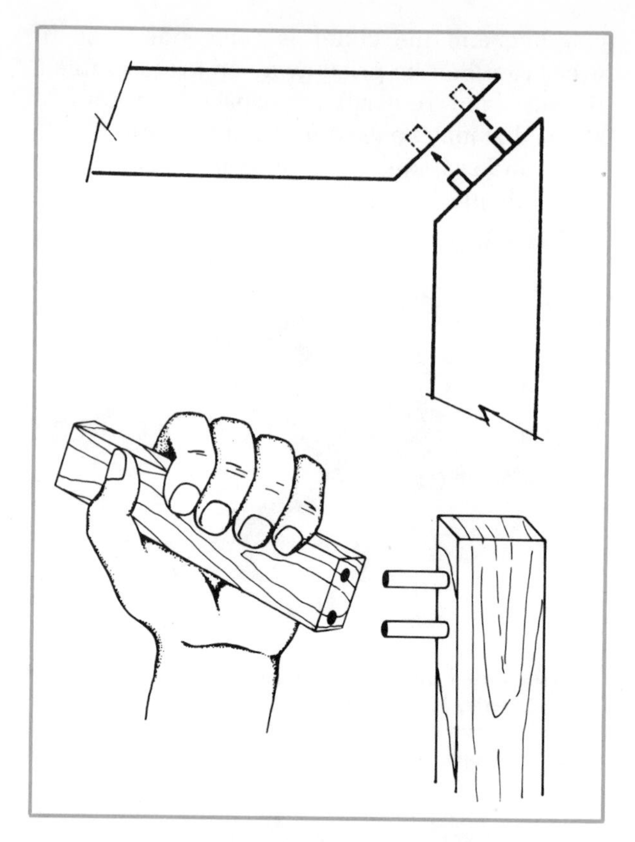

Blind doweling shown in cross-section.

blocks of wood to the drill-press table to create a locating-jig. Then all the other parts will be placed under the spindle correctly. In other words, locate the holes on a "mass production" basis as commercial companies do, and eliminate errors.

An incorrectly located hole can be fixed by gluing a dowel into the hole, allowing it to dry, and redrilling another hole in the right spot.

Blind Nailing

Blind nailing is a method of concealing nailheads in wood to give a smooth, finished appearance to its surface. One method of blind nailing involves lifting a small chip of wood from the surface with a chisel, driving the nail into the recess, and then gluing the chip back into place. Another commonly used method is to drive and set the

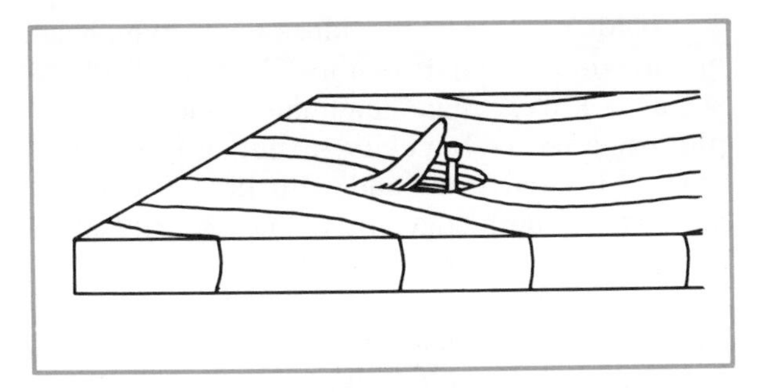

Blind Nailing

nail below the surface of the material, and then fill the opening with a wood filler. *SEE ALSO NAIL HIDING.*

Blind Stop

A member (usually a 3/4 by 1 3/8-inch strip of wood) which is attached to the exterior edge of the side and head jamb of a window is called a blind stop. It serves as a stop for the top sash, and also forms a rabbet against which blinds, screens, shutters or storm sashes are fastened. Sometimes the blind stop is milled as an integral part of the outside casing.

Blistering

Blistering, as the term applies to painting, is the name given the enclosed raised spots which sometimes appear on painted surfaces. These spots are the first signs of most water-caused paint failures. Blistering is not linked to excessive water on the finish, but is the result of moisture in or behind the wood trying to escape in the form of moisture-vapor. When the vapor meets a vapor-barrier material, it puts forth sufficient pressure to push the paint off the wall.

Before you repaint, locate and eliminate the source of moisture. It may be necessary to provide an escape for the water through vents. Blistering is usually localized and does not generally present the problem of removing the paint from the entire structure. Remove the loose, flaking paint with a wire brush, putty knife or scraper, and feather the edges with sandpaper so that they will not show when you repaint. When blistering is extensive, remove the old film down to the bare wood before priming and repainting. We recommend the use of a latex acrylic paint, which permits the passage of moisture-vapor while blocking moisture in liquid form. *SEE ALSO PAINTS & PAINTING.*

Block, Cinder

[SEE CONCRETE BLOCK.]

Blocked Sewer

Occasionally, sewer lines beyond the walls of the house become blocked. This is commonly caused by tree roots penetrating sewer pipe joints, but it can also be caused by an accumulation of waste and grease in the lines.

The first step in cleaning out a blocked sewer line is disposing of the sewage accumulated in the pipe above the clean-out plug (the place your tape will enter). You should drain all sinks and fixtures and bail the water out of the toilet to a normal level. Place a large container under the clean-out plug to catch the spillage. Loosen the plug just enough to let the fluid in the pipe run into the container at a moderate rate.

When the container is full, tighten the clean-out plug to stop the flow. Empty the container and repeat the process until all the fluid has been drained, then remove the plug to permit the insertion of the special clearing rod (either a plumber's snake or clean-out tape or auger). These rods have an assortment of end attachments to aid in boring or cutting through the obstructions.

Uncoil the tape into the sewer line and clear the blockage, then recoil the tape. If tree roots are causing the blockage, they may be repelled by flushing the sewer line with a solution of copper sulfate. All snakes and tapes should be uncoiled again out of doors and thoroughly hosed down to remove dirt and bacteria, then recoiled for future use. Care should be taken while using the tape not to let either end spring out and strike you. *SEE ALSO PLUMBING REPAIRS.*

Block Flooring

[SEE FLOOR CONSTRUCTION.]

Blocking

Blocking is the process by which wood blocks are glued to a particular section of furniture to build that section up to necessary size. Leg turnings, for example, sometimes have a square section which is smaller than the diameter of the largest turned area. It is possible to add bulk to the smaller square section by blocking. A good wood match, a good glue job and attention to grain direction are necessary for complete success. The same system, incidentally, can be used to bulk out areas on a cabriole leg so that considerably less wood is used than is the case when starting with a solid block large enough to do the job in itself.

Blocking is also a means of creating inlay effects on turnings. This is accomplished by gluing together contrasting woods to form the turning blank. Walnut and maple or birch and mahogany are examples of combinations that would produce obvious contrast.

Block Plane

The block plane is the smallest (anywhere from 3½ inches to 7 inches long) of the planes used in home workshops. Its size makes it easy to handle, especially when one hand is needed to hold the work and the other is needed for planing.

The blade or cutter of the block plane, which can be anywhere from 1 inch to 1¾ inches wide, is set at a lower angle than the blades in most planes, and its bevel is turned up. For this reason, it cuts faster and with little resistance, making a smooth edge, but not necessarily a true one because it is short.

The block plane is used to trim just a little from a board or an edge, and will produce a smooth cut for moldings, sidings and trim; or corners and chamfer on small pieces of wood. Because of the shallow angle of the blade, it is very good for planing end-grains, or "blocking-in," which is where the plane gets its name. *SEE ALSO HAND TOOLS.*

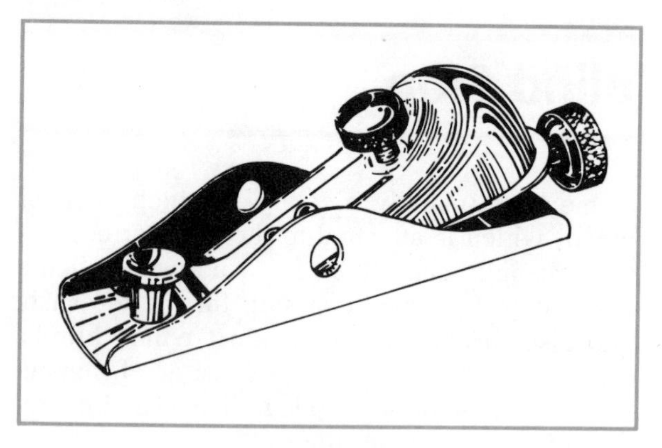

Block plane

Blocks, Concrete

[SEE CONCRETE BLOCK.]

Block Walls

Block walls can be built for houses, patios, fireplaces, fences or other areas inside or outside. Before actually building, plan the wall so that the block size can be determined. By planning, block cutting can be reduced and such items as doors or windows can be placed correctly. Check the local building codes to make sure the construction and design are in compliance with them.

Concrete blocks are laid in a similar way to bricks, except for three major differences: dry laying, joint size and bonding. When concrete blocks are laid, they must be dry. To prevent the blocks from getting wet, keep them covered to protect them from rain and stack them on boards or planks to prevent ground contact. The mortar joints between concrete blocks must be 3/8 inch rather than the 1/2 inch of bricklaying. Instead of continuously bonding long block walls, at each 20 foot interval there must be a control joint running the height of the wall, to keep the wall from cracking. Door and window openings, intersections of two walls and wall and column intersections should have control joints also. Use elastic caulking compound to seal the joint.

A control joint is needed at the intersection of bearing walls. Metal tiebars which are spaced no more than four feet apart, tie the walls together. The two inch bend at the tiebar's end must be embedded in cores which are filled with mortar or concrete supported by metal lathe.

To support floor beams or slabs, the courses must be solid masonry. Blocks which have the hollow cores filled in or ones with solid tops may be used. A metal lathe is embedded in the course underneath which supports the concrete or mortar filling the cores. This solid course may also be built as a capping on garden walls to keep water out.

A wall supporting a frame roof will need 1/2 inch anchor bolts 18 inches in length embedded in the mortar-or concrete-filled cores of the top two courses. Do not space the bolts more than four feet apart.

Cavity walls, such as the ones for houses, need 4 x 6 inch wall ties made of noncorrosive metal which are placed 32 inches apart in every other course.

Insulation of block walls can be strengthened by packing vermiculite, a granular insulation, in the cores.

Two coats of either portland cement plaster or a 1/2 inch coat of the mortar used to lay the blocks may be troweled on the blocks to make them watertight. *SEE ALSO CONCRETE BLOCK.*

Blonde Finishing

Blonde finishing is done either by rubbing a cream-colored paint on the unfinished wood before applying a protective coating, (such as lacquer, varnish or shellac) over its surface, or by removing color from the wood with a bleach and applying the protective coating. There was a period when blonde finishing was more popular than it is today.

To blonde finish with paint, begin by sanding the wood to a smooth finish. Mix equal parts of an oil-base paint with paint thinner or turpentine. The paint should be a light color, such as white or yellow. After the paint and thinner are mixed well, brush them on the wood and wipe it off with a dry cloth. The blonde effect is produced by the amount of paint which is left on the wood. Let the paint dry for about six hours and complete the procedure by putting a protective coating on top. The first protective coat must be shellac so that the thin paint film is not dissolved.

Bleaching is the second method of blonde finishing. Most of the wood's pigmentation is removed by bleaching: walnut turns a cream color, mahogany turns a pale rose color and other light woods sometimes turn white. Bleaching causes the wood's color tone to remain the same but decreases its intensity.

Clean or sand the wood before applying any bleach. Any grease, oil, old finishes or dirt remaining on the wood will cause resistance to the bleach, producing uneven bleaching. Although bleaches may be purchased at any paint or hardware store, the best ones are normally found in paint stores, in either one or two solution products.

To begin the bleaching, very carefully apply the first solution which chemically changes the pigments onto the surface, evenly saturating or wetting the wood. A clean white rag or a nylon brush may be used. If the wood repels the wetting, use fine steel wool to help work the bleach into the wood. Leave this first solution until it has dried about 15 minutes or longer. Then brush the second solution on top, making sure that it saturates evenly also. Allow the second solution to dry at least 12 hours before continuing to the next step. If a lighter color is wanted after the second coat dries, another coat of the second bleaching solution may be applied. When the desired color has been obtained, wash the bleach off with clear water while scrubbing with a brush, or neutralize the bleach by rubbing a mixture of white vinegar and water onto the wood surface with fine steel wool. Allow 24 to 48 hours for drying, then lightly sand the surface.

A less efficient method of bleaching is to combine the two solutions for one application. Two parts of the first solution to five parts of the second solution are normally combined. Because application methods do vary with different brands, be sure to read the directions carefully.

When using the strong bleach solutions, wear rubber gloves to keep from irritating the skin. Empty the solution amounts to be used into glass containers to prevent discoloring of the unused material. Safety goggles or some kind of eye protection should be worn while applying the bleach. An old pair of sunglasses may be used if your face is kept away from the wood.

After the bleach has dried completely, apply a protective coating. For the lightest result, clear lacquer which is brushed or sprayed on may be used. Thin coats of white shellac or a pale-drying varnish may be applied also. *SEE ALSO WOOD FINISHING.*

Blowtorch

A torch which provides extreme heat is known as a blowtorch. Two kinds are available: the gasoline type and the alcohol type which is smaller and works on pressurized petroleum. Blowtorches are mainly used for solder-joint work, such as sweating brass and copper pipes and fittings, for removal of old paint and for larger jobs, such as thawing pipes.

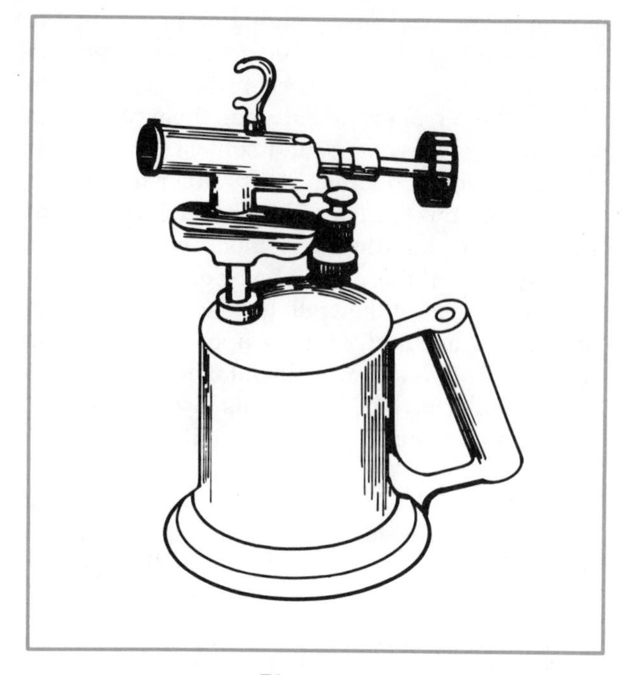

Blowtorch

The manufacturer's instructions should be read before using the torch because operating information may vary with different makes. Be cautious at all times when working with a blowtorch. Try to prevent filling it with fuel in a closed room. If the torch is to be stored for an extended time, it is best to empty the gas to prevent gummy deposits from forming.

Generally, the operating procedure for blowtorches begins by filling the fuel container of the torch about three-fourths full. If possible, white or non-leaded gasoline is used to lessen fumes. Once the valve is closed, the plunger is usually pumped about fifteen strokes. Next, the iron cup beneath the burner is filled with gasoline or alcohol, which can be done by holding one's hand over the end of the combustion chamber with the torch valve on. This permits some gas to dribble into the priming cup. Before lighting the cup, be sure to wipe the torch body dry. A less messy way of filling the cup is to slowly let denatured alcohol flow into the cup through a small syringe. This will produce an almost smokeless flame instead of a sooty gas flame. In either method, do not overflow the cup with gas. Light the fuel in the cup with a match, letting it burn until almost dry. Turn the torch valve on, holding the lighted match beneath the burner shell's holes. When the vaporized gasoline ignites, the torch is ready to use. By operating the control valve, the flame size can be increased or decreased.

The torch may be turned off by gently closing the valve opening. The filler should then be partially opened to release the air pressure so that the torch may be stored safely. As soon as the air quits hissing, the valve must be tightened again. *SEE ALSO PLUMBER'S TOOLS & EQUIPMENT.*

Blueprints

Blueprints and drawings (plans) are the chief means of conveying an idea for a new product to the workmen who produce it. Often several copies of a drawing are needed for a job, and since it would be too expensive to supply an original drawing to everyone, duplicates in the form of prints are made. Such prints are often called "blueprints", because the original type of print was blue with white lines. A blueprint is the least expensive print to make; it holds up well under continuous use, and it is resistant to fading. It is difficult, however, to make changes or notes on the prints because of the blue background.

Before prints can be made, tracings of the original drawing must be made on thin, transparent paper or cloth. This tracing serves the same purpose as a negative in photography. It is placed over light-sensitized, chemically-coated paper and exposed to a strong light which produces an exact copy of the drawing.

The process of drawing an object or objects larger or smaller than actual size is called "drawing to scale", (or making the drawings in a relative proportion). All blueprints and drawings mush have on them the scale used. Scales are designated as follows: 1/4″ = 1′0″; or 1/4″ = 1′3″; or 1″ = 3″; or 1/2″ = 1′, etc.

A set of house plans contains floor plans, elevations, site plan, roof layout, a legend (definition of all symbols used on the print) and elevation in section, together with some details of important parts of the structure. Two or three sheets are needed to detail the smaller parts of the structure. Many details are shown in full size while others are drawn to scale.

Reading blueprints is a matter of understanding the types of drawings, lines, symbols and notes used. It is valuable to the handyman to have some knowledge of the terminology used by architects on prints. The ability to check your blueprints thoroughly permits you to make changes before the work has started, as changes in plans after the work has begun can be very costly. Basic architectural symbols are uniform in meaning, enabling you to read any set of plans, as well as to draw your own, once you are familiar with the "blueprint language".

Dimension lines on blueprints are continuous unbroken lines with the size noted near the line. Generally, all dimensions over one foot are expressed in feet and inches. Dimension lines are easily read, but can be misinterpreted. An exterior frame wall is measured from the outside face of a stud to the next outside face of a stud. Masonry walls are dimensioned from the outside face of a wall. Brick veneer walls are measured from the face of the studs just as frame walls are, but the distance from the stud facing to the outside face of the brick is dimensioned separately. These same rules apply for interior partitions, with one exception. Stud partitions are dimensioned to the center line of the partitions. All others are dimensioned to the masonry face. Vertical dimensions are always measured from the finished floor line.

Abbreviations are commonly used in blueprints, such as "o.c." for on centers, meaning that all framing is measured from the center of one framing member to the center of the next; "wc" means water closet or toilet; "mc" is used for medicine cabinet; "t&g" indicates tongue-and-groove, applying to sheathing, flooring and paneling; "gi", galvanized iron; and "ds" is used to show a downspout. Circled numbers indicate the type of door to be used.

Blue Stain

Blue stain is a blue-black wood discoloration which is created by a fungus growth in sapwood. It is most commonly found in pine wood. Excessive moisture, such as moist ground, rain, dew or water vapor, causes blue stain to develop. Even though this stain is not decay, the moist conditions can lead to development of decay-producing fungi.

Applying a liquid chlorine bleach or sanding the wood can reduce blue stain if it has not already penetrated too deeply. The bleaching process is not recommended for oak or poplar wood. Keeping moisture out of the wood will help produce a more permanent cure. Unpainted wood may be treated with a preservative which is water-repellent. *SEE ALSO LUMBER.*

Board

A board is a flat rectangular piece of wood which is less than two inches thick and more than four inches wide. *Board* is a technical term which describes narrow sections of lumber as opposed to strips or planks. A board can be made from various kinds of wood. *SEE ALSO LUMBER.*

Board Foot

A board foot is a measurement of lumber, which is 1 inch thick, 12 inches wide and 12 inches long and is equivalent to 144 cubic inches. Since lumber is priced and billed by the board foot, it is to the handyman's advantage to become thoroughly familiar with figuring board feet. Naturally, all lumber that you purchase will not be these exact dimensions, but *will* be a portion of a board foot and will be priced accordingly.

You can calculate the board feet in *any* length of lumber by multiplying the nominal thickness in inches by the nominal width in inches by the length in feet and dividing by twelve. Lumber that is less than 1 inch in thickness is figured as 1 inch.

Boat Anchors & Anchoring

[SEE RECREATIONAL BOATS & BOATING.]

Boat Design & Construction

[SEE BASS BOAT; SAILING PRAM.]

Boathouses, Docks, Piers & Floats

[SEE PIERS; FLOATS; DOCKS & BOATHOUSES]

Boat Ladders

[SEE RECREATIONAL BOATS & BOATING.]

Boats & Boating

[SEE RECREATIONAL BOATS & BOATING.]

Boiled Oil

Boiled oil is named inaccurately, since the oil is *not* actually boiled. It is the result of adding certain chemical agents called driers, such as manganese oxide, to linseed oil while the oil is still hot from processing. Boiled linseed oil dries in less time than either raw or refined oil and is added to varnishes, enamels and oil-base paints to facilitate drying. *SEE ALSO LINSEED OIL; PAINTS & PAINTING.*

Bolt Cutters

Bolt cutters are specially designed to make quick work out of the toughest cutting jobs, like concrete form ties, wire mesh, rods, cables and bolts. They are available in over-all lengths of 14 inches to 42 inches and will cut pieces anywhere from 1/4 inch to 1/2 inch in diameter. The density of the material to be cut determines the needed strength of the blade, or jaws. The blades are available in styles that make either a center or flush cut, and because they will break before they will bend, replacements are available for these. *SEE ALSO HAND TOOLS.*

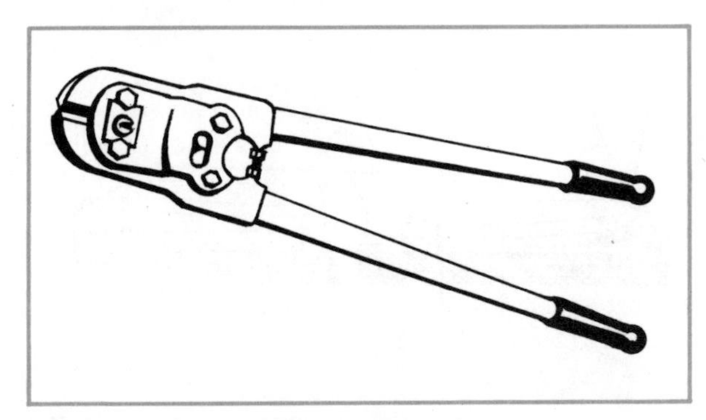

Bolt cutters

Bolts

[SEE FASTENERS.]

Bonnet

The upper section of a faucet through which the stem or spindle passes is called a bonnet. Frequently referred to as a packing nut or cap nut, this bonnet contains the interior working parts of a faucet assembly.

Remove the bonnet for faucet repairs by turning it counterclockwise with a pipe wrench. To avoid marring a chrome-plated bonnet, wrap it with adhesive tape, or pad the jaws of the wrench with felt. It isn't necessary to remove the handle screw; once the bonnet is loose, you can lift out the entire assembly. If the bonnet seems to jam during removal, it can usually be freed by turning the faucet handle in the direction you turn it to turn on the water. *SEE ALSO FAUCETS & FAUCET REPAIRS.*

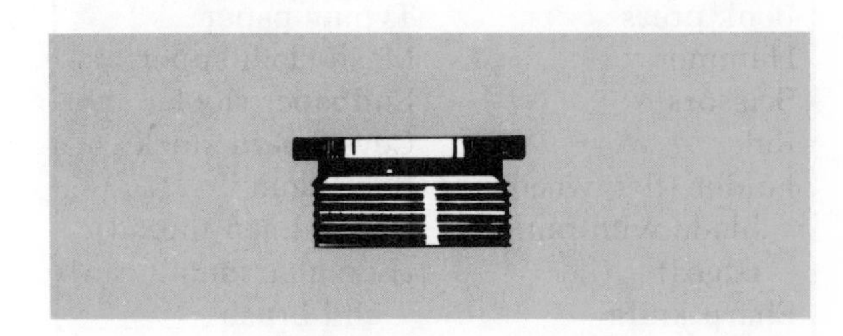

A packing nut or bonnet.

Bookbinding

Is your favorite book falling apart from old age and hard use? There is no need either to throw it

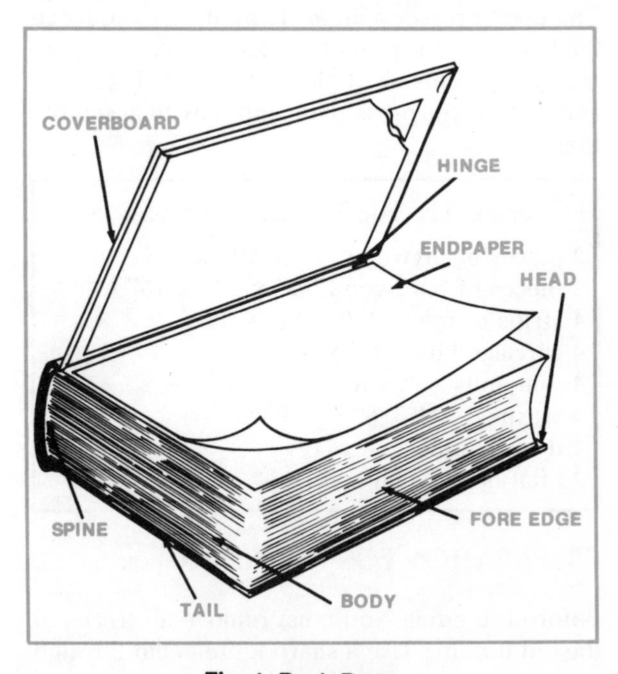

Fig. 1. Book Parts

out or keep it in its tattered condition. You can give the book a new life by removing the old binding and replacing it with a handsome new one (see Figure 1).

MATERIALS LIST

Except for an easy-to-make book press, bookbinding requires only common, inexpensive tools. You can buy the materials at a bookbinder's supply store.

Book press	Typing paper
Hammer	Mesh-cloth super
Scissors	Endpaper stock
Ruler	Coverboard stock
Folder (flat, wooden blade with rounded edges)	Book cloth
	No. 25 linen thread
	Hide glue (small can) and brush
Sharp knife	
Dull, fine-toothed saw	Library paste (small jar)
Large needle	
Crochet hook	"Liquid Cloth" (or other flexible glue)
Waxed paper or aluminum foil	

MAKING THE BOOK PRESS

The book press is a large clamp used to squeeze the book into the proper shape and to assure that the glued joints are tight and strong. Figures 2 and 3 show the press parts and how to assemble them.

Materials List For The Book Press

2 pieces of plywood, $^3/_4$" x 10" x 15"
2 pieces of hardwood, $^1/_4$" x 10" x 15"
4 strips of metal, $^1/_8$" x $^3/_4$" x 15"
4 carriage bolts, $^1/_2$" x 6"
4 wingnuts, $^1/_2$" x 6"
4 washers, $^1/_2$" x 6"
1 drawer pull
20 flat-head wood screws

PREPARATION FOR REBINDING

Before rebinding, you must remove all traces of the old binding. Use a sharp knife to cut through the endpapers at the hinge, both front and back.

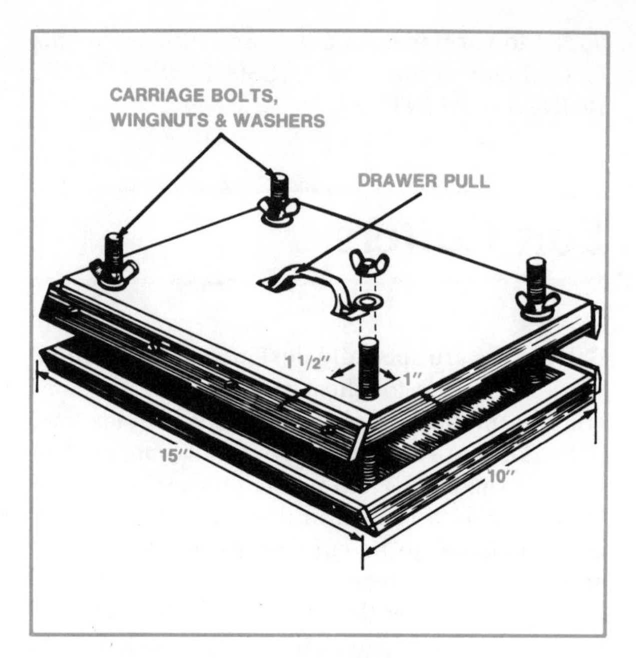

Fig. 2. Book Press

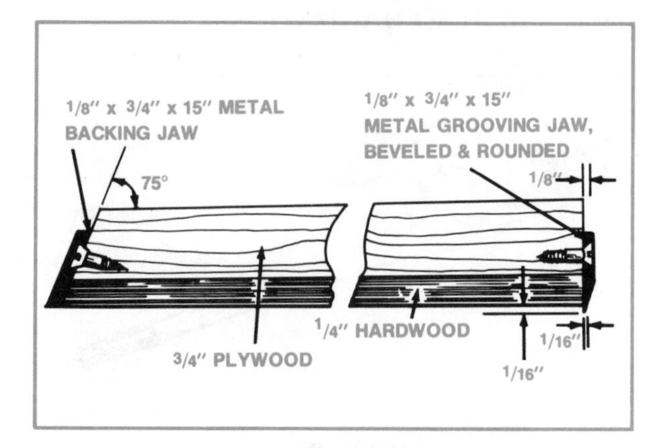

Fig. 3. Cross section of press jaw.

Carefully tear the endpapers from the body of the book and discard them. Next, clamp the body of the book between the backing jaws of the book press so that the spine is exposed. Wet the glue, then gently scrape it off with a knife. Remove all of the paper, glue and mesh, taking care not to damage the folded groups of pages (signatures).

When you have cleaned the spine, remove the book from the press and open the first signature to expose the threads at the center. Cut all the stitches in each signature, and then carefully separate the signatures from each other.

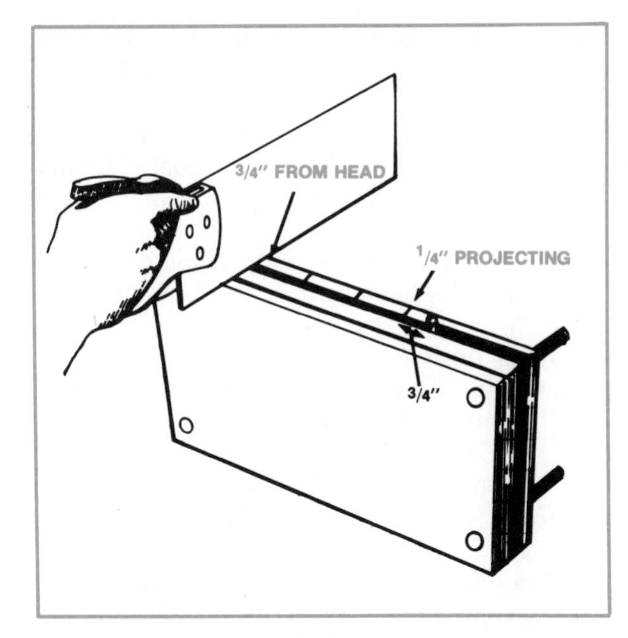

Fig. 4. Cut at least four grooves at uneven intervals across the backs of the signatures. Each cut should go just deep enough to penetrate the innermost sheet of each signature. The end cuts should be 3/4" from the head and tail of the book.

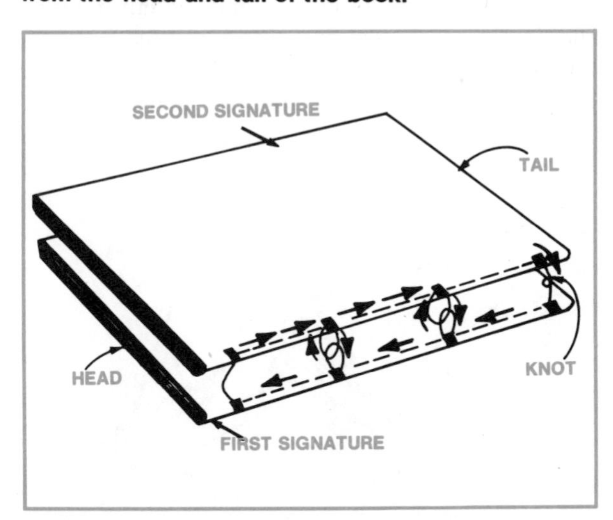

Fig. 5. In sewing the second signature, pass the needle out, down and then upward through the loop protruding from the first signature. Pass the needle back into the same saw cut from which it came in the second signature.

You will see that each signature has a crease from head to tail near the fold. This crease must be hammered out. Cover the signature with a sheet of waxed paper to protect it, and hammer gently along the crease.

You may have torn some of the pages along the fold when you separated the signatures. If so, paste a 1/2" strip of typing paper down the inside of the fold of the page, from head to tail. Place each repaired page in the press, inside of fold up, and squeeze for 3 to 4 minutes. Collect the signatures and let them stand in the press overnight.

MAKING A NEW BINDING

The new binding should be assembled carefully in the order of the following steps to make the finished book as strong and attractive as possible. When gluing or hammering various parts, protect the book and cover with sheets of waxed paper or aluminum foil.

Step 1: Assemble the signatures in the correct order. Clamp the signatures in the press with about 1/4" of the folded edges projecting from the backing jaws. Use a dull saw to cut at least four grooves across the exposed fold edges of the signatures, as shown in Figure 4.

Step 2: You are now ready to sew the first two signatures together. Thread the needle with about two feet of linen thread. Pass the needle into the saw cut at the tail of the signature. Run the thread along the inside fold and out at the saw cut at the head. Then, using a crochet hook, pick a loop of thread out through each of the other saw cuts. Next, lay the second signature on top of the first, and pass the needle into the saw cut at the head. Sew the signatures together with a lock stitch, as shown in Figure 5. As you sew, pull the loops just tight enough to hold the signatures without buckling. When you have finished sewing the signatures together, knot the free end of the thread (from tail cut of first signature) to the remaining thread length (from tail cut of second signature).

Step 3: The remaining signatures are added one at a time, using a continuous length of thread as shown in Figure 6. When you come to the end of the thread, tie on another length and continue. Make sure the knot is *inside* the signature. When all of the signatures are sewn together, secure the thread with two or three extra kettle stitches and cut off the thread about 1" long.

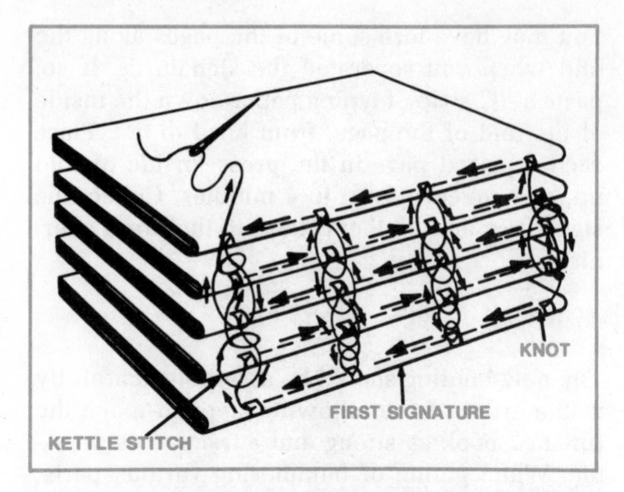

Fig. 6. To sew on the remaining signatures, pass the thread out of each saw cut, down and behind the stitch below and then back into the same saw cut. At the end of each signature, make a kettle stitch by passing the thread one more time through the loop formed in making the regular lock stitch. This stitch will hold the signature to the one below.

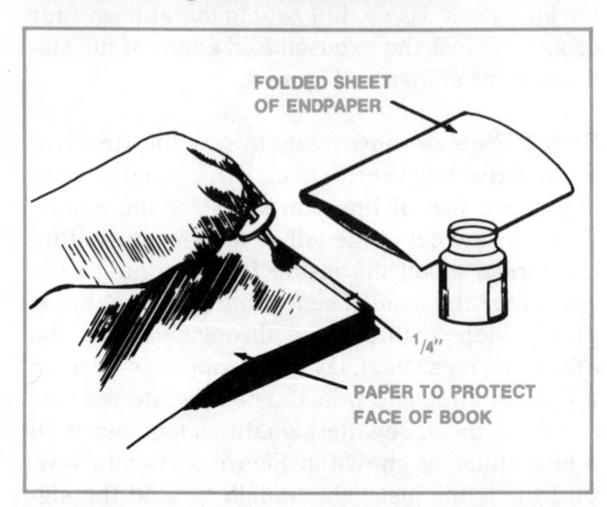

Fig. 7. To attach the endpaper, apply a strip of library paste 1/4" wide down the fold on an outside signature. Then press one endpaper in place. Turn the body over and attach the other endpaper in the same way. Place the book, with endpapers in place, in the press and let the paste dry under pressure.

Step 4: After sewing, the book's spine (the folded signature edges) will be thick. Hammer the spine until it is only as thick as the rest of the book.

Step 5: To make new endpapers, cut endpaper stock or a sheet of strong paper to exactly the size of the book body (both sides and spine). Attach the endpapers as shown in Figure 7.

Step 6: You are now ready to shape the spine of the book. Begin by applying a thin coat of Liquid Cloth to the spine and tapping the spine into a rounded shape with a hammer. Push in the fore edge with your thumb to help shape the spine. Then place the book in the book press, leaving about 3/16" exposed at the backing jaws. Shape the spine further as shown in Figure 8. After shaping, apply more Liquid Cloth and work it into the spine with your fingers.

Step 7: Finish the spine by cutting a strip of meshcloth super long enough to span the distance between the kettle stitches at the head and tail. The super should be wide enough to extend 1 1/4" beyond each side of the spine. Rub the super onto the glue on the spine. Then cut a strip of typing paper as wide and as long as the spine, and glue it over the super, as shown in Figure 9.

Step 8: To cover the book, begin by cutting two pieces of coverboard exactly as long as the body and 1/4" wider. Cut a piece of book cloth large enough to wrap around the book with 3/4" over-

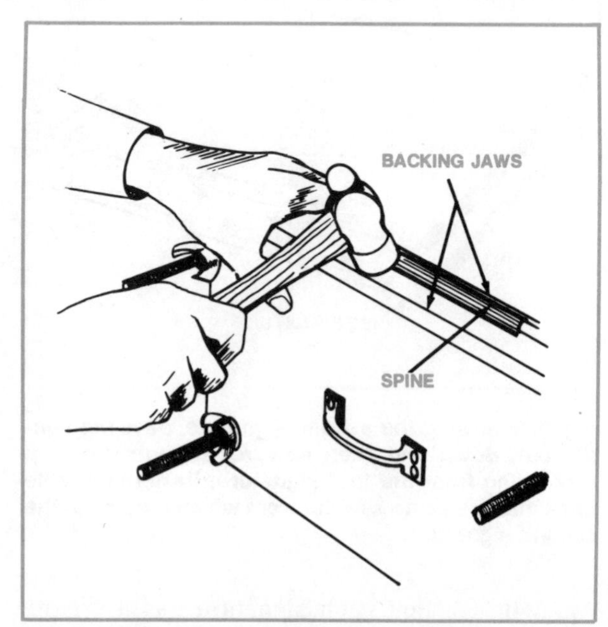

Fig. 8. In shaping the spine, gently hammer the spine with glancing blows to turn each side over against the backing jaws. Hammer the full length of the spine to produce a smooth, well-rounded spine.

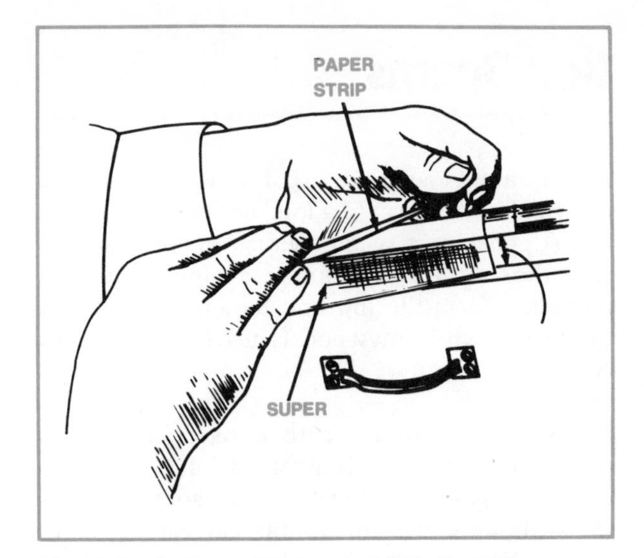

Fig. 9. Apply the super to complete the spine.

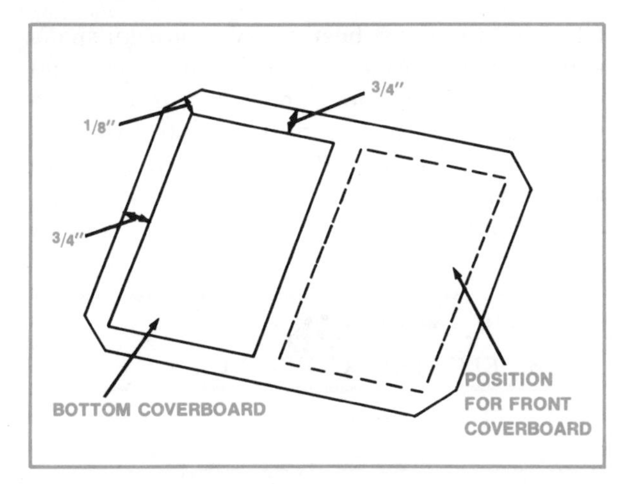

Fig. 10. To build the cover, first place the back coverboard to the on the rectangle.

lapping on all edges. On the inside of the book cloth, mark two rectangles showing exactly where the front and back of the body will fit. Cut off each corner of the book cloth to within $^1/_8$" of the corners of the rectangles. Coat these two rectangles with thin, runny hide glue. Heat the glue in a pan of water if necessary to make it thin enough. Then attach the bottom coverboard and spine-sized paper strip as shown in Figures 10 and 11.

Step 9: Place the other coverboard on top of the body so that it overhangs the body by $^1/_8$" at the fore edge, the head and the tail, leaving $^1/_8$" of the body exposed at the spine. Then, holding everything tightly, fold the book cloth up and over the top coverboard and rub it down firmly with the folder. Work the excess glue from between the coverboard and the book cloth. Rub down the back of the book in the same way. Then open the book and remove the body.

Step 10: Fold the edges of the book cloth neatly over the coverboards, and rub them down to squeeze out the excess glue. Then place the body back inside the cover, and clamp the book in the book press with the spine protruding from the

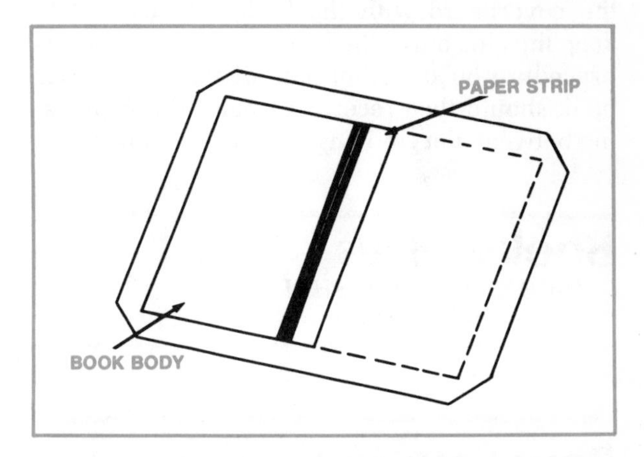

Fig. 11. Position the body of the book on the coverboard and add a strip of paper, cut to spine size, along the inside of the book cloth where the book's spine will hit.

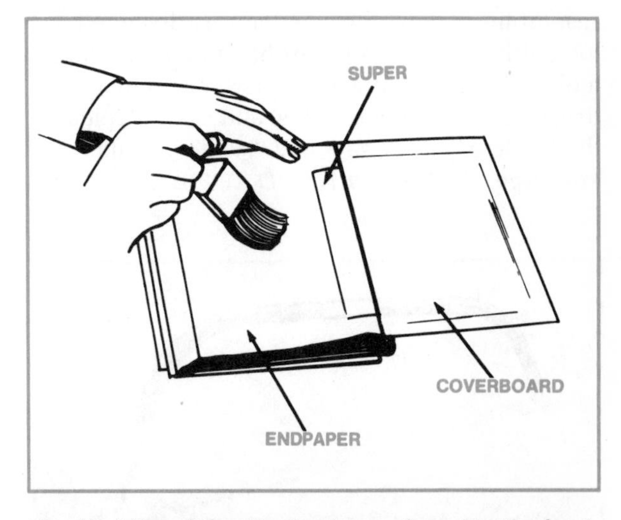

Fig. 12. After gluing the front coverboard to the book cloth, attach each exposed edge of the super to one of the endpapers, and glue the endpapers to the coverboards.

grooving jaws. Tighten the book press to create the hinge groove along the spine. Leave the book in the press overnight.

Step 11: Remove the book from the press. Open the cover, and trim the turned-over edges of the book cloth to a width of 3/8″ from the edges of the coverboards. *Do not* trim across the spine.

Step 12: Spread a thin layer of glue on the outside flap of the endpaper. Attach the exposed edge of the mesh super to the endpaper as shown in Figure 12. The press the endpaper onto the coverboard with the folder. Be careful to keep the glue out of the hinge groove. Repeat this procedure on the other side of the book. Your book should then receive a final 24-hour pressing between the grooving jaws of the book press.

Bookshelves

[SEE SHELVES & SHELF CONSTRUCTION.]

Bow Saw

Characterized by a tubular steel frame which resembles a bow, the bow saw is designed for log cutting and pruning. Although a light weight tool, it is strong and can, therefore, cut green, dry, soft and hardwoods fast and easy. Typically, the blade of a bow saw is 3/4″ wide and its teeth are large. *SEE ALSO HAND TOOLS.*

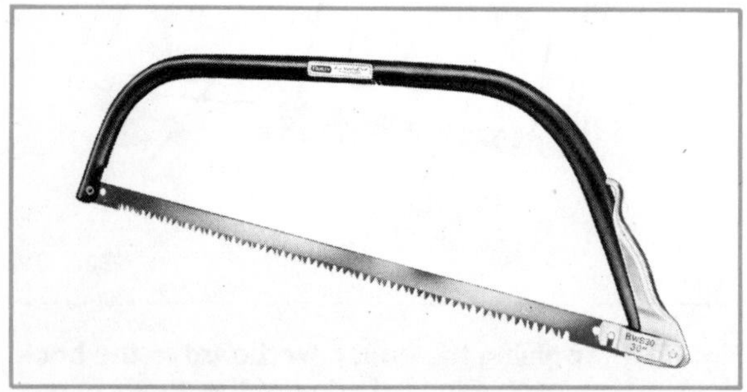

Courtesy of The Stanley Works

Bow Saw

Box Beams

Box beams are built up from lumber and plywood in the form of a long hollow box, which will support more weight across an opening than will the individual members alone. Lumber members form the top and bottom (flanges) of the beam, while plywood is used for the sides (webs).

Economical and easy to construct, nailed plywood box beams offer a good solution in residential construction for problems such as framing wide openings for double car garage doors and fabricating ridge beams.

Glued plywood box beams, having greater spans and heavier loadings, are used in commercial structures where wide, unobstructed areas are needed. These beams must be carefully designed and constructed under controlled conditions. *SEE ALSO WALL & CEILING CONSTRUCTION.*

Boxes, Wiring

[SEE ELECTRICAL WIRING.]

Box Sill

A box sill is a type of sill assembly, which is the base member of a house frame structure which supports all the frame weight, except the load carried by the inside bearing walls. A box sill is commonly made of wood, and is not needed when the outside walls of the house are made of brick or concrete. A box sill consists of a header, a horizontally-placed supporting member, placed along the edge of a sill plate, which is fastened to the foundation wall with bolts. Joists are placed at right angles to the header and rest on the sill. One type of box sill has brick fill placed between the joists, which acts as a retardant to fire and draft. Another type has no sill plate, but

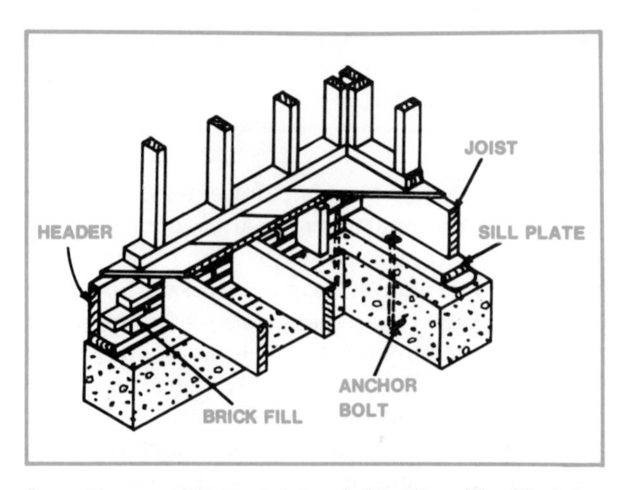

Box sill assembly containing brick fill, with sill plate.

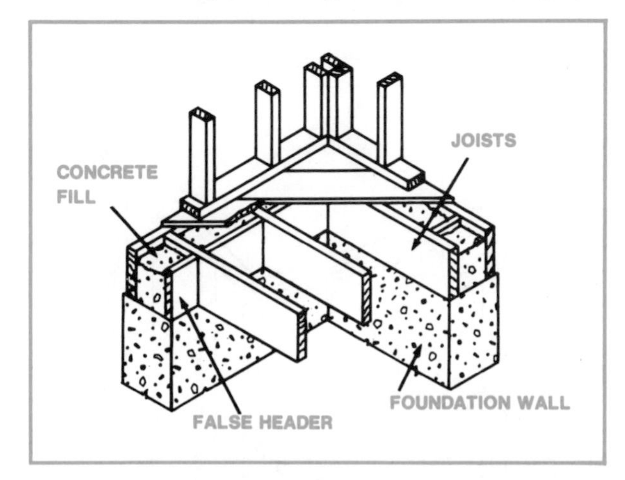

Box sill assembly with concrete fill, no sill plate.

a header placed directly on the foundation and concrete fill between this header and other shorter, false headers attached between the joists by nailing. This concrete fill also acts as a shield against fire, draft and termites. *SEE ALSO FLOOR CONSTRUCTION.*

Boxwood Rule

The boxwood rule is made mainly in 1′ and 2′ lengths. Its folded or extended position is held by the friction of its hinged joints. Extended, it has a smooth, flat surface to lay on the work — handy when a line must be drawn along it. Available with numerals running from left to

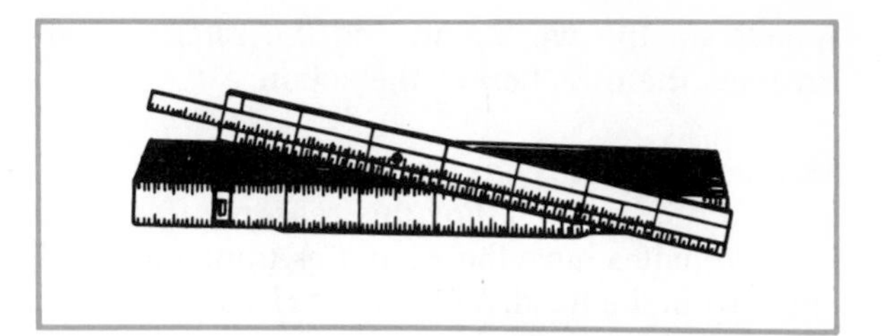

Boxwood Rule

right (standard), its numerals may also be positioned parallel to the rule length, running in both directions. This double calibration makes it easy to take quick readings from either end in difficult locations, as in overhead work. *SEE ALSO HAND TOOLS.*

Box Wrenches

Box wrenches have an advantage in their great strength. The box construction, composed of a 12-notch circle, is sturdier than the open-end wrench. It is also thinner, which allows the wrench to fit into tighter places than an open-end wrench. Also, the box wrench will not slip off the head of a nut or bolt the way an open jaw wrench will.

In making a turn with a box wrench, the wrench must be picked up and repositioned before it is turned again. This process is slower than working with an open-end wrench, and for this reason, there are combination open-end box wrenches. The box end can then be used for the tougher jobs, like breaking loose tight nuts, and the open-end for the easier jobs. These wrenches also come in ratcheting style, which

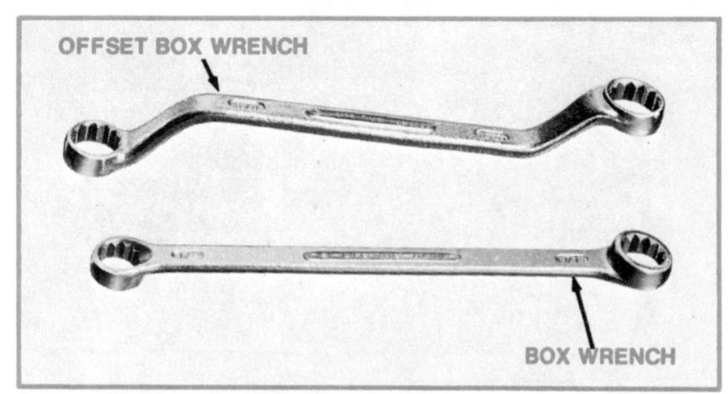

Courtesy of The Cooper Group (Crescent Tools)

speeds up the work. Turning the ratchet over reverses the direction of the action.

Skinned knuckles are a common problem in using a box wrench. For this reason, offset box end wrenches have their handles tipped at a 15° angle from the head. *SEE ALSO HAND TOOLS.*

Braces

A brace, when the term applies to a hand tool, is a hand-held, crank-type drill. Braces are used to bore through all the materials for which a power drill is used, but have the advantage of not requiring electricity. They are also much less expensive and operate almost noiselessly. They do, however, take longer to do the job and require a great deal more energy on the part of the worker. Some braces are fitted with a ratchet to increase the ratio of drill revolutions per handle turn.

The corner brace has the handle bow set at an angle to facilitate boring holes in close quarters and close to walls.

The short brace has a horizontal handle which, when turned back and forth, activates the drill.

The term *brace* also refers to a method of holding building materials in place, often by nailing them in the form of a triangle. *SEE ALSO HAND TOOLS.*

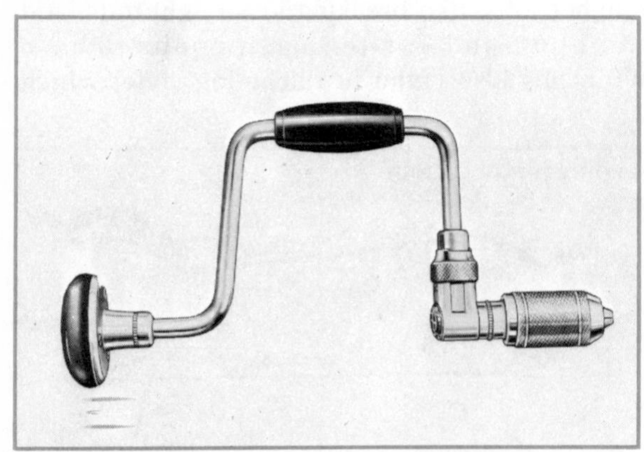

Courtesy of The Stanley Works

Brace

Bracing

Bracing is a type of support for exterior walls of a house frame, particularly at corners, to help decrease lateral stress and give the framework a more rigid structure. Bracing involves fastening a wood or metal brace between, across or against the frame members; 1 x 4 lumber cut to the necessary length is commonly used for brace construction. Bracing is especially needed when an opening, such as a window, interferes with the diagonal course of the framework. *SEE ALSO WALL & CEILING CONSTRUCTION.*

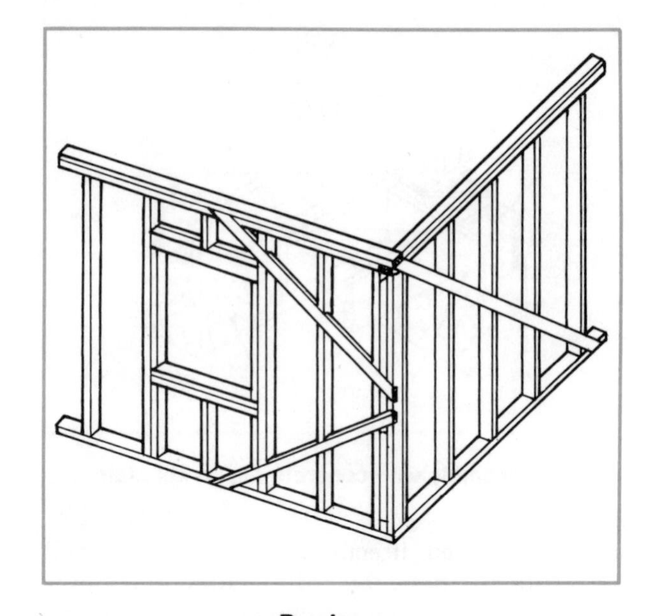

Bracing

Brad Awl

The brad awl is smaller than the common awl, but like the awl, is used to make starting holes for screws. The brad awl has a flat tip like a very small chisel. It should be started into the wood with the edge across the grain, thereby cutting the wood fibers. This allows the brad awl to make a deeper hole than the scratch awl. *SEE ALSO HAND TOOLS.*

Brads

A brad is a thin nail with a small round head. This head is much smaller than the head of a finishing nail. Brads are sold by length ranging from 3/8" to 1 1/2". Usually they are used in fine woodworking jobs, such as nailing parquetry to the subfloor, cabinetmaking and fastening wall and furniture molding, where countersinking the nailheads is necessary. *SEE ALSO FASTENERS.*

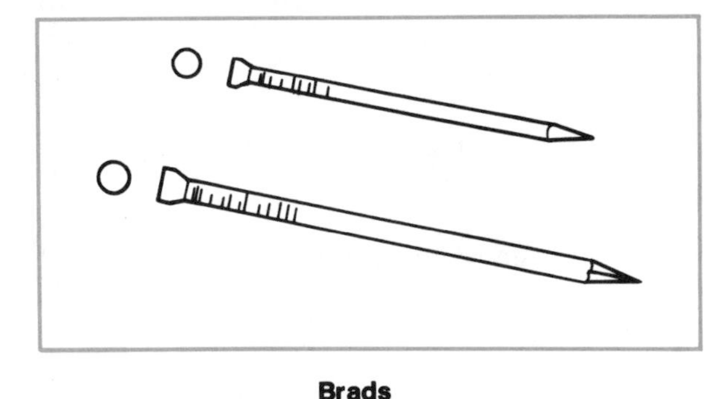

Brads

Brazing

Brazing is a metal fastening technique similar to soldering. Two metal pieces are welded together through the use of a brazing alloy, usually a copper-zinc compound. A brazed bond is much stronger than a soldered bond because the brazing alloy has a high melting point and will withstand higher operating temperatures before weakening. To braze two metal parts together, clean their surfaces thoroughly, removing all rust. Clamp the parts together tightly with metal clamps, and apply the brazing alloy to the joint. Heat the parts and the alloy to a red heat, using an electric or acetylene torch. To insure a solid joint, make sure the brazing alloy completely covers the joint before beginning the melting process. Cool the brazed joint completely before removing the clamps. Brazing is usually done in metalworking shops.

Breast Drill

A breast drill is a larger form of hand operated crank drill which contains a concave breastplate at the top of the drill. By resting one's chest or shoulder on the breastplate, greater pressure can be exerted on the drill. Some breast drills have two speeds and others have an adjustable ratchet on the spindle which allows the bit to turn in either a clockwise or counterclockwise direction. *SEE ALSO HAND TOOLS.*

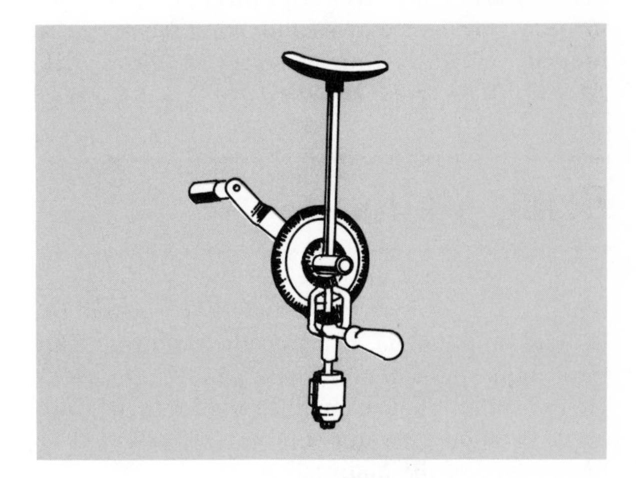

Breast drill

Breezeway

A breezeway is a roof-covered passageway connecting a house and garage. The breezeway may be converted into a room by enclosing the area with walls.

Bricklayer's Tools

[SEE CONCRETE & MASONRY TOOLS.]

Brick Molding

Brick molding is a molding used for window and exterior door frames. It serves as the boundary molding for brick or other siding material, and it forms the rabbet for a screen, storm sash or combination door. *SEE ALSO MOLDING & TRIM.*

Brick Sealers

Brick Sealers are transparent silicone solutions. Applied with a paintbrush, the clear sealer aids in keeping moisture and stains from permeating masonry. Paint may be used as a brick sealer to help prevent excessive build-ups of dirt or mold in grout. By forming a solid bond, sealers are helpful in controlling masonry erosion. *SEE ALSO BRICK & STONE WORK.*

Brick Stains

Brick stains are changes in color caused by various compounds affecting the material. The four major types of stains are soot, grease, mortar and efflorescence, a white powder formed by crystallization of water-soluble salts washed to the surface of the material.

Before beginning to remove stains, rubber gloves, eye shield and a stiff-fibered scrub brush are needed. Some stain removers are dangerous and the gloves and eye protectors are needed for safety.

The first step is to try and remove the stain with soap and water. If soap and water does not work, harsher compounds are needed. Most stains on stones will react with caustic soda mixed in three or four parts of water. Brick, flagstone or tile stains are usually removed by a one-to-one ratio of muriatic acid and water. Garage and driveway concrete grease and oil stains are removed by a solution of trisodium phosphate.

Marble stains are easily bleached by a paste made of hydrogen peroxide and powdered whiting. The first of these products can be obtained from a drugstore and the other found in a paint store.

After spreading the paste on the stain, add a few drops of ammonia and cover with a piece of plastic for a few minutes. Rinse with hot water and wipe dry. If the stain persists, repeat the procedure.

Rust stains on marble can be removed with ammonia or if stubborn, a solution of equal amounts of amyl acetate and acetone. Using powdered pumice, light rubbing removes smoke stains.

By rubbing a medium grade of abrasive paper over slight burns on limestone or sandstone, the discoloration will disappear. Using a wet scrubbing brush dipped into hydrated lime, rub vigorously to remove moss or lichen stains on outdoor ornaments.

Place commercial cleaners in the fire to remove excess soot from a chimney.

Whatever stain remover is applied, caution must be used. Do not use carbon tetrachloride. Its fumes are extremely dangerous. *SEE ALSO BRICK & STONE WORK.*

Brick & Stone Work

WORKING WITH BRICK

Brick is made in large factories by pulverizing clay and shale, tempering with water and forming the raw material into molds. It is then cut and dried in special kilns which reduce cracking and greatly speed up the drying process. The brick is finally placed in another, much hotter kiln, for *burning.*

Some brick is colored on the facing surface by glazing. Whether the glaze is applied before or after the brick is burned depends on the color. If applied after, the brick is again returned to the kilns for low-temperature firing.

Experienced bricklayers can do many more things with brick than the homeowner, but you can learn the basics easily and do simple projects yourself. Most of the projects illustrated here are basic ones. Start off with them, and do not attempt anything more complicated such as an archway until the fundamentals are fully mastered. You should gradually improve your skills so that you can do most home brick jobs.

Types of Brick

There are many more varieties of brick than the homeowner would think possible, and almost as many sizes. Some of the better-known types are Norman brick (2 3/4 x 3 3/4 x 12 inches) and Roman brick (1 1/2 x 3 3/4 x 12 inches), but the kind most often used by the homeowner is *common* or *standard* brick, which measures 2 1/4 x 3 3/4 x 8 inches. The projects discussed here assume the use of common brick in the size mentioned. Always measure brick before planning the layout as sizes and terminology may vary in some areas.

Brick may be either solid or cored (with several holes in the center section). The holes make the brick cheaper and lighter without losing strength, but the coring should not exceed 25 percent of the volume of the brick.

Natural colors in fired brick are a variety of reds, buffs and creams, depending on the type of clay and the processing. Glazes, of course, can produce almost any color imaginable.

A good trowel is the indispensable bricklayer's tool.

A bricklayer's hammer has chisel back for chopping off projections.

Tools Needed

The indispensable bricklaying tool is the trowel. Even if the project is very small, get a high-quality trowel that can be handled easily and that will stand up under hard use. A 10-inch length is best for most people.

In addition to the trowel, you will need a broad-bladed brick chisel or bolster, a hammer (preferably a brick hammer, although a mash or ball peen type will suffice), a good level, the longer the better (a mason's type is best), a folding rule, a length of tough string and a pointing tool. You can substitute a length of 5/8 inch copper pipe, bent into an S-shape, for the pointing tool.

A square-end short-handled shovel for mixing mortar and a container in which to mix it are also necessary. A wheelbarrow makes a convenient, movable mixing container. A mortar board can be used as well. This can be just a scrap piece of plywood or other clean surface.

Other tools, scaffolding for example, might come in handy, but are best rented because of their high initial cost.

Layouts and Materials

When planning any brick project, be sure to plan for the mortar in your layout. One way to do this is to establish an approximate size, convert feet into inches and divide each dimension by the size of the brick plus a half inch for each mortar joint. If you are left with anything other than a whole or half brick, adjust your plan so that bricks will not have to be cut.

Actually, there is no need for this except in a situation where the brick must fit exactly into a certain dimension. With most walls, patios and other small projects, size can be flexible. Use rough dimensions when ordering brick, and make a trial run with the first row to establish the precise finished length.

When ordering, figure roughly seven brick per square foot of wall layout and 4 1/2 brick per foot of flat installation like a patio. *The accompanying chart* gives the actual numbers, but add 5 to 10 percent to these figures for waste. Brick can be bought at all masonry and most building supply dealers.

NUMBER OF BRICK NEEDED

Area	Walls (single)	Paving Brick
1 sq. ft.	6.16	4.5
5 sq. ft.	30.80	22.5
10 sq. ft.	61.60	45.0
25 sq. ft.	154.00	112.5
50 sq. ft.	308.00	225.5
75 sq. ft.	462.00	337.5
100 sq. ft.	616.00	450.0

Add 5-10% for waste and breakage

Mortar

Brick mortar consists of portland cement, hydrated lime, sand and water. You can buy it premixed, if you wish, or mix your own in proportions of one part portland cement, 1/2 part lime and four parts clean sand.

Mix mortar thoroughly, using a shovel and turning the batch over and over, preferably in the pattern shown.

Begin by thoroughly blending the cement, lime and sand with your shovel. Then scoop out a hollow in the middle of the mixture and slowly add water until it is the consistency of soft mud. Unlike concrete and some other mixes, it is better to err on the side of too much water than too little, since the brick will absorb much of the moisture anyway.

Make sure that there are no dry spots in the batch, and mix only as much as you can use in 30 minutes to an hour. To prevent too rapid drying out of the mortar, wet the brick with the garden hose about an hour before using. The surface of the brick should be dry when laying up, so that the mortar does not slip off, but the interior will still be wet to help avoid premature mortar stiffening. It also helps to dampen the foundation before laying the first course.

Laying the First Section

Brick is heavy material, and when combined with mortar it weighs about 120 pounds per cubic foot. Therefore, a brick structure must have a strong foundation. A brick barbecue, for example, should rest on footings or reinforced concrete. Any brick wall should bear on concrete footings at least twice as wide as the brick itself. Smaller, less massive structures like garden edging can be set in mortar on top of a sand bed, but

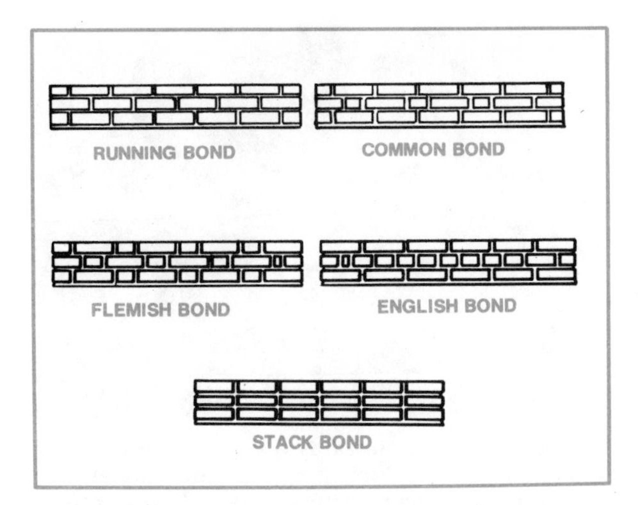

Some of the more traditional bonds are shown.

most brickwork demands at least a four-inch slab underneath.

Brick patterns are called *bond,* and there are many choices. The most common and easiest is *running bond,* in which each brick is placed so that it straddles the two bricks below it (half on each side of the joint). No matter which bond you choose, lay out the first course row without mortar beforehand so that you wind up with a whole or half a brick at each end. You can usually avoid cutting brick by adjusting the length of the row a little or, if necessary, using tighter mortar joints (as little as 1/4-inch is acceptable). Whether the structure is one or two bricks wide depends upon the particular project. A high wall should be two tiers wide for extra strength, but there is no need to use more than a single width for a small project like a planter.

Begin laying brick at a corner, building it up three or four rows high, dovetailed with the adjacent wall (if any) at right angles. Make frequent use of the level and square to keep things in true. When you have built up one corner, go on to the next, lining it up with the first by means of a straightedge or line level.

With at least two corners in place, push nails into the soft mortar between the first two courses and run a line between them. The line should be almost, but not quite, touching the front and top of the first course. Use this string as a guide for placement of the rest of the bricks in the first row.

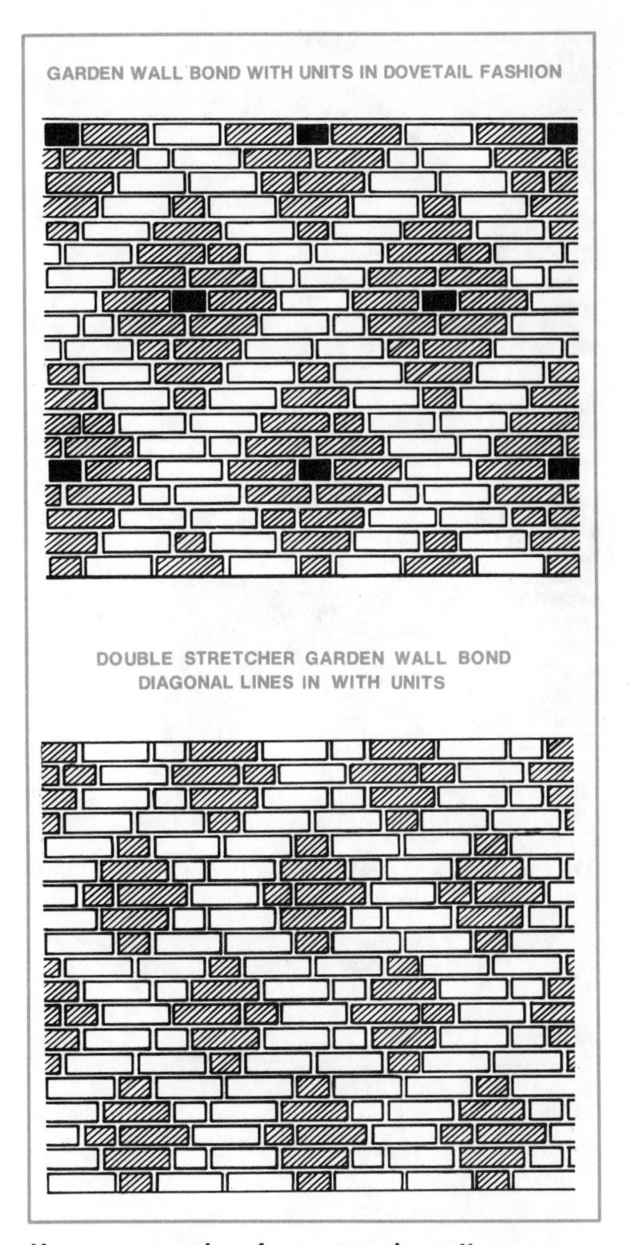

Here are examples of more complex patterns.

Each brick should be individually lined up the same distance from the line about 1/16″. You should be able to do this by sight, but it will help if you measure the first few. After the first course is laid, move the string up to the row above and repeat for each .ourse.

The technique of bricklaying is simple, as long as you take your time in the beginning. Take a slice of mortar on the trowel and lay it along the

Lay down a heavy bed of mortar over two or three bricks. (the man in photo is experienced and is working with four or five.)

After making a shallow furrow in the mortar, "butter" the next brick to be laid.

Set the brick in place, using the string line as a guide. Push down gently to the line with your hand or the side of the trowel.

Shove brick gently towards the others until you've squeezed all but 1/2 inch of mortar. (Measure at first; later you'll be able to estimate the right distance.)

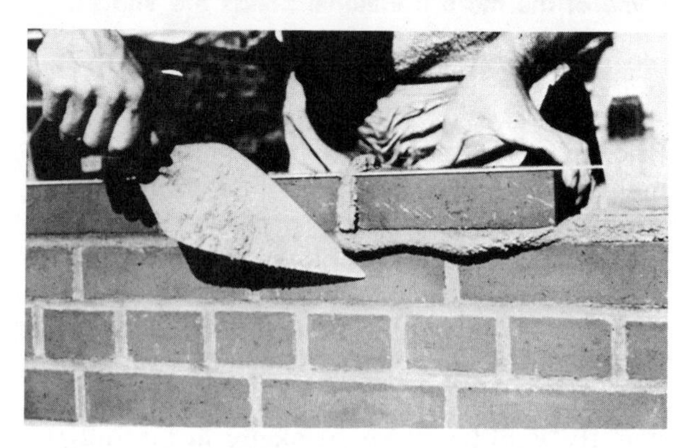

Strike off the excess mortar with side of trowel and return it to the mortar board for reuse.

foundation about a half-inch thick and long enough for two or three bricks (later you can stretch to four or five). Furrow the mortar a little bit with the point of the trowel, making sure it extends the width of a brick. Then *butter* the end of a brick and set it firmly into the mortar bed. Some mortar should be squeezed out of the joints. Trim off the excess mortar and return it to the mortar board, butter the next brick, set it against the previous one, and continue. With the first few joints, you may want to measure the mortar (half-inch thick is best), but you will soon learn to estimate this, too.

If you have made the dry run correctly, the last, or closure, brick should fit perfectly. When laying this brick, butter *both* ends of the brick as well as the flanking bricks on either side. Lower this brick carefully into the gap, taking care not to knock off the mortar, and press it into position.

Any brick that is set too high can be tapped down into position, but you cannot tap up a brick that has been set too low. Pull up the brick, scrape off the mortar, lay down more mortar and set the brick again.

Build your corners carefully, making sure of alignment in all directions. A long mason's level is your best tool here.

Keep working on the intermediate bricks between corners until you reach the highest course, then switch to laying corners for three or four more courses. Go back to the middle sections, then the corners, and so on, until you reach the top.

Completing the Project

As you move along, don't forget to keep checking for plumb, level and alignment. If you find your wall is bulging, dipping or otherwise running out of true, do not attempt to tap bricks into place once the mortar sets up. Take up the brick, (and those on top, if necessary) scrape off the old mortar and add new, then reset it. Any tampering with the mortar once it starts to harden is sure to cause cracks or hollows in the joint, weakening the entire structure and inviting leakage.

Sometimes, in spite of good planning, you will find you have to cut a brick. Put the brick on a solid surface, preferably sand. With the brick chisel and hammer, tap a line all around with the bevel facing inwards. Then give the chisel a sharp blow and the brick should break clean. Don't try to break bricks with a trowel. Do use the chisel back of the hammer to chip away rough edges or protrusions.

As each course is completed and before the mortar has hardened, run the 5/8-inch pipe or pointing tool across the joints to produce a smooth and uniform appearance. Other types of tooling are often used, but the concave joints produced by the pipe is the best for producing a water-tight seal. While tooling or pointing, also fill in the holes left by the line nails, and any other imperfections, with dabs of mortar.

Finishing Touches

Like all cement compounds, mortar should be allowed to mature for at lease 2 or 3 days. Hot, dry weather will accelerate the hydration process, which should take place slowly. During such days, give it an occasional watering. Be gentle to the project for a week or two until the mortar is good and strong. If you have built a barbecue, wait at least two weeks before firing it.

Meanwhile, clean up any mortar stains with damp burlap or other coarse cloth. If the stains have set, remove them with a solution of 1 part muriatic acid diluted with 10 parts of water. Wet down the brick and scrub on the liquid with a stiff brush. Wear gloves and goggles when using this solution, and wash off any acid immediately and thoroughly with cold water.

After the mortar has completely cured (at least a week), you may want to coat the brickwork with a colorless masonry sealer. This provides a transparent, water-repellent surface that protects against crumbling mortar for many years.

"Tool" joints when they are hard enough to show the imprint of your thumb. Use a special pointing tool or a piece of pipe 1/8-inch wider than the joints.

Patios and Other Flat Surfaces

The techniques described above apply to walls, barbecues and other upright structures, but brick sidewalks, patios and other flat surfaces require slightly different treatment. The only

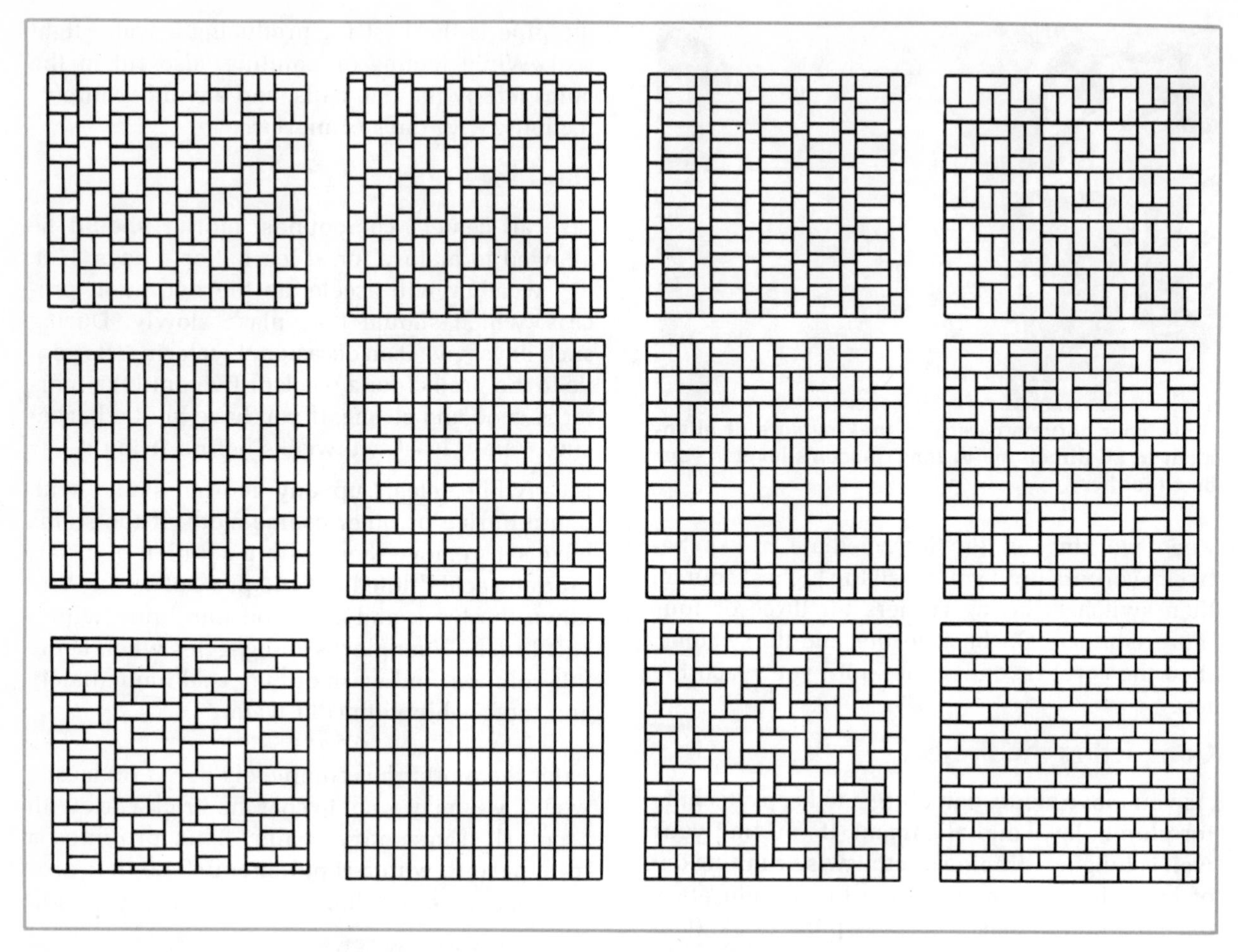

Some of the many patterns possible for patios and walks.

weight on the brick here is that of the people who walk on it.

In most cases, the best and by far the easiest method is to apply mortarless paving. To do this, excavate to a depth of about 4 1/4 inches. Lay down a two-inch level bed of sand and simply set the bricks in the sand. Fine sand is then swept over the surface, filling the joints and locking each brick in place.

The whole surface is than watered down, re-sanded and watered again. The watering forces the fine particles of sand downward, filling gaps in the bed and between the bricks.

If you are using a running bond, common brick can be used. Any modular pattern, however, is difficult to achieve with common brick because there will be uneven gaps between the bricks. For other patterns, use special paving brick, which comes exactly 4 x 8 inches and falls easily into any type of bond.

In areas of severe winters, the mortarless method may result in heaved bricks and uneven pavement. Actually, this is not a serious problem, because a little waviness is not unacceptable in a rustic setting. Furthermore, the heaved brick can be returned to position by digging out the sand beneath it and replacing it.

Frost problems can be eliminated by digging six inches below the frost line and filling in with gravel approximately 6 3/4 inches below the intended surface of your patio. Then lay a concrete slab about four inches thick. Spread a 1/2 inch mortar bed on top of the cured concrete and lay common brick in the mortar with 1/2 inch mortar joints in between. This is, of course, a lot more work, but it is much more durable.

A double-tiered wall is much stronger than a single wythe (tier).

Header course spans two wythes and binds them together.

Larger Brick Walls

Large Brick walls and load-bearing walls are built with the same basic techniques as the smaller wall previously described, but they must be stronger and more durable. Sometimes a double brick wall is built, or other materials such as concrete block, wood or clay tile are used for a back-up wall, and the brick is veneered in front.

When a double brick wall is built, *headers,* or brick laid lengthwise across both walls, are provided in regular sequence but no less than every seven courses. Various patterns can evolve by alternating the bond and position of brick as illustrated. English bond, for example, has one course of stretchers followed by one of headers. Flemish bond alternates headers and stretchers in each course. Occasionally, rowlock *headers* are used, which means that the crossing brick is laid on the narrow side instead of the wider dimension.

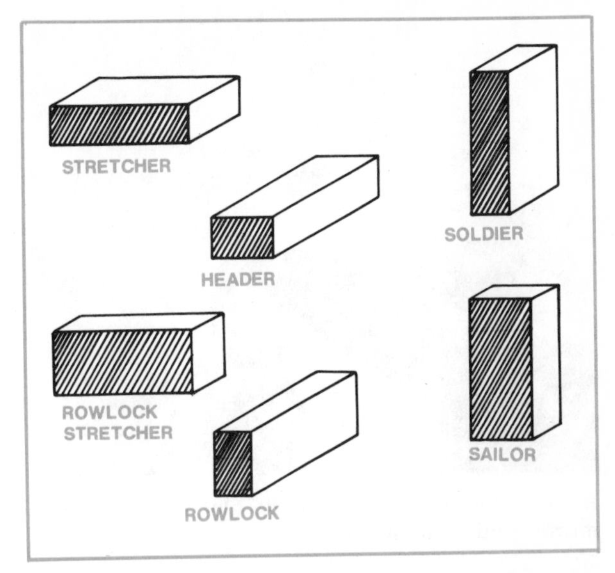

Bricks are given names according to how they lay in the bond. The different positions are shown here.

When good insulation, strength and weather resistance are a factor, a *cavity* wall with metal ties is recommended. In this type of wall, a hollow is left between the two tiers for insulation and metal ties hold them together. The ties not only bind the two tiers, or wythes, but they allow slight movement in one wythe without affecting the other. This type of wall is also relatively easy to build.

With a double wall, the brickwork should be *parged* (plastered with mortar) on the inside to provide additional moisture protection. When laying up a cavity wall, be careful not to allow

Parging or plastering with mortar on the back of one tier, increases wall's resistance to weather.

Brick veneer is tied to concrete block back-up with mortar and metal hangers.

mortar to fall down into the hollow area. The hollow will be filled either with insulating materials such as perlite or with a cement grout so wet that it can be poured out of a bucket into the hollow spaces. An easy way to make grout is take leftover mortar and mix it with lots of water.

Brick veneer is the most common type of brickwork used for the walls of homes and buildings. In this instance, the back-up material provides most ot the stability for the structure, with the brick being mostly decorative, although it does increase building strength and provide weather resistance.

Concrete block is used most often as backing, but almost any framing material can be used. In

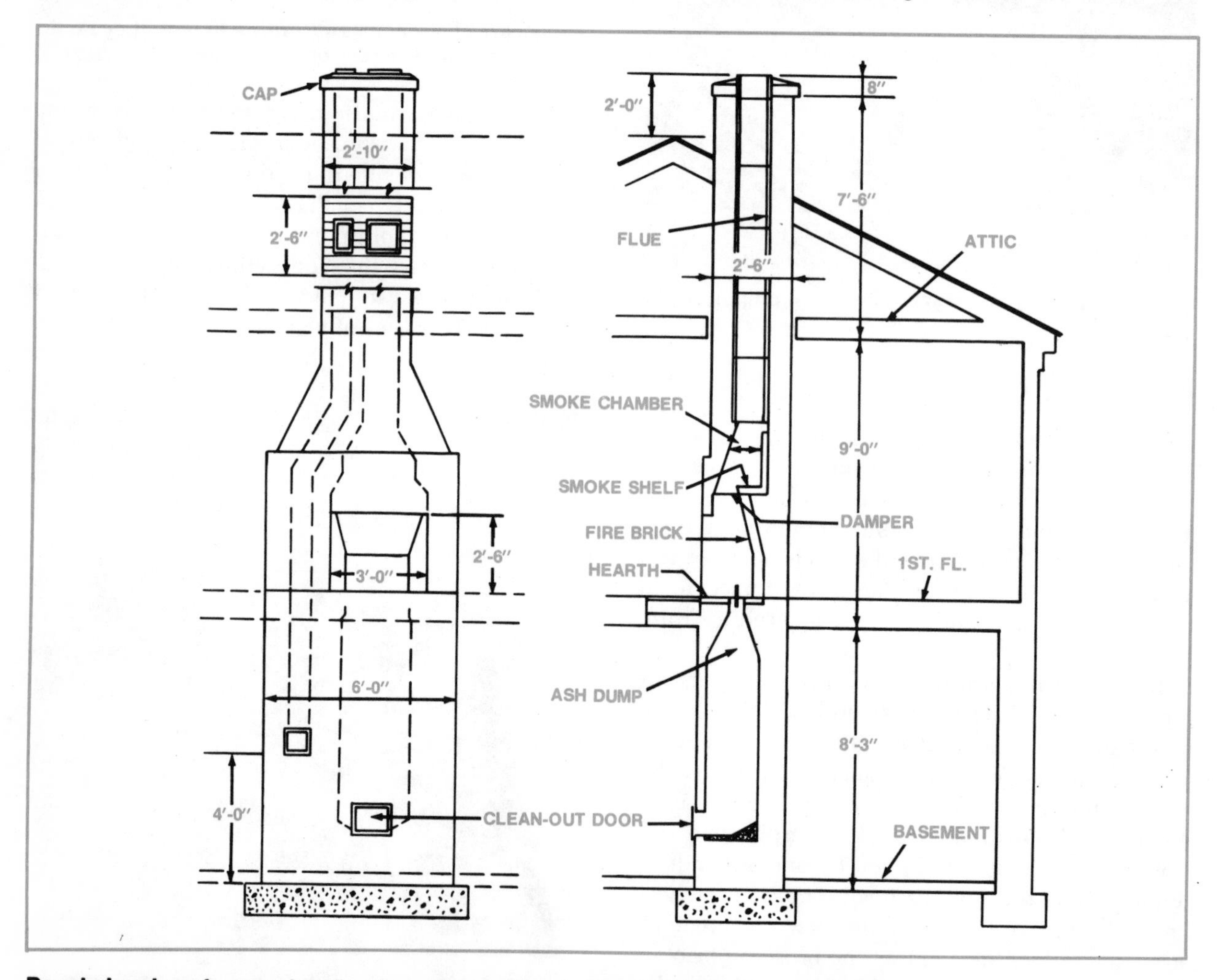

Rough drawing of a complete fireplace. Some of the intricacies such as "corbeling" (building out or cantilevering) illustrate why this type of job should be left to professionals.

homes, standard wood framing is often used, and clay tile is another common back-up material. Metal hangers are attached to the block or wood with appropriate nails, and the other end is positioned so that it will be embedded in the brick mortar between head joints.

Fireplaces and Arches

The beginner should shy away from complex and potentially dangerous brickwork such as fireplaces and archways. An exception is the outdoor fireplace, or barbecue, designed for cooking. Indoor fireplace design is quite intricate and if poorly built can result in backed-up smoke or even a house fire.

Arches are designed to carry heavy load on top and must be constructed with great care. The novice mason is urged to try his luck on a non load-bearing partition, in a spot where not too much brickwork is laid above. Arches need temporary shoring, and this is done by the use of *centers,* wood structures which hold up the brickwork until it hardens to maximum strength. Centers must remain in place for at lease ten days before moving.

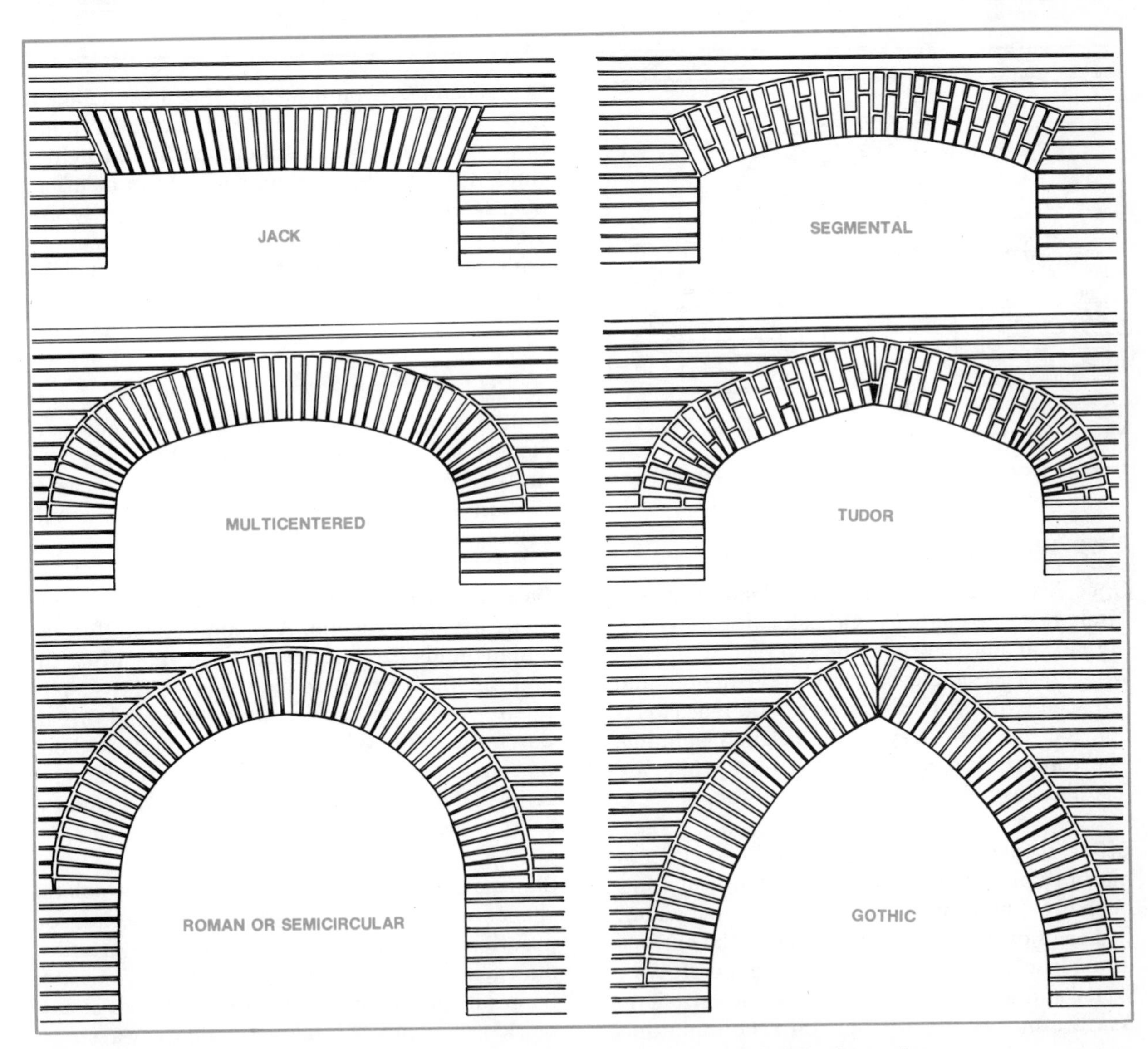

Some of the most common types of arches. Arches are not recommended for the novice.

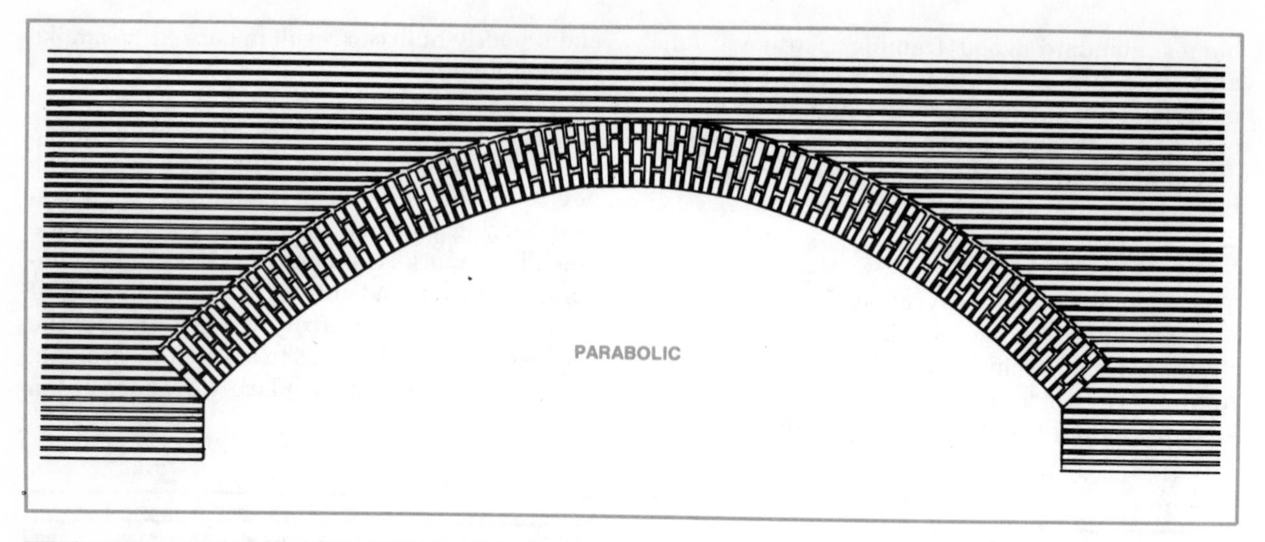

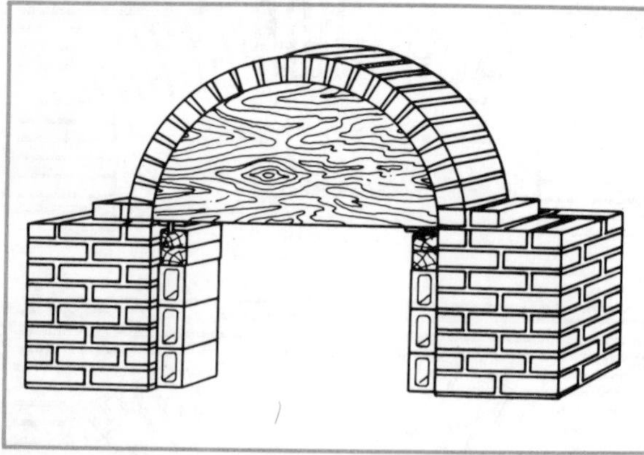

Using a wood "center" to support a Roman arch.

Care and Maintenance

Once brick has been laid and cleaned, it will rarely need further care. Occasionally, however, the mortar may become cracked or crumbly, in which case it should be scraped or dug out and replaced with fresh mortar, or re-pointed. This is done in the same way as the original pointing. There are some ready-mixed products which are fast and easy to use for such small jobs.

Efflorescence is the presence on the surface of masonry of a white powdery substance that has been brought to the surface by evaporated water. If these salts should be deposited on the surface of the brick, they can usually be cleaned off with water and a stiff brush. If this is not sufficient, use the muriatic acid solution recommended previously for cleaning mortar from the brick.

Stains can occur on brick and the cleaning agent depends on the sources. For many of them however, a poultice of fuller's earth and lighter fluid, naptha or some other solvent can be effective. If and when brick becomes generally unsightly for any reason, professional cleaning with steam or sandblasting equipment will be needed.

Using Building Stone

Unlike brick, concrete block or other masonry, stone does not require mortar to bind building units. The builder has the option, in most cases, of building his wall *wet* or *dry*, and he will usually choose dry because it is so much easier.

Ease of construction is not the only reason for using dry construction. A retaining wall, for example, holds back hundreds of pounds of earth, and the extra pressure exerted by rainwater is often enough to crack the mortar and break down the wall. When the wall is built without mortar, water seeps through every chink and relieves the pressure that would build behind a solid, mortared surface.

Stone can be bought in many different colors, shapes and textures. The suggested materials for practically all stone installations are granite, limestone, marble, sandstone, slate or quartzite. Some of the potential uses for attractive stonework are patios, barbeques, walkways, steps, planters and walls of all sorts. Do not neglect stone for indoors, either, as it is most striking in a fireplace or planter.

If stone is easy to lay, it is very hard to cut. For this reason, many people buy stone pre-cut into squares, rectangles and circles. The cost is considerably more, however, than buying stone by the ton and doing the cutting yourself. Actually, if you use random or rustic patterns, you can take advantage of the fact that stone *breaks* easily, (just drop on hard pavement) and keep cutting to a minimum.

You won't need any more tools to work with stone than you use for brickwork. In fact, you need very few tools at all if you stick to dry construction. A cold chisel, a heavy mash hammer and a long level are all you will need.

Wet construction requires the addition of a trowel, shovel and wheelbarrow for mixing the mortar.

Ordering Materials

Garden supply houses are usually the most available sources for cut stone in regular sizes. Virgin stone can be found at stone or masonry dealers. Look in the yellow pages under "Stone—Natural," for a local supplier.

You will find that stone is very heavy and that you may need a ton for even small projects. The retaining wall shown in the photos required over three tons of rough stone plus another half ton of squared materials for steps and coping.

Since stone is relatively expensive, don't use it any thicker than you have to. A high retaining wall may need to be 12 to 18 inches thick, but small ones do not, especially if laid dry. Your stone dealer will be be best judge, but it should not be necessary to lay stone any more than six inches thick for a moderate sized wall. In some cases, four or five inches will be enough. Actually, you should resign yourself to wide tolerances, because of the difficulty in cutting the stone to exact measurements.

Where a wide wall is desired, it may be best to use stone as a veneer rather than a mass. A stone veneer wall is built in much the same way as brick veneer, with concrete footings and block back-up. The stone is attached by metal ties or clips. Lay the stone with the flat side out and use mortar between pieces. Tell the stone dealer that you will be using the material as veneer so that he can sell you stone of the same thickness (usually four inches) and the proper attachments.

Building a Stone Wall

A convenient factor in working with stone is that you can afford to be somewhat casual in the layout. With drywall construction, you will be putting up the stone piece by piece (all varying sizes), with no permanent ties, and you can pull down the whole project and start over if you wish. Even with mortar, the pieces are so irregular that accurate planning is impossible.

If you plan on stairs, save some large pieces for treads. When the stone arrives, however, don't be distressed if the truckdriver dumps the load and smashes up most of it. He is saving you a lot of future work.

In some cases, a concrete footing will be necessary. It, like all footings, should be placed six inches below the frost line and at least two feet below the surface. You should not need a footing with a mortarless wall unless the soil is very mushy.

When you build with mortar, the technique is much like bricklaying. Lay down a bed of mortar on the footing, butter one end of a stone piece, place it and strike off the excess. Butter another piece, press it firmly against the first one, and so on.

You will run into trouble with stone if you try to make even courses and neat mortar joints. There is no way (or need) to achieve the kind of exactness necessary with brick. Just put up a piece of stone with the straightest edge out, fill all joints with mortar and go on to the next. The only bond you should be concerned with is not letting any joint fall directly on top of the one beneath. Try to use stone of the same thickness for each course and keep the tops generally level, but you

Stonework can be a family project. The young man should be wearing goggles to protect his eyes.

In spite of uneven sections, wall should be level overall. Use a long 2 x 4 with level to check.

can adjust unevenness as you go along. Use varying size mortar joints to fill in the extra spaces.

For dry construction, start one or two courses below the surface, making the joints very tight and the tops level. Use extra-large, thick pieces of stone for this, which is in essence your foundation. The soil should be dug out with a square-end garden spade to a depth of about four inches and a bed of sand laid first (unless the soil is sandy anyway, in which case this step is unnecessary).

As long as you aren't using mortar, you can be even less particular about fitting the pieces. Stone is very massive and the surfaces are all essentially abrasive. When stone is laid on stone, the little projections lock against each other and are very difficult to dislodge. For that reason, try to get as much bearing surface between each surface as possible. Don't worry about gaps or uneven courses unless the stones tip and lose contact with the ones above and below. Use a long mason's level or a 2 x 4 with a carpenter's level to keep the top of the wall relatively even.

It doesn't matter what the sides and back of each piece look like, since no one sees them. Actually, the back should be as jagged as possible to provide better ties with the soil.

Eventually, you will have to start breaking or cutting the stones. For a truly rustic look, just drop the stones on a hard surface and they will break in lots of pieces. You should be able to get a relatively straight surface on one of the edges and, if you don't, you can always cut the piece in half, thereby getting straight edges on two pieces. But try using the uneven pieces without cutting. You will be surprised how straight and pleasing the wall will look overall, even though individual pieces are rather jagged.

If you prefer straight edges, tap a line on the surface with a mash hammer and cold chisel. For a higher degree of accuracy, tap all around the stone, including the edges. This is very time consuming. Most of the time, you can get a relatively straight cut by scoring just the top. Once the top is scored, give the chisel some heavy blows up and down the line, and eventually the whole line will crack and fall into two (or more) pieces.

For greater wall strength, taper the wall backward two inches for every foot in height. Also tie the wall into the soil behind it by inserting a long piece sideways every 24 to 36 inches. The best pieces for this are shaped like an isosceles triangle.

Backfill when the wall reaches six inches in height and every six inches thereafter. If your soil is highly organic, use a layer of sand directly behind the wall about six inches deep. Tamp down firmly and soak with water. When dry, tamp again and fill with more water, packing the dirt tightly so that it will bond with the jagged edges of the stones.

Backfill when your wall gets six inches high and every six inches thereafter. Tamp and wet down to provide solid bond behind stones.

As you work, set aside thicker pieces with squared ends to be used in the topping course or stairwell, if any. Some stone dealers advise mortaring this course even if the others are dry, but chances are that the mortar will crack with the frost anyway. It is better to simply butt the ends together and pack in the soil behind. These pieces may get knocked off, but you can simply set them in place again.

To build stairs, make small retaining walls in front and on each side to hold each large stone tread.

Curved stairwell makes pleasing design.

Stairs

An easy and economical way to make good-looking stone steps is lay a veneer over existing concrete. If you like the rustic steps in the photos, however, they must be built from the ground up. (They can be built as part of a retaining wall or separately.)

Stone stairs should be built into the grade rather than projecting from it. Thus, the sides of the stairwell and the risers are miniature retaining walls and should be constructed as such. The stairwell should be dug out in its entirety before starting and, if combined with a retaining wall as shown in the photos, built along with the wall. Outside corners should be constructed of large, heavy, triangular or rectangular pieces, and inside corners should be dovetailed as with brick.

When your wall gets to the height of the first stair tread (six to seven inches), build a small wall on either side, and another foundation wall underneath the front of the tread. The side walls should go back far enough so that you have a solid foundation for the tread on both sides. If you don't have enough large, squared pieces for treads, you can buy them extra from the stone dealer.

Walks and Patios

Stone has long been a favorite for handsome patios, sidewalks and other horizontal applications. Flagstone is nothing more than any hard stone that will split into pieces suitable for paving, which most of the stone mentioned will do.

Again, it is easier and less expensive to lay this type of stone dry, which is accomplished in exactly the same manner as mortarless brick. Here, of course, bond is meaningless, even with cut stone. If you prefer, use mortar for the bed instead of sand, and fill up all chinks, too.

A common and worthwhile variation is laying stone over poured concrete. It is usually unnecessary to put down a slab underneath the stone, but if the slab is already there, you can lay stone on top. Apply it as described under brickwork.

Flagstone terrace is made from cut stone, providing an elegant, formal look.

Other Uses

Stone makes an exciting fireplace or house front, and there are countless other applications limited only by a dull imagination. The methods of applying the stone, however, are no different from the technique previously described. Stone is used either in its natural position (as in walls or patios) or as a veneer. Follow the instructions above for the specific application.

You can create a handsome fireplace yourself by using a prefabricated metal design and flanking it with stone.

Brick Veneer Construction

In this construction method, masonry (usually brick) is used for siding the exterior surface of a building. It supports no weight other than its own. This masonry siding can also be made of concrete units or stone, and can be applied in combination with other materials for a "wainscoting" effect.

Brick veneering, which can be applied to almost any new or existing structure, is a fairly simple process, even for an amateur bricklayer. *SEE ALSO BRICK & STONE WORK.*

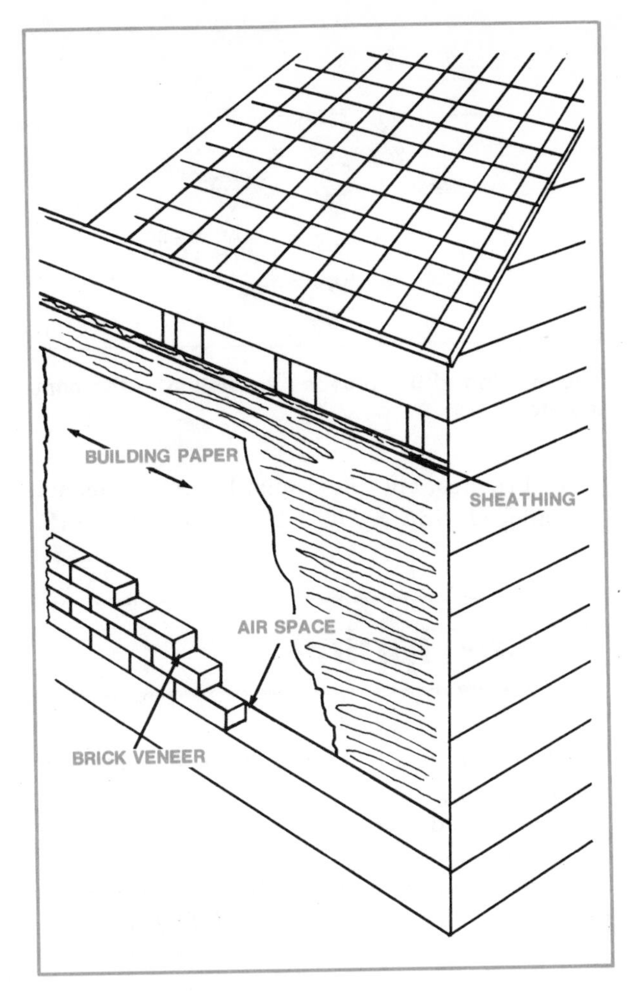

Brick veneer construction.

Bridging

The wooden or metal bracing nailed between the floor joists is termed *bridging*. Its purpose is to distribute floor loads evenly and stiffen the floor joists, which would otherwise be free to move from their vertical position. The result would be a saggy or squeaky floor and twisted joists.

There are two common methods of bridging; solid and diagonal. Solid bridging must be cut squarely and accurately; diagonal bridging requires angle cuts. Metal bridging, which saves time and labor, on angle cuts particularly, is also available, but it costs more than the scrap stock

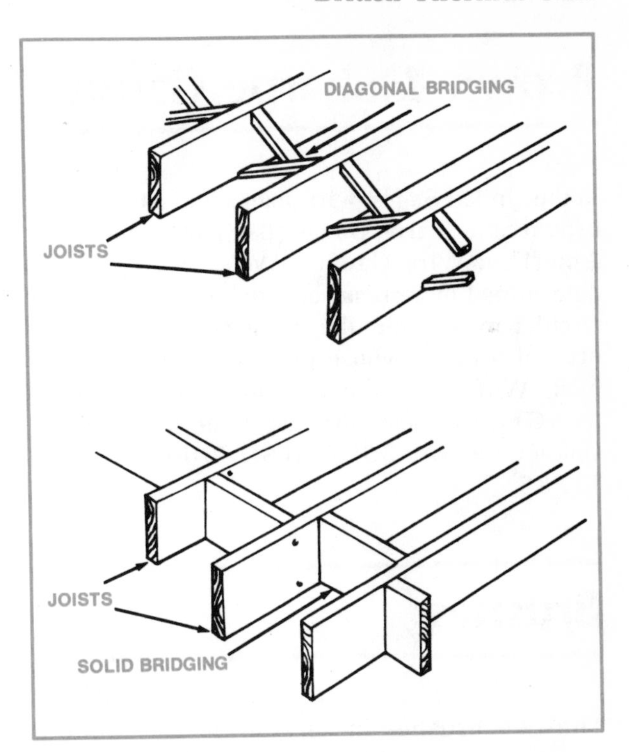

Bridging reinforces joists.

used for wooden bridging. *SEE ALSO FLOOR CONSTRUCTION.*

Brightwood

Brightwood is a term applied to varnished or clear wood finishes rather than painted ones. It is most often applied to marine finishing or coachwork.

British Thermal Unit

The British Thermal Unit, or BTU, is the standard of measure that indicates the amount of energy necessary to raise one pound of water one degree Farenheit. This heat energy, about 252 calories, is often used when planning air conditioning and heating systems in the house.

Brown & Sharpe Gauge

In the United States, wire size is indicated by the Brown and Sharpe Gauge (B&S), also called the American Wire Gauge (AWG). Wire size is determined by a cross-sectional measurement in circular mils. A circular mil is equivalent to the area of a circle whose diameter is $^{1}/_{1000th}$ of an inch. Wire sizes range from 40 (B&S) or 60 (AWG) up to 0000; the larger the number, the smaller the wire. *SEE ALSO WIRE SIZES & TYPES.*

Brushes

The two brushes in certain electric motors, which lead current to the coils of the commutator, consist of a spring and a rectangular or cylindrical block of soft carbon. When the current is turned on, current moves through one brush, through one of the many commutator bars under the brush, then through the armature windings. Next, the current flows out through another commutator bar and through the other brush. This action supplies the current that maintains the magnetic current that keeps the armature rotating.

If a commutator motor either fails to start, hums or clicks, the problem is often a result of dirty or worn brushes, and they must be either cleaned or replaced. *SEE ALSO ELECTRIC MOTORS.*

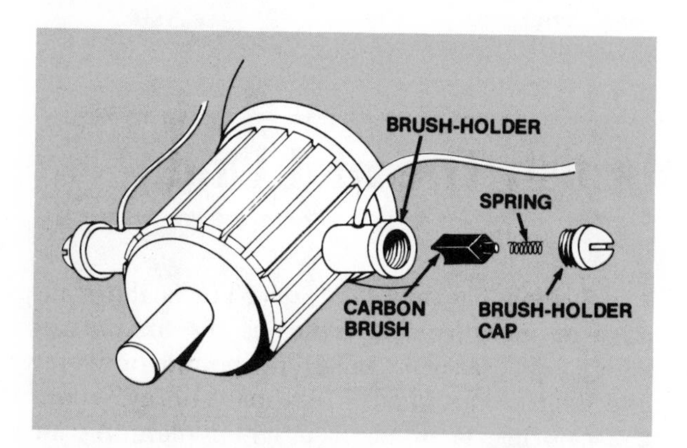

The assembly of a brush and brush-holder.

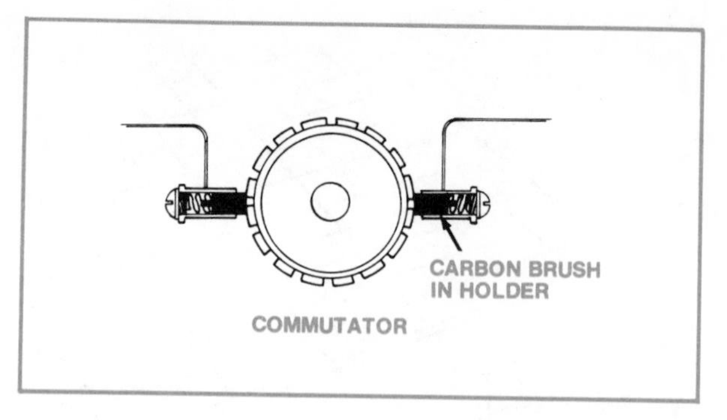

The location of the brushes in relation to the commutator.

Brush-Tipping

Brush-tipping is a technique used in glazing, or antiquing, to produce a wood grain appearance in the antiqued piece. This effect is achieved by applying a moderately stiff brush or steel wool to the object in straight long strokes after removing most of the glaze. *SEE ALSO ANTIQUING.*

Builder's Level

[SEE TRANSIT.]

Building Code

A building code is a set of regulations that controls the method of construction and specifies the quality of materials (lumber, electrical wiring, etc.) used in building. The codes are often set up as supplementary codes to those derived nationally by certain groups. Most codes differ from city to city which makes it necessary for the builder to check the local codes of a particular area or community before attempting construction.

Building Inspector

The purpose of the building inspector is to enforce the local building codes by inspecting methods and materials to decide whether or not they comply with local code specifications. Often this inspector is supported by the Federal Housing Authority or other federally-funded agencies, although he is usually appointed by civil courts.

Building Line

Building lines form the outline of a foundation after the building site has been determined and cleared, establish the level height of the foundation and designate the limits of an area that can be used as a construction site, according to law. Building lines must be established at right angles, locating corners formed by the outside walls of the building. Batter boards make up the framework built around the corner stakes, which contain tacks for attaching builder's line. The correct square layout of building lines is of basic importance throughout the construction process.

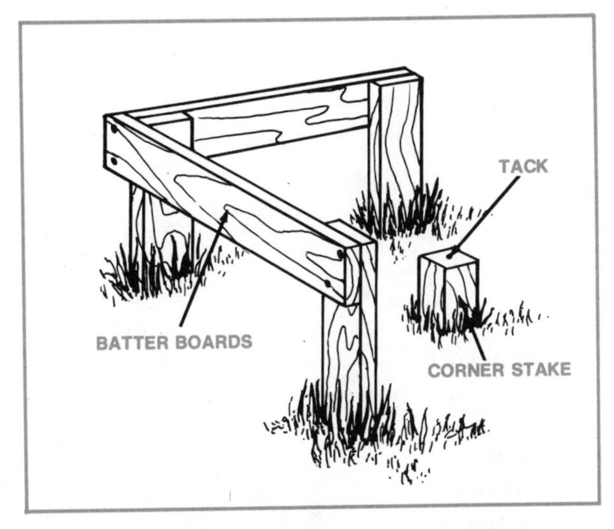

Right-angle batter board frame for building line layout.

Building Permit

A building permit must be issued to the contractor or landowner before building may begin on a site. The permit is deemed as proof that the property has been registered and that plans and methods of construction comply with local requirements prior to and during construction. Civil authorities issue the building permits.

Building Terms & Abbreviations

Acoustical Tile	AT
Aggregate	Aggr.
Air Conditioning	Air Cond.
Air Dried	AD
Alternate	Alt.
Alternating Current	AC
Aluminum	AL
American Institute of Architects	A.I.A.
American Institute of Electrical Engineers	A.I.E.E.
American Society for Testing Materials	A.S.T.M.
American Standards Association, Inc.	A.S.A.
Apartment	Apt.
Approximate	Approx.
Architectural	Arch.
Asbestos	Asb.
Average	Av.
Average Length	Av. L
Bags	Bgs.
Basement	Bsmt.
Bathroom	B
Beam	Bm.
Better	Btr.
Beveled	Bev.
Blocking	Blkg.
Board	Bd.
Board Foot	Bd. Ft.
Brick	Brk.

British Thermal Unit	BTU
Building	Bldg.
Bundle	Bdl.
Cabinet	Cab.
Casing	Csg.
Cast Iron	CI
Ceiling	Clg.
Cement	Cem.
Cement Floor	Cem. Fl.
Cement Mortar	Cem. Mort.
Center Line	CL
Center Matched	CM
Closet	Cl. or Clo.
Column	Col.
Common	Com.
Concrete	Conc.
Concrete Block	Conc. B
Conduit	Cnd.
Construction	Const.
Counter	Ctr.
Cubic Foot	Cu. Ft.
Cubic Inch (or cubic inches)	C. In.
Cubic Yard	Cu. Yd.
Degree	Deg. or °
Diagram	Diag.
Diameter	Dia. or Diam.
Dining Room	DR
Dimension	Dim.
Direct Current	DC
Ditto	Do.
Double Hung Window	DHW
Double Strength Glass	DSG
Drawing	Dwg.
Dressed and Matched	D & M
Drop Siding	DS
Edge	Edg.
Edge Grain	EG
Entrance	Ent.
Excavate	Exc.
Exterior	Ext.
Factory (lumber)	Facty.
Fahrenheit	Fahr. (or F)
Federal Housing Authority	FHA
Finish	Fin.
Fixture	Fix.
Flashing	Fl.
Flat Back	F. Bk.
Flat Grain	FG
Floor	Fl.

Flooring	Flg.
Fluorescent	Fluor.
Foot or Feet	Ft. (or ')
Footing	Ftg.
Foundation	Fdn.
Framing	Frm.
Furring	Fur.
Gallon	Gal.
Galvanized Iron	GI
Glass	Gl.
Hardwood	Hdwd.
Horsepower	HP
Hose Bib	HB
Hot Water	HW
Heart	Hrt.
Hundred	C
Heartwood	Hrtwd.
Inch (or inches)	In. (or ")
Insulation	Ins.
Interior	Int.
Kiln-dried	KD
Kitchen	K
Knocked Down	k.d.
Lavatory	Lav.
Length	Lgth.
Light	Lt.
Linear Foot (12 inches)	Lin. Ft.
Linen Closet	L Cl.
Linoleum	Lino.
Living Room	LR
Lumber	Lbr.
Masonry Opening	MO
Material	Matl.
Maximum	Max.
Medicine Cabinet	MC
Mill Run	MR
Minimum	Min.
Miscellaneous	Misc.
Mixed Width	MW
Modular	Mod.
Molding	Mldg.
Multiplied By	X
Nail Size (penny)	D
Net Weight	Nt. Wt.
Nosing	Nos.
Number	No. (or #)
On Center	OC
Opening	Opng.

Ounce (or ounces)	Oz.
Partition	Pn.
Pattern	Pat.
Plaster	Plas.
Plate	Pl.
Plate Glass	Pl. Gl.
Plumbing	Plbg.
Precast	Prcst.
Prefabricated	Prefab.
Quart	Qt.
Random	Rdm.
Random Length	RL
Random Width	RW
Refrigerator	Ref.
Reinforcing	Reinf.
Revolutions Per Minute	RPM
Revision	Rev.
Ripped	Rip.
Roofers	Rfrs.
Roofing	Rfg.
Rough	Rgh.
Rough Opening	Rgh. Opng.
Round	Rd.
Schedule	Sch.
Screen	Scr.
Seasoned	Sd.
Select	Sel.
Service	Serv.
Sheathing	Shthg.
Shelving	Shelv.
Shipping Dry	Sh. D
Siding	Sdg.
Single Strength	SS
Softwood	Sftwd.
Specifications	Spec.
Square	Sq.
Square Edge	Sq. E
Square-edge Siding	SESd.
Square Feet	Sq. Ft.
Squares	Sqrs.
Stairway	Stwy.
Standard	Std.
Standard Bead	SB
Standard Matched	Sm.
Steel	St. or Stl.
Stock	Stk.
Structural	Str.
Surface Feet (an area of 1 sq ft)	SF
Surface Measure	SM
Surfaced and Matched (surfaced 1 or 2 sides, and tongued — and grooved on edges. The match may be center or standard)	S&M
Surfaced Four Sides	S4S
Surfaced One Side	S1S
Surfaced One Side and Two Edges	S1S2E
Surfaced Two Sides	S2S
Switch	Sw. or S
Temperature	Temp.
Terra Cotta	TC
Thermostat	Thermo.
Timbers	Tbrs.
Thousand	M
Tongue and Groove	T&G
Top, Bottom, and Sides	TB&S
Typical	Typ.
Unexcavated	Unexc.
Ventilation	Vent.
Vertical Grain	VG
Water Closet	WC
Water Heater	WH
Weight	Wt.
Wider	Wdr.
Wider, All Length	WL
Width	Wth.
Wood	Wd.
Wrought Iron	WI
Yard (or yards)	Yd.

Built-Ins

The ideal built-in occupies space that is otherwise wasted. Literally, the term refers to anything that is permanently attached, or the opposite of furniture that you can move at will. In essence, existing closets and kitchen cabinets are *built-ins*.

Most times, the project is done to provide additional storage space. The design may occupy an entire wall, be a unit that hangs on a wall or even

Courtesy of Marlite

Open shelving may be viewed as a built-in especially if the pattern creates nooks for pieces of furniture. The span of the shelves depends on the weight they must support.

be a divider that contributes to traffic direction or provides a screen in a room.

Some built-ins may take away from actual floor space, but the results make better use of what remains. For example, a wall unit can be a bookcase, a telephone table, a hi-fi cabinet. It can contain closed cabinets for storage and open areas

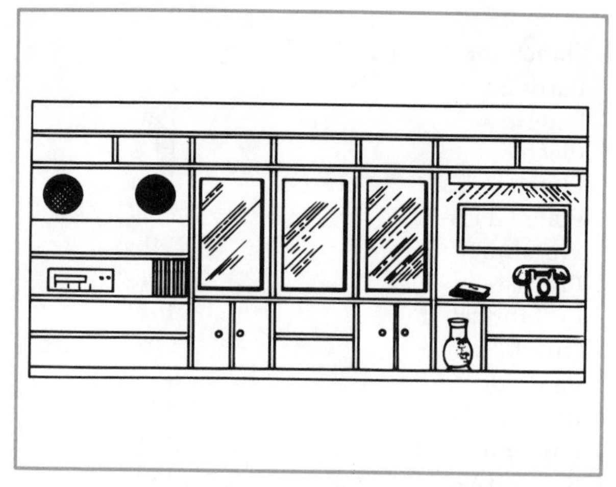

A built-in around a window can be very attractive and can supply plenty of storage space. It can include open shelves, plus a music center with built-in speakers, cabinets, decorative detail areas, a telephone desk, a bulletin board and built-in lighting.

for decorative touches even a "built-in" television set. When comparing a built-in with individual accommodations, you find that you gain usable space when part of it is designed for maximum utilization.

A wall project that is high enough that furniture may be placed beneath takes away none of the floor space. By substituting a ceiling-high unit for a table-high cabinet, you can double or triple the available storage space without using additional floor space.

Built-in work also includes making better use of existing storage space. You may never build a complete project, but merely redesigning the interior of existing closets and cabinets effectively increases the amount of usable space.

Many clothes closets are nothing but space wasters. The single shelf-and-pole design is not engineered for the many items you may wish to store. There is usually a lot space between the shelf and the ceiling but it means the inconvenience of stacking items. A second shelf, perhaps narrower than the first, will be helpful, but it is only a step in solving the overall problem.

Dresses need more vertical space than coats, shirts and sweaters, yet the closet is designed for

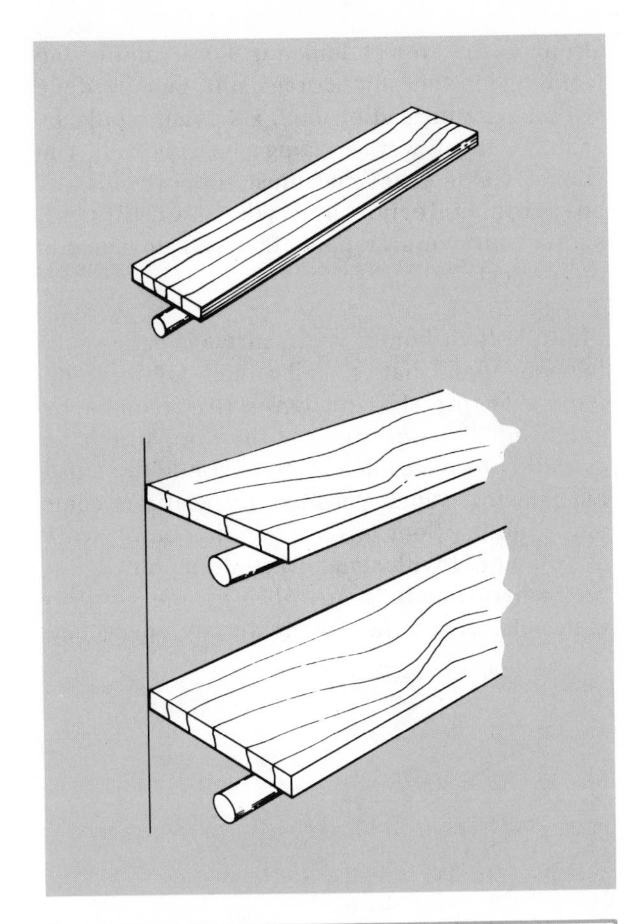

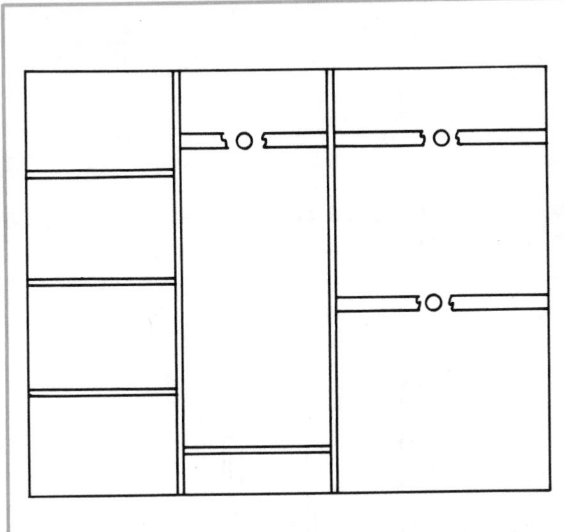

The single shelf and pole in the average closet is very poor design since it provides but one storage height. Adding another shelf and pole is an improvement but installing vertical dividers is better. Then, you can add poles for different heights and shelves. Also utilize space near the floor.

the dresses only. A good answer is to install vertical dividers so you can hang a length of pole at dress height and add others to accommodate items that need less room. When you view the closet as *space* and design it specifically for those articles you wish to store there, you will include additional poles, shelves, drawers, and racks. Good engineering may result in as much as twice the *usable* space.

This also applies to kitchen cabinets. The standard, equally spaced, straight shelves are inconvenient and waste space. Using a method that enables you to change shelf heights is a help, but only a step in the right direction.

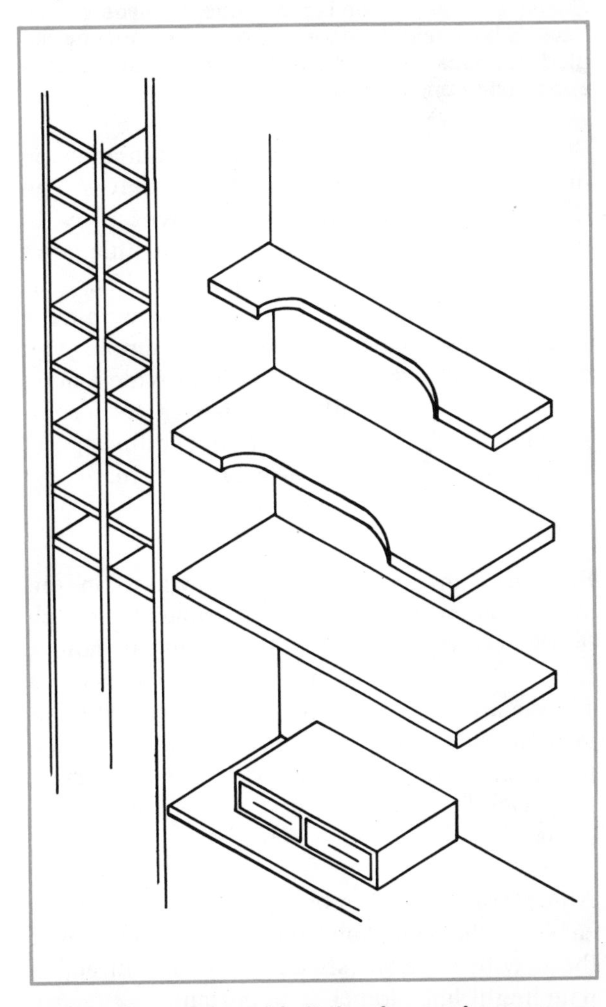

Design the *interior* of built-ins for maximum space utilization and convenience. Ideas shown here are for a built-in bar: bins for storage of wine bottles, narrow balcony shelves, wide balcony shelves, full shelves, case with small drawers for bar equipment.

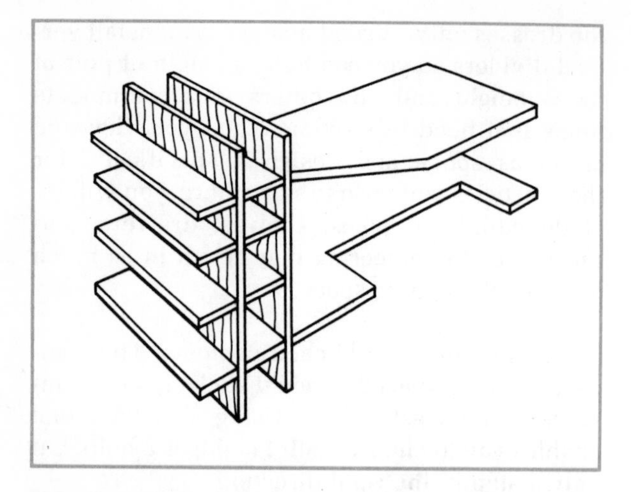

Check shelves in existing built-ins. Shelves do not have to be straight pieces of wood. They can be angled, set back, notched which provides more usable space and convenience.

Shelves can be cut in a basically triangular shape or they may be cut back as balcony shelves. The point here is that the novel shelves provide different heights for storage. There is little point in having a shelf 12 inches high for a coffee pot if the rest of the shelf will be occupied with cups and saucers. For this particular example, you could install a vertical divider to provide a nook for the pot plus additional shelves to accommodate the low items. You are not adding space, but you are using more of what is there.

PLACES FOR THE BUILT-IN

Built-ins can be put almost anywhere in the average home. Cut an opening through the siding in the crawl space of a basementless house, frame it, and hang a door that will conceal a storage area for long pieces of lumber and similar materials. Racks for the storage items can be pieces of lumber nailed across posts or piers or they can be U-shaped assemblies hung from joists.

Attic storage units can be made by erecting vertical studs that run from floor to roof joists. Cover these with drywall (sheetrock) or an attractive paneling if appearance is important.

As these projects are not bearing structures, that is, they are not needed structurally, the homeowner can choose materials that are only as strong as the project demands. For example, the framing for the attic storage unit can be done with 2 x 2's instead of the 2 x 4's that would be required if you were erecting a bearing wall. The frame is a skeleton that must support only the covering materials and whatever internal shelves, drawers or poles that you design into the project.

Multiple floor homes with stairways have space beneath them that is well suited for built-ins. Add a frame that outlines the area to be enclosed. The perimeter at the floor line is an assembly of plates that are nailed into the existing flooring. When possible, try to direct some nails into the floor joists. From this point, work as you would with standard studding but, again, be aware that it is possible to use smaller materials. When the understairway space per-

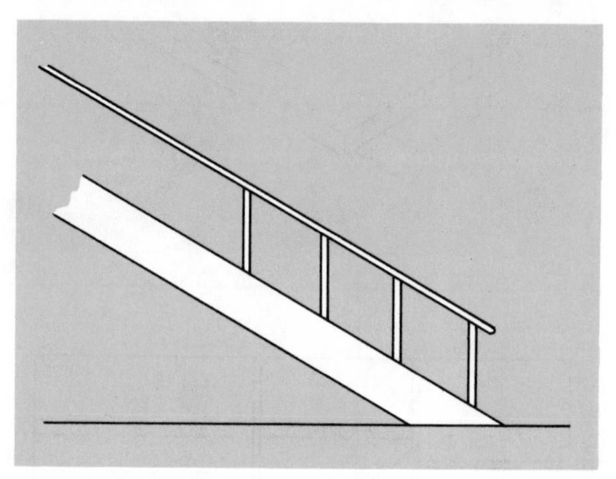

Make use of wasted space under a stairway by adding a built-in.

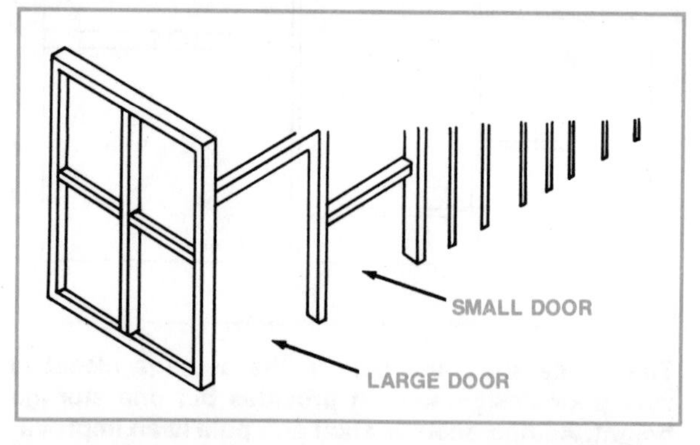

This project requires open studs for attachment of wall paneling. Design interior to suit. The size of doors depends on the space that is available.

mits, you can use a full-size door and have, in effect, a walk-in closet. If this isn't possible, utilize small doors that conceal reach-in storage space.

Look for places to install very shallow cabinets. An example would be a cabinet for canned goods in which the shelves have to be only as wide as the largest can to be stored. Possible locations are walls in a kitchen or a utility room, or even an extra-wide hallway where reducing the width by five or six inches wouldn't be critical. Other possible places for built-ins include: the space above the bowl and basin in the bathroom, the walls above the laundry appliances in the utility room, areas under sinks, the corners of any room, the exposed rafters in a garage and rooms that are so large that covering an entire wall will not restrict the living space.

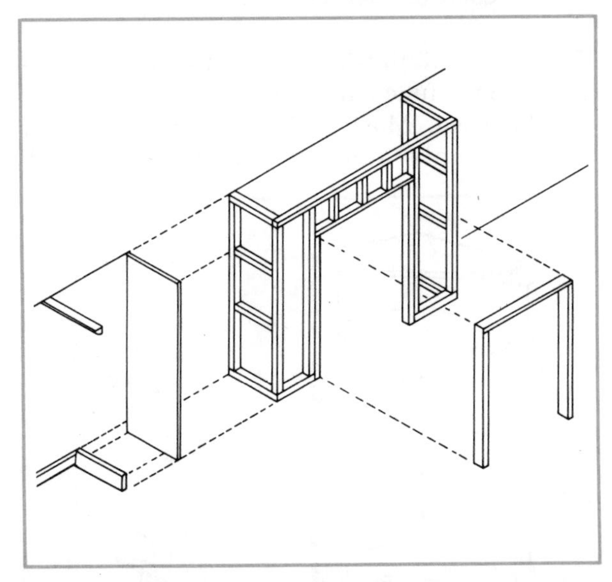

Attach parts of new frame to existing studs, and joists wherever possible. Place double studs at door opening. Cover molding, baseboard, door frame.

Remember that the walls of the average house are hollow (although they might be filled with insulation). If you add up the total number of cubic feet that are between the outside wall and the inside wall you come up with a rather startling accumulation of unused space. Some of this space can be used.

The basics for such a project involve cutting through the existing wall covering to open up a

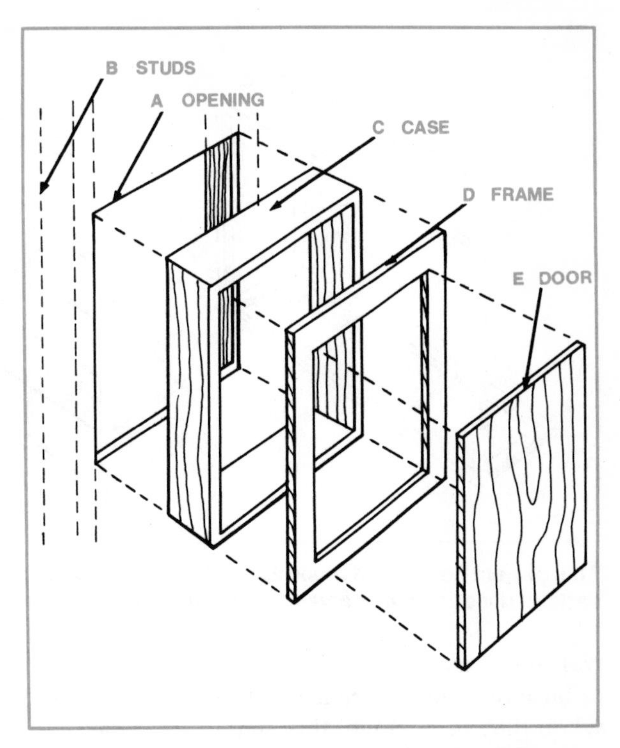

Cut an opening in the wall to reveal the space between the studs. Make a "case" with or without a back to fit the opening. Secure it by nailing into the studs. The case may have shelves. Add a frame that will hide the front edges of the case. The project may be left open or it may be closed by hanging a door on the frame.

space between the studs. This limits the width unless you wish to cut through the studs and install a header as substitute support. The only thing that interferes with the height of the project is the fire blocking that is in the wall.

Make a case to fit; its depth should equal the width of the studs plus the thickness of the wall covering. You can choose whether to put a back on it or not. Secure this case in the opening by nailing through its sides into the studs. Make a frame (preferably with mitered corners) so it will hide the edges of the case and the joint between the wall coverings and the case. Nail this into the case-edges. All that is necessary now is hang a door. If you want shelves, install them in the case before you put the assembly in the opening. Leave the shelves exposed if you wish. If you have the plans of the house, check them before doing any cutting to be sure you do not encounter wiring or plumbing. Most such in-the-

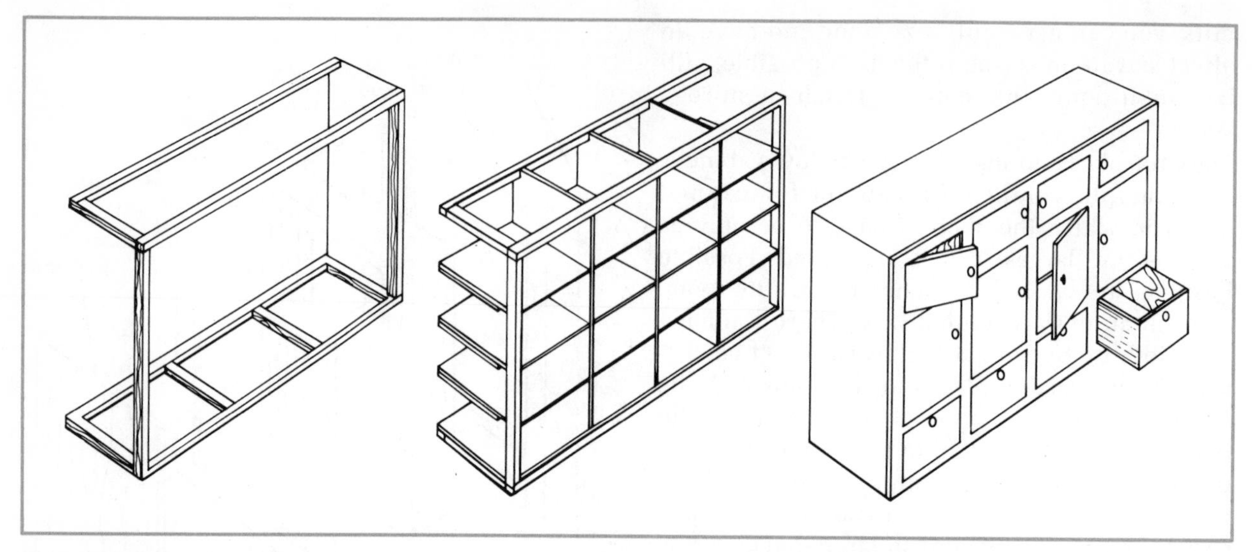

This project consists of basic 2x3 or 2x2 framing attached to floor, walls, and ceiling. Add vertical dividers and shelves. Finish with a facing to which you hang doors or insert drawers.

wall items come directly up from a crawl space or basement and are reasonably close to the floor when they must travel through a wall. One way to find these is to check the locations of sinks, outlets and ceiling fixtures.

MATERIALS TO WORK WITH

Plywood is often recommended for built-ins. Often, 3/4 inch panels require only a minimum of framing. A project that juts out from a wall or a corner can actually be preassembled of plywood panels and then pushed into place. For security it can be toe-nailed at strategic places into floor, walls, and ceiling. The joints between the new unit and existing surfaces should be covered with a suitable molding.

The thinner the cover material, the more framing will be needed. This also applies when the cover material cannot be assembled with standard joints such as drywall materials. The framing does not have to conform to the standards established for house framing. You can work with 2 x 2's or 2 x 3's instead of 2 x 4's unless the project requires the heavier material.

Shelves can rest on cleats or special perforated strips and brackets that are made for the purpose. In either case, the support materials should be firmly attached to the wall. When possible, attach these directly into the existing wall studs.

The degree of finishing (total appearance) depends on the function of the project and where it will be used. Most shelves in the house for clothes, books and kitchenware should be

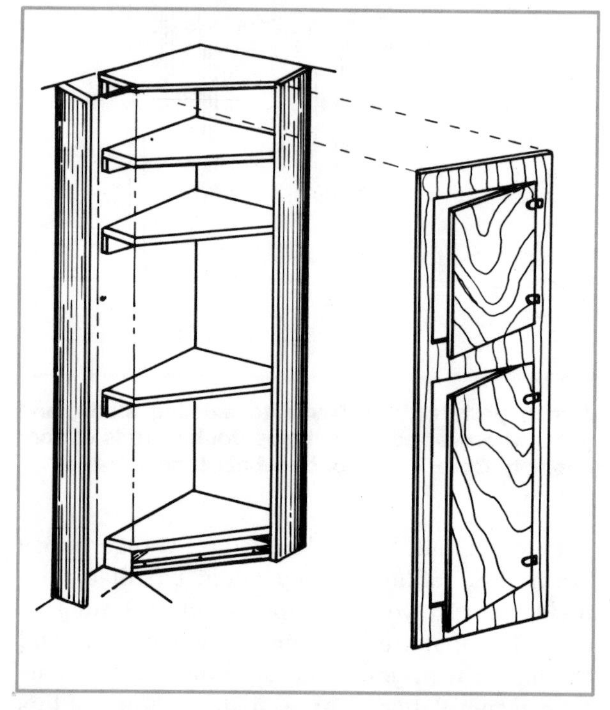

Corners are ideal for built-ins that utilize waste space. Set triangle shelves on cleats. Add sides if any of the bottom shelf rests on cleats. Finish by attaching front facing and hanging doors, or leave shelves open.

By-pass sliding doors are good for large built-ins since they do not need the room that is required for swing doors. These solid lumber doors are floor-to-ceiling and move on rollers hung from special tracks.

smooth and have solid front edges. With solid lumber give them a good sanding. If plywood is being used, either band the exposed edges or glue on strips of solid lumber. This kind of care is not necessary if you are installing, for example, paint shelves in the garage. Plywood edges are no problem when the material is used for internal components on a project that will have a facing frame. Here, you would use solid lumber for the facing and this would conceal the plywood edges.

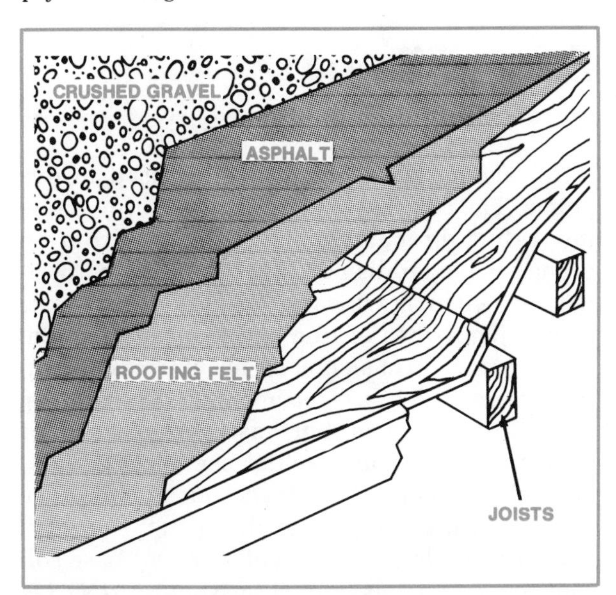

Cutaway of a built-up roof.

Built-Up Roof

A built-up roof, for use on low-sloped roofs, is composed of several layers of roof felt or jute treated with asphalt or coal tar. The top layer of crushed gravel or marble, usually light colored to reflect sunlight, is an attractive feature of this type of roof. *SEE ALSO ROOF CONSTRUCTION.*

Bullet Catch

A bullet catch is a type of hardware used to keep swinging doors, such as cabinet, bi-fold or drop doors, closed. The catch consists of a rounded, protruding end which can be snapped into a concave holder. *SEE ALSO KITCHEN DESIGN & PLANNING.*

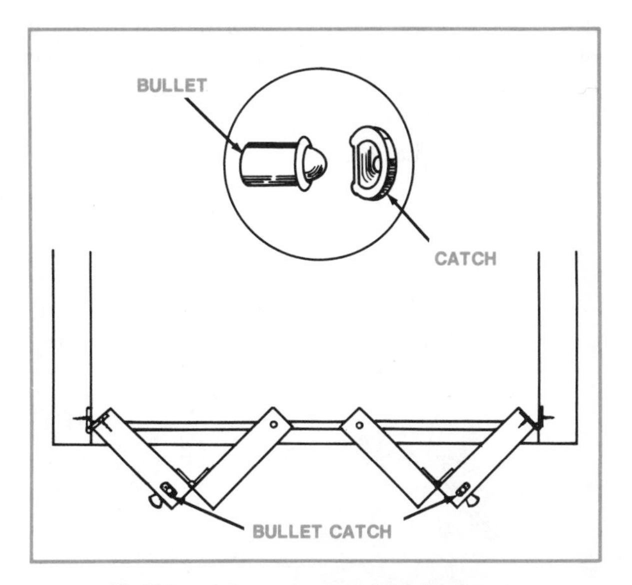

Bullet catches used on bi-fold doors.

Bullnose

Bullnose is the term used to describe a surface that has been rounded to eliminate a sharp corner. The front edge of most stair treads has a bullnosed finish. Generally, the first step in a stairway has a bullnosed corner to lend a finished appearance for decorative purposes. A bullnosed plane is a small hand plane with a rounded nose that has the iron set near the front end of the stock for close corner work.

Bunch Splice

A basic electrical wiring technique, bunch splice is the name often given to the pigtail splice when it joins more than two wires. It is made in much the same way as the usual pigtail. Twist the three wires simultaneously so they will fit together like the strands in a rope. If two strands are twisted first, then over-wrapped with the third one, the splices will not be as secure.

In taping bunch splice, start tape on one branch and run onto bare section. Tape a little way beyond the end of bare wire, then back onto other branches. Fold over excess at end of splice and use a separate piece of tape to make an extra turn or two. Rubber tape is best for complex splices. *SEE ALSO ELECTRICAL WIRING.*

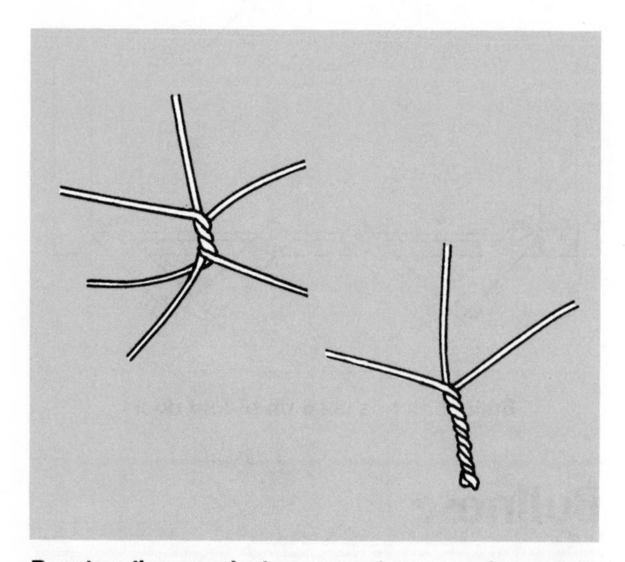

Bunch splice, used when more than two wires are to be combined, starts like this (left). All wires are twisted together like strands in a rope. Completed bunch splice is shown at right.

Bunk Rooms

[SEE REMODELING.]

Burglar Alarms

[SEE HOME ALARM SYSTEMS.]

Burglar Insurance

[SEE INSURANCE PROTECTION.]

Burls

Burls are hard, woody outgrowths, often of a flattened hemispherical form, which occur on trunks or branches of trees. Although they are associated with adventitious buds, they also serve as a protective covering for an injured area. The large, knurled, wart-like growths are removed from the tree and peeled like an apple to produce a valuable and attractive veneer which is also referred to as *burl.*

Burnt Sienna

Burnt sienna is a pigment (color) used to dye paints. The colorant is classified as a brown pigment, but the color actually ranges from an orange red to reddish brown. It is made by roasting raw sienna, which is an earthy substance containing oxides of iron and manganese. Paint stores carry burnt sienna in the "universal" tinting colors which are recommended for dyeing vinyl, acrylic or rubber-base paints; also for coloring alkyd or oil-base flat, semigloss or gloss enamels, linseed oil or alkyd house paints. The pigment is also available in oil and in this form, it is recommended for use in oil or alkyd-base solvent reduced paints only. *SEE ALSO PAINTS & PAINTING.*

Burnt Umber

Burnt umber is a brown pigment (color) used to dye paints. It is darker in color than either ocher or sienna. This pigment is made by roasting raw umber, an earthy substance containing a high content of manganese and iron oxides. Umber is highly valued as a permanent color in either the raw or burnt state. Burnt umber may be purchased from paint stores in either the "universal" form or in oil. Use the "universal" tinting colors for dyeing vinyl, acrylic or rubber-base paints; also for tinting alkyd or oil-base flat, semigloss or gloss enamels, linseed oil or alkyd house paints. The colors in oil should be used only to dye oil or alkyd-base solvent reduced paints. *SEE ALSO PAINTS & PAINTING.*

Bushings

Whether it is a plumbing job, mechanical work or electrical wiring, bushings can assist you in your labor.

Although different in design from a reducer, a bushing in the plumbing field serves the same purpose as a reducer. It is a standard plumber fitting used to join two pipes of different diameters. The threaded, larger end of the bushing fits into a plumbing fixture or coupling, while the threaded opening is a smaller hole which will allow the smaller of the two pipes to be fitted into it.

A bushing, used as a mechanical part, is a removable cylindrical lining for an opening. Besides limiting the size of the opening, it helps resist abrasion and serves as a guide.

In electrical work, the small fiber insulated lining inserted in a hole to protect a through conductor is referred to as a bushing. Preventing the cut metal edge from rubbing against the insulated wires is very important. Therefore, electrical wiring codes specify that bushings must be used with BX cable as protective insulators.

Butt Chisels

Butt chisels are designed with short blades (about 3 inches long) for working in tight places where a longer blade would not give the control needed. Although blade widths range from 1/8 to 2 inches, the home handyman will find that four sizes (1/4, 1/2, 3/4, and 1 inch) will serve practically every requirement. Butt chisels are so named because they are primarily used for making mortise cuts when installing butt hinges. *SEE ALSO HAND TOOLS.*

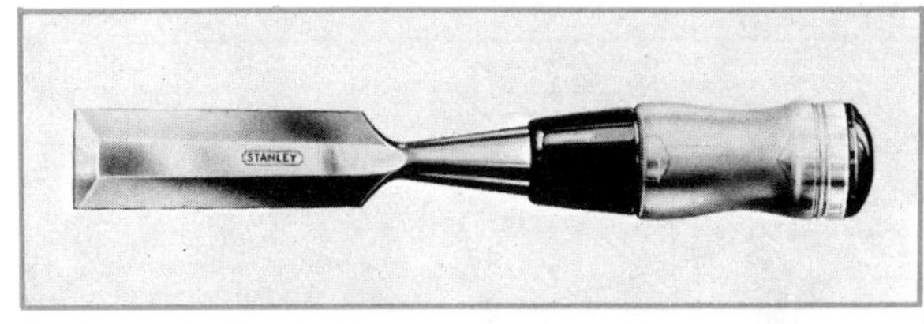

Courtesy of The Stanley Works

Butt Chisel

Butterfly Roof

A butterfly roof is a double-surfaced shed roof, pitched or sloped so that water sheds toward the center. Improvements in drainage and waterproofing methods have made this type of roof practical. The tendency of the butterfly roof to accumulate snow and ice limits its use to areas with warmer climates. *SEE ALSO ROOF CONSTRUCTION.*

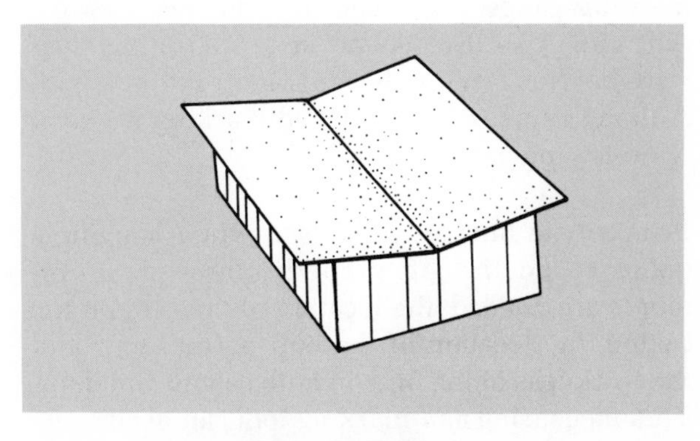

Butterfly Roof

Buttering

Buttering is the process of spreading mortar on a block. This process secures a block to the surrounding blocks.

Besides buttering the projecting ends of the block that will join with the block already in place, butter the top of the block on which this one will be placed. The layer of mortar formed by buttering the top of two or three blocks is called a bed. *SEE ALSO CONCRETE BLOCK.*

Buttering

Butt Gauge

A double-bar gauge for marking two parallel lines at any given distance from the edge of a board is termed butt gauge. This miniature metal marking gauge is used to indicate recesses for butt hinges so that the surface of the hinge leaf will be flush with the surface of the wood. Although smaller than a wood marking gauge, it operates much the same.

Primarily, a butt gauge is used when hanging a door. To do the job properly, three measurements are needed: the location of the butt on the casing, the location of the butt on the door and the thickness of the butt on both casing and door. This measuring and marking tool can accurately gauge all three.

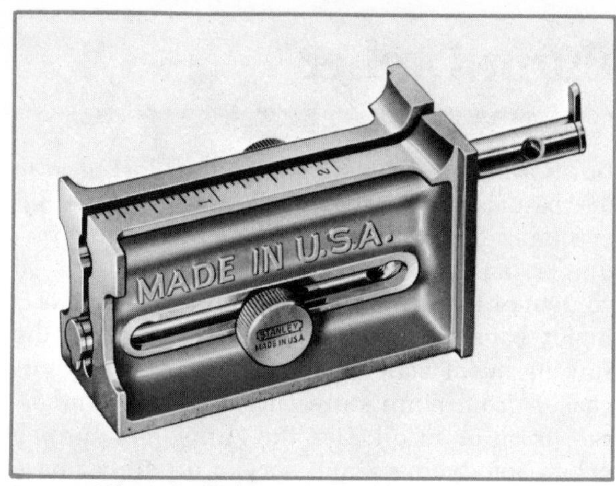

Courtesy of The Stanley Works

Butt Gauge

Square with the base, the ends of a butt gauge serve as a marking square. A pointed "cutter" is adjusted to mark the rectangular outline of the recess to be made and the depth to which it is to be cut. When setting the cutter bar so that the cutter will scribe the hinge width on both door and jamb, allow for the usual setback. The squared flange on the marking gauge permits its use as a try square for marking the end lines of the hinge recesses. *SEE ALSO HAND TOOLS.*

Butt Hinge

A butt hinge is a type of door hinge that has one leaf fastened to the edge of a door and the other leaf fastened to the side of the door-frame jamb. A butt-style hinge usually requires a mortise and

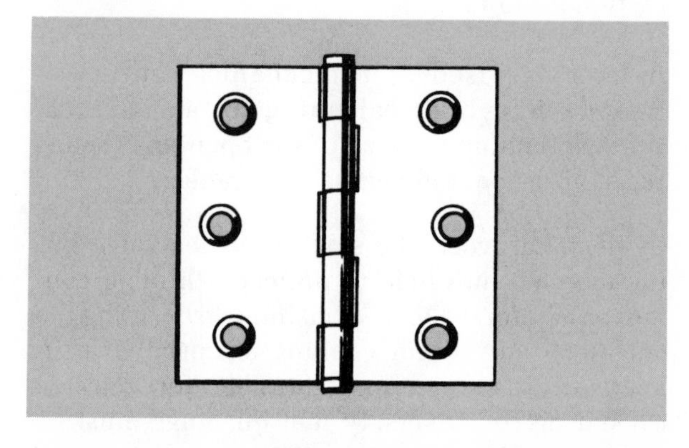

Butt Hinge

gain, but there is the no-mortise type that is flush-mounted with one leaf folding over the other. A simple butt hinge cannot be taken apart, but is reversible — that is, it can be used with either a left- or right-handed door. If carpeting interferes with opening the door, use a rising butt hinge that allows the door to rise slightly to clear the carpeting when the door is swung open. *SEE ALSO HINGES.*

Butt Joint

The most common of joints, a butt joint is a simple joint made by abutting one member against another, end to end, end to edge or edge to edge. Adequate for most edge-gluing work, it is usually a right angle or 90° joint where the two pieces are perpendicular to each other.

Because the butt joint is the weakest of all types of joints, its strength depends upon the kind of mechanical fastener that is used. Nails, screws, glue, bolts, anchors and rivets may be utilized to secure a butt joint.

Although most frequently used in "rough" construction, a butt joint is suitable for some commercial pieces of fine furniture. A craftsmanlike finished appearance can be obtained by sanding, filing and painting the exposed end sufficiently to give it a slick look. Cutting a shallow kerf just below the edge also helps to improve the joint. To construct a butt joint, you need only a try square, crosscut saw, hammer and either a screwdriver or drill, depending upon the fastening method desired.

Several methods of fastening a butt joint are possible. Adhesive fastening will hold the joint. However, by combining it with another fastening method such as blind doweling, the joint can be made much stronger. Driving nails in at an angle, a technique called toe-nailing, and end-nailing through one piece of wood into the end grain of the other are used to secure a butt joint. If a finishing nail is used, the nail head can be countersunk to conceal the fastener. Roundhead and flathead screws are inserted similarly.

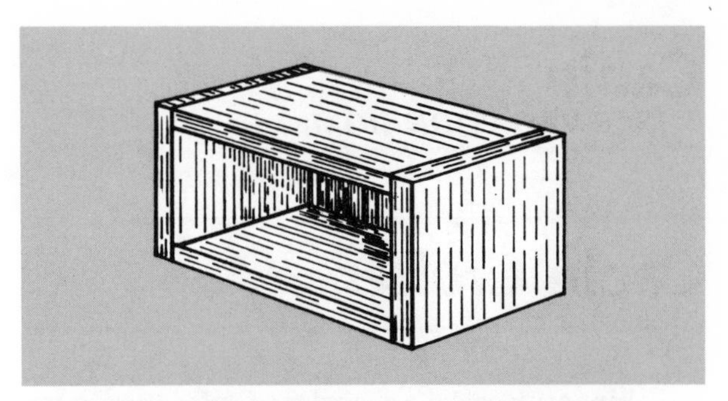

In the simple construction of butt joints, edges to be joined must be perfectly square with the try square before they are fitted together.

Another way to hold a butt joint together is with corrugated fasteners placed on both sides of the joint. These are mainly for use when flat pieces of wood are joined together. For additional strength, angle irons at each corner of the butt joint, or T-straps placed on both sides, have more holding power than most of the other methods of fastening. *SEE ALSO FURNITURE MAKING; WOOD JOINTS.*

Buzzers

[SEE DOORBELLS, CHIMES & BUZZERS.]

BX Cable

BX is the trade name for an extensively used flexible armored cable. It contains two or more insulated copper wires which in turn are wrapped with stiff paper and enclosed in spiraled galvanized steel. There is also a small uninsulated ground wire inside the cable which the handyman may ignore; the metallic armor of BX cable acts as a grounding conductor. BX cable can be used for both concealed and exposed interior wiring and with steel junction and switch boxes. *SEE ALSO WIRE SIZES & TYPES.*

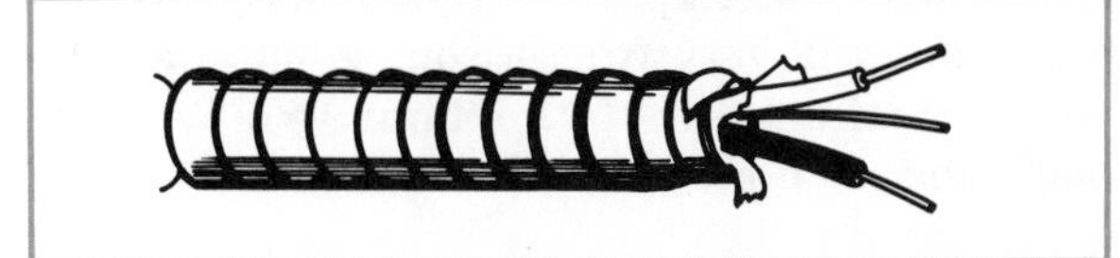

BX Cable

Cabin

[SEE VACATION HOMES.]

Cabin Cruiser

A cabin cruiser is an enclosed pleasure boat powered by a gasoline or diesel marine engine. Cabin cruisers may be used for fishing, day or overnight cruising, or, particularly in the larger sizes, as a temporary or permanent home.

Cabin cruisers range in size from about 20 to more than 60 feet in length. Most cabin cruisers presently being built are made of fiberglass, although wood, steel, aluminum, and ferrocement are also used in boatbuilding.

All cabin cruisers contain six standard areas: bridge, lounge deck, salon, galley, stateroom, and head. The bridge is the location of the main power and steering controls. Depending on the size of the boat, the bridge will usually be located in the salon or the cockpit. Fishing cruisers may have a secondary set of controls located on an elevated flybridge.

The lounge deck is the large open cockpit at the rear of the boat. Depending on the size of the boat, this area may vary from a workmanlike fishing platform to an elaborate entertainment area.

The salon is the living room of the boat. In smaller boats, settees in the salon will convert to berths for two to four persons. The galley, a compact kitchen, often occupies a portion of the salon.

In larger cabin cruisers, sleeping accommodations are moved from the salon to staterooms. Again, depending upon the size of the boat, the stateroom will vary from a somewhat cramped room in the bow of the boat to spacious bedrooms with private baths.

Marine bathrooms, or heads, are also items that vary with cruiser size. In smaller cruisers, the head will be a small portable toilet concealed in the forward stateroom. In larger boats, the head will have a pressurized water system, flush toilet, and possibly even a showerbath.

Photo Courtesy Trojan Yacht

A cabin cruiser provides an ideal way to enjoy water sports.

All cabin cruisers come equipped with standard Coast Guard safety equipment. The remaining equipment installed upon the boat is largely at the whim and pocketbook of the prospective boat owner. SEE ALSO RECREATIONAL BOATS & BOATING

Cabinet Making

[SEE KITCHEN DESIGN & PLANNING.]

Cable

Cable consists of separately insulated wires wrapped together inside a protective covering. Cable can be installed in both finished and unfinished buildings because it threads easily through walls and floor joists. The main types of cable are flexible armored cable, nonmetallic sheathed cable and plastic-covered cable.

FLEXIBLE ARMORED CABLE

Flexible armored cable can be used for both concealed and exposed interior wiring, but only in permanently dry locations. It consists of two or more insulated wires covered with a spiraled steel armor which permits flexibility and makes the cable a grounding conductor. Flexible armored cable should be used with steel junction and switch boxes.

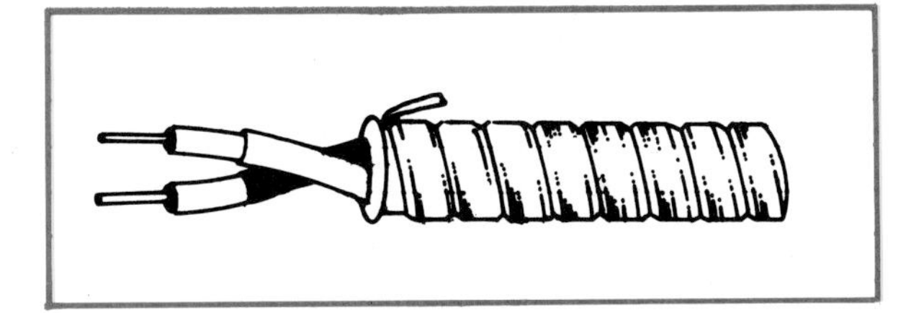

Flexible Armored Cable

NONMETALLIC SHEATHED CABLE

Nonmetallic sheathed cable is encased in a moisture- and fire-resistant braided fabric covering. Since its covering would rot if exposed to moisture, nonmetallic sheathed cable is used only in permanently dry locations. Nonmetallic sheathed cable is extensively used in ordinary house wiring.

Both flexible armored cable and nonmetallic sheathed cable are installed to distribute electricity from the fuse or circuit breaker box to household switches and outlets.

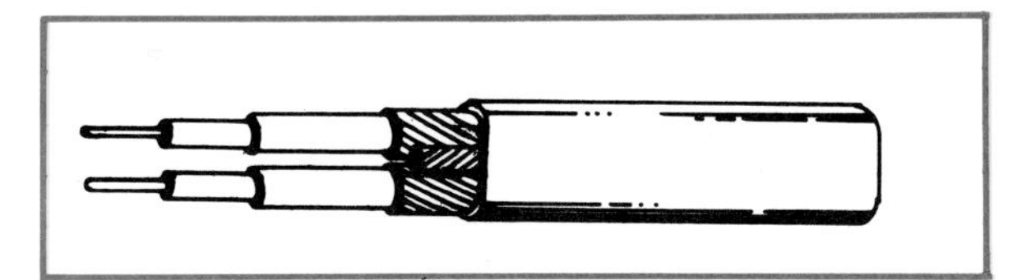

Nonmetallic Sheathed Cable

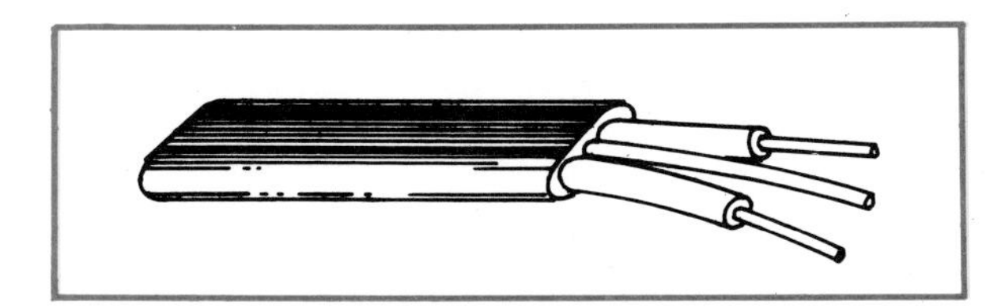

Plastic-Covered Cable

PLASTIC-COVERED CABLE

Plastic-covered cable is coated with a tough, waterproof plastic so that it can be used underground without further protection. Plastic-covered or underground cable is used in damp locations, out of doors and underground to wire a driveway light or an outbuilding or garage, for example. Plastic-covered cable may also be used indoors. Lead-encased underground cable may be substituted for plastic-covered cable if local electrical codes demand it. Underground wiring provides a safer installation because the cable is not exposed, reducing the danger of lightning.

If the handyman is confused as to which cable to use, he should consult his local electrical supplier indicating the purpose for which it will be used. An electrical supplier will know which cables local codes require. *SEE ALSO WIRE SIZES & TYPES.*

Cable Cutting

Cable cutting is often necessary when installing house wiring, and should be done with the proper tools and procedures. Armored or BX cable is cut with metal snips and a turning action of the hands. To begin the process, grip the cable with both hands about two feet apart and bend it toward the body. The armor should then buckle. With one hand on either side of the buckle, twist the cable in the direction opposite the spiral. The cable will begin to break at the point of the buckle. Slip a pair of metal snips into the break and snip all the way around the armor without cutting the wires. The section to be removed can then be slid off the end of the cable. The large recesses of the jaw of the metal snips may be used to reshape the cable after the cut has been made.

Nonmetallic sheathed cable or rigid cable (like surface wiring) is cut with a hacksaw in much the same manner as cutting a board. Either a cable ripper or a multipurpose cable cutter will cut flexible nonmetallic sheathed cable. To cut these types, slide the rippers over the cable and squeeze the handles together. Then, the rippers can be used to strip the insulation from the wires. *SEE ALSO ELECTRICAL WIRING.*

Cable Designation

Cables are designated with letter names by the National Electrical Code according to their prescribed use; however, trade names are probably used as much or more than the letter designations. In the national code, armored cable (BX) is referred to as Type AC. Nonmetallic sheathed cable (Romex) is designated as Type NM, but if it is exposed to weather its designation is Type NMC. Underground cable is called Type USE (Underground Service Entrance); a newer underground cable UF (Underground Fused) is similar to USE, but it must be protected by fuses and circuit breakers at the point of origin. Type UF is identical in appearance to Type NMC, and Underwriters' Laboratories have approved some brands as Type UF-NMC for use in interior and underground wiring. *SEE ALSO WIRE SIZES & TYPES.*

Cable Ripper

The cable ripper is a flat wedge-shaped instrument used for "ripping" or separating the strands of a cable. The cable ripper, lighter and faster than a jackknife, is used for extensive wiring jobs such as wiring a house. *SEE ALSO ELECTRICIAN'S TOOLS & EQUIPMENT.*

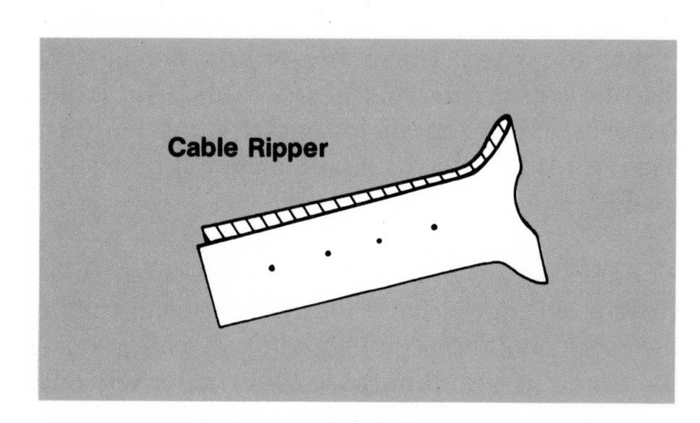

Cable Stringing

[SEE ELECTRICAL WIRING.]

Cable Support

Cable support is necessary to anchor cable as it is installed behind baseboards, along the roof, in meter sockets and in other areas. Armored cable, enclosed in galvanized steel, is supported by long staples. Nonmetallic sheathed cable, covered in a special fabric braid, is supported by metal cable straps which fit over the cable and are fastened to the wood or other surface by long screws on either side of the cable. All parts of the cable should fit easily behind the baseboard, without causing the baseboard to protrude from the wall. If there is unnecessary pressure on the cable, a recess should be made in the back of the baseboard to accommodate proper cable placement and support. *SEE ALSO ELECTRICAL WIRING.*

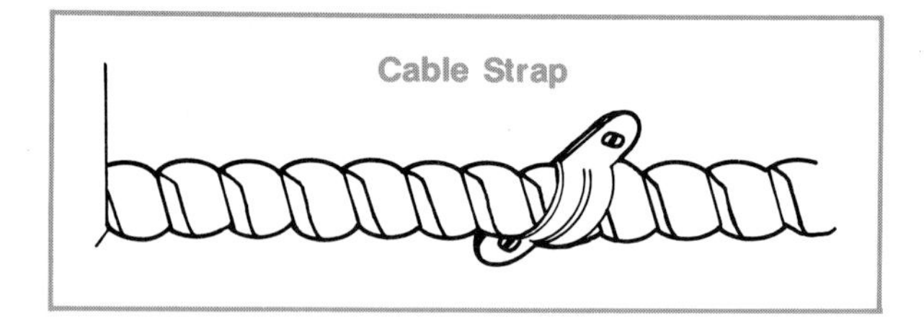

Cable, Waterproof

Waterproof cable is a plastic-covered cable used in wet, outdoor and underground locations, as in wiring an outbuilding, basement or driveway light. *SEE ALSO WIRE SIZES & TYPES.*

Cafe Swinging Doors

A familiar sight at cafes and bars for many years, the swinging door has become quite popular as a means of interior decorating in the home. Besides introducing a different touch to interior design, cafe swinging doors provide additional privacy between rooms.

Either a single door or a pair of doors is considered a swinging door. Double cafe doors enable a room to be semi-closed off without reducing its total size. To break the endless tunnel effect of long, narrow hallways, place swinging cafe doors a portion of the way down. This placement divides the more public open doorway or entrance from other areas, such as the bedroom, bath or kitchen which tend to be more private.

Although these doors should measure approximately half the length of the doorway, they are hung so that there is more clearance at the bottom than at the top. Double hinges are required to hang the doors, enabling them to swing in and out.

Cafe Swinging Doors

Calculators

[SEE HOME CALCULATORS.]

Calculator Tricks

[SEE HOME CALCULATORS.]

Caliper Rule

A boxwood type folding rule with a built-in caliper is known as a caliper rule. This measuring instrument quickly gauges the thickness of lumber or the diameter of round stock like a closet pole or dowel. Usually 1-inch long, it is made up of a graduated bar, one fixed jaw and one moveable jaw.

Caliper rules are designed to provide both inside and outside dimensions of cylinders. Simply close the caliper against the stock to be measured and take the reading directly from the brass slide in thirty-seconds of an inch. When figuring an outside measurement or thickness, stock must be placed between the jaws of the tool. Readings should be taken from the scale on the rule marked *out*. The scale marked *in* is used when measuring the width of an opening or figuring an inside measurement. Place the head of the caliper rule inside the stock to accurately gauge inside dimensions. Remember that a caliper rule should be kept folded to provide a wide base in caliper operations.

Quite accurate as a measuring tool, the caliper rule can also pinch hit as a marking guide for angle lines when the legs are set with a protractor. *SEE ALSO HAND TOOLS.*

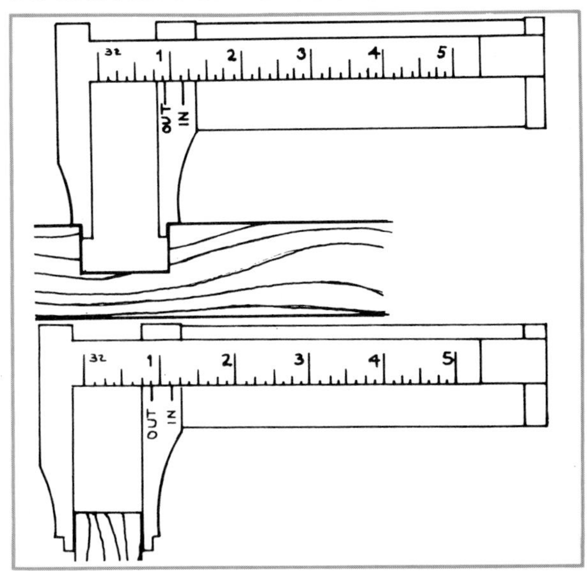

Using a caliper rule.

Calipers

Calipers are measuring instruments with two legs or jaws that can be adjusted to determine thickness, diameter and distance between surfaces. There are three different types of calipers: inside, outside and hermaphrodite. All are basic devices used by machinists and carpenters when accurate measurements are required.

OUTSIDE CALIPERS

External measurements of rounded stock are taken with an outside caliper. Taking an accurate measurement with an outside caliper is easy as long as the legs are not forced over the stock. Place the caliper at right angles to the center line of the cylinder to be measured, pushing it gently back and forth across the diameter of the work. When it moves over the surface with a minimal amount of resistance, the outside caliper is adjusted correctly.

INSIDE CALIPER

An inside caliper is used to determine inside diameters. It must be placed in the opening to gauge accurately. When the caliper slips into the opening with a very slight drag, it is adjusted properly.

HERMAPHRODITE CALIPER

Hermaphrodite calipers, so called because they are half caliper and half divider, are used to measure and mark from an edge. They can be used to locate the centers of pieces of cylindrical stock to find centers for drilled holes and to mark parallel lines. *SEE ALSO HAND TOOLS.*

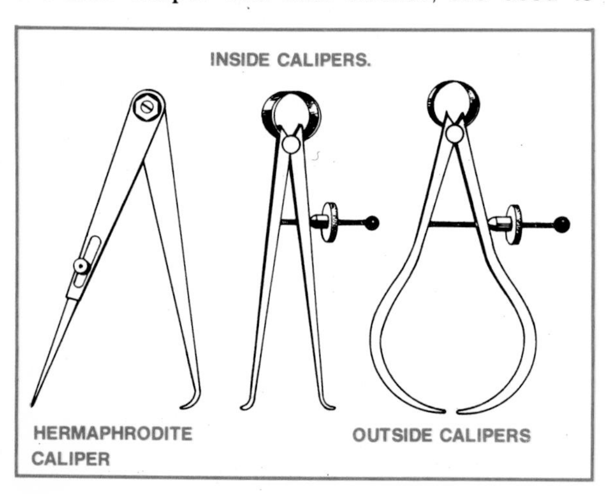

Camber

Camber is the in and out tilt of a wheel. It is referred to as the amount of angle made by the center line of the wheel and the true vertical of the wheel. Proper camber allows even contact with the road to prevent excessive pressure on any portion of the tire.

Improper camber can be caused by wear or damage to spindles, control arm bushings and ball joints. These parts connect the car body and the wheels. If not set at the correct camber, uneven tire wear will result. By placing thin spacers or shims at control areas or by using adjusting bolts, proper camber can be restored.

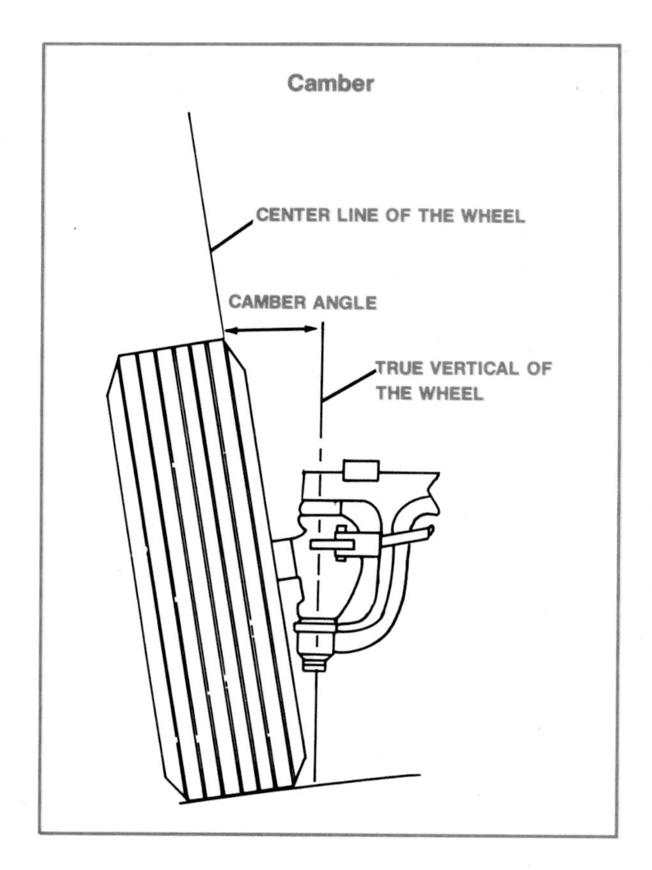

Camping Equipment

Camping can be a bargain vacation. But it takes know-how, or a campout can exceed the cost of a vacation at an expensive resort.

The cost lies in the words *camping equipment.* Sleeping bags, tent, fancy cooking equipment and gadgets can run the bill up to hundreds of dollars. If the camping vacation is rained out, or the great outdoors turns out to be not all that great for a family, they may be stuck with a lot of expensive items to never use again.

Here are a couple of ways to try out camping before investing in equipment. Start by camping overnight, or for a week end, at a campground near home. For a short trip in ideal weather, make-do with blankets and kitchen equipment from home supplies. Sleep out under the stars, as real campers do. If no one complains about bugs or scarey night noises, you are ready to try a longer trip.

This time go to a rental agency, and get a tent, sleeping bags, stove, and perhaps heavy clothing. Ask for the option of applying rental fees to purchase price if you like the equipment well enough to want to make it a permanent part of a camping outfit. It may be possible to select camping equipment by buying at the end of the season when rental dealers often get rid of this year's stock. You will need sharp eyes. Rental items often get mistreated (a main reason for the high cost of renting). Check the intended buys for tears, ripped seams, unworkable zippers, or lost parts. Be a tough bargainer. Be sure to figure in what it will cost for repairs and cleaning.

There are unforseen problems, too. A used tent may have leaks that may not show until a sleeping bag is soaked next summer. Take this precaution. By erecting a used tent in the backyard, and dousing it with a hose, you can find any leaks. During the off-season they can be waterproofed or repaired.

DO-IT-YOURSELF CAMPING EQUIPMENT

Courtesy of Frostline Kits

Every item shown here was a part of a sewing kit. All items of ripstop nylon have been designed for maximum comfort in wind and rain as well as this sunshine.

Save one-third to one-half the cost of buying similar equipment in a store by making tents, sleeping bags and heavy down clothing from ready-to-sew kits. Materials and instructions are first rate. Good results are possible even on a portable sewing machine. The home effort may be a better job than available on some store

Courtesy of Frostline Kits

Bike-camper carries all necessary gear in a seat bag, panniers, and handlebar bag with plastic-window map pocket to keep it dry and dust free. All items shown here were made from ready-cut kits and are of urethane-coated nylon. The straps are nylon and the zippers are Delrin plastic. The rider is wearing a safety vest over his ordinary clothing. For safety all items are highly visible blaze orange.

Courtesy of Frostline Kits

Making camping equipment can be a winter family activity. One person reads and interprets instructions while another does the sewing.

equipment, because you will have time to do the job meticulously, using strong thread and small stitches. Items available in kit form include everything from easy to make hoods and sleeping booties to backpacks, arctic-weight sleeping bags and down jackets.

Companies which sell the kits offer expert assistance by mail, phone, and now through high school classrooms, where they are setting up home economics courses for students who make outdoor equipment in class.

CAMPING EQUIPMENT IS EMERGENCY EQUIPMENT

Well-chosen outdoor equipment is no extravagance if used year around. Sleeping bags which unzip all the way make extra bedding for cold weather or for guests. Good quality camp pans, griddle, dishes work equally well in a home kitchen. A camp lantern, catalytic heater and flashlights can take over when the electricity is out. A tent in the backyard can double as a guest room for visiting children. An icebox or cooling chest will hold ice cubes and drinks for a party, or will stow the most perishable frozen foods should the freezer break down. Good quality equipment, kept clean and well cared for, should last 20 years.

HOW TO BUY IT

Reliable manufacturers of outdoor equipment have been in business many years and they guarantee satisfaction on their products. They put out specification sheets which help to decide which models suit the camper's needs. If their equipment is sold by mail, get a free catalog. Once you buy something, an updated catalog will usually arrive each year. Every item is described in detail. The design, the way it is constructed, exact size, life expectancy, where and in the type weather it can be used, how it compares with other versions, and maintenance cleaning are usually included in the description.

A discount or drug outlet which sells no name-brand tents and sleeping bags is not a good place to shop. The price may be attractive, but the durability of the item is usually low. Also, there will be difficulty exchanging it or getting a refund when the store no longer handles the item.

If you do make such a purchase, try reading the directions for use before buying. Even well made items such as a tent may come with vague directions.

A good precaution on any tent is to use a permanent ink marking pen and print directions clearly and in large letters on the side of the bag which holds the item. Small papers or booklets are easily mislaid and it can become amazingly difficult to erect a tent, for example, after a year has gone by, even if one did the job many times the previous summer.

HOW TO BUY A TENT

This is the most expensive item for most campers. It is an item which should last many years, provided it is cared for properly once chosen.

1. Size

A big-family tent may have several rooms — bedrooms as well as dining-cooking units. If you backpack, you will want a tent big enough to hold sleepers plus gear. If you plan to camp in one area for a week or more, a large tent will be more comfortable. It will be sturdy and need not be moved until vacation ends. It will also be heavy, take up a lot of luggage space and will

Courtesy of Hirsch-Weis White Stag

This lightweight flame retardant explorer tent is tall enough so campers can stand up to put on clothing or stretch legs, a feature not provided by most backpack tents.

Courtesy of Hirsch-Weis White Stag

The sloping walls of this cabin tent give excellent wind resistance. The easy to erect aluminum frame is color coded.

need several people to handle it. If possible, buy your tent from a store which has samples erected on the floor so you can compare sizes and to see how well sleeping bags and other equipment will fit.

If choosing a tent from a catalog, or without seeing it other than in a box, look for the words *finished size*. This gives the actual measurement of available space as opposed to the words *cut size* sometimes given on a less expensive tent. Cut size merely means that seams have not been allowed for and the finished tent will be smaller than the dimensions given.

Before buying, mark out the size considered with string on the living room floor, or with chalk on the driveway. Try fitting in sleeping bags, and see whether the tent which is advertised to sleep four will really do that without inconvenience. A family tent must be large enough for clothing and other equipment too. Some tents come with an area that may or may not have a floor, but with a roof, so wet or muddy gear can be stowed without being brought into the sleeping area.

Look for the amount of headroom available. Be sure that the figure given does not mean a person can stand up only in one small spot at the center of the tent. If excess weight is a concern, you will probably get a tent that requires dressing while sitting down. Claustrophobic persons may find this tent design bothersome because the sides slope until they are only a few inches above you as you sleep.

2. Kind of Fabric

Cotton drill, or better yet, poplin, is best. A 6 ounce or heavier fabric with a 200, or more, thread count per inch, is excellent. These figures are found in the catalog description or on the packing box in the store. Look also for the descriptive word *combed* which means a high quality fabric with no short fibers to weaken it. Army duck is a durable tent fabric, but it is extremely heavy and rarely used for family camping tents. More frequently found are tents made of cotton-dacron or cotton combined with some other synthetic. Adding a synthetic thread adds to fabric strength and also helps cut the cost.

If weight of the tent is important, such as for backpacking, choose ripstop nylon, or nylon taffeta. The taffeta is abrasion resistant and heavier than ripstop, but a tear can run the width of the fabric. It is safe to get the ripstop fabric in about a 1.9 ounce weight.

3. Kind of Waterproofing

Look for the words *dry finish*. This means that fibers have been chemically treated before the tent fabric is woven to give a soft feel, but a resulting material which, once wet, is as waterproof as rubber. Cotton fibers, so treated, swell when they are wet, but the tent breathes so occupants are comfortable. A treated fabric lets in a fine mist for a few minutes as rain starts, ceases once the fibers are thoroughly wet. Equipment or human touch against the fabric can start a leak, but this will cease when contact is removed.

Semi-dry, another tent finish commonly used on cheaper tents today, gets its name from the slightly damp tacky feel of the fabric. The finish wears off seams and places where the fabric has been folded after a few years and repairs may be necessary.

A tent made of nylon fabric poses quite a different problem. Since nylon threads do not expand when wet the fabric is a sieve. If waterproofed, the tent will not breathe and occupants suffer from their own moisture. The usual solution is to waterproof the floor and about 10″ up the sides of the tent. The remainder of the tent is protected by a separate waterproofed vinyl fly which is pitched several inches above the roof to keep water off the tent and at the same time allow air to circulate. A fly may extend to the ground all around the tent and be staked to keep it in place.

Courtesy of Coleman Co., Inc.

This backpack tent is roomy enough for two, has a waterproof fly to keep rain from soaking through nylon roof. Although the catalytic heater is shown inside the tent, the door is open. When the door is closed, provide adequate ventilation through screened window.

Whatever fabric and finish is chosen, look for a *flame* or *fire-retardant* feature. Many such tent treatments are appearing and may be required in the near future.

Plastic, as a tent fabric, has the advantage of being inexpensive and light weight. It can be folded without damage, easily wiped off. However, even with both ends of the tent open (a safety necessity) moisture condenses on a sleeping bag and makes it almost as wet as if it had been out in a rainstorm. Choose a plastic tent primarily as an emergency extra. One of the more desirable models comes with supports which can be inflated by mouth, and the tent more than eight feet long, weighing under two pounds, sells for about $8.

4. Tent Construction

Tent should be double-lapped with no raw edges on either side. There should be no puckers or missed stitches. The thread used should be heavy and the stitches (about 12 to 15 per inch) should be far enough from the seam edge so they will not pull out. Points of stress and strain (where poles or stakes are inserted and around door or window openings) should be reinforced with double fabric and extra stitching. Grommets should be rustproof and placed in a double fold of fabric. Loops or tape ties should be double-stitched.

A synthetic fabric, vinyl-coated for waterproofing, makes the best floor. A floor that is merely water-repellent will soon be hard to clean because of abrasion from ground materials, and it may mildew from continued dampness.

Check the door and window openings for such features as good screening and protective flaps which fasten easily with zippers or velcro fasteners which are better than ties which tend to tear off or become knotted. Zippers in doors should have both in-and outside tabs for easiest use. A recent innovation, the D-shaped door, is quite an improvement over the conventional door which needs one vertical and two horizontal zippers to work conveniently.

A heavy duty nylon or Delrin plastic zipper with large teeth seems to be the choice of most campers. The zippers work easily in all kinds of weather, are warm to the touch, and do not gum up easily. Try out the zippers while still in the store to make sure they work easily. A self-healing zipper which goes back together without repair is a definite advantage should the zipper get caught.

5. Design and Model to Choose

The camper will have to choose from a wide-range of shapes and pole arrangements. The choice depends on the planned use of the tent. The cabin tent, though it weighs more than other types of tents which use less material, is a first choice for camping families. The side walls slope slightly which is a good design to shed water and resist wind. Most models now have the desirable lightweight external aluminum frame which is strong, rustproof and easy to assemble. Size range is usually 8 x 10 feet, 9 x 12 feet, and 9 x 14 or 16 feet and prices start around $80 and go up to about $150 depending upon whether there is also an enclosed nylon screened patio.

This ripstop nylon tent comes in kit form and weighs less than 6 pounds including poles, fly, and stakes. Fly, vestibule, rear end, floor and the lower 9" of the sidewalls are waterproof. The tent poles are strung on shock-cord; a flick of the wrist and they snap themselves together. Unassembled each pole is 20" long. Zippers are non-corroding Delrin plastic, and doors and windows have nylon mosquito netting. No tools are needed to assemble the tent. A rock can hammer in stakes. The cost of the kit is about $70 as compared to a similar ready-made tent that would cost about $115. The tent holds two people comfortably; three in an emergency.

Umbrella tents, once very popular, are not as roomy as the cabin tents, nor as easy to pack and put up as the backpacking tents. They no longer have the inconvenient internal pole system, but have adjustable aluminum poles which provide a sturdy external support. Some use dry-finish poplin fabric, others use nylon. Poplin is the better choice since nylon presents so many waterproofing problems, especially in the umbrella shape where so much fabric is exposed. Expect to pay about $100 for a wellmade umbrella tent.

Backpacker, or trail, tents are available in a hundred sizes and shapes. Decide on the model by comparing weight (with poles), ease of putting it up, and how well it is protected against all kinds of weather. Be sure to consider head room since most barely permit the sleepers to sit up comfortably while slipping on trousers. If you do not have to count every ounce, a 3-man tent is a good idea for two persons. Just that little extra space gives maneuverability and room for gear. Fabric will probably be ripstop nylon, and therefore it should come equipped with a waterproof fly floor and about a third of the sidewalls should also be waterproof.

The bowed frame of this tent provides tension that holds walls and floor taut, makes it unnecessary to stake it. Shock cords absorb wind and rain strain. In addition, the lightweight dry finish poplin makes this camping structure very easy to lift.

If standing-up space is important, then there are several tents which range from 60 to 88 inches high in the center.

If the camping area is in rocky or sandy country where stakes cannot or will not go in easily, look for a free standing tent which is supported entirely by its frame. In a crowded camp, or where a spot of level ground is difficult to find, the camper can pick up the erected tent with one hand and move it to another spot.

Courtesy of Frostline Kits

This camper and his pack are protected from weather by a poncho, with extension, made of totally waterproof urethane-coated nylon. The garment shown here was made from a do-it-yourself kit, total cost under $15. This poncho is the equivalent of a turtle's shell, and may be converted into a tent.

Courtesy of Frostline

This camper is relaxing in a shelter made from the poncho. Poncho-tent conversion includes floor, pole sleeves, pole set, guylines, snap sets for attaching floor to poncho and total weight of the kit is only 2 lb. 5 oz. A couple of backpackers caught in a shower can shelter under the one poncho without adding more than a pound a piece to their total load.

New on the market is a poncho tent-conversion kit. The poncho which protects the camper by day as he hikes or bikes can, with three poles and a cross-rod hold, become a shelter for one — or even two in an emergency. The total weight of this outfit is 2 lb. 5 oz.

Turn your car into a comfortable campground by adding a roof top tent unit. The 115 lb. unit is a flat package that opens in two minutes to become a comfor-tent for two adults and a child.

A built-in ladder is first used to erect the cartop camping unit, then serves to assist campers into their bedroom.

If tent camping is not appealing, and the budget forbids a more expensive outfit, strike a compromise with a fabric shelter which travels in a neat flat package on top of the car. There is one which pops up into a roomy two-person tent complete with floor and mattress with the release of a few catches. This one weighs about 100 lbs., has a clothes bar and dressing room, zippered closures, screening and is weatherproof. When you get home, unclamp it and hang it on the garage wall.

Another version weighs about 115 lb., is a full size tent on a platform and is big enough for two adults and a child. It pops from a compact package into an outdoor home in two minutes. The unit comes with an attached lightweight ladder that serves as a staircase to the bedroom-tent.

The camper that owns a camping bus without camping interior, may add a bedroom. Many auto dealers sell a screened waterproof unit which converts the rear portion of the bus into a 7′ long double bed. The mattress and platform stow away completely within the car while traveling. Other companies make tents and conversion units for vans and minibuses.

Courtesy of CarBak Camper Co.

Another cartop unit designed for compact cars has a sleeper section weighing only 52 lbs. in addition to a double bed on foam mattress for two people. The unit includes a dressing room that doubles as a bench seat for lounging or dining.

Courtesy of Volkswagen of America

Owners of some bus-vans can now easily add a screened waterproof sleeping unit to the rear of the vehicle. Inside there is a 7′ long double bed on a solid platform. When not in use, the unit stows compactly inside the bus.

Courtesy of DorMobile, Ltd.

Flip up the fan shaped top on this camping car for standing room to prepare food or change clothing.

Courtesy of Hirsch-Weis White Stag

This van tent is designed to be used with a slideaway side door camping bus. Magnetic tape holds door extension to side of tent. The tent is free standing so van can be driven away without taking down the tent.

CHOOSING A SLEEPING BAG AND AIR MATTRESS

Small children and many teenagers sleep well on hard ground while more mature people may need the cushioning provided by an air mattress. When weight of the mattress is a factor, choose a half-mattress, about 50″ long which will cradle head and hips, and use a duffle bag or rolled-up clothing to support legs and feet.

The best choice of material, whether half, or full length mattress, is vinyl bonded to nylon (weight about 3 lbs. in a backpacking narrow width model). Look for a king-sized model if extra heavy or very tall. A built-in pillow is a comfort available on some mattresses. The most comfortable shape has waffle or quilted-type construction with no-roll-off tubes at the sides. The least comfortable is the long narrow tube type.

A polyurethane foam pad 1½″ thick protected by a nylon coating or cotton/nylon cover provides enough bed comfort for many campers. Try it out at home before taking it on a trip. Such a mattress has the advantages of needing no blow-up, light weight and usefulness to insulate food or protect breakables around camp during the daytime.

CHOOSING A SLEEPING BAG

Warmth

The warmth provided by a sleeping bag depends upon where it was designed to be used. The salesman or camping catalog will give you some help by providing suggested comfort ratings. If you will never camp in cold weather you hardly need the extra heavy Arctic bag which protects an individual down to 30 degrees below zero. Choose one suggested for normal summer weather and plan to add extra warmth, when necessary, with a blanket, a padding of newspapers, or one of the lightweight space blankets. A space blanket has a reflective aluminum coating on one side. When placed under a sleeping bag, aluminum side up, it reflects back most of the body heat. When you are too warm turn the dull side toward the bag. (The blanket is also useful for sunning on a beach, as insulation around food, or to sit on.)

Also consider the heat requirements of the potential campers. Some people need a sweater in mid-summer while others are comfortable in shirt sleeves. Choose a heavier bag if a camper's needs demand one.

Types of Insulation

Prime white northern goose down is the most expensive and luxurious sleeping bag filler. Synthetic fibers can be equally effective. Unless light weight is of primary importance a sleeping bag filled with a synthetic fiber will be less expensive and will retain its resiliency and insulation qualities even when wet. Goose and duck down are expensive and must be handled with care to keep their *loft*, the fluffiness which traps air cells and makes them warm. Cheaper bags with a filling of cotton kapok or recycled wool fibers are neither as durable or as warm as the synthetics.

Courtesy of Frostline Kits

The ultimate in comfort, shown here, is a down-filled sleeping bag. This one was made from a kit. The outer fabric is ripstop nylon. This one can be paired with another to form a double bag.

It is impractical to tear open a bag for a look at the contents, therefore the buyer will have to rely on the manufacturer's tag and the catalog or salesman's word. Occasionally a manufacturer will provide the store with a sample of the filling in a bag, but it really won't tell the buyer very much about the warmth or wearing quality. Price is usually a reasonable indication of quality.

Kind of Cover and Liner

Downproof ripstop nylon is the cover fabric to choose on a backpacking bag. Duck and poplin are excellent fabrics which are used as covers on good quality bags. The fabric should be firmly woven, heavy enough to withstand rough use and resist moisture. Plain cotton flannel makes a more comfortable liner than nylon which does not absorb body moisture.

Bag Construction

The quilting should go through the cover, insulation, and liner in order to keep the filling from shifting and leaving thin spots. Cheaper bags may have little or no quilting. Check the stitching. There should be about 10 stitches to the inch, and the thread should be heavy or it will soon break. A down bag will be sewn in a baffle system to keep the down from shifting or lumping in one area.

The zippers should be sturdy industrial type nylon or Delrin, firmly sewn in with some sort of baffle cover to keep air from coming in through and around the zipper. A two-way zipper which operates from either top or bottom is a help if feet get too warm and need to get a little cool air.

The camper does not need either an air mattress pocket or a waterproof panel on the bottom of the bag. They will keep body moisture from evaporating and make the bag less comfortable.

Shape of Sleeping Bags

A tapered rectangular bag which unzips so two bags can be zipped together to make a double is a first choice. Feet don't need as much room as head, so weight and extra fabric expense are reduced by the tapering. Choose an extra-length model if you are six feet tall or more or an extra wide one if you are heavy. Child or youth-model bags, soon outgrown, are a poor investment. Although mummy-shaped bags are light, most people find them confining, too warm in summer, and impossible to turn over in.

Bag Washability

A sleeping bag is washable only if the tag says that it is and tells how it should be done. Poor stitching and cheap insulation will not stand up to machine washing. A down bag can be washed best in a double or triple load machine at a laundromat and dried thoroughly in an extra large dryer. Dampness in the down would cause matting and mildew.

A professionally dry cleaned sleeping bag will probably carry a warning tag saying that the bag must be aired for 24 hours before it is either carried in a car or used. Failure to heed such a warning has resulted in death from breathing solvent fumes remaining in the insulation.

Courtesy of Hirsch-Weis White Stag

Mummy bags weigh less than other bags, but can be too confining for most people, unless the choice is a pair like these which zip together to make a cozy double.

CAMP COOKING EQUIPMENT

Kind of Stove

Because fire danger and wood scarcity prevents open fires in many camping areas, the camp cook will have to bring the range along. Look first in the garage. Many families still own an old gasoline fueled campstove. New models are much like the old ones, and replacement parts are usually available. A gasoline model may be converted to a propane-fueled stove by buying a special adapter from the manufacturer which will permit use of a bulk-filled propane tank. It might also be able to be adapted for use with disposable metal cylinders of bottled fuel. Bottled gas has the advantage of being clean, convenient, and safe. However, it is more expensive than using a special fuel from the manufacturer, or buying white gasoline which is less desirable because it may eventually produce clogging of the mechanism.

The most practical stove is a two-burner model large enough to hold a big frying pan and a large pot.

Courtesy of Coleman Corp., Inc.

This stove has a waist-high foldable stand which stows away compactly when it is not in use. Table is also a handy compactable type.

However, a small family, or backpackers, may want one of the single burner small stoves, large enough to accommodate a medium-sized pan to prepare soup or a quick hot drink. Some of these small stoves weigh only a few ounces.

These stoves use a variety of fuels: bottled gas, alcohol, gasoline, or kerosene. The bottled gas unit is convenient, rather expensive to operate, and may not operate well in very cold weather or at a high altitude. Look for a model which permits disconnecting the cylinder after cooking. One widely used model inconveniently requires that the cylinder remain connected to the stove until all the gas is consumed.

Whatever the stove chosen, it should be equipped with a wind shield, be made of sturdy

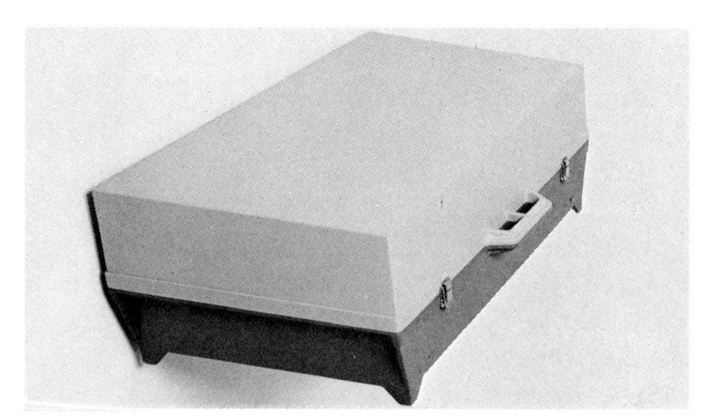

Courtesy of IHA, Inc.

This simple suitcase, made of high impact molded plastic, contains a complete trailcooker kitchen. Pull out folding legs, open the catches, and you will find stove, sink, work counter, and water tank with faucet.

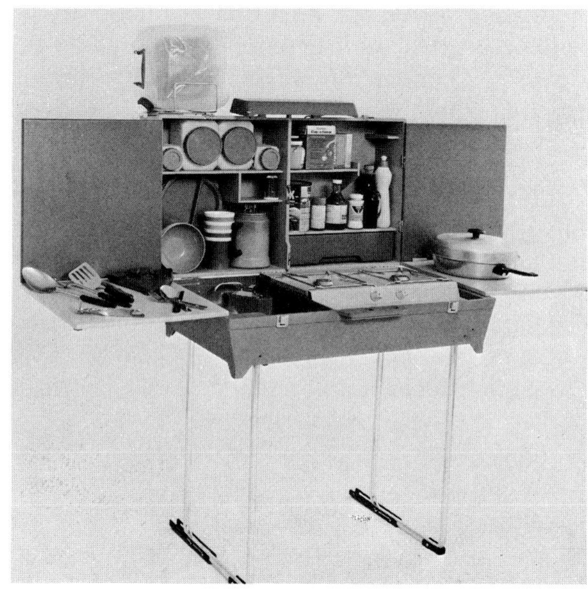

Courtesy of IHA, Inc.

Trailcooker kitchen from previous photograph is shown set up with space for dishes, food, and utensil drawer. A fluorescent lamp attachment which operates off a battery or auto cigarette lighter is also available. Recessed section to left of stove is a sink with built-in faucet and drain. Water flows by gravity from portable bag on shelf or can be connected directly to pressurized water system.

non-rusting metal parts, have no sharp edges, have parts that easily disassemble for cleaning, and have no cracks that trap grease and dirt. If the model requires liquid fuel, buy also a fuel flask, or can, designated as safe for the fuel you will be carrying.

No matter what type of stove used, it should be started and used with adequate ventilation. Never cook inside a tent. Refuel a stove only when the stove is cool.

Cookware

Nested sets of pans and pots with removable handles can be useful if they are made of heavy duty aluminum or stainless steel and have sturdy easy-to-remove handles. Bottoms should be extra thick to keep food from burning. Teflon lining on at least one skillet and a pan will permit wiping the item clean with a paper towel if water is scarce. Plastic handles such as bakelite are a better choice than metal ones which scorch fingers. Look for a set with low, flat pans that do not tip easily. Cups should be strong plastic or enameled metal, not thin aluminum.

A really good set of pans will come apart and go back together easily (try it out before buying). It will run about $40, but it will be handsome enough to use at home, too, so it will not have to be hidden away until the next trip.

An old cast iron frying pan and heavy, no longer attractive kitchen equipment from the kitchen are better than any cheap new items. Do not buy the clipped-together sets of eating tools as they are too much trouble to reassemble. Plastic jars with screw top lids saved through the year will do nicely for camp food. Tape the lids on securely, to prevent lids from coming off during travel. Heavy duty aluminum foil is a useful camp kitchen item. It can be shaped to fit inside a pan or molded around a dish to form another dish. Since it won't burn or disintegrate and should be carried back to a suitable disposal can, if there is none in the camping area.

Flexible plastic pans of all shapes and sizes are sold in supermarkets or drug stores at very low prices. Buy them in different colors to differentiate which pan is used for a particular job. Rectangular pans, all the same size, stack and store easily, and will double as containers in the car for food and dishes.

Kitchen gadgets for the camper are endless. The necessary items are a good can opener, a bread knife, and a bottle opener. A Swiss army knife which comes with every attachment from a Phillips screwdriver to a small saw is a very convenient addition.

COOLER AND REFRIGERATOR

Unless a person is doing a lot of camping, staying in one area for quite a while, or catching a lot of fish that need good refrigeration, there is no need for an expensive refrigerator that operates on bottled gas or a battery. These cost upwards of $200. Instead, get a large, well-insulated cooler for around $30, or less, at summer's end. These are the features to look for: A steel or aluminum exterior. A plastic exterior is a second choice, and may be somewhat cheaper than metal type. While the cooler should have a generous size, be sure it will fit easily into your car. The lid, as well as interior of the box, should be insulated with an efficient material such as urethane foam.

Check to see if the lock or catch closes the lid securely, and whether there is a well-fitted gasket around the lid. Close the lid on a piece of string or slip of paper and see if it will pull out easily. If it does, the lid does not fit tightly enough.

There should be recessed drain spout at the bottom, and a built-in bottle opener, placed where it will not catch on clothing or cause injury. The interior should be smooth, with rounded corners and no cracks. Additions such as trays, a divided area for ice or a built in water container are nice to have, provided they do not add much to the cost.

Finally, check the weight. If it is difficult to lift when empty, think of the difficulty of lifting it when it is loaded.

A polyfoam cooler (some cost but a dollar or two) is a fine extra for carrying drinks or stowing overflow food from a better cooler, but they are not worth paying much for. One handy type, however, holds a six-pack of drinks, and has a lid which contains a sealed-in refrigerant liquid. Put the lid in the freezer until ready to go, and there is no mess as the liquid thaws. Foam coolers can be annoying in a car as they squeak loudly if they rub against any solid object. Campers need a good big water jug. A five-gallon one will be necessary if going where water either is scarce or may be unsafe. Get a jug with a mouth wide enough to accept whole ice cubes. It should have a faucet located at the bottom, rather than top, of the jug. One type of jug is divided in two compartments which allows a camper to carry water and fruit juice or a hot and cold drink in the same jug. Another handy type of container is the expensive, but unbreakable, steel thermos bottle which is available in pint, quart, or widemouth half-gallon size. In one of these, coffee made at night will still be steaming hot for breakfast.

CHOOSING A LANTERN

A new camper will need to decide whether to buy the time-tested gasoline fueled lantern, one fueled by bottled gas, or one of the new types which operates from either a rechargeable battery, or regular house current when needed at home.

The lantern which operates on white gasoline (or the manufacturer's special fuel) gives excellent light, and should last for a good 20 years. With it, buy a reflector-handle and one of the new chain-plus-a-hook hangers which wraps around a tree and hangs the lantern safely without damaging tree bark.

A lamp fueled by bottled gas (or the more expensive metal cylinders of gas) is convenient and easier to operate than the liquid fuel type. It can be balky at a high altitude or in cold weather.

The deluxe lighting item, however, is the electric lantern which operates from a wet-cell battery which can be recharged from either house current or the car cigarette lighter. This lamp gives 14 to 20 hours of light on a charge, depending upon whether low or high intensity is used. The lantern uses a standard 8-watt fluorescent tube and has a dial which can adjust the degree of light. The bulb has a 1000 hour life expectancy, and the battery can be recharged up to 150 times.

This last type of lantern is rather expensive, but it will probably be used throughout the year in the home or yard, especially under emergency situations, since a person can recharge it from the car should electricity fail.

HEATERS

Since most camping takes place in summer, there is little need for a heat source other than good warm clothing and sleeping bags. In mountain country or when camping in fall, the camper might want a safe quick source of heat. If needed, the best bet is to choose a catalytic heater which burns either liquid fuel or bottle gas without an open flame. The top of some heaters can double as a stove for heating soup or drinks. GOOD VENTILATION IS ESSENTIAL. This heater cannot be used in a tightly closed car or tent without suffocating the occupant.

CAMP CLOTHING

Most campers prefer jeans, a soft cotton flannel shirt, a down jacket, and a stretch nylon athletic, or jogging suit, with zippers at the ankles and at the neck. Woolen items, though warm, can be scratchy. Cotton flannel will absorb moisture and keep you more comfortable than a synthetic fabric would.

In spite of its high cost there is nothing lighter, cozier or more satisfying for pure comfort than a down jacket. One type which uses ripstop nylon for its outer cover sheds soil, repels water, and compacts into a tiny bundle. (One model fits into a belt-pouch. Another kind compresses and fits into one of its own pockets) Make a small pillowcase and stuff it with the jacket at night. The chief disadvantage to the down jacket is that once it gets really wet, it is hard to dry. As for the high cost, get one of the ready-to-make kits and make your own luxury garment for a third to half of the cost for the same item in a store.

For children, or for economy-minded campers, there are excellent jackets insulated with the same synthetic fibers you will find in a sleeping bag. Though not as lightweight as the down, this jacket will dry out quickly, keep its fluffiness, and can be machine washed and dried.

Jogging suits have become camp uniforms throughout the world, because they look neat,

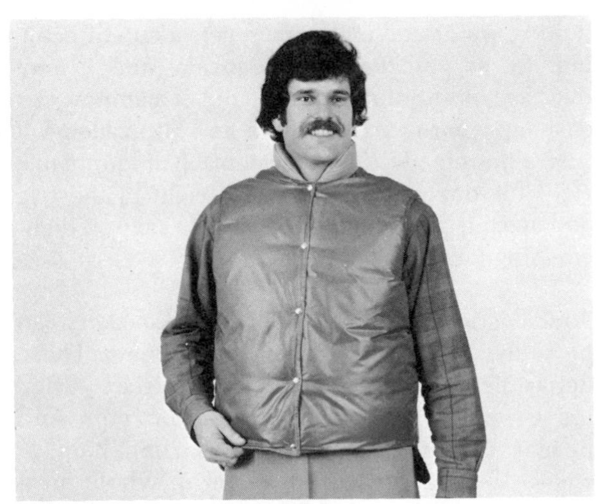

Courtesy of Hirsch-Weis White Stag

For warmth, choose insulated clothing. The layer system is a good one used by many campers. This camper is wearing a dacron-filled vest which can be worn under another jacket in extreme weather or with a light jacket in warm weather. Anyone who goes hunting or fishing should take the safety precaution of choosing a garment in a bright color such as this one.

never wrinkle and are comfortable because they stretch. They can be worn all day long, and many people use them for sleeping garments as well. They machine-wash and dry and look like new for years.

Most essential and most personal when it comes to comfort is the choice of shoes or boots. One camper's footwear choice may be another camper's agony. Lightweight canvas shoes do nicely in a civilized camp, but they are hazardous for climbing and soon get wet or torn. Ankle-high leather boots, well broken in before the trip, are a better choice. They protect the wearer from insects and snakes, and the foot is less likely to be injured in a fall. Choose a type with a waterproof sole and leather top that has been treated to resist moisture.

There are hundreds of other items from which to choose — hoods, special pants filled with down, even something called "itchy-scratchy" underwear, guaranteed to keep you warm by friction created as you wear it. Unless you are very rich or are a dedicated outdoor family, the best camping clothing is the same clothing which can be worn at home other times of the year.

HOW MANY AND WHAT GADGETS?

Most people buy too many. Here is just a partial list to suggest a few items to make an outdoor vacation more comfortable or interesting: air mattress pump, nylon blowup pillow, rucksack, backpack, fanny pack, rain parka, fishnet under-

Courtesy of Hirsch-Weis White Stag

A large nylon pack on an aluminum frame is a first choice for the serious backpacker. Each section is zippered separately so items in one compartment can be extracted without disturbing other sections.

Courtesy of Coleman Co., Inc.

Fix a flat tire the easy way with a midget air compressor that plugs into the car's cigarette lighter. On a camping trip the compressor will also blow up an air mattress or a beach ball.

wear, down booties and mittens, down hood, folding saw, hatchet, axe, folding table and chairs, portable toilet, candle lantern, repair kit and spare parts for all equipment, hand warmer, laundry bags to hold gear, cube fire-starter, friction type lantern and stove lighter, squeeze tubes of plastic to hold jam or peanut butter, portable shower, pressure cooker, compass, survival kit, pencil sized flashlights, nylon tarp, folding plastic water jug, plastic sink which doubles as a water container, electric inflator for air mattresses.

SAFETY EQUIPMENT

Any camper should have a first-aid kit. The best kind is assembled to suit a family's particular needs. It will not only include routine items such as bandages and suntan lotion, but special prescriptions and items needed because of the particular nature of the outing — snakebite kit, for example, needed especially in desert country. Also carry bug spray (don't use it on tent fabric) and an insect repellent, safe to put on the skin. If someone in the family is allergic to bee stings, a doctor will provide a special kit to use as an emergency lifesaver should you be far from a doctor.

Carry along a lightweight all-purpose fire extinguisher, one that is rated to put out any type of fire — in a tent, in the car's electrical system, or one caused by burning gasoline or cooking grease. A box of baking soda, packed with the kitchen equipment, is one simple fire extinguisher which should be a part of any camper's gear. Bring a small shovel (some are folding) and an axe or hatchet for emergency.

WHAT KIND OF FOOD TO BRING

Camp meals should be uncomplicated. One way of keeping them so is to take along some of the meal-in-a-package foods which supply potato, rice or a pasta, a packet of seasoning, sometimes gravy and even a little dehydrated meat, so all that is needed is to add water and heat. There are also such quick cooking items as quick rice, instant potato, and dehydrated soups, none of which need refrigeration and all of which are easy to pack. Some of the new dried soups come in individual foil-sealed envelopes. Add a cup of boiling water and one person gets a cup of bean, tomato, or chicken soup. Pancake and biscuit mix are other time savers, but a camper can easily prepare mix at home and prepackage it (use a double plastic bag system) in amounts just right for one meal. Add water right in the bag and use the bag for a mixing bowl to save on dishwashing.

Foods especially developed for backpackers can be found in sporting goods departments. These departments provide such things as freeze-dried ice cream, freeze-dried strawberries and peaches, and delicacies such as shrimp, ham, or steak. Some items are packaged in whole meal form, enough for two or four people.

Here's a sample dinner: two boneless pork chops, hash brown potatoes, applesauce, green beans. The price is $3.40 at one camping outlet. This food is excellent, but — as are all these special foods — expensive and not too generous for hearty appetites. Gourmet main dish meals run from about a dollar for a one person serving to several dollars for two who want steak and the trimmings. There's a great deal of variation in the taste and quality of the food.

The only way to be sure before camping is to try a few samples.

If the camping area can be reached by car, the camper will be better off bringing in ordinary packaged and canned foods. The first day's meals can be brought frozen or chilled in a cooler, and cooking will not be necessary.

CARE AND OTHER USES OF CAMPING EQUIPMENT

All camping equipment, including clothing, makes good emergency or survival gear. If the electricity goes out, use the camp lantern, stove, and warm sleeping bags. In a real disaster, a tent may be a necessity. Year-around, camping equipment comes in handy for extra guests. Sleeping bags are deluxe extra bedding. A cooler holds ice cubes or drinks. The stove can be set up for an outdoor picnic. Down clothing and a heat-reflecting space blanket will keep the family warm at a sports event.

Do-it-yourself camp storage box made of plywood is out of the way on a garage wall when equipment is not needed. With everything stowed in the same place, it is easy to find and remove items needed for guests or emergency use, after the camping season is over.

When family arrives at a campground one end of the box flips down and becomes a cooking counter or serving table. Surface is easy-to-clean laminated plastic. Chains hold up the counter and do away with need for legs.

The box holds all basic camping equipment for a family of six. All items, with exception of food, are a permanent part of contents — sleeping bags, table, stove, lantern, stools, and cushions. Best of all, the box comes off the wall and fits perfectly in the back of the family station wagon. Then there is room to tuck in all the groceries and pans that are seen on top of the table.

Courtesy of Coleman Corp., Inc.

Gasoline burning camp appliances should be cleaned after each trip, fueled and tested in open air, as shown here. Should electric power fail during winter, they are ready for use.

How long these items last will depend entirely upon whether someone chooses well in the first place and whether the camper cleans and repairs them after each trip and stores them in a dry place. A camper can figure on a quarter of a century's use under these circumstances.

Can Opener

[SEE ELECTRIC CAN OPENER REPAIR.]

Canopy

A canopy, like an awning, is a rooflike cover that shields a doorway or window from rain and intense sunlight. By blocking the sun, it keeps adjacent rooms cooler and reduces glare. A canopy also provides shelter at a doorstep when unlocking doors or raising umbrellas.

Canopies are made usually of corrugated fiberglass or aluminum. They are attached flush to the house exterior with brackets or are supported on pillars. *SEE ALSO AWNINGS.*

Cantilever Joists

Cantilever joists are used to provide floor support in a house construction design that includes a flooring section protruding beyond the lower level of the house. Cantilever joists are only used when the regular floor joists run parallel instead of perpendicular to the foundation walls. They are usually extended inwardly at least twice the projection length beyond the wall. The weight of the outer wall to be supported will determine the specific length and spacing of the joists. *SEE ALSO FLOOR CONSTRUCTION.*

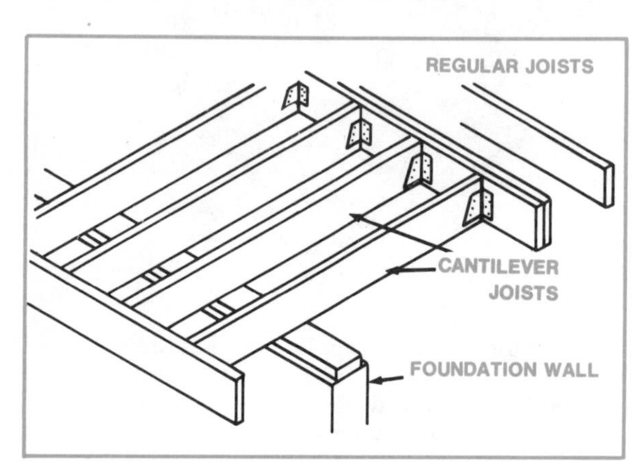

Cantsaw File

The cantsaw file, named after the saw for which it was designed, is used for sharpening circular and crosscut saws with less than 60° teeth in an "M" shape. If there is a job, however, that requires a file with narrow, triangular cross sections, a cantsaw file can be used. *SEE ALSO HAND TOOLS.*

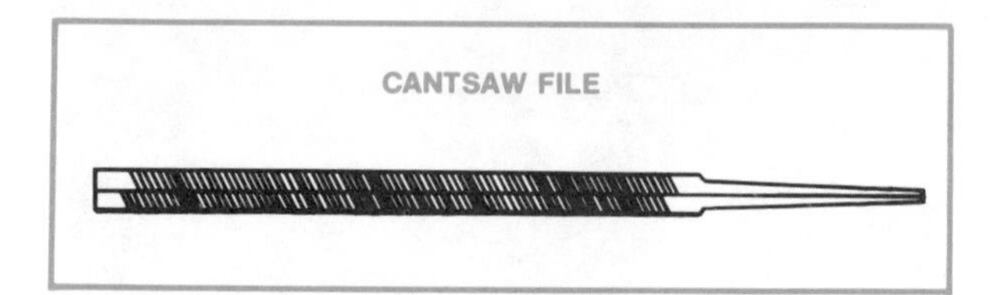

Cap

A cap is a galvanized steel pipe fitting with internal threads used for water and vent pipes. Fitting into the open end of a pipe, a cap completely closes the pipe's end. A cap performs the same function as a plug. *SEE ALSO PIPE FITTINGS.*

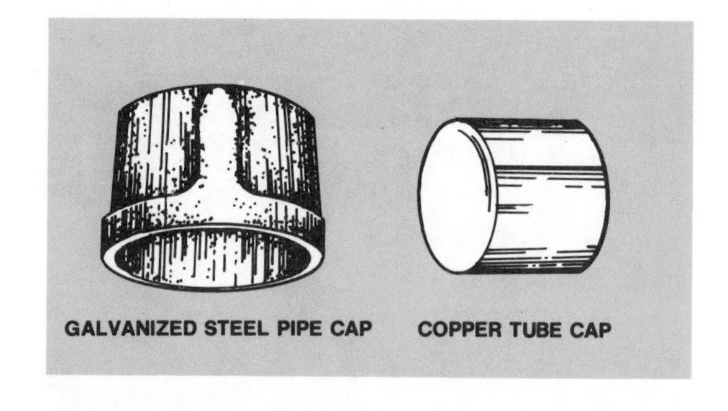

Capacitor

A capacitor, found in electric motors or electronic equipment, holds or stores electrical charge. Although there are many differences in types of capacitors and their construction, all have two main features: plates, or metal surfaces for conducting electricity, and a dielectric, the insulation separating these surfaces. There are many sizes of capacitors that range from the giants in industrial electric generators to the tiny paper capacitors in a radio.

The capacitor is used as a reserve for electricity in an electronic or electric motor circuit. This reserve helps to stabilize the charge throughout the circuit by increasing or decreasing current where needed. They also provide short circuits in alternating current and open circuit for direct current, keeping the type of current uniform throughout the circuitry.

Capacitors should never be tested by the home craftsman, as they require special equipment for this purpose. Rather, a faulty capacitor should be taken to a repair shop where professional experience is available. *SEE ALSO ELECTRIC MOTORS.*

Cape Chisels

One of the four general types of cold chisels, a cape chisel is specifically designed for cutting narrow grooves. This is the chisel used to shear off rivet heads, by driving a groove through the center of the head and chipping off the rest. As with all other cold chisels, use a ball peen hammer to drive a cape chisel, and always wear goggles while working. *SEE ALSO HAND TOOLS.*

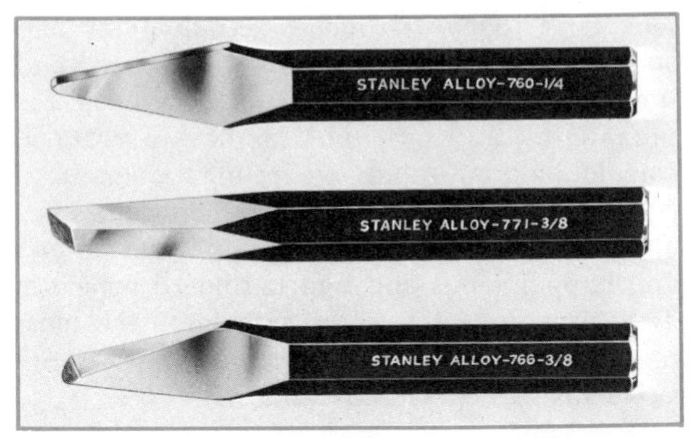

Courtesy of The Stanley Works

Cape Chisel

Cap Molding

Cap moldings or *wainscot caps* are used with wainscot paneling (paneling on just the lower part of the walls), or as caps for baseboards. Defects in craftsmanship can be concealed by using cap molding with a wraparound lip. *SEE ALSO MOLDING & TRIM.*

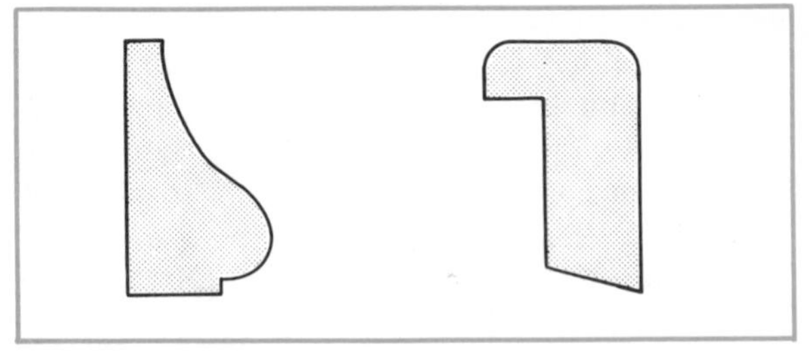

Cap Molding

Cap Screw

A cap screw is a non-conductive cover for a solderless connector with set screw. After the stripped wires are pushed into the connector and the set screw is tightened, a cap screw is placed over the connection and tightened. A cap screw forms a firm, safe shield. *SEE ALSO ELECTRICAL WIRING.*

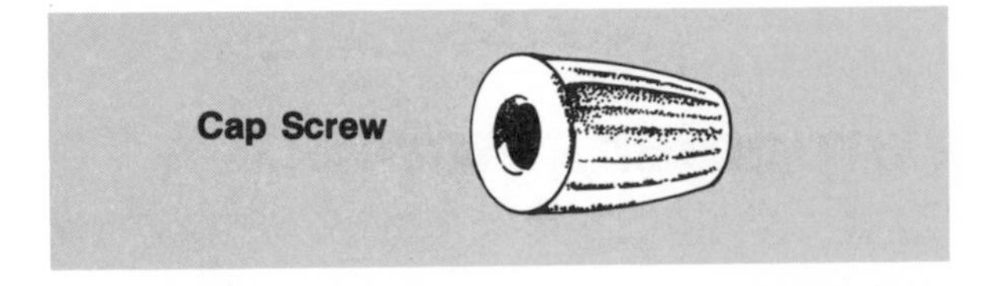

Carbide Bits

Carbide bits have a tip made of tungsten carbide, one of the hardest man-made metals. These bits will drill through concrete, brick, stone and other hard materials. You can get sizes up to ½ inch that will fit a ¼ inch chuck, and up to ¾ inch that will fit a ½ inch chuck. The common overall length is from 4 to 6 inches. Sharpen these bits on a bench grinder using a silicone-carbide grinding wheel. *SEE ALSO HAND TOOLS.*

Carbide-Tipped Blades

Carbide-tipped blades are used for cutting plywood, masonite, aluminum, brass, large amounts of lumber and other tough or abrasive materials. These blades, with small pieces of carbide welded to the tips, are used primarily because they hold an edge much longer than regular steel blades (from 10 to 150 times longer). The cost is determined by the number of teeth rather than its size. Generally, a good one costs about $2.00 per tooth. *SEE ALSO HAND TOOLS.*

Carburetor

The carburetor is designed to provide and control the mixture of air and fuel that is burned in the combustion chamber of an automobile engine. *SEE SYSTEMS, AUTOMOTIVE.*

Car Care
[SEE SYSTEMS, AUTOMOTIVE.]

Carpenter's Apron

The carpenter's apron is an apron made of heavy duty material designed for holding a carpenter's tools in separate pouches. Most carpenter's aprons have a nail pouch, loops on either side for hammers and "T" squares and smaller sections for pencils, folding ruler and tape ruler. The style of the apron generally stays the same, but depending on the job to be done, the size and placement of the pouches may vary (for instance, a dry wall hanger's apron will not be exactly like a carpenter's apron). Although most professionals now prefer carpenter's overalls, the carpenter's apron is still quite common. *SEE ALSO CARPENTER'S TOOLS & EQUIPMENT.*

Carpenter's Level

The carpenter's level, usually made of wood, aluminum or magnesium, is used for checking the alignment of a structure. Ranging in sizes from 9 to 12 inches, the carpenter's level has both plumb and level vials. The level vial in the center is used for checking horizontal surfaces. The plumb vials measure the "trueness" of vertical surfaces (from this comes the expression "plumb true"). The carpenter's level is essential in major projects like construction of homes, setting vertical fence posts and making drain pipe pitch at the right slope. *SEE ALSO CARPENTER'S TOOLS & EQUIPMENT.*

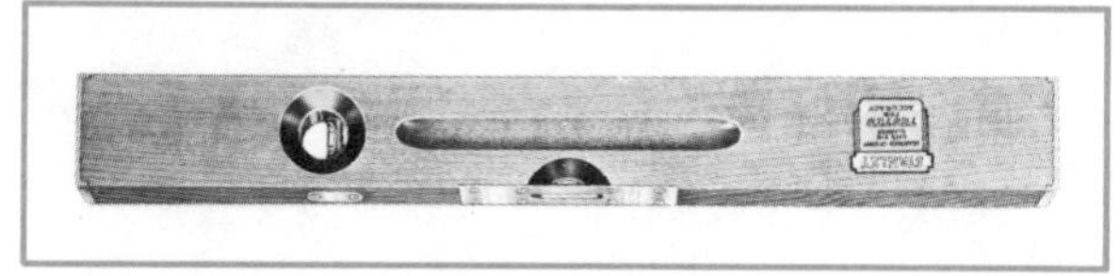

Courtesy of The Stanley Works

Carpenter's Level

Carpenter's Square

The carpenter's square (also called framing or rafter square) is a big, flat piece of L-shaped steel. The body measures 24 by 2 inches, and the tongue is 16 by $1^1/_2$ inches. Graduations and special tables are marked on both the body and tongue. The carpenter's square is used for measuring and cutting braces and rafters, calculating proportions, converting timbers from squares to octagons, finding the circumference and center of a circle, laying out ellipses, miters and hopper joints and figuring board measure. The carpenter's square is considered the most important and useful of all squares. *SEE ALSO CARPENTER'S TOOLS & EQUIPMENT.*

Courtesy of The Stanley Works

Carpenter's Square

Carpenter's Tools & Equipment

There are many tools useful in carpentry work, but the home handyman, as an amateur carpenter, may want to invest in only the very basic ones. You may already have acquired some of these basic tools through the years, but if buying a few more is necessary, select only those of high quality that will serve you well for many years.

First of all, measuring tools are needed. One of the most common is the bench rule. Select one of hard wood that is divided into fractions and has markings on both sides. Later, you may want to acquire a zig-zag rule with extensions for measuring up to six feet.

The steel or rafter square is considered a basic tool in a carpenter's box for measuring almost anything. The steel square is a steel right angle approximately 1/8 inch thick with a 24-inch long body and a tongue 16 inches in length. This square has marked graduations and special tables that enable you to accurately calculate rafter cuts and notches that require a perfect fit.

The bell-faced hammer is considered by many to be the "first" hammer you should buy for carpentry work. Because of its slightly convex face, a nail can be driven flush without leaving hammer marks, even when the striking angle is not perpendicular. The claw of the hammer chosen depends on what job needs to be done. The straight claw is good for ripping boards apart, while the curved claw is better for removing nails. The head of the hammer has to be safe and durable. Cast heads tend to chip or break. Drop-forged steel heads are the best and will last longer. Hammer handles are primarily made of steel or hickory. Most woodworkers prefer tubular steel or solid steel shafts with rubber grips to prevent slips.

The level is a necessity for carpentry work. A 24-inch aluminum-frame level is a good buy, but always check the accuracy of the vials before purchasing any level. Lay it on a flat, horizontal surface, and if it doesn't register level, try putting folded paper under one end. If the vials still don't register properly, check the vials — some are adjustable. Make sure the level gives correct readings on both ends. For use in tight spots, try a nine-inch level. There are many levels available for a variety of jobs, but at first buy only those for which you can see an immediate need.

Crosscut saws are usually considered a "basic" hand saw for a carpenter. Its small, knife-like teeth are set parallel, far enough apart to prevent binding. The crosscut saw, designed for cutting across the woodgrain, does 75 per cent of its cutting on the downstroke and 25 on the upstroke. Check the blade for flexibility, the wooden handle for a comfortable grip. The top edge should be thinner than the cutting edge. File the crosscut saw to maintain sharp teeth. As you progress in woodworking, you may want to buy a portable power saw.

Two common drills used in carpentry are the hand drill and push drill. Push drills are operated by forcing the bit chuck down into the wood, and are used by carpenters to make holes for nails and screws. Special fluted bits ranging in size from 1/16 to 8/16 are used in push drills.

The crank-operated hand drill is used for forming small holes in wood. The size of the hand drill is determined by the capacity of its chuck, generally 1/4 to 3/8 inch. Twist drills are used in hand drills with the practical set for carpentry ranging (by thirty-seconds) from 1/16 to 1/4 inch. After achieving accuracy in your work, try an electric drill for speed.

Planes are used for truing the edges of wood after it has been cut. The smooth plane is probably the most useful for the carpenter's tool kit. Ranging in size from four to ten inches long, the smooth plane has a 1 3/4-inch blade and is the smallest and lightest of available planes. You may also want to purchase a jack plane. It is larger than the smooth plane (12 to 15 inches long) and can be used to rough down edges before truing with the smooth plane.

For shaping the wood, a wood file is necessary. You may first want to get the dual-purpose, half-round file. The flat surface of the half-round is used for making sharp corners, while the rounded back is handy for forming smooth, inside circles. Later, you may want a round file and pillar file.

Like planes and files, sandpaper is used in smoothing wood. It comes in different degrees of coarseness and you should keep a varied selection handy. The best sandpaper is made of tough, prepared paper coated with glue, then sprinkled with bits of flint, quartz or garnet. Garnet is considered the best to use in woodworking.

The awl is a useful item for every carpenter because its sharp point makes small pilot holes for screws, nails and brads.

Screwdrivers are necessary, also, and the two commonly used in driving wood screws are the standard and Phillips.

There are a wide variety of wrenches a carpenter can use. Some of the more common are open-end, box and socket, any of which you may already have acquired for general house repairs.

A utility knife can be used in numerous ways. The knife selected should be made of good, solid steel with a retractable blade that locks for prevention of unintended slides.

Power tools are good investments, but if you can't obtain them at first, you do have an option. Portable circular and sabre saws, electric drills, disc, belt and pad sanders and routers are a few you may be able to rent for a few dollars a day. *SEE ALSO HAND TOOLS; PORTABLE POWER TOOLS.*

Carpet, Indoor-Outdoor

Indoor-outdoor carpet is a surface covering suitable for use in and out of the home. Available with a rubberized self-backing, this carpet is made from olefin or polypropylene. Indoor-outdoor carpet can be purchased in rolls, tiles or peel-and-stick tiles. Companies produce great varieties of colors, designs and textures in this type of carpet.

Indoor-outdoor carpet may be used in any room of the house. Because it is water repellent, this carpet can be used outside on patios, around pools, or as the floor covering for an animal shelter. *SEE ALSO CARPETING.*

Carpeting

Buying carpet for the home is a step which requires much forethought for the homeowner. For example, he should consider the specific needs of his own home, the size and activities of each room to be carpeted, the amount of sunlight each receives, the traffic each room receives and the styles and colors of the furnishings in each.

Before purchasing carpet, keep in mind the importance of choosing the correct color for each room. Light shades make rooms appear larger, whereas dark ones make them seem smaller. Bright colored carpet can intensify the brightness of a room or a subtle shade can tone down one which is too bright or too sunlit. Areas

Courtesy of Ozite

The focal point of this decorating scheme is a lush deep green grass look-alike carpet with the look and feel of a country club green.

which receive more traffic naturally soil more quickly. Therefore, you should consider for these areas a darker shade or a color blend which will not show dirt readily. In matching carpet to furniture, it is a very good idea to choose a color that matches at least 30% of the furnishings.

In choosing carpet texture, make sure that you choose one which is suitable to the activity of each room. For example, shag carpet, a long-haired carpet, gives an instant appearance of comfort and relaxation. It seems to go best in bedrooms and recreation rooms.

Plush carpet, on the other hand, has a very sophisticated appearance which adds appeal to living rooms or any room of the house which is frequently used for entertaining guests.

For areas which endure much traffic and frequent soiling, such as the kitchen or hallway, consider a carpet with a texture which will wear well and one that is easy to clean, possibly one of the many brands of indoor-outdoor carpet.

After making these very important preliminary decisions, visit many carpeting stores, get as much information from salesmen as possible, read literature on the different types of carpet available and price carpet carefully to make sure that you are getting the best buy for your home.

An excellent type carpet to consider before purchasing is the modern do-it-yourself carpet.

Courtesy of Armstrong

Laying a do-it yourself carpet.

Courtesy of Ozite

This versatile indoor/outdoor carpet can take all the wear of kitchen traffic.

Many reputable companies manufacture carpet which can be installed by the homeowner. This type of carpeting comes with a complete set of instructions,

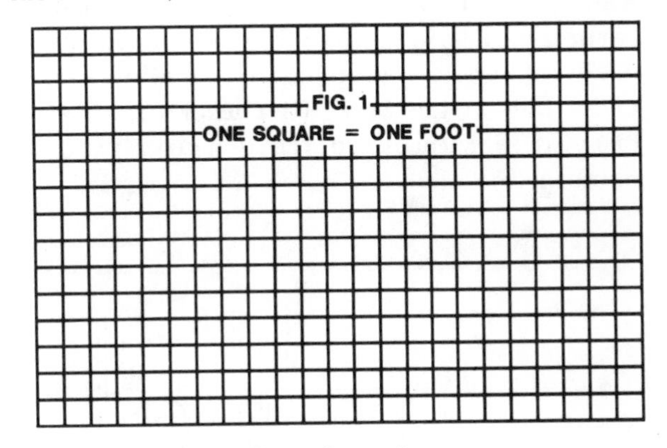

Room Layout

HOW TO INSTALL DO-IT-YOURSELF CARPET

Use the room layout (Fig. 1) to draw your room dimensions. Be sure to include all doorways and offsets such as closets or dormer-type windows.

Read these instructions completely before starting work.

Prepare the Floor

Before installing do-it-yourself carpet, check your floor area to make sure it is clean, dry and warm (preferably about 70 degrees, but definitely more than 55 degrees). Pressure-sensitive tapes will not bond readily to concrete floors or other floors that are dusty, cold, rough or oily. Concrete should be vacuumed (or washed with water, then allowed to dry) before installation. Note: All do-it-yourself carpet is unsuitable for areas that are continually wet with no chance to dry out.

Remove all the furniture and movable objects before starting.

For all carpets except shag, remove quarter-round molding before installing the carpet. The molding should be replaced after the installation is completed. It will help secure the edges of the carpet and give the installation a more professional appearance.

Single-Piece Installations

Roll out the carpet wall to wall and roughly cut to size, allowing 3 to 4 inches excess to run up each wall and out each doorway (Fig 2). Position carpet, and using sturdy household scissors, make relief cuts at room corners to allow carpet to be flat on the floor. (If corner or offset is curved, a number of relief cuts will be necessary.)

Allow 3 or 4 inches excess to run up wall.

To trim excess, start at one wall and fold back carpet to expose wall and floor joint. Using an ordinary soft chalk stick held at a 45 degree angle to the joint, make a chalk line by moving the point down the length of the joint (Fig. 3). (Two lines will actually appear — one on the wall and one on the floor.)

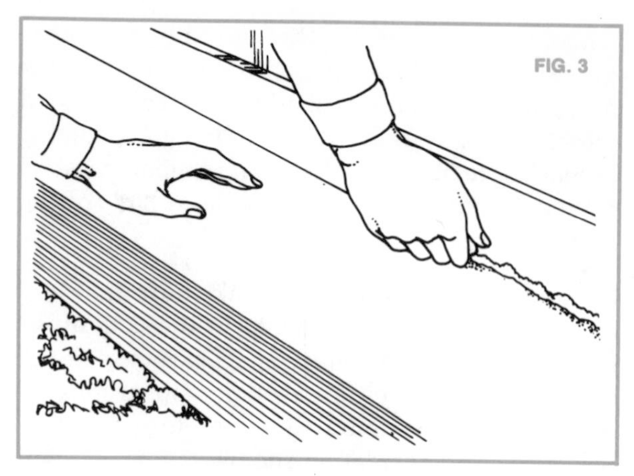

Make a chalk line.

On wall surfaces that won't mark with chalk, such as ceramic tile or high-gloss enamel, apply a strip of 1-inch masking tape (not carpet tape) where the surface meets the floor. Make sure you remove the masking tape after the carpet is fitted.

Be sure to continue the chalk line around obstacles such as door jambs and offsets. (The chalk lines will serve as your trim lines.)

Carefully unfold the carpet, allowing excess to run up the wall. Force the carpet into the wall-floor joint with firm finger pressure and transfer the chalk line onto the back of the carpet.

Fold the carpet back away from the joint and make sure the two chalk lines are reproduced on the foam rubber back (Fig. 4). Make your trim cut on the line nearest to the edge of the carpet (the line made by the wall).

Look for chalk-line reproductions on foam rubber backing

Unfold the carpet and allow it to fall into position on the floor. The trimmed edge should just touch the wall or molding. If the fit is too tight at any point, carefully trim off the slight overcuts. Trim excess from other walls, using the same technique.

To trim around obstacles in an open area such as a support beam, toilet, pipe, etc., cut toward the obstacle from a convenient edge of the carpet. If necessary, rough-cut to allow 3 to 4 inches of excess around the base of the obstacle and follow the above technique for trimming.

Installing Two or More Pieces

Unroll the first piece of carpet in the area. (Note the directional arrow on the foam-rubber back. All pieces should have the arrow pointing in the same direction so the lay of the pile is uniform.) In some cases, particularly with shag carpet, it may be possible to butt one of the long sides of the first piece against a straight wall that has no doorways (with the short ends turned up the walls). If this is done and the fit along the wall is satisfactory, check the opposite edge of the carpet (seam edge) to make sure it is straight. Do this by stretching a cord from one end of the seam edge to the other. If the seam edge is bowed or curves away from the line, the carpet cannot be installed properly by butting the first piece along the wall. Instead, it will be necessary to move the piece toward the wall until approximately two inches of the long side is uniformly turned up the wall rather than butted against it. The carpet will also have to be turned up any walls that have doorways in them.

Turn up approximately two inches of carpet against the wall.

Make sure the main portion of the carpet is lying flat with no wrinkles or buckles.

Make a small pencil mark on the floor at each end of the carpet edge where the first seam will fall. Fold back the carpet and strike a chalk line on the floor between the two pencil marks. Start 12 inches away from one end wall and apply a strip of double-faced carpet tape along the chalk line, stopping 12 inches short of the other end wall. With the protective liner still on the topside of the tape, press tape down firmly. Apply a second strip of tape on the other side of the line the same length. The chalk line should just be visible. Press down firmly.

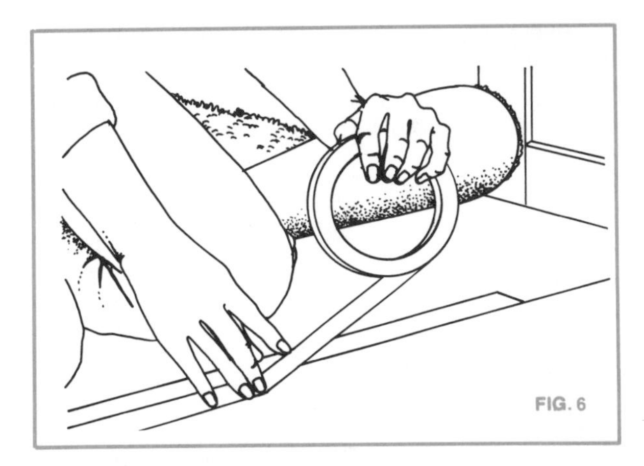

Apply carpet tape along the chalk line.

Unfold carpet to make sure the edge covers one tape strip completely and is against the chalk line along the entire length of the seam.

If you are installing shag carpet, brush all shag pile up and away from the seam edge.

Now, slowly pull off the protective liner from the top side of the tape strip beneath the carpet edge. As you pull off the tape liner, gently press the carpet down onto the exposed tape with the carpet edge against the chalk line. When carpet edge completely covers the length of tape, walk on it to insure a good bond.

Roll out the second piece of carpet and butt it against the first piece at the seam edge. Make sure the directional arrow on back is pointing in the same direction as the first piece. Rough-cut,

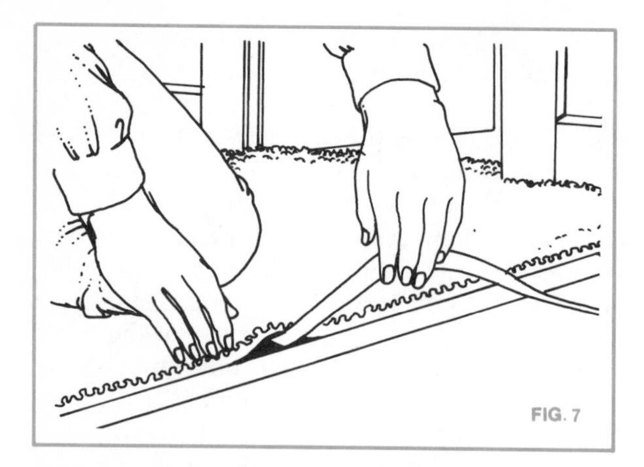

Pull protective liner from tape strip.

if necessary, and allow the excess to run up walls and into doorways. Keep the second piece butted firmly against the seam edge and make necessary relief cuts (Fig. 8). *Do not trim.*

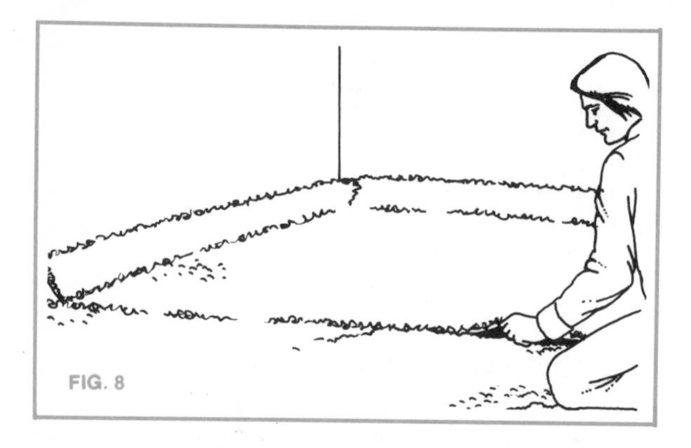

Roll out second piece of carpet to overlap first piece.

If you're installing shag carpet, brush back all shag pile from both carpet edges, making sure you don't trap any tufts in the seam.

Beginning at one end, carefully remove the tape liner beneath the second piece of carpet, pulling the liner out through the seam. As you pull the liner out, butt the carpet firmly in place down onto the exposed tape and against the first piece. When the carpet edge completely covers the tape strip, walk on the seam to insure a good bond.

Rub the seam lightly with fingertips and free any pile that is pinched in the seam. Carefully trim any frayed pile from the surface of the seam with scissors.

Trim the excess from the wall edges on both pieces, using the chalk-line technique described under single-piece installations.

Remove tape liner beneath second piece of carpet.

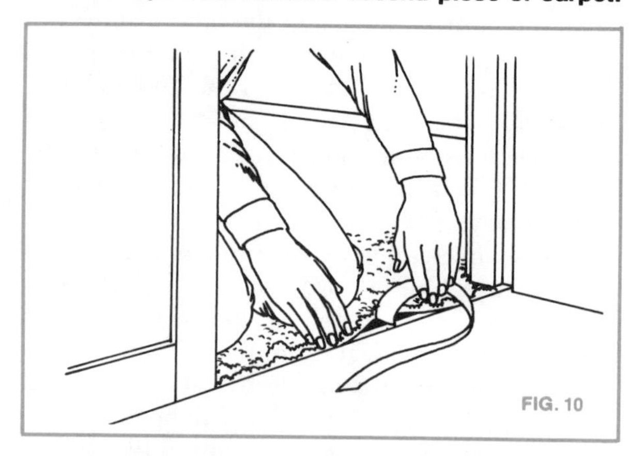

Remove tape liner from carpet at doorways.

CLEANING

Whether you install carpet yourself or have it installed professionally, you will want to do everything possible to keep the carpet you choose clean and beautiful as long as possible. Read all the available material from your manufacturer concerning proper cleaning methods. Most manufacturers suggest daily care, weekly cleaning and seasonal cleaning. For each of these, they list the needed equipment and methods.

However, you still must also consider those needs particular to your own home. For example, day-to-day care depends upon a number of factors: the walking traffic the carpet receives (one that receives more traffic will require more cleaning); the color of the carpet (bright colored

STAIN REMOVAL CHART

STAIN	CLEANING MATERIAL	METHOD
BUTTER GREASE OIL MILK INK	A SOLVENT CLEANER (a home dry-cleaning product)	Using a sponge, blot the stain with the cleaner. Then blot with paper towel. Repeat until stain is gone.
GRAVY CHOCOLATE STAINS TEA COFFEE	DETERGENT SOLUTION AND SOLVENT CLEANER	Sponge the stain first with a detergent solution several times, then with a solvent cleaner.
LIPSTICK CANDY PAINT GLUE CRAYON	SOLVENT CLEANER AND DETERGENT SOLUTION	Sponge solvent cleaner first. Then use a detergent solution. Repeat as many times as necessary. Blot excess moisture with paper towel.

If home remedies for carpet stains fail, do not chance ruining your carpet with too much sponging and blotting. Consult professional cleaners immediately.

or light colored carpet shows dirt more readily than tweeds or other color combinations); and the location of the home (carpeting in a home located in an urban area may require more care than that of one located in a rural or suburban area).

Dirt can cause more than just an unsightly appearance on carpet. If not removed in time, it can actually scratch the carpet fibers, giving them a dull or faded appearance. If the carpet is not cleaned before this is allowed to happen, the resulting damage may be irreparable, even with the assistance of professional cleaners. Make sure, therefore, that carpeting which receives heavy traffic in your home gets vacuumed daily. (Note: Always check the underside of a vacuum cleaner for sharp objects. If these go unnoticed, they may pull or snag carpet loops.)

Weekly cleaning and seasonal cleaning, again, depend upon the carpet's exposure to dirt. Some areas will need heavy cleaning more often than others. For the more thorough types of cleaning, there are many machines, materials and methods to consider. Many brands of carpet shampoo are available. Their accompanying instructions usually direct you to apply shampoo to the carpet, rub in with a damp sponge, let dry and vacuum. This method is inexpensive and simple enough to be done by almost any member of the family.

There are also shampooing machines available for either purchase or rent. These machines have foamer attachments with brushes which may rotate up to 200 RPM's. The foaming method is frequently preferred over the liquid shampoo method because the carpet dries in 30 to 60 minutes instead of the usual 4 to 6 hours.

One other type of cleaning which can be done by the homeowner is steam cleaning. It is especially recommended for carpet dirtied with greasy soil. Steam cleaning equipment is costly, but it is available for rent in most areas.

The process of steam cleaning involves dispensing a detergent mixed with hot water through water jets. The detergent mixes with the soil in the carpet and holds the dirt in suspension until it is picked up with a vacuum tank. This method is favored because it does not involve scrubbing, and the carpet dries quickly.

If you wish to employ professional cleaning, you have a choice of on-location cleaning or plant cleaning. Plant cleaning, which involves having your carpet removed from your home and cleaned, is absolutely the most thorough type of cleaning available. The rinsing operations used in plant cleaning completely remove all soil and detergent, which on-location cleaning cannot do. However, due to the complicated process of removing carpeting for plant cleaning, the homeowner more frequently favors on-location cleaning.

REMOVING SPOTS AND STAINS

When spilling occurs, follow this simply procedure: Soak up the spill immediately with tissues or paper towel. (DO NOT RUB.) Make a solution of warm water, mild detergent (never use soap, ammonia or any cleaning element intended for hard surfaces), and a teaspoon of white vinegar. Using a sponge, blot the stained area gently. Avoid soaking the carpet. If the carpet absorbs too much water, it may mildew.

Note: It is a very good idea to keep in your home scraps of your carpet, and use these scraps to test this cleaning procedure and any other cleaning methods you wish to use to make sure that your carpet will not be damaged.

For removing specific types of stains, refer to the removal chart. However, if home remedies for carpet stains fail, do not chance ruining your carpet with too much sponging and blotting. Consult professional cleaners immediately.

Carpet Pads

Carpet pads are used as a separate backing for carpet to aid in carpet maintenance. Pads provide for longer lasting, more soundproof carpet and also increase walking comfort. Some commonly used padding materials are rubber padding, available in sponge or foam, and a felted type of cushioning, made from animal hair and/or jute. *SEE ALSO CARPETING.*

Carpet, Self-Backing

Carpet with self-backing or cushioned-backed carpet contains a pad of backing material made into the floor covering. This type of carpeting is simple to install. Before beginning work, be sure to read the manufacturers instructions for special techniques for the particular carpet being used.

INSTALLATION

After cleaning the floor, apply two inch wide double-faced tape flush with the wall. Do not remove the protective covering. Next, lay the carpet on the floor and cut it to fit room dimensions. After the carpet has been sized, remove the protective stripping and press the carpet firmly to the tape. Trim excess with a sharp trimming instrument.

To make a seam, adjust the edges to form a peak. Fold back one side and make a chalk line or draw a pencil line along the edge of the other section of carpeting. Centering five inch wide tape over the line, apply an activator to the tape and let the carpet edge fold back. After applying seam adhesive along the edge of the first section of carpet, let the second section ease down gently until it drops in place. By patting or rolling an object over it, smooth the seam edges. To close gaps, simply push from the sides toward the seam. Rubbing a solvent over excessive seam adhesive will remove it. A metal binder strip or aluminum saddle placed at doorways are safety features and prevent raveling.

By cutting a slit and trimming the hole to fit the outline of the object, protruding pipes and other objects may be carpeted on all sides.

Taking up this type of carpet is quite simple. Start at a corner and pull the carpeting up. Be sure that the adhesive is still attached to the carpet. Put toilet paper on the tape to prevent it from attaching itself to other objects. *SEE ALSO CARPETING.*

Carport

A carport is a part of a house design commonly used as an open-sided substitute for a garage, providing economical shelter for automobiles or other vehicles as well as convenient storage space. Carports may be simply an extension of the roof, or a more subtle, elaborate plan of horizontal design. Formerly considered rather makeshift structures, modern carports are sturdily built, and may easily be converted into an enclosed garage. *SEE ALSO GARAGE & CARPORT CONSTRUCTION.*

Carriage

The carriage, also termed stringer, is the framing along the sides of stairs that supports the treads, the horizontal stair members, and the risers, the vertical stair members between the treads. *SEE ALSO STAIR CONSTRUCTION.*

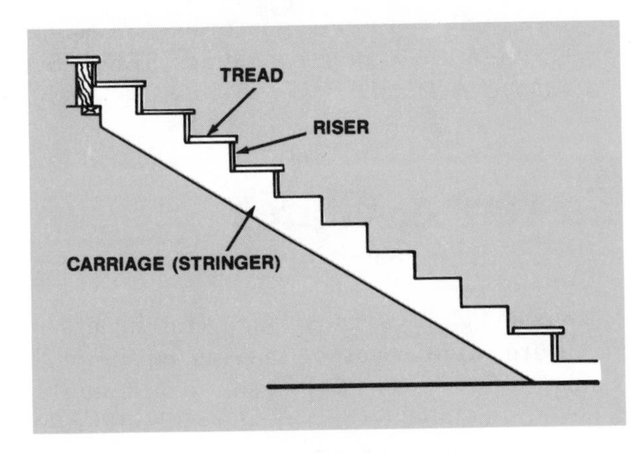

Carriage Support

Carriage Bolt

A carriage bolt has coarse threading on one end. The bolt head can be either round or countersunk flat-topped. A shoulder located just below the head aids in preventing the bolt from turning as the nut is tightened. *SEE ALSO FASTENERS.*

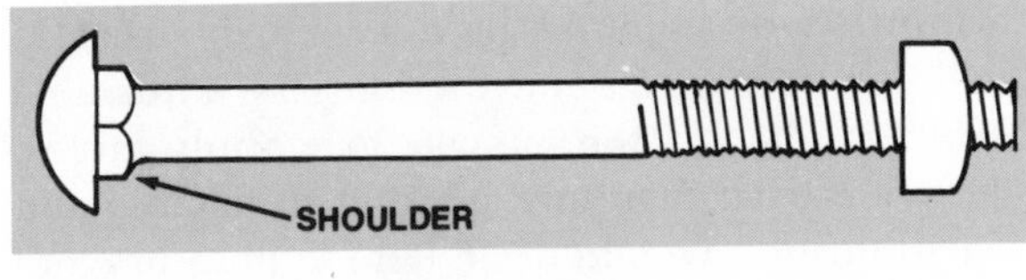

Carriage Bolt

Cartridge Fuse

A cartridge fuse, like a plug fuse, "blows" when an overload of current passes through it. But, the cylindrical-shaped cartridge type is most commonly used where high amperage is needed. One style of cartridge fuse has round metal cap terminals at each end and has an ampere rating of 15-60. The other type, with an ampere rating of 60-600, has flat metal terminals extending from the ends. Both types fit into a clip device in a fuse panel. There are one or two large cartridge fuses in a household service panel, one for each "hot" service entrance wire (120-240 volts) coming from outside. These fuses may be rated at up to 200 or more amperes, and they are an indication of how much total electric power is available in the house. *SEE ALSO FUSES & CIRCUIT BREAKERS.*

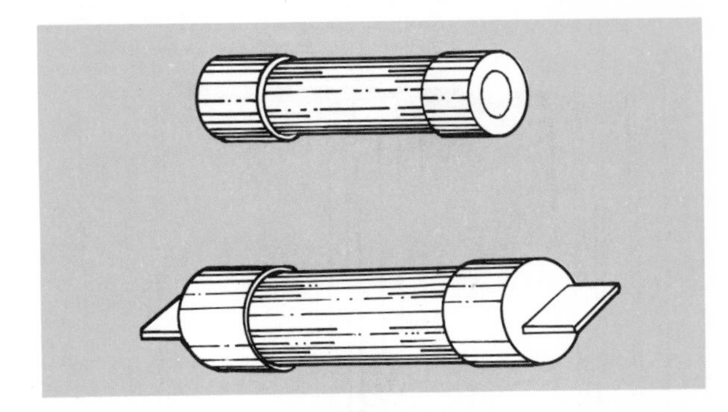

Cartridge Fuses

Casein Glue

Casein glue is an adhesive for general woodworking, most especially, furniture making. The base of the glue is skim milk curd. Lime and other materials are added to make the mixture usable.

Casein glue is made by mixing equal amounts of powdered casein and water. It must be used within seven hours after mixing or it will harden to the point it is no longer usable.

Casein glue is especially useful on lemonwood, teak and other woods containing oil. It should not be used on oak or maple since stains will result. Although resistant to moisture, casein glue is not waterproof. *SEE ALSO ADHESIVES.*

Casement Window

The casement window sash is hinged on the side and pivots out from the window frame on a vertical axis. The sash, which can be metal or wood, is opened and closed by a cranking lever that is mounted to the frame, and shuts tightly against the weather stripping with a latch. The storm sash and the window screen are located inside the casement, but do not interfere with the action of the window. The operational casement units are usually installed along with fixed units, each being separated by mullions.

Case Molding

Case moldings or casings are similar to baseboards in design, although they are usually smaller. They are used around doors, windows or for other trim purposes. *SEE ALSO MOLDING & TRIM.*

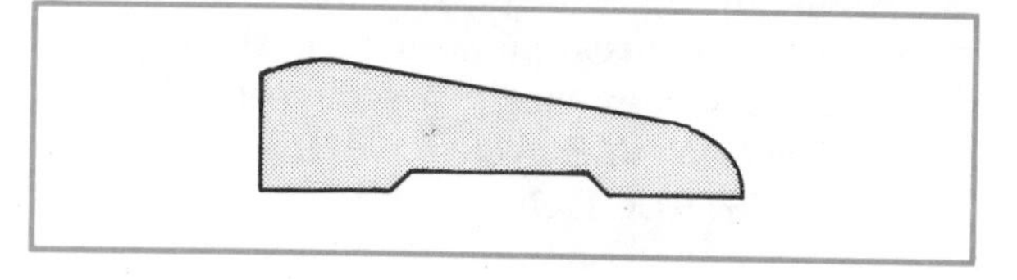

Case Molding

Casing

Casing is the trimming around a door or window, either on the outside or inside, or the finished lumber around a post or beam. Casings are also referred to as case moldings. *SEE ALSO MOLDING & TRIM.*

Casters & Glides

Casters and glides are attachments for the legs of furniture, appliances or moving equipment. Their purpose is to more evenly distribute the weight of the item or give greater mobility without marring the floor surface.

GLIDES

Glides are discs attached to the foot of a leg. They may be driven, screwed or slipped on the leg. They distribute weight as well as slide over surfaces. These are especially good for furniture on carpeting or soft wood floors.

The rubberized-cushion glide is used on furniture such as occasional chairs and dining room tables. The hollow-shafted glide is designed to fit furniture with tapered legs. Primarily used to level furniture on an uneven floor, the adjustable furniture glide is the answer to wobbly tables. The wide-base furniture glide is adjustable and distributes the weight of an item to help prevent marring of the floor surface.

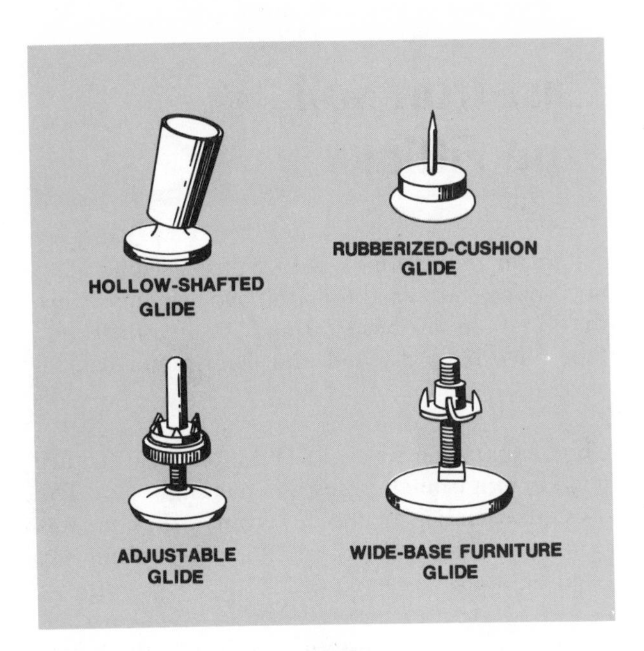

Glides

CASTERS

Casters are rollers attached to leg ends. The ball-type casters are used for furniture moved across carpeting. Adjustable casters are excellent to level furniture on uneven flooring. General purpose casters are for both light- and medium-weight furniture. Heavy duty flat-plate swivel casters are used on hand trucks and dollies.

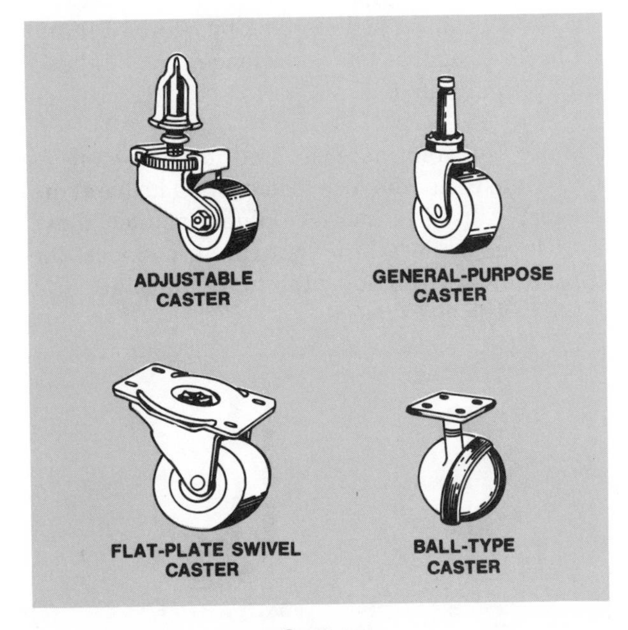

Casters

Casters attach to the leg in several ways. While the flat-plate swivel and ball-type casters are affixed by bolts or screws, the adjustable and general-purpose casters slip either into the center of a hollow tube leg or a drilled hole in the center of a solid leg.

Cast-Iron Pipe

Cast-iron pipe is most commonly used as a drainage pipe. In older homes the entire waste system used cast-iron pipe. Available in both service-weight and extra-heavy weight, cast-iron pipe may come with a preservative coating. Due to its durability, this pipe is widely used. The distinguishing feature of a length of cast-iron pipe is that one end has a hub or collar and the other end has a spigot or neck. The spigot fits into the hub to form a joint.

Cutting cast-iron pipe is not as easy as cutting other pipes. Using a hacksaw, a $^1/_{16}$ inch deep cut should be made all the way around the pipe. Position the cut just over the edge of a sawhorse or workbench, then tap near the cut on the overhanging portion with a hammer until the pipe breaks away. *SEE ALSO PLUMBING MATERIALS.*

Cast-Iron Pipe Adapter

A cast-iron pipe adapter is a copper pipe fitting. The cast-iron pipe adapter joins cast-iron pipe to copper pipe. *SEE ALSO PIPE FITTINGS.*

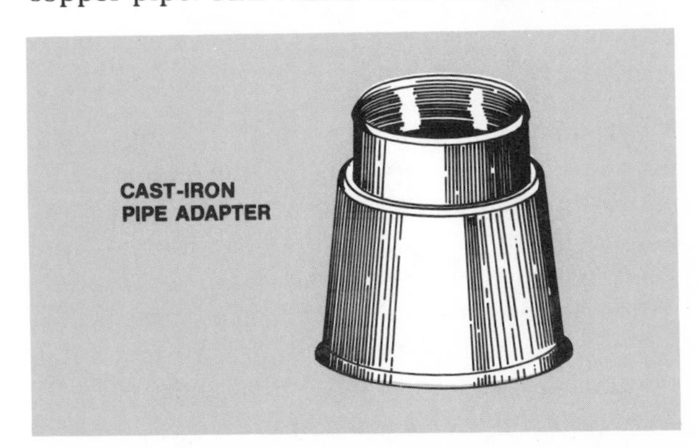

Cast-Iron Pipe Joints

Cast-iron pipe joints are the sealed union of two cast-iron pipes. The two types of joints are the vertical and horizontal.

VERTICAL JOINT

A vertical cast-iron joint is formed in a series of steps, the first of which is centering the spigot end of the pipe in the hub end. Next, wrap oakum around the spigot inside the hub and pack it tightly with a yarning iron. While the home craftsman is doing this, lead should be melting in an iron pot.

The pot should be heated by a blow torch beneath the pot. An iron ladle is needed to scoop the molten lead from the pot, and a pair of heavy gloves is needed to handle the hot ladle. The ladle should be held momentarily in the flame to remove any moisture. The slightest amount of moisture on the ladle will cause the lead to spatter. Heat the lead just beyond melting as molten lead will burn the oakum if the lead is too hot. A yarning iron can be used to tightly pack the oakum into the joint as it is twisted around the pipe.

When the oakum is packed and the lead is melted, ladle the molten lead into the space above the oakum. After the lead has cooled, use a caulking tool to chip the lead. This is done by driving the end of the tool into the cooled lead and spreading the prongs. The chipped lead is then smoothed around the edges to form a watertight seal.

HORIZONTAL JOINT

A horizontal joint may be made by placing a joint runner around the top of the oakum. A joint runner is a piece of fat, asbestoes rope with a clamp to hold the ends together. Pour the molten lead into the joint runner using the clamp as a funnel. After the lead has cooled, chisel off the bump left by the clamp and smooth chipped lead around the edges as described before. *SEE ALSO PIPE JOINTS.*

Cast-Iron Soil Pipe Fittings

Cast-iron pipe fittings, which are various sizes and shapes, are used for drainage systems. Since the functions of these fittings are also different, they have been divided into eight major categories.

The sanitary tee with side inlet and test tee are used to join branch pipes into a straight run. The second division is the Y branch. It connects pipes at an angle. A Y branch is most commonly used on a 45 degree angle.

The soil p-trap, provides a liquid seal which prevents passage of air from the pipes to an opening. The fourth division, a reducer, joins pipes of different sizes such as a 3/4-inch to a 1/2-inch pipe.

Fifth is the cleanout ferrule, a threaded plug used to cap a pipe at strategic points such as corners and vents. When removing clogs, this allows easy access to the inside of the pipe.

The caulking spigot, the sixth division, is used to join straight run pipes of the same size. Next is the floor drain which permits the flow of liquid from floor surface to the drainage pipes. It has a p-trap to eliminate pipe odors.

Finally, the vent increaser and the hub-vent fittings make up the last category. The vent increaser is used to increase pipe diameter above roof level while a hub-vent fitting connects the hub of a cast-iron soil pipe to a vent pipe. *SEE ALSO PIPE FITTINGS.*

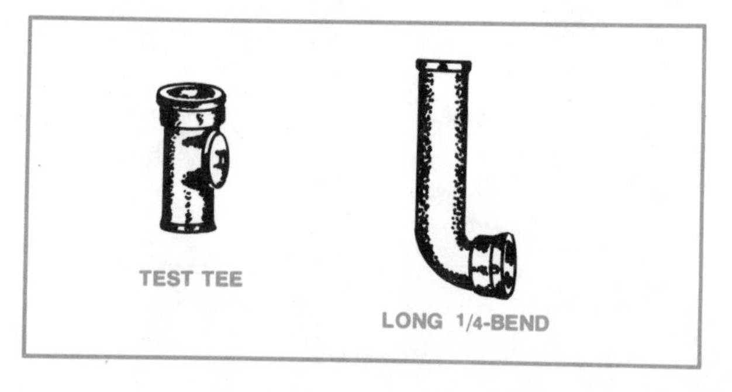

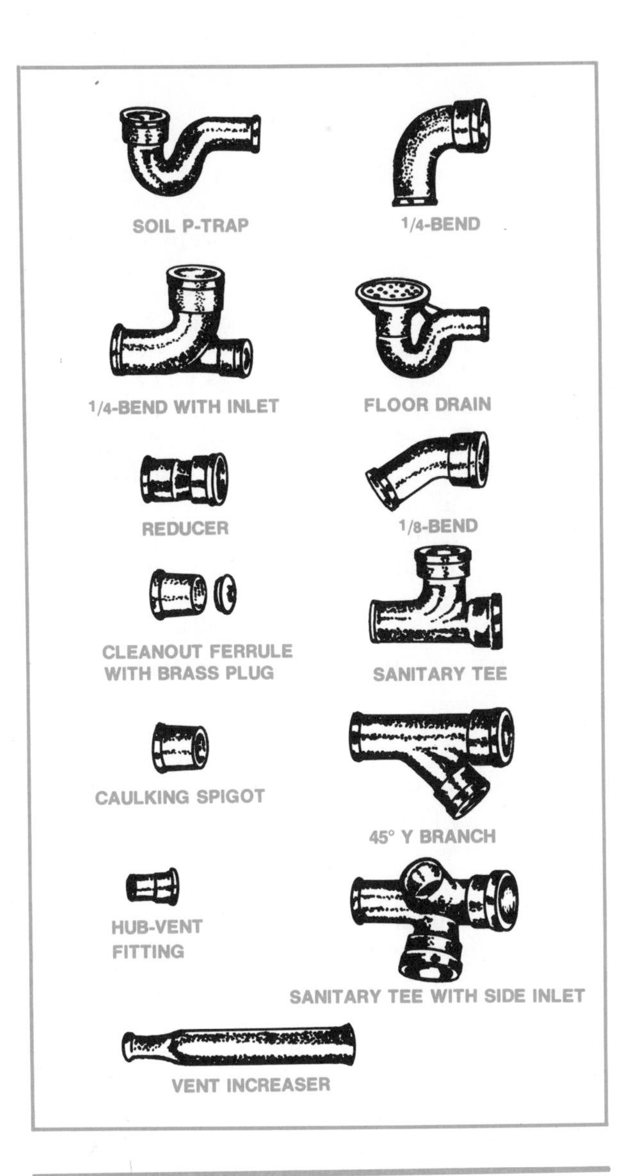

Castle Nut

A nut commonly used to secure an automobile's front wheel drums is a castle nut, also known as a castellated nut. It was so named because its upper face has radial grooves and resembles a castle. A cotter pin can be slipped through a hole in a bolt to prevent the nut from turning. *SEE ALSO NUTS & BOLTS.*

Cotter pin keeps nut from turning.

Cast Thermostatic Heating Appliances

Most of these appliances differ from each other only in the shape of the main casting or container. A separate thermostatic control is used to sense the heat within the casting. This control is in the probe that inserts between the two electrical terminals when the control is put into place on the unit. The control is marked in degrees of heat and temperature is sensed rather accurately.

Courtesy of General Electric Company

Dutch Skillet performs many food preparation duties.

The heating element is made into the base casting and is completely enclosed. It is not serviceable and not visible. Luckily, this is seldom the cause of problems in these appliances unless they are very old.

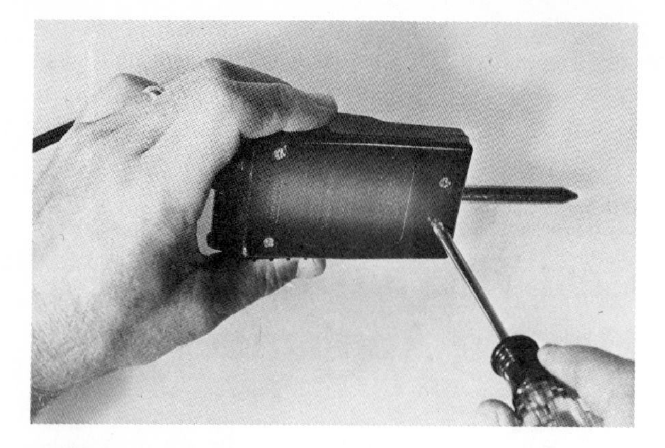

Temperature probes on most cast appliances can be serviced by removing screws underneath probe. Be sure that unit is unplugged before handling temperature probe.

When the appliance is turned on, the element begins to heat the base casting. As the temperature increases, a bimetal wire within the probe begins to move a set of contacts back in the detachable control body. When these contacts open, the heating element turns off. As the appliance begins to cool, it turns back on. This on-off cycling varies with the temperature set on the control by the user, and temperature is maintained quite accurately.

If a problem arises with the frypan, the fault will usually be within the control itself. The best way to prevent problems is to use proper care when using the appliance. Keep grease away from the control section and never immerse this section in water.

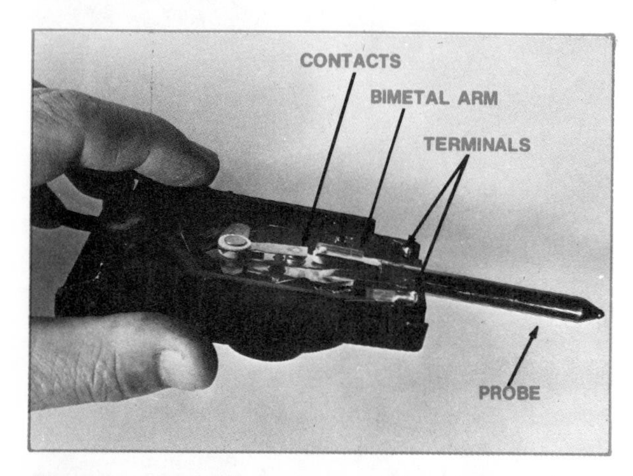

Bimetal arm can be seen extending from probe to contacts which are in base of the control.

If the frypan doesn't operate, check the receptacle first with a table lamp to see if voltage is reaching that point. If it is, check around the plug and the point where it enters the control. A special flexible heat-resistant type cord is used for these appliances. When replacement is necessary the same type cord should be used.

The detachable control normally has a small neon pilot light which also gives you an indication as to whether or not voltage is reaching the control and whether contacts within the controls are closing. If the light doesn't come on, you know something is wrong. If it is necessary to disassemble the control, unplug it and look carefully around the outside housing for any screws that may come loose. On some models, it is necessary to remove a small disc in the center of the temperature knob to remove the knob, before the cover can be removed. Be sure and mark the position of the knob before lifting it from the shaft. This is often a calibration point and if it is put back on in the wrong place, temperatures will be incorrect.

To check the temperature setting of these controls, put about one inch of water in the pan. Set the control to 212 degrees. The water should begin to boil at this point (let it heat for about five minutes before making observations, allowing the temperature to stabilize). When the temperature setting is raised, the water should reach

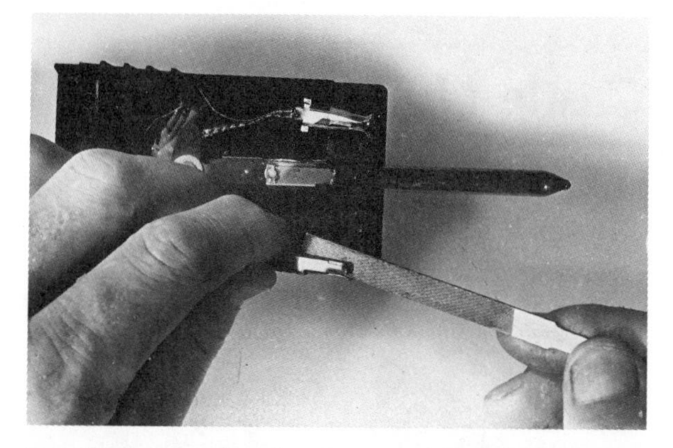

Terminals can often be cleaned and repaired if they are defective. Be sure to clean the male portion on the pan as well as the portion within the control. Make sure that all connections are tight before reassembling.

Television tuner spray is handy for cleaning control section.

a heavy boil. When it is reduced below 212 degrees, it should stop boiling. Allow for a 20 degree tolerance.

Look closely at the condition of the control contacts and the connecting wiring, making sure that all terminals are fastened well. If the contacts have to be cleaned, filing with an automotive point file followed by burnishing with a hardwood stick or the striking surface from a book of matches should take care of the problem. If the control has collected a lot of grease, it's wise to clean it with television tuner contact spray available from any radio and TV parts supplier.

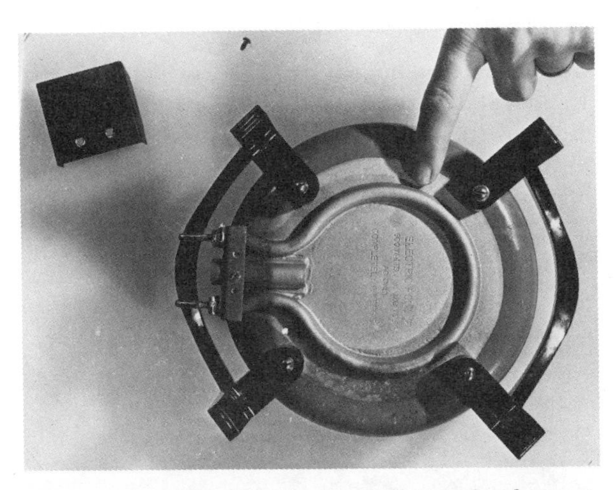

Element is visible in the base of this fondue pot. Since element is molded in, it isn't serviceable as a replacement part. However, it is one of the least likely components to fail.

The heating element will have to be checked with a VOM or continuity tester and should also be checked for grounds to the frame of the housing. If the element has failed, it would probably be wise to purchase a new appliance since the base casting will likely cost practically as much as a new frying pan, if it is available at all.

If the appliance overheats, the control section is likely inoperative. Possibly the contacts are sticking or welded together. You can inspect visually for this problem. If it's defective, it would be best to replace the entire control section.

A frying pan that shocks the user could have a grounded heating element, but it could also be caused by operating it with a thermostatic control that has been immersed in water and is still damp. If this is the problem, you can dry it out by opening the control carefully, then placing it in an oven at about 140 degrees. After an hour or so, the moisture should be eliminated and the control can be reassembled. Be sure to test the unit with a VOM before putting it back into operation. *SEE ALSO APPLIANCE REPAIR, SMALL.*

Be sure to check for ground or have base tested at an appliance shop with VOM. Terminal area must be dry before this test is made. Meter is set to highest resistance scale. One probe is placed on housing and other probe is placed to each terminal in turn. If ground is indicated, appliance should be discarded.

Catalytic Coatings

Catalytic coatings offer maximum protection for problem areas such as heavy equipment, structural members and around sinks. These enamel coatings are heavy-duty epoxies or urethanes which require a curing agent (catalyst) for drying. Made up of a resin and a hardner, the enamel is mixed immediately before use. It sets chemically rather than by evaporation of thinners, and produces a continuous film about 2 milligrams in thickness, so a three-coat application provides a dry film 6 milligrams thick.

Mix only the amount needed for each job as it will not store after mixing. Spraying or rolling is recommended, but it may be brushed on also. It may be applied over old catalyzed finishes, from which the gloss has been sanded. Old, unknown finishes should be spot tested to avoid possible wrinkling and lifting. Apply the enamel to a clean surface in as many coats as needed to achieve required film thickness. Use an undercoater before applying to bare wood, but the coatings may be applied directly on new metal. Fill masonry blocks with a block filler before the first application. Other new masonry should be primed first. *SEE ALSO PAINTS & PAINTING.*

Catch-All Shelf Units

Select one 8′ board for right side standard. Measure 12″ up from bottom and draw a line across the face of the board. Measure 12″ up from this line and draw another line across the face of the board. Repeat this until 6 lines are drawn across the board. These lines indicate where top edge of cleats will be placed. Check to be sure there is 24″ between last line and top of the board. Nail cleats into place.

Select one 6′ board for left standard. This piece stands on top of plate (or bottom piece), adding ¾″ to its height. Left standard must be cut off before attaching cleats. Attach first cleat 11¼″ from the bottom. Measure 12″ up for position of each succeeding cleat. Only five cleats are needed on this board. Drive nails into cleats in slightly downward position for added shelf support.

Select another 8′ length for the left side of the unit. Measure 2′ down from the top of the board and attach cleat.

At this point, start assembling the framework. Nail the outer sides into the ends of two 8′ lengths selected to form the top and bottom.

Next, put in the top shelf an 8′ board running horizontal 2′ below the top piece. Place it on top of the cleats and nail through the sides into the ends of the board. Then nail the shelf into the cleats. To install the left standard, measure plate 6¼″from the right side (to insure that the shelves will slide in easily) and draw a line. Duplicate this measurement on the underside of the top shelf, then slide the standard into place, keeping right edge of board on the drawn lines. Nail through top of shelf down into standard. Toenail bottom of standard to plate.

Now take the unit to its permanent site. Set against the wall and anchor into place by toenailing upper half of unit into studding in the wall. Use masonry nails if anchoring to brick or masonry wall.

Five 6′ shelving boards can now be installed; but first cut six braces 11¼″ long. Insert lower shelf and nail into cleats. Insert bottom brace about midway between shelf and bottom (plate). Nail through shelf into brace, then toenail lower edge of brace. Repeat working from the bottom up. Put in upper 2′ brace and the unit is complete. *SEE ALSO PROJECTS.*

MATERIALS LIST

5 pieces 1 x 12, 8′ long
6 pieces 1 x 12, 6′ long
1 piece 1 x 12, 2″ long
5 pieces 1 x 12, approx. 12″ long
12 pieces 1 x 2 for cleats, 11⅝″ long
½ pound 4d common or box nails (4d finishing nails may be used for better appearance)

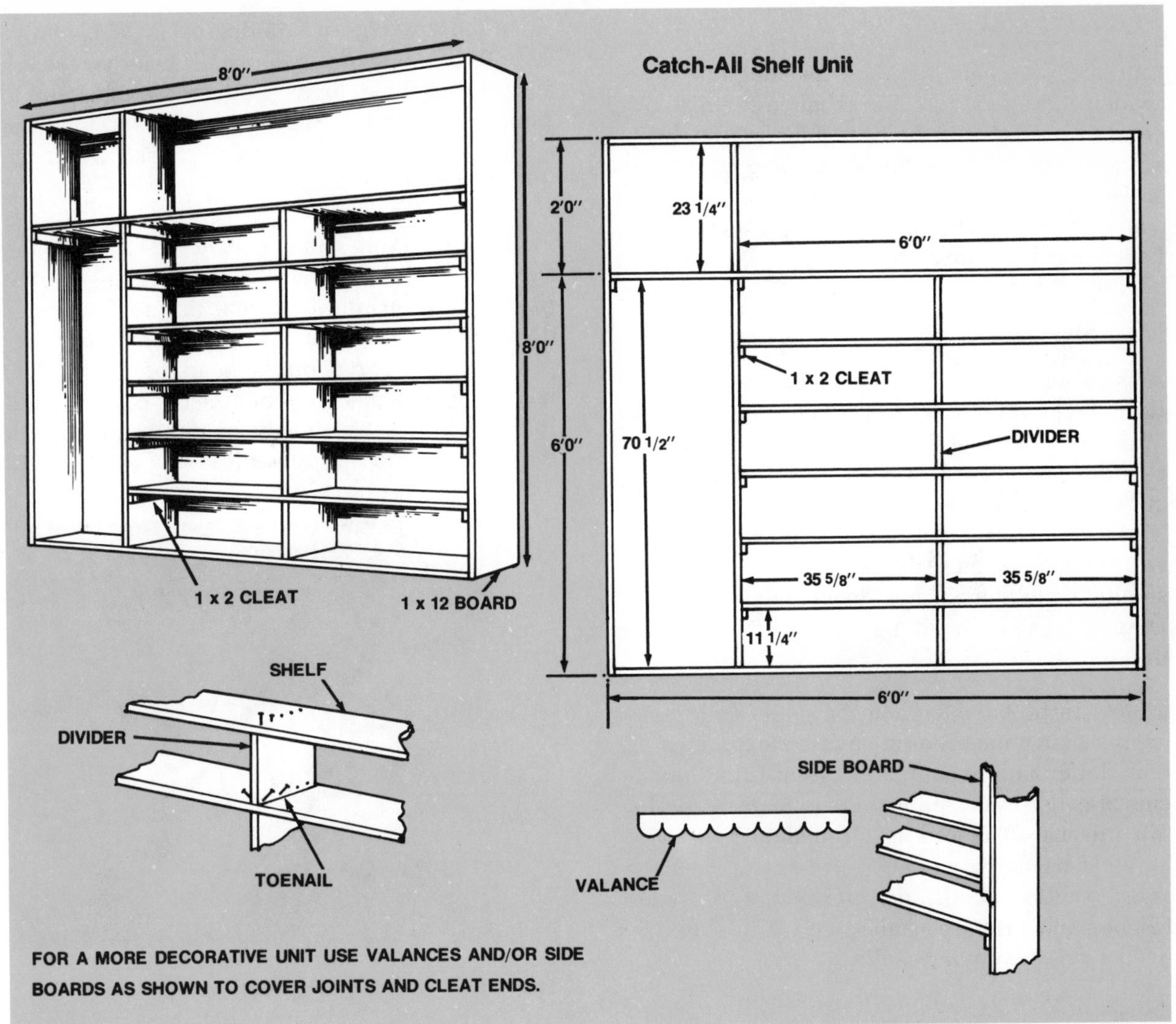

Courtesy of Western Wood Products Association

Catch Basin

A catch basin is an artificial reservoir positioned to trap materials which would not flow easily through a sewer. It is placed where a street gutter empties into a sewer. *SEE ALSO DRAINAGE SYSTEMS.*

Caulking

Although caulking materials have changed through the ages from clay to modern plastics, the reasons for caulking remain basically the same. By filling the cracks in a house, cold is kept outside and heat is held inside, thus saving money and fuel. Caulking is an important step in preparing a house for painting. Caulking comes before painting and should not be neglected.

Caulks are also used to seal against rain, moisture, and rot. It is needed wherever there are gaps in the exterior or interior walls, joints that need to be moisture or water sealed, and areas where different materials meet. Notice the presence and condition of the old caulking. If it is dry and cracking, then the house is unprotected. The old caulking should be chiseled out and new caulking applied.

HOW TO CAULK

Caulking, like painting, requires adequate preparation for a good job. The label on the caulking you have selected is the best guide to joint preparation. Some caulks need priming of certain substrates such as wood and masonry. Most caulks need a clean, dry surface for application. Latex caulks, however, may be applied to slightly damp surfaces.

Joint Size

All old and cracked caulk should be removed from the joint with a chisel, screwdriver or putty knife as dried caulk makes an unsatisfactory base for new. Check to make sure that the joints are wide and deep enough to do the job properly. Most materials need 1/4 x 3/8 inch minimum width-depth joints. Any joints smaller than this should be widened and deepened if possible. Otherwise, use a caulking material designed for undersized joints.

Joints can be too deep and too wide. Any joints deeper than 1 inch should be filled to the ideal 1/2 inch depth using a compatible joint-filler. One is closed-cell vinyl or polyethylene foam made for this purpose. The joint material should be twice as wide as the crack, so it presses against the sides. Another joint-filler, rope oakum, is used to fill beneath oil-base caulks and should not be used with most other caulks.

Adhesion

Because of the expansion and contraction of housing materials, caulk needs good adhesion to all surfaces, otherwise it would soon loosen its grip. To ensure a tight grip, clean all surfaces with a rag soaked in mineral spirits to be sure the surfaces are free of grease. Bond-breaking dust should be brushed off with a stiff-bristle brush. Apply a coat of primer to the substrate (if required), and let it dry. Wood should be primed with an oil-base primer; steel with a rust-inhibiting metal primer. A suitable day above 40°F should be chosen for caulking. If it's rainy, save the job for another day. Only latex caulks will adhere well in damp weather.

Application

To begin caulking, first cut off the tapered plastic tip of the cartridge at a 45-degree angle, leaving a hole the right size for the caulk bead you want. Insert a large nail or wire down into the spout to puncture the inner seal to prevent bursting the cartridge by internal pressure caused when the gun is triggered.

Hold the caulking gun at a 45-degree angle to the surface, and parallel to the crevice. Engage the pushrod by turning it so that the notches point downward. Squeeze the trigger to move the pushrod and force out a bead of caulk. The neatest bead is made by moving the caulking gun forward in the direction the spout is aimed. Fill the joint, but do not over-fill it.

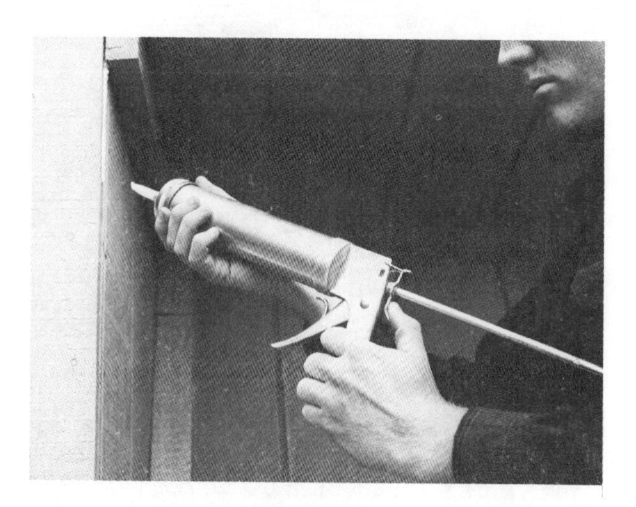

The correct position for caulking.

To stop the caulk flow, stop triggering and disengage the pushrod by turning its notches upward. Pull the rod back an inch or two to release the pressure on the cartridge. Some caulking cartridges come with dome-shaped plastic followers, a piston inside the cartridge that drives caulk out as you gun. Shaped followers prevent most after-ooze so that you need not retract the pushrod to stop caulk flow. Tool the bead smooth after application. A common tool for this is the smooth handle of a spoon or an ice cream stick.

To store a partly used cartridge or tube, cover the end with masking tape to prevent the remaining caulk from hardening. An even better trick is to gun out a little caulk and leave it as a beginning to get the flow going when you next use the cartridge.

After caulk has dried for a week, most types can be protected with a coat or two of paint. This reduces the weathering they have to endure. Latex caulks, however, can be painted with a latex house paint after only 30 minutes of drying.

CAULK GRADES

Caulks should always be used as they come from the container. Thinning causes excess shrinkage and loss of adhesion. Caulks are offered in three grades: gun-grade, knife-grade, and weather-strip caulking cord form. Gun-grade caulks in their handiest form come packaged in cylindrical, fiberboard or metal cartridges with plastic cut-off tips at one end. These cartridges fit the drop-in caulking guns with large triggers that permit dispensing the caulk in a uniform bead. Each one contains 11 fluid ounces of material.

CAULK CARTRIDGES PER 11 FL. OZ. CARTRIDGE (LIN. FT.)

JOINT DEPTH	JOINT WIDTH				
	1/4″	3/8″	1/2″	5/8″	3/4″
1/4″	25-1/2	15-1/2	12-1/2	10	8-1/2
3/8″	15-1/2	11	8-1/2	6-1/2	5-1/2
1/2″	12-1/2	8-1/2	6-1/2	5	4
5/8″	10	6-1/2	5	4	3-1/2
3/4″	8-1/2	5-1/2	4	3-1/2	2-1/2
1″	6-1/2	4	3-1/2	2-1/2	2

Gun-grade caulk is available like toothpaste in metal or plastic roll-up tubes. Gun-grade caulk is well suited for small projects where a whole caulking cartridge would be wasted. You can get gun-grade caulking in cans for filling of bulk-type caulking guns. This is a messy job and one that is not recommended.

Knife-grade caulk, best for small joints and cracks, comes in cans to be applied with a putty knife or spatula. Fill the joint using pressure on the putty knife to force caulk in and then go back over the joint smoothing the surface with the knife. Actually, caulking tubes and cartridges are so easy to use that there is little reason for the homeowner to take the extra trouble to use canned caulks.

Weatherstrip caulking cord is sold in rolls. It is the easiest of all caulks to use, but offers only temporary sealing. All that is necessary is to peel off a strand and press it into the joint. Caulk cord is nondrying, and, therefore, is unsuited to painting. It is used mostly for sealing around storm windows and room air conditioners.

The ideal caulk would adhere to any unprimed surface. It would be easy to gun and tool smooth. To minimize dust pickup, the ideal caulk would become tack-free quickly. It would shrink only a little, cure in a rubbery plastic form, and stay that way. It would also clean up with just water. It could be painted but need not be for maximum weathering. And a single application would last the life of the house. A few caulks approach the ideal. Good caulk sense requires knowing about the various caulking materials.

CAULKS VS SEALANTS

The word *sealant* once meant a high-performance elastomeric (stretchable-compressible) material that could be used in moving-type joints. Moving joints are ones in which the joint expands and contracts with temperature, moisture and load. Most house joints are non-moving. Those that do move are joints between dissimilar materials such as glass-to-sash joints

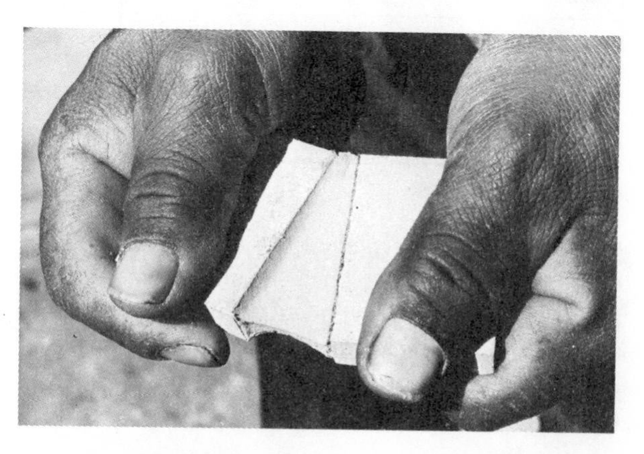

A non-hardening caulk is best for moveable joints.

between wood and brick or house and siding. Other moving joints are the ones between the house and a sidewalk slab, joints in walkways and pool deck joints. Expansion-and-contraction joints in masonry walls and slabs and in metal guttering are moving joints, too.

All moving joints require sealants. But the word *sealant* has been tacked onto materials that are in no way elastomeric, until today it means little. For that reason, we will call them all simply *caulks*. Moving joints thus require high-performance elastomeric caulks.

The chart lists the kinds of caulks that are available for home use and their expected life. Priming and paint-over requirements are shown, as well as best uses and costs. Actual prices for typical 11-fluid-ounce cartridges vary from about 50 cents to $4 each. Your own caulk selection is actually much simpler than it would appear from the chart.

HOMEOWNER CAULKS

MATERIAL	LIFE (yrs.)	PRIMING NEEDED?	MOVING JOINTS?	PAINT NEEDED?	IN COLORS?	BEST USES	COST
Urethane	20+	No	Yes	No	Many	Any joints, horizontal and vertical. Close to being the ideal caulk.	Moderate
Hypalon	15-20	Porous surfaces	Yes	No	Some	Any joints. Runner-up as the ideal caulk.	Moderate
Silicone rubber	20+	Porous surfaces	Yes	No	Some	Tub-and-tile, metal-to-metal, and undersized joints that move.	High
Acrylic latex	2-10	Porous surfaces	No	When exposed	Some	Nonmoving joints that are painted over or not exposed to weathering.	Low
Butyl rubber	7-10	No	No	Is best	Many	Narrow openings in nonmoving joints.	Low
Oil-base	1-7	Porous surfaces	No	Yes	A few	To get by cheap. Not recommended.	Very low
PVA tub/ tile	3-10 (indoors)	Usually, no	No	For best results	No	Hole-filling, indoors only. Not recommended.	Low
Neoprene rubber	15-20	No	Yes	No	A few	Driveway and wall cracks and narrow joints.	Moderate
Nitrile rubber	15-20	No	Yes	No	A few	Small joints in metal, masonry	Moderate
Polysulfide rubber	20+	Special one	Yes	No	Many	Any joints. Hard to work with for beginners. Not recommended.	Moderate
Weatherstrip Caulking cord	to 20	No	No	No	No	Temporary draft-sealing and hole-plugging.	Moderate

Oil based caulks are cheapest and most popular caulks on the market. They are short lived and as soon as their oil solvents dry out, they shrink away from the substrate and lose their pliability. All that can be done is to remove them out and recaulk.

The average time for this is two to three years. Your labor considered, oil-base caulks are the poorest buy.

The caulking cost comparison shows why a low-cost, short-life caulking material is not economical. The net annual cost for oil-base caulks works out to approximately $9.67 compared to $2.25 for a new high-quality, long-life caulk. This

ANNUAL COST COMPARISON						
MATERIALS AND LABOR	OIL-BASE			URETHANE		
	COST PER UNIT	COST PER CAULKING	NET COST PER YEAR	COST PER UNIT	COST PER CAULKING	NET COST PER YEAR
10 cartridges caulk	$ .50	$ 5.00		$2.50	$25.00	
10 hours preparation	2.00	20.00		2.00	20.00	
2 hours priming	2.00	4.00		none	—	
TOTALS		$29.00 =	$9.67		$45.00 =	$2.25
Years of life (divide by)		3			20	

is assuming that your time is worth $2 an hour and that you can do the whole caulking job in just 10 hours. At higher rates of pay and longer times to complete the job, the comparison would favor the better material even more. Additionally, the better material looks and does the job better.

Next are the *acrylic latex caulks*. These are the very lowest priced materials you should consider putting on a house. They clean-up easily with water, like the latex paints they resemble chemically and can be painted over quickly if latex paint is used. A longer waiting period is required if you are painting with an oil-base paint.

Latex caulks come in three forms: economy, quality and tub-and-tile. The tub-and-tile latexes often are packaged in squeeze-tubes and should be used for tub/tile purposes only. If the label on the cartridges, does not read *acrylic latex*, you're looking at the economy or quality, but a price of less than $1 denotes the economy grade. Higher quality latexes are recommended over the economy ones.

Polyvinyl acetate (PVA) tub-and-tile caulk is disappearing because manufacturers are converting to acrylics, but it is still available. PVA is strictly for indoor use. PVA caulk is similar to PVA white glue with fillers added. It sticks well, but is not very flexible when hardened. Using other, more flexible tub-tile products makes sense.

Butyl rubber caulk is a borderline elastomeric. As it stretches and compresses well enough for most home uses, it once was recommended as an all-around home caulk. Butyl rubber shrinks on curing, leaving less of it in the joint. Therefore, it's tolerance for joint-widening is limited.

Polysulfide was the first of the high-performance elastomerics. It is widely sold for home use, but is hard to handle without experience. Moreover, it is toxic, therefore, it is not recommended.

Silicone rubber is the highest-performing of all elastomerics. Cure by chemical reaction to moisture in the air. Since it stretches up to 7 times its initial width, use silicone for very narrow, shallow, moving-type joints that cannot be widened enough for another caulk. Joint depth need be only 1/4 inch. Its disadvantages are that it is expensive, cannot be painted over, and, once applied, hard to smooth. Silicone is also good for caulking of metal gutters and downspouts. There is one brand which is a paintable silicone rubber caulk. And another is available in popular bathroom colors that do not need painting.

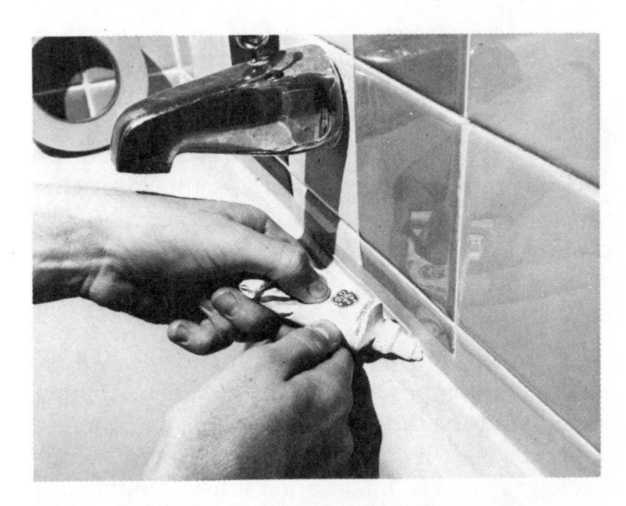

Tub-and-tile sealer comes in convenient tubes.

Any silicone caulk can be painted by first brushing a coat of contact cement onto the cured bead. The contact cement sticks to the caulk and, in-turn, the paint sticks to the contact cement.

Hypalon, is easy to run into the joint, and is easily tooled. Once a professional caulk, it is now widely marketed at a reasonable price. It is definitely recommended as a high-performing elastomeric home caulk. Few homeowners have been told about Hypalon, and not many store clerks know to tell you, even if they carry it.

Short for polyurethane, *urethane caulk* is relatively new to the home-handyman market. It was originally a two-part mix-together product like epoxy glue. A one-part formulation has been developed that comes closest yet to being the ideal homeowner caulk.

Urethane caulk sticks and bonds to any surface around the house without priming. It guns and flows extremely well. Urethane's weathering is superb, whether painted or not. A wet finger is all that is needed to tool urethane caulking. Urethane is also considered nontoxic.

Urethane caulk comes in nonsag for use in most joint and in a pourable form for sealing of horizontal joints. To obtain urethan caulking, look in the local Yellow Pages directory under "Calks" (different spelling) and find the nearest distributor of *Vulkem* caulking products.

Shelf-Life

The shelf-life of all elastomeric caulks is limited. You should buy only what you will need within a year. After that the caulk may spot-cure in the cartridge. Resist the temptation to squeeze the cartridge to see whether it is still soft. This makes tiny openings that hasten the spot-cure process.

SPECIAL-PURPOSE CAULKS

A number of caulking materials are now marketed for specialized uses. Cement-patching compound is used for filling cracks in concrete and masonry. It comes in cartridges and is concrete gray or black and often it has a butyl rubber base.

Special caulks are available for special jobs such as cement patching.

Masonite has developed a simulated mortar which is vinyl-based to be used with its imitation brick and stone panels.

A low-cost asphalt-base caulk is made for resealing roof flashing and shingling. Avoid using anything with asphalt for new work because, once you do, it is the only product that will stick. For initial use on flashings try any of the elastomerics instead.

Nitrile/neoprene rubber caulks are for specialized uses in driveways and on masonry and metal. They work in joints only 1/8 inch wide. Gallon plastic jugs of driveway crack-sealer with a cutoff plastic pour spout are now on the market. Fill horizontal cracks with the caulk and water is kept on the surface.

Sealing between two sheets of metal or plastic roofing material calls for a caulk that does not stay elastic. Butyl gutter and lap seal does this. Do not use them as ordinary caulks, though, as they would attract too much dust.

Glue-gun caulks, called *sealers,* cannot replace good caulking compounds. They are suitable for small-job sealing of non-moving joints when it would be necessary to buy a regular caulk and the glue-gun sealer is already on hand.

Many caulks are toxic. These should not be swallowed or gotten into the eyes. Some, like nitrile rubbers, should not be used in closed quarters because of their solvent fumes. All of these carry the required label warnings. Some of the clean-up solvents called for on the labels, such as trichloroethylene and methylethylketone, are toxic or flammable or both. Therefore, store both caulks and solvents where children cannot get at them.

Caulks come in natural whites and grays. Some are colored in metallic and architectural colors such as aluminum, bright white, browns, beiges, pink, blue, green, bronze, black, yellow, mahogany, redwood and clear.

When all the facts are considered, an economical program of home caulk-buying would be like this: Use a quality acrylic latex for nonmoving, nonweathering joints; use urethane caulk for all moving joints and all those exposed to the weather. For a premium job, use it for all joints (Hypalon may be substituted). Use either an acrylic latex tub-and-tile caulk or silicone rubber caulk for tub-tile purposes, which one depends on the desired life of the product. Finally, if not handled better by one of the above, use a specialized caulk for the specific purpose intended.

Caulking Guns

Caulking guns are used to lay caulking compounds. The two types of guns are the drop-in or half-barrel and the full-barrel.

Loading the full-barrel is quite simple. After removing the nozzle of the gun, fill the tube with caulking material and replace the nozzle. The half-barrel is equally as simple to load. After cutting off the nozzle tip of the cartridge containing the caulking material, break the inner seal. Insert the rear of the cartridge into the tube of the gun and snap the front portion into place.

Pressing the trigger of the gun releases the caulking material in a measured amount. Best results are obtained by holding the gun at a 45 degree angle to the surface. The slanted portion of the nozzle should be pointed in the direction of movement. *SEE ALSO CAULKING.*

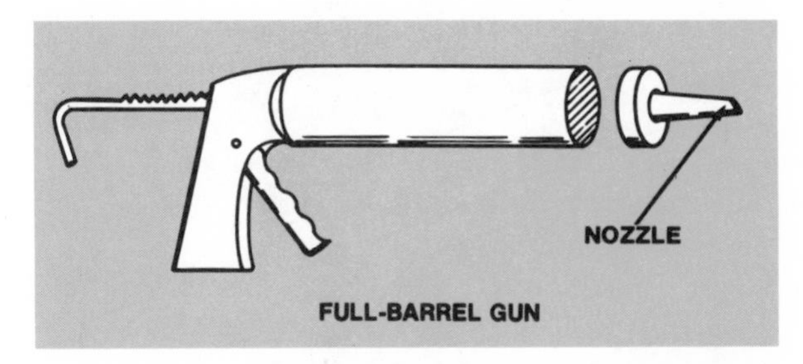

Caulking Gun

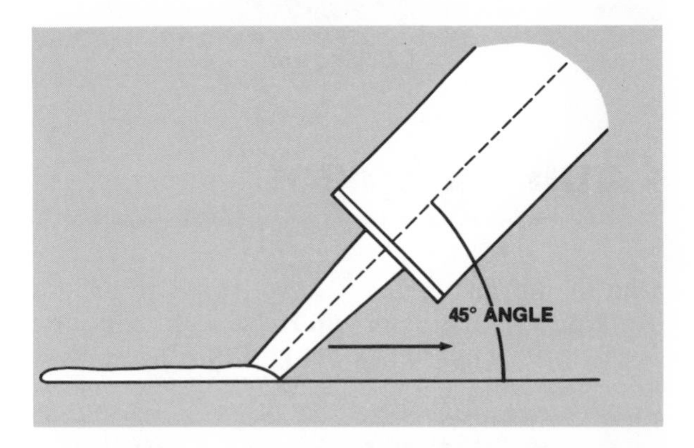

Slanting base in direction of movement, hold gun at a 45° angle.

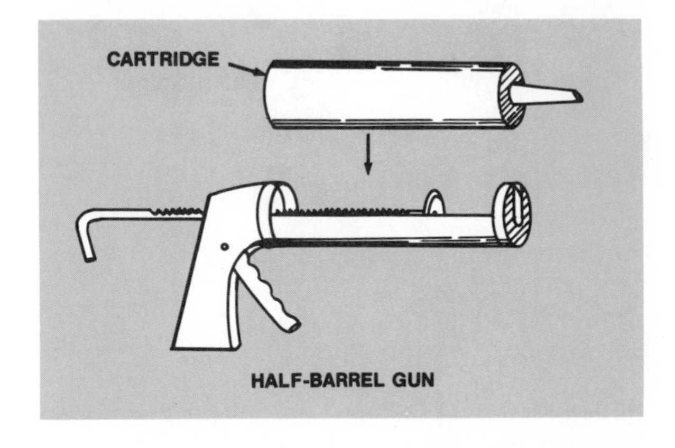

Caulking Iron

A caulking iron is a tool used in plumbing to insert and spread caulking into pipe joints after the joint has been sealed and cooled. The working end of the iron is offset so that it may be pressed flat against the pipe to pack the lead and oakum into the bell-shaped end of the joint. *SEE ALSO PLUMBER'S TOOLS & EQUIPMENT.*

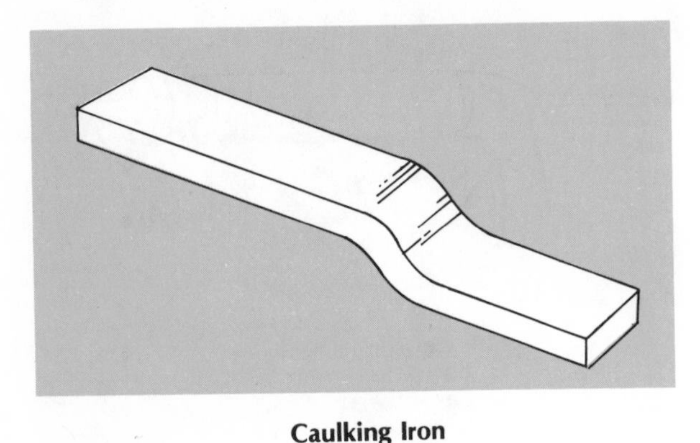

Caulking Iron

Caulking Spigot

One of the many cast-iron soil pipe fittings, a caulking spigot is used to form straight-run pipe joints. *SEE ALSO PIPE FITTINGS.*

Caulking Spigot

C-Clamps

One look at these clamps and you'll know how they got their name. Sizes, based on the maximum opening, range from the lightweight, 1-inch ones to the big, heavy, iron ones that open 8 inches. The depth of the back of the clamp ranges from 1 to 4 inches. There are also deep-throated c-clamps available from some manufacturers.

Primarily designed for metalworking, these adjustable, screw-type clamps have many uses including the clamping of wood. When used on wood, it is recommended that pads of scrap wood be used between the clamp jaws and the work to protect the wood's surface against marring. These protective pads also serve to distribute pressure uniformly. To insure a secure clamp on work which is not flat, the ball joint at the foot of the clamp is designed to swivel. *SEE ALSO HAND TOOLS.*

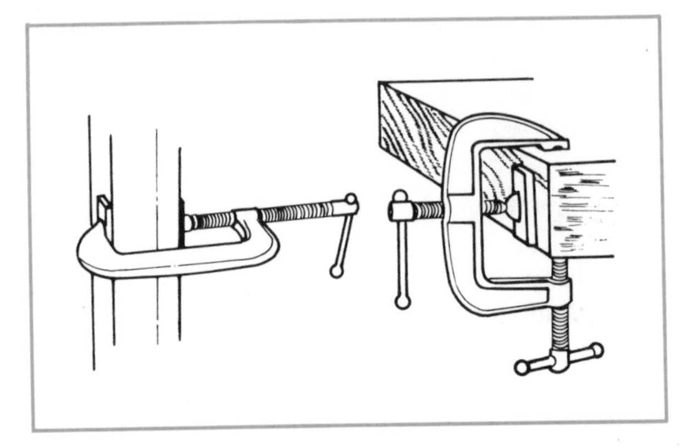

Protect wood finish by using pads of scrap wood between work and clamp. Apply pressure in two directions for edge gluing.

Cedar

Cedar is a softwood with a fresh, sweet odor, reddish color, resistance to decay and uniform texture. Produced from two species of a cone-bearing tree, both eastern red and western red cedar are used in construction and furniture making.

EASTERN RED CEDAR

Eastern red cedar is a medium density wood. While the heartwood is red, the sapwood is white. Since its distinctive odor inhibits the growth of moths, eastern red cedar is used in the construction of chests, closets and novelty items.

WESTERN RED CEDAR

Western red cedar is quite similar to redwood except for its distinctive cedar aroma. This variety is widely used for siding, structural timbers, shingles and utility poles. *SEE ALSO WOOD IDENTIFICATION.*

Courtesy of George C. Brown & Company, Inc.

This convenient and attractive closet, lined throughout with cedar wood, provides maximum protection for woolens and other clothing which are subject to moth damage.

Cedar Closet

Installing a cedar closet in your home will pay dividends over the years by keeping all woolens in a convenient location well protected against moths, dust and light. You can either line an existing closet with cedar, or build an extra closet in the basement, attic or bedroom and line the walls with cedar paneling.

Use cedar wood throughout the closet for maximum protection — floor, ceiling, shelves, cabinets and even the inside of doors. Fragrant and pleasant to people, cedar is extremely unpleasant to moths and it paralyzes their larvae.

If you decide to build a new closet, all you have to do is frame it with 2 x 4s. Space these the usual 16 inches apart, on centers, and put in horizontal cross pieces about half way up to keep the studs from twisting or warping. The strips of cedar can be nailed directly over the open framework, eliminating the need for gypsum board or other paneling. If the outside walls will be exposed, then the studs can be hidden by nailing up sheets of wallboard, plywood or hardboard and then painting them to blend with the surrounding room walls.

Red cedar for lining closets comes in strip form. The boards are 3/8 inch thick, 2 to 4 inches wide and 2 to 8 feet long. For interlocking construction, strips are tongue-and-grooved along edges and ends.

Before applying cedar lining, remove all shelving and other trim from the inside of the closet. Locate the studs with a stud finder, or by driving experimental nails along the bottoms (don't worry about the holes; they will be covered by the cedar). Plan your nailing so that you tie into studs whenever possible. Joints need not occur over studs, as the tongue and groove binds the pieces together.

Install the strips by working from the bottom up, starting in one corner. The location of all studs should be marked beforehand, and the first strip should have the grooved end butted into the corner. Use four-penny finishing nails driven through the face of each strip wherever it crosses a stud, and space these nails approximately 3/4 inch down from the top edge. Then drive a second nail into each stud about 3/4 inch up from the bottom edge. Where pieces meet end-to-end, force them tightly together so that the tongue-and-groove joints interlock tightly. Corner pieces should be scribed to fit, unless quarter-round or cove molding will be nailed up later to hide the joints.

After the first row along the floor is complete, install the other rows by tapping each piece down tightly against the one below it. Only one nail in each board, about 3/4 inch from the top, is needed at 16-inch intervals. The bottoms will not have to be nailed as long as they interlock with a strip below. Line the floor the same way, starting in one of the back corners and working your way across the back to front.

After lining the closet, apply rubber or vinyl weatherstripping around the door to make the closet as air-tight as possible. Nail up shelves, hanger poles and other hardware last.

Before placing clothing or other woolens in the closet, be sure they have been dry cleaned and thoroughly aired. Wipe cedar occasionally with a dry cloth to remove dust which may clog pores. Never use varnish, shellac or other finishes, thus sealing up pores and the aroma. If the aroma fades slightly with the years, rub the surface lightly with fine sandpaper or steel wool to open the pores and renew the fragrance. *SEE ALSO STORAGE & STORAGE AREAS.*

Ceiling Beams, Polyurethane

[SEE DECORATING.]

Ceiling Construction

[SEE WALL & CEILING CONSTRUCTION.]

Ceiling Joists

Ceiling joists are the principal framing members of a ceiling frame, the structure directly below

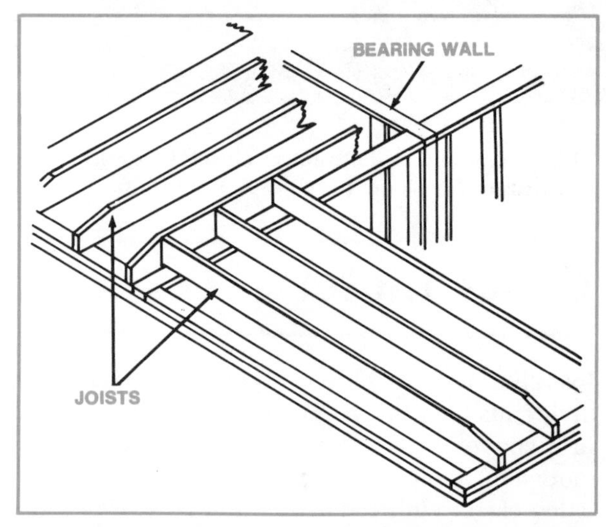

Joists placed at right angles reduces their overall span.

the roof that bears the surface of the ceiling. The joists themselves rest on larger girders or bearing walls. Ceiling joist construction is similar to floor joist construction, and in a structure of two or more stories, the ceiling joists are also the floor joists of the above level. Ceiling joists are sized according to local building code requirements as well as the load they must support and the length of span. Joists placed at right angles reduce the overall length of their span. Ceiling joists are put in before rafter installation, and are toenailed to the top plate of the roof, the structure that supports the rafters. *SEE ALSO ROOF CONSTRUCTION.*

Ceiling Repairs

[SEE PLASTER & PLASTER PATCHING.]

Ceilings, Suspended

[SEE SUSPENDED CEILINGS.]

Ceiling Tile

Ceiling tiles can add a decorative touch to new construction, conceal old, unsightly ceilings, absorb noise and reflect light. They are available in different colors and textures made of fibers, cork, asbestos or wood and can be installed to form decorative patterns. Ceiling tiles are inexpensive and easy to install, making them ideal for the do-it-yourselfer. Many kinds are also fire resistant.

Ceiling tiles can be installed directly to the ceiling with adhesives or stapled to furring strips that run at right angles to the ceiling joists. If the ceiling is smooth and undamaged, the tile can be applied directly with a special adhesive (mastic). When the ceiling is uneven, cracked, peeling or covered with old wallpaper or water soluable paint, the tile may be attached to furring strips with staples or special fasteners along either a tongue and groove edge or side flanges.

Ceiling Trim

Soften the break between wall and ceiling with the use of ceiling trim. In both size and design, the array of available molding is sufficient to satisfy almost every need and taste. Crown, bed and cove moldings are popular for trimming the ceiling, but flat trim moldings or quarter-round moldings are also used in newer homes with dry-wall construction.

Cut the molding to size, mitering corners as needed. To apply ceiling trim, use finishing nails driven through the trim into studs. Finish by countersinking nail heads and filling with wood putty. *SEE ALSO MOLDING & TRIM.*

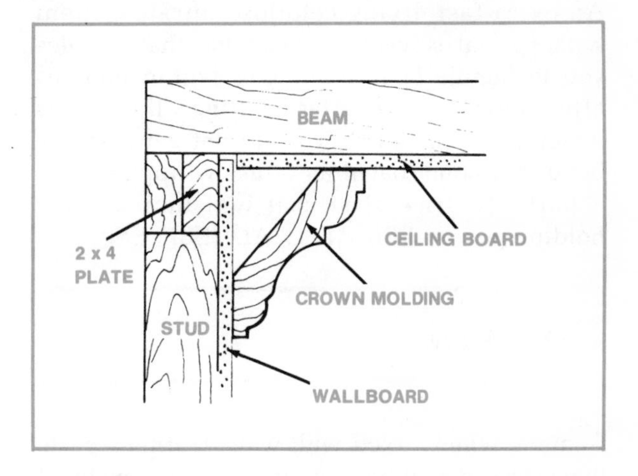

Cellar

[SEE FOOTINGS & FOUNDATIONS; REMODELING.]

Cellulose Nitrate Cement

Commonly known as household cement, cellulose nitrate cement is a good adhesive for repairing porous and semiporous materials. It can also be used for nonporous material provided there is a way for the solvent to escape. Trapped solvent will cause a weak joint.

Cellulose nitrate cement, which comes in clear form or amber-dyed, may be purchased in either tubes or cans. Used in clear form, repairs are practically invisible, while the use of amber-dyed cement will permit you to distinguish two-coat applications.

The acetone-type solvent evaporates quickly, bringing a joint to one-quarter strength in two hours. Full strength (about 3,500 pounds per square inch) is achieved in twenty-four hours. Due to the low solids content, evaporation causes shrinkage which draws the joints tightly together for a fine glue line. This shrinkage can cause distortion on large thin sections.

An extra-fast-drying cellulose nitrate cement with special solvents is available that enables you to handle light assemblies within minutes after gluing, but the fast setting allows less penetration; therefore, you do not get a strong bond. A second coat of the adhesive applied over a partially-dried first coat will increase the holding power. *SEE ALSO ADHESIVES.*

Cement

Cement, when mixed with water, forms a paste that acts as a binding agent in concrete, causing it to harden. Cement is made from a mixture of limestone, shale and clay. It should be protected from moisture to maintain its dry powder form. Any cement with lumps that are not easily crumbled between the fingers and thumb is not usable. Portland cement, the most commonly used, is manufactured in 94 lb. sacks, each sack equivalent to one cubic foot. *SEE ALSO CONCRETE.*

Cement-Base Paints

Cement-base paint is used on concrete or concrete block walls, basements and foundations. It is a long-lasting paint and helps prevent dampness.

Cement-base paint comes powdered, a mixture of Portland cement, lime, pigments and other ingredients, and has to be mixed with water. It can only be used on previously unpainted masonry surfaces or surfaces that have been painted with the same type of paint. Loose dirt, cement, grease, and oil should be removed from the painting surface before applying cement-base paint. The prepared surface should be dampened thoroughly before painting and kept damp by sprinkling while the paint is drying. *SEE ALSO PAINTS & PAINTING.*

Cement Mixer

[SEE CONCRETE MIXER.]

Cement Patching Materials

The standard formula for a cement patching material is 1 part portland cement, 2 parts sand and 3 parts pea gravel. This formula is for the larger cracks and depressions in concrete, but one rule of thumb in patching concrete is that no coarse ingredient (such as the pea gravel) should be bigger than one-half the minimum dimension of the crack. Therefore, many experts recommend for cracks up to 1-inch wide that a sand mix, consisting of 1 part portland cement and 3 parts sand, should be used.

All the ingredients should be what concrete material suppliers term *washed;* in other words *clean,* because any fine silt, clay or other soil material coating the sand, gravel or stone occupies space that should be taken up by cement, resulting in a loss of strength. Also, all of the elements should be thoroughly mixed, for an absolutely homogenous mixture. Even the conveniently and efficiently premixed cement products need a thorough remixing because they settle into layers during transportation.

Also available are the quick-drying patching compounds that are fortified with latex, vinyl or epoxy. These are more expensive than the materials already discussed, but they are worth the extra cost because they make a stronger patch. The latex patching materials are packaged with two parts: a powdered cement and a liquid latex binder. The two ingredients should be blended into a smooth, workable consistency, as package directions indicate; but these directions are general and may be varied to suit the job at hand. A thicker mixture may be used for molding a piece that must keep its shape, and a thinner mixture that will flow easily may be used for small chips and fine cracks.

The epoxy compound gives the strongest possible bond, and can be used either for patching or for setting brick, flagstone, tile or slate, and for bonding glass, steel or ceramic tile. The kit contains a bag of dry cement and two bottles, one containing an emulsion and the other a hardener. The liquids are mixed in the proportions specified on the package and are then stirred into the dry cement. The vinyl patchers come premixed in a dry compound to which only water is added. This material may also be used in setting brick, stone, tile and glass. It is not affected by winter freezing and thawing, and it resists chipping and cracking. Unlike the standard cement formula, which should be applied only as thin as 1/2 inch, these fortified patching materials may be spread in layers as thin as 1/16 inch, and "feathered out" on the edges to meet existing surfaces.

For ordinary concrete floor and wall repairs requiring a cement mixture, it is probably cheaper and easier to use one of the patching materials covered above, particularly on larger repair jobs. But certain jobs call for special cement patching materials. Some of the most useful include hydraulic cement, air-drying cement and expanding cement.

Hydraulic cement is a modification of an ordinary cement-based mix, except that it hardens in only a few minutes. For this reason, it is the right patcher to use when a foundation or floor is actively leaking. Because this compound sets so rapidly, no more than can be used in three minutes should be mixed at one time. It is not recommended for cracks less than 3/4-inch wide, and, like putty, it must be pressed into place with a minimum of troweling or rubbing.

Air-drying cement defies the law that says a patch must be kept wet. Because it is not truly a cement product, air-drying cement will not set under water. It handles like a sandmix and hardens in a few hours. It forms a tight plug in cracks and holes, but should not be used where there is an active leak.

Cement Products

[SEE CONCRETE.]

Cement Tile

Cement tile or concrete tile pipe is used on the outdoor portion of a septic tank in a drainage system. Although very durable, cement tile is the least expensive of the tile pipe group. Before selecting cement tile or any other tile, check the local code to be sure it is approved for the drainage system being installed.

By leaving a space of 1/8 inch to 1/2 inch between the cement tiles, the liquid material which flows through the tiles will be able to seep into the ground. It is essential to place small pieces of tar or roofing paper over each joint so that earth will not sift into the spaces between the tiles.

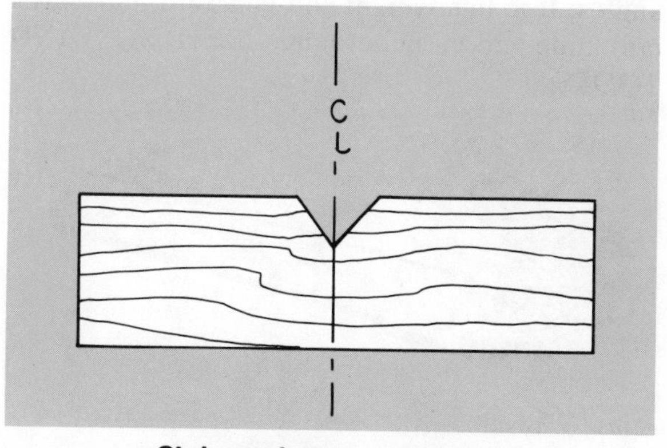

CL is symbol for center line.

Center Line

A center line marks the center of an object. In drafting, it is usually shown as a series of dots and dashes.

Center Punch

A center punch is used to make a starting indentation or hole in a metal surface, prior to drilling, so that the drill point won't slide on the surface. A center punch can also be used for making alignment marks on metal parts before disassembling them. *SEE ALSO HAND TOOLS.*

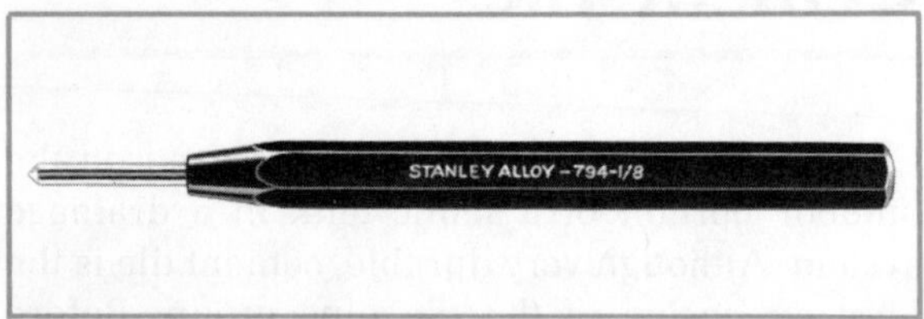

Courtesy of The Stanley Works

Center Punch

Center Square

The center square is used primarily for locating the center of round objects as large as tables and as small as a dowel. The center square is also useful for drawing straight lines and marking angles. It is lightweight and generally measures only nine and 1/4-inches long. *SEE ALSO HAND TOOLS.*

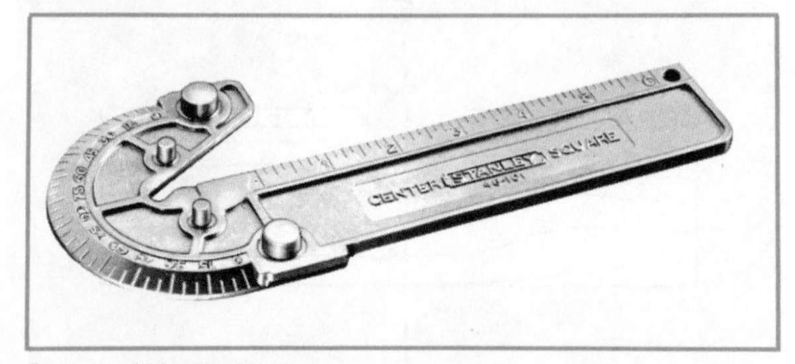

Courtesy of The Stanley Works.

Center Square

Central Air Conditioning

[SEE HOME AIR CONDITIONING.]

Central Electric Heating

[SEE HEATING SYSTEMS.]

Ceramic Adhesives

A ceramic adhesive is a heavy paste adhesive which is used to secure ceramic tile to a surface. This mastic is spread with a notched trowel over a small area so that the adhesive does not dry before the tile is in place. Although the thick glue must be waterproof, it can be removed with a damp rag before the tile has set. Petroleum solvent may be used to remove the adhesive after it has hardened. *SEE ALSO ADHESIVES.*

Ceramic Tile

Ceramic tile is most often used for walls and floors in bathrooms, laundry rooms and kitchens. It comes in many sizes, shapes and shades of glazed and unglazed varieties. The glazed variety, which resembles polished chinaware, is considered wall tile; the unglazed tile, with its flat luster, is usually considered floor tile. Because ceramic tile is very hard, it is rarely damaged and will probably last the life of the house. Modern methods make replacement easy if a tile should get scratched or chipped.

Cesspools

Cesspools, which are an outdated, unhealthy version of septic tanks, are being outlawed in more and more areas because they are extremely unsanitary. The raw sewage collects in the cesspool and percolates into the ground, without being broken down or treated. For this reason, cesspools are especially dangerous if they are located near a water supply because they will ultimately pollute the water, making it unfit for use. Also, the sewage may rise to the ground level, decompose and cause foul odors. *SEE ALSO SEWAGE & DISPOSAL.*

Chain Saw

A chain saw is basically a motor, either gasoline or electric, and a saw chain with guide bar. Gasoline-powered saws use two-stroke cycle engines in which a little oil is mixed with the gasoline. An automatic clutch lets the engine idle without moving the chair. Throttling is done by a trigger. Razor-sharp cutter teeth slice through the toughest wood. A chain saw eliminates hand-sawing and chopping, allowing the homeowner to direct the cut where he wants it. A chain saw can be used for backyard pruning, felling trees, cutting firewood and even rough carpentry.

Most chain saws today are the direct-drive type which are lighter and easier to use than gear-drive ones and have fewer moving parts to wear out. A sprocket on the engine moves the chain. Gear-drive saws are used almost exclusively by professionals for big work.

Selection

The kind of chain saw you buy should center on the amount and type of use it will get, where it will be used, and, of course, the size budget. Chain saws range in price from $35 to more than $200, less expensive ones being electric. A professional gasoline-powered model offering more controls, power and features sells for more than $400.

Size

For easy use at home, an electric chain saw is an excellent choice. It is quiet, and can even be used indoors. There is no danger of a hot muffler with an electric saw. However, your range is limited to an extension cord and 120-volt electrical outlets.

With a gasoline-powered saw there are limitations as to where it will be used. You will have to mix the fuel with oil according to the manufacturer's specifications and periodically clean the air filter, however. You will also have to start the engine each time you use it.

The size chain saw to buy depends on the size logs you will be cutting. Chain saw size goes by length of the guide bar. These range from 10 to 24 inches and more. A chain saw will cut through a tree up to twice its guide bar length in diameter. A 12-inch guide bar can handle a 24-inch diameter tree, but no larger. If you will just be trimming limbs or felling small trees, then a 10- to 14-inch superlightweight chain saw, either gas or electric, is your best choice. These weigh as little as 8 pounds (gas-powered), which is definitely an advantage for pruning above your head. These amazingly light saws usually have 1/4-inch pitch narrow kerf chains that make them cut rapidly and smoothly. With narrow chains, the tiny 30cc displacement gasoline engines cut almost as fast as the big chain saws. These are excellent saws for all light cutting. Prices are about $100 and up depending on features.

For trees more than 2 feet in diameter, you will need a chain saw with a longer guide bar and more power than the superlightweights offer. These, called lightweight saws, weigh about 12 pounds and generally feature 16-inch guide bars. The larger 50cc to 70cc engines have more power for heavier cutting (No electrics come this large.).

For really heavy work on larger logs, a standard-size model with 24-inch guide bar is necessary. The newer models range from 15 to 25 pounds and engine sizes are from 70cc to 125cc.

Features

Most large chain saws have many desirable professional features such as: An all-position carburetor lets you work with the saw in any position, even upside down. In these, a weighted fuel-pickup hose in the gas tank falls to the bottom no matter what position the saw is held in. To determine if a saw has this special carburetor, shake the saw. If it rattles, it has the "fuel-finder" hose and an all-position carburetor.

All chain saws provide some means of oiling the chain while you cut. A worthwhile feature is an automatic chain-oiler which eliminates the job of pushing an oil plunger every five seconds while cutting. A small amount of oil is metered steadily onto the chain as it runs, to ensure long chain and guide bar life. The best chain-oiling feature offers a combination of automatic and push-button oiling. With it, you can manually supplement chain-oiling during hard cutting.

All-important carburetor air cleaners have been made easy to clean on some saws. On many, all you need do is unscrew a cap, pull out the filter element, clean and replace it. During heavy work when the filter needs frequent cleaning, you will appreciate this feature. Good air filters prevent sawdust-fouling of the spark plug.

To reduce operator fatigue, some manufacturers mount the saw handles in rubber and provide rubber-padded grips which cut down on vibrations reaching your hands. If you use your gasoline-powered saw at home and don't have a silencer muffler on it, your neighbors will suffer. Both you and your neighbors will be happier if you choose a model with a silencing muffler or order one as an accessory.

Chain tension adjustment is important to long chain and guide bar life. A few chain saws have semiautomatic chain tension adjusters. After loosening the guide bar clamping nuts, the guide bar is held downward and a spring brings the chain to the right tension. Tighten the nuts and it is ready to cut again.

Other chain saws come with self-sharpening chains. A knob on the side of the saw is pulled out and turned until a hone just touches the moving cutters. The chain is sharpened while the saw runs, and the 20-minute manual chain-filing chore is eliminated.

A friction-free roller-nose guide bar tip extends guide bar life and frees additional power for cutting. The roller nose has lubricant fittings that need daily greasing with a special low-cost grease gun which can probably be supplied by your dealer.

Surprisingly, most saws don't come equipped with a bucking spike. This spike, mounted at the base of the guide bar, lets you lever the guide bar through the wood faster and easier. Bucking spikes are available as accessories to fit most chain saws. Other accessories which your saw should have are a tool kit containing spark plug wrench, combination screwdriver/guide bar wrench and a chain file and guide.

Additional chain saw features to look for are: external carburetor adjustment screws that facilitate turning; a recessed spark plug and an adjustable throttle latch for easier starting.

Spark-Arrester Mufflers

Using your chain saw in a dry-timber area poses a real fire hazard. If you use it in a forested area, it should be equipped with a U. S. Forest Service-approved spark arrester. This device is required if the saw will be used in or near any National Forest and a new federal law states that a saw dealer must show you the law if he delivers a saw to you without this vital safety feature. If you choose not to have a spark arrester on your

Every gasoline-powered chain saw should have an approved spark arrester screen. Minimum screen opening should be 0.23" (0.58mm).

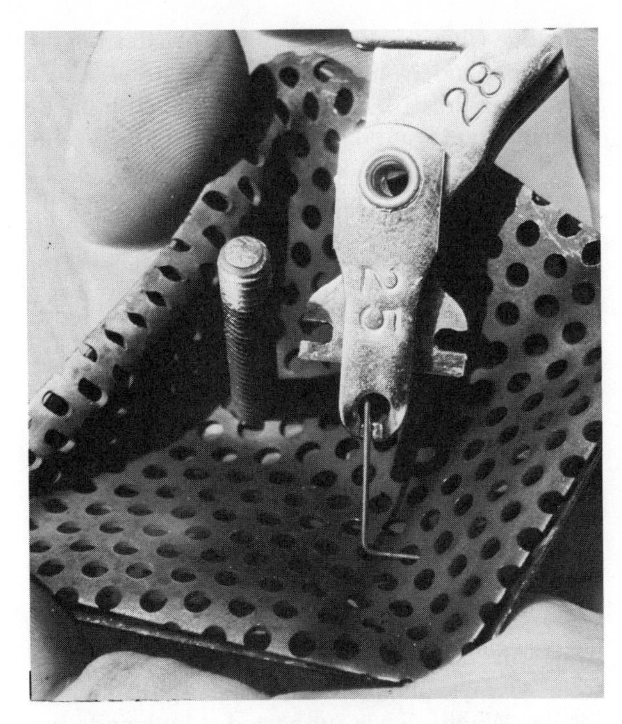

This is not an approved spark arrester screen because the openings are too large. A fire-starting spark could easily pass through them.

saw, you must sign a statement that you have read the law.

A USFS-approved spark arrester contains a metal screen with openings no larger than 0.023 inch. The screen fits inside the saw's muffler. To make sure that you get one on your saw, ask the dealer. Better yet, take the muffler apart and see. Some chain saws still don't come with approved spark arresters and a few aren't even available with them.

USING THE SAW

First, thoroughly read the owner's manual. It contains the safety, operational, and maintenance instructions for your saw. The manual will tell you how to assemble the guide bar and chain (often they come unassembled), mix the fuel and adjust chain tension. It also gives useful wood-cutting tips.

If you have chosen an electric saw, you will need an extension cord as most come with only a 2-foot lead. For sizes and amp ratings see Chart A.

An electric chain saw draws 6.2 amperes for each horsepower it has.

Chain Saw Safety

Chain saw operation is probably more dangerous than most work you do. Always have a helper with you as accidents can happen unexpectedly, especially in felling trees. Recommended safety equipment includes hard hat, nonslip gloves, boots for a good footing, safety goggles and some sort of hearing protection for big, unmufflered saws. When cutting in a dry area, you should also have a shovel for putting out a fire.

Properly dressed and equipped for chain-sawing, this worker is wearing nonslip boots, cuffless pants, gloves, goggles, and a hard hat.

Keep everyone a safe distance away whenever you are operating the saw. When felling a tree, they should be completely clear of anywhere the tree could fall.

When starting the saw's engine, make sure you have moved at least 10 feet from where you filled its fuel tank. Never fuel a running saw.

Proper chain saw starting technique ensures control of the saw while starting it. Brace the rear handlegrip against one knee and hold the handlebar tightly while you pull sharply on the starting cord.

After filling it, place the saw solidly on the ground, kneeling behind it. Steady the saw with the side of your knee against the rear handle and hold the saw to the ground firmly with one hand on the front of the throttle grip. Pull the starter cord sharply. Once the saw is running, keep both hands on it.

When moving with the saw, switch it off. A warm chain saw engine is easy to restart. Carry the saw with its guide bar to the rear to keep from getting snagged by the sharp cutters. As you cut, control the saw with both hands, but do not fight it. Let the weight of the saw carry the chain through the log. When cutting a log on the ground, always stop before the chain touches the ground. Roll the log over if possible and finish cutting. Nothing dulls a chain faster than running it in the dirt.

Tree-Felling

Before felling a tree, consider wind, natural lean, balance, the wood's soundness and all their influences on direction of fall. If anything valuable, such as a house, could possibly be damaged by an unplanned tree fall, stop and call a professional. It isn't worth the risk. Plan your path of retreat before you start cutting. Check the tree for dead branches or loose bark that could fall on you while cutting, and eliminate these, if possible. Clear away all the underbrush from the tree base and from your path of retreat. Cut a notch one-third the diameter of the tree in the direction you want it to fall. On the opposite side of the trunk make a back-cut parallel to the notch, but 2 inches higher up. Cut in about halfway, leaving a hinge of uncut wood to direct the fall. When the tree begins to move, switch off the saw and retreat opposite to the direction of fall at a 45-degree angle.

When making the back-cut, if the tree looks as though it might not fall in the desired direction, pound a plastic or wooden wedge in the back-cut to try to tilt the tree in the desired direction. Never use steel wedges. They can ruin chain saws.

Bucking the Tree

The term *"bucking"* refers to slicing up the felled tree. Always buck-cut from the uphill side of the log. When a log is supported at both ends, cut first from the top side down about one-third the diameter. Finish the cut from the bottom up. This avoids getting the guide bar pinched in the log.

To limb a fallen tree, start to cut on the narrower, angled side of the branch. Rev the engine up slightly before the chain touches the wood, then bring it in and cut the limb off clean. Be careful of the lower limbs toward the bottom of the log. They are under tension and can spring at you when cut.

Sharpening

The first time you run a saw chain in the dirt, or after many hours of sawing, the chain's cutters become dull. Don't run a saw with dull cutters. It over-stresses the saw *and* you. To sharpen, use the recommended size of round chain file (1/8 inch for most superlights). Use it in a file guide that shows the correct filing angle for the chain you have. Follow the chain-sharpening instructions that come with your saw. *Never* touch or sharpen a chain on a saw that is running.

Always unplug an electric chain saw before doing any work on it, sharpening included. Although most electrics are double-insulated, it

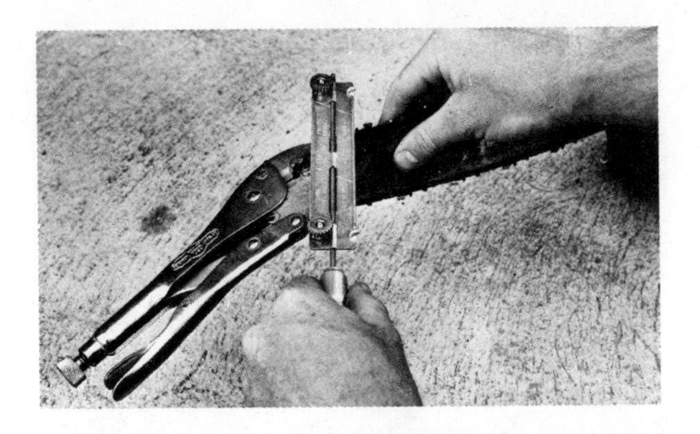

Sharpening of other saw chain teeth is done with a small round file mounted in a special guide. The guide shows the proper angle for filing left-hand and right-hand teeth. It helps to clamp the tooth being filed in a pair of locking pliers.

is best not to use them in wet locations or while barefooted.

The use of your chain saw can be fun. Once you have practiced wood-cutting techniques, you can try to tackle more complex projects such as rail-splitting, boring and carving.

Table A

EXTENSION CORD AMPERE CAPACITY (115-VOLT)				
CORD GAUGE* (AWG)	LENGTH 25′	50′	75′	100′
No. 18	7 amps	4.5 amps	3 amps	2 amps
No. 16	10 amps	7 amps	5 amps	3.5 amps
No. 14	15 amps	11 amps	7.5 amps	5.5 amps
No. 12	20 amps	18 amps	12 amps	9 amps

*2-conductor cord, Types ST, SJT

Chain Wrench

A chain wrench is used on fittings, tubing, and pipes either too large or inaccessible for a standard or Stillson pipe wrench to fit. It gives a vise-like grip on pipe without crushing or marring the pipe. One of the best advantages of a chain wrench is its capacity. A chain wrench with a 12″ handle and a 15″ chain can be used with pipe anywhere from 1/4″ to 4″ in diameter.

Chain wrenches vary according to manufacturer, but the procedure for using one is basically the same. Begin by setting the toothed, or business end of the wrench handle against the pipe. Then wrap and pull the chain tightly around the pipe and hook it onto the nib at the tip of the handle. The fit will not be snug until the handle is pulled and the toothed end rocks up on the pipe to tighten the chain so that the teeth take a non-slip hold on the pipe. *SEE ALSO HAND TOOLS.*

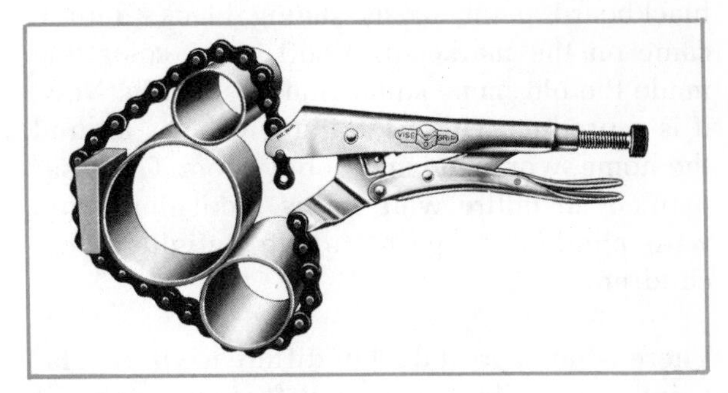

Courtesy of Peterson Tool Company

Chain Wrench

Chair Construction

[SEE FURNITURE MAKING.]

Chair Rail

Chair rails are moldings about 4 inches wide and 1/2-inch thick, attached to interior walls about 3 feet from the floor to protect the wall covering from damage caused by the backs of chairs. If chair rails are used solely for decorative purposes, they should be attached several inches lower than the chair back (about 2 1/2 feet from the floor). *SEE ALSO MOLDING & TRIM.*

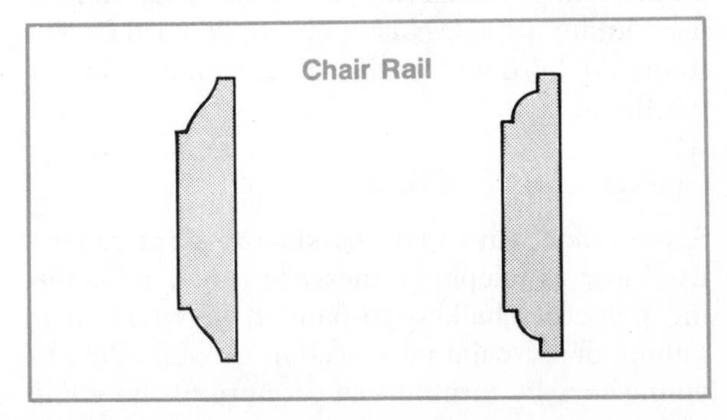

Chalet

[SEE VACATION HOMES.]

Chalkboard Paint

Chalkboard paint was more often known as blackboard paint, or as slating black, until it came on the market in a soft green color that made the old name somewhat unsuitable. Now, it is a product with a multitude of uses around the home, workshop and hobby room. One user painted an entire wall in his recreation room with chalkboard paint to the delight of his children.

There is not a great deal of difference in regular paint and chalkboard except from the point of view of the chemist developing the rather demanding formula. A chalkboard paint must be a highly durable (against abrasion), flat paint suitable for interior use and which offers enough roughness to take the chalk readily.

Chalkboard paint can be either brushed or sprayed on. A single coat will usually be sufficient on a sealed or previously painted surface, but to produce a good, long-wearing writing surface a second coat is advisable. The second, or a third, coat can be added at any time later, too.

On some exceptionally porous surfaces, such as some composition boards, it is advisable to use three coats. The first coat could be a primer designed for walls on interior trim, flat white or an enamel undercoat, rather than chalkboard paint. When primer is used, especially if it is used under a single coat of the chalkboard finish, it should be tinted to the approximate color of the finish coat.

CHALKBOARD IDEAS

Some other ways that chalkboard paint can be used are: as telephone message center by hanging piece of chalkboard-painted plywood near phone, or by painting a section of wall. Delight youngsters by turning one or more of the walls of their room into a giant chalkboard. Paint the inside of steel or wood cabinet door and make an ideal place for market lists and chore assignments. Make a front door chalkboard, and in your absence; callers or delivery men find your messages or leave their own. A workroom tool cabinet, chalkboard-painted, serves for designs and calculations, or an entire shop wall can become a design board. In photographic darkroom, a chalkboard takes film notes, holds equipment messages and notes of needed supplies.

Gifts can be made with chalkboard paint too. A scrap of plywood or hardboard becomes a slate. The addition of colored chalk makes a welcome surprise. A permanent scoreboard can be made by painting or taping white or colored lines across a chalkboard. A discarded picture, glass, frame and all, becomes a bulletin board, since chalk paints take nicely on glass.

HOW TO MAKE A FRAMED CHALKBOARD

A really big chalkboard like this is a great gift for a child, yet easy and inexpensive to make from a sheet of hardboard, a little lumber and some chalkboard paint.

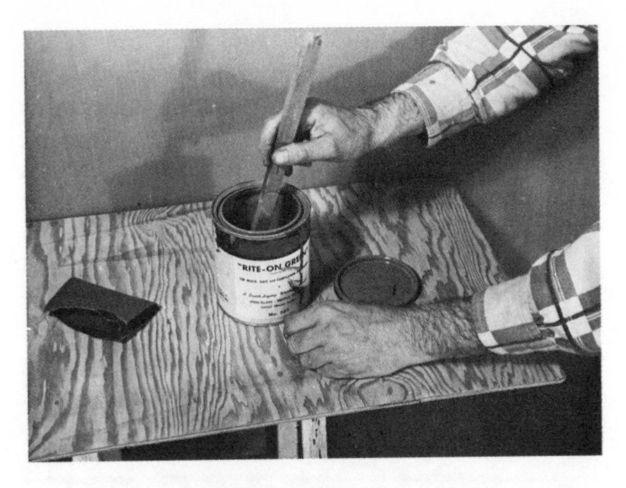

Thorough mixing is especially important since chalkboard paint contains fine grit to bite the chalk.

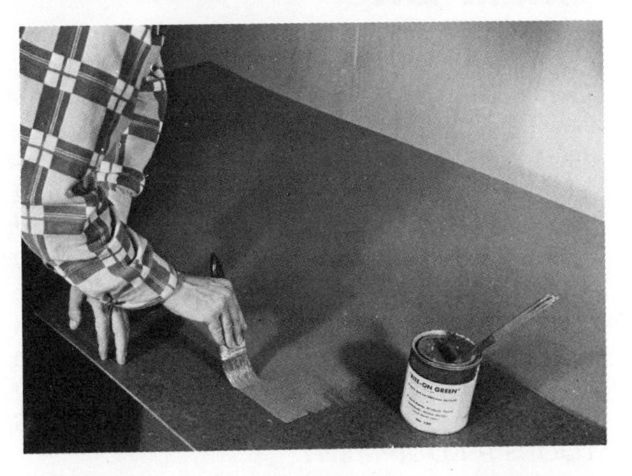

Brush or spray chalkboard paint onto smooth surface of hardboard, other composition board or plywood.

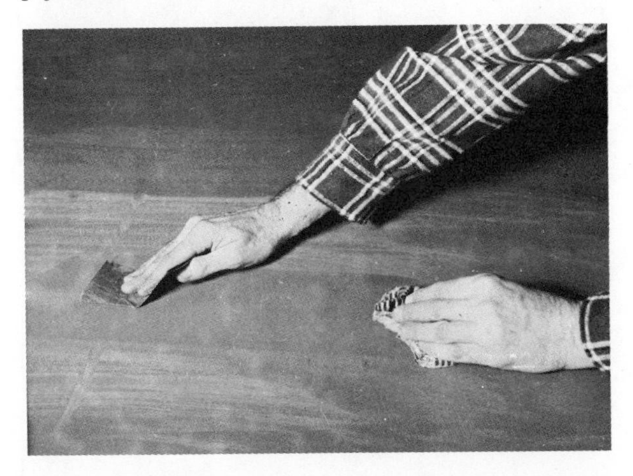

After overnight drying, sand and apply second coat. Let dry, then wet-sand final coat with water sandpaper.

Make a frame. For a big chalkboard use 1¼" x 2" stock, rabbeted the thickness of the hardboard panel.

By using a radial saw with blade set slightly askew, you can cut chalk groove along inner edge of bottom framing member before completing assembly, of course.

Prepare the board by rubbing with side of chalk and then wiping or erasing before its first use.

Hang a big board like this one with 6 screws or toggle bolts. Weather permitting, an outdoor location is good.

A picture frame can become an unusual gift.

Chalking

Chalking, as the term applies to painting, is the process by which a painted surface develops a powdery exterior. Good outdoor paint is designed to chalk so that rain will wash away surface dirt. Manufacturers try to incorporate this self-cleaning feature in paint formulas. Without a degree of chalking, years of paint buildup would eventually form a thick coat that would crack or scale. However, early or heavy chalking, which is often the result of moisture affecting the painted surface before it has dried or paint too thinly applied, may be a problem. Remove all chalk before repainting by scrubbing with water or brushing with a stiff brush. *SEE ALSO PAINTS & PAINTING.*

Chalk Line

The chalk line is used as a means of making a very long, straight line when no other measuring device can be used. Forming a chalk line is simple. Using two nails as anchors at either end of the area to be measured, draw a chalk-coated cord (reels are available that automatically apply chalk to the cord) taut around them. With the thumb and forefinger, pull the cord up, then let it snap back. The chalk will mark the surface. The chalk line is an easy measuring guide for laying tile or shingles. *SEE ALSO CARPENTER'S TOOLS & EQUIPMENT.*

Courtesy of The Stanley Works

Chalk Line Reel

Chamfer

A chamfer is a bevel cut which removes or flattens only the sharp edge of a piece of stock, rather than the whole side. A stop chamfer is one that does not continue the whole length of the edge. A chamfer is used for prevention of splintering and for decoration. It is made with a plane saw or power saw or by hand or machine sanding. *SEE ALSO BEVELS.*

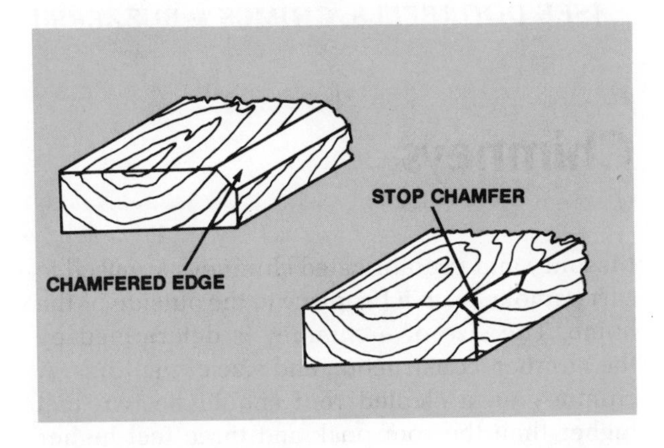

Chamfer Bit

A chamfer bit is used with a router to form decorative edges on stock or funiture. It is also used to make angle cuts to fashion concealed joints.

A chamfer bit can also be used with a hand drill to sharpen the ends of dowels which are intended as plugs or used for blind doweling. The sharpened edge prevents the lumber from splitting.

Channel

A channel is a concave groove cut into wood furniture for decorative purposes. Channels are more common on end tables, chests and cabinets, coffee tables and dressers. A router with special bits are generally used for making channels.

Chassis

[SEE SYSTEMS, AUTOMOTIVE.]

Checking

Checking, as the term applies to painting, is the appearance of a network of small, hairline cracks, either parallel to one another or in the shape of bird footprints. The cracks may also appear in the shape of many minute squares. Checking is usually a minor defect and can be ignored if it is slight. However, the cracks do occasionally extend down to the bare wood and flake off as the paint ages and weathers. This problem, common on plywood veneers, is caused by expansion and contraction as the paint and wood age. The fault can also be traced to insufficient drying time between coats and the use of an improper primer or finish coat.

To repair a checked surface, first determine if the paint is loosened enough to be removed entirely. If this is practical, use a scraper, sandpaper, paint remover or power sanding equipment, making certain that the area is sanded smoothly. If the checking is less severe, blend the base and sound areas together with fine sandpaper and fill deep cracks and joints, as needed, with a good-grade caulking compound. Spot prime or apply a coat of primer to the entire area which is thoroughly clean and dust-free. Allow the primer to dry according to manufacturers directions and proceed with the finish coat.

To prevent a painted surface from checking, start with a surface that is smooth and free of all contaminating substances, such as grease, dirt, dust, mud, etc. Make sure that the wood is completely dry before painting. Use the primer that is recommended for the finish chosen. Two full coats of primer are recommended for plywood and even with this, plywood is prone to check with age. *SEE ALSO PAINTS & PAINTING.*

Checkrails

Checkrails are meeting rails which are sufficiently thicker than a window to fill the opening between the top and bottom sash. They are usually beveled. *SEE ALSO MOLDING & TRIM.*

Check Valve

A check valve controls the direction of water flowing through a pipe. A hinged, metal flap on the inside of the valve permits water to run through a pipe in a specified direction, but will not allow any backflow. For example, if a sump pump is used in a basement, a check valve is placed on the outlet or exhaust line so that after the pump has been shut off, the water cannot back up into the pump. *SEE ALSO PLUMBING SYSTEMS.*

Cherry Wood

Black cherry, the only species of cherry used commercially, is a moderately hard, close-grained wood that machines easily and can be sanded to a very smooth finish. The beautifully grained heartwood ranges from light to dark reddish brown with the narrow sapwood almost white. Few woods age more gracefully than cherry; only its scarcity prevents it being used extensively in the manufacture of fine furniture and interior trim. *SEE ALSO WOOD IDENTIFICATION.*

Chestnut Wood

Chestnut is a soft, firm, durable wood that looks like, and has open pores similar to oak. Its heartwood is grayish brown and the thin sapwood is almost white. Resistant to warpage, chestnut is used for flooring, but because it shrinks or swells very little, it is used principally for veneer cores. Due to the chestnut blight at the turn of the 20th century, wormy chestnut is the only grade readily available. As with other open-pore woods, chestnut may be finished with a penetrating or surface finish. *SEE ALSO WOOD IDENTIFICATION.*

Chimes

[SEE DOORBELLS, CHIMES & BUZZERS.]

Chimneys

Masonry and prefabricated chimneys are used to carry smoke from a fireplace to the outside of the home. The size of a chimney is determined by the number, construction and size of the flues. A chimney on a slanted roof should be two feet higher than the roof peak and three feet higher than a flat roof. The taller the chimney, the better the draft and removal of smoke. A chimney near a tree with over-hanging branches or on a down-sweeping hill seldom has proper ventilation since winds in these areas form eddies in wind currents and can force smoke back down the

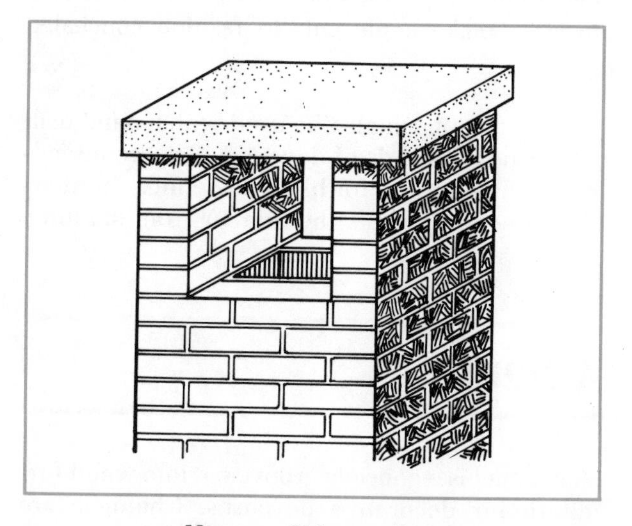

Masonry Chimney Cap

chimney and into the room. Masonry chimney caps can be installed so that smoke emerges only at the sides, to help this problem. They also prevent a vertical downdraft.

Masonry chimneys are usually free standing so they add no support to, nor receive any support from the house frame. Prefabricated chimneys are generally manufactured of metal, vermiculite concrete or a mixture of cement and asbestos. These chimneys are set on top of the house around the flue.

Metal chimney caps can also be set on top of a chimney to eliminate downdrafts. There are several styles from which to choose: wind-activated caps with a rotating, bladed turbine, weathervane types which turn in the wind and plain metal caps with a shaft that has three vents circling it.

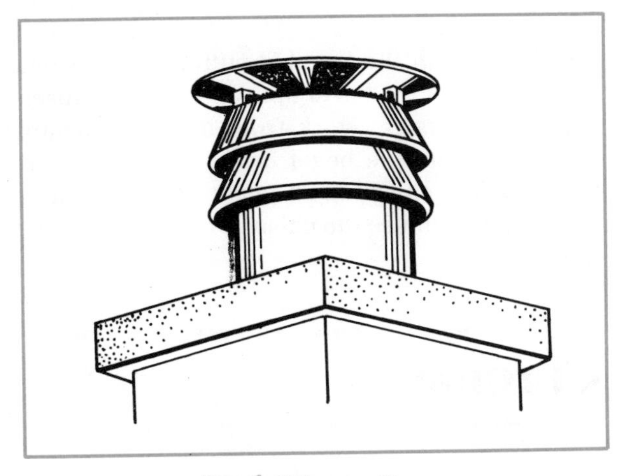

Metal Chimney Cap

CARE OF CHIMNEYS

Every few years a chimney will need cleaning to remove soot and creosote. This is a simple operation that practically any homeowner can do. Place a covering over the fireplace and seal it at all edges to prevent ashes and soot from entering the home. Partially fill a cement or burlap sack with straw or rags so that it fits easily into the flue, but is snug enough so that it touches its sides. Tie the top of the sack and attach a long rope to it. Standing on a ladder, slide the sack up and down the chimney to knock loose excess soot and creosote. When this is finished, remove the fireplace covering and clean out the ash pit with a brush or broom. Check the damper and oil it, if necessary.

Masonry chimneys should be inspected externally every year for chinking, and internally for loose flue units and clogs. Mortar can be applied around bricks or stones to patch loose joints. Flue units can be replaced easily, and clogs are removed by cleaning them with the same method mentioned previously. *SEE ALSO FIREPLACES.*

Chinking

Chinking is the process of filling chinks, or open spaces, with material such as chips or mud when the holes are too large to be filled with caulk. In log cabins, chinking is used when the logs are irregular and large gaps occur. Materials, such as wood pieces, metal lath, small poles or oakum, are driven into the hole until the gap is sealed. Chinking is recommended to fill holes between chimneys and walls, under eaves and at edges of floors. *SEE ALSO CAULKING.*

Chip Groove Bit

A chip groove bit is a machinist's variation of the conventional metal cutting bit used in lathe

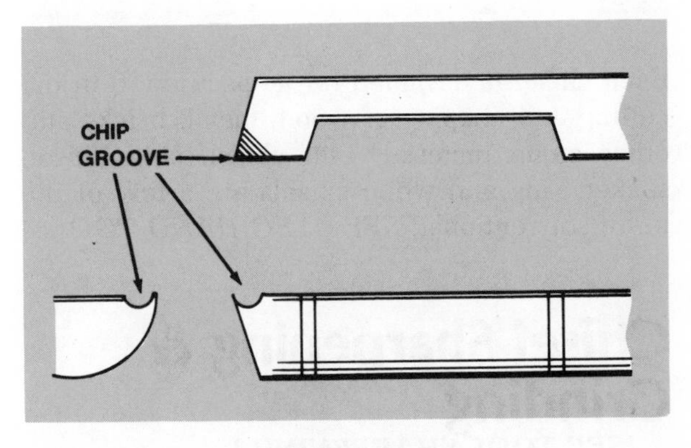

Chip Groove Bit

work. Experienced machinists will supplement the cutting edge of the bit by grinding a groove slightly behind it. This enables the waste chips to spiral upward and away from the work preventing binding of the bit. Chip groove bits are used primarily in working with steel, aluminum and certain plastics.

Chipping

Chipping is caused by a blow to a surface finish and results in a small portion of the finish flaking off. Usually the wood underneath the finish is not damaged. On painted surfaces, chipping leaves a sharp edge which must be smoothed with fine sandpaper before the damaged spot can be primed and painted. On clear finished surfaces, the chip may be repaired by a shellac or wax stick or filled in with plastic varnish. If patching will show, the entire surface should be stripped and refinished. *SEE ALSO PAINTS & PAINTING.*

Chisel Mallet

A chisel mallet is a type of hammer made of wood, plastic or rubber, used to strike the head of a chisel in order to drive the chisel. *SEE ALSO HAND TOOLS.*

Chisels

Each chisel is designed for a specific job in the cutting and shaping of wood, metal, bricks and other stone material. Butt chisel, cold chisel, socket, tang and wood chisels are a few of the more conventional. *SEE ALSO HAND TOOLS.*

Chisel Sharpening & Grinding

[SEE TOOL SHARPENING.]

Chisels, Tips On Using

Work only with sharp chisels; discard any chisel with a chipped, battered or mushroomed head. If only the handle is damaged, replace it with a new handle.

Use chisels only for removing material that cannot be removed with another tool. Take out the bulk of wood with a saw, drill or plane. Don't rush; take small cuts to minimize the risk of splitting the work.

When hand-powering a chisel, control the cut with one hand, using the other to supply the power. To avoid an injury in the event the chisel slips, always keep both hands behind the edge of the blade.

Rough cut with the beveled cutting edge down, finish cut with the bevel up. When you're chiseling along an edge, work from the edge toward the center with the bevel facing out toward the waste. When chiseling an enclosed area, it may be necessary to use the chisel with the bevel facing inward.

Chroma

Chroma is a term used in painting to describe quality of color combining hue (graduation) and saturation (intensity). *SEE ALSO PAINTS & PAINTING.*

Chuck

A chuck is a part of an electric drill that is geared with teethlike devices to hold bits and arbors turned by the drill. Other attachments that may be chucked are grinding wheels, wire wheels, and sander, buffer or polisher attachments.

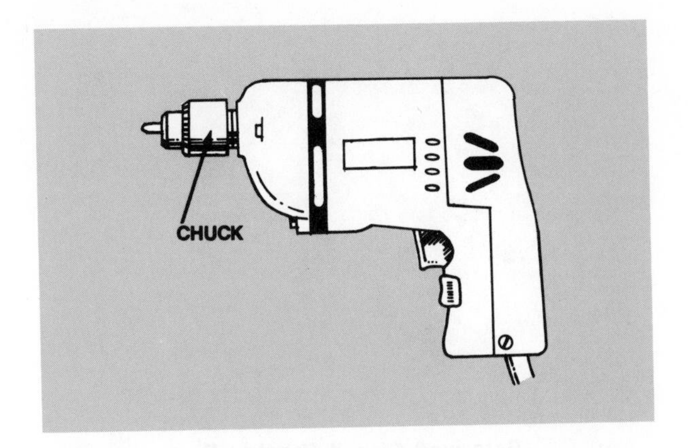

Chucks are also manufactured for use in hand drills, drill presses, braces, lathes and other power tools.

The type of chuck commonly used with hand drills, braces and some electric drills is tightened or loosened by revolving the outside shells with the hand, causing separation or contraction of the inner jaws surrounding the attachment. Some types of chucks require a key which rotates to lock or unlock the teeth, and an Allen wrench or setscrew is used with other models to release or tighten the geared part. *SEE ALSO HAND TOOLS; PORTABLE POWER TOOLS.*

Cinder Block

Cinder blocks differ from concrete blocks only in the mixture of materials; cinders are used instead of gravel or other aggregate. *SEE ALSO CONCRETE BLOCK.*

Circle Cutter

The circle cutter is used with a drill press or portable hand drill to cut holes in wood or nonferrous metals. The circle cutter, also referred to as a fly cutter or circle inscriber, works on the same principle as a pencil compass. The center pilot drill of the tool has a special side-cutting drill bit that rotates on the end of an adjustable

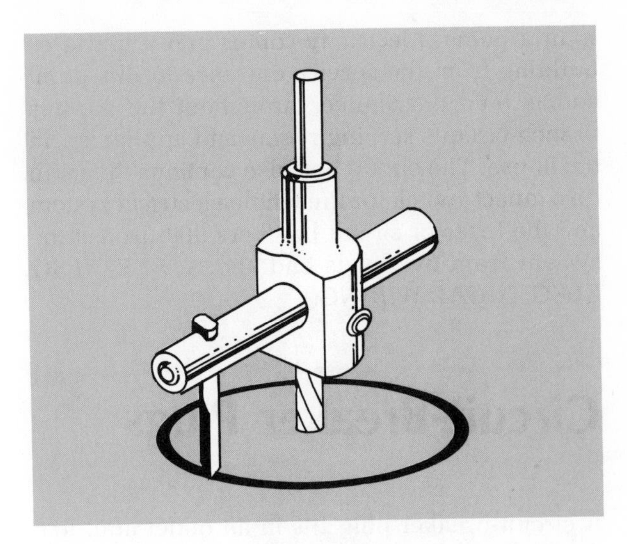

Circle Cutter

arm when the drill is activated. This single cutter can be started on any point of the circle's circumference, carving a hole that is anywhere from one half to 12 inches in diameter. At least 5/32 of an inch must be allowed for blade width when cutting. *SEE ALSO HAND TOOLS; PORTABLE POWER TOOLS.*

Circuit Box

The circuit box, also known as the electric service panel, is the distribution point of the electrici-

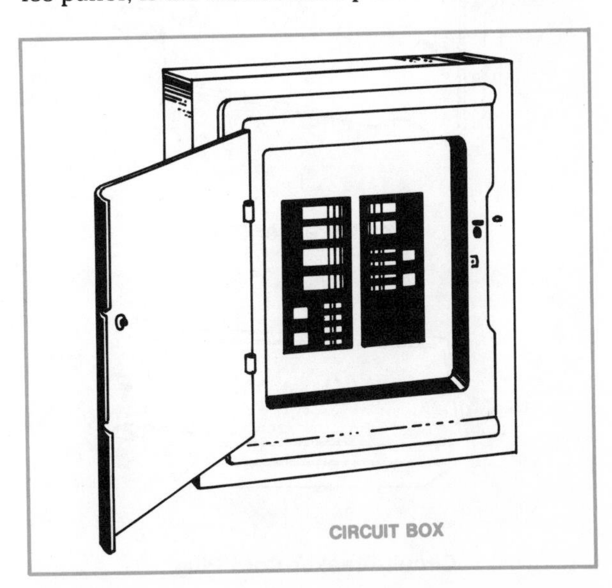

CIRCUIT BOX

ty in a home. Electricity comes into a house or building from the service entrance to this point and is then distributed throughout the various branch circuits serving rooms and appliances in the house. The circuit box also contains the main disconnect switch for the whole electrical system and the fuses or circuit breakers that protect the system from overloads and shorts. *SEE ALSO ELECTRICAL WIRING.*

Circuit-Breaker Plugs

A circuit-breaker plug fits in an outlet and, like an adapter, accepts plugs from tools or appliance cords. If an overload occurs, a button on the plug pops up and the tool or appliance is automatically disconnected.

A circuit-breaker cord plug can be used in place of an ordinary plug on an appliance cord. If an overload occurs, the plug automatically disconnects the attached tool or appliance. The plug is reset by a lever.

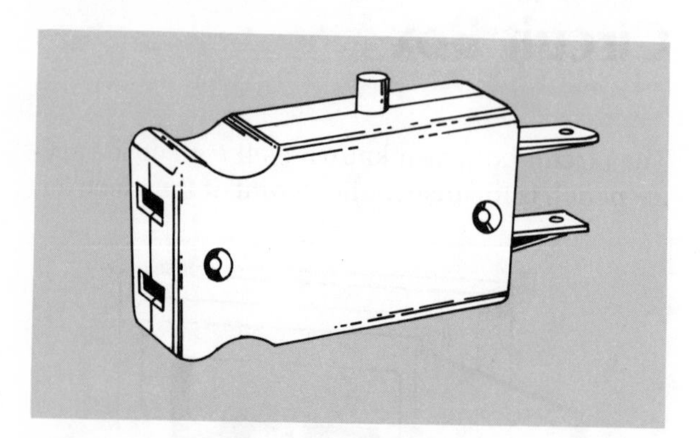

Circuit-Breaker Plug

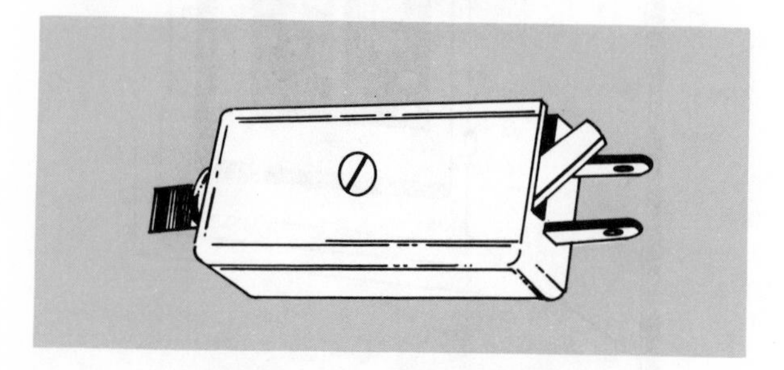

Circuit-Breaker Cord Plug

Polarized Circuit-Breaker Plug

A polarized circuit-breaker plug is a three-prong grounded plug that automatically stops its attached tool or appliance if an overload occurs. It can be reset by a button. *SEE ALSO PLUGS & CORDS.*

Circuit Breaker

A circuit breaker is a device which automatically shuts off when a circuit is overloaded. Although a circuit breaker has the same function as a fuse, the convenience of resetting the switch rather

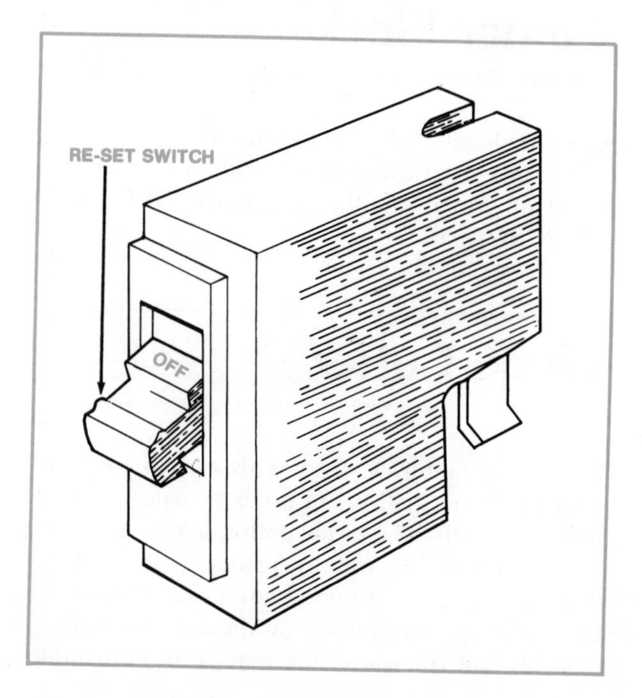

than replacing the fuse has made the circuit breaker panel more popular. *SEE ALSO FUSES & CIRCUIT BREAKERS.*

Circuits

The purpose of the circuit is to provide a means by which electricity can flow between two points. Electrical devices work when the circuit is *closed* or uninterrupted. A "break" in the circuit means that electrical flow stops at the point where the wire or other conductor is discontinued. This condition is also called an *open circuit.*

Usually two wires create a circuit. There are some instances, however, where a three-wire circuit is necessary for installing high voltage wiring. One wire circuits are made to demonstrate models dealing with basic electrical principles.

House wiring is done with two-wire circuits. A distribution panel or entrance panel will have circuit diagrams for the house in which it is being installed. The wires of the circuit are usually color coded black and white, or labeled. By following these circuits diagrams, the homeowner will have no trouble in wiring or repairing his house circuitry. *SEE ALSO ELECTRICAL WIRING.*

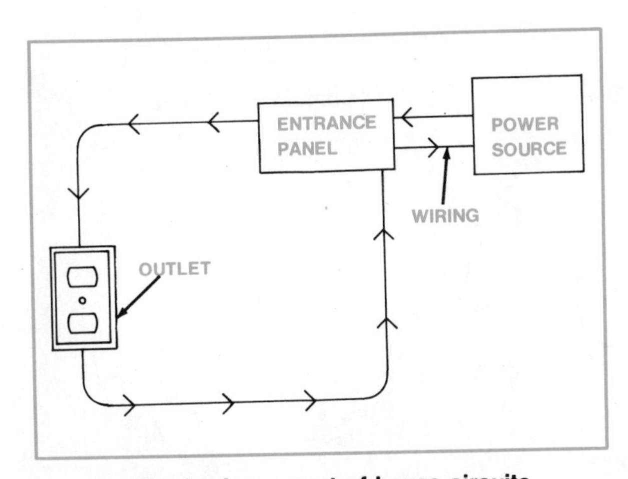

The basic concept of house circuits.

Circuit Tester

The circuit tester is used to check electrical current flowing through such conductors as wires, appliances, and electronic equipment. The simplest circuit tester is a small neon lamp with two wires leading from it. These wires are attached to the switch, outlet, or other conductor to see if a current is present. For example, after installing an outlet, the circuit tester should be attached to it. The outlet is "on" if the lamp glows. *SEE ALSO ELECTRICIAN'S TOOLS & EQUIPMENT.*

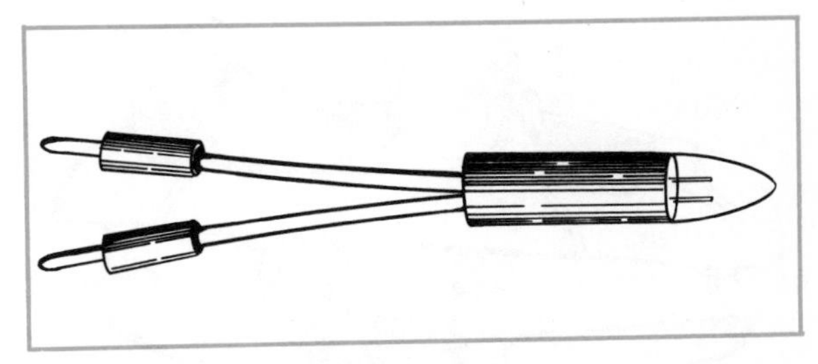

The circuit tester may be used to find a short circuit.

Circuit Tracing

Circuit tracing is useful in determining which outlets and switches in a circuit are operative when the current is flowing through its wires. It is also helpful in identifying which fuses control what outlets and in labeling them, which is a convenience when replacing blown fuses.

Circuit tracing is a simple procedure. With the main switch in the "on" position, plug a lamp or circuit tester into each of the outlets in the various rooms of the house. Unless the outlet is faulty, the lamp should light up. Then, one by one unscrew the fuses. By relating the fuse to its particular set of fixtures, the homeowner can label his fuse box accordingly. If he knows the relationship between his fuses and outlets, he can easily trace and examine the condition of the wires connecting them.

Circular Plane

The circular plane is characterized by a flexible steel bottom that can be bowed to a wide range of curvatures to fit a concave or convex surface to be planed. An adjusting screw varies the curvature, as required, and holds it as set. Once adjusted to the surface, this tool is capable of planing down to a minimum radius of 20″. *SEE ALSO HAND TOOLS.*

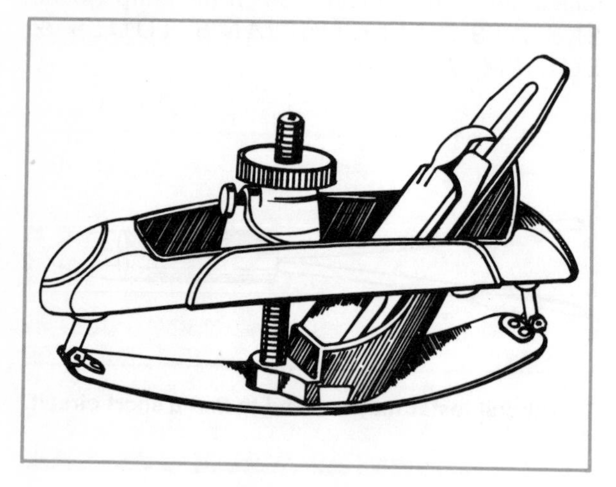

Circular Plane

Circular Saw

[SEE PORTABLE POWER TOOLS.]

Ripping Blade

Cut-Off Blade

Plywood Blade

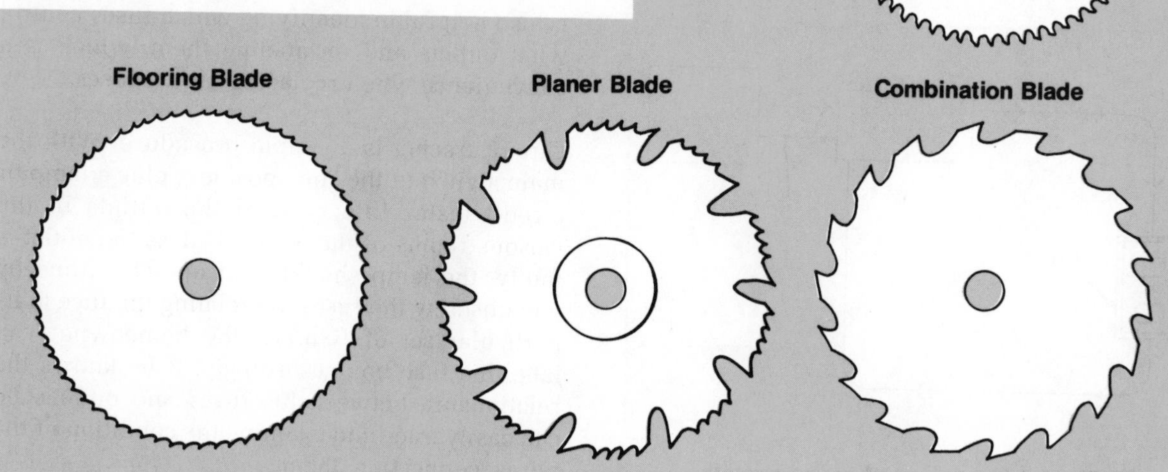

Circular Saw Blades

Circular saw blades are the same ones used in a table saw with the exception of one that is especially designed to cut concrete blocks, stone and brick. Nonferrous blades can cut any metal except iron or steel. Carbide-tipped blades cut hardboard, plywood, plastic, aluminum, brass and asbestos. The blades used in a circular saw are the combination blade, which is used for mitering, crosscutting and ripping. The planer blade makes the same cuts as a combination blade, but leaves a cleaner edge that doesn't require sanding. Flooring blades are designed of a special steel unaffected by cutting knots and nails in used lumber. A plywood blade leaves a smooth cut in any direction relative to surface overlay. Used in crosscut squaring and trimming, the cut-off blade holds a sharp edge through long periods of heavy work. The ripping blade is similar to a combination blade except that the back of its teeth is not beveled. *SEE ALSO HAND TOOLS; TABLE SAW.*

Circulating Fireplaces

[SEE FIREPLACES.]

Circumference

Calculate the circumference (perimeter) of a circle by multiplying the diameter by 3.14, or for greater accuracy, 3.1416.

Clamps & Clamping

Although the single most important use for clamps is in gluing, the other home and home-workshop uses are so many that they add up to at least equal importance. (Uses with adhesives are described under *GLUES AND GLUING.*)

In metalworking, clamps are essential for holding work in place while it is being milled, cut, drilled, polished, or welded. In some of these situations, clamps are functioning essentially as a third hand where two are not enough.

Third hand describes the value of clamps in many construction situations. Where a journeyman carpenter or construction worker would call for a helper, the home carpenter or craftsman would often find himself helpless to continue without the aid of a clamp. Clamps also operate to multiply human strength, as when they are used to pull two studs together for nailing or to force timbers apart to allow insertion of a brace. To appreciate the value of a clamps utility, suppose that a 16 foot heavy timber is to be held in place to be nailed to the ends of supporting rafters. How can you hold up both ends at once while you climb a ladder and nail it at one end? In the absence of an assistant with a second ladder, the solution might be to clamp a small scrap board to the underside of one rafter so that it extends a few inches beyond it. While the clamped scrap supports one end of the timber, lift and nail the other end. This done, adjust the scrap-supported end into perfect position, nail it permanently and then remove the clamp and the scrap.

Essentially a woodworking jig is a temporary device created to make a task easier, safer or more accurate or to permit quick repetition of identical cutting or shaping chores. In its simplest form, it might be just a block of wood nailed to a bench top as a stop to insure that the pieces you are cutting one after another will be precisely the same length. The same stop will be neater and stronger, and possibly quicker to arrange, if you use a clamp instead of a nail to hold it. Since you can clamp a jig or fixture to a metal saw table as easily as to a wooden bench, clamps make jig arrangements far more versatile.

Other uses for clamps are among the following:

To install wooden window stops or floor or ceiling trim, as when paneling a room, the quickest way to make the cuts is by using a miter box. Instead of returning to the workshop to make each cut, clamp the miter box to a saw horse and make the cuts right on the job.

When traveling, and especially when camping, carry along one or two pairs of small C or short bar clamps. A pair of them on two trees will support a stick used to convert a tarpaulin or ground sheet into a tent or eating shelter — or to hold up a kettle for campfire cooking.

USEFUL TYPES OF CLAMPS

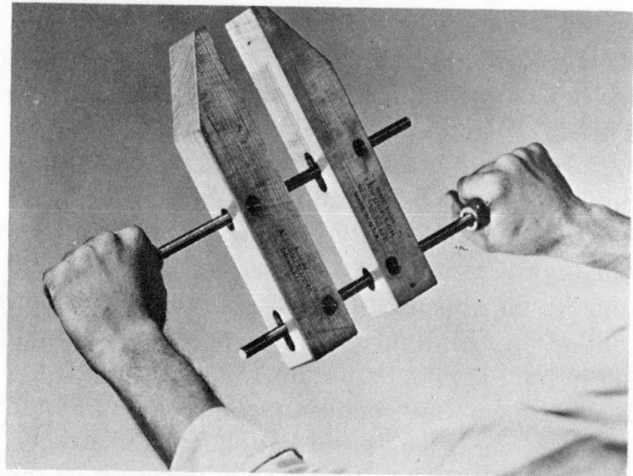

Courtesy of The Adjustable Clamp Company

Handscrews of hard maple are less likely than metal clamps to mar wood surfaces, have great reach, hold cylinders and other odd shapes well.

Courtesy of The Adjustable Clamp Company

Hold-down clamps are a relative newcomer but have proved almost indispensable in home and industrial shops. By use of a removable bolt they can be inserted at any point on a workbench top as well as within a slot in a steel table, as here.

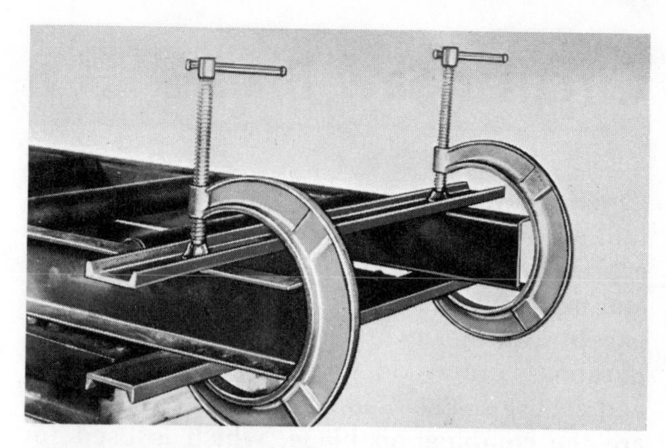

Courtesy of The Adjustable Clamp Company

"C" or carriage clamps are popular because they are highly adaptable and inexpensive. This fully curved shape gives greater throat depth than the more usual flat shape, seen in some of the illustrations.

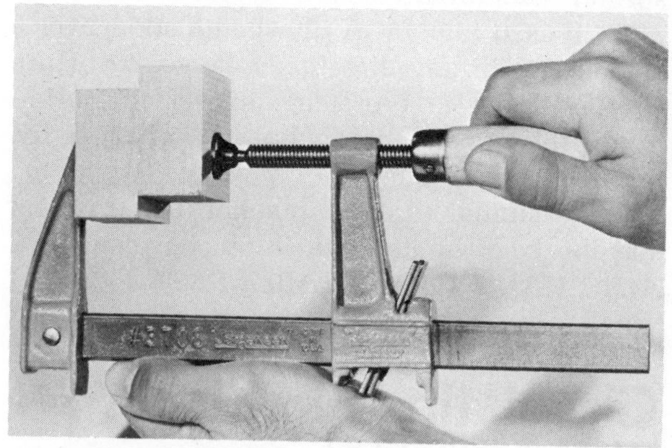

Courtesy of The Adjustable Clamp Company

Bar clamps are offered from 6 in. to 8 ft. in length. Short ones do the work of "C" clamps and do it faster. Long ones handle building chores, large furniture assembly.

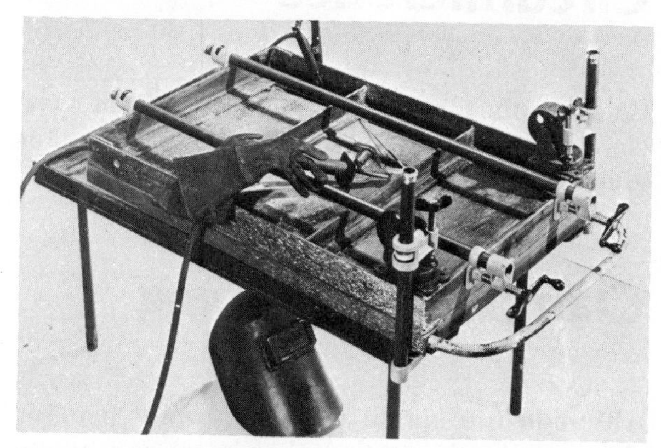

Courtesy of The Adjustable Clamp Company

Pipe clamps do the work of bar clamps, for economy may be purchased as "fixtures" (no pipe) and used with ordinary $^3/_4$-in. black pipe of any length.

Courtesy of The Stanley Works

Band clamps are straps that can be wrapped around objects of irregular shape—such as furniture frames, assemblies, tanks, columns. For round shapes only, a type with a steel band may be used instead of the canvas-band type shown here.

Courtesy of The Adjustable Clamp Company

Spring clamps are inexpensive and quick to use, suffice where only relatively light pressure is needed. They sometimes have plastic-protected tips and handles. They are used to hold materials for gluing, soldering, welding—and for miscellaneous chores as disparate as holding memos, drying photographic negatives, clipping a blanket to a trotting horse so he doesn't cool off too fast.

CLAMPS IN METAL WORKING

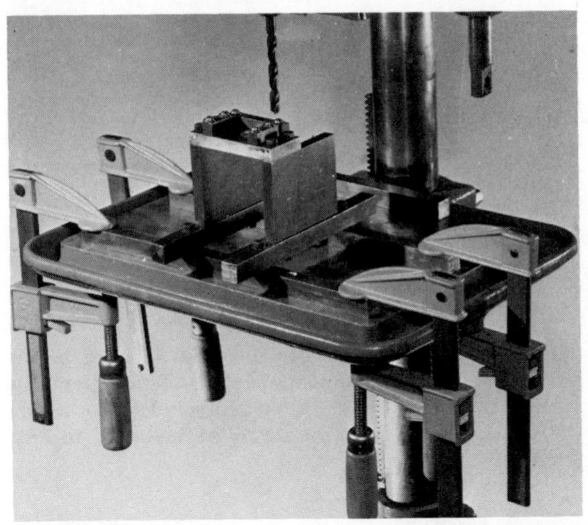

Courtesy of The Adjustable Clamp Company

Ordinary bar clamps—short sizes are the handiest—are an excellent complement to a drill press, where they serve as third hands and add greatly to the precision of the workmanship.

Courtesy of The Adjustable Clamp Company

The special heavy-duty type of hold-down clamp differs from ones shown previously in having a $^5/_8$ in. steel machine bolt for extra hold-down strength. Bolt head fits T-slot or hole in wood or steel bench or table.

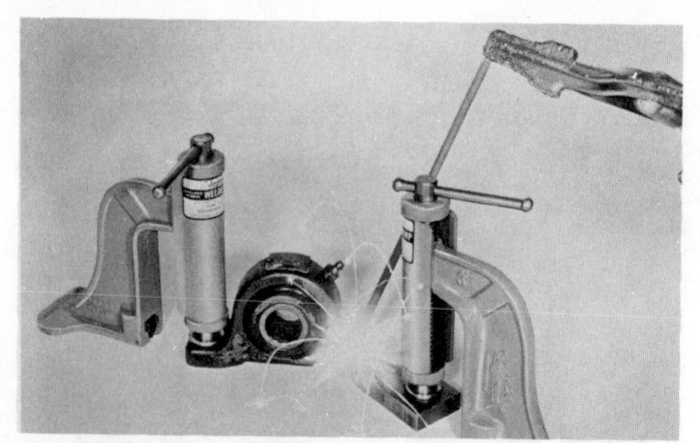

Courtesy of The Adjustable Clamp Company

The hold-down clamp shown earlier is here being used in a special version for metal shops, especially where welding is done. Shield protects against welding spatter, hold-down bolt may be installed in any surface.

Courtesy of The Adjustable Clamp Company

What will hold a piece of steel in your vise when it's far too long for the vise jaws and has to be fully exposed for working? Answer: a steel bar clamp, as auxiliary to the vise.

Courtesy of The Adjustable Clamp Company

Ingenious holding jigs are easily worked out with an assortment of "C" clamps, two styles of which are used here both to hold two strips of steel together and to fix them rigidly in place. Long type being applied here is called "carriage" clamp, round type is called "body".

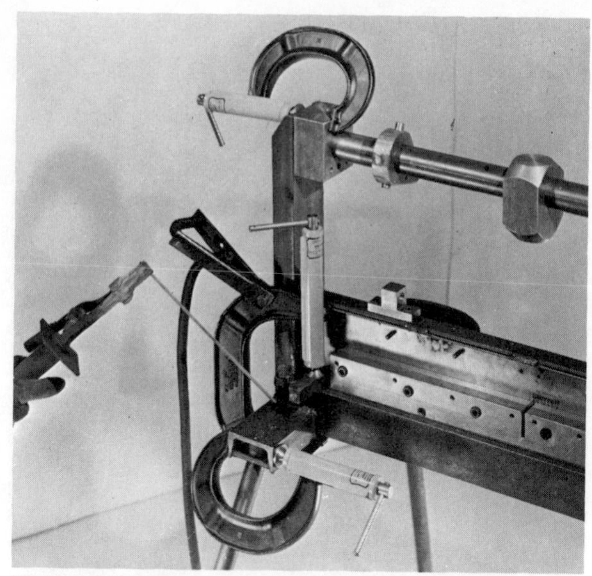

Courtesy of The Adjustable Clamp Company

Shields adapt ordinary "C" clamps (both of the most popular shapes are seen here) to welding, protecting the threads against spatter and other damage.

CLAMPS IN WOODWORKING

Courtesy of The Adjustable Clamp Company

A single "C" or short bar clamp becomes a woodworking jig for disc-sanding curves. Inner edge of work rides against pointed stick clamped in place, duplicating the shape of the outer edge of the work.

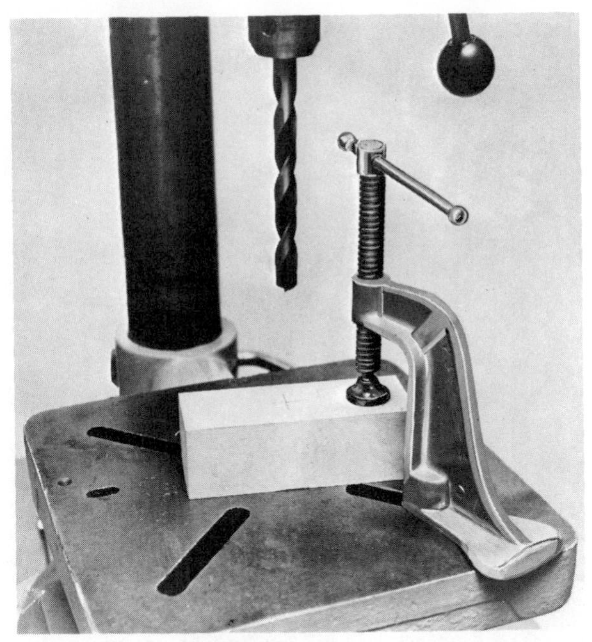

Courtesy of The Adjustable Clamp Company

Fitted to the slots in the drill-press table, hold-down clamp aids in precision drilling of wood parts. Same clamp may then be shifted to any position on workbench where a hole has been made for the hold-down bolt.

Courtesy of Black and Decker

Here again a wide board is substituted for normal fence and another scrap piece blocks the work to desired height. As saw is elevated by cranking right number of turns, holes can be drilled in a straight line at precisely equal intervals. Clamp has helped create a vertical boring machine.

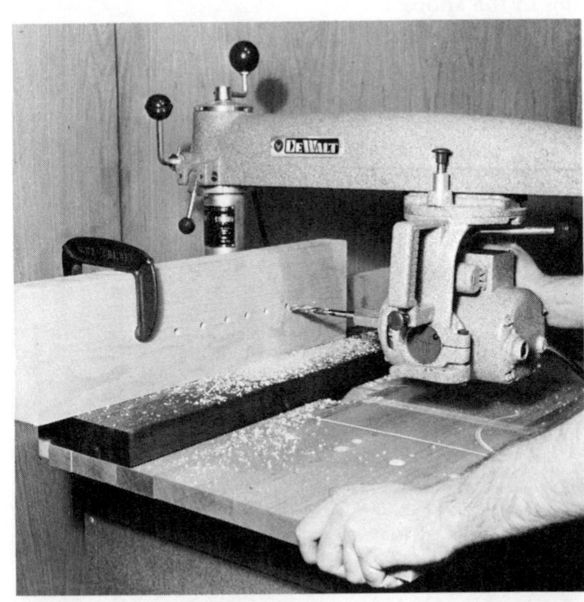

Courtesy of The Adjustable Clamp Company

For straight-line or parallel boring with radial-saw adaptation, install wider board in place of normal fence. Insert a board to bring work to desired height, sliding the work along it. Same board, if clamped tightly, serves also as depth gauge when hit by bell of motor.

Courtesy of Black and Decker

An instant jig made from clamps and lumber turns taper cutting, a difficult job when done freehand, into a cinch without need of constructing a complicated fixture. Set the blade to the edge of table. Cut the stock by clamping it to a straight board and letting the jig ride against the edge of the saw table. The same set-up is great for ripping irregular pieces of lumber or raw edges.

Courtesy of Shopsmith

Clamp method permits automatic cylinder turning on any lathe with tool rest. With sliding tool rest and eccentric mount by which cup center may be offset, it allows automatic taper cutting as well, for legs, lamps, and so on. This permits accurately duplicated legs for furniture. It is best to rough-out the work to approximate shape first, using the jig only for the finishing cut.

Courtesy of The Stanley Works

Here is a novel use for the band clamp shown earlier. A heavy-duty web clamp is useful for security tie-down of boating or camping equipment on car or trailer, as well as luggage. The maker, The Stanley Works, recommends this 600-lb. test nylon type for lifting and moving heavy equipment and refrigerators and trunks, as well as during gluing and welding in the shop.

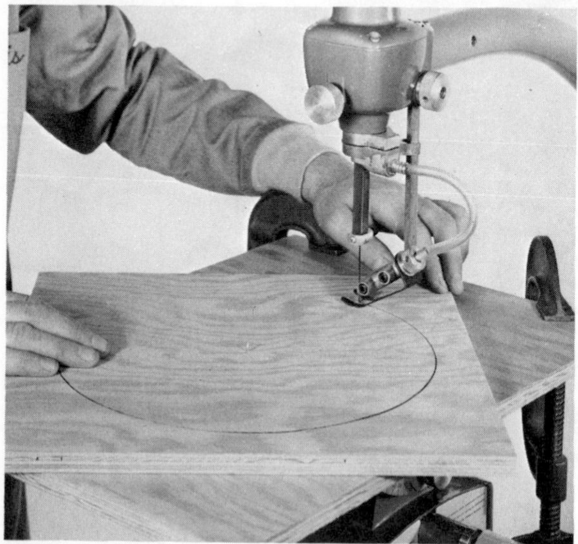

Courtesy of Shopsmith

Circle-cutting jig for jig saw is easily rigged by use of a pair of clamps. Drive a nail through an odd piece of plywood, turn it over and clamp it to the table, then use it as a pivot to get an accurate circle. By starting the circle along an edge of the stock, this method works equally well on a band saw.

Courtesy of The Adjustable Clamp Company

Holding a tray of parts or materials for tooling is a final auxiliary service a handscrew or other woodworking or metal working clamp can offer. A pair of clamps might equally well be arranged to perform the service shown here, in the absence of a vise.

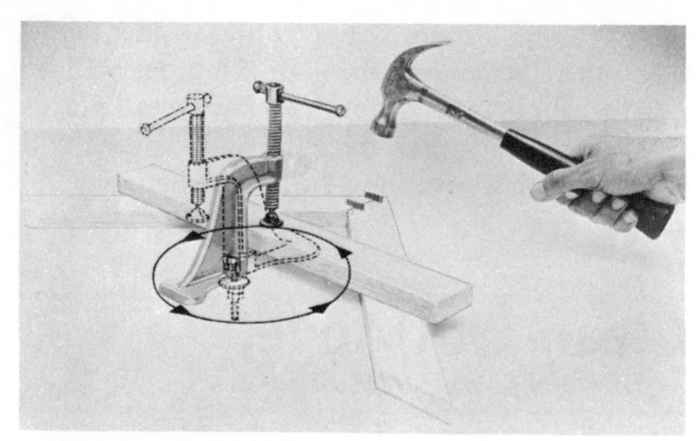

Courtesy of The Adjustable Clamp Company

One of the trickier operations in woodworking is holding a miter joint together, as in picture-framing while securing it with corrugated fasteners. Here a hold-down clamp solves the problem and can be instantly swiveled out of the way while the next joint is positioned.

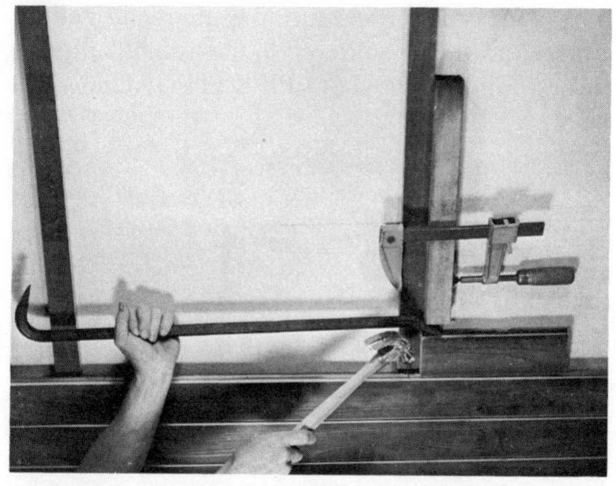

Courtesy of The Adjustable Clamp Company

When placing roof decking, subflooring or paneling (as here) with tongue-and-groove lumber, use this arrangement where it's not possible to pull up the pieces with a long clamp. A long, stout screwdriver is a good alternate pry bar, although tool makers will hate you for using it this way. Note how panel scrap with groove protects tongue of paneling.

Clamps & Vises

Clamps and vises are for holding materials tightly together in gluing, sawing or drilling. The most popular are the C-clamp, band clamp and corner clamp. *SEE ALSO HAND TOOLS.*

Clapboard

Clapboard, which is usually six to twelve inches wide and 1/2-inch thick, is used as an exterior siding on homes. Most modern clapboard siding is made of wood fiber products that look like wood but have no splinters, knots or internal grain to twist and warp. These boards are straight, flat and square, and some varieties are vinyl coated.

Clapboard is applied from the bottom to the top of a wall frame with aluminum sinker nails. The first board is nailed to the lower edge of the frame, and the next board is placed so that it laps one inch over the top of the first board. Repeat this process up the framing members driving the nails in either the top or bottom edge of the board. *SEE ALSO SIDING.*

Clapboard Siding

Claw Hammers

Claw hammers are available in two designs: curved claw and straight or ripping claw. The curved-claw hammer is the tool to use for nailing or nail pulling and for general carpentry work. Weights, based on the head weight, range from 7 ounces for light work to 13, 16 or 20 ounces for general carpentry. The straight-claw ripping hammer is designed for rough work and dismantling. The straight claws fit easily between boards for prying, as in opening crates. Weights range from 20 to 32 ounces.

When purchasing either type, be certain that the head is made from deep-forged steel rather than brittle cast iron. A cast iron hammer will lose a claw if you yank too hard on a nail; further, it is seldom balanced properly. A good hammer has a head that is beveled so the edges won't chip. The striking face has a slightly crowned surface to provide a square, true blow and to minimize marring when nails are driven flush. Handles made from tubular steel, solid steel or fiberglass will hold up better when subjected to excessive heat or humidity than one made from hickory. *SEE ALSO HAND TOOLS.*

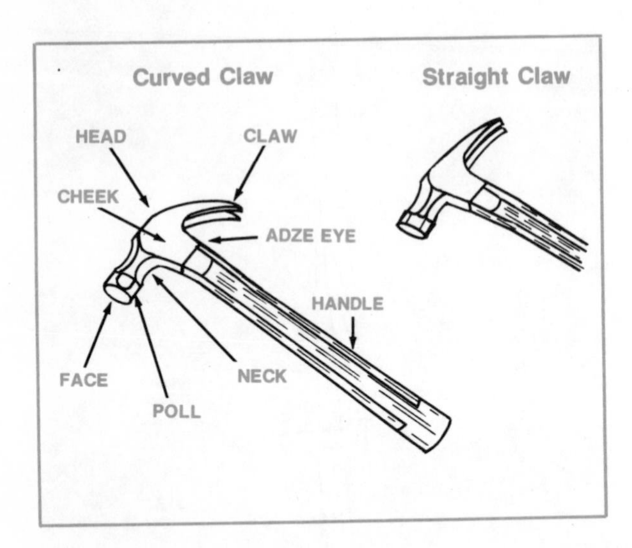

Clay Tile

Clay tile is the red or yellow kiln-hardened tile used for building the outdoor part of a drainage system. Available in one foot lengths with four inch diameters, clay tile is slightly more expensive than cement tile. Before purchasing, check the local code to see if clay tile is approved for the drainage system being constructed.

Allow a 1/4 inch space between tiles so that the liquid material flowing through the pipes will be able to seep into the ground. Placing small pieces of tar or roofing paper over the open spaces will prevent earth from filling the spaces between the tile.

Clean-Out Auger

[SEE SNAKE, PLUMBER'S.]

Clean-Out Ferrule

A clean-out ferrule is a cast-iron soil pipe fitting which allows easy access to the inside of the pipe. This type of pipe fitting is characterized by a threaded sleeve soldered to the hub of a pipe to form a joint. *SEE ALSO PIPE FITTINGS.*

Clean-Out Ferrule

Clean-Out Plug

The use of clean-out plugs at intervals along the drainage system permits easy access to the inside for removal of blockage. One is usually placed in each horizontal run of drainage line, and every right-angle turn should definitely include a clean-out plug. Use an adjustable wrench for removing and replacing the plug. A thin layer of grease over the threads of the plug will facilitate removal. *SEE ALSO PLUMBING SYSTEMS.*

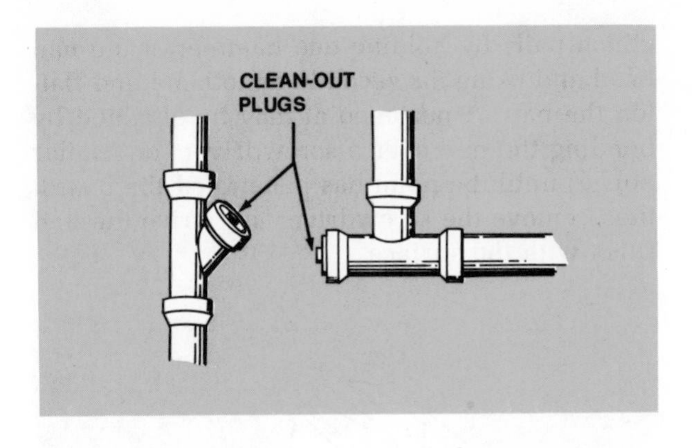

Cleanouts

Used primarily on copper and cast-iron pipes, cleanouts are a type of pipe fitting used for quick access to the inside of a pipe. Placed at traps and corners of pipe, they can be removed easily to help in clearing clogs and debris that normally collect in these places. *SEE ALSO PIPE FITTINGS.*

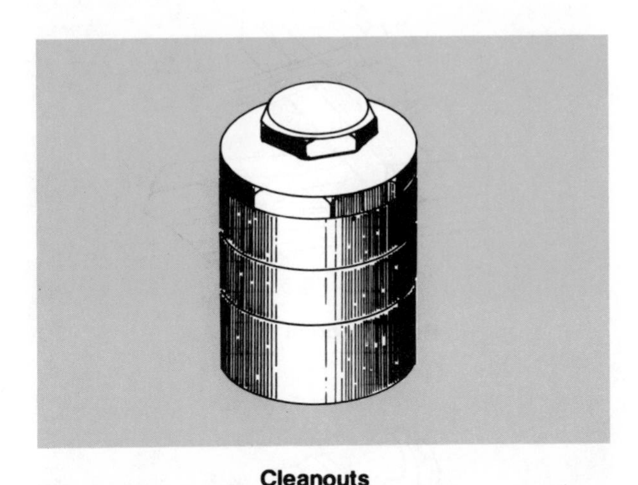

Cleanouts

Clear Finish

A clear finish is applied to a surface when a protective but transparent, colorless coat is required. Of the several types of clear finish, varnish is the most popular because it dries very hard and resists water. Shellac is easier to apply and dries faster than varnish, but is soft. Lacquer requires more skill to use and dries very fast. Some handymen prefer to use a penetrating sealer for a clear finish because it protects by sealing the pores, but retains the natural look of the wood.

Cleat

The term cleat has a double meaning to the home handyman. It is applied to a strip of wood or metal which is screwed or nailed to the back of a panel to brace it against buckling or to add strength. When used this way, the term cleat is synonymous with batten. A short piece of wood fastened to a wall to support the end of a shelf or other fixture is also called a cleat. In boating, a cleat is a wood or metal object with projecting ends around which a rope may be tied.

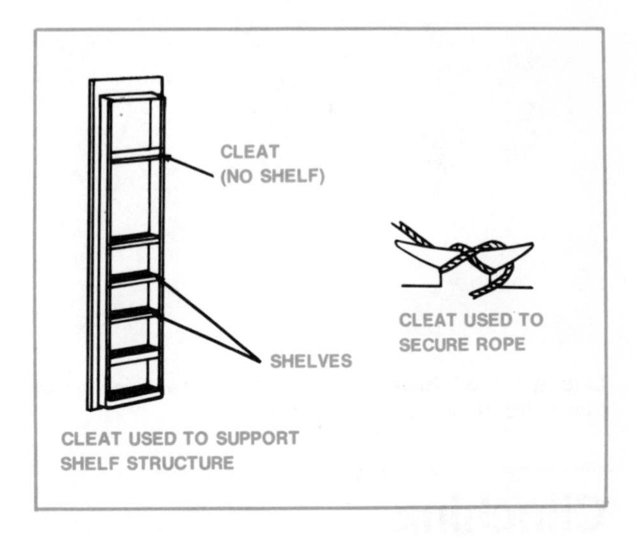

Clicktester

The clicktester is a device used in testing the continuity of a circuit. Easy to make, the clicktester consists of a set of earphones (single or double earphones will do), a flashlight battery, some wire and test prods. Connect one end of a length of wire to the top center of the battery and the other end to a flexible test prod. Splice another wire, about 4″ in length, to the wires leading from the earphones and connect it to the bottom of the battery. A third length is then connected to this splice and another test prod. The test prods are then tapped against the object being tested. If a clicking sound results, the circuitry of the object is closed. Caution: No circuit should be tested while connected to a power source. *SEE ALSO ELECTRICIAN'S TOOLS & EQUIPMENT.*

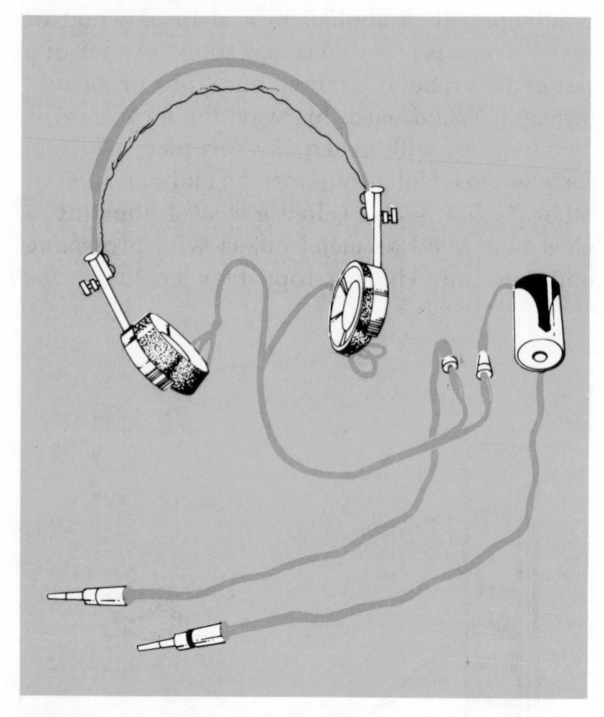

Like a circuit tester, the clicktester will verify an open circuit.

Clinching

Clinching, a method of nailing wood to wood, is generally used in rough or rustic construction where strong joints are needed and appearance is not important. Drive the nail through the boards so that approximately one-third of the sharp end is exposed. Then hammer the exposed point over so that it is flush with the board's surface. You can use two hammers to clinch nails by holding one hammer at the nail head and using the second one to bend and flatten the nail. A neater joint may be obtained by bending the nail over a screwdriver (or similar object) until the point has penetrated the board; then remove the screwdriver and drive the nail flush with the surface.

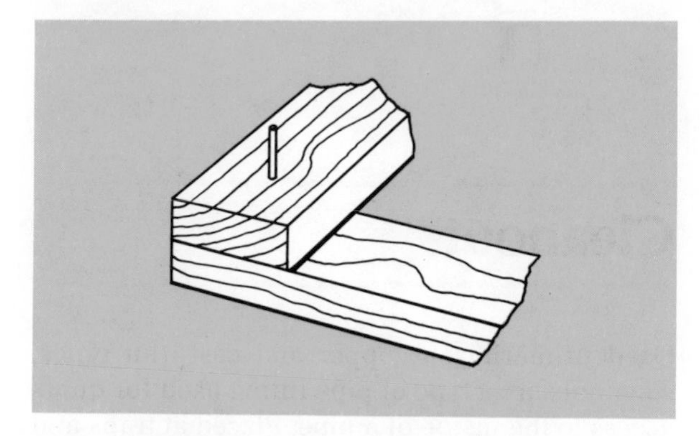

Drive nail through both boards.

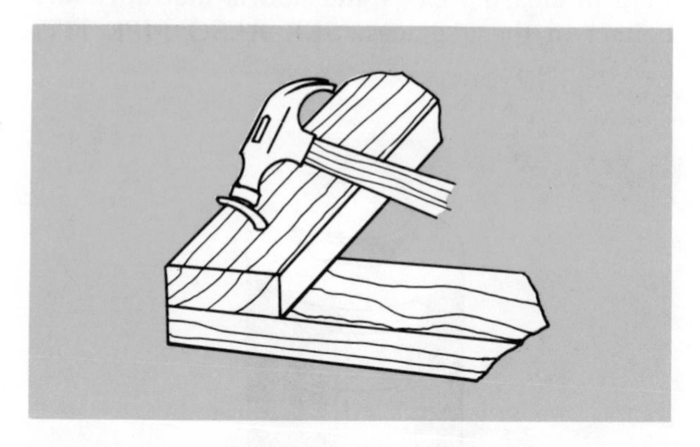

Hammer point over.

Bend nail over screwdriver.

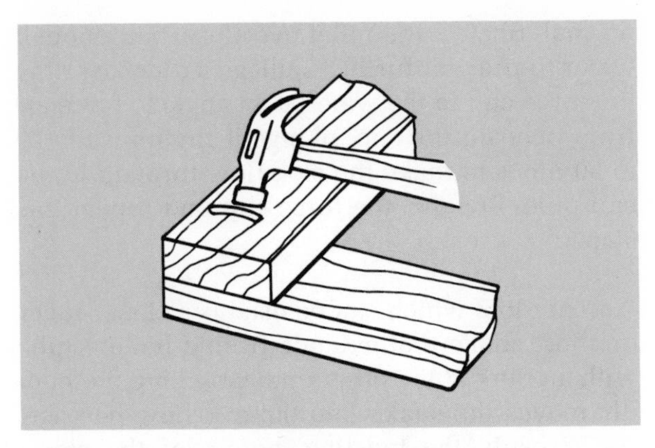

Flatten nail.

Clock Hanger Outlet

The clock hanger outlet is a special outlet for installing wall clocks. The cover plate houses a recessed receptacle for the clock plug and a hook upon which the clock is hung. This specialized device will fit into any standard outlet. *SEE ALSO SWITCHES & OUTLETS.*

The clock hanger outlet fits into any standard outlet.

Clocks, Electric

[SEE ELECTRIC CLOCKS REPAIR.]

Clock-Timer

A specialized cousin of the portable timer, a clock-timer is an aid in the kitchen and the workshop. Use it for controlling cooking appliances in the kitchen and heat lamps in your shop. It is easy to set and offers the added bonus of a quickly-read electric clock. Limited to timing intervals of a few hours, a clock-timer requires resetting for repeated use.

Clockwise

Clockwise is the direction in which the hands of a clock rotate.

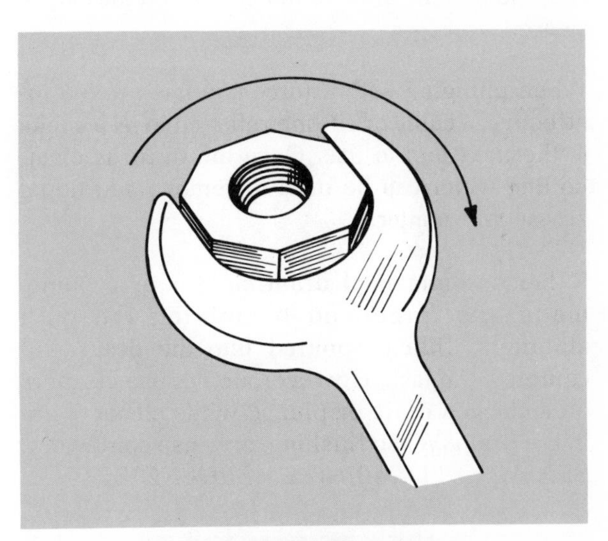

Arrow indicates clockwise turn.

Clogged Drains

Clogged drains are often an urgent problem, caused by dropping things into drains or by build-ups of grease, dirt and other matter. There are two basic corrective procedures that can be handled by the handyman.

Should the basin be nearly full, bail out some of the water to prevent splashing. Leaving enough water to cover the rubber portion of the force cup, the tool to use first on clogged drains, insert it into the water at an angle that will force out air trapped under the cup. If the work being done is on a double sink or a wash basin with an overflow opening, it would be wise to place a stopper or sponge over the drain and hold it securely. This is to prevent a stream of dirty water from shooting out when the clogged drain is being plunged. After making sure that the stopper has been removed from the sink to be plunged, place the cup over the drain and plunge 20 to 30 times. Feeling the rhythm of the water being forced through the drain and plunging with this beat will produce maximum results. Occasionally remove the force cup from the drain to allow material to flow into the basin and help clear the clog. This matter may be disposed of by flushing it down the toilet. Watch for a sustained whirlpool in the drain to indicate when the clog is cleared.

When plunging with a force cup has proven ineffective, a cable or ribbon referred to as a snake is the next tool to use. Once the drain is clear, boiling water can be used to remove additional grease and matter.

Either a commercial drain cleaner or a homemade one, produced by mixing lye with aluminum fillings, poured into the drain will complete the task. However, do not use cleaners on a clogged drain or plunge while cleaners are in the drain. When flushing, only use cold water. *SEE ALSO PLUMBING EMERGENCIES.*

Clogged Toilet

A clogged toilet is cleared by either a force cup or a closet auger. Before attempting to open the bowl stoppage, take a careful look at its outflow passage. If the clog is caused by a large object stuck at this point, remove the obstacle.

If an over-sized object is not causing the clog, then proceed by filling the water level above normal. Should the toilet overflow, bail enough water to prevent further spillage. After inserting the force cup in the water at an angle to force air from beneath the cup, plunge it rhythmically 20 to 30 times to make the clog flow through to the soil pipe. Remove the force cup and repeat this step.

Another tool which can be used is a closet auger or short snake that extends from a hollow tube with a crank at the other end. Cranking the handle moves the snake into the overflow passage. As a result, the twisting motion of the closet auger breaks or loosens the clog. If an object such as a diaper is causing bowl stoppage, the snake will twist into the object without releasing the flow of water. Periodic removal of the closet auger will remove these objects or further loosen larger clogs. *SEE ALSO PLUMBING EMERGENCIES.*

Closer

A closer is the last brick or tile laid in a course or row. It may be a whole or part of a brick which must have mortar on both ends before it is placed in the course. *SEE ALSO BRICK & STONE WORK.*

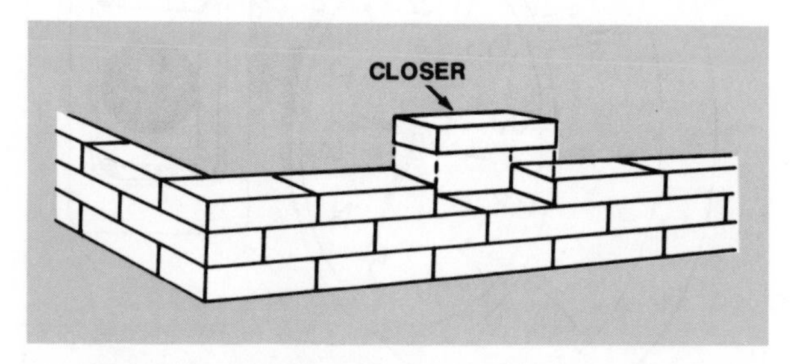

Brickwork showing placement of closer.

Closet Bend

The closet bend, a copper pipe fitting, hooks the closet flange to the sewer. *SEE ALSO PIPE FITTINGS.*

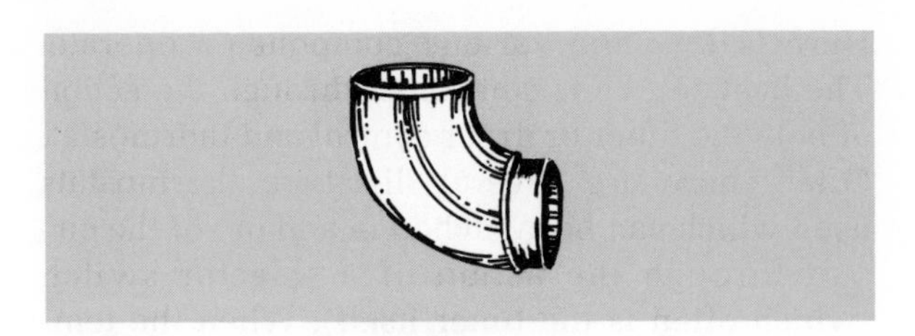

Closet Bend

Closet Flange

A closet flange, which is normally a copper pipe fitting, can be made of cast-iron. When attaching a toilet bowl to the floor, a closet flange is fitted into the closet bend, which is at floor level. *SEE ALSO PIPE FITTINGS.*

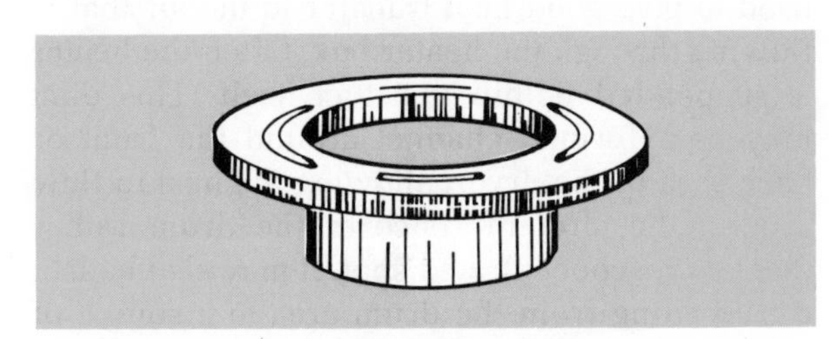

Closet Flange

Closet Pole

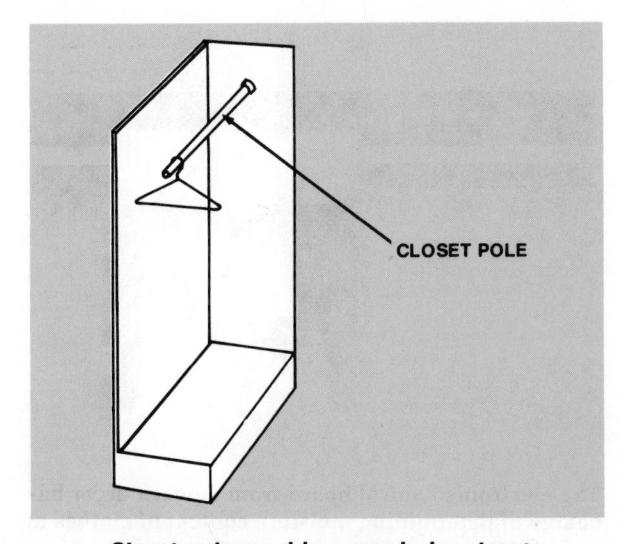

Closet pole used in a wardrobe closet.

Closet poles fit into the functional-type molding category and are ready-made spindles or shelf supports. They can be turned on a lathe or used as they are inside closets to hold clothes hangers. *SEE ALSO MOLDING & TRIM.*

Closets

[SEE CEDAR CLOSET.]

Clothes Dryer

[SEE APPLIANCE REPAIR, MAJOR.]

Clothes Dryer Repair

Basically, the function of the clothes dryer is to provide three necessary operations: heating, air flow and tumbling. They have been so well perfected that it has been said that drying clothes in modern dryers is safer for fabrics than drying them on a clothes line.

As with any other appliance, be sure to observe safety precautions when inspecting, checking or performing any maintenance repair on the clothes dryer. Never remove an access panel or handle any parts until the appliance has first been unplugged to remove all power from the machine. Also be wary of sharp edges behind the sheet-metal panels.

The heating action of a clothes dryer is provided by an electrical heating element or by a gas burner. The heat from the source is channeled into the drum area, usually by means of a duct. This action is enhanced by the second of the dryer's basic functions, air flow. In most dryers it is provided by an exhaust fan which pulls air through the drum. From the drum the only entrance (when the door is closed) is through the heater duct, which is open to room air at the end opposite the drum. The third and final function, tumbling, is provided by revolving the drum itself. This causes the clothing to tumble and to expose all of its surfaces to the heated air that is

The timer is a switch that is controlled by motor. This unit has two motors. One provides timing action during normal cycle; other motor is in charge of de-wrinkling function at end of cycle.

moving through the drum of the dryer. This allows the clothes to dry evenly and thoroughly. The drum usually has baffles formed into its outer edges to improve the tumbling action.

These functions can be modified to provide very close control of the drying effect upon various types of fabrics. Cottons and linens can be dryed at a rather high temperature. On the other hand many synthetics require low temperature to keep from removing the folds pressed into the fabric at the factory with heat and pressure in permanent press clothing.

Here is how the various components operate. The heat source is controlled through the action of both the timer or dryer control and thermostat. Often there are several disc-type thermostats used which can be switched in and out of the circuit through the action of a selector switch (which often is the timer itself). When the temperature in the drum has reached a certain level, the thermostat will open, breaking the circuit to the heat source. The dryer will continue to run and circulate air until the drum has cooled down to a level below that particular setting. Typical levels used are 155 degrees for high levels and 135 degrees for wash-and-wear or medium heat levels. This temperature can be checked by inserting a thermometer at the point where the exhaust vent is attached to the dryer.

The open-type heating element is most often used to give good heat transfer to the air that is flowing through the heater box. Often the heater is suspended within the duct itself. This duct may be a formed channel around the front or back area of the dryer, allowing the heat to flow around the circumference of the drum rather than at one concentrated spot. It may also be in a duct leading from the drum area to a source of outside air. The element is suspended upon porcelain blocks to insulate it from the adjacent cabinet. The element usually operates on a 230-volt circuit; however, some compact dryers have 110-volt elements that allow them to be used as

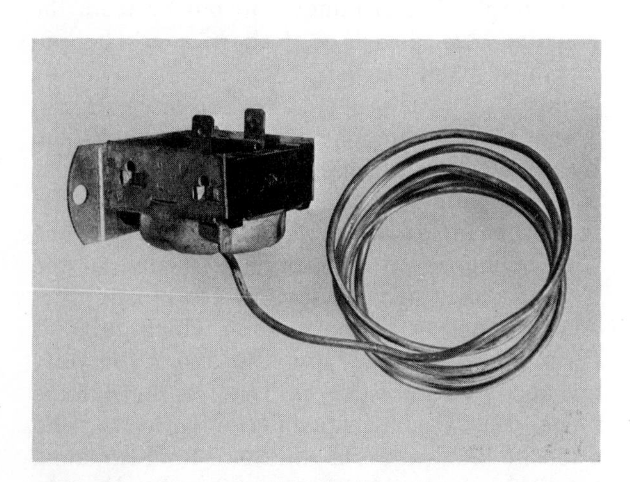

An adjustable thermostat is usually capillary-tube type. The thermostat body is located in console while sensing tube goes in exhaust duct.

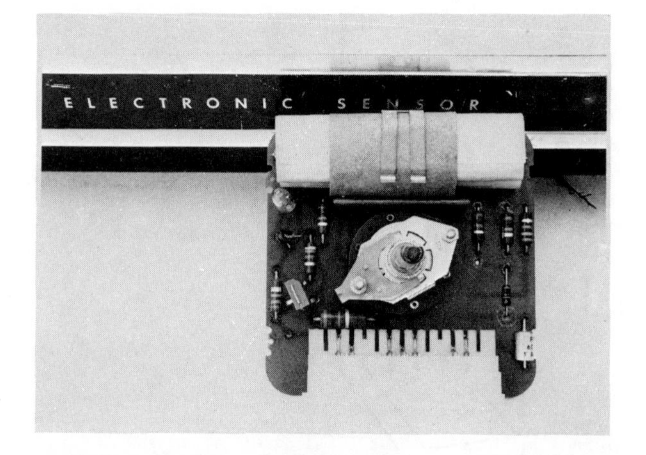

The electronic control board from modern dryer has charge of determining moisture content of clothes at end of cycle.

portable appliances and in apartments. The drying time is increased substantially when 110-volts are used.

In gas dryers, the burner can be either a standing-pilot type or an automatic-ignition type. Standing-pilot units are being phased out of dryer production lines. In the standing-pilot burner the pilot is in use during the entire cycle. Another type must be lit with a match at the beginning of each cycle.

Many gas burners currently in use utilize a *glow coil* to light the pilot. With this method a small filament is located directly beneath the pilot orifice. The filament is made of a material (usually an alloy of rhodium and tungsten) which glows white-hot when power is applied to it. This ignites gas flowing from the pilot orifice. When the pilot ignites, the flame heats a thermocouple which is connected to a switch on the burner. If this switch transfers within 30 seconds, the main burner valve is turned on. This ignites from the pilot and the main burner cycles through the action of the thermostat. If for some reason the pilot fails to ignite and does not heat the thermocouple within the prescribed amount of time, a special switch shuts the burner down completely. In this case the timer must be turned to the off position and the burner allowed to rest for about ten minutes before it can be restarted. If it should fail to ignite again, a problem within the burner itself likely exists.

The newest burners utilize direct ignition components, eliminating the pilot all together. This may consist of a small device similar to an electric motor which creates an electromagnetic field and causes two contacts to "chatter" against each other. As the contacts open and close quickly, an arcing occurs which gives a spark causing it to ignite the burner directly. On others a ceramic carbon or crystallized-carbon is located near the main burner orifice and becomes white-hot when power is applied. In either case, if heat from the burner does not open a thermostatic switch within a very few seconds the burner shuts down. Direct-ignition burners have the advantage of offering faster safety shut down than standard burners, as well as eliminating the pilot.

It is not recommended that gas burners be serviced by anyone other than authorized gas appliance technicians or the gas company. They are rather complex devices and special equipment is required to make necessary adjustments within the area. Many localities also require special licenses of anyone servicing gas equipment. Gas dryers should be checked thoroughly for leaks whenever they are moved for servicing or inspection.

One problem that you can correct occurs when the pilot burner becomes linted from the air that is pulled in to combine with the pilot flame. Use an old brush such as a toothbrush to remove the lint from around the pilot orifice. Sometimes contacts on direct ignition burners can become linted, also. If this occurs, the brush should eliminate the problem. Be sure to disconnect the power and turn off the gas before attempting either of these solutions.

The control system of a clothes dryer is of great importance since this is the system that controls all operation of the dryer. There are three basic methods that are used. The first and most basic of all, is the time and temperature method. This is the machine that has a simple timer with which you select the amount of time that you want the clothing to dry. Accompanying this is a thermostat, often the adjustable type, with various ranges of heat input. This is set when the running time is selected for the timer.

The timer itself is simply a group of switches that are combined in a housing. The switches are turned on and off by the action of cams upon which a movable section of the switch contacts rests. A mechanical gear train connected to a clock motor turns the cams and makes the switches open and close in accordance with the portion of the cycle remaining.

The programming of this type of dryer is usually quite simple. There is a long period of time, as much as 60 minutes or more, provided on the timer when both motor and heating element are turned on. During the last five minutes of the cycle, the heating element contact in the timer is opened. This breaks the circuit to the heater, but

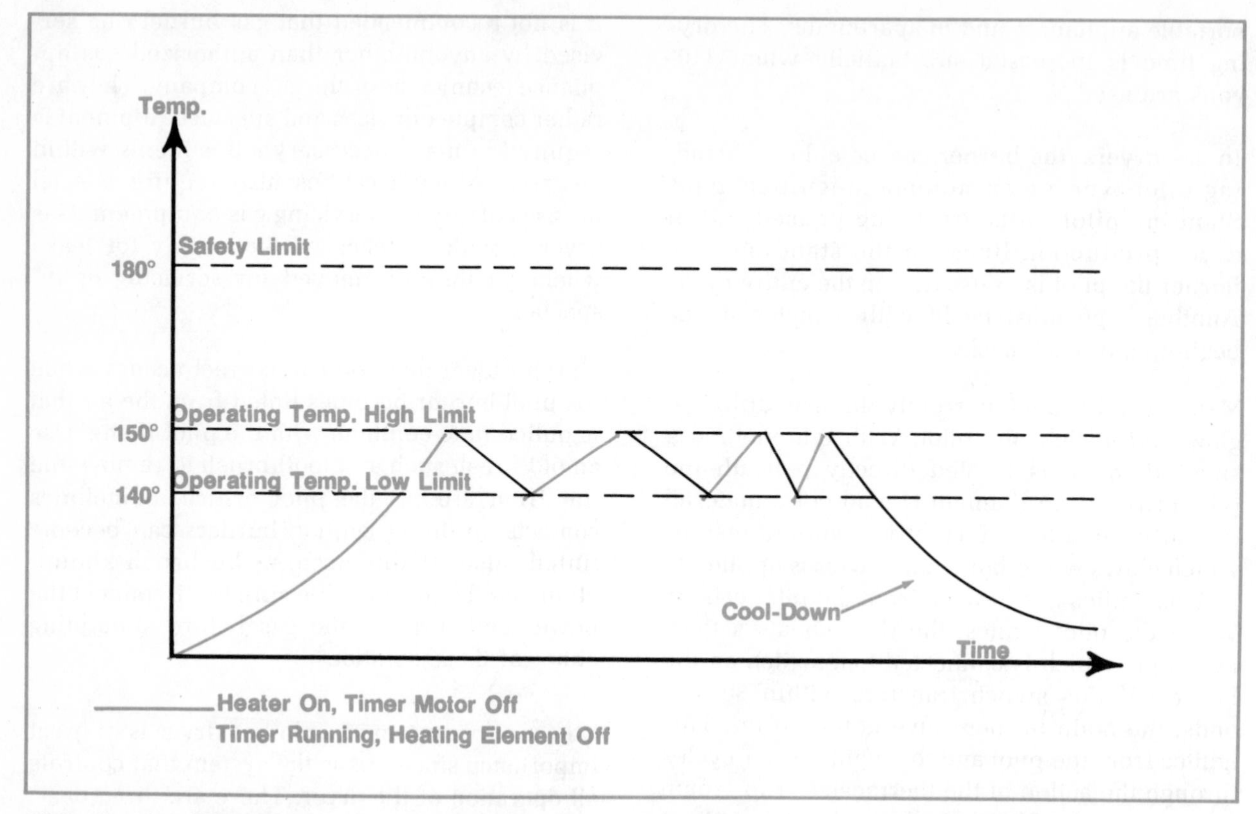

This drawing illustrates how an automatic cycle functions in a typical clothes dryer. At beginning of cycle, heat rises slowly due to large amount of moisture within air stream. When heating element cycles off, thermostat simultaneously turns timer motor on. As timer cycle progresses, heating and moisture levels become lower and heating element stays off a shorter period of time while timer is on for longer periods.

allows the motor and fan to continue to run. The clothes keep tumbling and air continues to circulate, but it becomes progressively cooler as the warm air within the heater box is used up. This provides a cool-down period which makes the clothes easier to handle when they are removed from the dryer and helps to prevent wrinkles from setting in synthetic fabrics.

During the time that the timer has the heating element turned on during the cycle, the element is also being controlled simultaneously by the action of the thermostats located within the dryer. As the temperature within the drum increases, the thermostats come into play to hold the temperature level at a particular point. This point depends upon the selection made by the user on an adjustable thermostat or upon the predetermined setting of a disc-type preset thermostat. The sensing point of these thermostats is usually in the outlet of the exhaust-air duct which carries the warm air away from the dryer.

You will rarely have to calibrate a thermostat on a dryer, but there is the possibility that a thermostat will sometimes have to be replaced. It can be the problem when an overheating condition occurs. But first be sure that the problem is not due to such factors as a grounded heating element or a lint filter or vent that has become clogged.

A second method of dryer control is the automatic cycle. In the automatic cycle, preset thermostats are used in the exhaust duct to sense the temperature. In addition to controlling the heating element, these thermostats also control the timer motor. Separate thermostats may be used or the same thermostat may serve both functions. When the clothing is placed in the dryer and the dryer is turned on, the temperature rises rather slowly at first because of the high moisture concentration in the air. The temperature in the exhaust duct gradually increases as the clothes become dryer. Finally, it reaches a point where it is sufficient to turn the heating element off. When this occurs the transfer also energizes the timer motor (which has not been running up until this point). With the heater off, the temperature cools rapidly. The element again turns on and the timer motor turns off. As the clothes become dryer, the exhaust temperature rises more quickly and falls more slowly, since moisture concentration in the air is being reduced. Finally the off periods have become sufficient to run out an amount of time allowed on a special timer, which is usually about 12 minutes. At this point the timer again controls the timer motor. The machine goes through cool-down with the heating elements off, then turns itself off. This method is somewhat more accurate than the time and temperature method since there is less guesswork

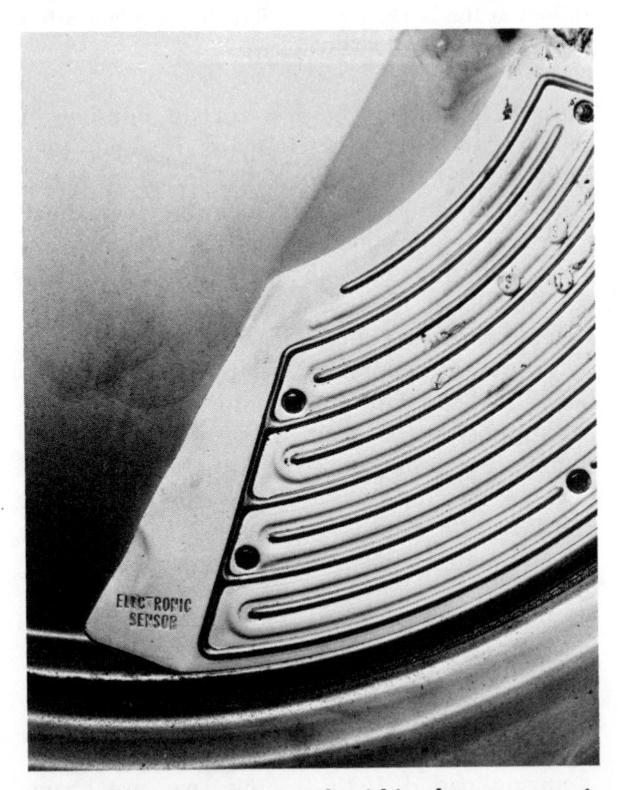

The sensing board located within drum compartment senses moisture level of clothes by passing small electrical current through them.

involved and it is variable to suit the type of fabric involved.

The ultimate in dryer controls today is the electronic control. With this method the drying of fabrics within the dryer can be controlled to a close range of moisture retention in the fabric itself. This is how an electronic control works. When the clothing is placed in the dryer its electrical resistance is lower than normal because it is damp. As the clothing becomes dryer, its resistance increases. A sensing device, located in the dryer drum, consists of metallic fingers which are interlaced but are not touching, being separated by a thin insulating board to which they are mounted. The clothes come in contact with these fingers and complete a circuit across them. In the console, the electronic control tries to build up a charge of some 72 volts which it needs to complete a circuit across a neon bulb, which in turn controls a master relay. This control current is also being fed to the sensing board within the drum. As the clothes brush against this board, they tend to reduce the charge which has been built up, since the clothing completes the circuit through the sensing board connected to the ground. This is an important reason to be sure that a dryer with an electronic control is properly grounded. The normal ground provided through the power supply on 230 volt electric appliances is not sufficient for an electronic control to function properly. It should also have an external ground wire run from the cabinet of the machine to a cold water line. This is not a bad idea even on those dryers which do not have electronic control.

As the clothes become dryer, the resistance of the clothing increases and this charge is not bled off so readily. Finally, when the clothes have reached a certain level of moisture retention (often adjustable by a dial on the electronic control), the circuit through the bulb is completed and the relay which controls the operation is opened. The heat shuts off. The dryer motor, however, continues to operate through the action of cool-down thermostat. This keeps it operating until the temperature reaches a low level (usually around 110 degrees). A similar function is sometimes served by an auxiliary timer which controls a cool-down cycle.

The drive system of automatic dryers is powered by a fractional-horsepower electric motor, usually a split-phase type. In most dryers a belt-driver system is used. Often a series of belts is designed to gear down the speed of the dryer drum. If the drum turns too fast, the clothing will stick to the edges of the drum and drying will be spotty. If the drum turns too slowly, the clothes will tend to mound in the bottom of the drum and will not be picked up and dropped through the air flow. Drum speed is normally from 48 to 55 rpm. You can check this by attaching a piece of tape to the top of the drum after the top panel has been lifted. Be sure that all power is turned off before attempting to do this.

Many tops on modern dryers are hinged so they can be raised when the front clips are snapped up. With the top propped up, plug the dryer in and turn it on. Keep hands off during this operation. Don't get near any electrical parts or revolving mechanical parts. Each time the tape comes up on the drum, count it for a period of one minute. This will give you a good indication of the drum speed for your particular dryer. However, unless you are having a problem with clothing sticking to the outer edges, there is little reason to question proper drum speed.

Some new dryers use a poly-V type belt which completely encircles the circumference of the

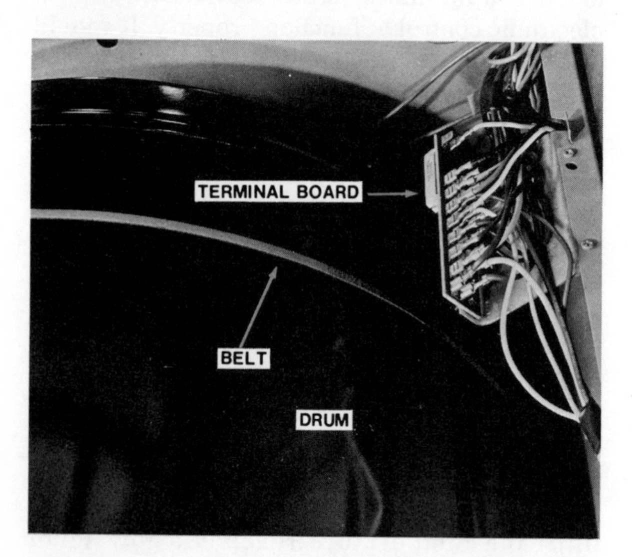

A ribbon-type belt with multiple V-grooves completely encircles the drum on many new dryers. The belt must be replaced with exact replacement.

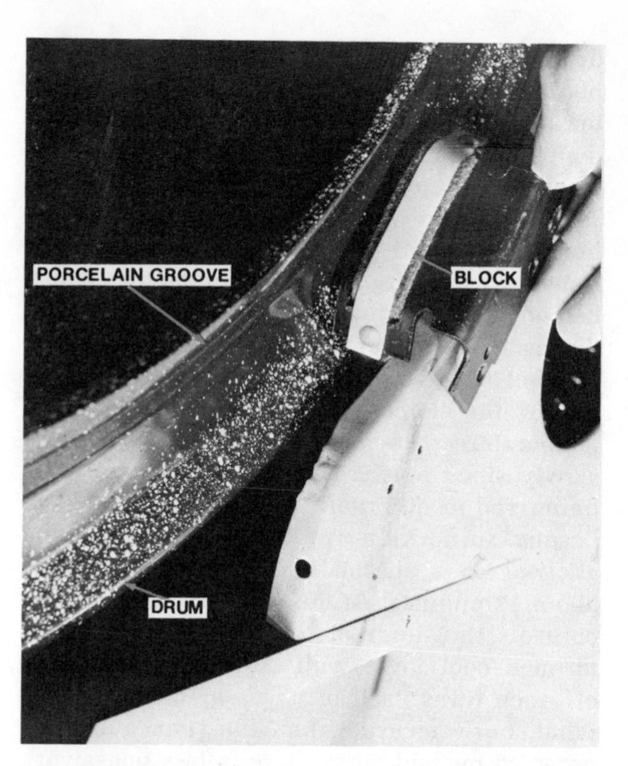

The drum is supported by blocks at the front and by rollers at the back. Be sure that the rollers are free and that they turn easily.

drum. These belts have a certain number of grooves, usually three, four, or five per belt. They are flat ribbon-like belts, and if an incorrect belt is used for replacement they can cause improper drum speed. Usually these belts are used in conjunction with an idler pulley to maintain tension on the belt. The basket itself can be suspended from a single bearing at the back or it may float on rollers which are attached to the back bulkhead. Often porcelain blocks are used for support at the front of these drums. When removing a dryer drum for any reason, be sure to check the condition of the bearings and clean and lubricate them with the particular lubricant recommended by the manufacturer.

To reach the drive mechanism or to replace belts on machines using the pulley drive method, it is usually necessary to remove the access panel at the rear of the dryer. Unplug the dryer first. Often an intermediate idler pulley is used which is spring-loaded. If this is the case, use heavy pliers to carefully lift and remove the spring. Wear goggles to protect eyes should the spring

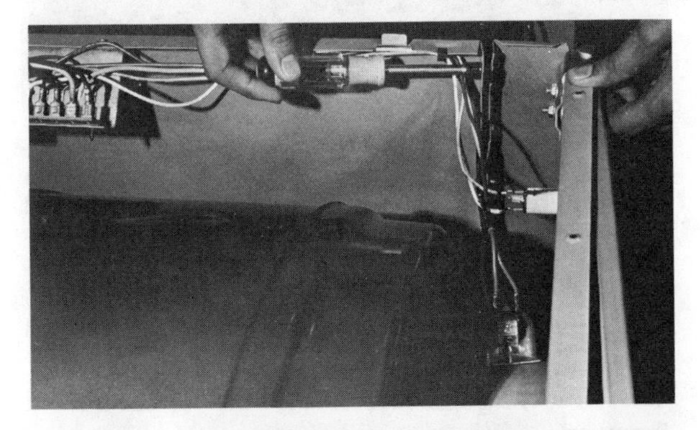

slip. The belts are then free for replacement. If it is necessary to remove one of the pulleys, be sure that it is in the proper position on the shaft before retightening the set screw that holds it in place.

Often the blower is driven through another belt from the rear of these particular machines. If a blower belt breaks for no apparent reason, check the condition of the bearing at the blower mechanism. This blower turns at high speeds and if the bearing is not lubricated regularly, it can fail. When it fails it usually locks the belt in place, damaging it at the point where it slips on the motor. Replacing a new belt without remedying the problem with the bearing will lead to another belt replacement very shortly.

Dryers using the poly-V type belt are usually serviced from the front. To reach this it is necessary to remove a toe panel that may be a separate part of the front panel, the upper support panel that supports the drum or the rear panel. Start by

Dryer front or rear panel is removed to service Poly-V type belts in most cases. First raise top. Be sure to remove any screws around vent opening. Then loosen any screws that are obvious near top or front of dryer. With these screws removed, dryer front can be pulled from clips that retain it at bottom.

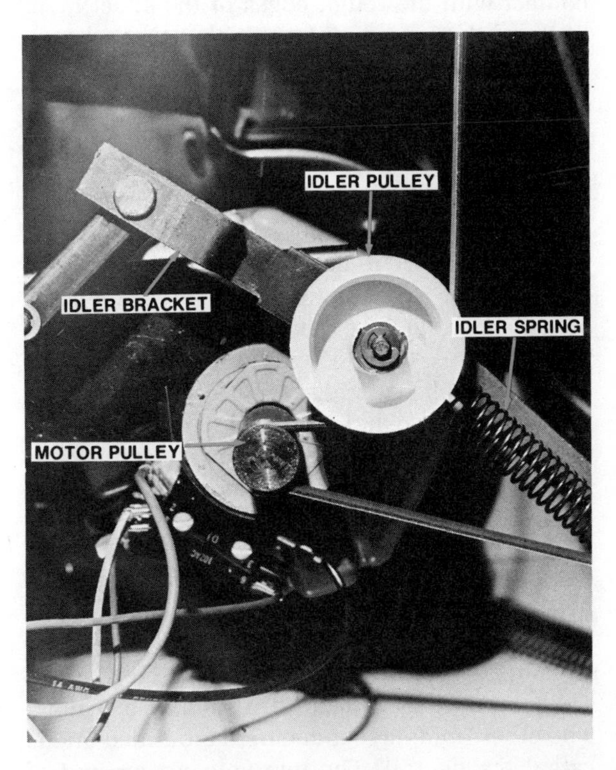

Note correct position of drum belt carefully. It can be tricky to replace otherwise. Spring-loaded idler presses against back of belt, maintaining proper tension.

unplugging the dryer and raising the top. Then look for any screws or clips that retain the front panel toward the front of the appliance. Remove these screws and the front panel can be removed without any problem. It is often necessary to lift it free from the retaining clips near the front of the panel. Once the panels are out of the way, the old belt can be removed by releasing the spring at the idler pulley or by releasing the tension on the idler pulley. The belt is then slipped off the motor pulley and off the front of the drum. The new one is installed in the same manner. Sometimes you have to look closely to see the way in which the belt threads over the motor shaft and through the maze of pulleys. This can best be done by looking closely before you remove the panel. If the belt has come off refer to the accompanying drawing for one typical installation. If you can understand how this operates, it is usually possible to determine the exact belt placement for your particular dryer.

When installing belts be sure that there is no contact with the rough edges of the sheet metal parts of the cabinet. Also see that the belts are lined up properly with their pulleys. Ribbon-type belts go around the drum with the grooves facing inward toward the center of the drum.

If a dryer fails to operate, inspect the fuses or circuit breakers before looking further. Turn the switch off before removing fuses and stand on a dry board or insulating support before touching a fuse box. Never expose yourself to live terminals. This simple test may pin-point the problem. If the cartridge type fuses are used in your panel, have them checked with a continuity tester to see that they are good as these fuses do not give any outward indication that they are blown.

On occasion an electric dryer may run but won't heat. This may be due to a power blown fuse. The reason is that the power supply to the dryer is comprised of three wires. Two of these wires are hot and carry voltages of 115 volts to ground. The other (middle) conductor is grounded and is called the neutral. The two voltages are out of phase with each other so that anything connected across these two lines is operating on the 230 volt difference in potential between the two. In an electric dryer, the only component connected across these two lines is the heating element. The motor, lights and controls are all connected from one of the 115 volt lines to the grounded neutral and operate on this 115 volt circuit. With this in mind, it is easy to see that if *one* of the fuses blows the dryer can run, lights will burn, and it will otherwise function normally, but it will fail to heat. When circuit breakers are used, they are joined together to form a double-pole type breaker, but even here it is possible for one side of the breaker to fail. If this occurs it will usually (but not always) trip the other side at the same time. Therefore, if a dryer runs, doesn't heat, or fails to run at all, check the fuse first.

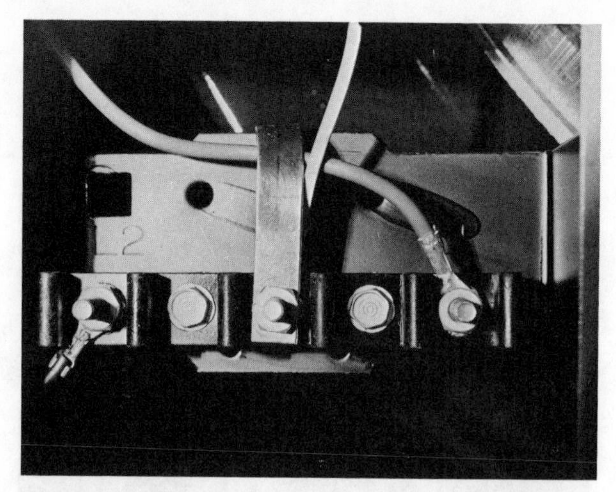

230-volt appliances have terminal block at cord connection. Be sure that grounding strap is in position to middle (grounded neutral) connector. It is required in most areas, but check with your utility before installing if it is not already connected.

After turning power off, the console of most modern dryers will lower after attaching screws are removed. Sometimes a simple inspection can reveal a loose terminal connection.

Use a terminal tool like the one shown to replace terminals. After the correct terminal is selected, the wire is stripped and terminal is crimped tightly in place. Be sure that the matching terminal is cleaned to a shiny appearance before installing new terminal.

There are a number of safety devices that are built into dryers which can sometimes cause problems. One of these is the door switch which turns off the machine whenever the door is opened. If the dryer continues to run with the door open or if the dryer doesn't run at all, make sure that the switch is adjusted correctly. The safety thermostat is usually placed on the heater box to shut the heat source off at a safe level before it reaches a point that it would damage the dryer or the home in case the fan doesn't come on or if for any other reason the machine overheats. If this thermostat fails or if a wire comes loose, the machine will operate but not heat.

The motors used on dryers contain a centrifugal switch to prevent the heat source from coming on in case the motor fails to operate. This is not only a safety device, but serves to allow the dryer to start properly as well. When the dryer is turned on, a large initial surge of current is required to start the motor. Since many dryers operate near the capacity of their 30-amp circuits, the surge of the motor starting plus the current load required to energize the heaters can easily exceed this limit. The centrifugal switch allows the motor to approach full running speed before the heating elements are turned on, thus reducing the momentary current surge in starting the equipment. Again, if a terminal or wire is not fastened properly to the centrifugal switch or if the switch fails to make contact, the heating

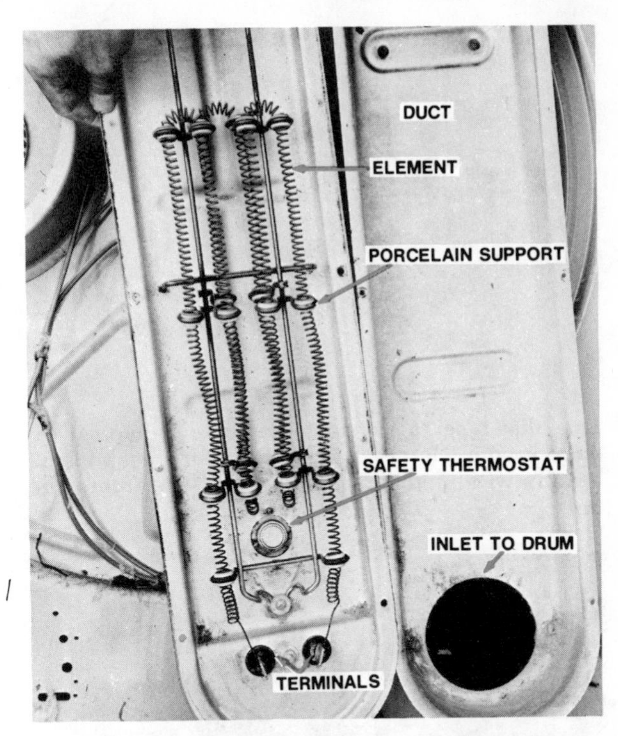

An open-type heater is used on most dryers to provide adequate heat transfer. It is usually located within a duct leading into the drum. The safety thermostat is mounted close to element.

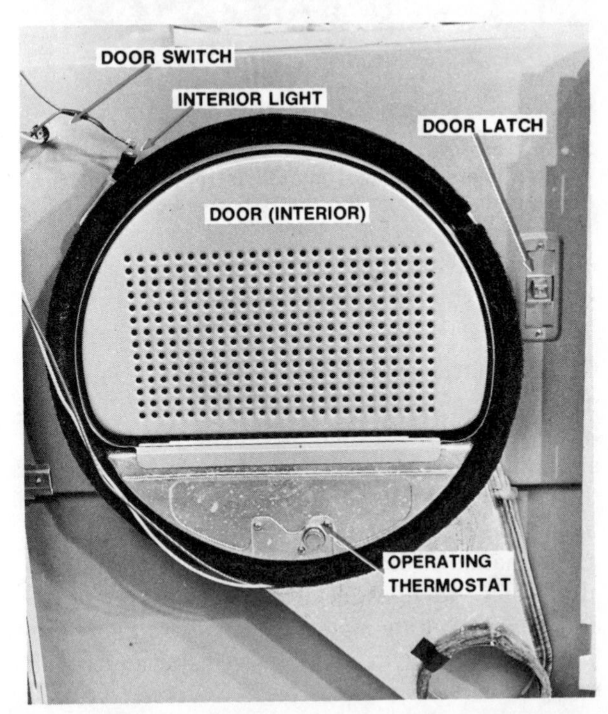

The operating thermostat is located in air flow that is typical of that circulating through clothing. Here, it is located in air passageway beneath door.

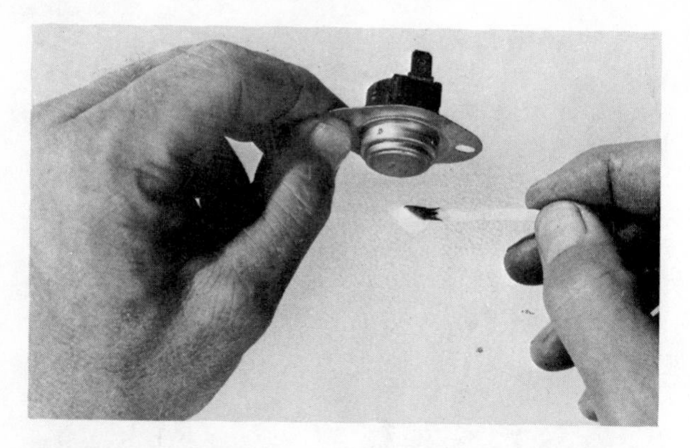

This disc-type thermostat seen here is typical of those used in clothes dryers. Listen for a snap when heating with match held at safe distance from control.

Sealed motors like this are used on many new dryers. The centrifugal switch is replaceable from the outside by removing the two screws shown.

element will not come on. Internal repairs of this type are a job for a motor shop.

On an electric dryer after unplugging the equipment, you can very often discover a break or loose wire or make an adjustment. That is often all that is necessary to make a repair. Very often the repair may be nothing more than replacing a blown fuse. Almost equally important, is proper maintenance of the dryer. Cleaning the lint filter after each usage, especially when new material and heavily-linting material such as blankets are being dried, can in itself reduce the source of many potential service calls.

Make it a part of a yearly check to inspect the condition of belts, to lubricate the motor if oil

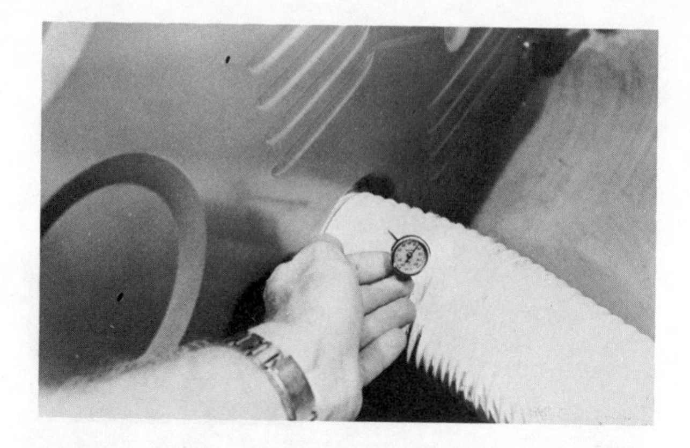

Check exhaust temperature of dryer by inserting thermometer in dryer where exhaust vent exists. Proper venting is important to dryer operation. Keep it short with as few bends as possible.

ports are provided on it. Only a few drops of SAE-20 non-detergent motor oil are necessary at the motor. On the blower bearing, it is a good idea to saturate the wick properly to retain the oil for the bearing.

While the access panel is removed from the machine, be sure that all lint is vacuumed away from the dryer motor. A fan built into the motor pulls air through to help cool it. This is important since the equipment operates in a high-temperature environment.

Finally, be sure that your dryer is properly vented outdoors, not just into a crawl space. The moisture in some cases could result in structural damage to the home when it is simply dumped into a crawl space. Secondly, lint (especially that from some synthetic materials) can be a fire hazard. If it is exhausted out of doors the hazard is eliminated. Follow closely the venting instructions recommended by the manufacturer of your dryer. Obtain the proper tubing from a dealer and be sure that you install a cap or hood which prevents birds and rodents from using the nice warm opening as a nesting place during cold weather. Most manufacturers recommend a maximum length of around 16 feet for aluminum duct, including two elbows and the exhaust hood. Deduct two feet for each additional elbow but in no circumstances exceed four elbows. Where flexible ducting material is permitted, the maximum length should only be about half that for aluminum. Keep the vent as short and

Blower units of many dryers have oil wick to feed lubricant to bearings. Soak wick yearly with SAE 20 oil. The telescoping-spout oiler is handy for reaching into tight spots.

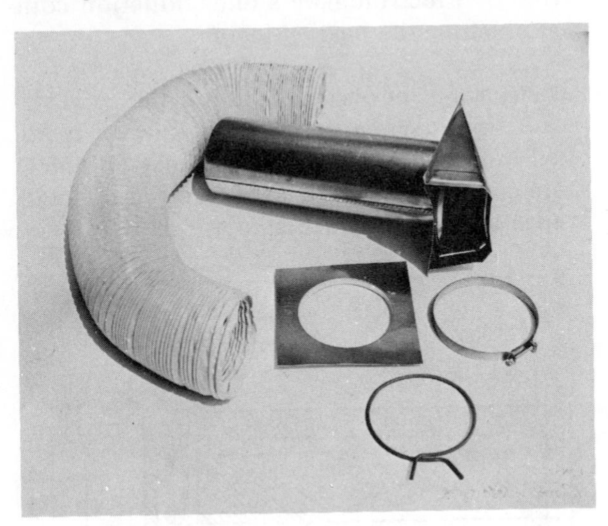

Vent kits such as this can do the entire job. They consist of the tubing, hood and clamps necessary for a normal vent operation. Check local codes before using flexible tubing like that shown.

straight as possible. Don't use screws when joining the pipe, for the projections into the pipe can cause quick lint build-up. Never try to operate a dryer without a vent. This will cause fast lint build-up within the machine and will also increase the temperature and humidity of intake air, limiting its ability to absorb moisture from the clothing. It will also cause the dryer motor to run hotter than it normally would. When the dryer is enclosed in a small utility room, be sure to provide proper ventilation into the room as well as exhausting the dryer out of the room.

Clutch

[SEE SYSTEMS, AUTOMOTIVE.]

Clutch Head Bit Screwdriver

The clutch head bit screwdriver is suited to clutch head screws only. The clutch head is classified as a "special" screwdriver, so there may be no immediate need for it around the house. The driving end of the clutch head will look like an hourglass, butterfly or blunt-tipped propeller. *SEE ALSO HAND TOOLS.*

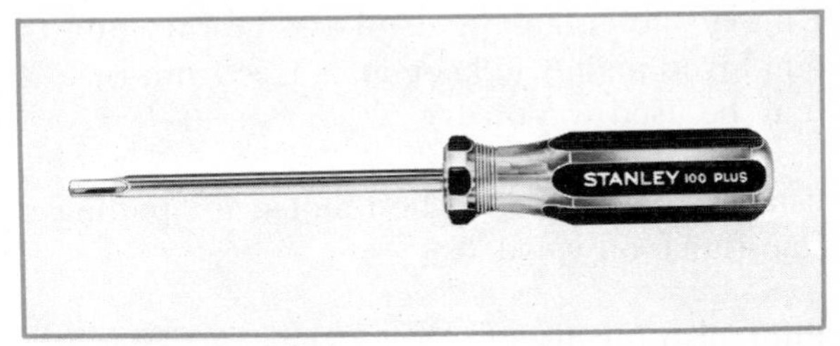

Courtesy of The Stanley Works.

Clutch Head Bit Screwdriver

Coated Abrasives

The coated abrasives, silicon carbide, aluminum oxide, garnet, flint and emery, are backed with paper or cloth. Those with cloth backing, which has more strength and flexibility, are used for machine sanding, while those with the paper backing are generally used for hand sanding. The grit particles of the abrasive coating may be closely spaced for extra durability and more cutting speed, or thinly spaced for decreased clogging action. The abrasives are graded on a scale ranging from very fine grit to very coarse grit. The abrasive material comes in dry types, or wet types, which may be used with a lubricant for cleaning off residue. Each abrasive is best suited for use on a particular material, but substitutions among the types can be made if the desired grit is not on hand. The manmade abrasives, silicon carbide and aluminum oxide, are more expensive although longer-lasting than the natural abrasives, garnet, flint and emery.

Silicon carbide, the hardest and sharpest of the abrasive coatings, may be used for either hand or power sanding. It is excellent for sanding metal, and can also be used on plastic, glass, ceramics, leather and stone. Silicon carbide is waterproof and may be used dry or lubricated.

Aluminum oxide also has a high degree of hardness and cutting ability and is used on metal, but is more durable than silicon carbide, which tends to have brittle cutting edges. It is used dry or wet for polishing stainless steel and on wood, plastics and fiberglass.

Emery can also be used on metal, but is employed mainly to keep tools free from rust. It may be used wet or dry.

Garnet, for dry use, is best suited for putting a fine finish on wood.

Flint, also for dry use, has a short working life, and is therefore used on work which clogs the grit rapidly, such as in removing paint layers and heavy gum or pitch deposits. *SEE ALSO ABRASIVES.*

Coated Box Nails

Coated box nails are box nails covered with a layer of resin that acts as an adhesive between the nail and the wood, after the nail is driven. They are classified as "tough-holding" nails but are generally used for light construction work. Coated box nails have either a smooth or barbed shank and are available in 3 to 8 and 10, 16 and 20 penny sizes. *SEE ALSO FASTENERS.*

Code Book

[SEE NATIONAL ELECTRICAL CODE]

Coffeemaker Repairs

[SEE AUTOMATIC COFFEEMAKER REPAIRS.]

Coil

Coils, essential to electric motors, vary in use from transforming voltage to turning armatures. Although there are as many types of coils as there are uses, the composition is common to all. Coils are made by wrapping wire around a cylinder. Electromagnets and induction coils best illustrate the basic principle.

An electromagnet is a soft-iron cylinder wrapped in wire. When an electrical current is applied to the wire, the cylinder is magnetized. A more complex system is used in electric motors to turn armatures which spin the shaft.

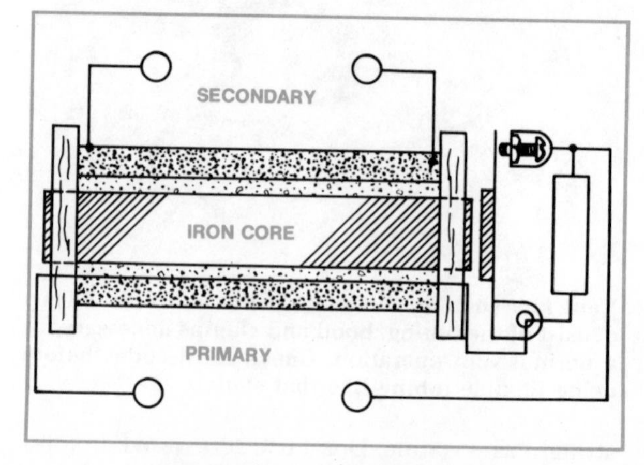

A diagram of an induction coil.

The induction coil is used in transformers and electronic components. A magnetic field is created by sending electrical current through the *primary coil.* The second or *secondary coil* is then moved close enough to cut across this field, "inducing" electricity through its turns. The resulting voltage will be in direct ratio to the turns of wire. For example, an induction coil allowing ten volts of electricity to pass into the primary coil of five turns and through a secondary coil of 50 turns will produce 100 volts of electricity. *SEE ALSO ELECTRIC MOTORS.*

Cold Chisel

Cold chisels are essentially designed for cutting and chipping cold metal (steel, wrought and cast iron, copper, brass, aluminum, etc.). They may be forged from round, square, hexagon or octagon steel stock with the heads and cutting edges heat treated. The blade sizes range from 1/4" up to 1 1/4" and the chisel sizes range from 5" to 18" long. Cold chisels are often misused for cutting and splitting stone and concrete.

In addition to the flat cold chisel, there are cape chisels, which clip rounded corners and cut narrow grooves; diamond-point chisels, which cut square-inside corners and V-grooves; and round-nose chisels, which chip round corners and trough-shaped grooves.

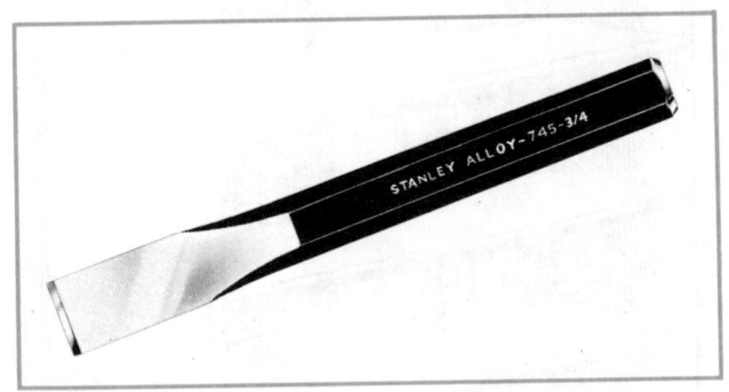

Courtesy of The Stanley Works

Heavy gloves should be worn in case the hammer misses the chisel, and goggles are needed to protect the eyes when cutting masonry. *SEE ALSO HAND TOOLS.*

Coldframes & Hotbeds

Coldframes and hotbeds are like miniature greenhouses, as they serve as a shelter for growing plants during the colder months. They are essential to the gardener who wants to grow seedlings or root cuttings early in the season. In constructing a coldframe or hotbed, it is best to use treated lumber to avoid decay.

COLDFRAMES

The standard coldframe looks much like a root cellar and is built three feet by six feet by two feet into the ground. Coldframes built well below ground level require less than ones constructed on the ground surface, but need proper water drainage to prevent flooding. The lid of the coldframe is hinged to the boarded walls and may be made of several materials. Most people prefer to use an old window or French door since the panes are inexpensive, easily replaced and allow maximum light penetration. Plastic-impregnated wire can be used, but it grows cloudy with age, reducing exposure to light. Flat or corrugated structural plastic costs more than glass, but is more durable. Notches should be cut into the mullions of the tilting lid so water will drain quickly. If the lid falls flush with the frame, attach a handle to the lid for easy lifting.

A coldframe is more convenient if it is near the house and a water source. Plants will receive maximum sun exposure and be shielded from north winds if the coldframe is facing south or southeast. However, sun can quickly reach 100 degrees in a closed frame, so special attention should be given to proper ventilation and shading. To control light, moisture, temperature and to maintain a coldframe, do the following: (1) Shade the coldframe from direct sunlight by covering the lid with whitewash, muslin or roller-type blinds. (2) Water the plants with a fine spray to avoid dislodging seedlings. (3) Raise the sash on warm days for ventilation. (4) Cover the coldframe with a blanket if temperatures are below 40 degrees. (5) Remove dead leaves from plants to keep the coldframe clean.

HOTBEDS

Hotbeds are coldframes with controlled heat. Although there are many ways to heat a hotbed, the most popular method is to attach 50-watt light bulbs at two foot intervals along the interior sash supports. Weatherproof bulb sockets and 10- or 15-amp fuses should be used. All wire splices require soldering and wrapping with both rubber and friction tape.

Outlets should be installed at an angle to allow moisture to drain. The warmth in a hotbed is regulated either by a thermostat or by the number of light bulbs used. Hotbeds should be heated to a temperature of no less than 35 degrees and no more than 100 degrees. *SEE ALSO LAWNS & GARDENS.*

Collar Beam

Collar beams, also called tie beams, connect pairs of opposite roof rafters high above the attic floor. Collar beams supply stiffening and bracing to reinforce the roof frame, but they are not roof supports. They also help hold together the ridge board and rafters. A common roof frame includes collar beams placed at every third pair of rafters. *SEE ALSO ROOF CONSTRUCTION.*

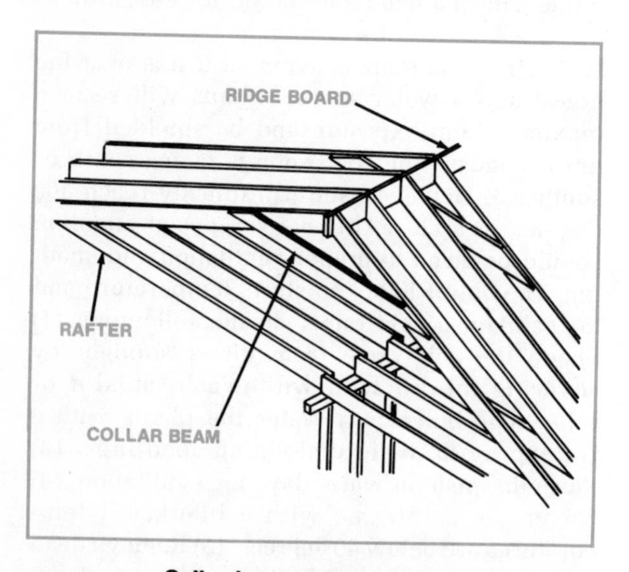

Collar beam reinforcement.

Collar Screw

Collar screws are designed with a long multi-sided head for easy removal and a flange that allows the bolt-like screw to fasten steel plates or coverings together without marring the metal. For this reason, collar screws are often found on electric motors. *SEE ALSO FASTENERS.*

Colonial Bookcase

The jigsawed plinth at the bottom and the valance at the top establish this as a Colonial piece. However, with a bit of restyling of these two features, the bookcase may be adapted to provincial, contemporary or any period you choose. The back is made from random width knotty pine (V-groove). The molding at the top is standard crown molding.

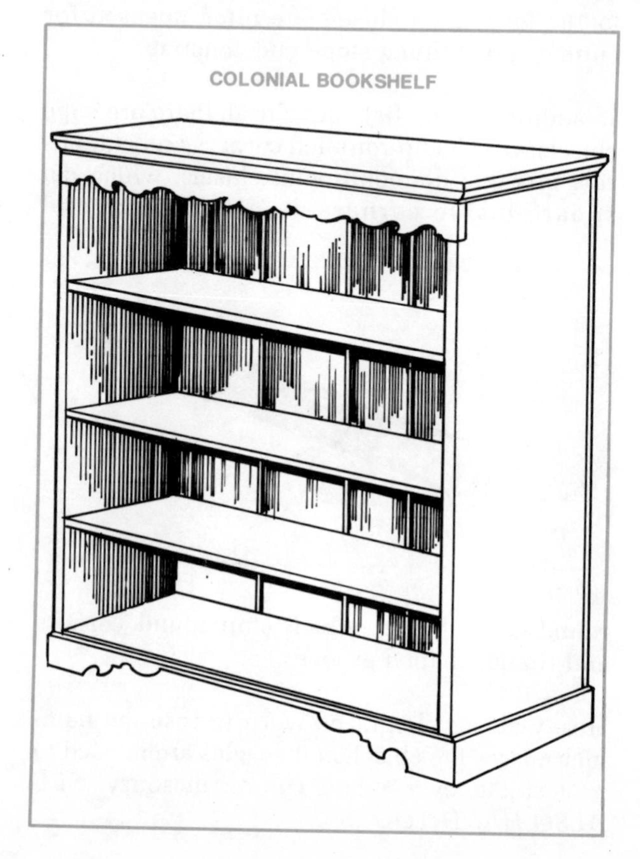

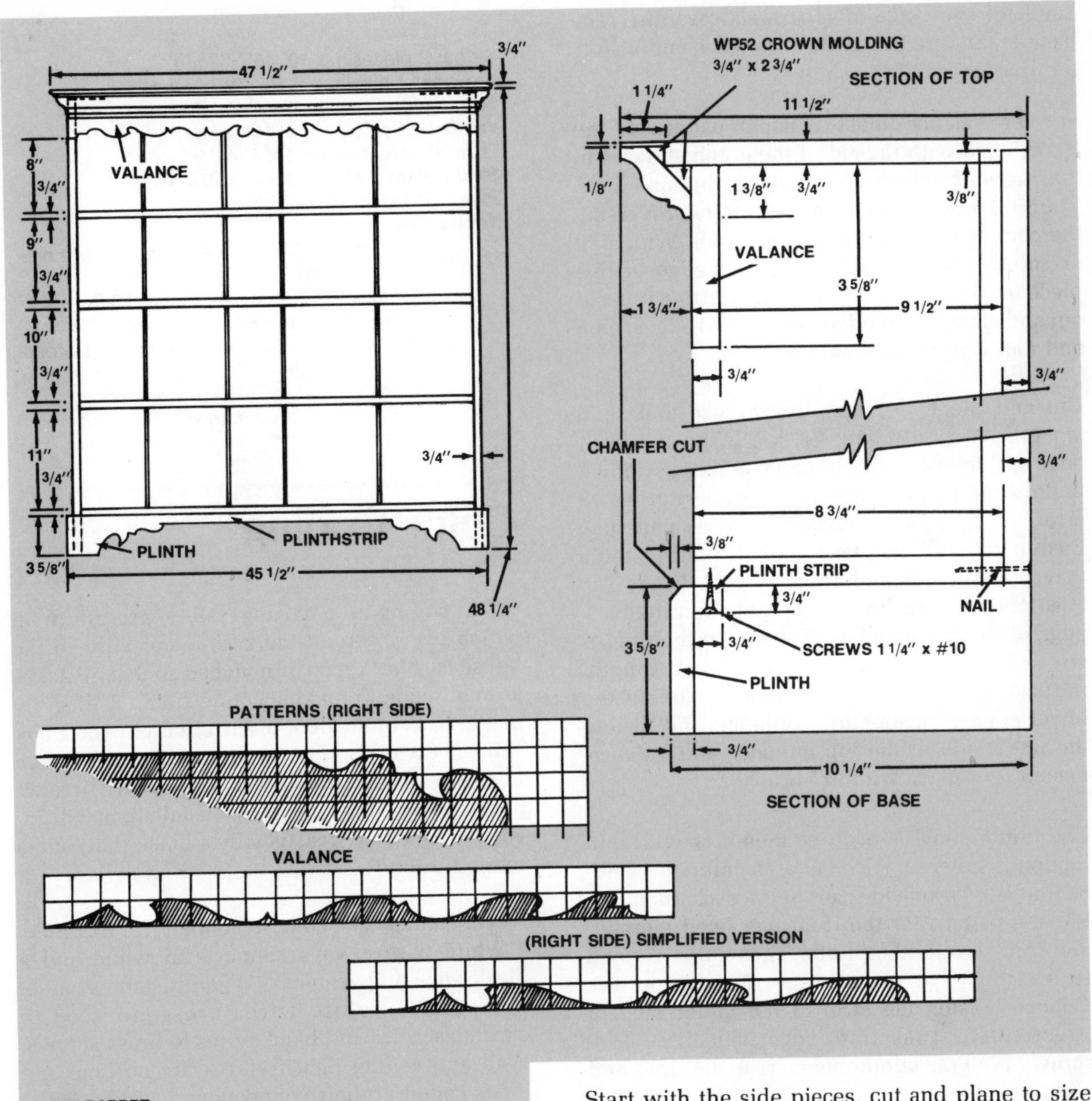

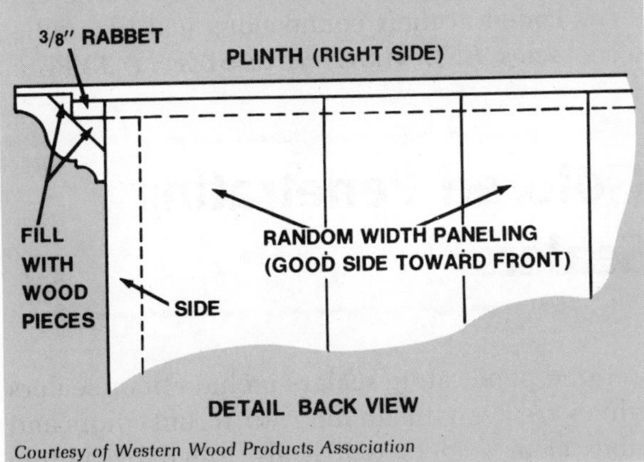

Courtesy of Western Wood Products Association

Start with the side pieces, cut and plane to size and sand both inside faces smooth. Mark the location of each shelf on the inside faces. Also mark and cut the notch on the upper front corner of each side to take the valance which is $^3/_4$'' x $3^5/_8$''.

Cut the four shelves, plane to size and sand. Fasten in place between the sides with glue and 8d finishing nails, setting the heads slightly. The back is made up of five pieces of matched knotty pine. Cut stock to length, then rip the two outer pieces and plane them to required net width.

Sand the face side of all panels carefully. The back is then nailed on the two sides and also to the rear edges of the shelves.

For the valance, make a paper pattern of the lower edge with the aid of the graph squares in the drawing which shows the right-hand half. Then trace the design onto the stock, reversing the pattern to mark the left-hand half. With a jig or scroll saw, cut away the lower edge of this piece on the outline of the design. After it is cut out and smoothly sanded on face and edges, glue and nail it in the two side notches.

Cut and plane the top piece to size and sand smooth. Work a rabbet 5/8" x 1 1/4" on the front edge and the two ends of this member as shown in the section detail; also, on the back edge, work a rabbet 3/8" x 3/4" to engage the back paneling. Fasten the top in place with finishing nails driven into sides and valance, with heads set. Also nail the paneling in the rabbet on the back edge of the top member. The crown molding is cut into three pieces of the proper length, mitered at the two front corners. Locate the lower edge of this molding on a line 1 3/8" below the underside of the top on sides and valance. Fasten it in place with 3/4" brads.

The plinth consists of three members with butting ends mitered. Also cut a chamfer 3/8" x 3/8" on the upper outside corner of each member. Make a pattern for the front jig-sawed member and trace it onto the plinth. Then cut it out and finish the edge in the same manner as the valance. Fasten the strip to the under side of lower shelf, at the front edge with three 1 1/4" screws. Nail the plinth members to the sides and along the strip.

When assembly is completed, sand surfaces and apply sealer coat or stain. Either pine or maple stain may be used to simulate the mellow tone of colonial furniture. Fill the nail heads and then apply several coats of white shellac or clear flat varnish. When hard, the final coat should be rubbed down with pumice stone or No. 00 steel wool. If varnish is not used, several coats of paste wax, well rubbed, should be applied over the shellac. The resulting surface will be quite durable. *SEE ALSO PROJECTS.*

MATERIALS LIST

Sides: 2 pieces 1 x 10, 48 5/8" long
Shelves: 4 pieces 1 x 10, 42 1/2" long
Top: 1 piece 1 x 12, 47 1/2" long
Valance: 1 piece 1 x 4, 44" long
Front Plinth: 1 piece 1 x 4, 45 1/2" long
Side Plinth: 2 pieces 1 x 4, 10 1/4" long
Plinth Strip: 3/4" x 3/4", 42 1/2" long
Knotty Pine:
- 1 piece 1 x 10" face x 45" long, groove one edge
- 1 piece 1 x 8 face x 45" long, T&G
- 2 pieces 1 x 10 face x 45" long, T&G
- 1 piece 1 x 10 face x 45" long, tongue one edge
- 6 lin. feet 3/4" x 2 3/4" Crown Molding
- 3 No. 10 flat head screws, 1 1/4" long

Color Coding

Color coding is a wiring safety procedure in which every connecting screw and wire in the house is color-keyed or matched so that mistakes are not made in making connections. A diagram on the back of the door of the circuit breaker box shows how to connect the wiring for each circuit to the terminal screws in the circuit breaker panel. From there on, most installation will involve only two wires, usually a black (hot) and a white (ground).

Never connect one color to another; for example, a white wire always connects to white and a black wire only to black. When installing outlet receptacles, white wires are connected to chrome screws and black wires to brass screws. Wall and ceiling light fixtures are chrome and brass coded at their connections just like outlet receptacles. *SEE ALSO WIRE SIZES & TYPES.*

Colored Penetrating Sealers

Colored penetrating sealers include floor sealers which are available in many different colors and other clear sealers which are tinted by adding oil-based colors or dyes to them. Sealers are painted on the raw wood or on top of the stain or filler to close the pores of the wood. They keep undercoats from bleeding and also prevent finishing materials from penetrating the wood. *SEE ALSO WOOD FINISHING.*

Colored Shellac

Colored shellac is used as a wood primer and sealer which can be painted or enameled. It comes in white and orange. Most commonly used is white shellac, which is bleached and creamy-white in color. White shellac may be tinted with aniline dyes to produce different coloring effects. Orange shellac is unbleached and is an amber color. *SEE ALSO WOOD FINISHING.*

Colored Varnish

Colored varnish is commonly used to stain wood floors and furniture. The colors range from shades of mahogany, maple and walnut to dark black. Without affecting the color tone, the varnish should be diluted with turpentine or paint thinner as much as possible, so that the varnish will penetrate the wood and carry most of the color into it. After the colored varnish has been applied, a top coat should be brushed or rubbed on top. Since colored varnish gets darker with each additional coat, a clear varnish is best to use for the top coating. *SEE ALSO WOOD FINISHING.*

Color In Decorating

[SEE DECORATING.]

Colors In Oil

Colors in oil are available in paste form (tubes) at paint stores, and are used for tinting oil or alkyd base solvent reduced paints. The paste is made by mixing a pigment (solid finely-ground particles of color) with linseed oil or other vegetable oils. Tinting colors are also available in liquid form for easier mixing. *SEE ALSO PAINTS & PAINTING.*

Column

A column is a vertical support either circular or rectangular in shape. In addition to providing support, columns add a decorative touch. In floor construction, columns help support beams and girders when floor joists are used over a long span. When determining correct column sizes, tables should be consulted. For best results, choose a column with the largest dimension equaling the width of the girder to be supported. *SEE ALSO FLOOR CONSTRUCTION.*

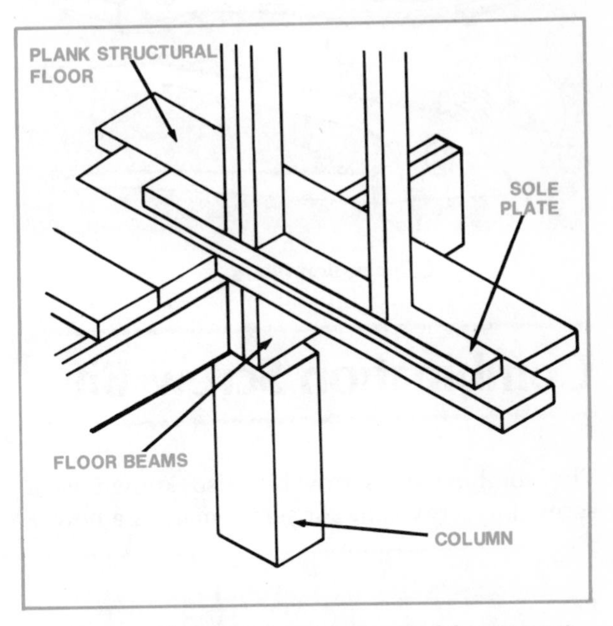

Framing section showing column used for support.

Combination Pliers

Combination pliers are used for holding materials with a firmer grip than the fingers can provide. Many possess a slip-joint or 8-shaped hole for grasping small or large objects. When grasping large objects, slip-joint handles do not have to be spread so far apart that a grip becomes difficult for the user. Another advantage of these handles is that they are usually serrated for an easy grip.

While they may scar or scratch some surfaces, the jaws have teeth for an improved grip. The nose length and shape of combination pliers may vary depending on the type of work needed to be done. Combination pliers with additional insulation on the handles may be used for electrical work. *SEE ALSO HAND TOOLS.*

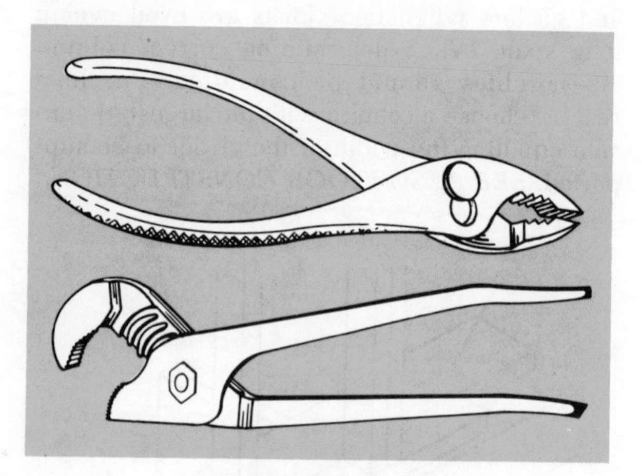

Combination Pliers

Combination Screw Bit

The combination screw bit, also known as a screw bit, screw-sink, or screw-mate is a newer type of drill which combines three jobs: drilling holes the correct screw size and depth, countersinking and counter-boring. It is used with an electric drill and comes in a variety of sizes. Combination screw bits may be purchased separately or in sets. *SEE ALSO HAND TOOLS.*

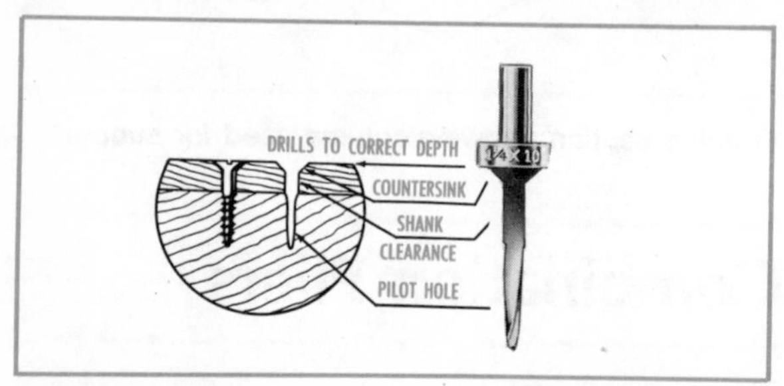

Courtesy of The Stanley Works

Combination Screw Bit

Combination Square

A combination of a protractor, ruler and moving head, the combination square can serve as a miter gauge, try square, depth and marking gauge, level and plumb, straightedge, foot rule and as a nail, screw and dowel gauge. The handle can be clamped to any point along the blade and it will automatically measure 90° and 45° angles by shifting the rule and using the edge of the handle. For using the combination square as a marking gauge, clamp the blade tip at any distance from the edge of the handle, hold a pencil point against it and make your mark. To judge the depth of a mortise, set the handle edge on the wood surface, slip the blade down in the mortise and the ruled edge gives the measurement. The combination square is highly valued by handymen because of its obvious versatility. *SEE ALSO HAND TOOLS.*

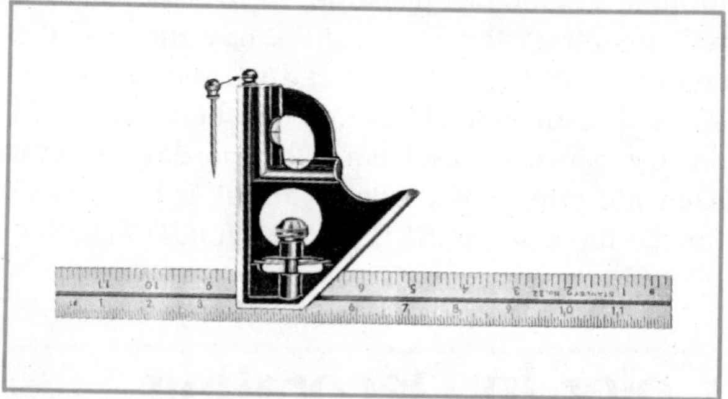

Courtesy of the Stanley Works

Combination Square

Commercial Standard

The commercial standard is a set of rules voluntarily adhered to by craftsmen of a particular trade. The National Electrical Code and Underwriter's Laboratories, Inc. are examples of the commercial standards for electricians. Building codes issued by the building department of local governments will have the necessary ordinances and codes that comprise the commercial standards for contractors and builders in their respective localities.

Common Nails

Common nails are wire nails used for doing basic rough work, such as framing or subflooring. They are round with flat heads and come in various sizes and gauges. The size (penny or d) comes from the old English penny system which was used to determine cost of the nails. Gauge is the same as wire size. SEE ALSO FASTENERS.

Common Rafter

A rafter, having the top cut supported by the ridge and the bottom (or seat) cut resting on the wall plate, is called a common rafter. *SEE ALSO ROOF CONSTRUCTION.*

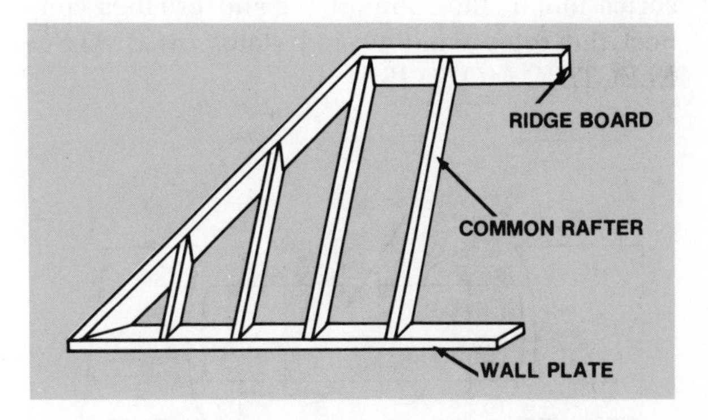

Part of roof showing common rafter.

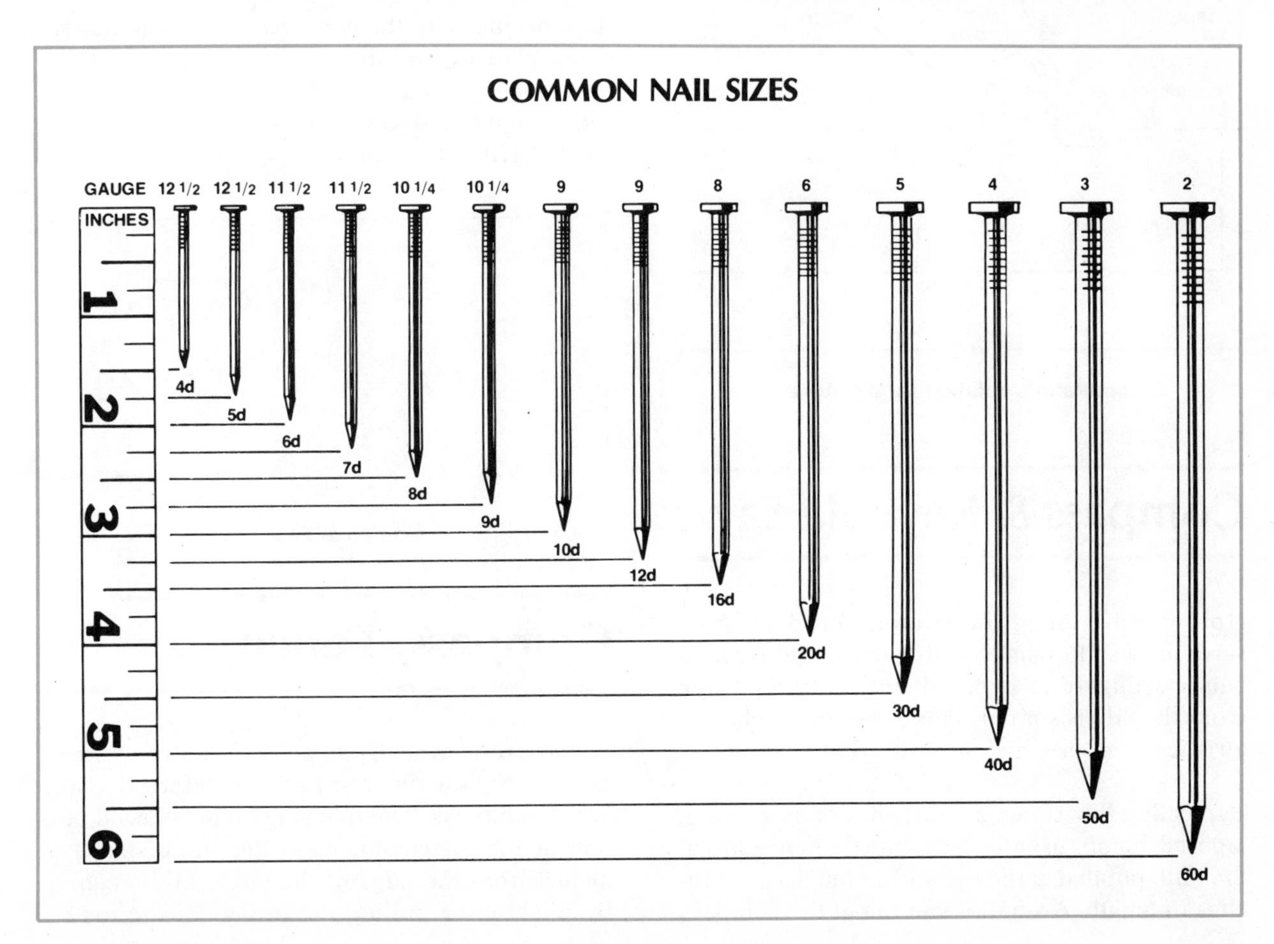

Commutator

A commutator is a device which changes the direction of current flowing through an armature. In so doing, the polarity of the poles is altered, and the armature continues to rotate. In a series motor, the commutator and brushes connect the rotor winding and stator. *SEE ALSO ELECTRIC MOTORS.*

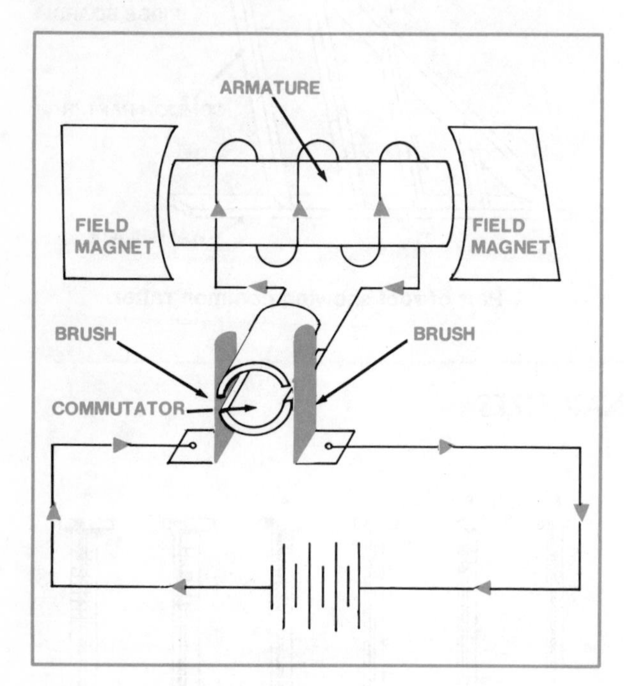

Commutator's relation to armature.

Compass & Keyhole Saws

Hole cutting tools, the compass and keyhole saws are used to make both curved and straight cuts starting from a bored hole. Although the work they do is similar, there are certain characteristics of each which are different.

Typically, the compass saw has a narrowed, tapered blade, usually less than 1 inch wide at the butt, pointed at the tip, and 12 inches to 14 inches in length. A smaller version of the compass saw, the keyhole saw has a narrower blade, usually 10 inches to 12 inches long.

While either can cut curves, the keyhole saw is for tight radius cutting of smaller diameters. As its name implies, it was once actually used to cut keyholes in wooden doors. Since compass saws cut faster and are better suited to working in thick stock, they are a favorite for making cutouts in floors or walls. Neither of these saws are frame types and therefore are not limited to working near the edge of a panel.

To start a cut from a hole bored through a panel, the compass saw can make an entire cut or make the first cut long enough for a larger saw to be inserted. Vertical strokes are used initially. Then as the cut progresses, tip the saw to about a 45° angle. For average curve cutting you can use the entire length of the blade. For small radius work use the narrower section near the tip.

In working with the compass and keyhole saws, keep your eye on the saw to avoid any flexing. The narrow blades bend easily, but can usually be straightened by hand or with pliers. *SEE ALSO HAND TOOLS.*

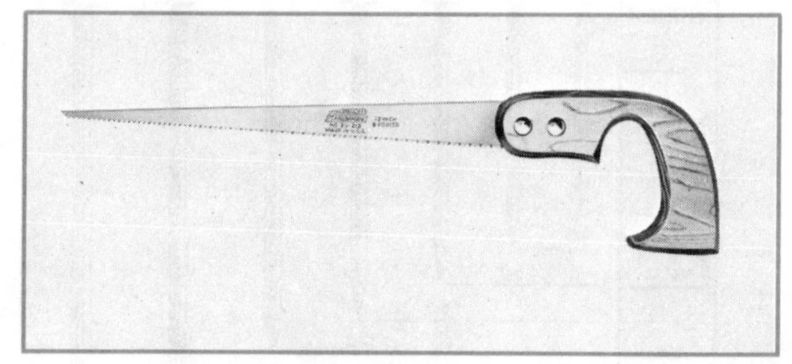

Courtesy of The Stanley Works

Compass Saw.

Compass, Pencil

A two-pronged instrument used to draw circles of a desired diameter or radius is referred to as a pencil compass. The marking on the curved portion of the instrument indicates the distance in inches from the edge of the circle to the center. By pushing or pulling the prongs of the instrument, both the radius and diameter can be changed.

To draw a perfect circle, the user can move the pencil portion in a circular direction without lifting the pointed metal end of the instrument from the point that is to be the center of the circle. *SEE ALSO DRAFTING EQUIPMENT; HAND TOOLS.*

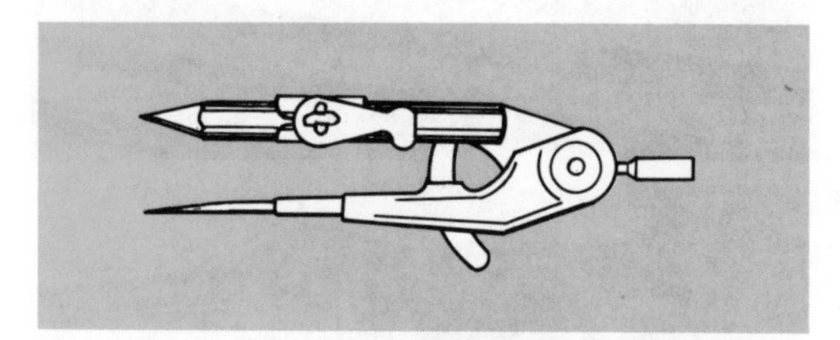

Pencil Compass

Components, Television

[SEE TV REPAIRS & TROUBLESHOOTING.]

Composition Board

Composition board, or hardboard, is a tough material composed of compressed sheets of wood fibers, used as finish material for interior paneling and siding. Tempered hardwood is treated with oils and resins to make it harder, darker and more resistant to moisture. Composition board is available with a variety of attractive surfaces, and is smooth on one or both sides.

Composition Sheathing

Composition sheathing is a structural covering for a house frame, and is attached to exterior studs and rafters of the house. It is made of wall boards or prefabricated panels of plywood shiplapped for watertightness, and is used for insulation purposes. Roof sheathing is used as a covering for rafters. The panels are usually one half inch thick and come in four sizes: four by eight feet, four by nine feet, four by ten feet, and four by twelve feet. *SEE ALSO WALL & CEILING CONSTRUCTION.*

Composition Shingles

Composition shingles are used as a protective and decorative material for roofs. They are usually made of asphalt and are laid in an overlapping fashion. Composition shingles are available in various colors, sizes and finishes, and may be laid individually or in strips which appear as individual shingles. Leak-causing loose nailheads in shingles should be hammered into the sheathing, and an asphalt roofing compound should be applied to them to act as a weather seal. Broken shingles are replaceable with new strips, and roof cement can repair either cracked shingles or those that have been lifted or curled by strong wind. *SEE ALSO ROOF CONSTRUCTION.*

Compost Heap

The compost heap is a bed of biodegradable material such as manure, plant matter or lawn and garden waste that is left to decompose and become a rich organic fertilizer. This fertilizer will greatly increase the efficiency of the soil of a lawn or garden by making the soil yield its own food. The compost is preferred over commercial fertilizer by many experienced gardeners because the material is inexpensive. Also, organic food growers recognize that compost increases the nutrient and taste value of vegetables without the use of chemicals.

The compost heap may be either a pit or a rectangular box into which the waste is placed. The dimensions of the heap will depend upon the amount of humus required. Start the compost heap with a layer of rich soil, like that found in wooded areas. Place a layer of plant matter and a plant-manure mixture proportioned in a ratio of one part manure to two parts plant on top of the first layer. Add another layer of soil to the pile and cover it with plant debris or lawn waste. Top the heap with a thick layer of soil in order to keep down the smell. These heaps build a temperature as high as 170 degrees during the maturation period. For this reason, they should be worked by shoveling the bottom of the pile to the top once a month. All layers of the heap should be moistened as they are placed and also during the monthly turning procedure. Basil or other insect-repelling herbs can be planted around the heap to decrease the attraction of flies and other pests. *SEE ALSO LAWNS & GARDENS.*

Compound Angle Sawing

[SEE TABLE SAW.]

Concrete

Contrary to popular belief, there is no such thing as a "cement" driveway. Cement is only one of several ingredients which make up *concrete,* the correct term.

As a matter of fact, cement is one of the lesser components of concrete, making up only 7% to 14% of the mix by volume. Because it is minor in that respect, however, does not mean it is unimportant. Cement is used quite literally in the usual sense, as a "glue." It is a compound that holds things together, in this case the other ingredients of the concrete mix — water, sand and coarse aggregates.

The cement used in concrete is portland cement, a soft, grayish-green powder packed in large bags of 94 pounds each (one cubic foot) or in Canada, 80 pounds (approximately $^7/_8$ cubic foot).

The term "portland" is not a brand name, but a term applied by Englishman Joseph Aspdin

Courtesy of Portland Cement Association

Concrete is highly durable and attractive, and can be used in a variety of applications such as driveways, patios and steps.

because concrete made from this cement resembled "Portland stone," a widely used building material in the early nineteenth century.

Modern portland cement is a fine pulverized material consisting principly of lime, silica and a sprinkling of metals. It is manufactured from limestone and other materials such as clay, shale or slag from blast furnaces. The ingredients are burned in a rotary kiln at a temperature of 2700 degrees Fahrenheit, which welds the materials into clinkers. The clinkers are then cooled and pulverized, with a small amount of gypsum added to regulate setting time.

In the late 1930's, it was discovered that microscopic bubbles of air greatly improved the durability of concrete, particularly in areas exposed to hard winters. In most parts of North America, it is advisable to use "air-entrained" portland cement, which contains an agent to create the necessary air bubbles.

Water forms between 15% and 20% of the volume in properly mixed concrete. The water combines chemically with the dry cement, forming a paste which holds the particles of aggregate together.

Aggregate is inert and plays no part in the chemical process of concrete. Yet it is the real basis for its durability and strength, constituting from 66% to 78% of good concrete. Two types of aggregate — fine and coarse — are used in concrete. The fine aggregate is always sand. Coarse aggregates are natural or crushed stone, gravel or slag.

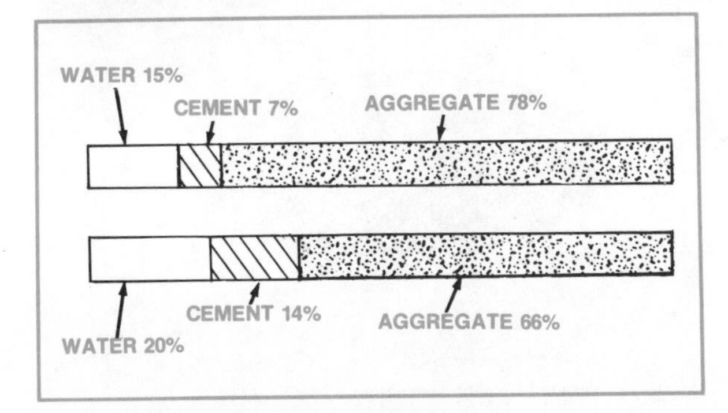

Graph shows range of good concrete mixes. Larger dots represent larger aggregates.

Aggregate comes in varying types and sizes, with bigger pieces used in bigger jobs like bridge pilings. The smaller the job, the smaller the aggregate size. For home use, varying-size, well-graded smaller aggregates make the best concrete and are cheaper than any one size.

All aggregate — including sand — should be clean and free of loam, clay or vegetable matter, since these organic particles prevent the cement paste from properly binding the aggregate. Concrete containing foreign matter will be porous and have poor strength. You can, if you wish, fill in a large excavation such as a house foundation with almost any inorganic material such as old concrete, broken bricks, rocks, iron, etc. This takes up space and saves money on concrete. It also gets rid of a lot of debris in the bargain.

THE PROPER MIX

It is vital that the concrete ingredients be in the right proportions. Too much or too little of any one ingredient will cause cracking, dusting, chipping, or some other imperfection. For larger jobs, it is best to order ready-mix from a local concrete service. The "cement" truck will not only bring a perfect mix, but save many hours of back-breaking work.

For very small jobs, a bag of premixed cement and aggregate will solve the same problems.

Courtesy of Portland Cement Association

To insure that you have the proper mix, order ready-mix concrete from a local supplier.

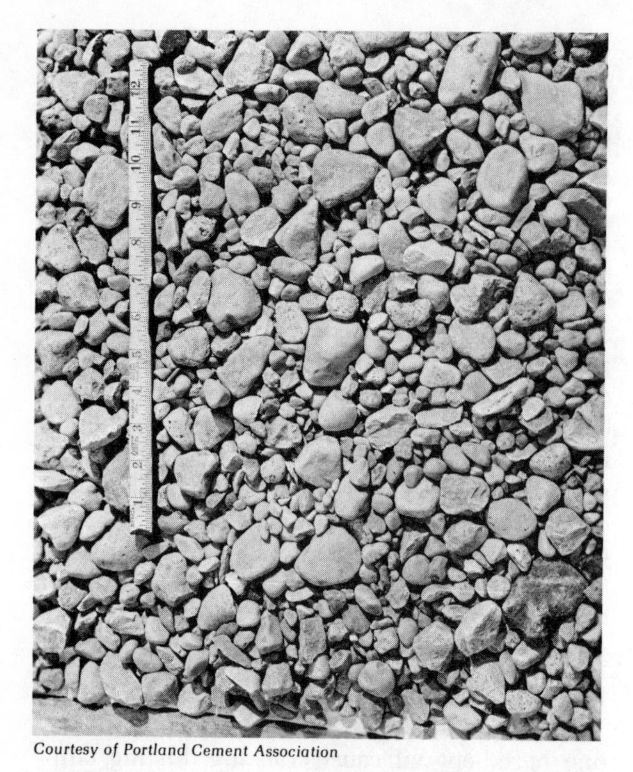

Courtesy of Portland Cement Association

A variety of coarse aggregates is best for most home projects. This well-graded mix contains pieces from 1/4 to one inch in diameter.

Courtesy of Portland Cement Association

A proper, workable mix trowels easily, with all spaces between coarse aggregate filled with sand and cement paste.

Here, just add water as directed on the package, and place the mix.

Most do-it-yourself jobs, nevertheless, fall somewhere in between large and very small. Sometimes, too, the area is inaccessible. For these applications, it is possible to mix your own. You can work up a good concrete mix by following two simple rules. First, always buy clean ingredients from a building or masonry supply dealer. (Sand or stones from the beach will contain organic matter and ruin the mix.) Second, use the proper formula. For typical home use, follow this guide:

94 pounds of cement (one U.S bag)
215 pounds of sand
295 pounds of coarse aggregate
5 gallons of water

A regular bathroom scale is accurate enough for weighing the materials. Use a large bucket to hold the material, but be sure to weigh the bucket first and deduct its weight from the weight of the material. Don't put any more in the bucket than you can handle. Load the sand and aggregate into three or four buckets of equal weight. Once you get the right weight established, mark a line on the bucket for each ingredient and put the scale back in the bathroom.

A simpler, but less accurate, guide is by volume. Use one part portland cement to 2 1/4 parts sand and three parts coarse aggregate. Add five gallons of water for each bag. These one-bag formulas should yield approximately 1/6 cubic yard of concrete.

Sometimes moisture in the sand or the size of the aggregate will throw off the above proportions,

Courtesy of Portland Cement Association

This mix is too wet, with too little sand and coarse aggregate for the amount of cement and water.

Courtesy of Portland Cement Association

This mix is too stiff. It contains too much sand and coarse aggregate and will be difficult to place and work.

Courtesy of Portland Cement Association

This mix is too sandy. It does not contain enough coarse aggregate and is subject to cracking.

Courtesy of Portland Cement Association

This mix is too stony. There is too much coarse aggregate and too little sand. It would be almost impossible to work and would produce porous concrete.

so be sure to make a test batch before forging ahead with the whole job. If the test batch is too wet, add about 5-10% more sand and aggregate and test again. If the mix looks too stiff, add proportionally more water *and* cement (never water alone) to the test batch. In subsequent batches, decrease the amount of sand and aggregate to accomplish the same purpose.

A mix that is too sandy requires a shifting of the aggregate proportions. Add about four pounds of stone to the test batch. In subsequent batches, decrease the sand by about two pounds and add the two pounds of coarse aggregate. If the mix is too stony, change the aggregate ratios in the opposite manner as the preceding (add sand and subtract stone in future batches). To save the test batch, add about four pounds of sand.

TOOLS YOU'LL NEED

Placing and working concrete is demanding physical work, so don't attempt it if you are in poor physical condition or if you have a medical problem like a heart condition.

Tools you will need depends on how much of this type work you plan to do. If a small slab or

Courtesy of Portland Cement Association

Photo shows the type of shovel used in concrete work. It has a square end and a short handle.

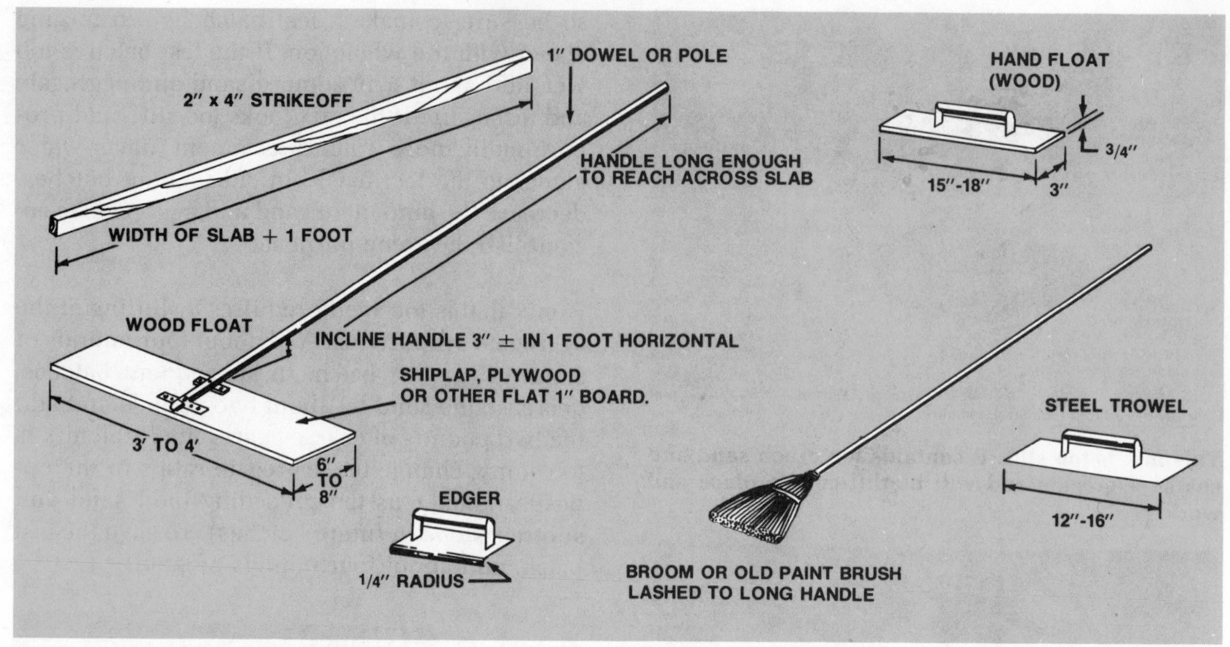

Courtesy of Portland Cement Association

Here are some of the essential tools.

some patchwork is all you have in mind, a piece of 2x4 and a pointed trowel will be about all you'll need. Jobs of any size, however, will also require the use of a wood hand float; a long-handled bull float; a rectangular steel trowel; an edger; a short-handled, square-end shovel (not a spade) and a concrete rake (a large hoe with a hole in the center of the blade). It also helps to have kneeboards, a mortar box, a wheelbarrow, a "darby" and a groover. For large areas when making your own concrete, a portable mixer is almost a must. (You can rent one or possibly buy a used one for $100 or so.) You will also need a garden hose, lumber forms, and some burlap or sheet plastic for curing. There are several other professional machines which may come in handy for special purposes. The uses for all these tools will be described as they fall into sequence.

Courtesy of Portland Cement Association

A "darby" is a handy tool used not only for floating and smoothing, but also as a strike-off tool.

SUBGRADE AND FORMS

The first step in concrete construction is to prepare the subgrade. All sod and vegetable matter must be removed, and any wet, soft or mucky places should be filled with a six-inch bed of gravel, thoroughly compacted. Exceptionally hard, compact spots must be loosened and tamped to provide the same bearing resistance as the rest of the subgrade.

If fill is required to raise the subgrade, it too should be of granular material like gravel, thoroughly compacted into layers of six inches. All filled areas should extend at least one foot beyond all sides of the concreted area itself. Steep grades should be avoided, since heavy rains can cause undercutting.

Forms can be of wood or metal. Most homeowners use 2x4s staked firmly with 1x4. On curves, use 1/4-inch plywood with the grain of the outside plies vertical for easy bending: 1x4 can be used if the curve isn't too sharp.

Steps and other more complex projects require more elaborate and rigid forming. When planning stairs, be sure to check local building codes regarding allowable dimensions and relationships between risers and treads. (See details on building stairs.)

A) SUGGESTED DETAIL AT JOINT BETWEEN STRAIGHT AND CURVED FORMS.
SMOOTH INNER FORM FACE
1/4" PLYWOOD
2 x 4 FORM
2 x 2 STAKE
B) USE 1/4" PLYWOOD OR HARDBOARD FOR SHORT RADIUS CURVES.
PLYWOOD GRAIN VERTICAL
STAKES AT 1 TO 2 FT. INTERVALS
1 x 4 FORM
C) USE 1" LUMBER FOR LONG RADIUS CURVES.
STAKES AT 2 TO 3 FT. INTERVALS
2 x 4 FORM
CUT 1/2 to 2/3 +
D) USE SAW KERFING TO BEND 2" LUMBER. BEND SO THAT CUTS CLOSE.

Courtesy of Portland Cement Association

There are several ways of forming curves, as shown. The easiest way is by using strips of 1/4 inch plywood.

There is no need for reinforcing wire in most home projects. The only exceptions are applications where great strength is vital, such as the foundation for an outdoor fireplace.

Courtesy of Portland Cement Association

For a level surface, line up the top of the forms with a line drawn taut between stakes.

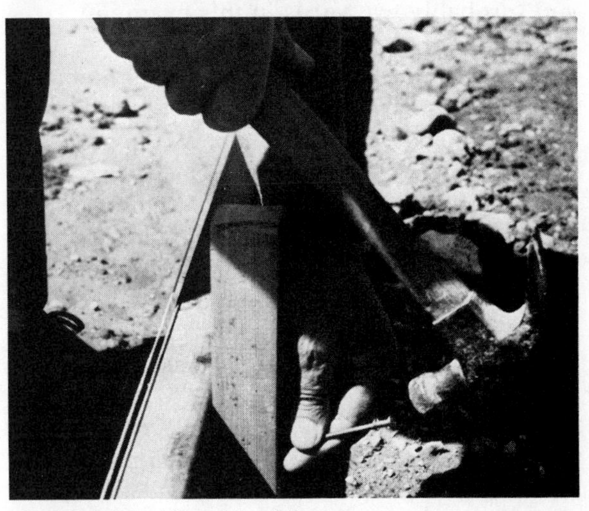

Courtesy of Portland Cement Association

Nail stakes to the outside of the forms, preferably using double-headed nails for easy removal.

ORDERING MATERIALS

Most home concrete projects are variations of a slab, which usually requires a four-inch thickness. To figure out how much concrete is needed, find the volume of your project (length x width x depth). Since there are 27 cubic feet in a yard, divide the result by 27 and you have the cubic yards needed. It is even easier to use the following chart:

Thickness, in.	Area in square ft. (width x length)					
	10	25	50	100	200	300
4	0.12	0.31	0.62	1.23	2.47	3.70
5	0.15	0.39	0.77	1.54	3.09	4.63
6	0.19	0.46	0.93	1.85	3.70	5.56

For a 6 x 20-foot walk, for example, multiply the dimensions to get 120 square feet. Using the chart, enter 1.23 for 100 square feet, then add .31 for 25 feet, the nearest amount to 20, and you get a sum of 1.58 cubic yards. Since your total reflects a 125-foot area instead of the actual 120, you may possibly rely on 1.5 cubic yards of concrete, but this assumes that you have graded and measured exactly, and that you won't waste a drop of concrete. It is much better to have a little more than you may need. If mixing it yourself, figure on 5-10% additional. For ready-mix, get whatever higher amount the supplier will sell you (probably two yards in this example).

A ready-mix dealer can give you more precision in the mix than you can achieve yourself, so you may as well take advantage of it. When ordering, specify at least six sacks of cement per cubic yard and five to six percent air entrainment. Ask for coarse gravel aggregate with 1 to 1½-inch maximum diameter, and request not more than a four-inch "slump" (a measurement of the workability). Tell the supplier you want the 28-day compressive strength to be 3500 pounds per square inch.

It is best to order ready-mix a day ahead, and be sure to direct the dealer exactly when and where to deliver it. When mixing your own, get all the materials ahead of time in the proportions mentioned earlier. Either way, don't be independent. It takes at least two persons to place and finish concrete. For larger jobs, three workers or more are recommended.

PLACING THE MIX

Before the concrete is placed, wet the surrounding earth and the forms with a garden hose. Have a wheelbarrow handy for both ready and home-made mix. (If there is much wheelbarrowing to be done, add still one more person to the two or three recommended above.)

Place the concrete in the forms to the full depth, spading along the sides to complete filling. Try to load the concrete as close as possible to its final position without too much dragging and spading. This will not only save your strength, but will prevent overworking the mix. Use your square-end shovel and/or concrete rake for this.

Do not pour too large a portion of your slab at one time. The mix should be placed and bull-floated as quickly as possible. After placing, strike off the surface with a 2x4 straightedge, working it in a saw-like motion across the top of the form boards. This "screeding" action will smooth the surface while cutting off the concrete to the proper elevation. Go over the concrete twice in this manner to take out any bumps or fill in low spots. Tilt the straightedge slightly in the direction of travel to obtain a better cutting effect.

Courtesy of Visqueen

It is best to have plenty of help when the ready-mix arrives. Shoveling concrete into the right place requires at least three strong backs.

The concrete slab is "struck off" using a 2 x 4 with a sawlike motion across the surface. The job goes much faster if two men are used.

Immediately after striking off, the surface is rough-floated to smooth it and remove irregularities. Use the small wood hand float for small or close work, and the large "bull" float (made of wood or steel) for larger areas. The "darby" is an excellent all-around tool that can be used as a straightedge as well as a float. The bull float is tilted slightly away from you as you push it forward, then flattened as it is pulled back. The darby is held flat against the surface of the slab and worked from side to side.

Do not overdo any of the preceding motions. Overworking of concrete causes excessive water and fine particles to rise to the surface, which renders the surface more prone to flaking and chipping.

Courtesy of Portland Cement Association

The bull float is tilted slightly away from the operator as it is pushed forward. On the way back, it should be perfectly flat.

Courtesy of Portland Cement Association

The darby is held against the surface of the slab and worked from side to side to float the concrete.

FINISHING

If you use air-entrained concrete as recommended, finishing can usually follow immediately after floating. However — particularly when the weather is cool and humid — check the surface before finishing. Make sure that there is no water sheen on the surface, and test proper stiffening with your foot. The indentation from your shoe should be no more than 1/4 inch before proceeding further. You can help ensure that the surface is dry enough by taking a little time before finishing to cut away the concrete from the forms. Work a pointed trowel along the forms to a depth of about an inch.

Courtesy of Portland Cement Association

Before finishing the surface, cut away the concrete from the forms by running a pointed trowel alongside.

Courtesy of Portland Cement Association

The edger gives the corners of a concrete slab a little extra dignity by virtue of a smooth and slightly rounded corner.

The first finishing step is edging, which should take place as soon as the surface is stiff enough to hold the shape of the edging tool. The edger is run between the form and the concrete with the body of the tool held flat on the concrete surface except for the leading edge, which is tilted up slightly.

Control joints are desirable if the slab is more than 10 feet in any direction. These joints help control large cracks. They are made with a "groover," which is similar to an edger except that it cuts down the middle. The tool should cut to a depth from 1/5 to 1/4 of the slab thickness. (A portable circular saw can be equipped with a masonry-cutting blade to accomplish the same purpose as the groover.)

Courtesy of Portland Cement Association

Redwood divider strips are attractive as well as functional, but the tops should be protected from cement discoloration by applying masking tape.

Courtesy of Portland Cement Association

Control joints are cut with a "groover" or double-edger.

Courtesy of Portland Cement Association

Finish floating is done with a wood float. This can be a final, non-skid finish, if desired, or it can be followed by troweling.

Isolation joints are similar to control joints, except that they are inserted before the concrete is placed. They are used whenever two surfaces join with potential stress, such as between a sidewalk and a driveway or building, and around obstructions such as manholes and poles. A 1/2 inch-thick fiber material is nailed to the forms about 1/4 inch below the surface and left there.

One excellent way to achieve the goals of control and isolation joints, plus a nice decorative touch, is to use redwood 2x4s at regular intervals. The redwood forms are left in the grass as divider strips, but should be protected by masking tape while working.

Finish floating is done with the hand float. This procedure eliminates any remaining imperfections — like the marks from the edger and groover — and produces a smoother surface, with large aggregates embedded and mortar consolidated at the top for further finish operations. If a rough surface is desired, as it should be for a non-skid surface, finish floating can be the final step. In that case, a *wood* float is essential, and a second floating may be in order after the surface has hardened somewhat.

Courtesy of Portland Cement Association

Troweling is the final step in smooth concrete finishing. The hand trowel should be held flat to the surface.

Courtesy of Portland Cement Association

The safest and most effective curing method for the homeowner is done by using clean, wet burlap bags.

Although the slightly rough surface created by floating is safer, many people prefer the smooth finish created by troweling. For this purpose, rectangular, steel-bladed trowels are used. At least two passes are necessary. Even if an automatic trowel is used for the first step, it is always followed by hand troweling. The final troweling should produce a ringing sound as the blade traverses the hardened surfaces.

CURING

The chemical reaction between water and cement is called hydration. This process must continue for several days to a week after the concrete is placed in order for the concrete to attain maximum durability. Hydration stops if too much water is lost by evaporation, or if the temperature falls below 50 degrees Fahrenheit.

Curing is an essential step and is designed to keep water in the concrete for the right length of time. To stop evaporation, several methods are used, the best of which is simply keeping the surface moist. To do this, wash out some burlap bags with a hose to remove any foreign matter that can cause discoloration. Place the bags on top of the concrete and wet them down, keeping them wet during the entire curing period.

Another way of keeping the surface wet is by running a sprinkler or soaking hose continuously over the surface. For small jobs, try "ponding," or dikes around the edges of the job which keep a pool of water on the slab.

An easier but less effective way to cure concrete is by spreading sheet plastic or waterproof paper over the entire surface. These materials form a moisture barrier and thus prevent evaporation. To do a proper job, however, the plastic or paper must be thoroughly sealed at joints and anchored firmly on all sides. The material must be laid perfectly flat to avoid discoloration.

The easiest way of all is to use a curing compound which is sprayed on the surface soon after finishing. Complete coverage is essential, and a second coat, applied at right angles to the first, is recommended when in doubt. Don't use curing compounds in cooler weather, since they may interfere with proper air-drying of the concrete and make it more prone to scaling.

It is best, as a matter of fact, not to lay concrete at all if there is any chance of the temperature falling below 50 degrees Fahrenheit. If you *must* place it during cooler weather, order heated ready-mix, and apply insulating blankets of straw one to two feet deep. Cover the straw with sheet plastic, waterproof paper or canvas. If a cold snap happens unexpectedly while concrete is curing, it is wise to cover the surface in the same way until warm weather reappears.

Curing time can be as little as three days, but at least five days are recommended in warm weather and seven in cold weather. During very hot, dry weather, hydration may occur very rapidly, and precautions should be taken to prevent excess evaporation while working. Be sure to wet the area thoroughly before placing, and work as rapidly as possible. Try to work in some sort of shade, and avoid the hot hours of late morning and early afternoon. (The cooler hours will be kinder to your body as well as the concrete.)

DECORATIVE FINISHES

Many people are perfectly content with typical light gray, rough or smooth-surfaced concrete. There are, however, a variety of specialized concrete applications which have more eye appeal than plain concrete.

Coloring — If you have ever tried to paint concrete, you know that all too soon the paint wears or starts flaking off, and the concrete becomes unsightly. Those who like colored concrete are well advised to pay the extra cost of having color worked into the concrete itself. If you simply want a nice white look instead of the usual concrete gray, order white portland cement instead of regular.

Other colors require the addition of a pigment, and this is done in several ways. A coloring agent (a mineral oxide made especially for concrete) is added to the mix before it is poured.

Guide to Coloring Compounds

To Obtain	Use
White	White portland cement, white sand
Blue	Cobalt oxide
Brown	Brown oxide of iron or burnt umber
Buff	Synthetic yellow oxide of iron or yellow ocher
Green	Chromium oxide
Red	Red oxide of iron
Pink	Red oxide of iron (in small amounts)
Dark Gray	Black oxide of iron

This can be done with ready-mix or in your own batch. White portland cement provides brighter tints than regular gray cement, and should be used unless you're working with the darker pigments. Coloring agents are available from most of the same sources as the cement. They should not exceed 10 percent of the cement by weight.

To save money on pigment, pour the concrete in two courses, using the coloring agent only in the top courses. If you do this, however, be sure to leave the surface of the first course very rough to provide good "tooth" for the second. The top course should be only ½ to 1 inch thick.

If you prefer to use the quicker but more costly one-course method, make sure to either soak the ground thoroughly the night before or to put down a moisture barrier like plastic sheeting under the slab. If you don't, some pigment may escape with the water and cause uneven coloring.

It is also possible to color the concrete with dry shake compounds, applied by hand to the surface just before final floating. Two applications are necessary, and the surface must be floated, edged and grooved after each one.

Courtesy of Portland Cement Association

One of the several ways of coloring concrete is done by applying a dry-shake material during finishing. (The least desirable way is to paint afterwards.)

Exposed Aggregate — This popular terrazzo-like finish takes extra time, effort and money, but the investment is worthwhile. The surface is anti-skid and highly durable, as well as very attractive. For best results, buy colorful, rounded pebbles of equal size. Adjust your usual concrete formula to provide a stiffer mix with more and larger aggregates (or request a three-inch slump with ready-mix).

Your concrete mix is placed in the usual manner, except that it should be leveled off at 3/8 to 1/2 inch below the top of the forms to allow for the extra aggregate. Screed and float in the usual way, then spread your rounded stones evenly over the surface with your shovel. Fill in the bare spots by hand until the surface is completly covered with aggregate. If the first few stones sink to the bottom, wait a half-hour or so until the mix gets a little stiffer.

Courtesy of Portland Cement Association

An attractive decorative finish is achieved with exposed aggregate, here demonstrated in random-size stepping stones with a white cement and beach pebble surface.

Courtesy of Portland Cement Association

Rounded aggregate is spread over surface with a shovel and by hand over the partially-set surface of concrete.

Courtesy of Portland Cement Association

Pat the pebbles into the surface with a darby or hand float.

Courtesy of Portland Cement Association

An hour or two after the aggregate has been embeded, the surface should be thoroughly washed and broomed. Shown is rentable "water-broom", but garden hose and stiff nylon garage brush will do almost as well.

When you have a good, even stone cover, tap it into the surface of the concrete with a 2x4, darby or wood float. Then go over the entire surface with your wood hand float, working the stones down into the concrete until they are entirely covered again by cement paste. The surface will look almost like it did before.

Wait for an hour or two, until the slab can bear the weight of a man on kneeboards without leaving an indention. Then brush the surface lightly with a stiff nylon-bristle broom to remove the excess mortar.

The final — and most difficult — job is hard-brooming the surface while washing the stones with a fine spray. Either have a helper for this, or alternately spray and broom. But brush hard enough to dislodge as much cement film as you can. Ideally, all you should see are the pretty, colorful stones. If the surface is too full, give it a bath with muriatic acid.

TEXTURED AND NOVELTY FINISHES

A textured finish is one in which the regular floated or troweled surface is altered in some way. The most common — and easiest — pattern is a broomed finish. Simply work a stiff-bristle broom back and forth over a newly floated surface. Either a straight or wavy pattern provides a good-looking, skid-resistant surface. An attractive "swirl" finish is produced by making semicircles with a hand float or trowel. To produce a uniform pattern, use your entire arm and keep the wrist rigid.

Courtesy of Portland Cement Association

Brooming provides an attractive, skid-resistant surface.

Another textured technique scatters rock salt over the top of the slab after hand floating or troweling. The salt is pressed into the surface so that it is almost invisible. After the concrete has hardened, washing and brushing dissolve the salt, leaving a pitted surface.

Courtesy of Sakrete

Wooden dividers enable this patio to be poured in two or three work sessions. The garden pool and fountain are a pleasant addition to the area.

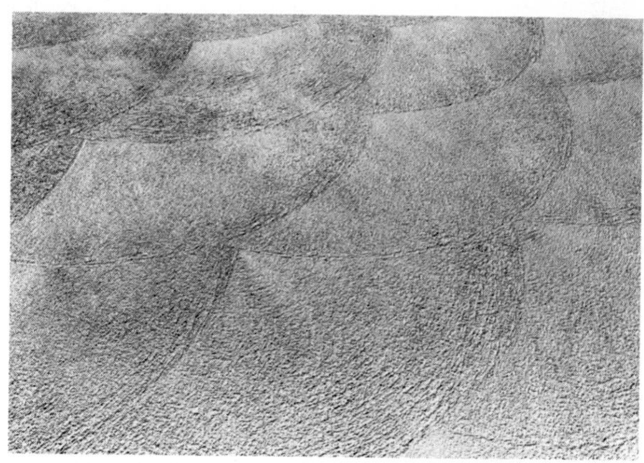

Courtesy of Portland Cement Association

A swirled finish is made with a trowel or hand float.

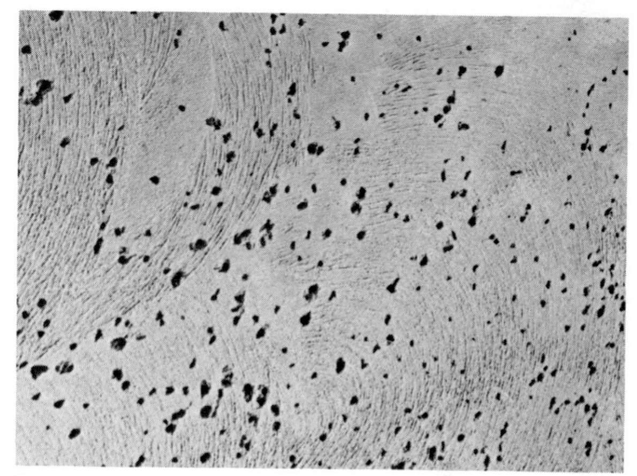

Courtesy of Portland Cement Association

This interesting texture was created by embedding rock salt crystals into the surface while finishing.

Geometric patterns can be pressed into the concrete surface using a variety of tools or instruments. A piece or curved copper pipe, for example, is used to produce a random flagstone pattern. The scored lines, which look like recessed joints, are made after bull-floating and while the mix is still plastic.

After hand-floating, the pipe should be run through again, and the joints cleaned of burrs with a fine broom and a soft-bristled paint brush. You can use empty cans of varied sizes to

create circles, or rent one of the devises shown in the photos to create brick and other patterns.

Another technique which is tricky but very interesting is a leaf pattern. Leaves are taken from nearby trees and pressed carefully into the surface with a trowel. The leaves should be completely embedded, but there should be no cement on top. After the concrete has set sufficiently, the leaves are removed. Thorough curing is especially important for this type of delicate finish.

Courtesy of Portland Cement Association

The random flagstone appearance can be created with a piece of copper pipe bent into a flat S-shape.

Courtesy of Portland Cement Association

This photo shows the pads used for the large area (note jointing tool used to dress grooves).

Courtesy of Sakrete

A variety of garden improvements can be made with concrete. A garden pool, a patio, and a group of stepping stones made with concrete add to the enjoyment of this yard area.

Courtesy of Portland Cement Association

Here a small hand stamp is used for the edges.

SIDEWALKS, DRIVEWAYS, PATIOS

The techniques described in detail above apply to the many varieties of concrete slabs. Sidewalks, driveways and patios differ only in their shape and size. Four-inch thicknesses are recommended for all these applications, unless your driveway is to be used for heavy vehicles, in which case a five- or even six-inch thickness is desirable.

Good planning is essential to any item of your home's landscape. Try, as best you can, to blend your concrete work into the setting and make it harmonize with, rather than intrude upon, the overall design.

Don't forget drainage. Handymen (even builders) sometimes build drives that drain into the garage, or patios that direct rainwater into the basement. If an area is already subject to erosion, be careful not to add to your problems by draining towards it. Remember that flat, impermeable areas — driveways in particular — act as conduits during heavy rains.

A driveway should be three feet wider than the largest vehicle that will use it. A one-car garage should have a driveway 10 to 14 feet wide, with 14 feet at the curves. Double garages should have a width of 16 to 24 feet at stretch. Short drives should be double width all the way. Maximum grade should be 14 percent (1-3/4 inch rise per foot) and changes in grade should be gradual to avoid scraping a car's undercarriage. There

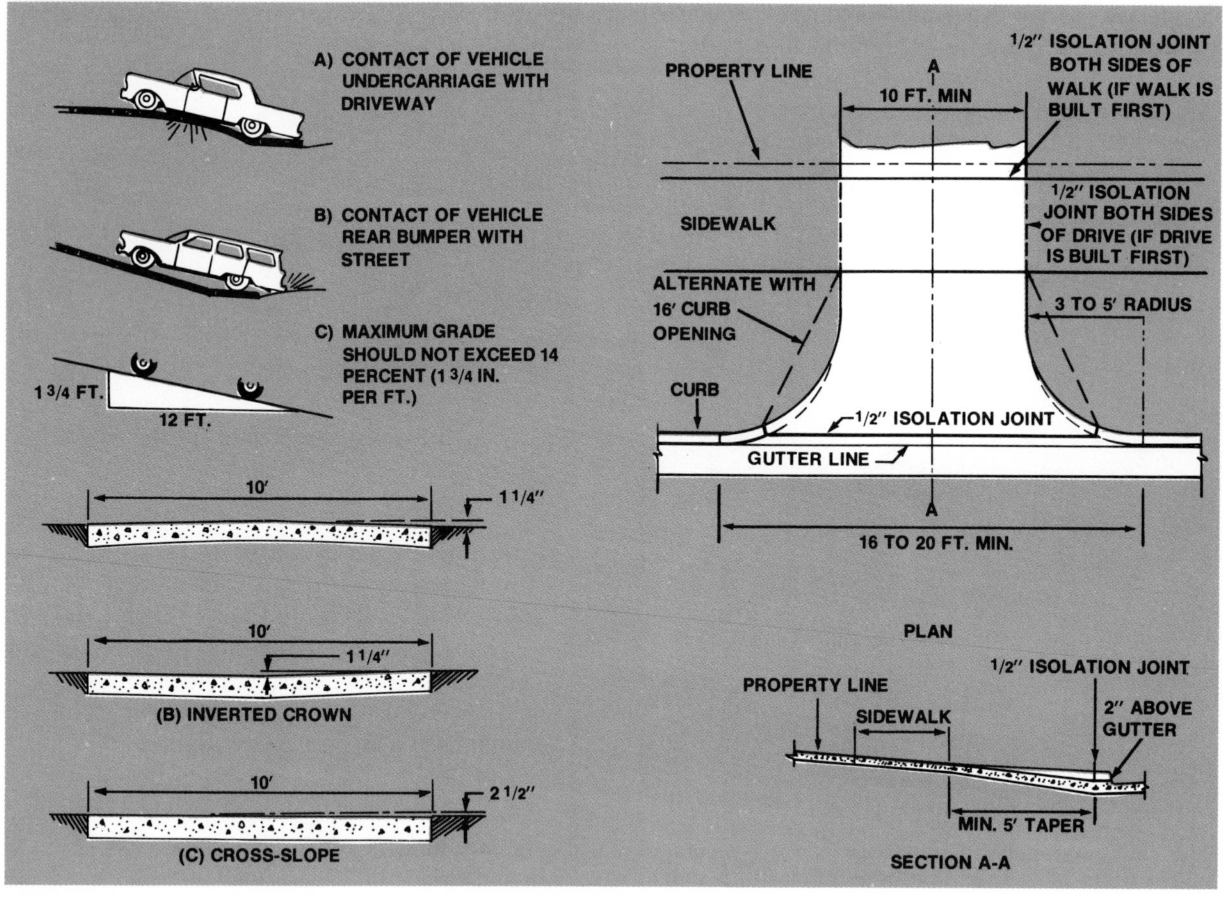

Courtesy of Portland Cement Association

Diagrams show (above left) good and bad driveway planning, (bottom left) methods of obtaining drainage and (right) details of typical driveway entrance.

Courtesy of Portland Cement Association

A driveway can be as simple or as complex as you like. Exposed aggregate and wood divider strips were combined here to make a very handsome approach.

Courtesy of Portland Cement Association

Use imagination when planning your front walk to make it as inviting as possible.

should be a minimum grade in the most favorable direction for drainage of at least 1/2-inch per foot. A driveway should be drained toward the street if at all possible.

Sidewalks leading to the front door of a home should be at least three to four feet wide; service entrances need only be two to three feet. Public walks along the front of your property should be four to five feet wide, or enough to allow two people walking abreast to pass a third person without crowding. In apartment, recreational or commercial areas, you may have to widen your driveway substantially to handle the foot traffic.

A concrete patio is no different from any other slab. There should be an isolation joint between the patio and the house or other structure. Sand boxes and planting areas can be built as an integral part if desired. Exposed aggregates and redwood control strips are especially effective in a patio setting. In areas where hot sun cannot be avoided, you may wish to add a roof.

MAKING CONCRETE STEPS

Concrete steps are a more difficult project for the homeowner than slab projects, but can be

built with proper care. You should not attempt to build more than a three-step project the first time.

Steps should be at least as wide as the sidewalk, and all risers should be exactly the same height (no more than 7 1/2 inches). Treads should be the same distance from front to back, at least 11 inches. Allow a 1/8-inch pitch on each tread for drainage. (Check local building codes.)

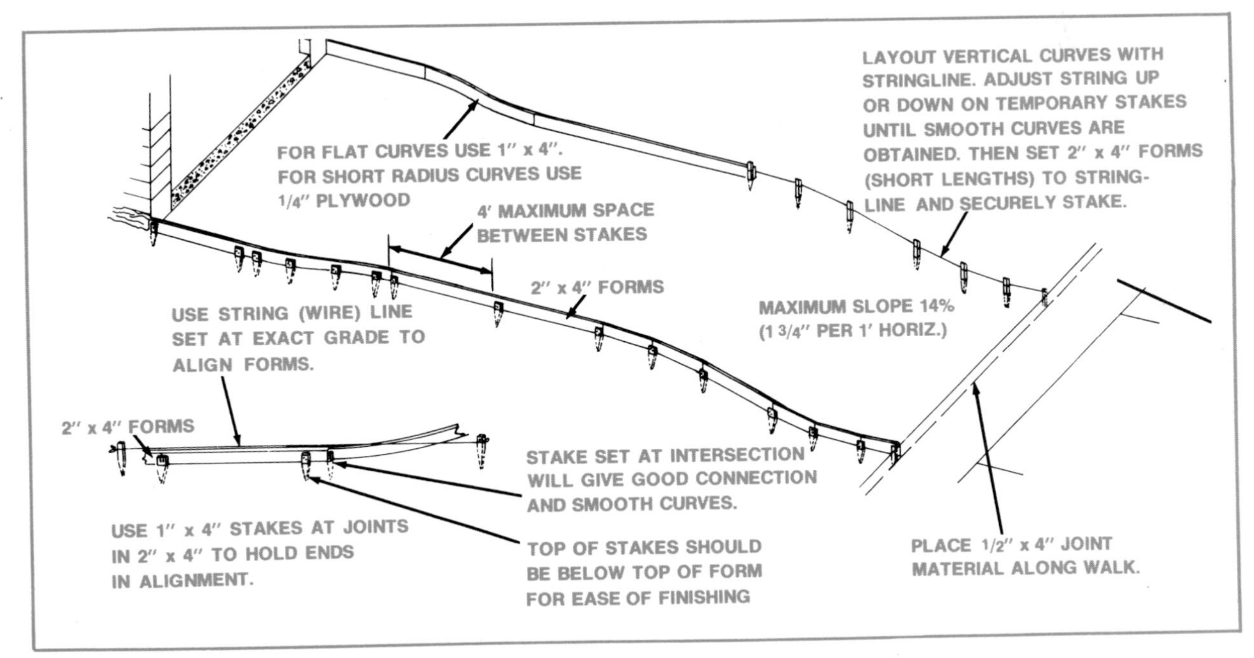

Courtesy of Portland Cement Association

Drawing shows formwork for typical one-car driveway.

Courtesy of Shakertown Corporation

The crisp line of concrete driveway blends with the formal crispness of the house design.

The best way to make a foundation for steps is to dig two of six- to eight-inch diameter postholes beneath the location of the bottom tread. The holes should extend at least two feet into the ground and six inches below the frostline. It is also advisable to tie the top step of the landing into the house foundation with two metal anchors. Drill a hole into the foundation and cement the anchor into the hole before pouring.

A simple step form is shown in the corresponding drawing. All forms must be rigidly braced, since the volume of concrete behind them is greater than that of a simple slab. Forms are usually made of one-inch boards, although sidewalls can be built of ³/₄-inch plywood if desired. The inside of the riser boards should be beveled toward the rear to allow tread finishing all the way back before the forms are removed. Forms should be oiled for easy removal.

You can save on concrete by filling the inside of the forms with old concrete or rocks. Concrete for this job is best ordered from a ready-mix dealer. Ask for a three-inch slump and one-inch aggregate. If mixing your own, make the mix stiff by using more aggregates.

Place the concrete in the post holes first, then spade the concrete thoroughly around the form edges of the bottom step. Proceed to each higher step, tapping the forms lightly to release air bubbles. Strike off the concrete at tread level, starting at the top and working down. Use kneeboards to prevent sinking into the lower steps. Float, edge and finish in the same manner as any other concrete.

The simplest procedure is to leave the forms in place until curing is completed as previously described. After curing, remove the forms and

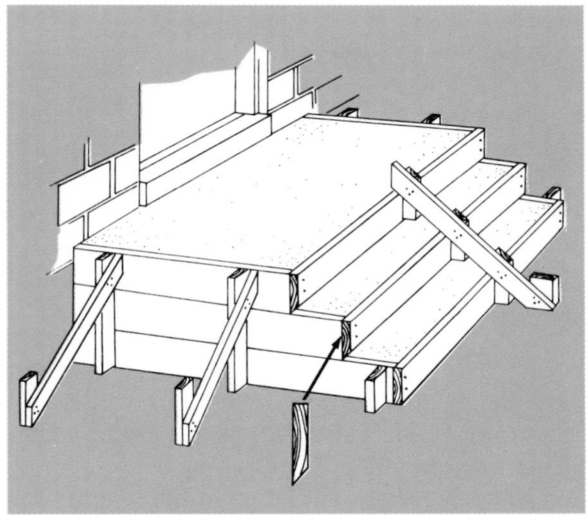

Courtesy of Portland Cement Association

Typical form arrangement for concrete steps. Note braces for side panels, and bevel on bottoms of rise forms which allows complete finishing of treads.

Courtesy of Portland Cement Association

Step treads are finished in the same way as a small concrete slab, while forms are kept in place until concrete dries. Here, an edger is used along rise form.

fill in any holes or voids with sandy patching cement. Projections are chipped or ground down.

Care in placing the concrete should keep defects down to a minimum, but if the job looks too bad after patching, go over the whole surface with cement grout to give it a uniform look. Make the grout with one part portland cement to $1^1/_2$-2 parts fine sand. Float vigorously to fill all voids. Rub with dry burlap to remove dried grout.

Courtesy of Portland Cement Association

Precast concrete comes in many forms, such as exposed aggregate rounds for informal gardens, or squares for more formal patios.

PRECAST CONCRETE

Precast concrete is available in a variety of applications, from an entire set of steps to small squares or circles. Precast steps, even though hollow inside, are very heavy and demand some sort of power lift for placement. Even precast sidewalk slabs are too heavy for hand work and require a vacuum lifting device.

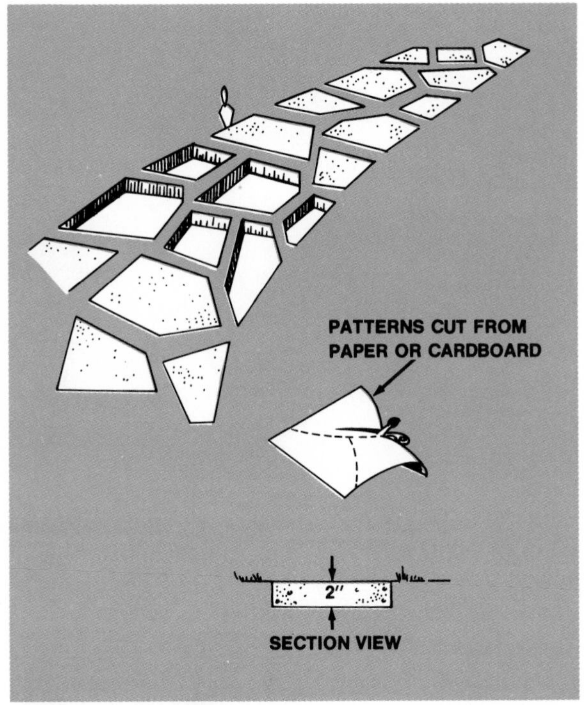

Courtesy of Portland Cement Association

Enchanting garden walks can be cast in place, as long as there is not heavy traffic.

Precast rounds come in regular, exposed-aggregate and other patterns. They are ideal for informal patios, garden walks and other uses. Blocks can be used in more formal settings as well as more rustic applications. For proper installation, the ground beneath precast blocks should be level, with a flat bed of sand or mortar on top of the subgrade.

Sometimes, as long as traffic isn't too heavy, you can get an excellent result by casting concrete in place. A flagstone-like walk can be built by carefully digging out sections of ground, using a sand bed up to two inches below the surface and pouring the concrete into the holes.

PATCHING AND REPAIRS

If a section of driveway or sidewalk is heaved and broken by tree roots, the best cure is to break up the section with a sledgehammer, remove the concrete and chop off the root. A tree with roots that big and powerful will be mature enough to survive, and you can simply replace the sidewalk section. Save the broken pieces, though, and use them as fill.

If the problem is flaking or other surface deterioration, you can probably do a quicker and easier job with vinyl patching cement. This type of patch can be "feathered" at the edges and will not wear like other cement compounds. Chip out the bad areas and apply the vinyl patch with a steel trowel.

When only certain areas are damaged, or if a large crack appears which should be filled, the deteriorated parts should be cut out with a cold chisel, undercutting the crack or edge in a "V" shape. Ordinary concrete, with finer aggregates, can be used for this type of patching, or premixed non-vinyl patch can be purchased at the hardware store. The undercut edges should hold the patch in the same way your tooth holds a filling.

FASTENERS

Fastening to concrete has always been a problem, but there are many devices available today which are quite effective. When concrete is fresh, masonry anchors can be set right into

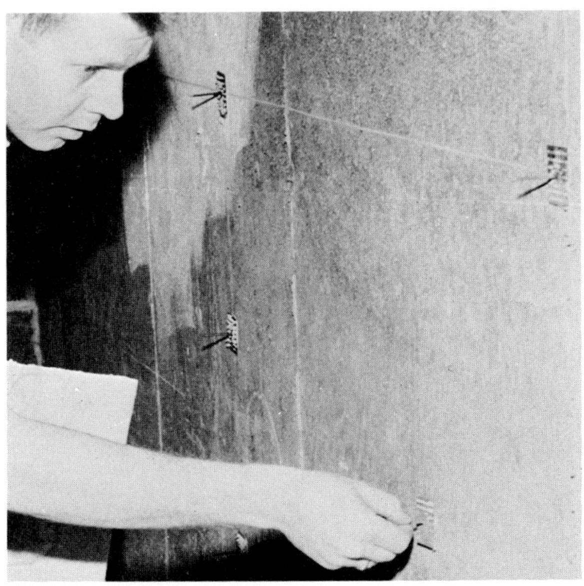

Courtesy of Portland Cement Association

The anchor nail is fastened to concrete with adhesive. Furring strips, 2 x 4, etc. are then pressed onto the protruding nail.

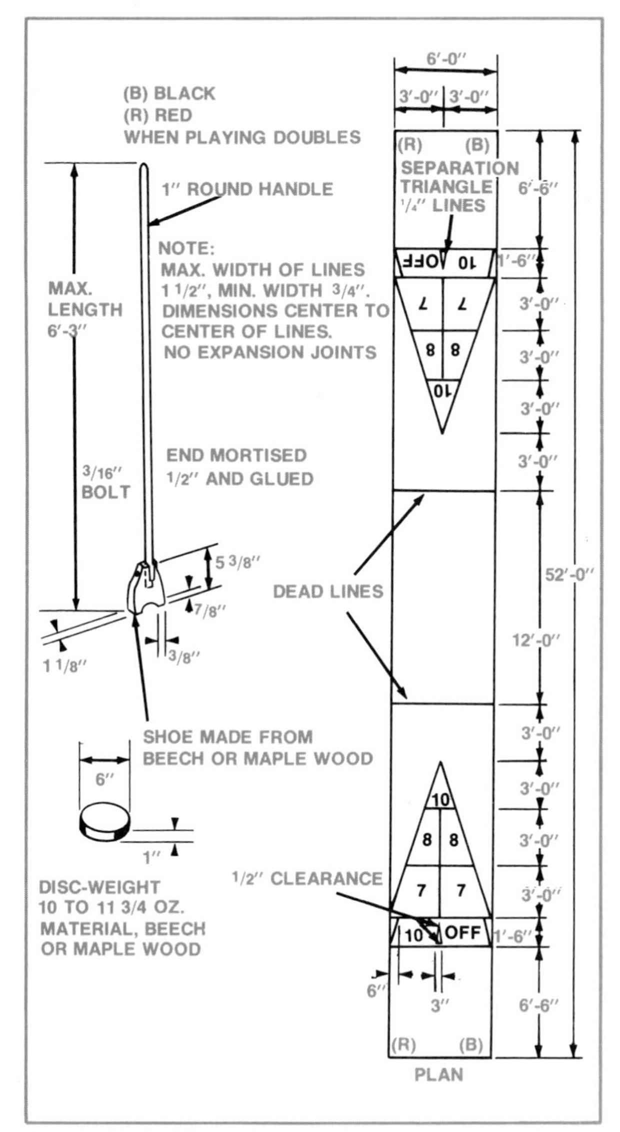

Courtesy of Portland Cement Association

Illustration shows a home-made shuffleboard, plus sticks and disc. Court is a simple slab, following dimensions shown.

the mix. Fastening becomes increasingly difficult as the concrete hardens and matures.

If the concrete is reasonably new, helical (spiral) concrete nails are the most efficient way to hold furring strips and other wood pieces. Make sure, however, that the nails are just slightly longer than the wood thickness, or they will not hold. Use a heavy mash or ball-peen hammer when driving concrete nails, and be sure to wear goggles.

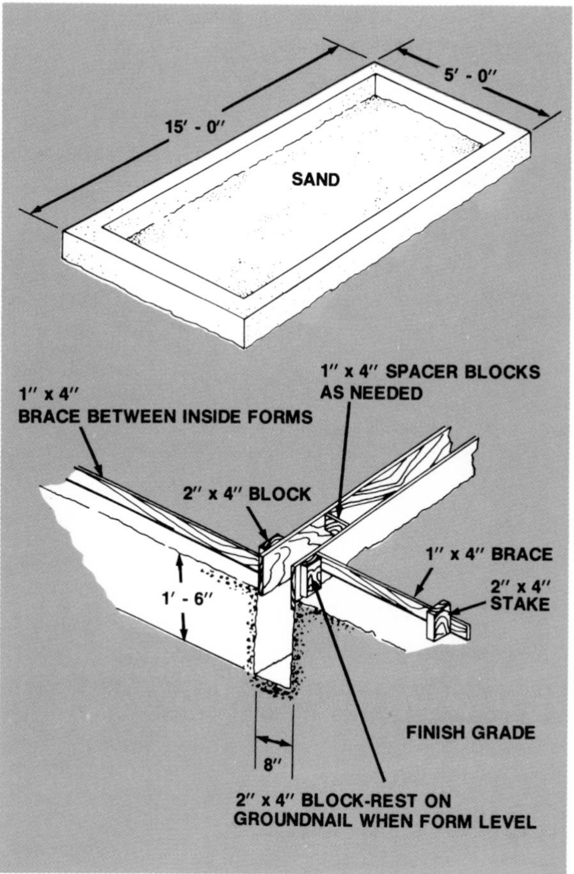

Courtesy of Portland Concrete Association

Here's an easy project that will delight the kids. For the size shown, you'll need $1\frac{2}{3}$ yards of concrete, but dimensions can be varied to suit your own needs.

When concrete has hardened for several years or so, it is best to make a hole with a star drill or ceramic bit in an electric drill at low speed. Insert a lead, fiber or plastic anchor into the hole. A lag or other screw expands the fastener and holds it tight.

There are several other types of devices that can be used for concrete fastening. One is the anchor nail or "spindle clip" that is attached to the wall with adhesive. Wood or other soft material is then pushed onto the protruding nail. If the nail is too long, it is bent over to further secure the material. There is also a pin device with varying types of plastic heads. Or, you can also buy a special type of "gun" which holds the fastening pin steady while you hammer the "trigger."

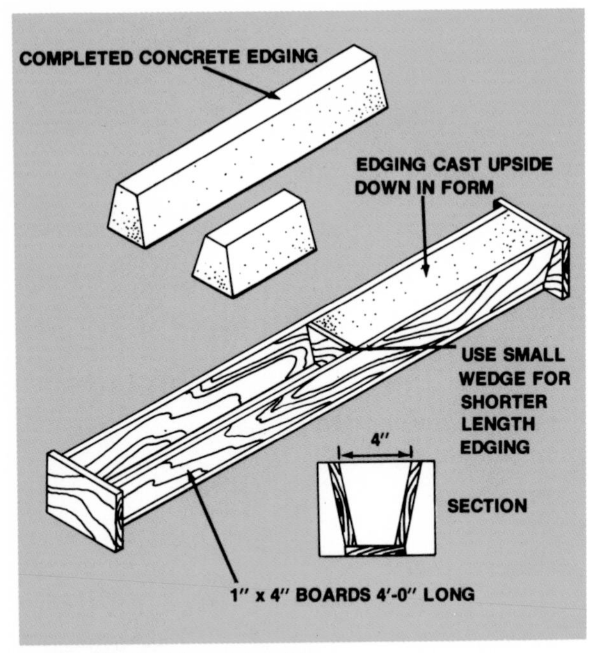

Courtesy of Portland Cement Association

Create your own precast garden edging with the simple wood mold shown in the diagram.

Concrete Block

Concrete block is commonly the preferred material for wall and building construction. It is easier to lay block on block than it is to erect elaborate forms for poured concrete. Once the technique is learned, a reasonably skilled handyman can put up concrete block in surprisingly short order.

Some of the projects that lend themselves to block, rather than poured concrete, are fireplaces, barbecue grills, retaining walls and walls of garages and homes, including additions. Handsome fences and privacy walls can be built with the many types of decorative masonry which are an ornamental form of concrete block. Even in-ground swimming pools can be built using concrete block, either with a vinyl liner or mortar "parge" coating. (The block alone is too rough and porous).

In addition to the decorative masonry mentioned above, there are also special facings made to blend with other types of materials such as *stone-faced* block, which is designed to blend with the stone foundations of older homes. Most "brick" walls are really brick veneer, with concrete block providing stability.

Tools needed for working with concrete block are: a pointed trowel, a mason's hammer (with a chisel point on one end for breaking the blocks), a brick chisel for fine cutting, and a good level, preferably a mason's level.

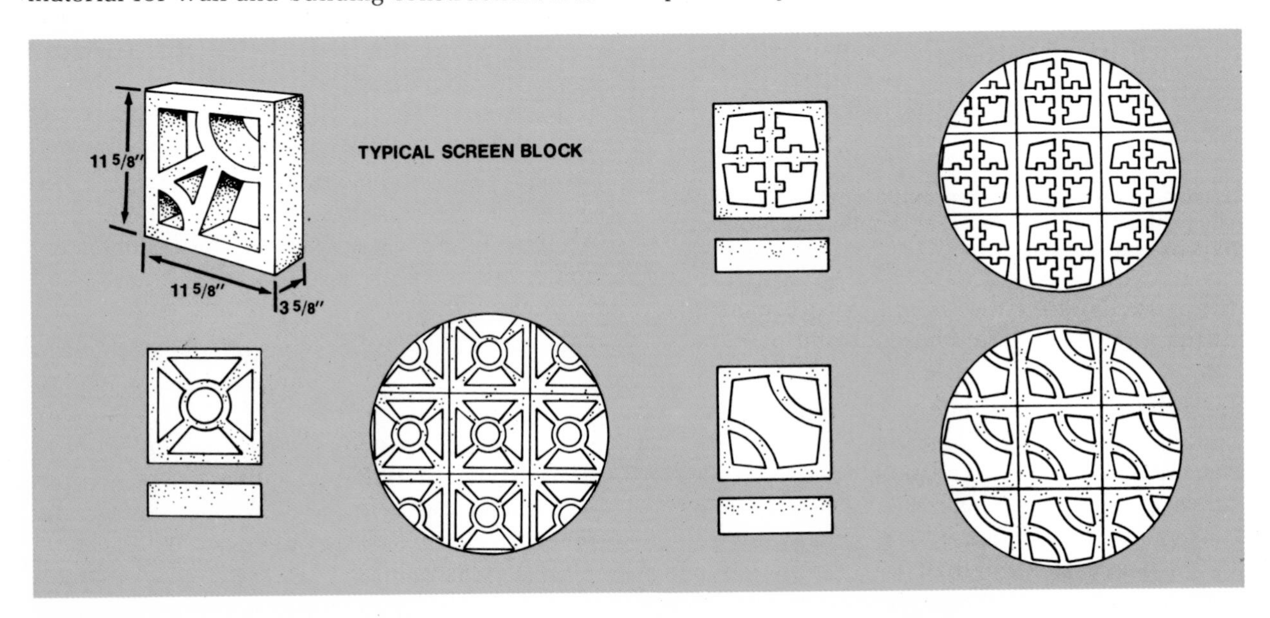

Decorative screen block is used for garden walls, to provide a barrier, yet allow the breeze through.

PLANNING

Be very exact when working with block. Depending on the needs of the project, it is wise to plan every dimension in multiples of eight inches. Standard concrete block is actually $7^5/_8''$ by $7^5/_8''$ by $15^5/_8''$, but the joint mortar brings the building units to exactly 8 x 8 x 16 inches. Half-blocks (eight-inch cubes) are used when 16 inches is too long. The closer the project comes to eight-inch modules, the simpler and cheaper it will be.

FOOTINGS

Block is always laid on a poured concrete footing. The footing must be at least two feet below the surface or six inches below the frostline. Footings should be twice as wide as the wall, so the standard footing is 16 inches. The usual footing is also as deep as the wall is wide, in this case eight inches.

For extra strength, key the footing with a groove down the center, so that the mortar fills in and creates a firmer bond between the footing and the first course. A 1 x 4 board embedded in the footing will accomplish this purpose.

No special finishing is necessary for footings, since no one will see them, but they must be as level as possible to provide a good start for the block. Retaining walls or other walls that will undergo a great deal of stress should be braced with steel reinforcing rods through the block cores. If rods are used, they should be embedded in the footings for maximum strength.

STARTING

Block is only one part of the equation. Good mortar is the other half. Masonry cement comes in several sized bags, the most common, one cubic foot. Follow manufacturers' instructions for the

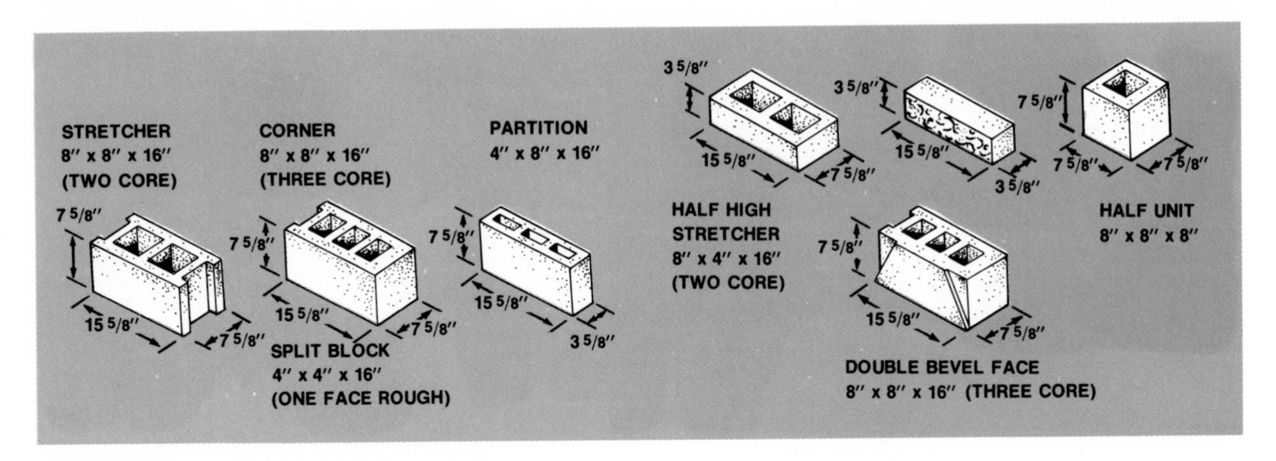

Concrete block is usually thought of as having three holes or cores, and ears at both ends. Actually, there are many types of standard building blocks, a few of which are shown. Three-hole stretchers are most common types.

best mix, but the usual is one part masonry cement to three parts sand, plus just enough water to make the mix workable. A mud-like consistency is best. Premixed mortar is easy to use and widely available. Simply add water as instructed.

For the first course, use a *full bed* of mortar, as opposed to *face-shell* bedding for the other courses. A full mortar bed simply means that the entire horizontal surface is covered with mortar instead of just the front and back. Footings should be wet down first to minimize absorp-

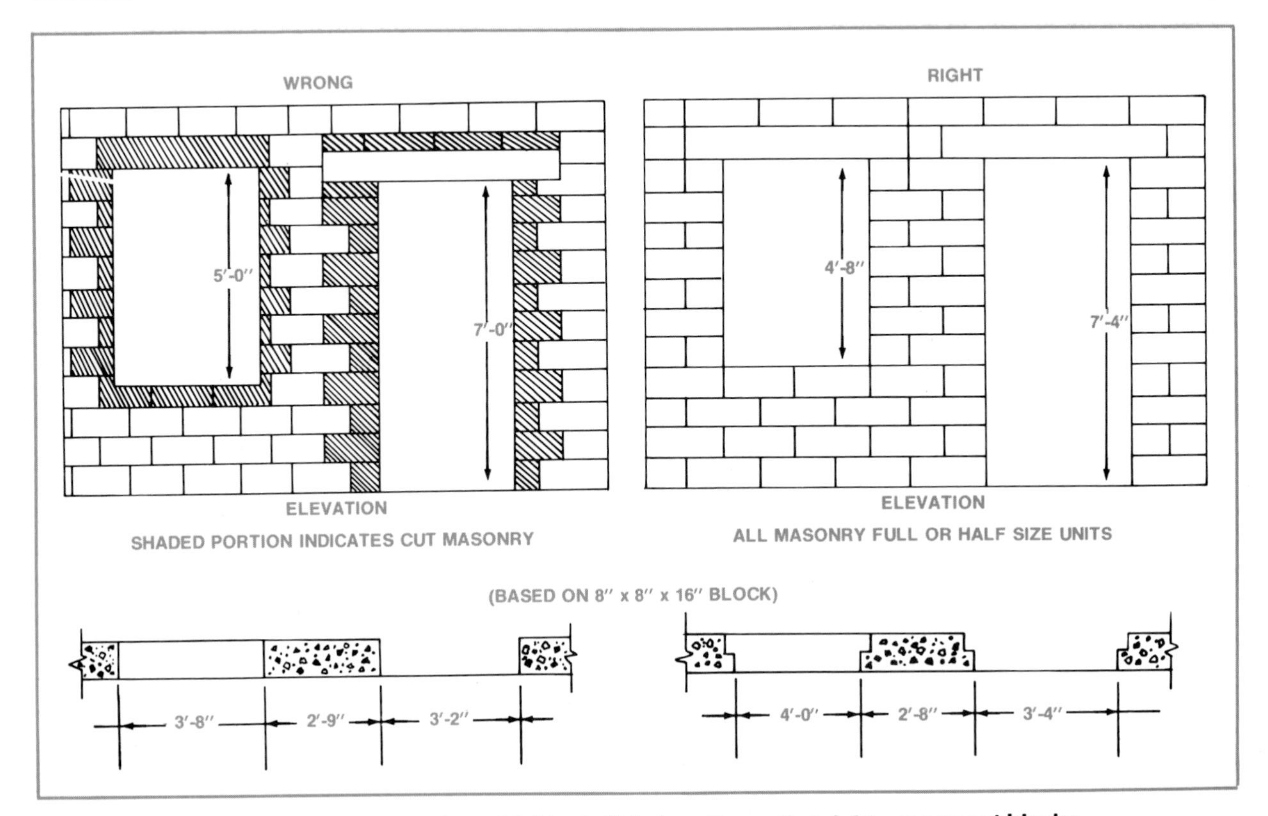

Good planning is essential when working with block. Note how the wall at right uses no cut blocks, while the illustration at left has cut-work surrounding both openings.

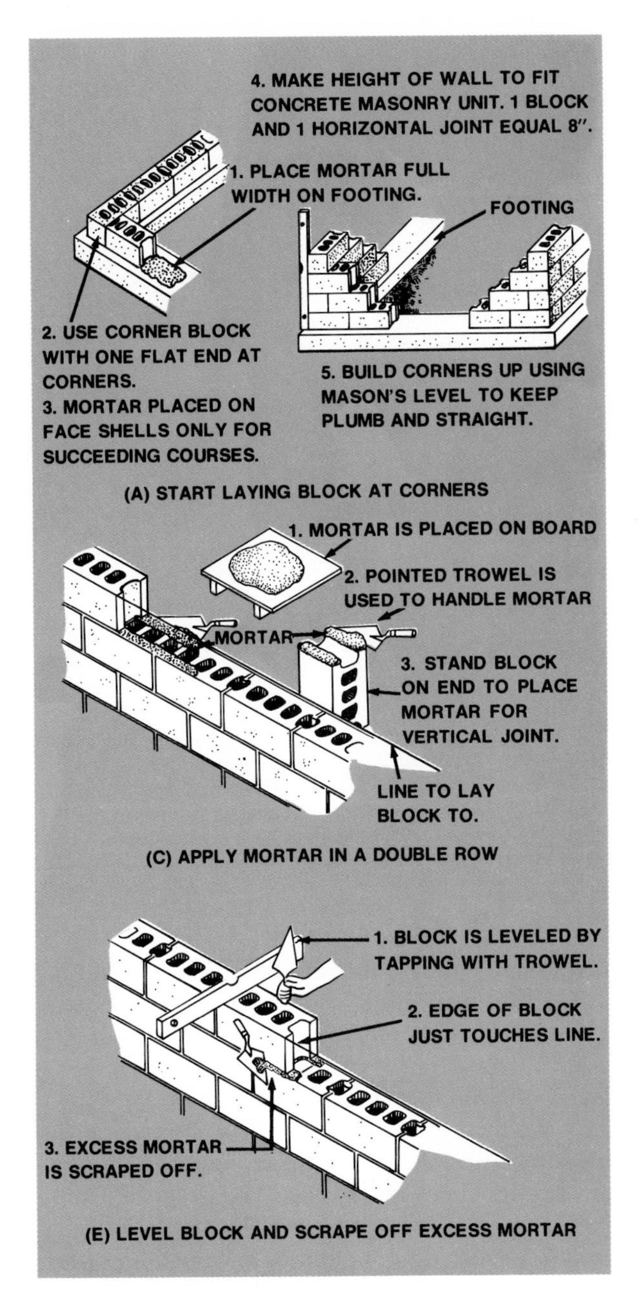

Step-by-step illustrations show how to build a wall with concrete block.

tion, (*Never* wet the block itself). The mortar bed should be laid over the center of the footing and furrowed down the middle with a pointed trowel, allowing the face shells of the block to absorb most of the mortar. When laying block, work from the corners toward the middle. Each block must be checked for level and plumb. Make sure that the mortar bed is approximately

3/8 inch at every joint and that the blocks are all aligned correctly. Work carefully but not too slowly, as all adjustments must be made before the mortar stiffens. Make sure to lay the block with the smaller ends of the core-holes up (to provide more space to lay mortar).

The vertical joints between each block should contain mortar at each edge. Set the block on end before placing and "butter" the other end with mortar. Press the mortar down onto each edge so that it will not fall off, then lift the block into place. If there is enough mortar, it should ooze out of all the joints. Cut off the excess mortar with the trowel and return it to the mortar board.

Hopefully, the wall is planned so that the closure block for the first course will be 16 inches counting mortar. If so, butter the "ears" on both sides of the last block, plus the edges of the blocks already in place on either side. Lay the closure block in from the top, being careful not to knock off the mortar from any of the edges.

Corners are laid up first, and accuracy is all-important. Use a mason's level for horizontal, vertical and course alignment.

If the space for the closure block is not exactly 16³/₈ inches (counting the joints on both sides), the home craftsman will have to cut block. Mark off the distance (subtracting ³/₄ inch for the mortar) on the closure block, and cut it with the brick chisel. To avoid fitting problems, it is a good idea to make a trial run of the first row and perform any adjustments before mixing the mortar.

SUCCEEDING COURSES

After the first course is in place, succeeding courses are laid up from the corners. It is particularly important that the corner blocks be accurate. Block is almost always laid in a *running bond,* in which the top block overlaps two bottom ones equally. Lay three of four courses in each corner before joining the bottom one. String a line from one corner to another to insure accuracy.

After the first course, face-shell bedding is used. Mortar is spread along the front and back of each row instead of over the entire surface. Except for this difference, the succeeding rows are placed exactly like the first.

Be careful not to spread the mortar too far ahead. Two or three blocks forward is plenty for the beginner. If it starts to harden, apply fresh mortar. Doublecheck the work as you proceed, filling in any open joints or holes in the mortar while it is still plastic. Do not attempt to change the position of any block after the mortar has stiffened for such movement will break the bond. If a block must be shifted, remove it entirely, scrape off the old mortar, and re-lay the block with fresh mortar.

Use special jamb blocks for doors and windows. Lintel blocks go across openings. No special techniques are needed for laying these blocks. Just make certain to follow the plan exactly. Where a partition meets a wall in a *T* joint, metal ties may be needed. Electrical wire or conduit can be run through the cores of the blocks and heating ducts can easily be set into non-load bearing partitions by using four-inch-thick blocks instead of eight.

If the exterior of the wall is to face the weather, dress or tool the joints in a concave or V-joint pattern. You can use a trowel, a special tool, or a piece of 1/2 inch copper tubing. Do horizontal joints first, then verticals.

It is difficult to clean mortar off concrete, so be careful not to spill too much, and wipe it off as soon as possible. If mortar hardens on the block, scrape it off with a piece of broken block.

DECORATIVE BLOCK

Masonry dealers have catalogs illustrating the wide variety of decorative or screen block. Some designs are solid, but others are designed to provide an open, airy effect. There are even precast concrete louvers which provide privacy, yet allow the breezes to blow through.

The choice of block is, of course, up to the home craftsman. Decorative block is laid in the same general way as standard block. Footings are required as always, and reinforcing rods or outside lintels may be in order if the wall is not sturdy enough on its own. A masonry dealer can best advise on details for a particular job.

USING DECORATIVE BLOCK — A BEGINNERS PROJECT

Set the block in place and mark borders with pencil.

Drill hole where three support blocks intersect.

Insert reinforcing rod in hole, lay down mortar bed.

Set first block, checking plumb with level.

Make sure that top of each block is level.

Butter touching sides of block with mortar.

Set both blocks together in mortar bed.

Line up both block.

Lay in third block, surrounding reinforcing rod, and check corners for square.

Set up other support in same manner.

Nail three redwood or cedar boards together for seat.

Cleats on inside of wood seat hold seat in place and prevent slipping. Sit down and relax. You've earned it. Courtesy of Sakrete, Inc.

Concrete Driveways & Walks

[SEE BRICK & STONE WORK; CONCRETE; CONCRETE BLOCK.]

Concrete Footings & Foundations

[SEE FOOTINGS & FOUNDATIONS.]

Concrete & Masonry Construction

[SEE BRICK & STONEWORK; CONCRETE; CONCRETE BLOCK.]

Concrete & Masonry Tools

A large number of concrete and masonry tools may be accumulated for all home construction and repair jobs. Many of these may be interchanged with those used for laying bricks and pouring slabs. Since nearly all of these tools are available for rent in most areas, purchase only those that you will most often use.

CONCRETE TOOLS

Having the necessary tools at hand when placing and finishing a concrete slab of any size is essential for the speed, efficiency and quality of the work. A shovel, tamper and even a heavy roller may be needed in preparing a level, compact subgrade for proper slab support after the area has been cleared. For building forms, you will probably need a hammer and saw, a level, a square, a 50-foot tape rule and mason's line for measuring, and a hacksaw, wrecking bar and some pliers for disassembly.

Mixing the concrete is probably the hardest part of the job, and for any space over one yard, it is advisable to have it delivered. When the mix arrives, you should be ready with rakes, shovels and wheelbarrows to spread and place the concrete. The typical home wheelbarrow will hold about 3 1/2 cubic' feet of concrete and, when full, will weigh about 500 pounds. So, although a contractor's barrow will hold more, it is wise to remember that it will weigh a lot more as well. After the concrete has been spread to the desired thickness, it must be leveled with a straight-edged 2' x 4' timber or metal screed. A metal or wooden tamper is used next, but only with a very stiff mix, to push the coarse aggregate below the surface, before floating. Because this step is unnecessary in most concrete work, a tamper is usually not needed at all.

When the tamper is not used, as with a normal mix, floating, which is a preliminary smoothing operation, follows the leveling. Floating is done with either a long-handled bull float (in large outdoor areas), or with a darby, which is best used in restricted or indoor areas, or an slab that may be easily and fully reached by hand. Either of these tools may be handmade with scrap lumber, unless renting or purchasing is preferable.

The next step is to finish the edges and groove the slab of concrete. Edgers are designed to finish the edges of any slab, such as sidewalks or driveways, and to form curbs, gutters and stairs.

Groovers are pushed along a straightedge to divide or pattern a sidewalk, and make contraction joints in a driveway. Both of these are used before the final floating, and sometimes again afterwards.

The wood float is the finishing tool for all concrete slabs, as it leaves a rough, nonslip finish which is especially good for sidewalks, garage floors and driveways. For a particularly smooth slab, such as one that is being prepared for flooring materials, a steel, or cement finishing trowel is used as a final finishing tool.

A good combination of tools is a mason's line and a line level. The line level hooks onto the mason's line when it is stretched tightly between corners of bricks or blocks; it is used as a guide for the line so that courses of masonry can be kept level and straight. The line is also used in laying out a project before the bricklaying begins, and then to check that the corners are

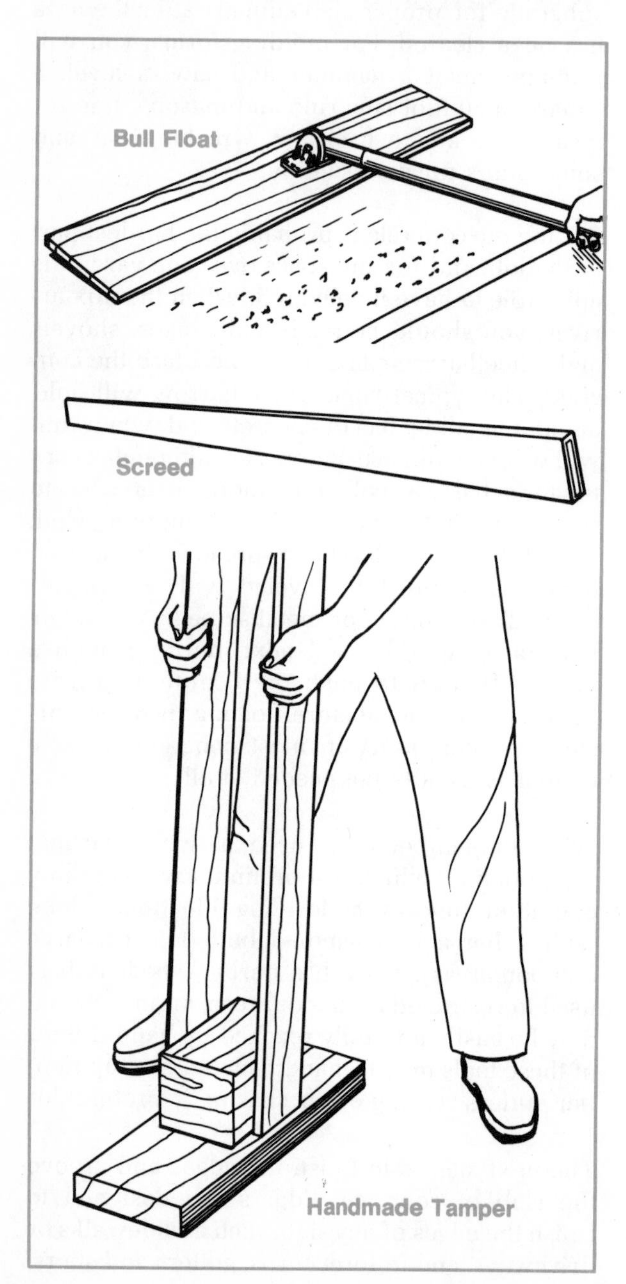

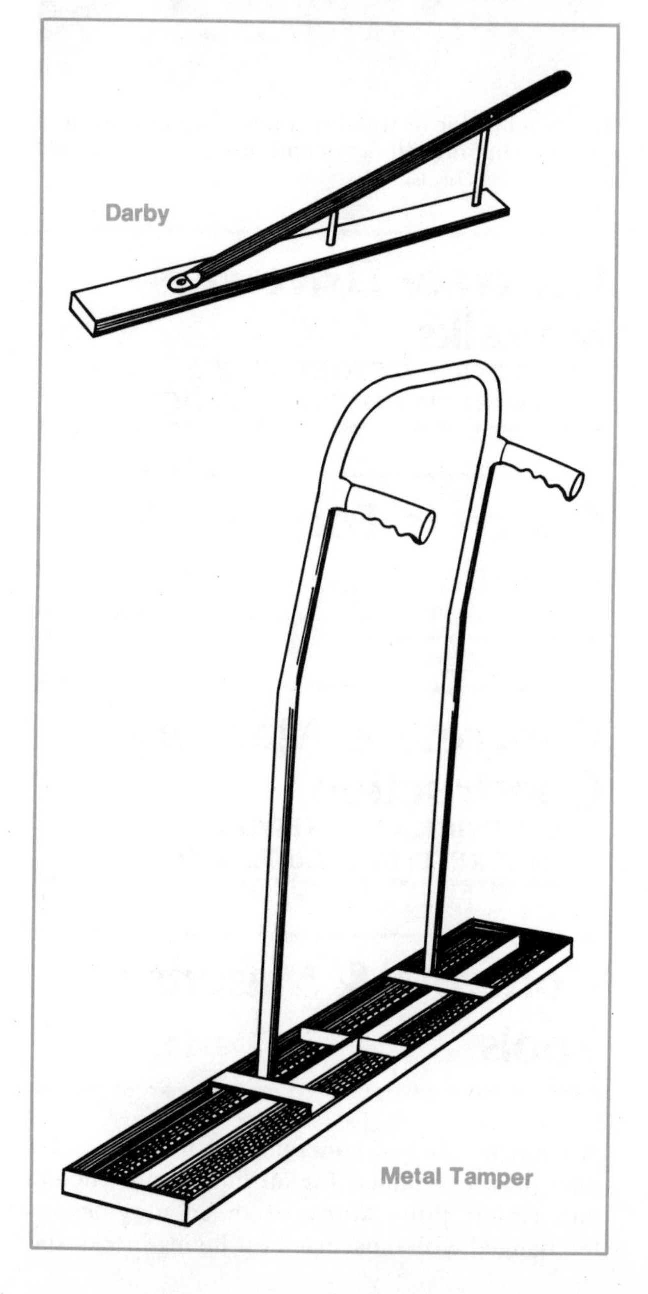

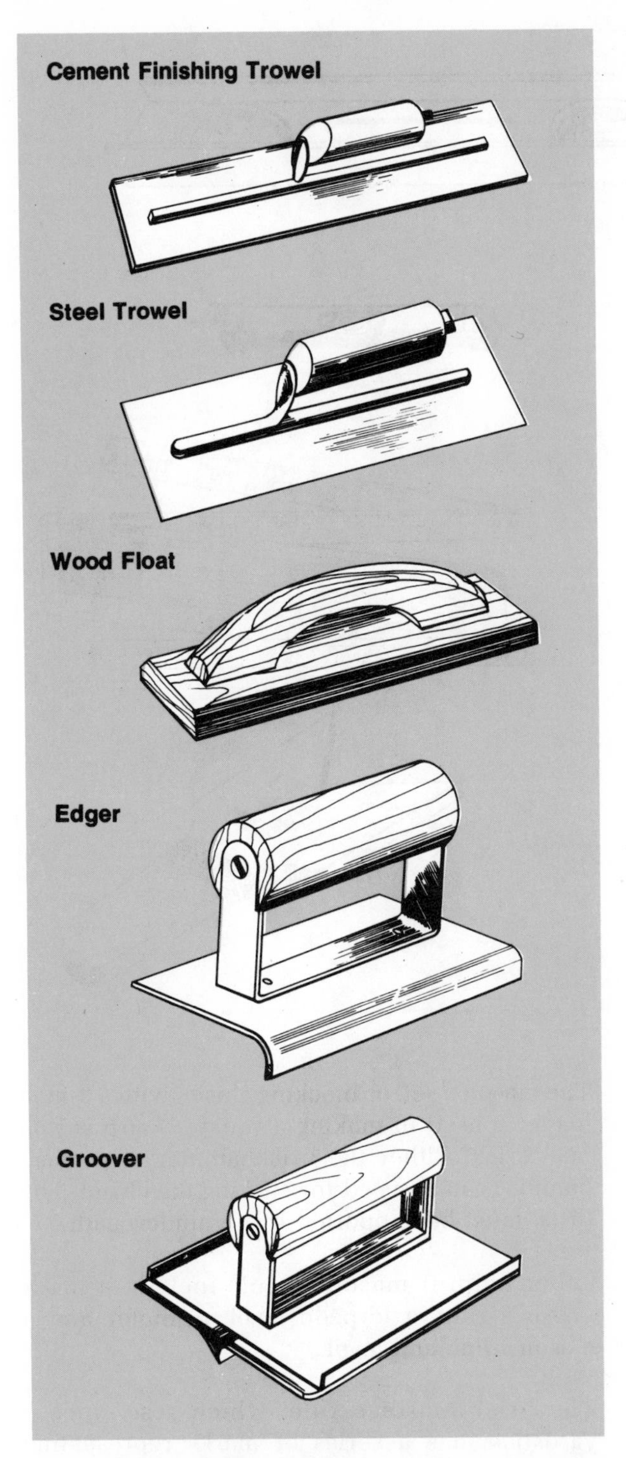

Jointers, used for forming the mortar joints, are shaped for easy hand use. They come in various shapes, each specially formed to make a certain kind of joint. The one most often used in bricklaying is an s-shaped jointer that combines rounded and v-shapes on either end of one tool.

MASONRY TOOLS

No matter how simple or small a masonry job may seem, tools made specifically for the job are a must if the job is to be done quickly and correctly. With most kinds of masonry work, only a few tools are necessary. The indispensable ones include a mason's trowel and a pointing trowel, a mason's brick hammer, a good level and a mason's set.

The brick or mason's trowel is used for carrying and applying the mortar to the bricks. It is available in several different sizes, but the most popular one is about 10 or 10½ inches long from point to heel, and 5 inches across the blade. The lightweight trowels are usually better and often more expensive.

The pointing trowel has a blade that is 5½ to 6 inches long and is useful for pointing up joints in a small space or doing most any kind of small job.

Most bricklayers prefer a 4-foot mahogany level. The 4-foot size is best because it spans over

Courtesy of The Stanley Works

Mason's Brickhammer

kept square. A pair of mason's line or corner blocks, either purchased or homemade, are used to hook around the built-up blocks or bricks at each end of a wall to keep courses straight. They are held in place by the tension of a well stretched mason's line between them.

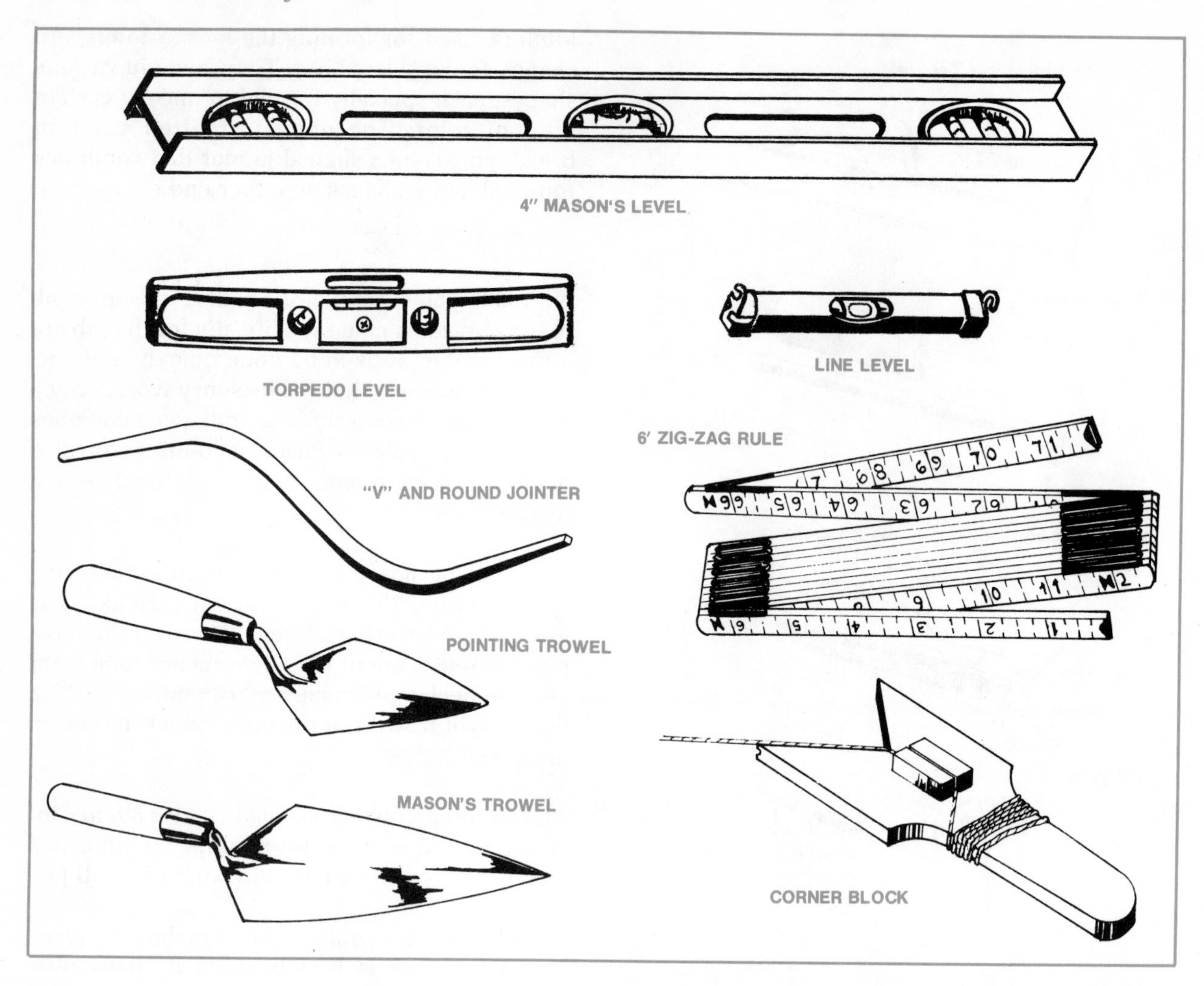

more units, and wood is more comfortable to the touch in any weather. A 2-foot level will work, and if necessary can be adapted by securely taping a good, straight 4-foot board to the side of it. However, be sure that the level and the board match exactly on bottom sides for complete accuracy.

A good brick hammer is made of hardened steel, and well-balanced so that it is easy to use. The head of the typical mason's hammer has a squared, flat face with sharp corners on one end and a chisel point on the other end. This hammer is specially designed for splitting and setting bricks, masonry tile and concrete blocks, and removing excess mortar from bricks. Either end can split a brick, but the face is especially good for removing irregularities.

The mason's set, or blocking chisel, with a 3-inch blade, is used in making a square, sharp cut on face brick. Either the brickhammer or a mash hammer can be used for striking the chisel. The brick must be supported firmly underneath.

Other helpful masonry tools include a brick mason's rule, a torpedo level, a jointer and a mason's line and level.

The brick mason's rule, which resembles a yardstick, has a series of marks representing course heights and aids in estimating where courses will fall. A 6-foot zig-zag rule, or a 6-foot roll-up tape rule is best for making vertical measurements. The torpedo level is similar in use to the 4-foot level, except in smaller areas.
SEE ALSO HAND TOOLS.

Courtesy of The Stanley Works

Blocking Chisel

Concrete Mixer

A reasonably large concrete job usually requires a cement mixer. The revolving-barrel machine does a better job of mixing, and saves more time and energy than hand-mixing concrete. These machine mixers are available in sizes that vary from small 5-gallon pails to 7-cubic-feet drums. While the numbers indicate the fluid capacity of the mixer, 60% of the capacity is usually the actual mixing capacity of the drum. Check the mixer for its limit because, if overloaded, it will not mix the batch thoroughly. Clean the drum when finished by throwing in some water and gravel while the mixer is turning.

These kinds of mixers are available with either a gas-powered engine, that gives greater flexibility of location, or an electric-powered motor, which is cheaper and easier to maintain. They can be hired by the day in most areas, but are a good investment for the man who does a lot of his own concrete work.

A manual or electric mixer-wheelbarrow combination is easier to transport and store than the separate items it combines to replace, and sells at about the price of a moderate-cost conventional mixer — or, it can be rented. Essentially, the combination mixer-wheelbarrow is a one-man machine, but it can keep two or three men busy on certain jobs. It saves labor and reduces getting-ready and cleaning-up time. It mixes a batch in one minute, and when cement must be mixed slowly, this mixer offers a convenience because one batch can be left turning while another is placed and tamped.

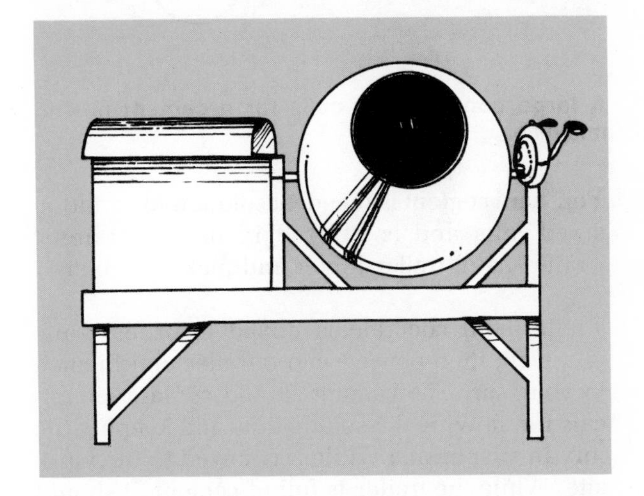

When wheelbarrow-mixer combination is used, concrete is usually dumped directly from mixer into forms, saving time and energy.

A trailer-mixer "cannon" keeps the concrete in suspension as it is towed. Using it requires skill in handling a trailer.

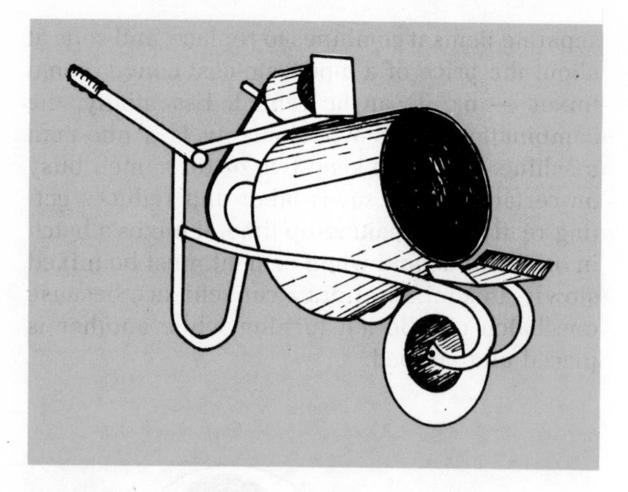

A large concrete job calls for a cement mixing machine.

You-haul cement is the ideal solution for middle-sized jobs and is offered in three versions: Trailer-haul, trailer-mixer and pick-up mixer.

Trailer-haul concrete is mixed to order while you wait, then poured into a trailer and hitched to your car. The cement should contain chemicals for slowing the setting time and keeping the mix in suspension while it is towed to the work site. While the trailer is full of cement, it should never be detached from the car bumper. The trailer-mixer, which also hooks onto the car bumper, resembles a cannon and keeps the concrete in suspension as it is towed. Note that both methods require some skill in handling a trailer.

The pick-up mixer, on the other hand, eliminates this problem because the "cannon" is attached to the back of a pick-up truck. With all three methods, the machine, as well as the cement, is hired for a fee. The dealer will often supply a wheelbarrow, tamp, shovels and other finishing tools, also for a fee. Whatever method is used, always be absolutely ready to pour the concrete. There will be no time for adjustments when a batch of concrete is waiting, and probably setting as it waits. *SEE ALSO CONCRETE.*

Concrete Painting

[SEE PAINTS & PAINTING.]

Concrete Patching & Repair

Concrete patching and repair involves certain fundamental procedures common to any patching problem. All cracks must be thoroughly cleaned before patching by rinsing them with water. The edges of the crack should be chiseled so that the patching material will not taper off and form a weak bond at the edge. The crack should be scrubbed with a wire brush to loosen jagged areas and then rinsed again to insure dampness before it is patched.

The typical patching material is a mixture of two parts pea gravel to one part cement to two parts sand. For narrow crack patching, use a mortar of one part portland cement to three parts sand or a dry-mix commercial compound that may be purchased in small bags at most hardware stores. Many cracks require a bonding coat called neat cement, which is composed of portland cement and sand mixed to the consistency of paint or cream.

Large cracks must be wet when the patching material is applied. However, be careful that no water is puddled in the crevice, or the concrete will not cure properly. Apply a coat of cement with a brush and let it dry until tacky. Puddle the patching material into the crevice and work it in with a trowel. Scrape off the excess material so that the patch is flush (even) with the structure's surface or slightly overfilled. The patch must be kept wet for a minimum of three days in order for it to cure.

Vertical crack patching is done similarly, but usually with a dry-mix, as this material has a fine texture for easy application. Vinyl base, epoxy, or hydraulic cement are also often used. Bond the crack in the usual way but let the bond dry longer. Working with as stiff a mixture as possible, start at the bottom of the crack and work upward. In this way, each addition of cement will be supported by the previous one. Sometimes a board or piece of plywood will be needed to hold the cement into place until it dries. Also, wet burlap may be used to keep the patch wet until it cures.

If the crack is narrow (less than 1/4") use the mixture of cement and sand or one of the trade name dry-mix compounds, as these work into a small crack more efficiently. Follow the mixing instructions stated on the package and apply the cement in the same way as for large cracks.

Sometimes, the crack may be in a surface that is constantly exposed to dampness. In these cases, the quick-setting compounds are especially handy because these materials (like hydraulic cement) will "set-up" or harden, even in running water. *SEE ALSO CEMENT PATCHING MATERIALS.*

Concrete, Reinforced

Concrete is reinforced with wire mesh or iron bars to provide a structure strong enough to resist great stress. The type of reinforcement needed will depend upon the type of pressure that the concrete is expected to undergo. Before laying the concrete, put the reinforcement in place. When a portion of the concrete is poured, lift the mesh or bar to the desired depth in the structure. Remember to keep it at least one inch below the surface of the concrete. *SEE ALSO CONCRETE.*

Concrete Texture & Color

[SEE CONCRETE.]

Concrete Tools

[SEE CONCRETE & MASONRY TOOLS.]

Concrete Walls & Steps

[SEE CONCRETE; CONCRETE BLOCK.]

Conductors

A conductor is any object or substance that carries electricity from one place to another. In an electrical wiring system, electricity is conducted through wires, which are usually covered with some type of insulation. These wires are usually composed of copper or aluminum. *SEE ALSO ELECTRICAL WIRING.*

Conduit

Conduit, a light steel tubing in which electrical wiring is installed, is required by the electrical codes in some localities. Although conduit leading through the house structure is tough, it is still flexible enough to be bent when necessary.

The conduit used for home work is 1/2 or 3/4 inch in diameter, and comes in easily handled 10-foot lengths. Ends are threaded so the lengths can be joined with threaded couplings, while section cuts with a hacksaw or wheel pipe cutter can be either threaded or locked into junction boxes with a clamping type connector.

The burr on the inside of the conduit must be removed with a reamer to allow free passage of wires that will be inserted, and to prevent the sharp edges from cutting into the wire insulation.

No more than the equivalent of four 90° bends in each run of conduit between boxes are allowed by the code. Conduit must be bent with a conduit bender to take the curves that lead it from vertical to horizontal runs, and it must be cut, fitted, and connected with couplings. It is held to the frame-work by special straps. After the conduit installation is completed, including the mounting and connection of the conduit to a metal electric box, the wiring is drawn through. A fish tape, or "snake," which is available in 50-foot and 100-foot lengths, is used to help pull the wires. The wires that will be needed are tied into a bundle

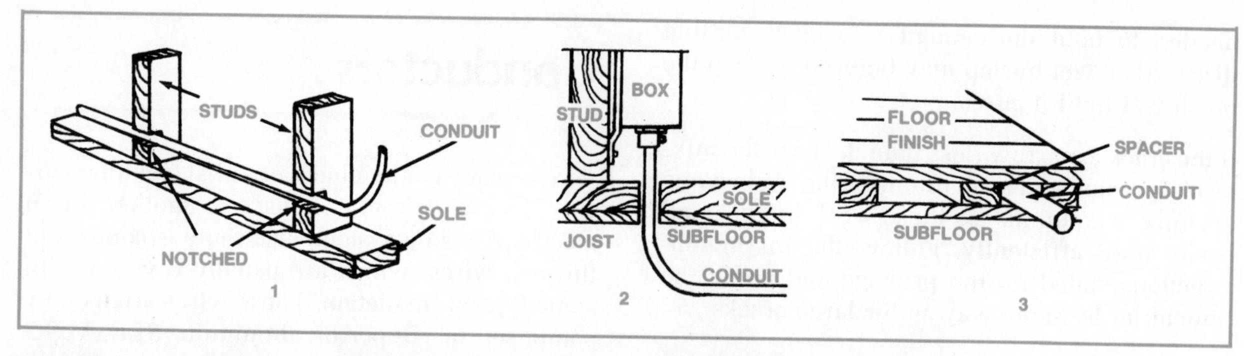

A conduit may 1) be mounted in notched framing, 2) run along joists and up through wall soleplate to boxes or 3) be installed between subfloor and finish floor with spacers.

and pulled through at one time, all tied to the fish tape. *SEE ALSO ELECTRICAL WIRING.*

Conduit Adapter

A conduit adapter is a threaded cylindrical connector for attaching thin-wall conduit to rigid conduit. The adapter is handy, for example, when thin-wall conduit must be bent to go to a receptacle outlet. The adapter will allow it to be connected to rigid conduit prior to the bend. *SEE ALSO ELECTRICAL WIRING.*

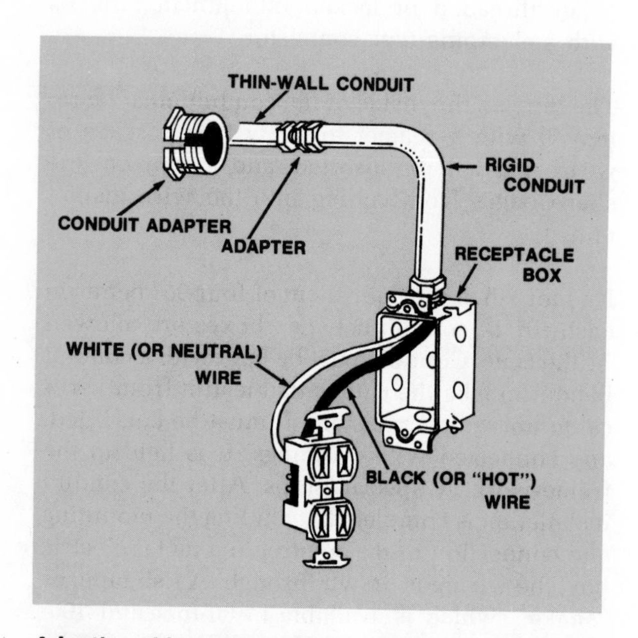

Adapting thin-wall conduit to rigid conduit is done with a conduit adapter.

Conduit Bender

A conduit bender, also known as an electrician's hickey, is a semicircular device with a length of pipe as a handle used for making smooth bends in conduit. Lay the conduit on the ground and hook it through the bender. Steady the pipe and pull the handle. The conduit will bend smoothly and easily at the point where the bender is placed. *SEE ALSO ELECTRICIAN'S TOOLS & EQUIPMENT.*

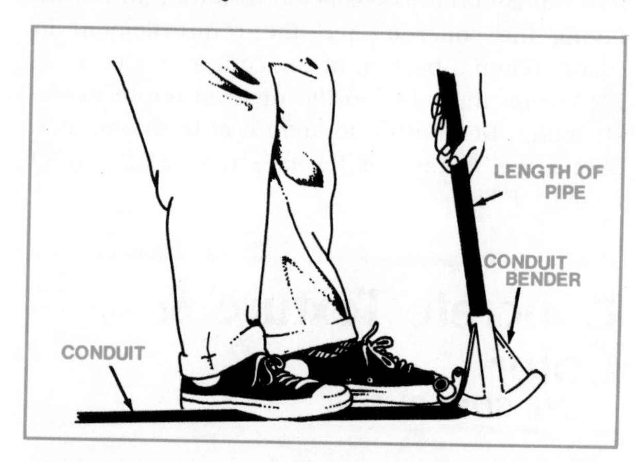

Smooth bends in the conduit are made with a conduit bender.

Contact Cement

As the name implies, contact cement bonds on contact, and requires no clamps or presses. Approximately 50 to 75 percent of full bond strength is reached on contact. Since formulas vary from manufacturer to manufacturer, be certain to read and follow label directions carefully. Although most contact cements are flammable and all fire hazards should be removed, there are contact cements on the market that are both waterproof and nonflammable.

Use this adhesive to bond plastic laminates to counter tops or to mount room paneling. It is also good for gluing plastic foam, hardboard, and metal to wood. The bond strength of contact cement is high (about 500 pounds per square inch), but it is not a "joint glue" and is not recommended for furniture building.

Before applying the cement, be sure that both surfaces to be joined are clean and dry. Paint or old finishes on wood should be removed before coating with cement. General instructions are to coat both surfaces with a thin, uniform coating and allow them to dry before positioning. Two coats should be used on porous surfaces; the second coat applied after the first coat has dried. To test for dryness, press a small piece of wrapping paper against the coating. If it does not stick, the surface is dry. Normal drying time ranges from 30 minutes to 2 hours.

Two surfaces which have been coated will bond instantly, but one coated surface and one uncoated surface will not, so use this advantage in aligning your work. Place a piece of wrapping paper between the members until you have a perfect alignment, then carefully pull the paper away. If the members *do* slip out of line, flush lacquer thinner into the glue line, then carefully and slowly pull the members free. Continue this process until removal is easy. Clean off any remaining cement with thinner, recoat the parts, let dry and reassemble.

Brushes or rollers used for coating can be cleaned with lacquer thinner. If you used a water-base type of cement, clean applicators with soap and water while they are still wet. Contact cement can usually be stored at normal room temperature for one year. *SEE ALSO ADHESIVES.*

Contact Printing

[SEE PHOTOGRAPHY.]

Continuous Header

A continuous header is made up of two 2 x 6 boards set on edge and placed end to end around the entire outside wall framing structure of a house. A continuous header may be used in place of a double top plate, and is sturdy enough to act as a lintel, the horizontal load supporting member over openings. The headers are toenailed to studs, and should be joined with metal straps at corners. *SEE ALSO WALL AND CEILING CONSTRUCTION.*

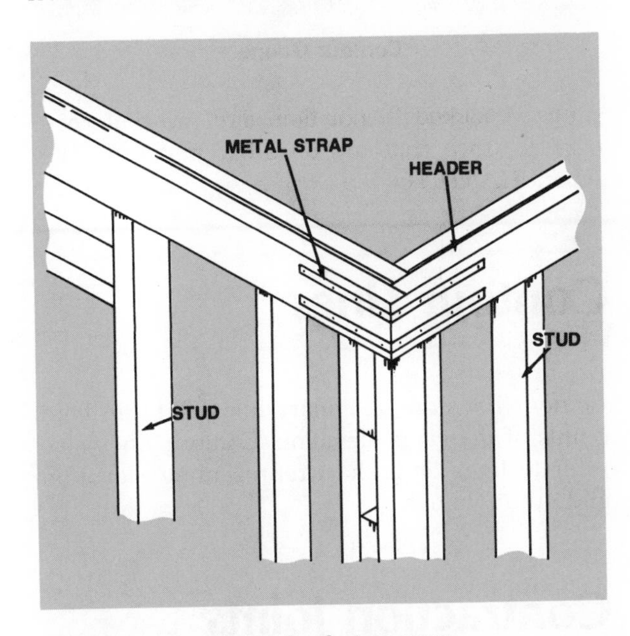

Continuous headers joined at corners.

Contour Gauge

A contour gauge is a device used for handling irregularities, such as fitting around moldings. Its adjustable wires will conform to any complicated shape. Once the profile is matched, the

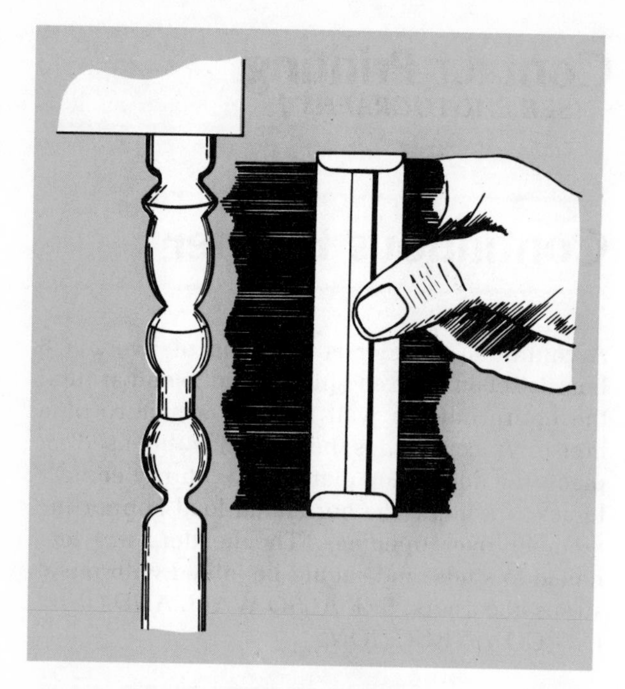

Contour Gauge

gauge is locked in position, and the pattern is used to trace contours on other material. *SEE ALSO HAND TOOLS.*

Contour Lines

Contour lines are imaginary lines that join land points of the same elevation. Contour lines also refer to lines on a chart representing elevation and ground slope.

Contraction Joints

Contraction joints are the horizontal or vertical channels in sidewalk and driveway slabs that give the slab room to expand and contract without cracking. Contraction joints are formed by placing thin boards inside the wooden framework so that they fit snugly against each side. After the concrete is poured and dried, these dividing boards are removed, leaving the contraction joints. *SEE ALSO CONCRETE.*

Convertible Tools

Convertible tools, because of their interchangeable parts, offer certain features not found in most conventional tools. The convertible tool can act as a horizontal or vertical drill press, a compound-angle drill, and with other attachments, as

Courtesy of Shop Smith, Inc.

Convertible Tool as a Lathe

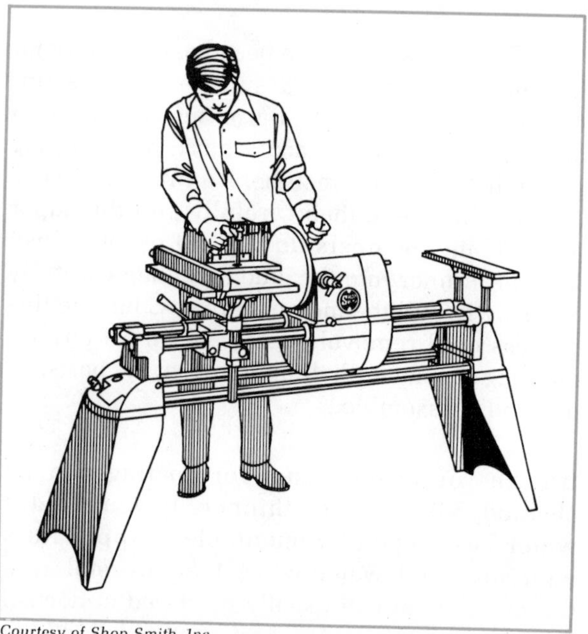

Courtesy of Shop Smith, Inc.

Convertible Tool as a Disc Sander

Courtesy of Shop Smith, Inc.

Convertible Tool as a Vertical Drill Press

Courtesy of Shop Smith, Inc.

Convertible Tool as a Horizontal Drill Press

a lathe, jigsaw, jointer, table saw and drum or disc sander.

Before purchasing a tool of this kind, visualize your general shop routine. In shops where hand fitting of parts is frequently required, or where different operations must be done in a particular order, individual tools may be better. On the other hand, if the shop is small and major projects using large-capacity tools are planned, a convertible tool may be a wise investment.

Where floor space is limited, measure the area to be occupied by the convertible tool (most are the size of a lathe) and the space required by individual tools. Then you can decide which will better fit your work methods.

With either arrangement, operating technique is similar whether you are using separate tools or a convertible. The special features on convertible tools depend on the make and model chosen and the manufacturer's owners' manual will help you decide which will best suit your needs. *SEE ALSO DRILL PRESS; JIGSAW; JOINTER; LATHE; STATIONARY BELT & DISC SANDER; TABLE SAW.*

Cooking Appliances

[SEE APPLIANCE REPAIR, SMALL; HOME APPLIANCE SELECTION.]

Cope

As the term applies to the handyman, cope means to cut or shape the end of a molded wood member so that it will cover and fit the contour of an adjoining piece of molding, forming a close joint.

Coping Saw

The coping saw is a special-purpose saw used for fine, ornate cutting of curves. Because of its small frame and very narrow blade, this saw can cut smaller-than-pencil diameter curves. Inexpensive, replaceable blades, usually 6 to 5 5/8 in-

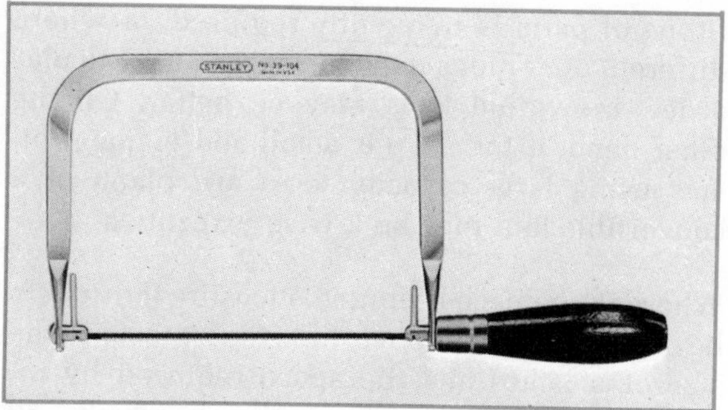

Courtesy of The Stanley Works

Coping Saw

ches long, are available in widths of 1/8 inch and less, with 10 to 20 teeth per inch. Wood, thin metal and plastics are all materials through which they can cut.

Blades for coping saws are mounted so the teeth slant to suit whatever work is to be done. For delicate ornamental scroll work, the blade teeth should point toward the handle so the cut can be made on the pull stroke. When a cut must be made on the push stroke, the blades are mounted with the teeth slanting away from the handle. This cutting stroke is used when work is placed vertically in a vise. The blade may be revolved in the frame by turning the end fittings. This keeps the frame clear of the edge of the material as the cutting direction changes. Usually, the depth between the blade and the back of the frame is from 4 1/2 to 6 1/2 inches. *SEE ALSO HAND TOOLS.*

Copper Pipe Fittings

A copper pipe fitting is usually designed with no ridges or pipe shoulders or with gentle curves. The flow of materials is not severely slowed and debris does not accumulate. The most common fittings are the tee, adapters, flange, trap, bends, couplings, cleanouts, branches and elbows.

The sanitary tee and the sanitary tee with side inlet fittings join straight run pipes with a branch entering at a 90 degree angle. The cast-iron adapter and the steel pipe adapter join copper pipe to cast-iron or steel pipe, respectively.

To fasten the toilet bowl to the floor, a closet flange is fitted to the closet bend. A closet bend is the fitting between the closet flange and the sewer lines.

The drum trap is connected to the bathtub drain at the bottom of the fitting and its side inlet is attached to a drainage pipe.

A bend, either 1/8" or 1/4", connects pipes the exact way a street elbow does except the bend does not have threaded ends.

While a coupling joins two same sized pipes to form a straight run, a slip coupling joins two different sized pipes in a straight run. A cleanout is placed at the end or a bend of a pipe to allow easy access to the inside of the pipe.

A Y-branch connects a pipe entering at an angle to a straight run pipe while a street elbow, threaded internally on one end and externally on the other end, joins pipe connecting at angles with a gentle curve to eliminate clogging of materials. *SEE ALSO PIPE FITTINGS.*

Copper Pipe & Tubing

Copper pipe costs more than galvanized steel but is much easier to use because it does not require threading. All that is involved in the assembly of copper pipe is cutting and reaming the pipe, slipping the fitting onto the pipe and sealing the joint with solder.

There are two types of copper pipe, the first of which is the rigid form. Because of the straight runs used in the construction of new homes, rigid pipe is sold in lengths of 20 feet. However, it can be purchased by mail order in ten feet lengths. Rigid copper pipe must be soldered to form joints.

Soft or flexible copper tubing comes in coils of 15, 30, or 60 feet. Because of its flexibility, it is especially useful in extending present water systems. Soft copper tubing needs connectors at both the beginning and end of the tubing. With

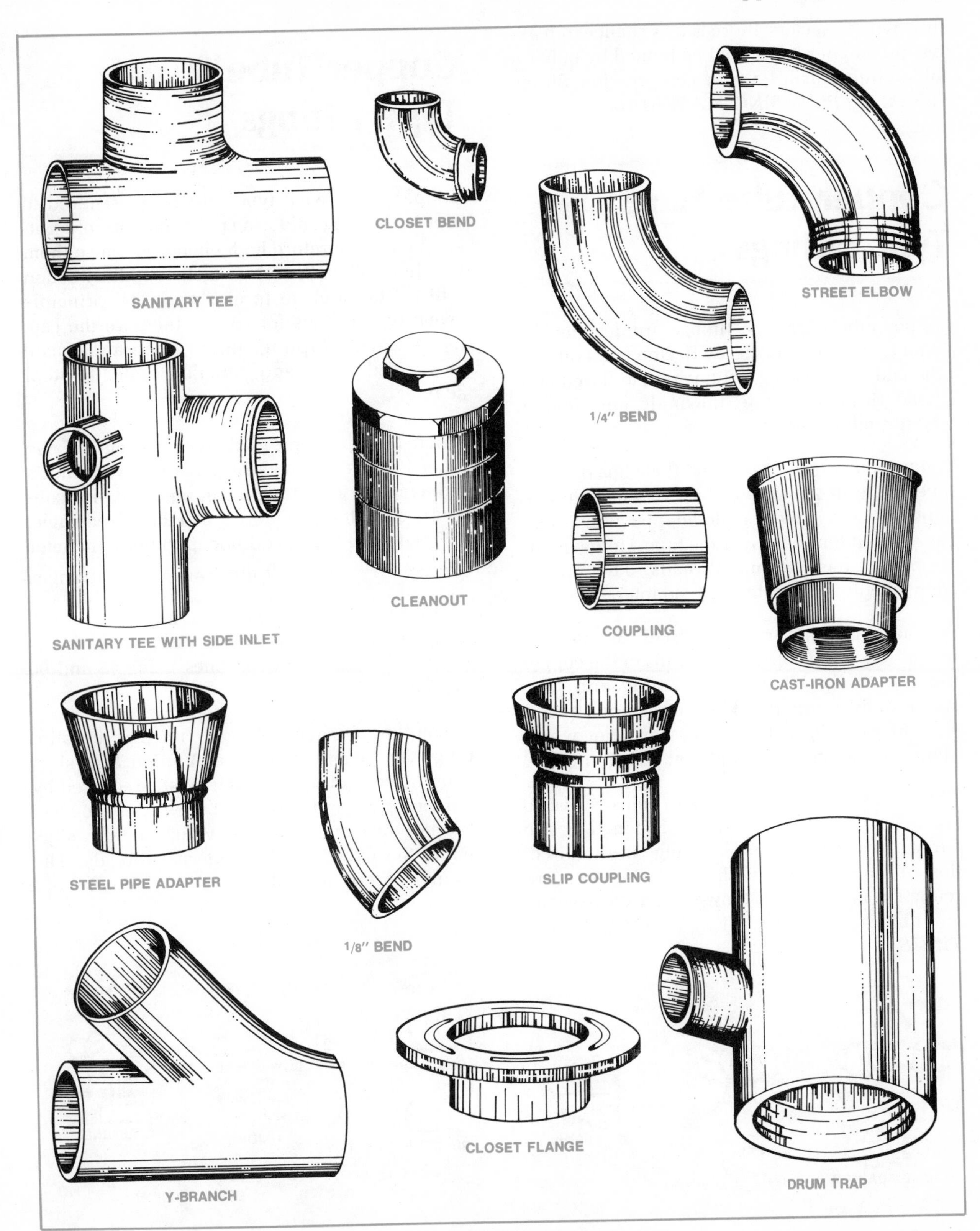

Copper Pipe Fittings

only two connectors, there is less chance of leaking. Soft copper tubing can be jointed by either a solder fitting or a flare or compression fitting. *SEE ALSO PLUMBING MATERIALS.*

Copper Tube Flare Type Fittings

Copper tube flare type fittings are designed so that a joint can be made by flaring one end of a tube and then placing a fitting on the flared end. These fittings include the male and female adapter, elbow, union and tee.

The male adapter has one end that slips over the tube while the other end has external threads. Quite similar is the female adapter which also has one end that slips over the tube. However, its other end has internal threads. The female adapter will receive the male adapter.

A union is a straight run fitting with an outer rim having a hex nut appearance. Ends of the copper tubes are slipped into this fitting and then secured by tightening the outer rim. Also a straight run fitting, the tee has an inlet which allows a branch pipe to enter at a right angle.

The elbow, on the other hand, joins tubes to create a curve or bend in them. Having a gentle curve, the elbow permits a change in the direction of material flow without causing a severe reduction in the rate of flow or an excessive accumulation of debris. *SEE ALSO PIPE FITTINGS.*

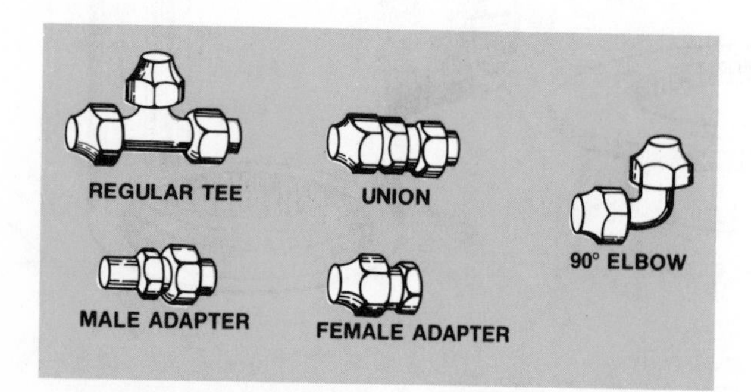

Copper Tube Flare Type Fittings

Copper Tube Sweat Type Fittings

Copper tube sweat type fittings are secured to pipe by heating soldering paste and the solder itself to a temperature high enough to cause them to soften. When the solder melts, capillary action will fill the joint to form a seal. The principle sweat type fittings for copper tube are the cap, tee, elbow, coupling, union, stop-and-waste valve and male and female copper-to-steel adapter.

When fitting a pipe flush with the end of the tube, a cap is used to seal it. A regular tee and a reducing tee join straight run pipe and also connect a branch pipe entering at a 90 degree angle. The reducing tee, in addition, permits a diameter change in straight run pipe.

Elbows connect pipes to form curves or bends. They are available in various gradations of curvature; the most common ones being 45 and 90 degrees.

A coupling connects straight run pipe by slipping over the end of the tube. A union, also, slips over the ends of a tube; but it must be secured by tightening the outer rim. A male copper-to-steel adapter has one end into which a tube slips while the other end has external threads. The counterpart of the male fitting is the female cop-

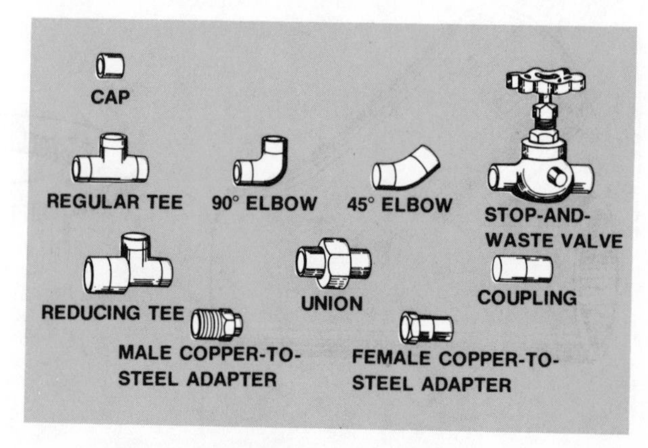

Copper Tube Sweat Type Fittings

per-to-steel adapter. It, too, has an end into which a tube slips, although the other end has internal threads to join with the external threads of the male adapter. These two fittings connect steel pipe to copper pipe.

Most helpful when working on tubing, the stop-and-waste valve is used to prevent freezing of outside pipe and faucets. If opened, a stop-and-waste valve will permit air to enter a pipe and drain water from that section, up to and including the outside faucet. *SEE ALSO PIPE FITTINGS.*

Cord, Asbestos-Insulated

Asbestos-insulated cord, or heater cord, is used with irons, toasters, portable heaters and other appliances that generate large amounts of heat. It contains two conductors made of fine, stranded copper wire covered first with a layer of cotton and then with rubber insulation. The conductors are then covered completely with a layer of asbestos before being twisted and wrapped in a final covering of either cotton, rayon or rubber.

Because of its asbestos insulation, the National Electrical Code allows the use of this type of cord for carrying a higher amperage than ordinary lamp cord. If an asbestos-insulated cord must be replaced, it should be matched with a cord with exactly the same outer covering, insulation, wire size and length. A cord that is too long has a greater resistance, which causes a voltage drop, making the attached appliance less efficient. *SEE ALSO PLUGS & CORDS.*

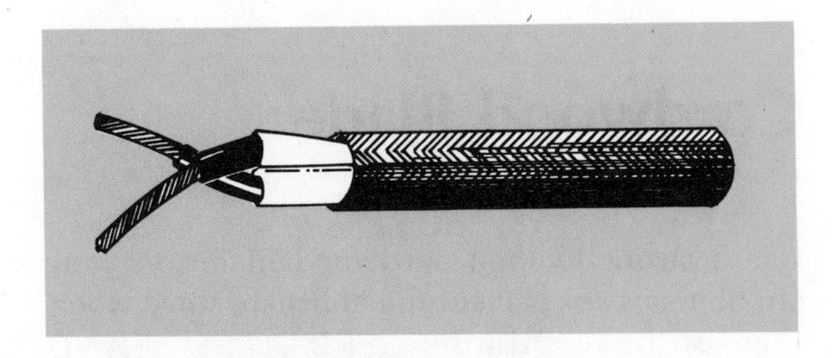

Asbestos-Insulated or Heater Cord

Cord Repairing

Cord repairing should only be done in an emergency. For safety's sake, the damaged cord should be replaced as soon as possible.

Most cord repairs involve cord that is frayed or has exposed wires. To repair a frayed cord, first disconnect it from the outlet. If the cord insulation is frayed near the plug, detach plug, cut away the damaged portion of the cord, and reattach the plug to the cord. When the cord is frayed near a molded plug, cut off the frayed section of the cord and the attached plug, then replace it with an ordinary terminal screw plug. If the cord is damaged near the appliance, unplug the cord, detach it from the appliance, cut away the damaged part of the cord, and reconnect the cord to the appliance. For a cord that is cracked or frayed in the middle, unplug the cord, separate its wires and wrap each of them with electrical tape, and then tape both wires together. Each wire must be first wrapped separately or a short will occur.

If there is no visible evidence that the cord is defective but the attached appliance does not function, an electrical tester can be used to determine cord damage. Unplug the cord and detach it from the appliance and twist each exposed wire of the cord around one of the tester's wires. Making sure the exposed cord wires do not touch, lay the combined tester and cord down and plug in the cord. If tester lights, the cord is not defective. *SEE ALSO PLUGS & CORDS.*

Cord Splices

Cord splices are not approved by the National Electrical Code and should be used only in an emergency. To repair a faulty cord, first disconnect it to avoid serious damage or injury. Cut away the worn-out area and separate the wires. Stagger the splices by making cuts not directly opposite each other. Make a pigtail splice in each wire, following the original twist so that the wires will not unwind. Use plenty of tape around each splice and then around the dual splice. At the first opportunity, the spliced cord should be replaced. *SEE ALSO PLUGS & CORDS.*

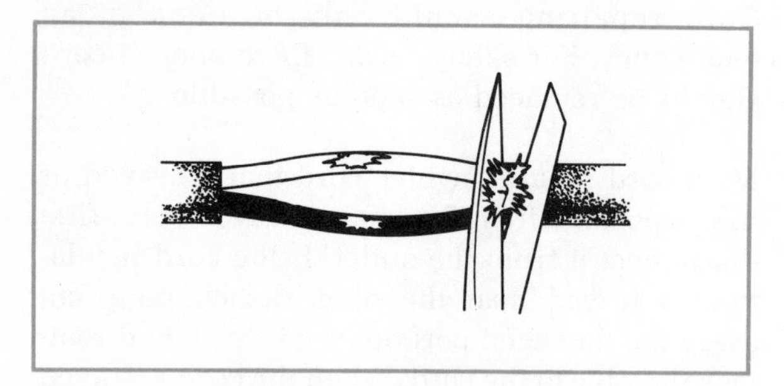

Cut away damaged area.

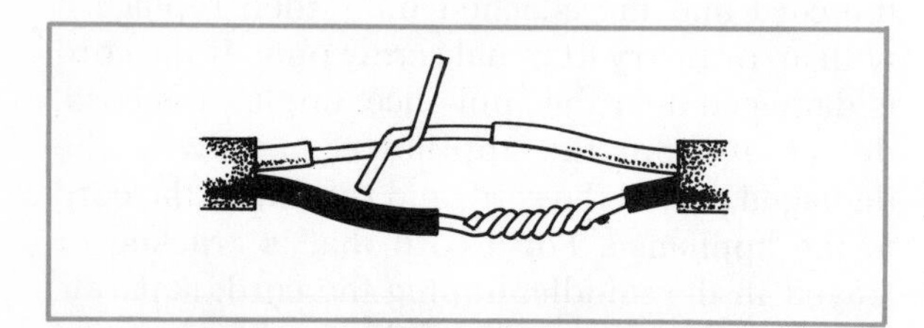

Make pigtail splices in wire.

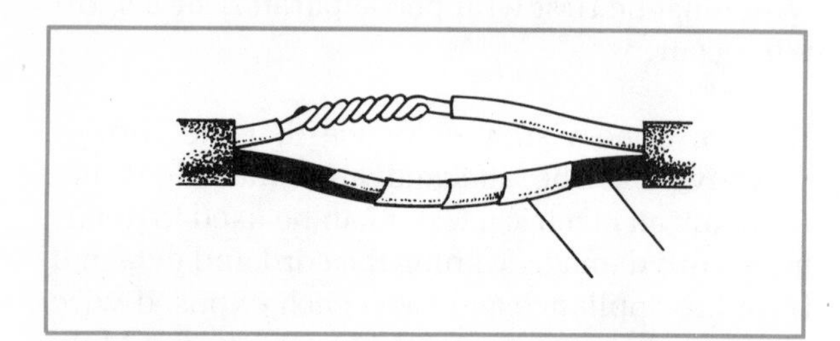

Cover individual splices with tape before wrapping wires together.

Cord Switch

A cord switch is a switch inserted along a lamp cord to permit more convenient control of an electrical appliance. For instance, with a bedside lamp, the cord switch can be placed on the cord within easy reach so that the light can be turned out from a reclining position.

To install, a cord switch opens in half with one of the cord wires running through the switch and the other one cut, so that it may be attached to the two terminal screws in the switch. Both halves are then screwed back together. Cord switches are made of brown or ivory plastic with either a rotary or rocker control knob. *SEE ALSO PLUGS & CORDS.*

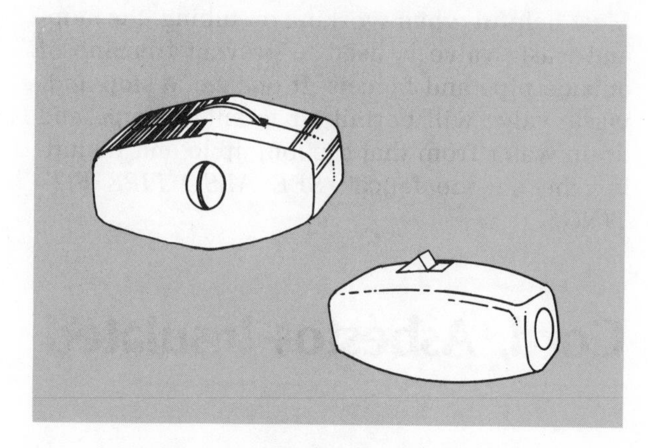

Cord Switches

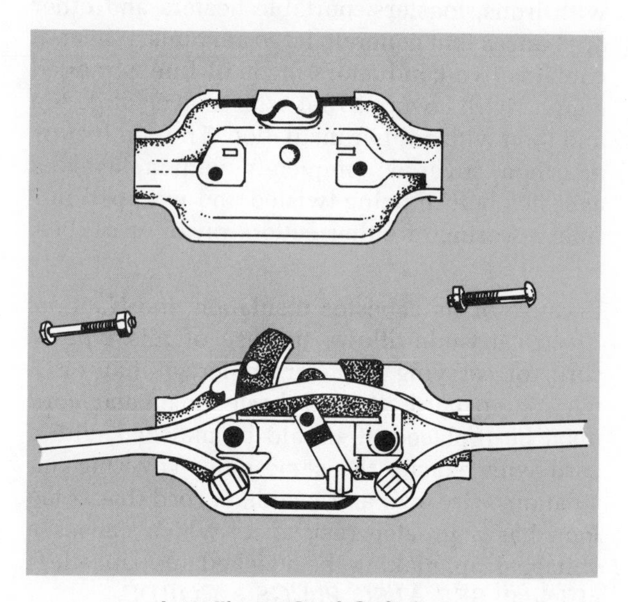

Installing a Cord Switch

Cordwood Blade

Use a strong-toothed cordwood blade on your circular saw for fast cutting of brush, stove wood logs or heavy timber. *SEE ALSO HAND TOOLS.*

Core Box Bit

A core box bit is a router bit which is used to flute flat surfaces. For free hand work with a router, it can also be used for recessing. The core box bit forms a groove which is primarily U-shaped, but has one side which is slightly more lateral. *SEE ALSO ROUTER.*

Core Box Bit

Corner Bead

Corner bead is a molding used to protect corners. Also, a metal reinforcement placed on corners before plastering is referred to as corner bead. *SEE ALSO MOLDING & TRIM.*

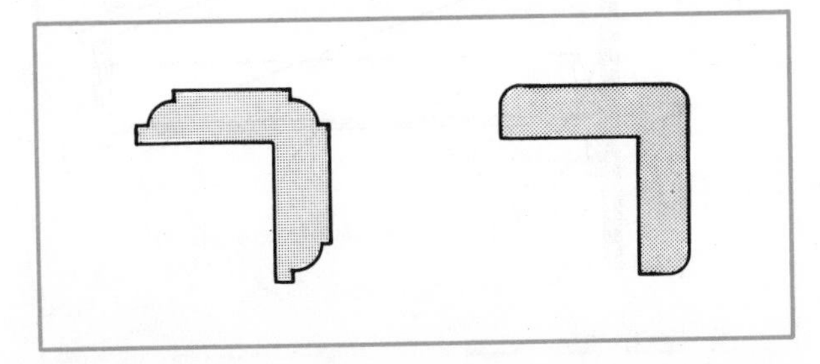

Molding used to protect corners is a corner bead.

Corner Brace

A corner brace in carpentry is a let-in brace placed diagonally across studs to help support corners in framing. In furniture making, a corner brace is a piece of fastening hardware used on

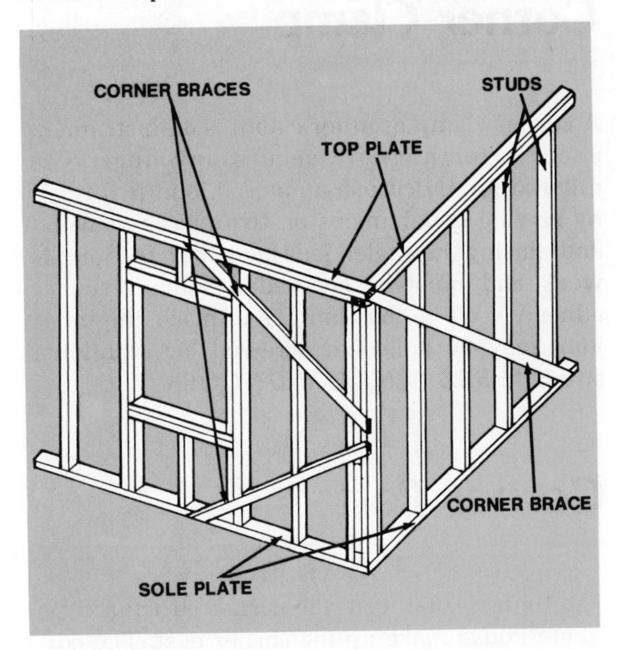

Corner braces used in framing.

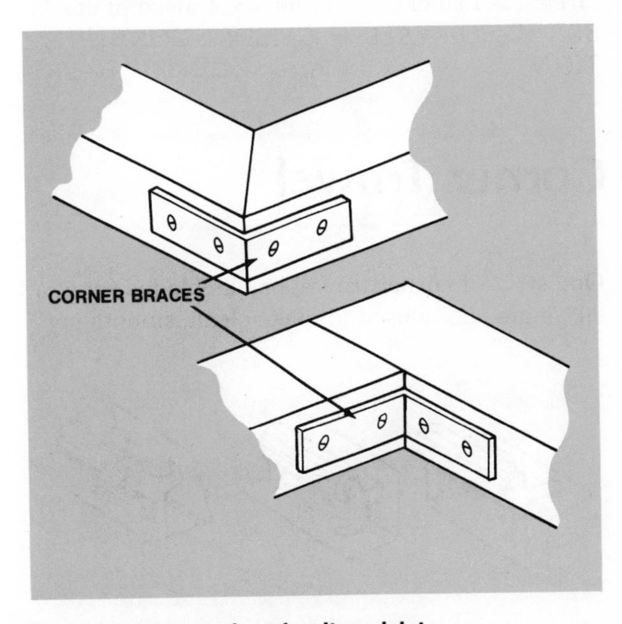

Corner brace used on furniture joints.

chairs or tables. This brace is a piece of steel bent to fit in or around a corner and used to assemble or reinforce a joint. In addition, a lag screw may be inserted through the corner brace and tightened to hold leg and rail furniture parts together.

Corner Clamp

A corner clamp or miter clamp is an instrument used to temporarily secure any degree of mitered joint. Because a mitered joint is formed by sawing equal angles on two pieces of wood and placing the angled sides together, the joint is weak and must be secured by some type of adhesive. While the clamp is in place, the miter joint may be nailed or screwed for additional strength. *SEE ALSO HAND TOOLS.*

Corner Post

The timbers that form the corner structure of a frame house make up the corner post. The corner post may be either solid or built-up using three 2 x 4 stocks or a solid 4 x 4 piece of stock. *SEE ALSO WALL & CEILING CONSTRUCTION.*

Corner Trowel

One style of corner trowel has its blades set at a 90° angle and is used to make clean, smooth corners in plaster walls. Another style offers a rounded shape that is used for making corners in concrete walls and steps, and is available in a pair of matched inside and outside corner patterns. *SEE ALSO CONCRETE & MASONRY TOOLS.*

Corner Trowels

Cornice

A cornice, sometimes called an eave, is that part of the exterior of a building where the roof and the walls meet. Cornices may be of different designs, such as open, closed or boxed, depending on the overall designs of the structure. Parts of the cornice include a frieze, which is the base for a molding, a fascia board, which is the trim attached to the roof edge and a ledger strip, which is nailed to the wall and forms a support for lookouts, or soffit rafters. A plancier or soffit, made of plywood, hardwood or plaster, is attached to nailing strips on the back of the fascia and to the lookouts and ledger.

Another type of cornice is a window cornice which is used in home decorating. This cornice is a piece of wood painted or covered with fabric and installed at the top of a window to conceal drapery rods and hooks. *SEE ALSO ROOF CONSTRUCTION.*

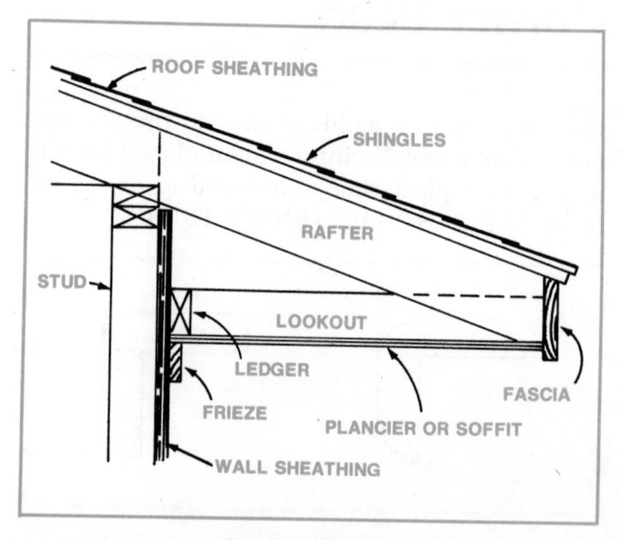

Cornice Parts

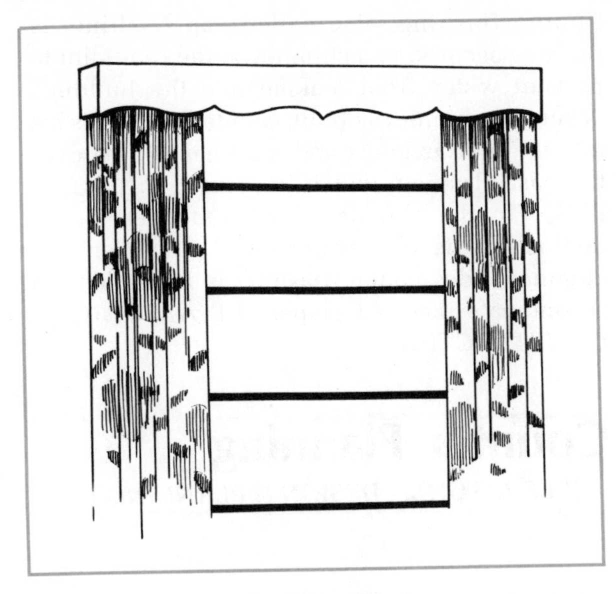

A Window Cornice

Cornice Board

[SEE CORNICE.]

Corrugated Fasteners

Corrugated fasteners or nails connect light-duty mitered joints such as picture frames and screens. These fasteners may also secure butt and end-to-end joints. Although usually placed where they are concealed or their appearance does not matter, corrugated fasteners can be driven below surface or covered with putty. To fix the fastener in place, drive it across the joint. *SEE ALSO FASTENERS.*

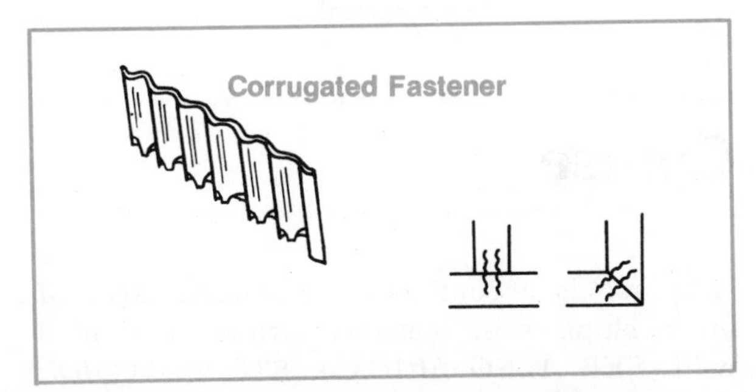

Drive corrugated fastener across the joint.

Corrugated Nails

[SEE FASTENERS.]

Cottage

[SEE VACATION HOMES.]

Cotter Pin

A cotter pin is used to fasten joints that will be taken apart at some later time. Joints formed by cotter pins are not rigid and both pieces are movable. Cotter pins may also be used as a locking device on fasteners.

Proper use of a cotter pin requires that the shank be inserted through a hole so that the arms may be spread in opposite directions. So spread, cotter pins prevent moving parts of various sizes from slipping apart and also may prevent a nut from working loose from a bolt. Cotter pins are available in various sizes. *SEE ALSO FASTENERS.*

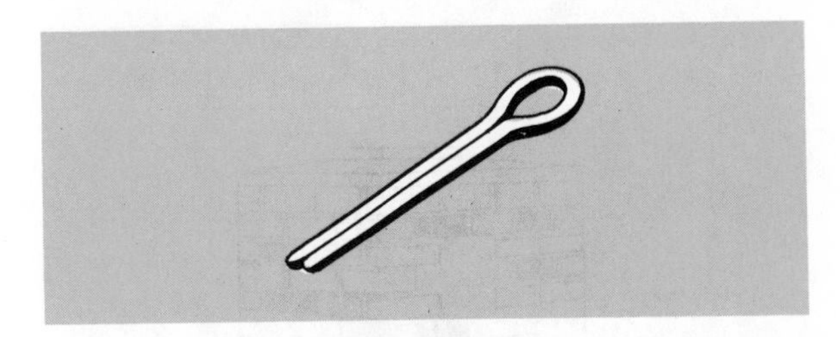

Cotter Pin

Cotter pin in use

Counterbore

Counterboring is much like countersinking except that the screw or other fastener is recessed deeper below the surface in order to conceal it. A plug of doweling or other material is used to fill the hole and complete the hiding process. *SEE ALSO HAND TOOLS.*

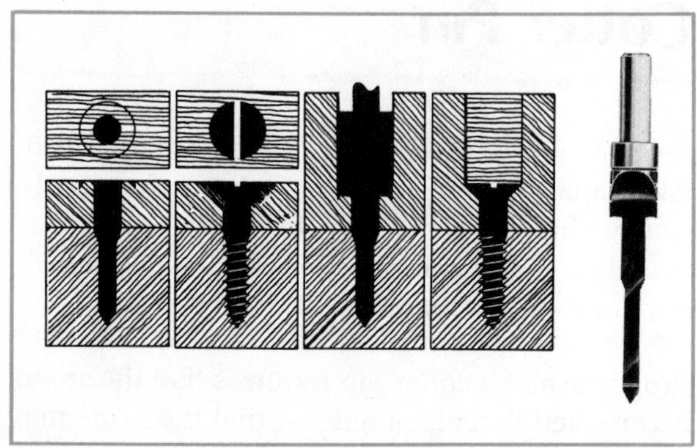

Courtesy of The Stanley Works

Counterbore

Counterflashing

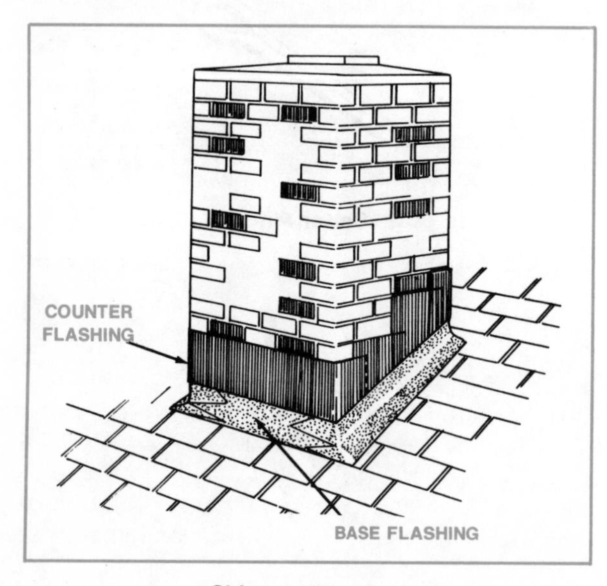

Chimney Flashing

Counterflashing, also called cap flashing, is flashing secured to a chimney at the roof joint to prevent water from leaking into the building. When the chimney is built, counterflashing is set into the mortar joints and later bent down over the base flashing, which is secured to the roof deck. On the chimney front and back, counterflashing is one continuous piece; on the chimney sides counterflashing is in sections to accomodate the roof slope. *SEE ALSO ROOF CONSTRUCTION.*

Counter Planning

[SEE KITCHEN DESIGN & PLANNING.]

Countersink

A countersink is a specialized type of conical reamer which is used to form a recess so that the head of a screw or other fastener will seat flush with the surface. It is available for use with a bit brace or a stubbier type which is used for hand and power drills. *SEE ALSO HAND TOOLS.*

Courtesy of The Stanley Works

Countersink

Course

A course is a continuous horizontal layer of brick, shingles or masonry forming part of a wall. *SEE ALSO BRICK & STONE WORK; CONCRETE BLOCK.*

Cove Molding

Cove molding is a three-sided molding with all or part of its face having a concave cross section. This molding is used wherever small angles are to be covered, and is beneficial in softening a wall-and-ceiling joint. *SEE ALSO MOLDING & TRIM.*

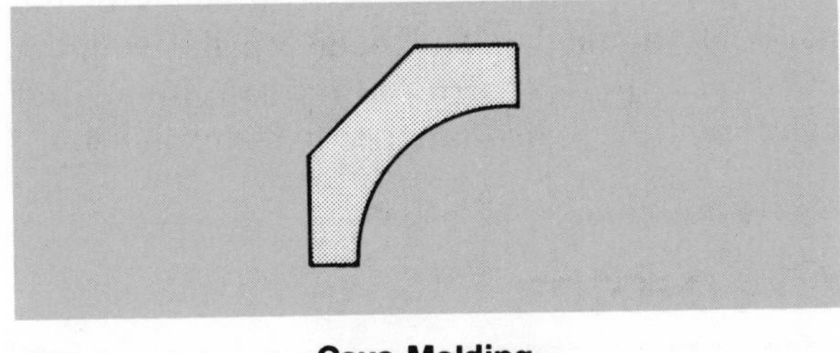

Cove Molding

Crabgrass

Crabgrass, a troublesome weed on lawns and agricultural land, was introduced into America from Europe. It spoils the beauty of more lawns than any other weed.

An annual, crabgrass develops from seeds produced the previous year. A single plant can produce as many as 50,000 seeds. The establishment of new plants continues from late spring until the first fall frost. The purplish seed heads that give lawns an unsightly appearance are formed as the plants mature from late summer to early fall.

There are several pre-emergence herbicides on the market which will often kill the crabgrass without causing injury to desirable lawn grasses. Since crabgrass germinates when minimum nighttime temperatures stay above 55 to 60 degrees, these pre-emergence herbicides should be used from late April to early May.

Siduron can be applied at the same time that lawn grasses are planted without harm. Also, DCPA has given excellent control of crabgrass without injury to most common lawn grasses. Bensulide helps control crabgrass, but lawn grasses cannot be seeded until 6 to 12 months after treatment. Other pre-emergence herbicides suitable for crabgrass control are benefin and terbutol.

Rooting at stem nodes can cause a two- to three-foot spread in a single crabgrass plant.

Once crabgrass has germinated, it becomes necessary to use post-emergence herbicides. DSMA and methylarsonate give good control if applied properly. It is usually necessary to make two or three applications at 7- to 10-day intervals.

Sold under various trade names, all of these chemicals are dangerous poisons and should be used only in accordance with manufacturer's directions.

Authorities agree that crabgrass cannot be eradicated with the use of chemicals alone. Crabgrass will not grow without light, so the best control is a dense, thick turf that is cut no shorter than 1½ inches. If seed production is controlled for several years, the viable seed supply will diminish to a point where it is no longer a serious threat to the lawn.

Reinfestation from seeds can be minimized if you rake the lawn to bring immature seed heads within the reach of the mower, then mow. Use a grass catcher on the mower if the seed heads have matured. *SEE ALSO LAWNS & GARDENS.*

Cracking

Cracking is a condition of a painted surface that is characterized by long narrow splits in the paint which reach to the bare wood. There are four basic reasons for this condition: the surface was not allowed to dry properly prior to painting; paint was used that was not suitable for the job; the paint was not adequately stirred prior to painting; the paint was inadequately brushed. Paint that has cracked should be removed with a paint scraper to expose as much of the wood as possible. Then, prime and repaint the area. *SEE ALSO PAINTS & PAINTING.*

Craft Shop

[SEE WORKSHOPS.]

Crawl Space

A crawl space is an area 18 to 24 inches in height which is located under the house. It helps make exposed flooring, pipes and wiring accessible if repair is needed. Insulation should be placed on walls and ceiling of the crawl space to prevent temperature extremes from affecting the inside temperature of the house. Fiberglass insulating boards should be used on the walls and rigid insulation used on the ceiling. Crawl spaces must be ventilated with a minimum of four louvered vents that are open all year to provide air movement.

Moisture is one of the major difficulties associated with a crawl space. Vapor rises from the excavated soil and saturates the floor. To prevent this, a layer of sand ballast should be placed on top of the soil which is then covered with heavy waterproof roofing material. The edges of the material should lap and bend up the walls at least six inches. Premolded vapor-sealed membranes can also be used to cover the soil.

Creosote

Creosote, a wood preservative, is an oily, brownish liquid made of aromatic hydrocarbons obtained from distilled coal tar. Designed to prevent decay and fungus growth, creosote is used on fence posts, telephone poles, trellis posts, railroad ties and any other wood in constant contact with the soil. Best results are obtained if the post is soaked or pressure-treated with creosote rather than having it brushed on.

Unpleasant features of creosote are the strong odor and the inability to paint treated areas in a normal manner since the brown stain will come through the paint. Creosote is also difficult to remove from hands and clothing. Although it is harmless to farm animals, creosote may kill plants that are near the post.

Cripple Jack

A cripple jack, or cripple rafter, is a type of rafter which does not intersect the plate or the ridge. It runs from a valley rafter to a hip rafter perpendicular to the ridge board. A cripple jack can be further identified as a hip-valley cripple jack or a valley cripple jack. *SEE ALSO ROOF CONSTRUCTION.*

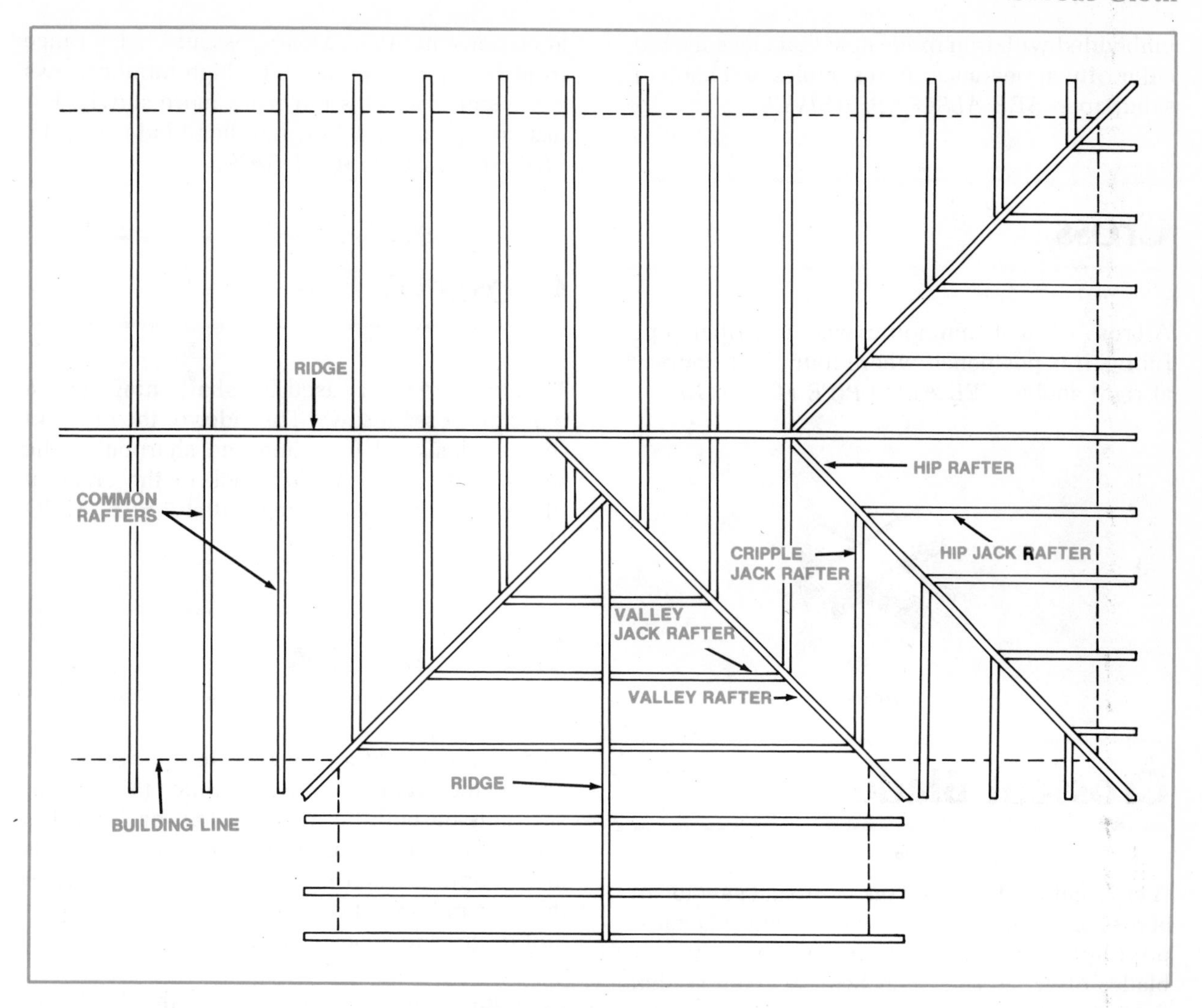

Plan view of roof frame

Cripple Stud

A cripple stud is a full length stud which has been cut for an opening, such as a window. When the opening is large, it is often easier and less costly to use a larger header rather than cutting and fitting numerous cripples. *SEE ALSO WALL & CEILING CONSTRUCTION.*

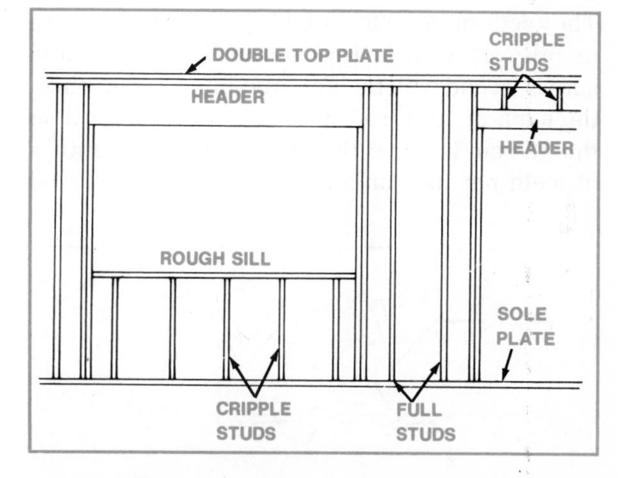

Larger header is used in window opening to save labor in cutting and fitting cripples.

Crocus Cloth

Crocus cloth is a cloth-back abrasive. Used to polish metals to a bright gloss, a crocus cloth is embedded with iron oxide dust that gives it a red color. In appearance it resembles a sheet of sandpaper. *SEE ALSO ABRASIVES.*

Cross

A cross is most commonly used as a fiber pipe fitting. It is positioned where four pipes connect at right angles. *SEE ALSO PIPE FITTINGS.*

Cross

Crosscut Blade

A crosscut blade is used on a crosscut saw to cut across or against the grain of the wood. The most popular blade size is 26 inches, but smaller blades of 22, 20 and 12 inches are made so that the saw will fit into toolboxes.

The teeth on a better quality crosscut blade are usually ground to tiny points for sharp cuts across wood fibers. For maximum efficiency, the teeth are alternately *set*, or bent, outward so that the cut is wider than the blade. The number of teeth per inch on a crosscut blade is referred to as point number. Most crosscut blades range from seven to 12 points. The high number saws make smoother cuts but work more slowly. For fast, rough cuts, a low number blade will do. *SEE ALSO CROSSCUT SAW.*

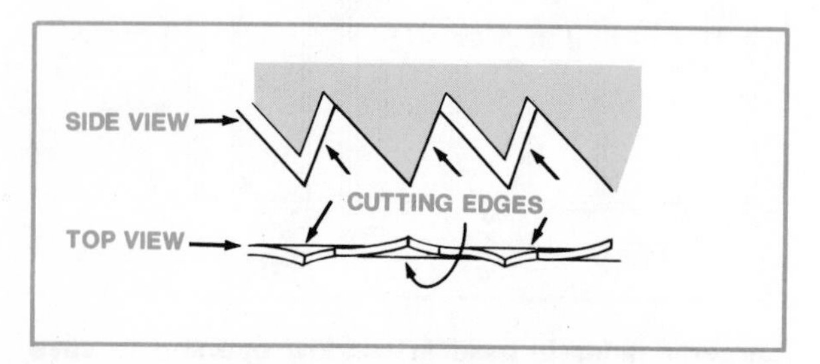

Teeth on a crosscut blade.

Crosscut File

The crosscut file is used for sharpening certain types of crosscut saws. The sides of the crosscut file are designed for filing and sharpening the saw's teeth. The rounded back of the crosscut file is used for deepening gullets. *SEE ALSO HAND TOOLS.*

Crosscut Saw

The crosscut saw is designed to cut against, or across, the grain of the wood. Since this type of saw cuts on both the forward and back strokes under its own weight, only light pressure needs to be applied when using it. Both the quality of the saw and how it is used are extremely important to this tool's performance.

In a high-quality crosscut saw, the teeth are usually precision-ground to tiny points that cut sharply across the wood fibers. Teeth on lower-quality models, though the same shape, are rarely precision-ground. This results in slower cutting with greater effort. In all grades alternate teeth are "set", or bent, outward about 1/4" the blade thickness to opposite sides, making the kerf wider than the blade thickness so the saw can move freely.

The most popular form of crosscut saw has a blade 26" long. However, smaller blades of 22", 20" and 12" are made to fit into toolboxes. These are slightly slower working.

Smoothness and speed of cutting also depend on the number of teeth per inch, referred to as points. The fewer teeth, the faster the cut; the

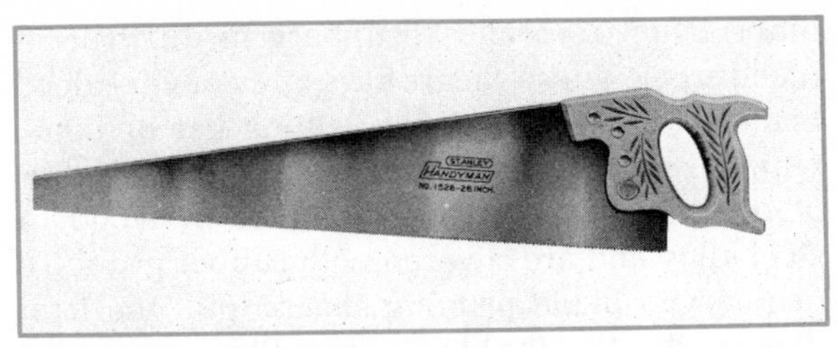

Courtesy of The Stanley Works

Crosscut Saw

more teeth, the smoother the cut. Crosscut saws commonly range from 7 to 12 points. The cutting is most efficient when the angle between the cutting edge of the saw and the work surface is 45 degrees. *SEE ALSO HAND TOOLS.*

Crossover Network

[SEE STEREO SYSTEMS.]

Crowbar

A crowbar is a straight, iron or steel bar, usually four to six feet long, which is used as a prybar or a lever. The working end is usually wedge-shaped. Crowbars are often used for prying out bolders or breaking up concrete. This straight bar offers better control than one that is angled. *SEE ALSO HAND TOOLS.*

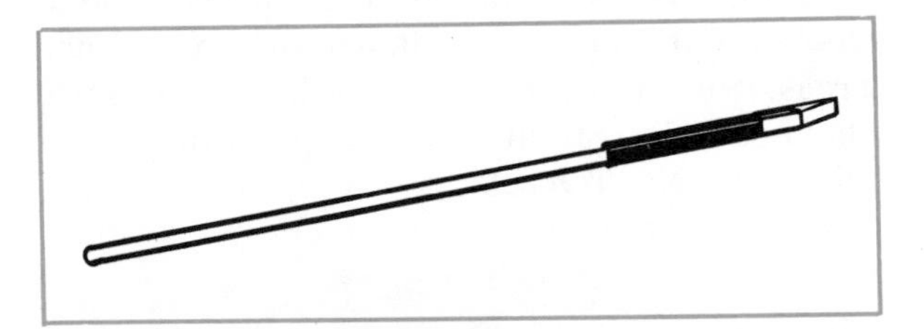

A crowbar is a useful prying tool.

Crown Molding

Crown molding is designed to be used at the break between ceiling and walls. It may be used indoors, or outdoors at the roof overhang, to make painting easier and to soften angle lines. *SEE ALSO MOLDING & TRIM.*

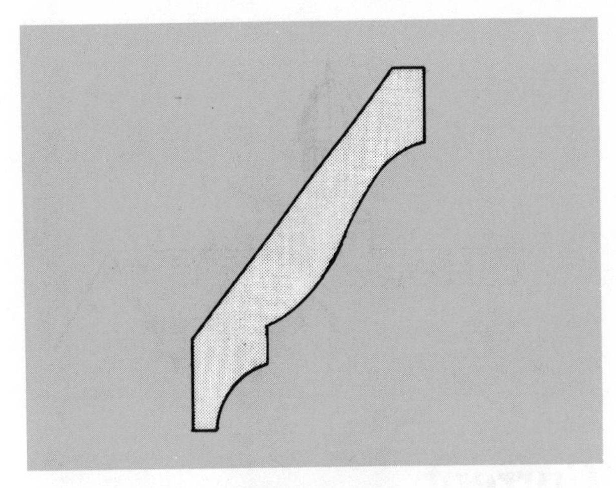

Crown Molding

Cubic Measure

Cubic measure computes the size and amount of liquid or space in three dimensions. To find cubic measurements, multiply the length, width, and heights of an area ($C = l \times w \times h$). This formula is frequently used in calculating house construction costs by finding the dimensions of a well that will produce a specific amount of water in U.S. gallons or for figuring the cubic yards of concrete needed for a foundation, basement or patio. Also the builder will need to know the cords of lumber required for framing, roofing and sheathing so he can calculate lumber costs.

Cupboard Devices

[SEE KITCHEN DESIGN & PLANNING.]

Cupola

A cupola is a small structure which is built or installed on the top of a roof. Both functional and ornamental, it can serve as a lookout, provide interior lighting and ventilation for the attic, or it can be used simply as a decorative addition.

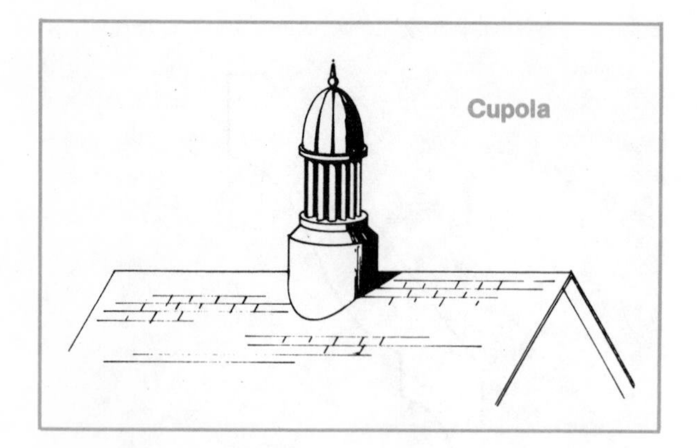

Current

Current is the transference of electricity through a wire or conductor from one point to another. *SEE ALSO ELECTRICITY.*

Curtains, Automatic

[SEE AUTOMATION.]

Curtain Wall

A curtain wall is a non-bearing wall usually structured between piers or columns. There is very little weight resting upon a curtain wall because the weight is distributed to the columns. *SEE ALSO WALL & CEILING CONSTRUCTION.*

Curved-Blade Pruning Shears

Curved-blade pruning shears, also called lopping shears or loppers, are used for cutting small limbs from trees and shrubbery in difficult-to-reach areas. These shears have one convex-edged blade that works against a cutting bar or hook, which is square and not sharpened. The handles of these pruning shears are made of wood or steel alloy and are covered with rubber grips. To use curved-blade pruning shears, pull the handles apart so that the blades open. Place the curved edge around one side of the limb and the opposite edge on the other side. By forcing the handles together, the blades will cut the limb. *SEE ALSO GARDEN TOOLS & EQUIPMENT.*

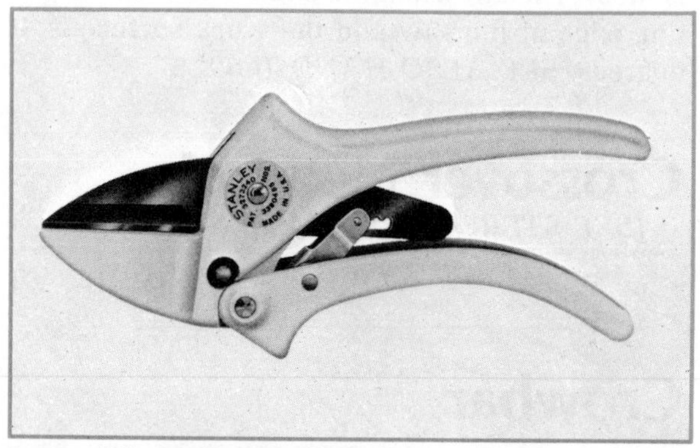

Courtesy of The Stanley Works

Curved-Blade Pruning Shears

Curved-Nose Pliers

Curved-nose pliers are fixed pivot pliers with a nose that bends or curves. This special type of pliers is extremely useful in working in confined areas, since they are able to reach into areas that the normal straight-nose pliers cannot. *SEE ALSO HAND TOOLS.*

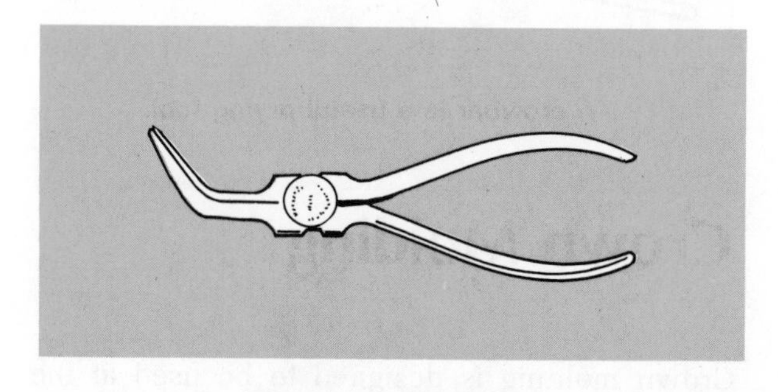

Curved-Nose Pliers

Curved-Tooth File

A tool widely used in the automotive industry, the curved-tooth file is designed for metal work. Available in both rigid and flexible styles, the flat-surface files shape convex surfaces, while the convex types are used on large, concave metal surfaces such as automobile bodies. Though the teeth are widely spaced, these files are stocky enough for sheet steel work, but can also serve well for filing softer alloys like aluminum. As they are used, curved-tooth files automatically discard chips, enabling the operator to work faster. *SEE ALSO HAND TOOLS.*

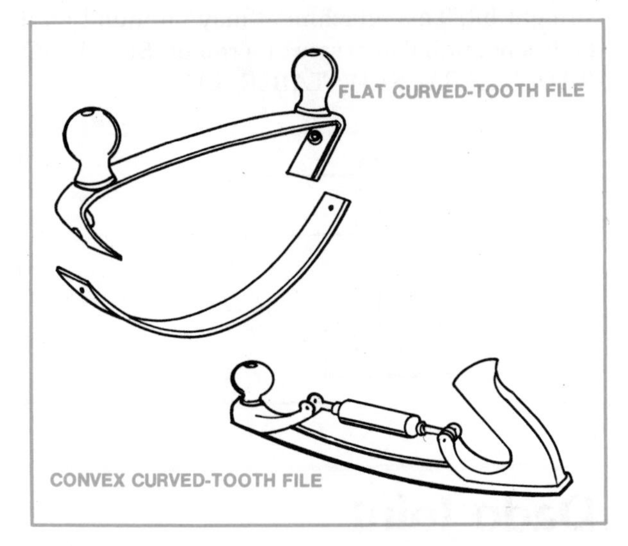

Cut Nails

Cut nails usually fasten tongue-and-groove flooring together or hold wood to brick or concrete. These are nails that are cut by machine and come in various sizes. *SEE ALSO FASTENERS.*

Cutting Guides for Sabre Saw

[SEE SABRE SAW.]

C-Washer

Made with an opening on one side, c-washers can be slipped on or removed from a bolt without taking off the nut. C-washers are also known as spring-lock washers, slip washers or open washers. *SEE ALSO WASHERS.*

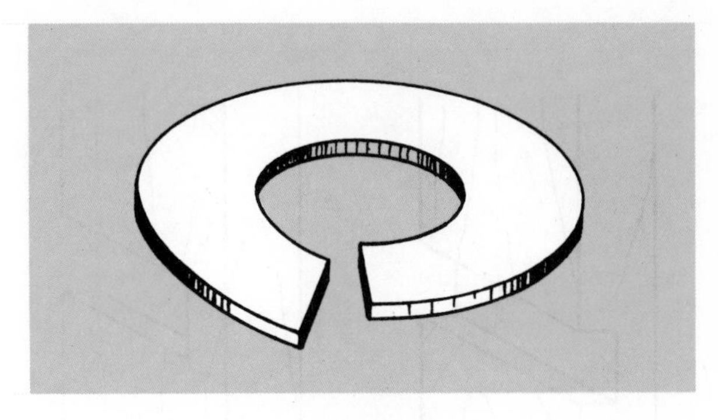

C-washer

Cypress Wood

Cypress wood is an easily-worked softwood which is one of the most decay-resistant lumbers. It is classified according to the region where it grows and may be known as red, black, white or yellow cypress. The sapwood is usually cream-colored, while the heartwood may vary from slightly reddish to a deep brown, or even black. Because of the durability of cypress wood, it is used primarily in outside construction, such as doors, steps, porches, tanks, vats and greenhouses. *SEE ALSO WOOD IDENTIFICATION.*

Dado

A dado is a square, flat-bottom groove. It is usually cut across the grain. The two types of dadoes are the plain and the stopped dado.

The plain dado is a cut extending the complete width of the joining member. A plain dado is used where the cross member will support considerable weight such as a bookcase.

A stopped dado extends only part way across the vertical member. It is cut when appearance is the major concern. It combines the finished appearance of a butt joint and the strength of a dado joint.

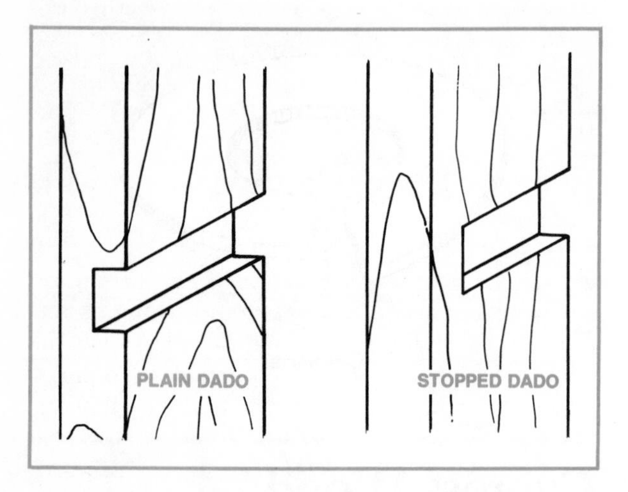

Dado Blade

The dado blade, an accessory for both hand and stationary saws, becomes essential when repeat passes of a regular saw blade are needed to widen the normal kerf of the stock. Varieties of dado blade sets are available. One of the best assemblies combines precision-ground blades and matched chippers. The number of chippers used determines the width of the cut that can be made. Especially important to the homecraftsman is a 13/16″ cut, which is the slot needed for 3/4″ shelving.

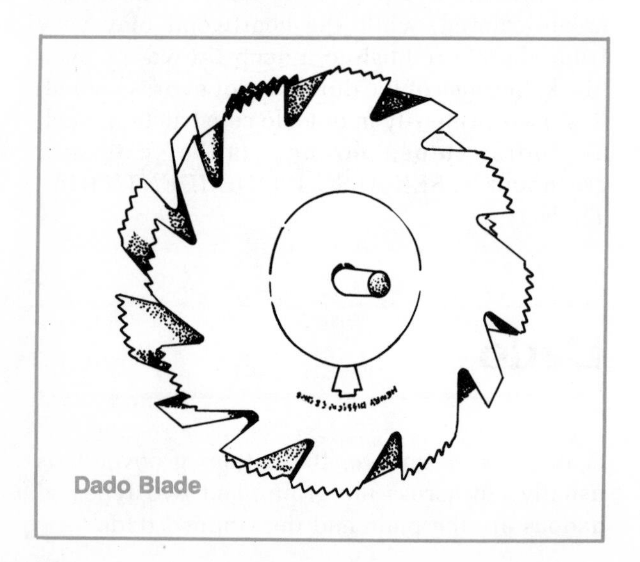
Dado Blade

Dado Head

A dado head is a tool attachment designed to cut dadoes. It is commonly called a single flute straight bit. This attachment may be found on a table saw, radial arm saw or a router. *SEE ALSO RADIAL ARM SAW; TABLE SAW.*

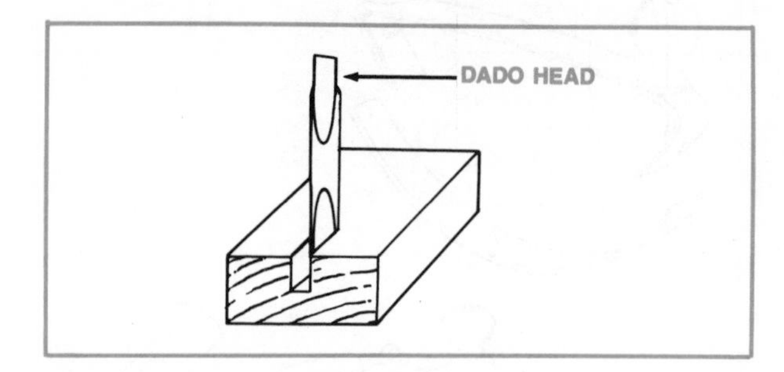

Dado Joint

A dado joint is made by cutting a dado and placing the cross member in the groove. There are two types of dado joints: the plain and the stopped.

PLAIN JOINT

A plain dado joint extends the entire width of the joining members. To make a plain dado joint, first place the board that will serve as the cross member on the vertical member and trace its outline to serve as a cutting guide. Saw to 1/3 the thickness of the cross member on both guide lines and chisel out the waste from the sides until the center is gone. Lastly, clean the groove

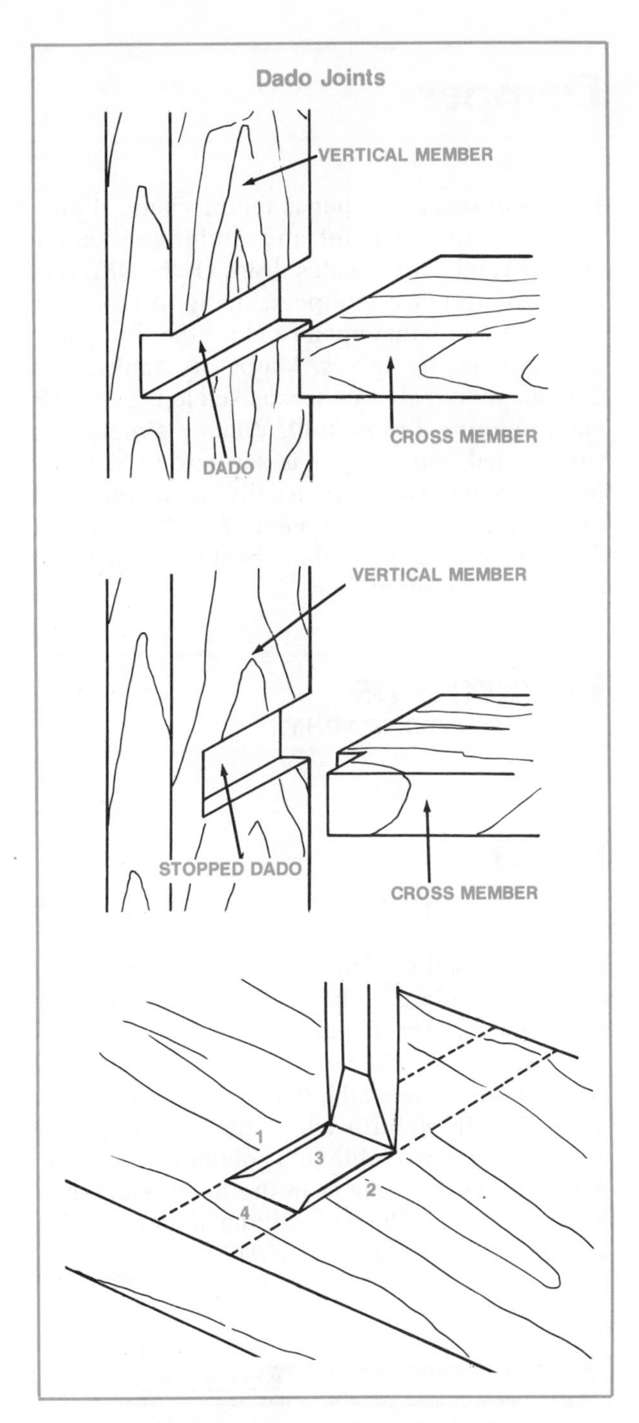

Use this order to chisel four cuts.

with a hand router or chisel. Then place the cross member in the groove to form the joint. The joint is very strong and capable of supporting considerable weight. Plain dadoes are often used in bookcases.

STOPPED JOINT

A stopped dado joint extends only part way of the members. To make a stopped dado, trace along the sides of the cross member to make cutting lines. Next allow space for saw movement by chiseling out a recess at the stopped end of the joint. Then saw along the guide lines to $^1/_3$ the thickness of the cross member. Chisel out the groove and clean it with a hand router or paring chisel. Lastly, notch the corner opposite the cross member to the depth of the dado. If both ends are stopped, cut the dado with a hand router or chisel.

Damaskeening

Damaskeening, also called spot polishing, is the process of forming smooth, overlapping spots on metal surfaces for decorative purposes. To make the spots, insert a solid steel rod into a drill press chuck so that it lightly touches the metal surface. Use a rip fence to guide the work in a straight line and apply a mixture of emery dust and light oil to the surface to act as abrasives in cutting the designs. Polishing rods can be hand made from hardwood and are covered with leather and either sandpaper or steel wool at the tip to act as an abrasive. This type rod can be worked dry

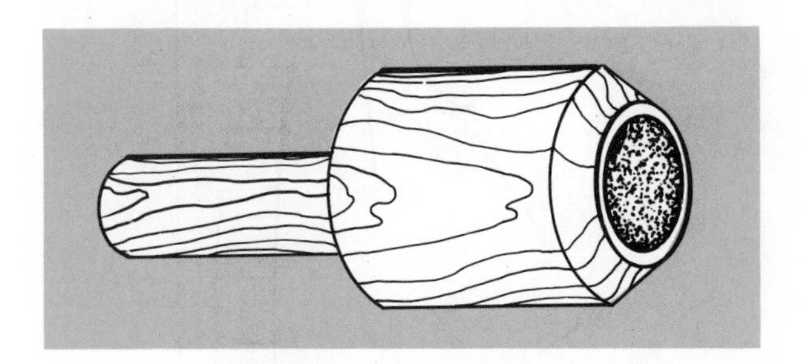

Wood Damaskeening Rod

since its abrasives are "built in". When damaskeening, start at a slow speed and gradually increase until the desired results are achieved. Overall speed is determined by the metal, the abrasive and the planned results being produced.

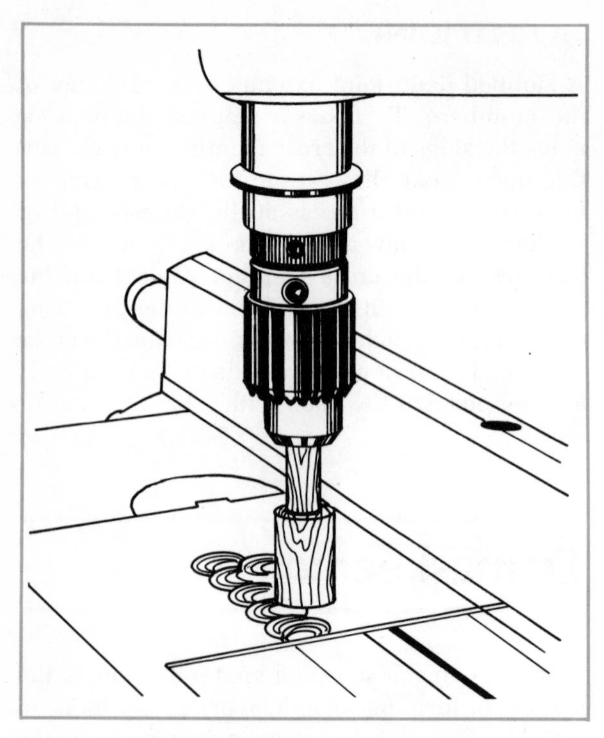

Damaskeening On A Drill Press

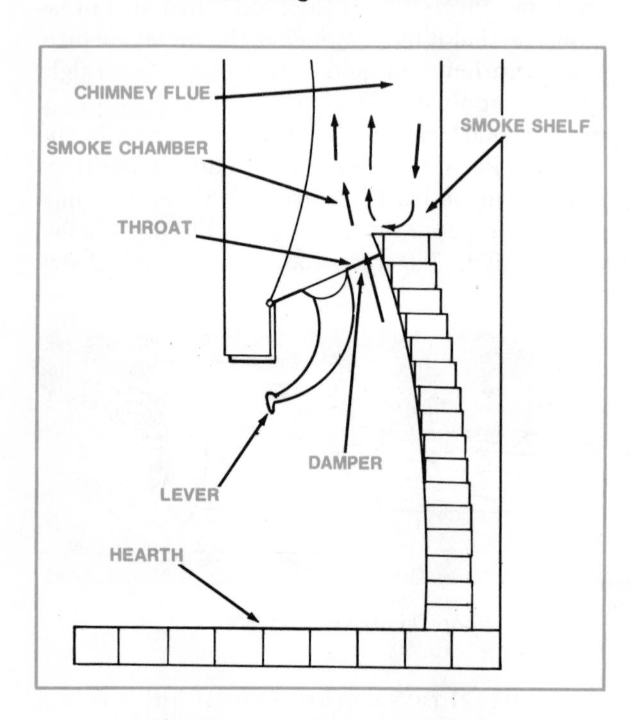

Side View of a Masonry Fireplace

Damper

In a fireplace, a damper is the mechanical part, located near the front and under the smoke chamber, which regulates draft. Of the different types of fireplace dampers, many are steel or cast-iron doors that open or close the throat and are operated by levers, knobs or cranks. The damper should always be checked to be sure it is open before a fire is built. When a fireplace is constructed, the damper is set loosely to allow for expansion. Dampers usually can be removed for cleaning or replacement. Another type of damper is used in certain heating systems to regulate the flow of heat.

Darkrooms

[SEE PHOTOGRAPHY.]

D-Bit

D-bits are used in conjunction with a drill press or lathe to enlarge a hole which was begun by another drill. The alignment necessary for this type work is made possible by the stationary nature of the lathe and the drill press. These bits are especially helpful when the exact hole size desired is not available in a commercially made drill. The D-bit is made in the home workshop by filing away almost half the diameter of a straight bit. *SEE ALSO HAND TOOLS.*

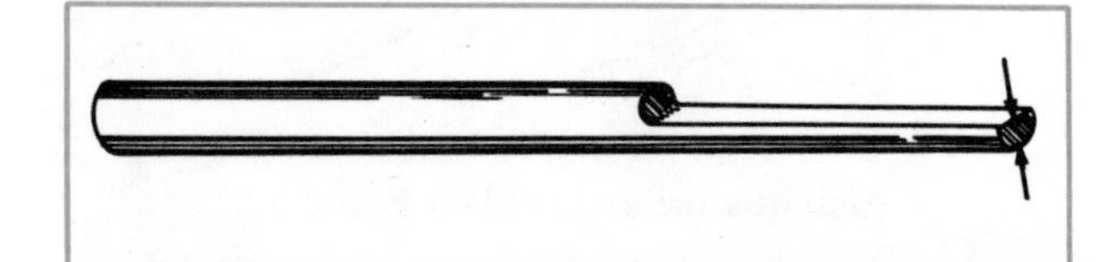

D-bit made to use in a lathe or drill press.